JAMES THOMSON

THE SEASONS

JAMES THOMSON

THE SEASONS

EDITED WITH INTRODUCTION
AND COMMENTARY
BY
JAMES SAMBROOK

OXFORD
AT THE CLARENDON PRESS
1981

Oxford University Press, Walton Street, Oxford OX2 6DP

London Glasgow New York Toronto
Delhi Bombay Calcutta Madras Karachi
Kuala Lumpur Singapore Hong Kong Tokyo
Nairobi Dar es Salaam Cape Town Salisbury
Melbourne Auckland

and associate companies in
Beirut Berlin Ibadan Mexico City

Published in the United States by
Oxford University Press, New York

British Library Cataloguing in Publication Data
Thomson, James, b. *1700*
    The seasons. – (Oxford English texts)
    I. Title II. Sambrook, James
    III. Series
    821'.5   PR3732.S4   79–41094
    ISBN 0–19–812713–8

Printed in Great Britain
at the University Press, Oxford
by Eric Buckley
Printer to the University

PREFACE

THOUGH critics from Johnson downwards have recognized the importance of Thomson's thoroughgoing and repeated revisions of *The Seasons*, no full collation of those revisions was published until a hundred and sixty years after the poet's death, when, in 1908, two critical editions appeared: Otto Zippel's in *Palaestra* lxvi (Berlin), and J. L. Robertson's in his edition of Thomson's *Complete Poetical Works* (Oxford). Both editions were reprinted in the 1970s, but, since both editors modernized their texts and both failed to take account of a number of editions or states revised by Thomson, there appeared still to be a need for a critical, unmodernized edition based upon a fresh collation of more extensive evidence. This I have attempted to supply. I have added, further, a commentary based in part on the explanatory notes in my edition of *The Seasons and the Castle of Indolence* (Oxford, 1972).

In the preparation of this edition I have received generous financial assistance from the British Academy, the Folger Shakespeare Library, the Leverhulme Trust Fund and the University of Southampton Research Fund.

I have drawn upon the patient and courteous services of librarians at Birmingham Public Library, the Bodleian, Brighton Public Library, the British Library, the Brotherton Library, Cambridge University, Cheshunt College, Edinburgh Public Library, Edinburgh University, Glasgow University, Hendon Public Library, the Royal Irish Academy, the John Rylands Library, St. David's College Lampeter, the National Library of Scotland, Reading University, Southampton University, the Victoria and Albert Museum, Winchester College, the Library of Congress, Columbia University, the Folger Shakespeare Library, Harvard University, the University of Illinois, Princeton University, Rice University, Swarthmore College, the Pierpont Morgan Library, and Yale University.

I have been greatly helped too by the following colleagues, other friends, and correspondents: Jacques Berthoud, Trevor Blount, Stanley Boorman, Dr Jean Bromley (Jean Robertson), Joel Egerer, Mrs Clare Kotch, John McGavin, John Swannell, Mrs Norma Martin, and, most especially, David Foxon.

CONTENTS

LIST OF ILLUSTRATIONS

SIGLA AND ABBREVIATIONS

1. KEY TO THE CRITICAL APPARATUS

OET the text of this edition.
    (*Note.* Plain line-numbers refer to the *OET* text. Line-numbers in round brackets refer to a specified early text cited in the apparatus.)

a   added to an *OET* line number indicates a variant reading in the apparatus.

+   precedes interpolated material in a collated text other than the *OET* or a specified early text.

/   end-of-line marker.

~   repetition of an identical word in variants of punctuation.

∧   omission of punctuation.

n.   editorial note in the Commentary of this edition.

Wi.26f *Winter*, folio 1726. Foxon T211.
    See pp. xxxvi–xxxvii below.

Wi.26o *Winter*, second edition, octavo 1726. Foxon T212.
    Winter, third edition, octavo 1726. Foxon T213.
    Winter, fourth edition, octavo 1726. Foxon T214.
    See pp. xxxvii–xl below.

Su.27 *Summer*, octavo 1727. Foxon T220.
    Summer, second edition, octavo 1728. Foxon T222.
    See pp. xl–xliii below.

Wi.28 *Winter*, fifth edition, octavo 1728. Foxon T216.
    See pp. xliv–xlv below.

Sp.28 *Spring*, octavo 1728. Foxon T227.
    Spring, second edition, octavo 1729. Foxon T229.
    See pp. xliii–xlvi below.

30q   *The Seasons*, quarto 1730. Foxon T236.
    See pp. xlvi–lii below.

Su.30p *Summer*, third edition, octavo 1730. Foxon T223.
    See pp. lii–lvii below.

Au.30p *Autumn*, second edition, octavo 1730. Foxon T233.
    See pp. lii–lvii below.

Wi.30p *Winter, a Hymn, a Poem to . . . Newton, and Britannia*, octavo 1730. Foxon T217.
    See pp. lii–lvii below.

Sp.31 *Spring*, second edition, octavo 1731. Foxon T230.
    See pp. lv–lvii below.

300   *The Seasons*, octavo '1730' (possibly a false date). Foxon
            T240.
            See pp. lvii–lx below.

Sp.34   *Spring*, second edition, octavo '1731' (actually published 1734).
            Foxon T231.
            See pp. lvi–lvii below.

Wi.34   *Winter, a Hymn, a Poem to* . . . *Newton, and Britannia*, octavo
            1734. Foxon T219.
            See pp. lvi–lvii below.

Su.35   *Summer*, fourth edition, octavo 1735. Foxon T225.
            See pp. lvi–lvii below.

38   *The Seasons* in *The Works of Mr. Thomson*, octavo 1738,
            vol. 1. Foxon p. 794.
            See pp. lxi–lxiv below.

44   *The Seasons*, crown octavo 1744. Foxon T243.
            See pp. lxviii–lxx below.

44Wks   *The Seasons* in *The Works of Mr. Thomson*, octavo 1744,
            vol. 1. Foxon p. 794.
            See pp. lxx–lxxi below.

45   *The Seasons*, crown octavo '1744' (actually published 1745).
            Foxon T244.
            See p. lxxi below.

46   *The Seasons*, duodecimo 1746. Foxon T246.
            See pp. lxxii–lxxiv below.

Note. Sigla representing early printed editions are set out in
the apparatus according to the order in which they are listed
above, with a dash to indicate a continuous series: e.g. *26f–38*
signifies a reading found in *26f, 26o, 28, 30q, 30p, 300, 34,* and
38. When variants within the same Season are listed (i.e. in
most textual notes) the prefix indicating the Season, e.g. *Sp*
or *Su*, is omitted.

MS   Revisions in Thomson's holograph on the interleaved copy
            of *Works* 1738, vol. 1, in the British Library (shelfmark C.28
            e 17).
            See pp. lxvi–lxviii below.

MSLytt   Revisions in Lyttelton's holgraph on this same volume.

            Note. Holograph revisions deleted by hand in the interleaved
            volume are, in this apparatus, placed in square brackets and
            followed by the symbol '*del.*'. Variants recorded as '*MS*' or
            '*MSLytt*' sometimes include, for the sake of clarity, printed
            words of *38* which Thomson or Lyttelton intended to retain in
            their revised text.

LH   extract from *Summer* in a letter from Thomson to Aaron Hill,
            *c.*June 1726, printed in *Letters*, pp. 38–9.

PS   extracts from *Spring* in *The Present State of the Republic of Letters*, May 1728, pp. 430–1.

WEP   extracts from *Spring* in the *Whitehall Evening-Post*, 16–19 March 1728.

2. KEY TO THE CRITICAL APPARATUS IN APPENDIX C

50   Cancel-sheet H in copies of *46* which were reissued with new preliminaries as *The Works of James Thomson. In Four Volumes. Volume the First. Containing the Seasons.* London: Printed for A. Millar . . . 1750. Demy 12°.
See pp. lxxiv–lxxvi below.

52 dd   *The Works of James Thomson. In Four Volumes Complete. With his last Corrections, Additions, and Improvements.* London: Printed for A. Millar . . . 1752. [volume i] *The Seasons.* By James Thomson. London: Printed for A. Millar . . . 1752. Demy 12°.
See pp. lxxvi–lxxvii below.

52 pd   *The Seasons.* By James Thomson. London: Printed for A. Millar . . . 1752. Pot 12°.
See p. lxxvii below.

57   *The Works of James Thomson. In Four Volumes Complete. With his last Corrections, Additions, and Improvements.* London: Printed for A. Millar . . . 1757. Volume the First. Containing *The Seasons.* Demy 12°.
See p. lxxvii below.

58   *The Seasons.* By James Thomson. London: Printed for A. Millar . . . 1758. Demy 12°.
See p. lxxix below.

62q   *The Works of James Thomson*, With his last Corrections and Improvements. To which is prefixed, An Account of his Life and Writings. In Two Volumes. Vol. I. London: Printed for A. Millar . . . 1762. 4°.
See p. lxxix below.

62d   *The Works of James Thomson.* With his last Corrections and Improvements. In Four Volumes. Vol. I. London: Printed for A. Millar . . . 1762. Demy 12°.
See p. lxxix below.

Note. Sigla are set out in the apparatus of Appendix C according to the order in which they are listed above, with a dash to indicate a continuous series: e.g. *58–62d* indicates a reading found in *58*, *62q*, and *62d*.

Lytt   Lyttelton's emendations for an unpublished edition of *The Seasons.*

Note. These emendations were made in Lyttelton's hand upon an interleaved copy of *The Seasons* 1752, the title-page date of which he altered, in manuscript, to 'MDCCLVIII'. This volume was found among the books of Lyttelton's friend Mrs Elizabeth Montagu when she died in 1800 and was given by her heir to Lord Spencer, who, in turn, presented it to the Lyttelton family at Hagley before 1845. A few of Lyttelton's emendations in this volume were printed by John Mitford (1781–1859) in the *Gentleman's Magazine* (Dec. 1841), pp. 576–8, and a few more by R. Phillimore in his *Memoirs* of Lyttelton (1845), i. 319–22. It may have been about this time that John Mitford transcribed all of Lyttelton's emendations onto his own interleaved copy of a 1768 edition of *The Seasons*, now in the British Library (shelfmark C. 134 c. 1, formerly 11632 c. 57). The readings printed in Zippel, pp. xxii–xxxi, were taken from Mitford's transcription in the British Library, but were 'verified' upon the original volume, marked by Lyttelton, at Hagley.

As the original is now lost, thought to have been destroyed by fire at Hagley in 1925, readings in Appendix C are taken from the Mitford transcript in the British Library, collated with the readings printed by Mitford, Phillimore, and Zippel. The list is complete for substantive variants but includes only the most significant of Lyttelton's nearly two hundred revisions of accidentals. Line numbers and lemmata refer to the *OET* text, though it should be remembered that Lyttelton entered his emendations on a copy of 52dd.

3. OTHER ABBREVIATIONS USED IN THE INTRODUCTION AND COMMENTARY

Arthos   John Arthos, *The Language of Natural Description in Eighteenth Century Poetry* (Ann Arbor, 1949).

Background   A. D. McKillop, *The Background of Thomson's* Seasons (Minneapolis, 1942).

Cas. Ind.   James Thomson, *The Castle of Indolence*, second edition (1748).

Foxon   D. F. Foxon, *English Verse, 1701–1750, a Catalogue* (Cambridge, 1975).

Grant   Douglas Grant, *James Thomson, Poet of 'The Seasons'* (1951).

Johnson   *A Dictionary of the English Language* (1755).

Letters   *James Thomson (1700–1748), Letters and Documents*, ed. A. D. McKillop (Lawrence, Kansas, 1958).

Lucretius   Lucretius, *De Rerum Natura*.

PL   Milton, *Paradise Lost*.

Sale   *A Catalogue of the Furniture* [*etc.*] *of Mr. James Thomson*
Catalogue   (1749) in *Sale Catalogues of the Libraries of Eminent Persons*,
             ed. A. N. L. Munby (1971), i. 47–66.

Zippel   Otto Zippel, *Thomson's Seasons, Critical Edition*, in
             Palaestra lxvi (Berlin 1908, reprinted, Folcroft, Penn.,
             1970).

INTRODUCTION

I. CONTENT AND FORM

THE subdivisions used in this section of the Introduction are not intended to be exhaustive, or even particularly methodical; but only to hint at the variety of subjects and attitudes to be found in a poem which has never seemed to be easily assignable to any one of the genres, and which in the eyes of many readers before and after Johnson has appeared to want method.

Devotional

When, in August 1726, Thomson wrote to Mallet 'My Idea of your Poem [*The Excursion*] is a Description of the grand Works of Nature, raised and animated by moral, and sublime Reflections . . . Sublimity must be the Characteristic of your Piece'[1] he was also giving the idea of his own recently published *Winter*, where description of the terrible beauties of that season prompts reflections upon God's powers and 'exalts' the poet's soul to heaven. The *Preface* to the second edition in June 1726 (see Appendix B below), with its references to ancient truth and purity and to Moses and Milton, not to mention Aaron Hill, links Thomson with contemporary efforts to write sublime poetry and with the advocacy of the religious sublime by such critics as John Dennis.[2] Hill's *The Judgement-Day* (1720), quoted in Thomson's *Preface*, is one of many early eighteenth-century attempts to versify with pleasing dread and due rhetorical sublimity the most exalted and affecting of all subjects; *Winter* itself ends, of course, with a prospect of the Last Day and a proclamation of faith. Before *Winter* was published Thomson had gone to the Bible to find the great and serious subjects which he was to call for in his *Preface*; like other aspirants after the religious sublime, he had subjected Psalm 104 and part of the sixth chapter of St. Matthew to paraphrase,[3] and in the *Preface* itself he praises that most frequented

---

[1] *Letters*, p. 40.

[2] Both criticism and poetry are well treated in D. B. Morris, *The Religious Sublime* (Lexington, 1972).

[3] 'A Paraphrase of Psalm civ', written about 1720, printed in William Goodhugh, *The English Gentleman's Library Manual* (1827); 'A Paraphrase on

resort of early eighteenth-century biblical paraphrasts, the Book
of Job. Using the phrase he would employ in his letter to Mallet,
Thomson reminds his readers that the Book of Job, 'that noble
and antient Poem', is 'crowned with a Description of the grand
Works of Nature; and that, too, from the Mouth of their Almighty
Author.'[1] The Book of Job communicates an awareness of the
inscrutable powers of God as revealed in external nature, and
dramatizes a faithful man's confrontation of the natural world's
rich beauty and unpredictable harshness. Employing description
rather than dialogue, but still assuming what a contemporary
hailed as 'the majesty freedom of an Eastern [i.e. Hebrew] writer',[2]
Thomson in *Winter* follows similar purposes.

Though the devotional conception of the first *Winter* survives
less and less strongly under the weight of secular accretions and
revisions which eventually brought Thomson's *Seasons* to full
growth twenty years later, the finished work of 1746 remains, in
intention, a religious didactic poem.[3] To the storms and wolves of
Winter were added the wild beasts and the typhoon, sandstorm,
plague and lightning of *Summer*, the insect-blights of *Spring*, the
floods and earthquakes of *Autumn*, and the storms which robe God
in the *Hymn*. The spectacle of uncontrolled power in nature evokes
salutary fear and reverential awe which turn the mind towards
God.[4] In a comparable vein, astronomical and geographical
excursions, particularly extensive in *Summer* and the later versions
of *Winter*, were intended to arouse that pleasure which the
imagination found in the vastness of the natural world, and thereby
to reinforce the reason's knowledge of God. References to astron-
omy by those influential philosophical popularizers Shaftesbury
and Addison showed that the huge distances revealed by
seventeenth-century telescopes had made the concept of God less,

the latter Part of the Sixth Chapter of St. Matthew', written October 1725,
printed in James Ralph's *Miscellany* (1729).

[1] It was customary (and decent) for critics to prefer descriptions of external
nature in the Book of Job to Homer's or Virgil's; see, e.g., Steele's *Guardian*
86 (16 June 1713).

[2] Patrick Murdoch, *Life* prefixed to Thomson's *Works* (1762), vol. i, p. iv.

[3] The most searching analysis of *The Seasons* as a religious didactic poem is in
Ralph Cohen, *The Unfolding of* The Seasons (1970).

[4] John Dennis had treated at length the poet's management of this 'en-
thusiastic passion of terror' for didactic ends in his *Grounds of Criticism in
Poetry* (1704), pp. 85–93. Thomson befriended Dennis (see Grant, pp. 140–1,
and *Letters*, pp. 50, 52, 86), and admired his criticism.

not more, incomprehensible; and Thomson's blank-verse 'Fragment of a Poem on the Works and Wonders of Almightly Power' (in Aaron Hill's *Plain Dealer* 46, 28 August 1724, and so the first work of Thomson's printed outside Edinburgh) was heavily indebted to some passages in *The Moralists, a Rhapsody* (1709) where Shaftesbury finds evidence of God in the vastness of the stellar universe.[1] Addison sang the spacious firmament on high in *Spectator* 465, and in *Spectator* 489 wrote: 'The imagination prompts the Understanding, and by the Greatness of the sensible Object, produces in it the Idea of a Being who is neither circumscribed by Time nor Space.' Shaftesbury's survey from the frigid to the torrid zone, showing that no part of the 'Map of Nature' was unworthy of man's reverence,[2] could almost be a programme for *The Seasons*. In *The Theory of the Earth* (English version 1684–90)—a major source for Thomson's *Seasons*—Addison's mentor Thomas Burnet had indicated the religious-cum-aesthetic value of the kind of imaginative experience Thomson sought to convey:

The greatest objects of Nature are, methinks, the most pleasing to behold; and next to the great Concave of the Heavens, and those boundless Regions where the Stars inhabit, there is nothing that I look upon with more pleasure than the wide Sea and the Mountains of the Earth. There is something august and stately in the Air of these things that inspires the mind with great thoughts and passions; we do naturally upon such occasions think of God and his greatness, and whatsoever hath but the shadow and appearance of INFINITE, as all things have that are too big for our comprehension, they fill and overbear the mind with their Excess, and cast it into a pleasing kind of stupor and admiration.[3]

Though Thomson's descriptions and reflections often come to rest in 'stupor and admiration' (notably in the classically sublime device of 'expressive Silence' at the end of the *Hymn*), his contemplation of God in external nature leads no less frequently, and more characteristically, to an active moral response. In the earliest version of *Winter*, Philosophic Melancholy, aroused by the inspiring scenes of autumn, bears the poet's swelling thought aloft to Heaven and prompts the spirit of social benevolence. This

---

[1] The debt is assessed in Herbert Drennon, 'The Source of James Thomson's "The Works and Wonders of Almighty Power"', *Modern Philology* xxxii (1934), 33–6.   [2] *The Moralists*, in *Characteristicks* ii. 383–91.

[3] Book I, chap. xi. On vastness and the religious sublime see Ernest Tuveson, 'Space, Deity and the "Natural Sublime"', *Modern Language Quarterly* xii (1951), 20–38.

passage was retained and enlarged in the final version of *The Seasons* (*Au.* 988–1029),[1] where it enjoyed the company of other Shaftesburian apostrophes to active charity (e.g. *Sp.* 867–903, *Su.* 1641–6, *Wi.* 322–88). Shaftesbury is introduced in person in the 1730 version of Summer as the 'Friend of Man'.[2] Like Shaftesbury and Hutcheson, Thomson believed that there is an innate 'moral sense', so he insists that social love is not merely a rational extension of self-love (see *Sp.* 878–903 n.). Thomson's ethics are Shaftesburian; so is his rhapsodic tone, and so at times, it seems, is his theology. That the orthodox Lyttelton was troubled by what he took to be Thomson's deistical inclination to identify God with Nature is evident from letters[3] and from Lyttelton's proposed revisions to *The Seasons* after Thomson's death: for instance the emendation of Thomson's 'Oh NATURE! all-sufficient! over all!' (*Au.* 1352) to 'Oh NATURE! Handmaid of Celestial Power' (see Appendix C below).

Scientific

The God of Job, actively present in the universe and directing its affairs, is apparent in the first versions of *Winter*, *Summer*, and *Spring*, but rarely appears in Thomson's additions and revisions from 1730 onwards. The insertion of a reference to God's Hand at *Su.* 41 in 1744 is uncharacteristic; other revisions made at that time (e.g. *Su.* 1131 and *Sp.* 860+) have the effect of removing the person of God from his machine. As Shaftesbury comes to contribute more than the Book of Job to Thomson's moralizing, so Newton and the Boyle lecturers come to contribute more to his descriptions.

Thomson could have studied natural philosophy at Edinburgh, and was certainly living among teachers of the 'Newtonian

---

[1] Unless otherwise indicated, all book and line references are to the *OET* text of *The Seasons*.

[2] Considerable claims for the influence of Shaftesbury on Thomson are made in C. A. Moore, 'Shaftesbury and the Ethical Poets in England, 1700–1760', *PMLA* xxxi (1916), 264–325; but for arguments that some apparently Shaftesburian notions came from writings by scientific rationalists see Herbert Drennon, 'Scientific Rationalism and James Thomson's Poetic Art', *Studies in Philology* xxxi (1934), 453–71; and 'James Thomson's Ethical Theory and Scientific Rationalism', *Philological Quarterly* xiv (1935), 70–82.

[3] Lyttelton's *Observations on the Conversion of St. Paul* (1747), a widely popular work of evengelical piety, was written partly with the intention of converting Thomson to Christianity (*Letters*, pp. 189, 210).

Philosophy' when he taught at Watts's Academy after May 1726.[1]
There are references to the percolation theory of springs and rivers
(cf. *Au.* 736–835 n.) in 'A Paraphrase of Psalm civ' and to etherial
nitre in the earliest edition of *Winter*, but Thomson's first sustained
effort to read Nature with a 'Philosophic eye' occurs in *Summer*
1727. Here we find Newton's notions of gravitation and projection,
and of light and colour, as well as a technical discussion of thunder,
praise of Bacon, Boyle, and Newton, and accounts of shooting
stars and the aurora borealis.[2] *Spring* 1728 has references to
animalculae (transferred in 1744 to *Summer*), plant physiology,
and Newton's explanation of the rainbow. *The Seasons* 1730 adds
a technical discussion of freezing in *Winter*; the aurora borealis
(transferred from *Summer*), wildfire, and a dissertation on the origin
of springs and rivers in *Autumn*; and lines on the simplicity of the
scientific laws of Nature in the *Hymn*. Additions and revisions for
the 1744 edition do not draw so heavily upon particular scientific
knowledge, except for the rewriting and enlargement of the springs
and rivers passage in *Autumn*. Such obviously 'scientific' passages
apart, the language of natural description elsewhere in *The Seasons*
is drawn freely from the regular, exact vocabulary of early
eighteenth-century scientific writing. Many words that are nowa-
days used in an extended, abstracted or metaphorical sense
(e.g. attraction, austere, bland, benign, concoct, exalt, insipid,
involve, refine, spirit, sublime, temperate, tincture) have in
Thomson's poem an exact, scientific significance—often close to
an original sense in Latin. Thomson's poetic periphrases are
formed on the analogy of scientific classifications (see *Sp.* 132 n.);
they serve to define particular characteristics or functions of a
creature or object, and if sometimes 'gaudy' they are never 'inane'.[3]
His language had for his contemporaries (and for Johnson when

---

[1] See Grant, pp. 56–8, 71–2, *Letters*, pp. 31, 214, and Herbert Drennon,
'James Thomson's contact with Newtonianism and his interest in Natural
Philosophy', *PMLA* xlix (1934), 71–80.

[2] For the influence of Newton and other scientists upon Thomson see the
articles by Drennon cited at p. xx n. 2, and p. xxi n. 1 above, and two further
articles by Drennon: 'Newtonianism: its Method, Theology and Metaphysics',
Englische Studien lxviii (1934), 397–409, 'Newtonianism in James Thomson's
Poetry', *Englische Studien* lxx (1936), 358–72. See also M. H. Nicolson, *Newton
Demands the Muse* (Princeton, 1946), and W. P. Jones, *The Rhetoric of Science*
(1966).

[3] See John Arthos, *The Language of Natural Description in Eighteenth-century
Poetry* (Ann Arbor, 1949); and Donald Davie, *The Language of Science and the
Language of Literature, 1700–1740* (1963).

he was compiling his *Dictionary*) a scientific precision which the modern reader can hardly appreciate.

Thomson admires the physical law and the hidden mechanism that, for instance, brought a rainbow into being, but he is equally excited by the human intelligence, 'the sage-instructed Eye' (*Sp.* 210), that could grasp this law and lay bare this mechanism. Addison's claim in *Spectator* 543 that Newton was 'the Miracle of the Present Age' was contested by few Englishmen, least of all by Thomson, whose influential panegyrical *A Poem sacred to the memory of Sir Isaac Newton* (1727) is an apotheosis of the great scientist.[1] Canon Rundle, recommending *The Seasons* to a friend in 1729, said that Thomson's themes were 'Nature and its explainer, and its author' and exclaimed 'what indeed could without prophaneness be joined to the praises of the Great Creator, but his works and Newton; his works are his words; he speaks his sublime wisdom and goodness to us in them, and Newton is his interpreter!'[2] Addison had declared in *Spectator* 543 that from the System of the universe Newton had drawn 'Demonstrations of infinite Power and Wisdom,' while Newton himself argued that 'So far as we can know by Natural Philosophy what is the First Cause, what Power He has over us, and what Benefits we receive from Him, so far our Duty towards Him, as well as that towards one another will appear to us by the Light of Nature.'[3] Newton's system required the belief that God had placed the planets in orbit and was constantly present within the universe to maintain its order (cf. *Sp.* 852–5, *Su.* 32–42), and Newton further conjectured that God was present in infinite space 'as it were in his Sensory' (his sensory being analagous to the percipient centre of a human brain to which sense impressions are transmitted). Such notions were given wider currency by Samuel Clarke, by Bentley in his Boyle lectures, and especially by Addison, whose *Spectator* 565 on the omnipresence and omniscience of God opens with references to Milton and uses the scientific findings of Newton to prove a text from the Book of Job. Religious hope and comfort was to be gained both from the increase in scientific knowledge and from the evident limitations upon such knowledge. Newton and his followers agreed

---

[1] For the sources and influences of T.'s praise of Newton see *The Castle of Indolence and Other Poems*, ed. A. D. McKillop (Lawrence, Kansas, 1961), pp. 128–47.   [2] *Letters*, p. 62.

[3] *Opticks* (3rd edn., 1718), Book III, Part i, Query 28, discussed in M. H. Nicolson, *Newton Demands the Muse* (Princeton, 1946), pp. 104–6.

that natural philosophy led men's minds by a chain of cause and effect towards a First Cause, but as earthly life is so short and man's view so limited it appears 'that our present state would be very imperfect without a subsequent one; wherein our views of nature, and of its great Author may be more clear and satisfactory.'[1]

Newton's discoveries and conjectures were used to support a physico-theological argument which was intended to demonstrate the existence and benevolent attributes of God on the evidence of the created universe; and this argument became the subject-matter of popular textbooks, such as John Ray's *Wisdom of God manifested in the Works of the Creation* (1691) and William Derham's *Physico-Theology* (1713) and *Astro-Theology* (1715), as well as of a succession of poems, beginning with Blackmore's much respected *Creation* (1712).[2] Blackmore sought inspiration in Newton and Milton, and must have been gratified by the notice of his *Creation* in one of Addison's papers on *Paradise Lost* (*Spectator* 339, 29 March 1712):

The Reader cannot but be pleased to find the Depths of Philosophy enlivened with all the Charms of Poetry, and to see so great a Strength of Reason, admidst so beautiful a Redundancy of the Imagination. The Author has shown us that Design in all the Works of Nature, which necessarily leads us to the Knowledge of its first Cause.

In their physico-theological passages then, *Summer* (1727) and Thomson's other *Seasons* to 1730 are unusually distinguished examples of a kind of verse already familiar and very popular in the 1720s and 30s.[3] For Thomson, as for other Newtonians, the natural world revealed to man's scientific understanding was both a system which evidenced God-given order and a body in which God, the 'Essential Presence', was immanent (cf. *Sp.* 556–71, 852–5, *Su.* 32–42, 1784–8, etc.). The poet, like Bacon, Boyle and Newton (*Su.* 1543–63), searches for the great Creator, traces his boundless works and points to Heaven.

Whereas in the 1726 version of *Winter* the reader, Job-like, is brought directly to face a mysterious, all-powerful First Cause, in the *Seasons* of 1727–30 he meets a host of second causes. Nevertheless

[1] Colin Maclaurin, *An Account of Sir Isaac Newton's Philosophical Discoveries* (1748), p. 391.

[2] For the generally favourable reception of this poem see Albert Rosenberg, *Sir Richard Blackmore* (Lincoln, Nebr., 1953), pp. 100–4.

[3] See W. P. Jones, *The Rhetoric of Science* (1966), especially chap. iv.

Thomson has not thrust 'some Mechanic Cause' into God's place; he is still pursuing the devotional end that prompted *Winter*, but is now bent on arousing rational delight in beauty and order. Science was certainly not out of place in sublime poetry. Dennis, arguing from the example of Milton, had even declared 'That Natural Philosophy is absolutely necessary to a Poet'.[1]

Georgic

The great classical model for the matter and method—though certainly not the theology—of early eighteenth-century scientific poems was, of course, *De rerum natura*. Thomson stands to Newton somewhat as Lucretius stands in relation to Epicurus, so it is not surprising to find on the title-page of *A Poem sacred to the memory of Sir Isaac Newton* (1727) some lines from Lucretius' panegyric to Epicurus which proclaim the poet's divine delight that the natural philosopher has opened every part of nature to him. *The Seasons* echoes *De rerum natura* in passages on science and social evolution and, notably, in accounts of human misery (e.g. *Sp.* 983–1112, *Su.* 1052–91, *Wi.* 311–21); furthermore Thomson seems to be striving in a general way after a Lucretian grandeur and passion; but as the arch-atheist is never mentioned by name he remains, as it were, a shadowy presence in the poem, behind Thomson's acknowledged Roman model, Virgil's *Georgics*.

In his *Preface* to the second edition of *Winter* Thomson refers, in successive sentences, to the Book of Job and to Virgil's 'Devotion to the Works of Nature', and then translates *Georgics* ii. 475–86, a passage in which the poet desires to know nature's secrets, or, failing this, simply to enjoy rural retirement. Virgil's thoughts on nature's secrets and rural retirement elsewhere in the *Georgics* are echoed in *The Seasons*, but Thomson also draws upon Virgil's practical advice on husbandry, his myths, his patriotism, his exotic excursions, his anthropomorphic, mock-heroic accounts of beasts, and much else. Material taken directly from Virgil's *Georgics* or from English georgical poems by John Philips or Gay appears in every one of the Seasons and in every considerably revised version from 1726 to 1744.[2] Thomson's loose linking of

---

[1] *The Grounds of Criticism in Poetry* (1704), p. 53.

[2] There is a good summary of Thomson's borrowings from the *Georgics* in John Chalker, *The English Georgic* (1969), pp. 93–126. See also Dwight L. Durling, *Georgic Tradition in English Poetry* (New York, 1935), chap. iii.

episodes, descriptions, and reflections along the narrative thread of a farmer's year from spring ploughing to winter sports is georgical, though *The Seasons* is not prescriptive quite in Virgil's way. Country lore from Virgil supplies descriptive detail (e.g. *Su.* 1116–25, *Wi.* 118–52) or a text for moralizing (e.g. *Au.* 1172–1207), but more significantly it serves a larger religious-didactic purpose (e.g. the description of animals mating in Spring and the poet's devotional reflection, *Sp.* 849–66).

Thomson's diction is highly latinate and often evocative of the *Georgics*; but it owes as much to *Paradise Lost*, the work which was Thomson's authority for his interchanging of parts of speech, his syntactical inversions, and his use of blank verse.[1] After the criticisms of Dennis and Addison, Milton had become the prime model of a sublime style, but Milton's manner was available to Augustan poets also as a reference point in mock-epic. The lines of Miltonic imitation in the eighteenth century began with the religious verse of Isaac Watts and the parodies of John Philips; and Thomson, for all his sublimity and gravity, belongs to both lines. There is obvious epic-burlesque in such an episode as the comic hunting and drinking of *Autumn* 470–569, but we find a hint of mock epic wherever Miltonic style is applied to creatures far less dignified than Milton's, e.g. when such a Miltonic word as 'diffus'd' is applied to a shepherdess (not Samson), or 'convolv'd' to bees and lambs (not Satan). The constant epical reference of Thomson's diction seems to be intended to throw lustre on the natural world which is God's handiwork, but also, by the contrary effect of mock-epic, to 'place' that natural world. The triumph of Virgil's *Georgics* lies in its perfect blending of the epical and the mundane: Thomson seems to have recognized this and to have sought to achieve a similar blend.[2]

The most noticeable influence of Virgil is, however, in the patriotic rhapsodies which rise expansively out of rural descriptions. For instance, referring to the activity which begins the

---

[1] On the Miltonic features of Thomson's style see R. D. Havens, *The Influence of Milton on English Poetry* (Cambridge, Mass., 1922), pp. 131–7. D. Nichol Smith, in *Some Observations on Eighteenth-Century Poetry* (Toronto, 1937), pp. 61–5, argues that the latinate diction was a consequence of Thomson's education in Scotland. There is a mainly hostile criticism of Thomson's diction in Arthur Sherbo, *English Poetic Diction from Chaucer to Wordsworth* (Michigan State U. P., 1975).

[2] See John Chalker, *The English Georgic* (1969), pp. 19–33, 134–9.

farming year (*Sp.* 32–77), Thomson first shows the oxen, faintly humanized, sharing the ploughman's joy in soft breezes and bird-songs and working in willing partnership with him; the earth too is 'faithful', and man, beast and soil exist in an ideal harmony. Thomson then goes on to elevate the ordinary labours of the field by referring to Virgil and recalling the Romans' respect for agriculture. As the poet's view expands, the plough turns from a thing into a symbol (*Sp.* 36, 58, 67), and the sharp particularity of the ploughman bending over and scraping his ploughshare yields to generalizations about Autumn's treasures and the better blessings of England's export trade. The implication of the whole passage is that the local harmony between the husbandman, his team, and his land is the foundation of the larger harmony of a wide mercantile empire which has cultural links with ancient Rome. A similar point is made in the similarly expansive account of hay-time and sheep-shearing (*Su.* 353–431). In these, as in Thomson's other highly charged descriptions of farming, we recognize Virgil's conception of the rural worker as a demiurge who follows the great Creator's purposes in bringing external nature to fulfilment. Such a conception coexists easily in Thomson's poem with other conceptions of man: as awestruck, Job-like worshipper, as physico-theologian, and as Shaftesburian rhapsodist. Like all English readers of the *Georgics*, Thomson is touched by Virgil's appealing myth[1] of the innocence, felicity, vigour, patriotism, and piety of the husbandman's life, and, like all English imitators of the *Georgics*, he offers his own version of the canonical *O fortunatos* passage (at *Au.* 1235–1373; also, in part, in the *Preface* to *Winter*, see Appendix B below).

Geographical, historical, and narrative

Idealization of rural retirement at the end of *Autumn* might appear inconsistent with another passage also influenced by Virgil, but modelled more closely on Lucretius, at the beginning of *Autumn* where Thomson praises civic and mercantile progress. Taking these passages alongside other historical generalizations in *The Seasons*, some critics[2] have claimed that Thomson's views of

---

[1] For an exhaustive study of the influence of this myth upon English literature down to 1760 see M.-S. Røstvig, *The Happy Man* (2 vols., rev. Oslo, 1962–8). Thomson is the subject of vol. ii, chap. v.

[2] See, e.g., *Background*, chap. 3; and R. D. Havens, 'Primitivism and the Idea of Progress in Thomson', *Studies in Philology* xxix (1932), 41–52.

'primitivism' and 'the idea of progress' are mutually contradictory; but one might argue, in reply, that unqualified exaltation of the primitive would be just as crass as a belief in universal progress. Thomson's reading of history and geography made him familiar with the notion that circumstances of time and place may cause societies to flourish or to decay; this, indeed, is the idea versified in *Liberty*. In the cyclical histories of various human societies it is possible to see a fall from golden-age innocence into iron-age experience (*Sp.* 242–335, *Su.* 850–5, *Au.* 1349–51), or a growth from sullen barbarism into animated civilization (*Su.* 1758–81, *Au.* 43–150, *Wi.* 936–87), or even a regeneration of corrupt civilization by vigorous barbarism (*Wi.* 834–42); some present-day primitive societies are happy and virtuous (*Wi.* 843–86), some are not (*Su.* 860–97).

Historical and geographical excursions embodying Thomson's notions about human progress are nearly all found in *Autumn* and in additions made to *Summer* and *Winter* in 1730 and 1744: this suggests that in the later stages of growth of *The Seasons* the poet became more concerned with public virtue than with the individual soul's devotion. The great stock of history and geography in Thomson's library at the time of his death[1] bears out Murdoch's declaration that the 'amusements of his leisure hours were civil and natural history, voyages and the relations of travellers, the most authentic he could procure,'[2] and such reading appears, for instance, in the catalogues of worthies (*Su.* 1479–1579, *Wi.* 439–554) and the tropical excursion (*Su.* 629–1102), each of which is four times as long as the corresponding first-edition passage from which it grew, and in the arctic excursion and account of Peter the Great (*Wi.* 794–987), which have no first-edition counterpart. Contemporary political affairs appear in the lines on Scottish industry (*Au.* 910–28) and the Jail Committee (*Wi.* 359–88) added in 1730; while compliments to Lyttelton, Pitt, Cobham, Hammond, and Chesterfield (*Sp.* 904–35, *Au.* 1048–81, *Wi.* 555–71, 656–90), added in 1744, even have a party-political edge not felt in addresses to friends and patrons in earlier versions of *The Seasons*. From 1730 more and more of the poem is dictated by that 'sage Historic

---

[1] *Sale Catalogues of Libraries of Eminent Persons*, ed. A. N. L. Munby, i (1971), 45–66.
[2] *Life* prefixed to Thomson's *Works* (1762), vol. i, p. xviii. For Thomson's efforts to borrow, then buy, Hakluyt's *Voyages*, see *Letters*, p. 181.

Muse' who tells why empires grew or fell and what makes present nations smile or pine (*Wi.* 587–93). Thomson's main career was now the writing of heroic tragedies, and it is not surprising that in his revisions of *The Seasons* he should be inclined to look on the whole earth as a 'moral Scene'.

In a different and narrower sense the notion of a moral scene could be attached to those little human dramas in Thomson's interpolated stories. The earliest of these, Celadon and Amelia (*Su.* 1169–222), which first appeared in 1727, complements, with its demonstration of God's power and of man's incomprehension of God's purposes, the Job-like devotion of *Winter* 1726. The story of Palemon and Lavinia (*Au.* 177–310) celebrates man's benevolence as it acts in a simpler, more comfortable, Shaftesburian moral world. In its first version, 1730, the salacious Damon and Musidora story (*Su.* 1269–1370) tells how a Stoic is humanized by the sight of woman's beauty, but this motive is discarded in 1744, so that the tale remains as the piece of playful rococo decoration which many later graphic artists recognized it to be.[1] Wordsworth testified that this was one of the most-read passages of *The Seasons*, but it is hardly that great and serious subject promised in the Preface to *Winter*. After he had spent nearly twenty years enlarging and revising his poem Thomson's grasp of his earliest purpose was inevitably, and perhaps deliberately, fainter.

Descriptive

One of Thomson's patrons, gathering subscriptions for *The Seasons* 1730, explained that the short stories were to the whole poem what figures were in a landscape painting, for they served to 'heighten and recommend' the 'various scenes of the year with all its contrasts of landskip' which made up the 'chief parts' of the composition.[2] Thomson's own earliest reference to his work on *Winter* described it as 'painting', and acknowledged that the design was suggested by 'some masterly strokes' in a poem by a friend of his youth, Robert Riccaltoun.[3] The list of 'Contents'

---

[1] There is a good discussion of illustrations to *The Seasons* in Ralph Cohen, *The Art of Discrimination* (1964), chap. 5.   [2] *Letters*, p. 62.

[3] *Letters*, pp. 16–17. Riccaltoun's poem has never been satisfactorily identified, though many later students have accepted Peter Cunningham's claim (*Gentleman's Magazine* xxxix, NS (1853), 368–9) that it is the brief heroic-couplet piece entitled *A Winter's Day*, printed over Mallet's name in Savage's *Miscellany*, i.e. *Miscellaneous Poems and Translations* (1726), pp. 309–12, then reprinted as

added by Thomson to *Spring* in 1729 implies, in such items as 'A Garden Flower-Piece' or 'A Landskip of the Shepherd tending his Flock', that poetic description is analogous to painting; while in the text of, or in the prose 'Arguments' to all four Seasons he uses the term 'Landskip' from time to time, though less frequently than its non-painterly equivalents, 'Prospect' and 'View'. It has been customary among Thomson's critics, from Joseph Warton downwards, to liken his verbal pictures to the work of specific painters, so that Claude Lorrain, Nicolas Poussin, Salvator Rosa, Jacopo Bassano. Guido Reni, Brill, and Elsheimer have all been drawn upon for parallels. The first three of these are, of course, the subject of a famous allusion in *The Castle of Indolence* (I. xxxviii) but their landscapes influenced *The Seasons* very little. Thomson's own quite considerable collection of prints and drawings, formed probably in the 1730s, consists almost wholly of historical, mythical, and religious subjects. The indications in *Liberty* and *The Seasons* are that Thomson's imagination was less deeply stirred by painting (landscape or otherwise) than by statuary—that 'living' marble which has its counterpart in strangely frozen or petrified or immobile human beings (*Su.* 1217–22, 1344–9, *Wi.* 930–5).[1]

Pope held that descriptive poetry is 'as absurd as a feast made up of sauces',[2] and Swift was not over-fond of *The Seasons* 'because they are all Descriptions, and nothing is doing';[3] but Thomas Blackwell, praising Thomson's poem in 1735, claimed that exended description of landscape 'nobly executed' opened the most promising possibilities for serious poetry in a modern age when epic could no longer be successfully attempted;[4] and soon it was generally agreed that *The Seasons* had proved the value of that relatively new species of composition—descriptive poetry. Critics from Joseph Warton to William Wordsworth[5] and on through the

---

'Written by a *Scotch* Clergyman. Corrected by an eminent Hand' in *Gentleman's Magazine* x (1740), 256.

[1] The best modern accounts of Thomson and the visual arts are A. D. McKillop, *The Background of Thomson's Liberty* (Houston, 1951), chap. 5; and Jean Hagstrum, *The Sister Arts* (Chicago, 1958), chap. ix. Hagstrum's arguments have been developed in Jeffry B. Spencer, *Heroic Nature* (Evanston, 1973), chap. vi. [2] Joseph Warton, *Essay on Pope* [i] (1756), p. 50.

[3] Letter to Wogan, 2 August 1732, in *Correspondence of Swift*, ed. H. Williams (1965), iv. 53.

[4] *An Enquiry into the Life and Writings of Homer* (1735), p. 35.

[5] Joseph Warton, *Essay on Pope* [i] (1756), 41–51; William Wordsworth,

nineteenth century agreed that Thomson's distinctive quality lay in his close observation and in the novelty, particularity and exactness of his paintings from external nature. So Hazlitt found Thomson 'the best of our descriptive poets' and 'perhaps the most popular of all our poets, treating of a subject that all can understand and in a way that is interesting to all alike, to the ignorant or the refined, because he gives back the impression which the things themselves make upon us in nature.'[1]

This said, one must remember that Thomson's descriptions of external nature are not always or wholly naturalistic. What we are called upon to 'see' at the beginning of each Season, and what William Kent's engravings for the 1730 quarto faithfully depict, is a mythological personification of the appropriate natural forces making its regal progress through the natural scene. Many of Thomson's most admired descriptions (e.g. *Su.* 46–55, 81–90, 1647–54, *Au.* 1083–1102) convey an effect of vitality not because the poet enumerates particulars, as if objects in a painting were being itemized, nor merely because he is describing natural objects in movement, but because he ascribes human activity to personifications, such as Morn, Day, Evening, Night, which are blended so fully with the natural scene that we are only half-aware of them as allegorical beings at all. Admittedly, for the most part Thomson's personifications no longer impress readers as vividly as they did in the eighteenth century.[2] Thus in a brief allusion to 'the Power of Cultivation' (*Su.* 1435–7) a modern reader might find only vague generalization, but a critic of the 1750s (possibly Goldsmith) observed:

We cannot conceive a more beautiful image than that of the Genius of Agriculture, distinguished by the implements of his art, imbrowned with labour, glowing with health, crowned with a garland of foliage, flowers, and fruit, lying stretched at his ease on the brow of a gently swelling hill, and contemplating with pleasure the happy effects of his own industry.

Essay Supplementary to the Preface (1815) in *Prose Works*, ed. W. J. B. Owen and J. W. Smyser (Oxford, 1974), iii. 72–5.

[1] *Complete Works*, ed. P. P. Howe (1930), v. 87–8.

[2] For the high value placed on personification by eighteenth-century critics and for modern assessments see: B. H. Bronson, 'Personification Reconsidered', *E.L.H.* xiv (1947), 163–7; E. R. Wasserman, 'The Inherent Values of Eighteenth-century Personification', *PMLA* lxv (1950), 435–63; C. F. Chapin, *Personification in Eighteenth-century English Poetry* (New York, 1954).

On this comment Donald Davie has rightly remarked that the writer 'probably contributes nothing that was not in Thomson's intention. For Thomson could count on finding in his readers a ready allegorical imagination, such as seems lost to us today. The loss is certainly ours.'[1]

Subjective

A landscape animated by personified abstractions is only part of what Thomson sees with reason's and with fancy's eye (*Su.* 1745). The reader is constantly being called upon to 'see' objects and events, physical and metaphysical, which are invisible to the corporeal eye, whether these be osmosis (*Sp.* 495–6) or the Second Coming (*Wi.* 1041–9), mountain-strata (*Au.* 779–810) or the smiling God (*Sp.* 859–62): when describing nature Thomson's 'eye' ranges freely over a Lockeian 'Kingdom' (or hierarchy) of ideas 'from plain Perception' up to the forms of Fancy, to abstract notions formed by reasoning and to higher religious intimations (cf. *Su.* 1788–98). In a letter of 1730 he wrote: 'Travelling has been long my fondest wish for the very purpose you recommend: the storing one's Imagination with Ideas of all-beautiful, all-great, and all-perfect Nature. These are the true materia poetica, the light and colours with which Fancy kindles up her whole creation, paints a sentiment, and even embodies an abstracted thought.'[2] He thinks of light and colours as the stores of his imagination because, in Addison's interpretation of Locke, light and colours are ideas produced in the perceiver's mind and not qualities that have any existence in matter.[3] Natural description in *The Seasons* is a frequent display of 'the fair Power / Of Light to kindle and create' (*Au.* 1143–4), and, in a very immediate sense, of what Coleridge would call 'the modifying colours of imagination'.[4]

We can watch fancy (or imagination, which is the same thing for Thomson) handling the true materia poetica in, for instance, the colourful 'Garden Flower-Piece' (*Sp.* 528–55) where the poet describes no specific garden but a process of Spring-and-Summer flowering (cf. 545–6), and what the reader is expected to sense is an informing 'Breath of Nature'. As the following lines (556–71)

---

[1] Donald Davie, *Purity of Diction in English Verse* (1952), p. 40.
[2] *Letters*, pp. 73–4.
[3] *Spectator*, 413, referring to Locke's *Essay Concerning Human Understanding*, Book II, chap. viii.
[4] *Biographia Literaria*, opening of chap. xiv.

indicate, this 'Breath' is at once the particular, infinitely varied scents, colours and 'Delicacies' produced as ideas in the poet's mind by such physical processes in external nature as 'Fermentation', and the single, unifying, 'Essential Presence' (literally the spirit) that orders this process and generates all being, including that of the poet. In recreating an experience in which sense-impressions are related to feeling and scientific understanding, which in turn are both related to religious belief, Thomson does, indeed, paint a sentiment and embody abstract thought. He is concerned less with natural objects 'themselves' than with the emotional, intellectual and devotional experience of a consciousness responding to those objects. So much is obvious at those points where Thomson explicitly refers to the thousands of 'Images' which throng 'Imagination's vivid Eye' (conceived of as passive, *Sp.* 459) or 'the Mind's creative Eye' (conceived of as active, *Au.* 1016) at times when sights and sounds of external nature have aroused him to heightened consciousness (*Sp.* 443–66, *Au.* 950–1036); and so much is obvious too on those less interesting occasions when he uses so conventional a term of imaginative projection as 'romantic' (*Sp.* 1027–8, *Su.* 459, *Au.* 880), but this distinction is also, I think, implicit in his natural descriptions generally.

Johnson wrote of Thomson: 'he thinks always as a man of genius; he looks round on Nature and on Life, with the eye which Nature bestows only on a poet; the eye that distinguishes, in everything presented to its view, whatever there is on which imagination can delight to be detained.'[1] Wordsworth, too, praised Thomson's 'genius as an imaginative poet', but, by adding that 'much of' *The Seasons* 'is written from himself, and nobly from himself', and citing *Summer* 977–9 as a 'beautiful instance of the modifying and *investive* power of the imagination',[2] he indicates that his concept of imagination is not Johnson's. In Thomson the 'creative' power of the 'Mind's eye' is related by way of Addison to Locke's psychology; and whatever notions Thomson had concerning the relationship between mind and external nature obviously do not anticipate those of Coleridge. Nevertheless *The Seasons* is remarkably self-conscious: 'The theme is not precisely

[1] 'Thomson' in *Lives of the Poets* (1781), iv. 272.
[2] *Prose Works*, ed. W. J. B. Owen and J. W. Smyser (Oxford, 1974), iii. 72, 74, 44.

working through the forces of Nature';[1] but there is a second actor in the person of a self-dramatized poet-philosopher who mediates between the reader and the great system of Nature. So, particular descriptions are characteristically organized in the form of a movement of Thomson's mind. The poet is his own subject. Standing alone, he finds in the shapes and sounds of unconscious external nature the self-conscious life of his own thought and feeling. Thomson may be far from anticipating Wordsworth's insight that movement of mind could be a principle of philosophic and artistic order, and even farther from seeing the growth of mind as his vital thread, but:

He foreshadows Wordsworth in giving himself up to a scene, accepting its mysterious power over him, describing with the exactness of awed attention the least movement he sees. All his best landscapes involve tension and movement. It may be the tension of anticipation, as all nature waits for the descent of rain or the breaking of a storm. It may be the movement into the deep recesses of shade and quiet. It may be the bursting force of a descending stream, roaring through a broken channel until it spreads over the valley below. What do these tensions and movements signify? It is hard to give them any simple moral import, or even a determinate psychological one. They accommodate meanings or feelings we bring to them. Like an abstract form—musical or pictorial— they articulate patterns of tension that underlie or are embedded in much of our experience.[2]

The sublimity of 'the varied God' may now excite readers as little as high-minded observations on 'the moral Scene' do, but the abiding success of *The Seasons* lies in the vigour and scale of Thomson's re-creation of his discovery that landscape can release and realize feelings, that landscape is the true *materia poetica*.

2. COMPOSITION AND PUBLICATION

WINTER 1726 (Wi.26f, Wi.26o)

When James Thomson landed in London in February 1725 it was with the professed intention of preparing himself for the Presbyterian ministry by completing studies begun in Edinburgh over nine years earlier. He wrote in April: 'succeed or not I firmly resolve to pursue divinity as the only thing now I am fitt for. now

[1] G. H. Hartman, *Beyond Formalism* (New Haven, 1970), p. 204.
[2] Martin Price, *To the Palace of Wisdom* (New York, 1964), p. 357.

science, philosophy, religion, nature, but a choice soul dwelling
on these high themes.'¹ The models for Thomson's manner of
proceeding are perhaps Milton's *L'Allegro* and *Il Penseroso*, which
were praised in the eighteenth century as 'Exquisite Pictures'² and
'the two first descriptive poems in the English language',³ and were
hailed by Johnson as 'two noble efforts of imagination' the design
of which is to show 'how, among the successive variety of ap-
pearances, every disposition of mind takes hold on those by which
it may be gratified.'⁴ There are echoes of Milton's companion-
poems in all four Seasons, particularly of *Il Penseroso* in *Winter*
(which was begun shortly after Thomson had completed a more
obvious imitation of Milton's poem in his octosyllabic-couplet
*Hymn to Solitude*⁵), but specific echoes are less significant than the
influence of Milton's general exploration of poetic consciousness
and his use of landscape description to evoke and define states of
mind.

Thomson's more obvious Miltonic debts are to the descriptive
and rhapsodic parts of *Paradise Lost*. A great deal of Raphael's
description of the creation in Book vii found its way into *The
Seasons* with the science modernized; the morning hymn (*PL* v.
153–208) could almost be read as a programme for Thomson's
poem; while the whole notion of a long, sublime devotional poem,
'the more / To magnify his works, the more we know' (*PL* vii.
96–7), is patently Miltonic. Raphael's conception of the relation-
ship between mind, matter and God, as outlined in *PL* v. 469–88
(and, significantly, placed at the head of Coleridge's chapter 'On
the imagination, or esemplastic power' in *Biographia Literaria*)
provides the intellectual framework for Thomson's procedure in
the Spring flower-piece, discussed above, and in many other of his
most effective nature-descriptions. Thomson obviously has no
epical plot or properly epical characters, for the ancient heroes he
mentions are not characters in the action of his poem. '*The Seasons*
is a visionary history without a hero—the hero being Providence

¹ *Background*, p. 26.
² Jonathan Richardson, *Life* of Milton (1734), in *The Early Lives of Milton*,
ed. Helen Darbishire (1932), p. 212.
³ Thomas Warton, in *Poems by John Milton* (2nd edn., 1791), p. 96; see also
Joseph Warton, *Essay on Pope*, [i] (1756), p. 35.
⁴ 'Milton' in *Lives of the Poets* (1781), i. 230, 227.
⁵ In a letter of 10 July 1725, see *Letters*, pp. 10–11. Thomson's *Hymn to
Solitude* was first printed in Ralph's *Miscellany* (1729) and achieved wide
circulation in vol. iii of Dodsley's *Collection of Poems* (1748).

if I can't accomplish the design on which I came up I think, I had best make interest and pass my tryalls here so that if I be oblidg'd soon to return to Scotland again I may not return no better than I came away.'[1] It is implied that the 'design' on which he came up to London was not divinity; so perhaps his intention was to support himself by poetry, since some of the devotional verse he had written in Edinburgh had been noticed in London by such influential critics as William Benson, who had promised encouragement should the young Scotsman come south,[2] and Aaron Hill, who had printed and praised Thomson's blank-verse 'The Works and Wonders of Almightly Power' in the *Plain Dealer* of 28 August 1724.

As late as July 1725 Thomson was reiterating his intention 'to consumate my original Study of Divinity'. At this time he was at East Barnet, supporting himself by the 'low task' of tutoring in the family of a Scottish nobleman, Charles Hamilton, Lord Binning; but in October he gave up his post and went down to stay with the friend of his Edinburgh days, David Mallet, who was then tutor in the Duke of Montrose's household at Shawford near Winchester.[3] There, according to Spence, 'he wrote single winter pieces; they at last thought it might make a poem'.[4] When, in a letter of 10 July, Thomson tells Mallet 'You may take what liberties you please with my poem', it is possible that he may be referring to one of these single winter pieces; but the earliest certain reference to *Winter* occurs in a letter to another friend, William Cranstoun, at the end of September:

Nature delights me in every form, I am just now painting her in her most lugubrious dress; for my own amusement, describing winter as it presents it self. after my first proposal of the subject,

> I sing of winter and his gelid reign;
> Nor let a riming insect of the spring
> Deem it a barren theme. to me tis full
> Of manly charms; to me, who court the shade
> Whom the gay seasons suit not, and who shun
> The glare of summer. Welcom! kindred Glooms
> Drear awfull wintry horrors, welcome all, & c.

[1] *Letters*, p. 7.
[2] Robert Shiels, 'Thomson', in Theophilus Cibber, *The Lives of the Poets* (1753), v. 194.
[3] *Letters*, pp. 12, 20.
[4] Joseph Spence, *Observations*, ed. J. M. Osborn (Oxford, 1966), i, 370.

After this introduction, I say, which insists for a few lines further
I prosecute the purport of the following ones

> Nor can I, o departing Summer! choose
> But consecrate one pitying line to you;
> Sing your last temper'd days, and sunny calms,
> That chear the spirits, and serene the soul.

Then terrible floods, and high winds, that usually happen about this
time of year, and have already happen'd here (I wish you have not felt
them too dreadfully) the first produced the enclosed lines, the last are
not completed.

Manuscript of lines about terrible floods and high winds has not
survived, but the reference is probably to forerunners of 133–85 of
the first edition (referred to as *Wi.26f* in the present edition and
reprinted in full in Appendix A). Lines on melancholy (cf. 33–79
in Appendix A) have some parallels elsewhere in the letter when
Thomson apostrophizes Cranstoun:

Now, I imagine you seized with a fine romantic kind of a melancholy, on
the fading of the Year. Now I figure you wandering philosophical, and
pensive, amidst the brown, wither'd groves: while the leaves rustle
under your feet. the sun gives a farewell parting gleam and the birds

> Stir the faint note, and but attempt to sing.

then again, when the heavns wear a more gloomy aspect, the winds
whistle and the waters spout, I see you in the well known Cleugh,
beneath the solemn Arch of tall, thick embowring trees, listning to the
amusing lull of the many steep, moss grown Cascades; while deep,
divine Contemplation, the genius of the place, prompts each swelling
awfull thought.[1]

It is not known when Thomson's poem was ready for the printer,
but Benjamin Victor, writing long after the event, recalled that
Mallet and he 'walked one November day to all the Booksellers in
the Strand, and Fleet-street, to sell the copy'.[2] Eventually John
Millan, a Scotsman who had recently set up business near the
Haymarket, accepted it and, according to Victor, gave three pounds
for the copy; but if this was so he had bought only very limited
rights, in view of the fact that Thomson was able to assign copy-
right of a revised *Winter* in 1729.

Publication of *Winter* was advertised in the *Daily Post* on 8
April 1726; Aaron Hill had seen a presentation copy before 2 April;[3]

---

[1] *Letters*, pp. 16–17.
[2] Benjamin Victor, *Original Letters, Dramatic Pieces, and Poems* (1776), iii.
27.
[3] *Letters*, pp. 22–4.

and the work was entered in the Stationers' Register to Millan on 29 April. Title-page and advertisements read 'printed for J. Millan and sold by J[ames] Roberts and N[icholas] Blandford', and state that the author is 'James Thomson, A.M.'; but as he had never taken his degree he was not entitled to use these letters after his name, and never did in subsequent editions of his poems. The format is folio, which was not unusual at that time for a pamplet containing a single poem of no great length: 'to put it more practically', as David Foxon writes of Pope's *Windsor Forest*, 'a format which would justify a price sufficient to make a profit—one shilling for . . . five sheets.'[1] On the evidence of ornaments it appears that the printer was Archibald Campbell.[2] Within three months there was a Dublin reprint in octavo by Thomas Hume for William Smith, probably unauthorized.

A fulsome prose Dedication of *Winter* to Sir Spencer Compton, Speaker of the House of Commons, was written by Mallet; but the dedicatee's permission had not been obtained and he did not make the accustomed recognition as quickly as Thomson and his friends had hoped, so it was hastily determined that ungrateful patrons should be satirized in commendatory poems which Hill and Mallet were writing to preface the forthcoming enlarged, revised, second edition of Thomson's poem. Thomson saw Hill's verses before 24 May and Mallet's on 3 June;[3] Johnson states that Hill's verses were printed in a newspaper,[4] but I have been unable to trace such a printing. A puff[5] contributed to the *London Journal* of 4 June in praise of *Winter* dwelt upon the question of patronage, named Compton, and delicately alluded to 'Want of Encouragement'; but the patron had already come alive to his duty, had asked the poet to wait upon him, and on that same morning of 4 June had given him twenty guineas. Thomson did not wish to snub the conspirators by now refusing to print what they had written, so he tried tactfully to persuade them to rewrite their verses. On 13 June the second edition of *Winter* was in the press, but as late as 17 June—on which day it was advertised in the *Daily*

---

[1] See D. F. Foxon's unpublished Lyell Lectures, 'Pope and the early Eighteenth-century book trade', the typescript of which is available for consultation in the British Library, the Bodleian, the William Andrews Clark Library in Los Angeles, and the Beinecke Library at Yale University.

[2] *Letters*, p. 37.   [3] *Letters*, pp. 28, 32.

[4] 'Thomson' in *Lives of the Poets* (1781), iv, 255.

[5] It is reprinted in *Background*, pp. 175–7.

Post as to be published 'Next Week'—Thomson was still waiting for the revised commendatory poems. In the event Mallet's verses were printed unaltered, while Hill's, revised, are no less severe then Mallet's in their satire upon patrons. A third, quite innocuous, commendatory poem is by 'Mira', who has been identified as Mrs Martha Fowke Sansom.[1]

On 23 June the second edition of *Winter* (referred to as *26o* in the present edition) was advertised again for publication 'Next Week' (*Whitehall Evening-Post*), but not until 16 July was it announced (in the *London Journal*) as published 'This Day'. The publisher was Millan again; the printer was Nicholas Blandford, who had been one of the retailers of the first edition and is named in advertisements, alongside James Roberts, J. Jackson, A. Bettesworth, and W. Meadows, as retailer of this edition too. The price was one shilling, the same as for the first edition, but the format is octavo in fours, and the irregular collation—π^1 A–B^4 C^2 D–G^4 H^1 (where π^1 is the title and H^1 an advertisement leaf conjugate with it and wrapped round the rest of the gatherings, while A–B^4 C^2 contain dedication, Thomson's new, long preface and the commendatory poems)—might indicate that the text of the poem on D–G^4 was set up before the preliminaries, and that the length of the preliminaries was overestimated, thus curtailing C. This could have come about because it was thought that revisions to Hill's and Mallet's introductory poems might increase their length, or more probably because space was being left for other commendatory poems. John Dyer was asked to contribute one, and his refusal was not communicated to Thomson until 13 June; while McKillop conjectures that Joseph Mitchell's 'To Mr. Thomson, the Author of Winter'[2] may once have been intended for inclusion. Perhaps the title-page and advertisements were printed on the same half-sheet as C and subsequently divided.

During the month or more when this edition of *Winter* was in the press it was subjected to some further revision. Press-correction affected the text of the poem significantly only on the inner forme of half-sheet F, where at line 308 (*OET Wi.* 426), half the surviving recorded copies have 'keen', following the first edition, and half have 'Ice', which is the reading of all editions after 1726; but in the

---

[1] See an anonymous review in the *Athenaeum*, 16 July 1859, p. 78, and *Letters*, p. 35. Correspondence about Hill's and Mallet's verses is in *Letters*, pp. 23–9. The poems of all three are reprinted in Appendix B below.   [2] *Letters*, p. 53.

preliminaries there was more extensive correction. On the two formes of half-sheet A are a dozen small variants of spelling and punctuation, a number large enough to suggest that printing of this half-sheet had perhaps begun before it had been properly proof-read. Half-sheet B survives in four states. In the first state a paragraph on p. 18 (B3ᵛ) reads:

I cannot put an end to this *Preface*, without taking the Freedom to pay my most sincere, and grateful, Acknowledgements to all those *Gentlemen* who have given my first Performance so favourable Reception; particularly, that *honourable Person*, under whose auspicious Name I have met with an Encouragement more answerable to his Generosity, than my Merit.

In the second state this paragraph is shortened, so that the author merely takes 'the Freedom to offer my most sincere, and grateful, Acknowledgement to all those *Gentlemen* who have given my first Performance so favourable Reception'. As a result of this curtailment three lines are transferred in a block from the top of p. 19 to the foot of p. 18 and the catchword of p. 18 changed; then all the following lines on p. 19, including the catchword, are closed up to the headline. Copies of the first state have on p. 15 (B2ʳ) the misprint 'how gay' where the second state is corrected to 'How gay'. Pages 15 and 18 would have been side by side on the forme, so that this misprint could have been easily detected and corrected. The third state is identical with the second except for the addition of the word 'a' before 'Reception', and the fourth is identical with the third except in that the catchword on p. 19 has been moved to the foot of the page. Though it might be conjectured that the reference to Compton's 'Auspicious Name' was inserted after payment of twenty guineas, the great rarity of this variant and the logical sequence of what I have described as the second, third, and fourth states argue that the chronological order of the four states is the one which I have just outlined; and therefore that the change at press was made in order to delete the compliment to the patron, in which case we might infer that the compliment had been ironic.

These changes are apparently unconnected with a further, and probably premeditated press correction on the title-page, where over half the surviving recorded copies read 'third' or 'fourth' edition, rather than 'second'. Typographical similarity of these title-pages (in broken letters, spacing etc.) and the fact that in all three so-called editions they are found to be conjugate with an

advertisement leaf of the same impression indicate that we have
press-variant titles, not cancels, and that Millan's intention seems
to have been to puff the book by creating three 'editions' from a
single impression. Similar examples of copies from the same press-
run with title-pages emended in the course of printing are the
third and forth editions of Pope's *Essay on Criticism*, the seventh
and eighth editions of Addison's *Cato*, and the second to fifth
editions of Thomson's *Poem to Newton*.[1] In the case of *Winter*
it is evident that sheets of various states were gathered indifferently
together to constitute the so-called editions: for 'keen' occurs in
copies of all three editions and so does 'Ice'; the corrected and the
uncorrected states of Sheet A may similarly be found in all three
editions; and the rare state of sheet B with its extra three lines is
found in one copy with a 'fourth edition' title as well as in two
with a 'second edition' title. These last two[2] happen to be the only
traced copies from any of the three editions with a title-page
printed in black only instead of the normal black and red, and may
therefore be proof-copies, even though, since they both have 'Ice'
on half-sheet F and a corrected outer forme of half-sheet A, they
perhaps do not show the earliest state of every sheet.

Although printed in the same press-run as the second edition,
the third and fourth editions appear to have been issued succes-
sively at decent and plausible intervals. The second edition, as
we have seen, was published on 16 July, 1726, but the third was
not advertised until September, when it was announced over the
names of Millan, Roberts, Meadows and Thomas Astley. Adver-
tisements for the third edition continued from the beginning of
January 1727 to 17 February; then on 23 February a fourth
edition was advertised by the same four booksellers (all these
notices being linked to announcements about *Summer*, which was
published on 16 February). The fourth edition was again adver-
tised alongside *Summer* on the title-page of the *Poem to Newton*,
published in May 1727.

SUMMER, 1727 (*Su.27*)

On 28 May 1726 Thomson had taken up residence in William
Watts's Academy, Little Tower Street, where he was to be private
tutor to one of the young gentlemen. He had probably already

---

[1] D. F. Foxon's unpublished Lyell lectures, 'Pope and the Early Eighteenth-
century Book Trade', fols. 31–2.   [2] One is at Harvard, one at Yale.

begun work on *Summer*, for in a letter of 13 June he referred to
Mallet's reception of the opening lines: 'If my Beginning of
Summer please you, I am sure it is Good. I have writ more which
I'll send you in due Time.'[1] In a letter accompanying the newly
published second edition of *Winter* Thomson transcribed a draft
of what would become lines 393–402 of the first edition of *Summer*:[2]
then in a series of letters in August he discussed his own new poem
and Mallet's work in hand, *The Excursion*. A draft of lines 183–306
probably accompanied his letter of 2 August: 'In the enclosed
Sheets of Summer, I raise the Sun to nine, or ten, o-clock; touch
lightly on his withering of Flowers: give a Groupe of rural
Images: make an Excursion into the Insect Kingdom; and con-
clude with some suitable Reflections—I have written a good Deal
more'. In the same letter he thanked Mallet for the 'Hints of the
Saphire, Emerauld, Ruby, &c', which would be worked up into
lines 132–44, and proposed some sublime scenes and amazing
prospects for inclusion in *The Excursion*.[3] From the next letter
on 11 August it appears that Mallet had questioned the original
plan 'to contract the Season into a Day',[4] but Thomson declares it
is now too late to change it because 'I am so far advanced, having
writ three Parts of Four.' He goes on:

We intirely agree from the Noon-Day Retreat to the Evening. I have
already writen of Shade, and Gloom, and Woodland Spirits, &c exactly
as You hint more than a Week ago. Verdure, and Flowers, belong to the
Spring; and Fruits to the Autumn; and therefore not to be anticipated.
I design toward the End of my Poem to take one short Glance of Corn-
Fields ripe for the Sickle, as the Limit of my Performance I thank you
heartily for your Hint about personizing of Inspiration. It strikes me.—
Next Post I will send you a Sheet, or two more.

In the printed text of the first edition personized Inspiration is
mentioned at line 15, and passages on the Noon-Day Retreat,
Shade, Gloom, and Woodland Spirits are found between lines 345
and 450. Sending drafts to Mallet towards the end of August,
Thomson wrote:

They contain a Panegyric on Brittain, which may perhaps contribute to
make my Poem popular. The English People are not a little vain of Them-
selves, and their Country. Brittania too includes our native Country,

---

[1] *Letters*, p. 36.
[2] The first edition is referred to as *Su.27* in the present edition and is
reprinted in full in Appendix A. [3] *Letters*, p. 40. [4] *Letters*, p. 45.

Scotland. After this I make an Excursion into Africa, which I inter-sperse, and conclude with some Reflections—What remains of My Poem is a Description of Thunder, and the Evening. Thunder I have writ, and am just now agreeably engag'd with the Evening. The Beginning of the Sheets I have sent You, at this time, connects with the Cataract.[1]

The description of the cataract begins at line 456 of the printed text, the description of thunder at 736, and the description of evening at 939. Hitherto Thomson's poetry on the Seasons had for the most part described native landscapes and had taken a devotional cast, but new concerns have become apparent with the lengthy panegyric on Britain (lines 498–609) and the longer excursion into Africa (610–735). The poem grows expansive in more senses than one, and with this growth Mallet's objections to the framework of the single summer's day appear more and more justifiable. Though Thomson tells Mallet he has already written of thunder he makes no specific mention of Celadon and Amelia (lines 827–76), so perhaps this, the first of the interpolated stories, was an afterthought designed to supply human drama and narrative interest hitherto lacking. Whatever Thomson's original intention, the poem he completed in the summer and autumn of 1726 was nearly three times as long as the first edition of *Winter*, and of a more mixed kind.

Thomson had intended to dedicate *Summer* to his former employer Lord Binning, but (Johnson writes) 'the same kindness which had first disposed Lord Binning to encourage him, deter-mined him to refuse the dedication, which was by his advice addressed to Mr Doddington; a man who had more power to advance the reputation and fortune of a poet.'[2] Spence quotes Mallet as his authority for saying that after the publication of *Winter* Dodington 'gave his services to [Thomson] by Dr. Young and desired to see him. That was thought hint enough for [a] dedication to him, and that was his first entrance to that acquain-tance.'[3] George Bubb Dodington, who was becoming a Maecenas to the Aaron Hill coterie at this time, promised and proved to be a more appreciative patron than Sir Spencer Compton.

The *London Journal* for 24 December 1726 carried the announce-ment from Millan that *Summer* was 'In the Press', and further advertisements in several newspapers indicate that the poem was

[1] *Letters*, p. 48.   [2] 'Thomson' in *Lives of the Poets* (1781), iv. 257.
[3] Joseph Spence, *Observations*, ed. J. M. Osborn (Oxford, 1966), i, 370.

published on 16 February 1727 and sold (at 1s. 6d.) by Millan, Roberts, Meadows, and Thomas Astley.[1] It was entered to Millan in the Stationers' Register on 20 February. The evidence of ornaments indicates that *Summer* was printed by Blandford. It is not a folio like the first edition of *Winter* but an 88-page octavo in fours:[2] the octavo format adopted in the second edition of *Winter* was to be used for all subsequent issues of single Seasons, so that sets of all four could be bound together. As usual, an unauthorized edition appeared in Dublin, in this case printed by S. Powell for Richard Norris, 1727.

SPRING and *WINTER*, 1728 (*Sp.28*, *Wi.28*)

Composition of the next of the Seasons was probably delayed by work on the *Poem sacred to the memory of Sir Isaac Newton*,[3] published at the beginning of May 1727; but in the summer of that year Thomson was writing *Spring* at Marlborough Castle where he was the guest of the Countess of Hertford, to whom he had been recommended by that pious and once famous poetess Mrs Elizabeth Rowe. There is no truth in the story told to Johnson, probably by Savage, that Thomson's carousing with the Earl of Hertford so offended the Countess that she never invited him to her house again.[4] Later in the year he was staying at Eastbury, Dodington's house in Dorset, and it may have been there that Edward Young saw the manuscript of *Spring* which he mentions in a letter to Thomas Tickell on 17 November.[5]

Back in London, Thomson wrote on 18 January 1728 to Sir John Clerk, a patron of his early years in Scotland: 'I am now almost done with the four Seasons; and by the Advice and Encourage-ment of several Friends have published Proposals for printing them by Subscription.'[6] These *Proposals*, which were published in various newspapers in January and also printed on a single leaf

[1] Copies at Yale and the University of Illinois have four pages of Astley's advertisements bound in.
[2] Half-sheet A is found in two states with unimportant variants affecting the layout of title-page and errata. T. R. Francis, *Book Collector* v (1956), 383, claims that these variants represent two distinct issues; but see Foxon, p. 798.
[3] Newton died on 20 March 1727.
[4] Johnson, *Lives of the Poets* (1781), iv, 258; see H. S. Hughes, 'Thomson and the Countess of Hertford', *Modern Philology* xxv (1928), 439–68, and xxviii (1931), 468–70.
[5] *Correspondence of Edward Young*, ed. E. C. Pettit (Oxford), p. 58.
[6] *Letters*, p. 59.

bound into *Spring* (1728), announce that the work, 'which is in great Forwardness, and will be published with all possible speed', will contain 'The Four Seasons, with a Hymn on their Succession. To which will be added a Poem sacred to the Memory of Sir Isaac Newton. And an Essay on Descriptive Poetry will be prefixed to the whole . . . N.B. The Pieces already published, viz. Winter, Summer, and a Poem on the Death of Sir Isaac Newton, will be corrected and enlarged in several places.' The entire price of the book in sheets—one guinea—was to be paid at the time of subscribing, and subscriptions would be taken in Edinburgh by the poet-bookseller Allan Ramsay and in London by the author and by three Scots booksellers—George Strahan, John Millan, and Andrew Millar. This is the earliest evidence of Thomson's association with Millar, who had only recently come south.

When the *Proposals* were reprinted in the *Whitehall Evening-Post* of 19 March 1728 (with Ramsay's name omitted and the London bookseller John Walthoe's added) they were prefaced by an article commending public taste in so readily approving of Thomson's poetry despite the disadvantage that it was the work of 'an Author altogether unknown to the World'. In similar phrases, in May, the *Present State of the Republick of Letters*, edited by Andrew Reid, took up the praise of Thomson. Both articles contained quotations from the forthcoming *Spring*, probably from manuscript or uncorrected proof, since the first edition of that poem published a few weeks later has substantive variants (including the addition and deletion of lines) from passages quoted in the journals. Possibly these puffs had some connection also with the issue of a fifth edition of *Winter* and a second edition of *Summer* which were both advertised alongside *A Poem sacred to the memory of Sir Isaac Newton*, fourth edition, in newspapers of 25 and 28 March.[1] *Summer* was merely a reissue of the first-edition sheets with a cancel title proclaiming the work as the 'second edition, 1728', and giving Millan's new address,[2] but *Winter* was reset, the

[1] Where titles are grouped in advertisements it is likely that one or more are listed subsequent to publication; see Foxon, p. 798. *Winter, Summer*, and *Spring* are listed in the two leaves of Millar's advertisements bound into a copy of *Spring* 1728 at Princeton; this copy includes also one separate leaf of advertisements by Millan.

[2] I have found copies of this 'second edition' only in Brighton Public Library and in Yale University Library. The title-page is in red and black, whereas the 1727 title is black only.

preface and complimentary poems deleted, never to reappear in
Thomson's lifetime, the text substantively revised and extended
to 478 lines (as compared with 463 in the second edition and 405
in the first) and its accidentals very extensively revised—probably
by the author. This edition (which is referred to as *Wi.28* in the
present edition) was last advertised on 9 March 1730 in the *Daily
Post*, shortly before the first edition of *The Seasons* was published.

Publication of *Spring, a Poem*,[1] described on its title-page as
'printed, and sold by A. Millar . . . and G. Strahan', and priced,
like *Summer*, at 1s. 6d., was announced in newspapers on 5 June
1728, but, despite the directive of the Copyright Act that books
should be entered in the Stationers' Register before publication,
the earliest reference to *Spring* in the Register is on 23 January
1729, when it is entered to Millar. Sheets of the 1728 impression
were reissued with an added contents-leaf and a cancel-title, dated
1729, reading 'second edition' and 'printed for A. Millar'.[2] The
alteration from 'printed . . . by' to 'printed for' and the dis-
appearance of Strahan's name (which had been dropped from
newspaper advertisements after 12 June 1728) appear to indicate
some shift in the business relationships of Millar with Strahan and
with Thomson. The poet had intended that *Spring* should first be
published in his subscription edition of *The Seasons*, but may have
been tempted by the success of *Winter* and *Summer* to order a
large[3] separate printing of his new poem and publish it on his own
account, employing Millar and Strahan as agents to sell on com-
mission. Perhaps sales were slow, and Millar may have shouldered
the risk and reissued the remainder sheets as a 'second edition'.
The Stationers' Register entry might arise from some such
transaction, though Thomson's formal assignment of copyright
was not made till January 1730. *Spring* (no edition number) was
advertised by Millar in the *Daily Post* on 8 May 1729, but the
earliest advertisement I have seen which specified 'second edition'
is in March 1730—probably post-publication since it is alongside
the announcement of a new work, *Sophonisba*.

Spring, at 1,082 lines, is nearly as long as *Summer*, for the poet

[1] Referred to as *Sp.28* in the present edition.
[2] Styled 'Second Edition A' by J. E. Wells in 'Thomson's *Spring*: Early
Editions True and False', *The Library* xxii (1942), 226–7. There is a copy at
Swarthmore with both 1728 and 1729 title-pages.
[3] I have traced many more copies of *Spring* than of any other book of Thom-
son's printed in the years 1726–8.

is now working to a larger scale than in 1726. For the first time
there is a verse dedication within the poem as well as the customary
prefatory prose dedication, in this case to the Countess of Hertford.
There is also an advertisement to explain why the poem was
published separately and not as part of the promised subscription
edition: see Appendix B below. This advertisement and the
proposals are found in both the 1728 and 1729 issues. The text of
the poem was reprinted in Dublin, without prose dedication,
advertisement, proposals (and doubtless without authority) by
S. Powell, for George Risk, George Ewing, and William Smith,
1728.

The subscription quarto *SEASONS*, 1730 (*30q*).

While Thomson continued to solicit subscriptions for *The Seasons*
he had other work on hand. *Britannia*, a poetical invective against
the pacific policies of Walpole's ministry and the only long work
of Thomson's to be published anonymously, came from the press
in January 1729;[1] and the tragedy of *Sophonisba*, completed in the
summer of 1729,[2] was first performed on 28 February 1730, thus
fulfilling Thomson's plan, formed as early as March 1728, to write
for the theatre.[3] Subscriptions to *The Seasons* came in slowly,
possibly because the whole price had been asked for at the time of
subscribing, rather than half in advance and half on publication,
which was a more common practice; Thomson wryly wrote to
Mallet on 20 September 1729: 'I have heard of an Agreement
among some of our modern Goths (who by the Bye are even
unworthy of that Name) by which they bind Themselves not to
encourage any Subscription what ever under a certain Penalty.'[4]
At this time Thomson was staying at Eastbury in Dorset, the seat
of his patron Dodington, so the description of Eastbury in *Autumn*
(cf *OET Au.* 652–82) may have been written then, though that
poem must have been complete in some form about five months
earlier if we are to believe an advertisement placed by Millan in
the *London Journal* of 26 April 1729 for *Britannia* and *A Poem
sacred to the memory of Sir Isaac Newton* by the 'Author of Spring,
Summer, Autumn and Winter, Etc.'

[1] J. E. Wells, 'Thomson's *Britannia*: Issues, Attribution, Date, Variants',
Modern Philology xl (1943), 43–56.
[2] *Letters*, p. 68.   [3] Grant, pp. 77–8.
[4] *Letters*, p. 65. Such an agreement is described by Fielding's Mr. Wilson
in *Joseph Andrews*, book III, chap. iii.

Whatever the poem's date of composition, the copyright of *Autumn* was sold on 18 July 1729, when, for £105, Thomson assigned to John Millan the 'Intire Right and Property' . . .

forever of the following Poems Bearing these following particular Titles viz Summer a Poem, Autumn a Poem, Winter a Poem, Britania a Poem, a Poem Sacred to the Memory of Sir Isaac Newton; a Hymn on the Succession of the Seasons and an Essay on Discriptive Poetry with all the Corrections, Alterations and Additions &c. that will be printed in the Subscription Edition of my forsaid Poems: as also in full for any alterations &c. that I may occasionally make hereafter.[1]

On 16 January 1730 Thomson assigned to Andrew Millar, for the sum of £137. 10s., the copyrights in perpetuity of *Spring* and the still unpublished *Sophonisba*, 'now in Rehearsal at the Theatre in Drury Lane', together with 'all additions corrections alterations and amendments whatsoever which shall or may at any time hereafter be made into or concerning' them. The printing of *Spring* 'once and no more in quarto as the same is now printing (and not otherwise) to go with other poems of the said James Thomson by way of Subscription to make a quarto Volume'[2] was allowed by this agreement, and presumably there was an understanding of the same sort with Millan over *Summer*, *Autumn*, *Winter*, the *Hymn*, the *Poem to Newton*, and the *Essay on Descriptive Poetry*. Though the last-mentioned *Essay* was never published under this title, and was probably never written (unless it is merely the *Preface* to the second edition of *Winter*), it looks as if Millan obtained more for his money than Millar did. Millar bought Millan's copyrights in 1738 and published many complete editions of *The Seasons* thereafter. When in 1769 he brought an action against another bookseller, Taylor, who had pirated the book, the jury found that the work was 'at first published and printed by James Thomson for his own use and benefit at several times between the beginning of the year 1727 and the end of 1729', and that 'Andrew Millar in the year 1729, purchased this work called the Seasons for a valuable consideration, of James Thomson the author and proprietor'. A note to the account of this case adds that Thomson 'reaped about a thousand guineas profit while the work was his own property; he sold it in 1729 to Millar for 160 pounds'.[3] Though this verdict and

[1] *Letters*, pp. 63–4.   [2] *Letters*, p. 70.
[3] *Speeches and Arguments in the Cause of Millar against Taylor* (Leith, 1771), pp. 2, 3, 53.

note are manifestly incorrect in some particulars they may provide reliable evidence that the early editions of *Winter*, *Summer*, and *Spring*, as well as the subscription quarto of 1730, were printed for Thomson's own use and benefit. If the profit was reported accurately then Thomson fared almost as well as Pope, who according to David Foxon's calculations[1] made a profit of about £5,000 from six volumes of the *Iliad* and about the same sum from five volumes of the *Odyssey*; and it is notorious that Pope's contracts with Lintot were sharply advantageous to the poet.

A last effort to attract subscribers to the quarto edition of *The Seasons* was made through an advertisement in the *Daily Post* of 11 April 1730, when booksellers prepared to receive subscriptions were named as Millar, W. Innys and George Strahan. It was promised that the book would be delivered to subscribers at the beginning of May, but further advertisements[2] indicate that publication was on 8 June. Subscription copies were delivered by the poet himself, by Millar, and by John Brindley a bookbinder who no doubt hoped that subscribers would employ him to bind their copies; Millar and Brindley also offered for sale at a guinea, in sheets, the copies not subscribed for. The printer was Samuel Richardson,[3] who had printed the first edition of *Britannia*. In the quarto he followed a new 'neat' style: he dispensed with the customary initial capital to every substantive and the customary italic for proper names, and instead printed all in roman, with large and small capitals for proper names and 'emphatical words'.[4] David Foxon showed in the 1976 Lyell Lectures that Pope was a pioneer in evolving this new style of typography. It is quite likely that Thomson insisted on this style for the quarto at Pope's suggestion, for it is quite foreign to the more old-fashioned styles usually employed by Richardson: all the other works of Thomson set up in Richardson's shop (*Britannia* 1729, *Winter*, etc. 1734,

---

[1] D. F. Foxon's unpublished Lyell Lectures, 'Pope and the Early Eighteenth-century Book Trade', fols. 77, 112.

[2] *The Craftsman*, *St. James Evening-Post*, *London Evening-Post*, *Whitehall Evening-Post*, *Daily Post-Boy*, and *London Journal*.

[3] W. M. Sale, *Samuel Richardson: Master Printer* (Ithaca, 1950), p. 87.

[4] John Smith, *The Printer's Grammar* (1755, repr. 1965, ed. D. F. Foxon), p. 201. A few initial capitals creep in, though; cf. p. lviii n. 1 below. Italic is used for the Arguments, for direct speech in the *Poem to the Memory of Newton*, and for titles in the list of subscribers. It also appears, probably by oversight, in the first paragraph of the *Hymn*. There are two small press-variants affecting subscribers' titles on p. vii.

Summer 1735) were for booksellers, and were printed after the old fashion. I do not know how many copies were printed, but it must have been many more than the 457 which had been ordered by 388 subscribers. We do not know how many copies were taken up by the multiple-copy subscribers, or how many subscribers' names were omitted from the printed list,[1] but, whatever the precise number of subscribers, it is evident that Queen Caroline, to whom, by gracious permission, *Sophonisba* had been dedicated, headed a subscription list crowded with names bespeaking wealth or genius or taste: Dodington subscribed for twenty copies, Pope for three, and Burlington for five. Ten copies were subscribed for by John Conduitt, Newton's nephew, whose projected *Life* of his uncle is mentioned in new lines added to the text of Thomson's *Poem to Newton* printed in the quarto. Presumably Burlington was interested as patron of William Kent, who had drawn the designs (engraved in Paris by Nicolas Henri Tardieu) which illustrate each of the four seasons. The upper half of each design represents an allegorical 'progress' of the personified season as described in the opening lines of each book, while the lower half illustrates naturalistically, upon different planes, several episodes and scenes from the book. Such multiple action and mingling of natural and supernatural accords well with Thomson's text. A fifth plate was engraved by Pierre Fourdrinier from Kent's preliminary design for the Newton monument in Westminster Abbey, and the title-page vignette was engraved by Fourdrinier after Kent.[2] The five plates are not part of the collation.

The text of the quarto is considerably, but unevenly, revised from earlier editions of the individual Seasons. In S*pring* there are substantive changes affecting about eighty lines of the 1728 text, and total length is increased by five lines to 1,087. In *Summer* over 150 new lines are added, including descriptions of a petrified city in North Africa and of English haymaking and the Damon and Musidora episode in its first version; there are substantive changes

<hr />

[1] In a Bodleian copy the extra name Charles Mellish Esq. is written in. Two persons named in the list of subscribers are known also to have received copies as presents (*Letters*, pp. 72–3). Subscription lists can rarely be wholly accurate: see P. J. Wallis, 'Book Subscription Lists', *The Library*, 5th series, xxix (1974), 255–86.

[2] Kent's designs are discussed in Jeffery Eicholz, 'William Kent's Career as a Literary Illustrator', *Bulletin of New York Public Library* lxx (1966), 629–35.

in another 150 lines; about seventy lines on the autumnal topics of Scotland, wildfire, and meteors are revised and transferred to *Autumn*, and other lines deleted completely, so that the length of the whole poem is increased by only sixty lines over the 1727 text—to 1,205 lines. Changes to *Winter* are far more considerable. Over four hundred new lines are added, including the episode of the shepherd perishing in the snow and humanitarian reflections upon it, exotic descriptions of northern wastes, a compliment to Alexander Pope, and scientific speculation upon the nature of frost; there are substantive changes in over a hundred lines of the 1728 text; a hundred lines of autumnal description are revised and transferred to *Autumn*, other lines are dropped, and the description of the redbreast is unaccountably shortened by six lines.[1] The result of all these revisions is to make *Winter*, at 781 lines, over 300 lines longer than the 1728 version and markedly different in scope and intention. *Autumn* is entirely new, except for the passages transferred and revised from *Winter* and *Summer*, and at 1,269 lines is the longest of the four Seasons. A prose 'Argument' is now inserted before each season. All the earlier prose dedications are deleted because every Season now has a verse dedication to its original patron; *Autumn* is dedicated to Arthur Onslow, who had become Speaker of the House of Commons when the dedicatee of *Winter* was raised to the peerage as Lord Wilmington. The *Preface* to *Winter* which had been deleted in 1728 is not restored, nor does Thomson pursue any designs he might have had to rewrite and print it as an 'Essay on Descriptive Poetry'. Despite the *Hymn* (121 lines), now added for the first time, the overall effect of revisions and additions in 1730 is to increase the 'georgical' and lessen the devotional character of *The Seasons*.

On 8 June, the day that subscribers' copies were delivered, Millan advertised in the *Daily Post* a second edition of *Britannia*, 'in Quarto, proper to be bound with the Subscription Edition of Mr. Thomson's Four Seasons, &c.', price one shilling. In November he advertised 'a small Number over what were subscribed for' of the quarto *Seasons* together with the quarto second edition of

[1] Actually five lines and two half-lines (cf. *OET Wi.* 250–6). As the omitted passage begins and ends in mid-line and occurs in the middle of D3ᵛ of *Winter* 1728, in a section six pages long (D1ᵛ–D4ʳ) reprinted in the quarto mostly word for word, I am unable to conceive how these lines could have been omitted accidentally. They were restored in the octavo pamphlet of *Winter* 1730, and retained in all subsequent editions.

Britannia, 'not delivered to the Subscribers', for sale 'bound and gilt' at a guinea. In publishers' announcements 'small' is no less relative a term than 'new', and this issue of the quarto *Seasons* with *Britannia* was on sale by both Millan and Millar through the next eight years.[1] Some surviving copies also include four leaves, without title-page or publisher's imprint, containing four short poems by Thomson.[2] Perhaps this represents some effort of sales promotion, but I have found no advertisements specifically for this issue. It is probable that one of the attempts to dispose of remainder sheets of the subscription quarto is recorded by Millan's notice in the *Daily Advertiser* of 8 January 1733 advertising an issue in fortnightly parts, the first to be published on 22 January. Millan quoted a price of '2*s*. or 3*s*.' for each fascicule and declared that paper, print, and plates were 'full as good' as in the edition published by the author for a guinea. David Foxon observes: 'Though no copies of these parts have been identified (once bound they would form a copy indistinguishable from any other), there seems no reason to doubt that they were sheets of [the 1730 quarto] edition.'[3] In 1736 unsold copies of the subscription edition with *Britannia* were reissued by Millar, without alteration of the 1730 title-page, alongside another quarto volume which bore the title *Works* volume ii and contained reissues of the five parts of Liberty

[1] Advertisements by Millan appear in newspapers of November 1730, February 1731, and November 1735 (price, bound and gilt, a guinea), and in the catalogue printed with *Winter*, etc. 1734 (no price given). The latest Millan advertisement I have found is in the *St. James's Evening-Post*, 16 August 1737, where there is no mention of a binding and the price is reduced to 15*s*. Advertisements by Millar are in newspapers of December 1734, January 1735, and June and July 1737, and in lists attached to most of the works by Thomson which he published between 1731 and 1738. The latest advertisement of all I have seen is in Millar's catalogue printed with Mallet's *Mustapha* in February 1739. The five engravings by Kent were advertised separately in 1731 and 1734 for 2*s*. 6*d*.: 'they are very beautiful, and fit to be framed.'

[2] 'A Paraphrase on the latter part of the sixth Chapter of St. Matthew', 'The incomparable Soporifick Doctor', 'The Happy Man', 'Hymn on Solitude'. (They had been first printed in *Miscellaneous Poems by Several Hands*, 1729, ed. James Ralph.) This same quarto type-setting, with reset titles and running-heads, was reimposed for an octavo issue of the four poems on four leaves bound into sets consisting of the 1730 collective title-page, *Spring* 1731, and the three Millan pamphlets of 1730. I have found only two copies of this octavo issue (at Swarthmore and Yale), and five of the quarto. See J. E. Wells, 'Thomson's Subscription *Seasons*', *Notes and Queries* (May 1941), p. 350.

[3] Introductory note to the Scolar Press facsimile of *The Seasons* 1730 (Menston, n.d.); see also R. M. Wiles, *Serial Publication in England before 1750* (Cambridge, 1957), pp. 127, 294.

(1735–6) and a new edition of *Sophonisba*. Though it is convenient to refer to *The Seasons*, quarto 1730, as the 'subscription edition', indications are that this, like Pope's Homer, was a joint enterprise between trade and author. In the case of Pope's *Iliad* the book-seller gave the author 660 copies for subscribers and had 2,000 printed in a plainer style and different format to sell on his own account, reducing the number to 1,250 after volume i. Trade copies of *The Seasons* were from the same impression as subscribers' copies, so that we have no means of estimating how many extra copies, over and above the 457 for subscribers, were printed for sale through the trade, but the long continuance of advertisements implies a large number, as does the fact that surviving copies (considerably more than half of them bound up with *Britannia*) outnumber surviving copies of any other issue of *The Seasons* in Thomson's lifetime.[1]

Pamphlet issues of the 1730s (*Su.30p*, *Au.30p*, *Wi.30p*, *Sp.31*, *Sp.34*, *Wi.34*, *Su.35*)

It would appear that after publication of the quarto Thomson was for a while satisfied with his poem, since in a series of octavo editions of all or parts of *The Seasons* through the 1730s major substantive revisions which one may confidently attribute to the author affect no more than six lines of *Winter* and two of *Autumn*. Except for those eight lines, together with a further handful of minor revisions which might be the author's and a few cases where corrections from the quarto errata-list are taken in, these octavos of the 1730s show the progressive corruption normal in a succession of reprints, though what exactly their succession was cannot easily be determined.

Closest to the quarto in text and time are three sepatate pamphlets published by Millan, printed by Blandford[2] and dated 1730. These are, firstly *Summer, a Poem* 'The Third Edition with Additions' (referred to in the present edition as *Su.30p*), secondly *Autumn, a Poem* 'The Second Edition' (referred to in the present edition as

---

[1] Among traced copies the quarto outnumbers the 1746 duodecimo by three to one, yet it is likely that 2,000 of the latter were sold. One grants, of course, that the survival rate of quartos would be higher than that of smaller, cheaper volumes; and that some surviving copies of the quarto would have belonged to subscribers who bought *Britannia* and had it bound in.

[2] As stated on the title-pages of *Autumn* and *Summer* and the separate title-page of *Britannia*; on the evidence of ornaments in the case of *Winter*, *Hymn* and *Poem to Newton*.

Au.30p), and thirdly, *Winter, a Poem, a Hymn on the Seasons, a Poem to the Memory of Sir Isaac Newton, and Britannia, a Poem* (referred to in the present edition as *Wi.30p*).[1] In this third pamphlet *Britannia* has separate signatures and pagination and a separate title-page describing it as the 'Third Edition'; it is, in fact, virtually a reimposition of the quarto second edition.[2] *Winter* was described as the 'Sixth Edition' in advertisements printed on the last leaf of text in *Summer*, third edition; the fact that these advertisements also list 'An Essay on descriptive Poetry' and '*Britannia* 2nd Edition' supports the inference that *Summer* was printed off before copy for the *Winter* pamphlet was ready. It is not clear why the quartos were taken into account in numbering the octavo pamphlet editions of *Autumn* and *Britannia*, but not those of *Summer* and *Winter*. Quarto errata are corrected in the text of the *Winter* pamphlet but not in the others, perhaps indicating that proof-sheets of the quarto were used as copy, and that *Summer* and *Autumn* were printed off before the last quarto sheet (which contained errata)[3] was to hand in Blandford's shop. Blandford's compositors may have been responsible for some or all of twenty indifferent, small substantive variants from the quarto in *Summer* and *Autumn*, nineteen of which were carried through into every later edition of the 1730s, and for the careless omission of a line in *Autumn* (corresponding to *OET Au.* 411). Variants in *Winter*, the *Hymn*, and the *Poem to Newton* are merely literals, except that the six lines on the redbreast left out of the quarto are here restored—to remain in every later text. Presumably Thomson ordered the restoration, and it looks as if he revised punctuation and tinkered a little with substantives on the first sheet of *Summer* (to *OET Su.* 280) and possibly elsewhere, but there is no indication

[1] *Summer* and *Winter* had been entered to Millan in the Stationers' Register on first issue, and *Spring* to Millar on perhaps second issue, but there is no entry in the Register for *Autumn* or the *Hymn*, even though Millan had bought copyright. *The Seasons*, entire, was not entered until 24 June 1738, when Millar bought Millan's rights.

[2] Evidently the type of the quarto *Britannia* was not distributed immediately; but a few small corrections were made in the metal, and then the lines of verse were releaded and reimposed with new ornaments, running-heads and line and page numbers so that the poem could be printed in octavo with a new title-page reading 'third edition'. See J. E. Wells, 'Thomson's *Britannia*: Issues, Attribution, Date, Variants', *Modern Philology*, xl (1942), 47 note.

[3] The quarto collation is π^4 A^2 B–Ii^4 Kk^2. A^2 (last page of subscription list, errata, *Spring* fly-title and argument) and Kk^2 (*Poem to Newton*, pp. 249–52) were printed together and then separated.

that he involved himself to any great extent in preparing the three Millan pamphlets for the press.

The three pamphlets were offered for sale separately at 1s. 6d. each and thus advertized by Millan (and Astley, Whiteridge, Jolliffe, and Worral) in newspapers from 13 June (less than a week after copies of the quarto had been delivered to subscribers) to 4 July.[1] Millan at the same time offered *Spring* at the same price, and all four pamplets, bound, for 7s. After 4 July there are no advertisements for separate pamplets but only for 'The Seasons Octavo', though we can be fairly certain in most cases that a set of four pamphlets is meant (see below, pp. lix–lx n. 1). Though Millan's advertisements between 20 June and 4 July describe *Spring* as a 'New Edition', I believe they refer to Millar's 'second edition' of 1729.[2] The fact of near-simultaneous publication suggests that the quarto *Seasons* and the three Millan pamphlets of *Summer*, *Autumn*, and *Winter* etc. were printed concurrently, with Blandford possibly taking batches of Richardson's quarto sheets as his copy, except in the case of *Britannia*, where the type of the quarto second edition was standing in his own shop. *Britannia*, which has separate pagination and signatures (A⁸ B²) and its own 'third edition' title-page, could have been printed at any point in the sequence; but if it was printed first, its italicizing of proper names and emphatical words might have influenced typesetting in the rest of the Millan pamphlets, where the large and small capitals of the quarto are consistently transliterated into italic.[3] On the other hand it might have been thought that while *cognoscenti* who could afford a guinea would appreciate the new style, the vulgar had better have the old and familiar. Such a reversion to italic in the octavos is paralleled in the small octavo *Works* of Pope from 1735 on.[4] Blandford followed the quarto

---

[1] *Daily Post, London Evening-Post* 13 June, *Universal Spectator* 20 June, *Craftsman* 27 June, *Whitehall Evening-Post* 30 June, *St. James Evening-Post* 2 July, *London Journal* 4 July, *Monthly Chronicle* June.

[2] The genuine 'New Edition' of *Spring*, i.e. a pamphlet containing those textual revisions which had been first printed in the quarto, is dated 1731 on title-page (see p. lv below), and I cannot see what motive Millar could have had for false-dating if this pamphlet was the one sold in June 1730 alongside Millan's three, all dated 1730.

[3] Except four words or phrases in *Summer*, set in roman in the pamphlet and all later editions through the 1730s.

[4] D. F. Foxon's Lyell Lectures, 'Pope and the Early Eighteenth-century Book Trade'.

fashion of setting common nouns without an initial capital, but did
so with a few deviations, the pattern of which shows that the quarto
provided copy for the pamphlets, not vice versa (see below, p. lviii
n. 1). Probably *Winter*, the *Hymn*, and *Poem to Newton* were
printed last. They appear in the pamphlet in that order, paged
consecutively on sheets A–D⁸ E³, with A1 the title-page listing
Britannia in addition to the other three. E4 was probably used for
the collective title-page,¹ '*The Seasons, A Hymn, A Poem to the
Memory of Sir Isaac Newton, and Britannia, a Poem*. Printed for
J. Millan and A. Millar, 1730.' This was separated after printing
and prefixed to a set of the three Millan pamphlets of 1730 and
whatever issue of *Spring* lay to hand in order to make a 'neat
octavo edition' sold for 7*s*. bound.

On 4 August Millan advertised² an octavo edition of *The
Seasons* 'With a beautiful new Set of Cuts design'd by the famous
Picart'³ and the *Hymn, Poem to Newton*, and *Britannia*, price 7*s*.
bound. 'N.B. to this Edition is added about 600 new Lines which
are all that is ever intended to be made.' I take it that these 600
new lines are the additions first printed in the quarto, and that
this advertisement refers to a set of the three Millan pamphlets of
1730 bound up with the 1730 collective title-page and (probably)
Millar's 1729 reissue of *Spring*.⁴ Picart's four engraved designs
depict each season symbolized by a single figure drawn from
'Marble Statues in the Garden of Versailles 7 foot high'.

For some time an unrevised text of *Spring* in octavo must have
been offered for sale at the same time as a revised text in quarto;
but when supplies of the 1728 and 1729 issues ran out, their place
in the octavo set of pamphlets was taken by a new 'second edition',
dated 1731, published by Millar and, on evidence of ornaments,
printed by Henry Woodfall.⁵ This reset edition (referred to as

---

¹ Foxon, pp. 798, 800.

² *London Evening-Post*: there was a similar advertisement in the *Daily Post*,
6 August.

³ Bernard Picart (1673–1733), a French artist working in Amsterdam in the
1730s. The engraver was J. Clark.

⁴ I have found no bound set of pamphlets which includes *Spring* 1728 and
the Picart engravings.

⁵ Styled 'Second Edition B' by J. E. Wells in 'Thomson's *Spring*: Early
Editions True and False', *The Library* xxii (1942), 230. I have traced forty
examples of an octavo set prefaced by the collective title-page dated 1730. All
have the three Millan pamphlets of 1730, three have the 1728 issue of *Spring*,
twelve the 1729 issue, and twenty-five the 1731 issue.

Sp.31 in the present edition) reproduces, with six substantive variants (all misprints) and a few accidental variants, the text of the quarto; in its use of large and small capitals rather than italics for proper names and emphatical words it follows the style of the quarto, not the Millan pamphlets. I have found no separate advertisement for *Spring* 1731, but its appearance is perhaps signalled by an advertisement for *The Seasons* octavo, 'with Cuts', bound 7*s.*, in the *Daily Journal* of 23 February 1731; for advertisements by Millar printed on the same sheet as the later part of the text of *Spring* include notices of Mallet's *Eurydice* and Frowde's *Philotas*, neither of which was advertised in newspapers before February, the month when these plays were first performed. This, the fourth issue of *Spring*, happens to contain a reprint of the second published version of the text, but one suspects that Millar called it the second edition not because it embodied Thomson's revisions of 1730 but because it was replacing the 'second edition' of 1729 in sets of pamphlets.

Three years later Millar published another, entirely reset, octavo of *Spring*, following the 1731 edition so closely as to reproduce all ornaments but one and all advertisements from the earlier volume, with 'second edition' and '1731' on the title-page.[1] 250 copies of this impostor (referred to as *Sp.34* in the present edition) were printed by Henry Woodfall and recorded in his ledger on 14 October 1734.[2] Presumably it was about the same time that Richardson reprinted for Millan an octavo *Winter, a Hymn, a Poem to Newton, and Britannia*, dated 1734, consecutively signed and paginated throughout, following the 1730 Millan pamphlet as copy but introducing new misprints. (It is referred to as *Wi.34* in the present edition.) Richardson also printed[3] a collective title-page—*The Four Seasons, and Other Poems . . . Printed for J. Millan . . . and A. Millar . . . 1735*—which is found prefixed to pamphlet sets consisting of *Spring* and *Winter*, etc. 1734 bound with *Summer* and *Autumn* 1730 and the four Picart engravings. Finally *Summer*, 'fourth edition' 1735 (refered to as *Su.35* in the present edition), was printed (with a shameful crop

---

[1] Styled 'Second Edition C' by J. E. Wells, art. cit. 232–5. Between the 1731 and 1734 texts there are a few trifling variants of spelling and punctuation.

[2] *Notes and Queries* (June 1855), p. 418.

[3] W. M. Sale, in *Samuel Richardson, Master Printer* (1950), p. 211, attributes *Winter*, etc. (1734) and *Summer* (1735) to Richardson's shop. On the evidence of ornaments the collective title-page was printed there too.

of errors) for Millan by Richardson, using the 1730 pamphlet as copy, and was bound with remaining copies of *Spring* and *Winter*, etc. 1734, and *Autum* 1730, under the 1735 *Four Seasons* title-page. There was no reprint of *Autumn*, so evidently the 1730 printing satisfied all needs. The price, 1*s*. 6*d*., is printed on title-page or half-title of all pamphlet issues of the separate Seasons, 1730–5, indicating that any one could be bought separately, but after July 1730 they were not advertised as separate items, and most surviving copies are found in complete sets of four, usually with the Picart engravings, under a collective title-page of 1730 or, less commonly, 1735.[1] It seems as if Millan and Millar were co-operating for five years or more from June 1730 to keep in print the Seasons of which each had copyright in order to maintain a common stock of *The Seasons*, etc. in octavo, with engravings, the text of which was (except for trifling variants and six lines on the redbreast) substantively identical with the quarto.

The consecutively paginated octavo *SEASONS*, '1730' (*300*).

Discounting a Dublin reprint, presumably unauthorized, of the three 1730 Millan octavo pamphlets,[2] and discounting R. Fleming's Edinburgh piracy of *Autumn*,[3] we are left with another edition dated 1730 for consideration. This is an octavo in fours published over the names of Millan and Millar. It consists of a half-title and title-page listing only *The Seasons, a Poem*[4] on two preliminary leaves (π^2), followed by the text of the four Seasons with the *Hymn*

---

[1] Among sets I have seen, all those with the 1730 collective title-page consist of *Summer, Autumn, Winter* (all 1730), and any one of three issues of *Spring* (1728–31), while all those with a 1735 collective title-page consist of *Autumn* (1730), *Spring* and *Winter* (1734), and *Summer* (either 1730 or 1735). This leads me to conjecture that most sets with a collective title-page were probably issued as sets, and are not chance accumulations by purchasers of various editions over the years.

[2] Octavo, printed by S. Powell for George Risk, George Ewing, and William Smith. The three pamphlets, separately paginated, are bound with the same booksellers' *Spring* 1728 and a collective title-page reading *Poems: viz. Spring, Summer, etc.* 1730. This title-page was printed as E4 of *Winter*, etc., as in the London edition; see Foxon, pp. 798–800. *Spring* and *Summer* were reprinted together, with continuous signatures, in 1740; the Dublin pirates evidently took no account of Thomson's revisions to *Spring*.

[3] Foxon, p. 800.

[4] This phrase 'The Seasons, a Poem' is, I think, never used elsewhere in Thomson's lifetime in title-page, half-title, contents list or advertisement. Perhaps Thomson and/or his booksellers usually thought of the work as five poems.

consecutively paginated on half-sheets A–Qq⁴, bound up, not always in the same order, with the *Poem to Newton* (A–B) and *Britannia* (A–B⁴ C²), each with its own signatures and pagination. Each of the Seasons has its own fly-title, but there are no title-pages or fly-titles for the *Hymn*, the *Poem to Newton*, or *Britannia*. No price or edition number is marked on the book or on any of its parts. There are no plates in any copy I have seen or heard of and no ornaments of any kind, not even a factotum. I have not been able to identify the printer. On evidence of traceable copies the print order appears to have been smaller than for any of the 1730 pamphlets.

Though dated 1730 on the title-page (and so referred to as *300* in the present edition) this edition was possibly printed later, since textual analysis (admittedly a far from mathematical science) suggests that copy for it consisted of four pamphlets, one of which was *Spring* 1731 or the textually almost identical *Spring* 1734.[1]

---

[1] In particular, the incidence of initial capitals for common nouns seems to point to progressive printers' normalizing from the quarto to the pamplets and thence to the consecutively-paginated octavo. The new 'neat' style of the quarto *Seasons* is to set common nouns all in lower case; but on a few occasions—apparently anomalously—initial capitals are set. David Foxon tells me that when Pope marked *The Dunciad* 1728 with his revisions his substitued nouns usually have initial capitals, though the 1728 text usually omits capitals. Something like this may have occurred in *The Seasons*, if we suppose that the initial capitals (being so few) came in at a late proof stage. Whatever the reason for its presence this initial capitalization is very sparse and unsystematic, with the result that in close on five thousand lines of the quarto *Seasons* and *Newton* there are only 172 occurrences of a common noun with initial capital. It looks as if compositors of the 1730–1 pamphlets (followed by those of the 1734–5 pamphlets) saw that the rule was to set lower case and so departed from the copy here and there in order to normalize. Consequently they reduced to lower case 40 of the 172 initial capitals of the quarto but retained the other 132. In the consecutively paginated octavo (*300*)—apparently after further normalizing—all these 40 remain in lower case while 34 of the pamplets' 132 capitals are also reduced to lower case (and two, in *OET Au.* 512, anomalously raised to large and small capitals). There is a clear pattern of progressive normalizing which is not significantly disturbed by 12 new initial capitals in the pamphlets (4 of which are retained and 8 reduced to lower case in the consecutively paginated octavo) and just one new capital in the consecutively paginated octavo itself. Thus, in perhaps eight to ten thousand occurrences of common nouns, there are 103 arbitrary capital letters in the consecutively paginated octavo, 98 of which are among the no less arbitrary group of 172 in the quarto, and 102 of which are among the 144 in the pamplets. The pattern is clear in all four Seasons, the *Hymn*, and *Newton*. *Britannia* is more heavily capitalized in all editions but the pattern is similar. Proper names and 'emphatical words' are set in large and small capitals throughout the consecutively paginated octavo, but we can infer that its compositors followed a set of pamphlets if we assume that they started with

This consecutively paginated octavo perpetuates all but four of the two dozen substantive variants first introduced, probably by compositors, in the 1730–1 pamphlets. There are eleven new variants, all of which could be errors, and one line of *Britannia* is omitted altogether. Of four errors in the pamphlets corrected here, three (including one noted in the quarto errata-list) could have been corrected unassisted by an alert corrector, but the fourth— 'unremitting' in *Spring* 854 (*OET*)—could, I think, only have come from the errata-list or by the author's intervention. All other quarto errata which had been ignored by the pamphlet compositors are also ignored here, and the incidence of misprints strongly suggests that this edition was not extensively corrected against the quarto text; nevertheless line 411 of *Autumn*, present in the quarto but omitted from the 1730 pamphlet, is here restored. Furthermore, lines 927–8 of *Autumn* are rewritten to eliminate a jingle, '*Britain Britain*', which had appeared in the quarto and pamphlet texts.

This last revision is surely authorial, but when it was made and when the consecutively paginated octavo was printed remain matters for conjecture, since there is no external evidence and it is difficult to determine when, or if, the book was advertised. All advertisements I have seen for an octavo edition of *The Seasons* earlier than August 1730 make it clear that the pamphlets are being offered (see above p. liv n.1), most advertisements from August 1730 to August 1737 state directly or imply that the edition offered has 'Cuts' (i.e. the Picart engravings), which are never found in the consecutively paginated octavo but appear in most surviving pamphlet sets; while the wording of all remaining advertisements does not rule out the possibility that engravings were still being offered.[1]

Spring and followed copy, and then, for the sake of consistency, transliterated italic in the other pamphlet Seasons into large and small capitals. Of course any conjectures based on textual analysis alone must be tentative, if only because it is possible that the author could have slightly revised accidentals at any point in any edition. Indeed, as there was authorial substantive revision to *Autumn* in the consecutively paginated octavo, the new large and small capitals to indicate personification of *Au.* 512 may be authorial.

[1] Millan's advertisements in various newspapers of November 1730 and November 1735 list the quarto 'with Copper Plates' and 'the Same in Octavo. Price 7s. bound', from which it is possible to infer that the octavo contained engravings. Millar's listings in *Liberty*, part iv, January 1736, and *A Poem to the Memory of Lord Talbot*, June 1737, read 'The Seasons [etc.] in Octavo, Price

Textual evidence, for what it is worth, suggests that the con-secutively paginated octavo is later than *Spring* 1731 and the 1730 pamphlets of other Seasons. It is more likely than not that all octavo *Seasons* in Millan's advertisements from June 1730 to August 1737 and all those in Millar's from June 1730 to January 1735 are sets, variously combined, of pamphlets. It is unlikely that Millan or Millar would go to the expense of reprinting until stocks of complete pamphlet-sets were running low. Of all the advertise-ments of the 1730s, Millar's in 1736–7 seem to be the only ones which could refer to the consecutively paginated octavo. In that case, at the risk of clutching at straws to build a bibliographical mare's nest, one might guess that the edition was printed for Millar to fill a gap between the sale of the last of the pamphlet-sets issued in 1735 and the publication of *Works* 1738.[1] The false date remains difficult to explain—though if the set of pamphlets used as exemplar was complete with a 1730 collective title-page then the date could have been copied from that, while if Millar handled printing arrangements he had already created his own precedent for false-dating with *Spring* 1734.

bound 6s, in Quarto, a Guinea', and advertisements are similarly phrased (except that prices are omitted) in newspapers of June and July 1737, but as the quarto always had engravings it is quite possible that the octavo referred to here was also illustrated. All other advertisements I have found from 4 August onwards clearly state that the octavo *Seasons* which is being offered contains 'Cuts' or 'Copper Plates'. Such advertisements are found in newspapers of August and October 1730, February and March 1731, and August 1737 over Millan's name, in newspapers of December 1734 and January 1735 over Millar's, in Millan's catalogue with *Winter*, etc. 1734, and in Millar's with *Spring* 1731 and 1734 and *Liberty* part i, January 1735. In two of his November 1730 advertisements Millan added a warning to hesitant prospective buyers: 'N.B. The Seasons will not be printed in any other Size for some Years to come.' In 1736 and 1737 Millar offers his octavo *Seasons* for 6s. bound, but in earlier advertisements states no price. Millan always quotes 7s. bound, except in the list attached to *Winter*, etc. 1734 and in the *St. James's Evening Post* of 16 August 1737, where the price drops to 6s. ('bound' in the first case, no reference to binding in the second). As this second advertisement (which is the last for an octavo *Seasons* which I have managed to find in the 1730s) also offers the quarto cut-price at 15s. it looks as if Millan was trying to move slow stock.

[1] It is possible to infer that Millar had in stock a 'small', i.e. octavo, edition in September 1737 when Thomson asked him to send 'a large Edition of the Seasons', i e. a copy of the quarto, for Stephen Duck, the Thresher Poet (*Letters*, p. 114), but we cannot tell whether any such octavo edition was consecutively paginated or a set of pamphlets. The printing of only 250 copies of *Spring*, probably as few of *Winter*, etc., and probably fewer of *Summer* in 1734–5 suggests that Millan and Millar intended to top up and balance stocks of the pamphlet Seasons so that all four might go out of print simultaneously.

WORKS, 1738 (*38*).

The new poems and plays which Thomson wrote after returning to England in the winter of 1732–3 from a two-year Continental tour were issued by Millar, whose position as Thomson's sole publisher was confirmed when, on 16 June 1738, he bought Millan's Thomson copyrights (except rights over the five plates of Kent's design and a portrait, in quarto size only) for £105, the price that Millan had paid Thomson in 1729.[1] 'The Seasons and Other Poems' were duly entered to Millar in the Stationers' Register on 24 June, and he lost little time in asserting his copyright. Before the end of the year he started an action[2] against twenty-nine Glasgow and Edinburgh booksellers whom he accused of selling pirated editions of Thomson's work (perhaps copies imported from Dublin, rather than Scottish printings) and from whom he tried to obtain damages in addition to the customary penalty, under Queen Anne's Copyright Act, of the seizure of copies found in their shops and the fine of a penny a sheet for copies seized.

A new edition of the complete works for which Millar now had copyright was being printed off before the assignment from Millan was actually signed, for on 26 June 1738 the first octavo edition of *The Works of Mr. Thomson*, Printed for A. Millar, was on sale in two five-shilling volumes.[3] Henry Woodfall was the printer; his ledger reads:

June 6, 1738.   Mr. Thomson's Works, vol. i. No. 1000, 8vo., 18 shts. Red title. Vol. ii., No. 1500, 15½ shts. Red title.

June 17, 1738.   1000 red titles for vol. i.[4]

The second charge for a thousand red (and black) titles is for a cancel, which was made necessary by the change in copyright ownership legalized on the day before they were printed.[5]

---

[1] *Letters*, pp. 120–2.

[2] The summons and pleadings, in the Scottish Record Office, Court of Session unextracted processes, under Adams/Dal M/3/4, were brought to my attention by David Foxon, who suggests that the 1738 case might have been by way of a sighting shot for the great copyright battles across the border in the 1760s and 1770s. Warren McDougall adds 'Probably Millar just wanted to warn [the Scottish booksellers] off; at any rate, he saw he was getting nowhere and dropped the case': 'Gavin Hamilton, Bookseller in Edinburgh', *British Journal for Eighteenth-Century Studies* i (1978), 7.

[3] It is referred to as *38* in the present edition.

[4] *Notes and Queries* (June 1855), p. 419.

[5] There is an uncancelled title in a copy of vol. i at Yale.

Woodfall's ledger does not account for the whole work as Millar issued it. The 18 sheets of volume i are A^4, containing half-title and title-page (both reading *The Works* . . .) and list of contents,[1] followed by B–S⁸ T⁴, consecutively paginated, containing the four Seasons (with a fly-title for each one), the *Hymn*, the *Poem to Newton*, *Britannia*, and a fly-title for *Sophonisba*. The volume, as issued, was completed by sheets of *Sophonisba* in a 1730 edition and by five plates re-engraved by Fourdrinier from Kent's designs for the subscription quarto. Similarly, volume ii contains new, reset editions of *Liberty*, in a revised version, and *A Poem to the Memory of Lord Talbot*, followed by reissued sheets of Thomson's plays *Agamemnon* (1738) and, in later copies of the *Works*, *Edward and Eleonora* (1739). Millar's print order seems to imply that he expected a larger sale for volume ii, which contained the first octavo edition of *Liberty* (in a revised text, too), or that he already knew that there was the prospect if a revised version of *The Seasons* which would supersede the edition of 1738. When such a revised edition at last appeared in 1744, surviving copies of the *Works* volume ii (1738) were mated with a new, enlarged volume i, and stocks of the two of them remained on Millar's hands until 1749 at least, in which year they were reissued with a new volume iii.

Nearly all features of typography and text indicate that Woodfall's compositors took a set of pamphlets as copy for volume i of the *Works* (1738). They departed from copy by placing an initial capital to every substantive (except in about 130 instances, over half of them in *Spring*, where lower case was used in error), but in setting proper names and emphatical words they employed large and small capitals throughout *Spring* and then switched to italic in *Summer* and the rest of the volume;[2] that is, they dutifully preserved a typographical discrepancy which had first come about accidentally when pamphlets printed at different times in different shops were brought together to make sets.[3] Where there is faulty

[1] Though newspaper advertisements for the *Works* list the contents of volume i as 'The Seasons', 'A Hymn', etc., the title-page, half-title, fly-titles, and contents-list of the book itself make no reference to 'The Seasons'.

[2] Except for the names of royal personages, dedicatees and Newton (in the *Poem* to his memory) and three possibly significant cases in *Autumn*; see below, p. lxiii, n. 1.

[3] Being a reprint and in verse, the work could have been cast off accurately, so one compositor could have set, say, E1–6 (last lines of *Spring*) while another

line-numbering in earlier texts the 1738 edition tends to follow corrections and mistakes in the pamphlets; when not introducing fresh errors it follows, for the most part, pamphlet punctuation; its spellings, though, are closer to the consecutively paginated octavo. All but one of two dozen substantive variants (certain or probable misprints) which first appeared in the 1730–1 pamphlets reappear in 1738, alongside three more from *Winter*, etc. 1734 and seventeen entirely new ones. Line 411, which had been accidentally left out of the *Autumn* pamphlet, is missing in most copies of the 1738 *Works* too; the error must have been discovered late, in view of the comparative rarity of a cancel leaf L4, pp. 151–2, which was printed to restore the line. The pattern of apparent errors, the omission of line 411 in *Autumn*, the punctuation and the otherwise inexplicable change in typographical style between *Spring* and *Summer* all indicate that copy for the 1738 edition was *Spring* 1734 (or 1731), *Summer* 1730, *Autumn* 1730 and *Winter*, etc. 1734, not the consecutively paginated octavo (*30*). Evidence that the consecutively paginated octavo was set from pamphlets and not from the 1738 edition is, if anything, stronger. Nevertheless these two texts which appear to descend independently of one another from the pamphlets have in common a few readings not found in any earlier text.

Some of these readings are undoubtedly corrections: both the consecutively paginated octavo and 1738 *Works* print *Autumn* lines 927–8[1] in their revised, improved version; both correct a wrong paragraph division at *Summer* line 677 and both correct misprints at *Summer* 452 and *Winter* 490. Seven other, indifferent, variants could possibly be authorial corrections too, despite the

was setting E8 (first lines of *Summer*); even so it is not easy to understand why one should use large and small capitals and the other italic, unless this happened to be what each man found in his copy.

[1] Line 928 of *Autumn* is the only place in the 1738 text after the end of *Spring* where 'Britain', or any other place-name, is set in large and small capitals. This might be taken to indicate that the 1738 compositor was at this point setting from the consecutively paginated octavo, where all proper names are printed in this style; but, from the corrections inscribed, probably in 1743, in the British Library interleaved copy, we know that Thomson's own habit was to double-underline 'Britain', so copy for the two revised lines in 1738 could equally well have been Thomson's manuscript in the form of an *erratum* or a 1738 proof-correction or, indeed, a hand-corrected copy of the 1730 pamphlet. In the twenty lines following 928 are two personal names italicized in the pamphlet but printed in large and small capitals in 1738—perhaps as the result of proof-correction.

fact that all but two are changed back to their pamphlet readings in 1744. One might conjecture that Woodfall was given as copy for the 1738 edition a corrected pamphlet set which had served as copy for the consecutively paginated octavo, or that he was given an unmarked pamphlet-set with a short hand-written list of errata covering *Autumn* 927–8 and perhaps some or all of the indifferent variants; but in either case such corrections apparently failed to take account of the omission of line 411 from the pamphlet *Autumn*. It is possible that Woodfall's compositors in 1738 used an uncorrected pamphlet-set but that his press-corrector referred intermittently to a copy of the consecutively paginated octavo which was known to contain authorial revisions. This would account for the presence of the revised *Autumn* 927–8, the indifferent variants, and the only undoubted error which is common to 1738 and the consecutively paginated octavo but found in no other edition, i.e. *Summer* 535, 'the turn to death' for 'to turn the death'. A press-corrector, not attending carefully to the syntax of a long Thomsonian sentence, might have thought that the wrong reading was the right one, and so imported it into the text he was correcting.

The descent of texts in the 1730s is not easy to trace, but it would seem that the pamphlets of 1730–1 were set from the quarto and, in turn, provided copy for the pamphlets of 1734–5; that the consecutively paginated octavo dated '1730' (perhaps published later) and *Works* 1738 follow the pamphlets by separate lines of descent; and that, after the quarto, Thomson himself made very few revisions and read no proofs carefully or completely, so that misprints accumulated and reached their highest concentration in *Summer* 1735 and *Works* 1738. There can be no doubt, though, that the author himself prepared the next edition of *The Seasons* for the press.

THE SEASONS and *THE WORKS*, 1744 (*44, 44Wks*).

Publication of this extensively revised edition in 1744 might appear to have been influenced by the 1710 Copyright Act, inasmuch as clause xi of that Act provided that, after the expiration of a term of fourteen years from first publication, copyright was to return to the author, if still living, for another fourteen years. If the Act applied, the first term of fourteen years after publication of *The Seasons* entire would have expired in June 1744, but there is no other indication that either Thomson or his booksellers thought that the Act had any bearing upon their dealings, since Thomson's copyright assignments in 1729–30 and Millan's to Millar in 1738 had been 'for ever' and had covered all revisions as well as the original texts. Clause ix in the Copyright Act had implied that the Act's provisions for statutory, limited copyright would not prejudice booksellers' rights under common law, and during the 1730s, through suits in the Court of Chancery, booksellers found that they could successfully claim perpetual copyright under common law.[1] In the two most celebrated copyright cases of the eighteenth century, both concerning reprints of *The Seasons*, counsel for Millar, his executors or assignees argued that Millar had bought a common-law perpetual copyright in the poem, and that the Copyright Act could not set aside such a common law right.[2] Counsel for publishers who had issued the allegedly offending reprints appealed to the Act and claimed that statutory copyright in *The Seasons* had finally expired in 1758, that is twice fourteen years from 1730. The first case, *Millar* v. *Taylor*, was determined in 1769 in favour of Millar and perpetual copyright; but five years later the second case, *Donaldson* v. *Beckett* (who had bought a share in the copyright from Millar's executors), went in favour of Donaldson, and effectively abolished common law copyright. Reports[3] of these cases make no mention of any reassignment by Thomson to Millar in 1744, but they are in may particulars vague and sometimes manifestly inaccurate—for instance about dates. Whether or not Thomson legally recovered copyright in 1744 and sold it again to Millar, it is unlikely that he would have carried out his extensive revisions for the 1744 edition

---

[1] A.S. Collins, *Authorship in the Days of Johnson* (1927), pp. 68–76; see also R. M. Wiles, *Serial Publication in England before 1750* (Cambridge, 1957), pp. 155, 158, 261–6. The eighteenth-century legal battle over literary property was, of course, fought between rival booksellers; any concept of author's rights was peripheral, if not outlandish. In May 1736, at the height of activity in Chancery, Thomson wrote to Aaron Hill, implicitly dismissing the 1710 Act, 'I wish we had one good Act of Parliament for securing to Authors the Property of their own Works' (*Letters*, p. 106; cf. *Castle of Indolence* II, ii).

[2] The summons for the 1738 case had referred to the statutory term of fourteen years, but of course at that date Millar's copyrights were well within the statutory term.

[3] *Millar* v. *Taylor*, 4 Burr. 2303–416, in *English Reports* xcviii, King's Bench Division xxvii (1909), 201–66; *Donaldson* v. *Beckett*, 2 Brown 129–45, in *English Reports* i, House of Lords i (1900), 837–49.

without at least an *ex gratia* payment from his publisher,[1] and it is certain that he needed money in 1743, when he had hopes of marrying.

It is in a letter to his intended bride, Miss Elizabeth Young, that we find the earliest reference to the revised *Seasons*. On 28 April 1743 Thomson wrote:

I am going, if I can, to put a finishing Hand to the Description of a Season now in high Song and Beauty, but to which I am dead. You alone I hear, You alone I see: all Harmony and Beauty are comprized in You. Those Parts, however, will be obliged to You which attempt a Picture of virtuous happy Love.[2]

The lines on virtuous happy love which were added in Thomson's hand near the end of *Spring* in the interleaved copy of *Works* 1738, volume i,[3] where he was making extensive revisions in 1743, and which reappear in the 1744 edition (*OET Sp.* 1158–62), are a paraphrase of part of his previous letter to Elizabeth Young on 19 April.[4]

On 14 July, accepting an invitation to join George Lyttelton at Hagley Park, Thomson wrote:

if you will be so good as to let me know how long you design to stay in the Country, nothing shall hinder me from passing three weeks or a month with you before you leave it. As this will fall in Autumn, I shall like it the better. . . . In the mean time I will go on with correcting and printing the Seasons, and hope to carry down more than one of them with me.[5]

---

[1] 'For though a Bookseller buys an Author's absolute Right, yet he pays him for his Trouble in correcting every Edition; and in those Works, (as most are capable of some Improvement) the Authors sometimes receive, in the Course of the Sale, as much Money for Corrections and Improvements, as was at first paid for the Copy.' (*An Account of the Expence of correcting and improving sundry Books* (1774) bound with Acts of Parliament in the British Library, shelfmark 215, i, 4 (93).) As this *Account* was written by booksellers, the case may be overstated.

[2] *Letters*, p. 154. Thomson probably met Elizabeth Young late in 1742; his first surviving love-letter is dated 10 March 1743 and his last, after she had repeatedly rejected him, 4 November 1745.

[3] Now in the British Library, shelfmark C. 28 e 17. It was previously owned by John Mitford (1781–1859), who described his purchase of it in the *Gentleman's Magazine*, Dec. 1841, p. 564. See also Robert Inglesfield, 'The British Library Revisions to Thomson's *The Seasons*', *The Library*, 6th ser., i (1979), 62–9.

[4] *Letters*, pp. 151–2.

[5] *Letters*, p. 163. Lyttelton and Thomson's friendship dated from the 1730s; see Grant, p. 170.

Thomson probably means 'correcting in readiness for printing', but if printing had actually begun in July 1743 we might have a ready explanation for the large bill which Woodfall sent Millar eleven months later 'for divers and repeated alterations'. That interleaved copy of the 1738 edition mentioned in my previous paragraph, is very probably the actual volume taken to Hagley in August 1743, since it contains corrections in Lyttelton's hand[1] as well as Thomson's. Thomson himself made revisions in this volume later, because one of his manuscript annotations (to line 929 of *OET Au.*) refers to the death of the Duke of Argyll on 14 October 1743. Copy from which Woodfall's long-suffering compositors set the edition which was finally printed off in June 1744 has, of course, not survived, but there can be no doubt that it contained many more authorial revisions. For instance, the story of Damon in *Summer*, untouched in the interleaved copy, is completely rewritten in 1744, with the bathers reduced to one and the moral changed.

None of the very long additional passages first printed in 1744 is found in the interleaved volume, but it is clear from marginal notes and other evidence that drafts of the lines on Hammond, on Chesterfield, on Stowe, and on a modern theory of springs and rivers (*OET Wi.* 555–71, 656–90, *Au.* 1037–81, 756–835) all existed before August 1743, written presumably on detached sheets which have not survived. Asterisks at various points probably indicate places where other new material on loose sheets was to be taken in. One new passage not referred to in the interleaved volume but probably first drafted at Hagley is a description of Hagley Park (*OET Sp.* 904–62), which contains distinct verbal echoes or anticipations of a letter sent by Thomson to Elizabeth Young from Hagley on 29 August.[2]

The interleaved volume was thoroughly worked over, so that corrections in Thomson's hand appear on all but 21 of the 240 pages of text and affect accidentals or substantives in over a thousand lines. Lyttleton's corrections, made usually in the interests of decorum or metrical regularity, affect about 150 lines, over half of them in *Autumn*, and are extensive only in the Palemon and Lavinia story in *Autumn* and the lists of worthies in *Summer* and

---

[1] The ascription to Lyttelton was made by C. G. Macaulay in the *Athenaeum* 1 Oct. 1904, p. 446, and further proof was offered in Zippel, pp. vii–ix; previously it had been thought that the hand was Pope's.   [2] *Letters*, pp. 165–7.

Winter. In nearly every case Thomson accepts the need for a correction, even if he does not take Lyttelton's emendation word for word into his own text. His compliance was remembered twenty years later when James Grainger sent a manuscript of *The Sugar-Cane* to two of his friends for correction: 'You will please to let Mr. Shenstone know, that I can bear to have my verses butchered, as Thomson used to call it, so that they need not stand on ceremony with me.'[1]

When Thomson had finished revising *The Seasons* its total length had been increased by about a quarter. Though many short passages are rewritten in *Spring* and *Autumn*, these two books are enlarged by only about a hundred lines each, the most considerable additions being descriptions of fishing and of Hagley in *Spring*, and a new theory of the origin of rivers and a panegyric on Stowe in *Autumn*. In *Winter* Thomson rewrites more, greatly extends his lists of ancient worthies and northern horrors, and adds compliments to James Hammond, Lord Chesterfield, and Peter the Great, so that the poem is nearly three hundred lines longer than the 1738 text. *Summer* is nearly six hundred lines longer than in 1738: there are new passages on tropical fruits, beasts, sandstorms, hurricanes, and plagues, though the story of a petrified city, added in 1730, is deleted; while to the English scenes are added a sheep-shearing and a summer-evening walk and view from Richmond Hill with an address to 'Amanda' (Elizabeth Young, who is complimented in lines added to *Spring* also). The catalogue of English worthies is lengthened and transposed, a passage on microscopic nature is rewritten and transferred from *Spring*, and the story of Damon is much altered. Such additional material intensifies Thomson's problems of organization,[2] but hundreds of small revisions throughout all parts of *The Seasons* are nearly always improvements in precision, harmony, or vividness.

The revised edition (which is referred to as *44* in the present edition) was published by Millar in July 1744[3] as a 'neat pocket

---

[1] Grainger to Thomas Percy, 5 June 1762, in Nichols, *Illustrations of the Literary History of the Eighteenth Century* vii (1848), 279.

[2] The poet himself admits his difficulty in making transitions between old and new when, after the passage on philosophic melancholy in *Autumn*, he introduces his description of Stowe with a bald 'Or is this gloom too much? Then lead . . .' (1037).

[3] *Daily Advertiser* 17 July. There is a presentation copy dated 23 June; see *Letters*, p. 172.

volume' in crown octavo (where previous Thomson octavos had
been the demy size), and, at 3s. bound, it was the cheapest English
edition of the poem so far. It was also the first time that *The
Seasons* complete had appeared in print unaccompanied by the
Poem to the Memory of Newton, and (apart from the earliest issue
of the quarto) the first time it had appeared without *Britannia*.
Woodfall's ledger entry reads:[1]

> June 19, 1744   Printing Thomson's Seasons, 8vo., No. 1500, 16¼
> shts. Title in red and black. 1500 erratas. For
> divers and repeated alterations, 2l. 4s.

These '1500 erratas' are errata slips, one for each copy of the book,
and not, as has been supposed,[2] the actual number of errors. The
high extra charge of £2. 4s. shows that Woodfall was put to a
great deal of trouble and implies that revision in proof went far
beyond an author's usual tinkerings: Murdoch's recollection that
'his printers were tir'd to death' with Thomson's 'deliberation and
care'[3] perhaps refers to the 1744 edition. Those 'divers and re-
peated alterations' were extra to five leaves of cancels which
must have been accounted for in the charge for 16¼ sheets, since
the book, as published, contains only 125 leaves, collating *A*
(3 leaves) B–Q⁸ R². The cancels[4] are K7, L2.3 and L5.6, containing
lines in *Autumn* corresponding to 189–239, 337–435, and 486–584
in the *OET* text. *Cancellanda* for these leaves have not survived.[5]
The *cancellans* of K7 and of L2.3 both reproduce a text very close
to the revised one in the interleaved volume, but L5.6 has a text
with many further revisions. In a copy at Columbia University
there is a reversed offprint of the plate to *Spring* on the verso of
K7, suggesting that the three leaves of *A* and the cancellans of K7
might have been printed together on the same half-sheet. Some
copies of *The Seasons* 1744 lack a few of the press-figures found
in others, but such differences do not appear to be associated with
any resetting of the text.

[1] *Notes and Queries* (June 1855), p. 419.
[2] Percy Simpson, *Proof-Reading in the Sixteenth, Seventeenth and Eighteenth Centuries* (1935), p. 166.
[3] John Wooll, *Biographical Memoirs of Joseph Warton* (1806), p. 254.
[4] Foxon, p. 794.
[5] In the Pierpont Morgan Library there is a scrap of manuscript in T.'s hand instructing the printer to correct 'embowering' to 'encircling' in *Autumn* (line 210 of the *OET* text). T.'s page reference indicates K7 in *44*; though the same correction appears among the errata in *44 Wks*.

To save expense, the four Kent–Fourdrinier plates which had been used in 1738 were reused, but, because the story of Damon had been revised, a small area of the plate for *Summer* had to be re-engraved to a new design, so that cross-hatched foliage now conceals three of the four bathers over-generously supplied by Kent—except for a ghostly foot, calf, and hand, and a streamer of ectoplasmic drapery. The plates were printed directly onto the ordinary sheets after printing of the letterpress had been completed, and so form part of the collation.

In all editions in the 1730s a patron's name had appeared on the half-title to each Season;[1] but in 1744 these names were dropped, though verse-dedication within the poems themselves remained; and *The Seasons* entire was prefaced by a short prose dedication to Frederick, Prince of Wales, who had earlier commanded performances of Thomson's plays, had received the dedication of *Liberty*, and had bestowed a pension on the poet in 1737. On the verso of the dedication-leaf was a short apology: 'This Poem having been published several Years ago, and considerable Additions made to it lately, some little Anachronisms have thence arisen, which it is hoped the Reader will excuse.' The round of nature is not subject to anachronism, but perhaps Thomson refers to the exploded theory of the origin of rivers which he retains in a shortened form in 1744 in order to refute it (*Au.* 743–837), and to his retention of compliments which address Lord Wilmington, formerly Sir Spencer Compton (*Wi.* 17–40), and the Duke of Argyll (*Au.* 931–45), as if they were still alive, when both men had died in 1743.

Before printing of *The Seasons* 1744 was completed, Woodfall had begun to print off for Millar a new setting of the poem as chief item in volume i of Thomson's *Works* in demy octavo (referred to as *44Wks* in the present edition). The ledger entry on 7 July 1744,[2] recording 1500 copies in 20½ sheets, was for printing *The Seasons*, the *Poem to Newton*, and *Britannia* consecutively paginated, but the volume as published included also a reissue of *Sophonisba*, separately paginated, just as in 1738. The text of *The Seasons* in *Works* 1744 is a reprint with small accidental variants

---

[1] Lord Wilmington's name was omitted, probably in error, from the half-title of *Winter* in *Works* 1738. There is no half-title in *Winter*, etc. 1734 and *Summer* 1735.

[2] *Notes and Queries* (June 1855), p. 419.

from the crown octavo, which it must have followed to press quickly, in view of the ledger date and the fact that seven of its errata (referring to misprints on sheets B to S) coincide with the first seven on the errata list attached to the crown octavo, and only the last three of the earlier errata (all referring to sheet T) are now corrected in the text. There are no cancels, since all material on *cancellantia* in the earlier edition is now printed on the main sheets. The place of a second volume in the set now advertised as *The Works of Mr. Thomson* in two volumes was supplied by remainder copies of the 1738 volume ii, unaltered; the two volumes were offered for 10*s*. bound, but, as in 1738, Millar sold the volumes separately too. Stocks were not exhausted until after both volumes had been mated in 1749 with a *Works*, volume iii, consisting of various issues of the later poems and plays.

THE SEASONS, 1745 and 1746 (*45, 46*)

Fifteen hundred copies of the pocket crown octavo edition (*44*) evidently sold much more quickly then the *Works*, because Woodfall's ledger records on 26 June 1745 the printing of five hundred copies of a new edition in the same format.[1] This new edition, entirely reset, is one leaf shorter than the earlier one because the *Hymn* ends on p. 242, not 243; there is no errata slip because all errata of *The Seasons* 1744 are corrected in the text; and, as there are no cancels, Woodfall charges for only 15½ sheets, not 16¼. The plates of *The Seasons* 1744 were touched up a little and reused, again printed on the ordinary sheets. The title-page is a reprint of the earlier title-page, even to the date 1744, but the text which follows is not a simple reprint. Most variants between this edition and the crown octavo actually printed in 1744 are accidentals, but there is authorial substantive revision in *Spring*, lines 208–455. J. E. Wells infers that Thomson had begun to revise the poem, and had gone through the first five hundred lines, when Millar's stock of the true 1744 edition ran low and a smallish edition was required to keep the book in print until a full revision was completed and a new, large edition could be launched. Alternatively, Thomson may have been tempted to a little more rewriting in proof, and tinkered with sheets B and C before he gave up, or was persuaded

[1] Referred to as *45* in the present edition, and styled '*1744 B*' by J. E. Wells in 'Thomson's "Seasons", An Unnoticed Edition', *Englische Studien* lxxii (1938), 221–2.

to keep his other revisions for the later edition. The 250 copies of *Spring* reprinted by Woodfall in 1734, but dated '1731', and perhaps also the consecutively paginated octavo dated '1730', provided a precedent for false-dating.

The last edition of *The Seasons* issued in Thomson's lifetime is referred to in the present edition as *46*. It was recorded in Woodfall's ledger on 9 May 1746:

> Printing a new edition of Thomson's Seasons, 12 mo., with alterations, No. 4000, 10 shts. Recomposing the first sheet. Title in red and black.[1]

Ten sheets are accounted for in the collation A^2 B–K^{12} L^{10} (A^2 and L^{10} being printed together). As there is a charge for recomposing the first sheet, we are not surprised to find in surviving copies of the 1746 edition two variant states of sheet B (lines 1–520 of *Spring*). However, the text of the rarer of these states differs from the other only in containing sixty-four errors (mostly dropped punctuation and literals), which suggests that the sheet was not read by the press-corrector. J. E. Wells conjectures that the first print-order was for less than 4,000, and argues that, after sheet B had been set, corrected, printed, and perfected, and the type distributed, Millar raised his order to 4,000. This total could be printed of the later sheets without resetting, but sheet B, Wells says, 'must be reset and copies from the new set-up must be run off to make a new total. This new work on the first sheet will be done hastily, for the rest of the book will be waiting.'[2] As a result the final heap of sheet B would contain a mixture of good early copies and faulty later ones, all to be gathered indifferently into individual copies of the book. Wells seems to assume that sheets were set and printed one by one in the order of signatures from B, but this is not necessarily the case. Many patterns of work-flow were possible, particularly with copy as easy to cast off as this was.[3] Nevertheless his hypothesis may be correct; there are parallel cases in the resetting of one sheet of *Roderick Random*, second edition 1748, and the resetting of nearly half of Prior's *Poems on Several Occasions* 1718,[4] in the first case probably and in the second case

---

[1] *Notes and Queries* (June 1855), p. 419.

[2] J. E. Wells, 'Variants in the 1746 Edition of Thomson's *Seasons*', *The Library* xvii (1936), 219.

[3] See D. F. McKenzie, 'Printers of the Mind', *Studies in Bibliography* xxii (1969), 1–75.

[4] See A. H. Smith, 'A Duplicate Setting in the Second Edition of Smollett's

certainly on account of an enlarged print-order. In both instances
the second setting has more errors than the first, and in the case
of Prior's *Poems* it has been argued that corruptions 'indicate
carelessness such as might be indulged in by a compositor who
knew that he was setting for a mere fill-in that would not be proof-
read by the author and would probably not be read against copy
even in the shop'.[1] It may be that the same considerations, or
inconsiderations, applied in Woodfall's shop in 1746.

The 1746 duodecimo contains the last revisions we can con-
fidently attribute to Thomson himself. They consist of sustantive
changes to fewer than a hundred lines of the entire poem, the
deletion of two lines from *Autumn*, and the addition of nine to
Summer and three to *Spring*. Compositors could have worked
from a not too heavily marked copy of the 1744 or 1745 editions.
J. E. Wells, claiming that the accidentals of lines 1–500 of *Spring*
are 'greatly closer' to 1745 while those in the rest of the poem are
'greatly closer' to 1744, argues that the 1746 edition was set from
a marked copy of 1744, perhaps the one prepared for the printers
in 1745 further corrected by hand; this would imply that author's
copy returned from the printing-shop in a fit state to be used
again.[2] However this greater closeness of 1746 to 1744 lies only in
thirty variants, which are cases of normalizing or correcting obvious
literals and faulty punctuation in 1745, resulting in readings
coincidental with 1744; and so the possibility remains that the
1746 edition was set from a marked copy of 1745, the sub-
stantively closer edition. The likelihood remains, too, that some of
the new readings of 1746 were not in any marked copy at all, but
were inserted by the author on proof-sheets, since Woodfall's bill
for 'alterations' suggests that there was revision in proof.

For the 1746 edition the Kent–Fourdrinier engravings were
reused, again printed on the ordinary sheets as in 1744 and 1745.
It seems that the copper plates, which, in various retouched states,
had yielded several thousand impressions since 1738, had become
so worn before the 1746 edition was completely printed off that

Roderick Random', *The Library*, 5th ser. xxviii (1973), 309–18; and H. B. Wright,
'Ideal Copy and Authoritative Text: The Problem of Prior's *Poems on Several
Occasions* (1718)', *Modern Philology* xlix (1951–2), 234–41. David Foxon drew
my attention to these examples.

[1] H. B. Wright, op. cit., p. 239.
[2] 'Thomson's "Seasons", 1744—An Unnoticed Edition', *Englische Studien*
lxxii (1938), 226.

a duplicate set had to be engraved;[1] the engraver mistakenly copied designs from the 1738 (or 1730 quarto) plates, and consequently produced a plate for *Summer* showing four bathers. There is an impression of such a plate, printed on the ordinary sheet, in a copy of *The Seasons* 1746 at Columbia University. It seems that when the mistake was discovered a corner of this plate was re-engraved to eliminate three redundant nudes, just as the 1738 plate had been re-engraved in 1744, though in this duplicate re-engraving the inevitable spectral hand and foot are less prominent than in 1744. Impressions of this re-engraved duplicate plate are found as a cancel-leaf D2 in some copies of the 1746 edition which were issued with new preliminaries and a cancel-sheet H to do duty as volume i of *Works* 1750 (cf. below p. lxxv).[2]

Posthumous editions to 1762 (*50*, *52dd*, *52pd*, *57*, *58*, *62q*, *62d*).

Thomson lived out his last years in easy circumstances with three hundred pounds a year from a government sinecure procured for him by Lyttelton in 1744. He completed two more plays—the highly successful *Tancred and Sigismunda*, acted 1745, and *Coriolanus*, acted 1749—and died in August 1748, three months after first publication of *The Castle of Indolence*. Lyttelton was an executor of the poet's estate and took full discretionary powers as redactor of the poems when preparing the edition of Thomson's *Works* published in four volumes duodecimo in 1750. The publisher was Millar, and the printer of volumes ii, iii, and iv was William Strahan, whose ledger contains a record of the job in September 1749: '34 sheets, no. 2000.'[3] Volume ii contains poems other than *The Seasons*, volumes iii and iv the plays. Textually volume ii differs from earlier editions in that two stanzas are deleted from *The Castle of Indolence*, *Britannia* is much revised, and *Liberty* reduced from five books to three, with the omission of 1,450 lines. The place of volume i in this edition was supplied by remainder copies of *The Seasons* 1746, two thousand of which

---

[1] At the Oxford University Press there are duplicate plates of Gravelot's tailpieces for Hanmer's *Shakespeare*, the second set engraved to replace the heavily worn first set: see Harry Carter, *A History of the Oxford University Press* i (1975), 305 n.

[2] In this issue plates for the other three seasons are cancels too, though their designs do not differ from those of 1738.

[3] Foxon, p. 794. Volumes ii, iii, and iv contain altogether 33⅓ sheets. The other two-thirds of a sheet might have been used for new preliminaries to volume i (four leaves), and for cancel plates (four leaves).

probably remained of the original printing since that was the number of cancels required (see next paragraph). Judging by survivors, most remainder copies had sheet B in its corrected state.[1] To adapt these copies to their new role, the preliminary leaves (A^2) were cancelled and replaced by two pairs of conjugate leaves containing half-title and title-page to the *Works*, volume i, dated 1750, a dedication to Frederick, Prince of Wales, of 'this complete and correct edition of all the works of the late Mr. Thomson, agreeably to his intention when living', and an unsigned, undated preface, reading:

This edition of Mr. Thomson's works was designed by him, and must be considered by the reader, as a collection of such of his works as he thought worth preserving, corrected and amended. . . . It is hoped, that all his writings will appear much more advantageously in their present form, (many redundancies being pruned away, and many faults of diction corrected) than they did in their first publication

As we have seen, *Liberty* in volume ii was heavily pruned; but in *The Seasons* shears were employed only on part of *Autumn* where a cut and some rewriting were effected by a cancel-sheet printed by Strahan and recorded in his ledger in February 1750: 'Letter H of the Seasons, no. 2000.'[2] This *cancellans* (refered to as *50* in the present edition) contains a scattering of substantive changes from the 1746 text but the most considerable revision is the deletion of burlesque descriptions of a fox-hunt and drinking-bout at lines 483–569 of *Autumn*. These lines were not lost but had gone before, inasmuch as they had been revised, supplied with a new opening and a title—'The Return from the Fox-Chace, a Burlesque Poem, in the Manner of Mr. Philips'—and printed off by Strahan five months earlier as the last item in volume ii of the *Works*; (see Appendix C below). An unsigned footnote explained that

The greater part of these verses were formerly inserted in Mr. Thomson's *Autumn*; but being of a different character and stile from the rest, and rather belonging to the Mock Heroick, or Burlesque way of writing, it has been judged proper to leave them out *there* in the present edition, and insert them here, by themselves.

---

[1] The only copy which I have traced of *Works*, vol. i (1750), with an uncorrected sheet B is in the National Library of Scotland. This copy is unusual too in that it retains the original sheet H of 1746, instead of the *cancellans* described in my next paragraph.   [2] Foxon, p. 800.

There cannot be much doubt that Lyttelton wrote this footnote and the preface to volume i, and was responsible for alterations in the text of the poems. Sending a complimentary, and self-complimentary, copy to a friend in March 1750, he declared that the edition had been made 'under my care', and went on:

You will find this edition much preferable to any of the former. . . . Great corrections have been made in the diction, and many redundancies have been cutt off, which hurt the spirit, and weak'ned the force of the more sublime and nervous parts; so that upon the whole I am persuaded you will think Mr. Thomson a much better poet, if you take the trouble to read over his works in their present from, than you ever thought him before.[1]

We know that Thomson discussed his work with Lyttelton and accepted many of his patron's proposed revisions into the 1744 text, but there is no positive evidence that he ever approved the changes made over his dead body in 1750.

Though an advertisement for the *Works* in four volumes appeared in the *Gentleman's Magazine* for February 1750, there was no entry for such a work in the Stationers' Register until 12 October 1751, so the entry may possibly refer to a reissue of volumes ii, iii, and iv of the 1750 impression, mated with a reset volume i, dated 1752, which contains new preliminaries[2] and a text of *The Seasons* reprinted from the 1750 issue of the 1746 text with its cancel-sheet H. The reprint (referred to as *52dd* in the present edition) is line by line, with the odd effect that twelve leaves of *Autumn*, from G10 to H9, have lines that are more widely spaced than in the rest of the volume because they carry the abbreviated text of the 1750 cancel-sheet; but page numbers do not agree with those of 1746 and 1750 because the engravings (apparently from plates in their latest re-engraved state of 1746) are now extra to the collation, not being printed on the sheet as in 1744, 1745, and 1746. Substantive changes between this text and

---

[1] R. Phillimore, *Memoirs of Lord Lyttelton* (1845), i, 322–3. Editions of *The Seasons* 1746–62 are described and discussed in J. E. Wells, 'Thomson's *Seasons* "Corrected and Amended"', *JEGP* xlii (1943), 104–14. Substantive variants in these editions are printed in Appendix C of the present edition.

[2] Copies with some or all of the 1750 as well as the 1752 preliminaries bound in together are found in the British Library, Bodleian, and Cambridge University Library, perhaps all deposit copies. A cancel-leaf H9 (to correct a single misprint) was printed on the same sheet as the 1752 preliminaries and is bound with them in the Bodleian copy, while the *cancellandum* remains in position.

that of 1746–50 are very few and could all be attributable to the printer. The preface to this volume is reprinted from the 1750 preface, with the omission of the words 'many redundancies being pruned away, and many faults of diction corrected' and the addition of a date, 1 Oct. 1751.

Sheets of this volume i, without the general *Works* title page, but with all the other preliminaries of the *Works*, were reissued with a cancel-title as *The Seasons* 1752. Millar at the same time published a reset, cheaper edition in the pot-duodecimo size—that is, smaller than his earlier Thomson duodecimos, all of which had been in the demy size. The pot-duodecimo edition of *The Seasons* 1752 (referred to as *52pd* in the present edition) has no preface, dedication or plates. Its text is a straight reprint of the demy-duodecimo of 1752 with a few printer's errors corrected and a few more introduced. Advertisements bound in at the end of copies of all these 1752 issues include one for Thomson's *Works* in three volumes octavo, price 15*s*., which must refer to sets made up of volume i 1744, volume ii 1738, and volume iii 1749; so, not for the first time, variant texts of *The Seasons* (and now, too, of other poems) were on sale simultaneously.

In 1757 Millar published another edition of the *Works* in four volumes demy-duodecimo. Volumes ii, iii, and iv were reprinted from the corresponding three volumes of the *Works* 1750. Copy for the text of *The Seasons* in volume i (referred to as *57* in the present edition) seems, from the pattern of printer's errors, to have been the pot-duodecimo of 1752; but the preliminaries of this volume, including the preface to, and dedication of, the *Works*, were reprinted from the 1752 demy-duodecimo. The 1757 volume i contains newly engraved plates copied from those of Fourdrinier in the editions of 1738–52, and, as in 1752, copies of this volume were supplied with a cancel-title so that they could be sold as a separate issue of *The Seasons*.

About this time Lyttelton must have been planning more corrections and amendments, for in the library at Hagley Hall there was once an interleaved copy of the 1752 volume i with the title-page date altered, in ink, to 1758 and the text riddled with revisions and deletions and plastered with additions in Lyttelton's handwriting.[1] A manuscript preface to this volume explains why

---

[1] R. Phillimore, *Memoirs of Lord Lyttelton* (1845), i, 319–22. It is thought that this volume was destroyed in a fire at Hagley in 1925, but its readings were

Lyttelton has made such sweeping changes as the deletion of the entire *Hymn*, and claims that in correcting what he calls Thomson's harshness and obscurity he is acting 'conformably to the intention and will of the Author', It seems that Millar, having been asked by Lyttelton to include these new emendations in a forthcoming edition, referred the matter to Thomson's close friend Patrick Murdoch, who wrote back to Millar, saying:

With regard to the alterations proposed to be made in Mr. Thomson's *Seasons*, having now fully considered that matter, and seen how few and inconsiderable his own last corrections were; I am confirmed in my first opinion—so much, that I shall retract most of my concessions, and even some of the alterations which I thought I had made for the better. In a word, I can have no hand in any edition that is much different from the small one of 1752, which I shall send you, with as many corrections as seem necessary, marked on the margin.

A detail of my reasons would be needless, it being agreed that an author's works should be presented genuine and entire. If he has written well, well: if not the sin lieth, and ought to lye, at *his* door. It is pity indeed that Mr. T. aided by my Lord L. did not correct and alter many things himself; but as that went no farther than a bare intention, 'tis too late to think of it now.[1]

Murdoch went on to defend the retention of the *Hymn*, which Lyttelton wanted to delete, and the restoration of the burlesque, which Lyttelton had deleted in 1750–7, and to justify one of his own alterations, which, at *Sp.* 65, restores the 1730 quarto reading. Critics[2] have assumed that this undated letter must refer to the two-volume subscription quarto edition of Thomson's *Works* 'with his last Corrections and Improvements', prefaced by Murdoch's *Life* of the poet, which Millar published in 1762 to raise money for a monument to Thomson in Westminster Abbey; but since the letter speaks only of *The Seasons* (not, for instance, of *Liberty*, where Lyttelton's revisions of 1750–7 had been so very much more considerable), and since the 1762 text is, in fact, a very

transcribed by John Mitford into an edition of Thomson's *Works* (1768) now in the British Library (shelfmark C. 134 c 1) and by Zippel in his edition of *The Seasons* (1908), pp. xxii–xxxi. See Appendix C of the present edition.

[1] John Wooll, *Biographical Memoirs of Joseph Warton* (1806), pp. 252–3. According to a story retailed by Mrs Elizabeth Montagu in 1773, it was Mrs Millar who objected to Lyttelton's revisions; see *James Beattie's London Diary, 1773*, ed. R. S. Walker (Aberdeen, 1946), p. 53.

[2] See Grant, pp. 277–8; and J. E. Wells, 'Thomson's *Seasons* "Corrected and Amended"', *JEGP* xlii (1943), 109–10.

close reprint of the demy-duodecimo edition of *The Seasons* published by Millar in 1758 (and referred to as *58* in the present edition), I think it likely that this duodecimo is the projected work under discussion in Murdoch's letter. Such a conjecture is supported by the fact that Lyttelton wrote '1758' on the title-page of his revised copy.

If Murdoch was editor of the duodecimo printed in 1758, as I believe to be the case, he evidently took the 1752 pot-duodecimo as the basis of his text, retored lines 483–569 of *Autumn* from the text of 1744–5 (not 1746), retained the other variants of 1750 together with most of the further variants of 1752–7, and introduced some thirty extra substantive variants from 1746, a few of which restore readings of 1744 or earlier and a few more of which are among Lyttelton's revisions for his proposed edition of 1758, but most of which are entirely new. This 1758 text was reprinted, with only a few slight changes, in the 1762 subscription quarto edition of Thomson's *Works* 'with his last Corrections and Improvements' and in the duodecimo reprint of that edition in the same year (referred to respectively as *62q* and *62d* in the present edition). Murdoch's text of 1758–62 seems to have been the model for most reprints of *The Seasons* until Bolton Corney in 1841[1] argued that the 1746 text was Thomson's final form of the poem, and should be preferred by editors.

However well intentioned Lyttelton and Murdoch may have been, their labours had, in Johnson's words, 'a manifest tendency to lessen the confidence of society, and to confound the characters of authors, by making one man write by the judgement of another.'[2] The latest text which certainly has Thomson's authority and cannot confound his literary character must be *The Seasons*, 1746.

3. THE PRESENT TEXT

An editor of *The Seasons* who held to Sir Walter Greg's classic theory of copy-text and accepted the prime authority of the first printed text in matters of spelling, punctuation, and other such 'accidentals' would produce a strange patchwork made up of the five different systems of punctuation and typography which are displayed in the first printings of each Season and in the copious

---

[1] 'Memorandum on the Text of The Seasons', *Gentleman's Magazine* (Feb. 1841), pp. 145–9.   [2] 'Thomson' in *Lives of the Poets* (1781), iv. 261.

additions of 1730 and 1744. There is, however, a stronger objection
to applying Greg's theory to *The Seasons*, for, whatever may have
been the habits of other eighteenth-century writers, Thomson,
like Pope,[1] attended to accidentals when revising printed copy for
the press. His sporadic attentiveness to accidentals in 1743-4 is
plain to see on the pages of the British Library interleaved volume,
while his earlier attentiveness may be inferred, firstly, from the
purposeful and progressive nature of revision to accidentals,
particularly punctuation, in substantively revised texts down to
and including *30q*, secondly, from a similarity between changing
habits in the revised printed texts of 1726-30 and changing habits
in Thomson's holograph letters of the same period, and, thirdly,
from the scarcity of variant accidentals in texts not substantively
revised. In a note at the end of this Introduction I offer more
detailed remarks on accidentals in the earlier editions and Thom-
son's hand in them. Between 1744 and Thomson's death variants
in accidentals are few. Most of those in *45* look like printers' errors,
but the majority of those in *46* (in copies with the 'good' sheet B)
are purposeful enough to suggest that they are authorial. The
trickle of small substantive revisions together with Woodfall's bill
for 'alterations' (revisions in proof presumably) are further
indications that the 1746 edition was proof-read by Thomson.

The text of the present edition, therefore, is *46* reproduced
literatim, except for the correction of obvious misprints, the
emendation of punctuation where it seems misleading, the inser-
tion of hyphens where necessary to indicate syntactical relation-
ships, and the provision of missing apostrophes for 'thro' and 'tho',
and of initial capital letters for single-word nouns on the few
occasions where *46* has lower case. Elsewhere the inconsistent
initial capitalization of *46* is allowed to remain, since I have found
no consistency in Thomson's own practice of sometimes giving
initial capitals to pronouns and adjectives (for emphasis or honorific
intent) and to hyphenated compound-nouns (which he evidently
regarded sometimes as two words, sometimes as one). All emenda-
tions, except the provision of initial capital letters for single-word
nouns and of apostrophes for 'thro' and 'tho', are listed in a table
in Appendix D as well as being recorded at the appropriate place
in the textual apparatus.

[1] See David Foxon, 'Greg's "Rationale" and the Editing of Pope', *The
Library*, 5th ser., xxxiii (1978), 119-24.

The apparatus records substantive variants in all editions earlier than *46*, in Thomson's letters, in newspaper announcements, and in revisions inscribed in Thomson's or in Lyttelton's hand upon the British Library interleaved copy of *38*.[1] For the purposes of the apparatus I treat this interleaved volume as I treat the printed texts: a full facsimile of the volume might be of considerable interest to bibliographers and to some students of Thomson but would be out of place in the present edition. My inclusion in the apparatus of revisions proposed by Lyttelton in the interleaved volume but not accepted into any printed text in Thomson's lifetime calls for comment. Admittedly, these revisions are not authoritative, but, since in many cases they form a necessary intermediate stage between *38* and *44*, I have thought it best to regard all of them as part of a collaborative authorial process of revision, and so record them in the main apparatus rather than in Appendix C, where I list substantive variants introduced by Lyttelton and Murdoch into the printed texts of 1750–62 and revisions drafted by Lyttelton in 1758 for an edition never printed. When recording both manuscript and printed variants I exclude obvious errors, such as dropped or transposed words or letters, or words which produce quite implausible readings or are corrected in errata lists.[2] My policy of including all other substantive variants must mean that a few probably unauthorial readings have been admitted to the apparatus; but they remain because some of what I guess are compositor's errors have influenced the course of Thomson's own revision (e.g. *Sp.* 728, 743) and because we cannot be absolutely certain that any one of them is not authorial.

Substantive variants in the apparatus are regularly reproduced

---

[1] Shelfmark C. 28 e 17; see p. lxvi n. 3 above. In the Dyce Collection there is a copy of *Wi. 26f* (*Dyce* 9893) with manuscript emendations on p. 9, never taken into any printed edition of *Winter*; in the British Library there are copies of *Sp.31* and *Su.30p* (bound together in 1486 b. 29) and in Edinburgh University Library a copy of *300* (*JA* 476) containing manuscript emendations which appear to be partial and not wholly accurate attempts to record the revisions of *44*. None of this manuscript is in Thomson's hand and none is taken into my apparatus. Furthermore, the apparatus excludes variants in the unauthorized editions printed in Dublin and in Edinburgh, and variants in the English texts printed, with B. H. Brockes's German translation, in Hamburg, 1740–5.

[2] One erratum for *30q* is keyed impossibly to 'line 284' on 'p. 169'. I conjecture that it was meant to refer to the line numbered 894 on p. 169 and called for an emendation (from 'the' to 'a') which was subsequently made at that point in the text in *MS* and *44–6*. Nevertheless I have allowed the original, possibly incorrect, reading to stand in the apparatus (cf. *OET Au.* 949).

with the accidentals of their first appearance (whether manuscript
or printed), but no attempt has been made to offer a complete
record of other accidentals. A selective record of variant accidentals,
which is printed in smaller type, takes no account of any spelling
variant which does not constitute a new word (as defined in *OED*),
any variant of hyphenation (except those affecting syntax), any
variant of initial capitalization (except those indicating a changed
part of speech or those associated with a change of punctuation),
any obvious error of punctuation (such as a dropped colon or full
stop), or any simple transliteration from italic to large and small
capitals or vice versa. So the record consists mostly of variant
punctuation and variations between the regular type (usually
roman) and an 'emphatic' or 'honorific' form (usually italic or large
and small capitals).[1] This selective procedure will, I hope, preserve
what is most significant out of ten thousand or more variant
accidentals among printings and manuscripts from 1726 to 1746.
A full history of, say, *Wi.* 406 (*Lyon 260* Lyon *28* lyon *30q 30p 34*
lion *300* Lion *38–46*), and *Su.* 58 (Forest-Glade, *27* forest ʌ glade ʌ
30q–35 forest ʌ Glade ʌ *38* Forest-Glade ʌ *MS* Forest-glade ʌ
44–46) and a few thousand comparable examples would not be
instructive enough to justify the expense of providing it in a printed
edition.

Throughout the apparatus authorities are ranked in the order
of the explanatory list on p. xi, so that, for example, the symbol
'*260–38*' in the apparatus to *Winter* signifies *Wi.260, Wi.28, 30q,
Wi.30p, 300, Wi.34,* and *38*. Literal prefixes are usually dropped,
so that '*28*' signifies *Wi.28* in the apparatus to *Winter* but *Sp.28* in
the apparatus to *Spring*. Headnotes list authorities for the *OET*
text and, where appropriate, authorities for any distinct section of
variant text printed immediately below in the apparatus. The
reader may assume that in each textual note the lemma is the
reading of all authorities listed in the immediately preceding
headnote except those specified in the note itself as reading other-
wise. However, where the *OET* text reading is found first in *MS*
or *MSLytt* and this information cannot conveniently be given in
a headnote it is given beside the lemma itself. Lemmata for variant

---

[1] Extracts from *Spring* in the *Whitehall Evening-Post* and *The Present State of
the Republic of Letters* were set in italic, with roman for emphasis; but these
styles are reversed in the apparatus to *Sp.* 340–70, 614–30, in order to bring them
into line with other texts where roman is the norm.

accidentals are usually omitted because each variant will indicate the relevant word in the *OET* text and in all texts which the appropriate headnote specifies as having the same substantive reading. However, a lemma is supplied when it is necessary to indicate that a variant accidental occurs first in *MS* or *MSLytt*. Where the variant is one of punctuation a caret indicates the absence of punctuation and a tilde does duty for a preceding word. Terminal punctuation is omitted, except to indicate a variant. All plain line numbers refer to the *OET* text; bracketed line numbers and numbers followed by 'a' refer to the variant text.

In setting out variants in a single apparatus keyed to the final authoritative text I have been obliged to rearrange the material of early editions in accordance with the order of lines in *46*, and consequently may have concealed from the reader significant differences of arrangement and of scale between Thomson's first and last versions of *Summer* and *Winter*. To make these differences clear the first editions of these two poems are printed *literatim* as Appendix A to the present edition. Consequently most of the text of both poems appears twice: *seriatim* in the appendix, and dispersed piecemeal in the main text and apparatus. However six distinct passages of some length (*Su.27*, 558–70, 803–26, 877–87, 1007–20, 1044–75, and *Wi.26f*, 17–111) which Thomson completely deleted before *30q* or transferred in a revised form to *Au. 30q* are not repeated in the apparatus to *Su* and *Wi*.

Appendix B contains prose dedications and other prefatory matter which Thomson discarded before *46*. Substantive variants in press-variant issues of *Wi.260* and later editions of Aaron Hill's commendatory poem are recorded; variants in accidentals are not, though emendations are noted in Appendix D. Appendix C, containing revisions to *The Seasons* by Lyttelton and Murdoch after Thomson's death, has already been referred to.

NOTE: ACCIDENTALS IN THE EARLY EDITIONS

I

In ascending order of importance accidental variants are of spelling, of italic or capitals employed for emphasis, and of punctuation.

Assuming that the unidentified printer of *Spring* 1728 was not Campbell, Blandford, or Richardson, we have first editions of the different Seasons each set up and printed in a different shop, so we are surprised to find many spelling variants between them, but there are inconsistencies within each first edition too. Thus *Wi.26f* has 'rolls', 'rowl', 'bless'd', 'vex'd', 'blest', and 'distrest'; *Su.27* has 'Musick', 'Music', 'Sithe', and 'Sythe'; *Sp.28* has 'mix'd', 'mixt', 'Choir', 'Quire', 'Musick', and 'Music'; *Au.30q* has 'rowl' and 'roll' on the same page, 'croud', 'crowd', 'mix'd,' 'mixt', 'checker'd', and 'checquer'd'. Such lists could be extended. We cannot know how many such doublets occurred in copy and how many were created by compositors' departure from copy, but it is worth noting that Thomson's manuscript draft of the opening of *Winter* has two spellings of 'welcome' in successive lines (see p. xxxv above).

30q was probably set up from the author's corrected copies of *Sp.28*, *Su.27*, and *Wi.28* together with manuscript inserts for *Autumn*, the *Hymn*, much of *Winter*, and some of *Summer*. It was very probably proof-read by the author, who may have been responsible for intermittent efforts to normalize spellings in both reprinted and new sections; so that a final 'k' is added to most, but not all, adjectives and nouns ending '-ic' in earlier texts, 'y' is usually preferred to 'i' or 'ie' (e.g. 'lyon', 'dy'd'), final 't' to 'd' (e.g. 'thatcht', 'tost'), and 'ou' to 'ow' (e.g. 'scouling'); but inconsistencies appear in the new material in the spelling of frequently repeated words, such as 'mix'd'/'mixt', 'croud'/'crowd', and 'lie'/ 'ly'.

Intermittent normalizing, probably mostly by compositors, in the series of reprints which stemmed from the quarto introduced about as many anomalies as it removed; so that, at the end of the series, the text of *38* in the interleaved volume upon which Thomson made revisions for *44* contained hundreds of spelling variants from the various first editions and some fifty doublets; but he seems not to have been greatly concerned by this. With his pen he changes 'Aether' in the 1738 printed text to 'Ether' on nearly every appearance, substitutes 'e' for 'ae' in '*Palaemon*', 'Chimaeras', 'primaeval', and twice corrects 'cheer' to 'chear', but he appears to have no settled views on the spelling of other words. So, for instance, though he corrects 'Clamour' and 'Rigours' to 'Clamor' and 'Rigors'[1] once each, he allows dozens of other

---

[1] As *44* has modern English spellings in both these cases (cf. *OET Au.* 360 and *Wi.* 424) it looks as if either Thomson had second thoughts or, less probably,

'-our' endings to remain, including another case of 'Clamour'.
He once corrects 'thatch'd' to 'thatcht', then deletes his correction
and writes 'stet'. In manuscript additions he has both 'fierce' and
'cheif', 'wrathfull' and 'skilful', 'Gothic' and 'Italick', 'its' and
'it's', 'Mix'd' and 'mixt'. He writes 'enchanting', but, in other new
passages of *44* which are not in the interleaved volume, we find
'inchanting' and 'inchanted'. This is in accordance with what
appears to be Thomsonian vacillation, since, in the earlier editions
and the holograph letters, there is a brisk alternation between the
'in' and the 'en' prefix for such words as 'inclose', 'increase',
'ingage', 'inlarge', 'inrich', 'intangled', 'intire'. In substantively
unaltered passages *44* prints most of the spelling revisions noted by
Thomson upon the interleaved volume, but otherwise reproduces
almost entirely the spellings, with their inconsistencies, of 1738.
So the doublet 'rowl'/'roll' reappears again on the same page of
Autumn, as elsewhere, and both spellings occur too in new
material. The evidence of the interleaved volume supports one's
inference from the printed texts, early and late, that Thomson had
opinions upon the way printers ought to spell his text, but that
these opinions were far from settled.

The first editions of *Winter*, *Summer*, and *Spring* are printed
after the customary manner with initial capitals to all nouns and
(except for a number of cases in *Spring*) to both elements in all
hyphenated compound-nouns. In the quarto all common nouns
are printed wholly in lower case except for a tiny number of
apparently random examples which may well be the result of
proof-correction by an author momentarily inattentive to the
typographical style of the sheets before him. Certainly the common
nouns with initial capitals do not appear to constitute a class of
particularly significant words. As I have explained on p. lviii n. 1
above, the *1730–5* pamphlets and *300* follow the quarto closely
except the they progressively reduce the capitalization to a very
small extent.

The rule in *38* is to set initial capitals to all nouns, but lower
case is set about two hundred times, some fifty of them occurring
at the second element in a compound noun where the first element
has a capital. In the interleaved volume Thomson occasionally

that the compositors did not endorse his latinisms here—despite their acceptance
of 'Splendor' (*Au.* 1210) and 'Ardor' (*Hymn* 88), both of which are so spelt in all
earlier editions.

marks the printed lower case of *38* for alteration to capital and once
asks for lower case instead of capital ('village-Dog' for 'Village-Dog'
at *Wi.* 734), but he tends to use initial capitals in new material, and
if he transcribes the printed text in the course of reworking a
passage of several lines he will generally give an initial capital to
any anomalous lower case noun he finds. So, for instance, in the
first rewritten passage of any length (*Spring*, 136ff., now at *OET
Su.* 295–307), he substitutes initial capitals for lower case in
'Sun-beams', 'Forest-boughs', 'green', 'millions' and 'taste'. He
tends to capitalize more consistently for single-word nouns than
for compounds; so he writes 'Wall-Flower' but 'Red breast', thus
continuing an inconsistent practice which was at least as old as
Sp.28 where we find, for instance, 'Black-bird' and 'Bosom-
slaves' alongside 'Rose-Bud' and 'School-Boy' etc. In *44* nearly
all the initial capitals of Thomson's MS are set, and over half the
l.c. initials of *38* are raised to capitals. In *46* a few more are raised.

Thomson's approval of his compositors' practice in capitaliza-
tion which I have just described may be inferred from his own
habits as a letter-writer. Though four dozen holograph letters
survive, they are mostly early or late, with only eight from the
1730s, but they indicate that before October 1725 and during the
period of at least two years from October 1730 it was not Thomson's
habit to put initial capitals to common nouns, whereas at other
times it was.[1] As the quarto was a subscription edition, printed
for the author, we may infer that Thomson approved the new,
'neat', lower-case style, particularly as he adopted this style
shortly afterwards for his private correspondence. In the 1730
printings of *Sophonisba* common nouns are in lower case too,
whereas in *Liberty* 1735–6 and all later works except *Alfred* (1740)
they have initial capitals as a rule. Possibly Thomson was not
consulted over the reversion to initial capitalization for *The
Seasons* in *38*, as that text was a mere reprint, but he had certainly
made the same reversion in his own letters several years before
and it is clear that the author intended to have consistent initial
capitals for common nouns in *44*.

In the first editions personal pronouns are set with an initial

[1] We cannot be certain as to when Thomson reverted to initial capitals for
nouns in his private letters, since there are no surviving holographs between
October 1732 (very lightly capitalized) and August 1735 (heavily capitalized).
Thomson would have been reading proofs of *Liberty*, and presumably approving
its capitalization, in the last weeks of 1734.

capital occasionally in *Winter*, consistently in *Summer*, and fairly frequently in *Spring*; while a few significant adjectives in *Winter* and *Spring* take an initial capital too. Nearly all these pronouns and adjectives are reduced to lower case in *30q* (though a few initial capitals for pronouns appear anomalously at the end of *Autumn*) and remain thus in *38*. In the interleaved volume both Thomson and Lyttelton occasionally place an initial capital to a pronoun or adjective. So, in his first rewriting of *Sp*. 861, Thomson emends 'thee, boon SPRING, to 'Thee Boon *Spring*', thus, as it happens, restoring the first edition reading. *44* has a few more capitalized pronouns (e.g. the mixture of 'Thee' and 'thee' at *Su*. 1730–74, in a substantively slightly revised passage), and capitalized adjectives (e.g. *Sp*. 908–58, in a new passage), which probably reflect—as many inconsistencies in *44* may reflect—Thomson's immediate subjective decision of what was appropriate in a given context.

II

Compositors customarily set in italic all proper names and any other words the author wished to emphasize, but if greater dignity were required for certain words these would be set wholly in large and small roman capitals with a space between every letter.[1] In first editions of *Winter*, *Summer*, and *Spring* names of the four seasons are sometimes dignified by large and small capitals (particularly in invocations) and sometimes by italic. The deity is italicized in *Wi.26f* and *Sp.28*, but appears in large and small capitals in *Su.27*, where the same respect is paid to such sublunary objects of worship as 'INSPIRATION' (personalized at Mallet's suggestion) and 'BRITANNIA'. Italic is employed in all three first editions for the names of persons and places and for adjectives derived from such names, it is used occasionally for an emphatic epithet such as '*little*' or '*soon*', but elsewhere it falls erratically. So in *Su.27* the names of precious stones are italicized, but flower-names in a comparable catalogue in *Sp.28* are set in roman; in *Wi.26f* such common nouns as 'Clouds', 'Hare[s]', 'Nature', 'Winds', 'Game', and 'Horror' are italicized at one appearance but set in roman at another, when the context calls for no different

---

[1] Joseph Moxon, *Mechanick Exercises* (1683–4), ed. H. Davis and H. Carter (1958), p. 216; John Smith, *The Printer's Grammar* (1755), ed. D. F. Foxon (1965), p. 14.

degree of emphasis, personification, abstraction, dignity, or what you will. If compositors closely followed copy it would appear that Thomson followed momentary inclination when he underlined common nouns. However, there is a clear and consistent pattern in the steady reduction of italic, so that its incidence is halved between *Wi.26f* and *Su.27*, and halved again between *Su.27* and *Sp.28*.

In the new 'neat' style of the quarto large and small capitals are employed consistently in both new and reprinted material for names of persons and places, for names and attributes of God, and usually for names of seasons, but other nouns and adjectives italicized for emphasis in earlier editions are now (according to no readily discernible principle) sometimes reduced to roman. For instance, in material reprinted from *Su.27*, the personifications *Day*, *Morn*, and *Night* near the beginning of the poem are normalized to roman, whereas *Evening* and *Night* near the end are transliterated into large and small capitals. On the first two sheets of *Summer* in the quarto 23 out of 31 commons nouns italicized in 1727 are now reduced to roman, but on the fifth and sixth sheets 27 out of 27 are transliterated into large and small capitals; on two pages of *Winter* all common nouns italicized in 1728[1] are similarly transliterated while in the rest of the poem nearly all are reduced to roman; in *Spring*, by contrast, all earlier italic is transliterated. There are similar inconsistencies and a similar clustering of emphatic words in the new material. *Autumn*, for instance, has at one point 'NATURE's common bounty' and at two others 'Nature's bounty'.[2] In ten lines of *Autumn* (95–104 of the present edition) there are eight common nouns in large and small capitals, but in the other two thousand new lines added to the quarto there are no more than fifty. If Thomson corrected proofs sheet by sheet in accordance with unsure and shifting opinions on the question of emphatic capitalization such inconsistency would be inevitable.

In the long process of revising copy and proof Thomson

---

[1] In *Wi.28* much of the italic of 1726 had already been normalized to roman.

[2] *OET Au.* 189, 398, and 1259. *Sp.28* betrays the same uncertainty over Nature's status. After shifting back and forth between roman and italic for the twelve appearances of this word in the first twenty pages (to C2^v) Thomson, or the compositors, settle consistently for '*Nature*' (seven times) from p. 22 to p. 45 (C3^v–D7^r), then no less consistently for 'Nature' (six times) from p. 46 to the end of the poem on p. 57 (D7^v–F1^r). This distribution of emphatic forms is very little altered until *44*, when the word is set consistently in roman.

probably took at different times differing views, or followed varying
whims, concerning which common nouns required emphasis. As
substantive revisions are most numerous in *Winter* so accidental
variants of all kinds between the quarto and earlier editions are
most numerous too; correspondingly both are least numerous in
Spring. I conjecture that Richardson's compositors faithfully
followed scanty underlinings in new manuscript and occasional
marginal directions to reduce to roman the italic of printed copy
(or the transliterated capitals of proof), and that, where they had
no specific instructions, they transliterated printed italic into
large and small capitals. Thomson presumably had given general
approval for this style, but probably used single underlining in
his own manuscript at least occasionally, since italic appears
anomalously in the first paragraph of the *Hymn* (perhaps resulting
from author's proof-revision).

   300, *Sp.31*, and *Sp.34* follow the quarto's typographical style,
but all pamphlet issues of other Seasons in the 1730s consistently
transliterate the quarto's large and small capitals into italic.[1]
Except for a few contemporary personal names in large and small
capitals, where the pamphlet *Summer*, *Autumn*, and *Winter* have
italic—a change which anticipates Thomson's practice in 1744—
and for one example of honorific 'BRITAIN' in a substantively
revised passage (first printed in *300*), the 1738 edition follows
pamphlet typography. Consequently Thomson wrote his revisions
for 1744 upon a text the first quarter of which had been normalized
in quite a different style from the rest. Though at this stage,
working through the interleaved volume, he made hardly any
attempt to harmonize the style of *Spring* with that of the other
Seasons he gave specific typographical directions at nearly two
hundred scattered places, either on printed text or manuscript
interpolations, by underlining, double-underlining, or writing
'Roman' or 'Italick' in a margin.

   From these directions it looks as if Thomson began his revisions
with no clearly formulated policy of capitalizing and italicizing.
Working through *Spring* he writes 'SPRING' when revising the
first line and writes '*Spring* 'and '*Summer*' in an interpolation
(*OET Sp*. 546), but does not mark any other printed names of
seasons, apparently resting content with the large and small
capitals of *38*. In the first paragraph of *Summer* he double-

---

[1] Except in the prose Arguments where the capitals of the quarto are retained.

underlines the printed words '*Summer*' and '*Spring*', but where
names of seasons occur in the rest of this book he allows the italic
of *38* to stand, and (except once near the end) he employs single-
underlining in manuscript interpolations. In *Autumn*, though he
still leaves unaltered most *38* italic, he begins to give more directions
than before. So he asks for italicized season-names to be changed
to large and small capitals at lines 627 (of the present edition),
674 and 143–8, but in this third case he changes his mind and
deletes the instruction; at lines 4–6 he calls, for the first time in
the poem, for a season-name in italic to be reduced to roman. In
Winter, fired by the spirit of innovation, he asks for over half the
season-names italicized in *38* to be altered, in roughly equal
proportions, to roman or to large and small capitals. Emending
the *Hymn*, where, perhaps, he wished to reserve the dignity of
capitals for the deity, he ordered all season-names to be set in
roman. In *44* the season-names of the *Hymn* are duly printed in
roman, but so too are nearly all those of the other four books
despite the italic and capitals of 1738; the only exceptions are one
or two in the opening lines of each Season, one near the end of
Spring and four near the end of *Winter* which are given the dignity
of large and small capitals. If the printed text of *44* fairly represents
Thomson's final intentions it would appear that he was at first
satisfied with the capitals of *Spring*, then was satisfied with the
italic of *Summer* and *Autumn*, but at last came to the view that
names of seasons should normally be set in roman except when
personified and invoked.

Thomson's manuscript directions concerning other classes of
potentially 'emphatic' words and concerning proper names are
no less scanty and intermittent, but, similarly, seem to reflect
changes if mind as the revision proceeds. Typography of emphatic
words or proper names in *44* differs from *38* at over five hundred
places where there is no manuscript instruction and actually
contradicts manuscript more than thirty times, but, as there were
many substantive changes and much authorial proof-revision
between *38* and *44*, Thomson could well have attended further to
the accidentals. Despite some anomalies the general tendency in
44 is to reserve large and small capitals for the names of persons,
of seasons when invoked as personages, and of the deity and his
attributes. Italic is preferred for place-names[1] (except such

---

[1] The rule in *Edward and Eleonora* (1739), *Alfred* (1740) and *Tancred and*

patently honorific ones as 'THAMES' and 'ENGLAND'), for some mythological personal names,[1] and for a small miscellany of other emphatic words found mostly in *Autumn*, where they could, in some cases, be chance survivors from earlier, more heavily italicized texts, since this is the most lightly revised of the Seasons.

III

Like the use of italic for emphasis, punctuation in *Wi.26f* and *260* is heavy and eccentric enough to suggest some closeness to manuscript. There is a noticeable dependence upon the dash, sometimes used in conjunction with another mark of punctuation but more often standing alone on duty as a full stop or comma or for some indeterminate purpose (if not to serve for what Cobbett was to call it—a cover for ignorance). Even more striking is the overall heaviness of punctuation, with, on average throughout the poem, one mark for every three words. Subordinate clauses of every kind are set off by commas, according to eighteenth-century usage, but single adjectives and adverbs are frequently placed between commas, giving a, jerky, parenthetic effect. The reader moves through *Winter* slowly against a driving hail of commas; and punctuation helps to define a syntax which, in Geoffrey Tillotson's words, 'fittingly contributes to rendering the external world in all its multitudiousness and turbulence'.[2] Thomson's earliest surviving holograph letters are lightly and haphazardly punctuated, but about the time that *Wi.26f* was being prepared for the press he began to punctuate much more heavily and carefully. Thus his first letter to Mallet and an enclosed poem, July 1725, contain altogether one comma and one semi-colon, whereas his second, October 1725, has over fifty commas and a dozen colons or semi-colons in roughly the same number of words and sentences.

In *Su.27* we again find little rows of commas for parenthetic effect, but, as the overall frequency of punctuation marks has been reduced by a third compared with *Wi.26f*, rhythmical

Sigismunda (1745) is italic for place-names and large and small capitals for the names of persons.

[1] In some of these cases (e.g. 'Aurora' and 'Philomela') both italic and roman forms are found in *44*, revealing, perhaps, a continuing indecision on Thomson's part.

[2] 'The Methods of Description in Eighteenth- and Nineteenth-Century Poetry' in *Restoration and Eighteenth-Century Literature*, ed. C. Camden (Chicago, 1963), p. 235.

movement is less slow and syntax less broken. Exclamation marks are no less frequent, but there are fewer colons and far fewer dashes.[1] In *Wi.28* parenthetic commas round single words disappear while most colons and half the dashes of 1726 are changed to full-stops, semi-colons, or commas, so that the page looks tidier and the verse sounds less vehement than in the first edition. As the thin, even spread of such small substantive revisions as 'who' for 'that' or 'Orb' for 'Eye' shows that Thomson's concern in this edition was to correct the style of his poem rather than add new material it is probable that he attended at the same time to the accidentals. This probability is reinforced by the fact that few further changes of punctuation were made in later editions during the poet's lifetime, and that all Thomson's subsequent new poems and additions to *The Seasons* have a weight and general character of punctuation very much closer to the 1728 text than to the 1726 texts of *Winter*. In the *Poem to the Memory of Newton*, printed in 1727 in the same shop as the first edition of *Winter*, and in *Sp.28*, punctuation marks appear scarcely more than half as frequently as in *Wi.26f*. In *Sp.28* commas are scarcer than in *Su.27*, the colon continues to lose ground to the semi-colon, and the dash occurs only three times in over a thousand lines. Only three holograph letters and one short note survive from the period August 1726 to October 1730, but—for what such evidence is worth—the frequency of all marks of punctuation is reduced by a quarter from that in the five letters of October 1725 to August 1726.

In *30q* the punctuation of *Summer* is appreciably lightened from 1727 (for instance three-quarters of parenthetic commas round single words now disappear), that of *Winter* is little altered from 1728,[2] while that of *Spring* is made slightly heavier than in 1728, though it is still the lightest of all four Seasons, so that the verse of this book has a fluency appropriate to its subject. This difference is felt most strongly at line-endings, for in *Summer* and *Autumn* three lines end with a punctuation mark for every one that does not, in *Winter* the ratio is as high as four to one, but in *Spring* it is only three to two. Apart from the relative lightness of

---

[1] 21 in the 405 lines of *Winter*, 15 in the 1,146 lines of *Summer*.

[2] In 166 lines substantively unaltered or hardly altered from earlier texts *30q* follows *28* in 124 lines, reverts to *26f* in 34 and introduces fresh punctuation in 8.

Spring, the system and weight of punctuation in both the reprinted and the new material in all parts of the quarto is now fairly consistent; and all dashes have disappeared—except for five in *Winter* and one in the *Hymn*. At the beginning of *Su.30p* there are signs of what appears to be a deliberate policy of removing parenthetic commas, but apart from this the punctuation of *30q* is preserved, with few, unimportant variants, through all editions of the 1730s.

Making his revisions in 1743 upon the interleaved 1738 volume, Thomson adjusted punctuation by adding about 130 commas, deleting about 70 and making some 50 other changes. Most of the increase is in *Spring* and *Summer*, but it occurs only in odd patches, with no changes for two hundred lines or more and then, perhaps, four extra commas in a few lines (e.g. *Sp.* 286–7, 641–6, *Su.* 343–7), for, in punctuation as in spelling, the author is tinkering with accidentals rather than revising them systematically. About two-thirds of the changes in punctuation called for in Thomson's annotations appear in the printed text of 1744, but in that text other changes are made so that punctuation is made heavier at a hundred further points and lightened at fifty. Though, as a result of these two stages of correction, *Spring* and *Summer* were slightly more heavily pointed in 1744 than in 1730, and *Autumn* and *Winter* a little more lightly, the overall weight and pattern changed far less after 1730 than before.

Punctuation in *The Seasons* seemed, and seems, heavy to later readers. Wordsworth was hard pressed to defend Thomson from the charge of having 'abused' punctuation.[1] George Saintsbury, taking up a hint in Johnson's *Life* of Thomson that 'His numbers, his pauses, his diction are of his own growth', wrote 'There is nothing more characteristic of Thomson's blank verse than its peculiarly broken character. The breakages are not such as cause roughness, but such as hinder continuity . . . His lines and sections of lines are not interfluent, but conjoined: the resulting structure is a sort of mosaic.'[2] Such a mosaic effect is particularly obvious when the semi-colon is repeatedly employed, for instance in *Sp.* 267–71, *Su.* 1446–51, *Au.* 118–23, and *Wi.* 809–15 in the present edition. Punctuation here is from the *44* edition, which in the first

---

[1] *Letters of William and Dorothy Wordsworth: the Later Years* iii (1939), 1114.

[2] *A History of English Prosody* (1908), ii, 480.

three passages is nearly identical with that of the first editions; the
fourth passage was first printed in *44*.

IV

That Thomson was an inveterate tinkerer is made abundantly
clear by the minor substantive revisions. His changes of mind are
shown, for instance, in the choice of relative pronouns. In both
Wi.26f and *260* and in *Su.27* 'that' outnumbers 'which' by five to
one; but in *Sp.28* 'which' outnumbers 'that' by three to one. In
Wi.28 every example but one of 'that' in the earlier editions is
changed to 'who' or 'which'; but, again with one exception, all are
changed back to 'that' in *30q*. In new material added to all Seasons
in 1730 'that' once again outnumbers 'which' (by three to one);
but in the additions of *44* the two forms are evenly mixed.
Thomson's revisions to *38* in the interleaved volume make four
changes of 'which' to 'that' and two vice versa. One is tempted to
speculate that Thomson had read Addison's *Spectator* 78 in 1727
and had forgotten it in 1729.

The interleaved volume displays Thomson's readiness to tinker
with accidentals and his desire to have some say in the typographical
style and punctuation of his printed work, but shows how impos-
sible it is for an author to make consistent decisions. During
revision even of a single book an author's intentions are likely to
change from time to time. In the case of that series of works which
grew in time into a full text of *The Seasons* we have first editions
spread through four years, 1726–30, and full revisions with great
expansion in 1730 and 1744, all of which are equally likely to
reflect the author's intentions in their accidentals. As it is known
that printing-house practice was changing quite rapidly at this
time in the direction of using less italic it is possible to take the
view that the reduction of italic, and perhaps also the steady,
progressive lightening and tidying of punctuation through the
succession of first editions and the further reduction of typo-
graphical emphasis and adjustment of punctuation in *44*, may all
have been due to progressive normalizing in the four or five
different printing-houses involved. In the absence of an author-
corrected final proof we have no absolute warrant for any particular
accidental in any printed text. Even Thomson's corrections in the
interleaved volume could have been (and I think in some cases

were) revised subsequently by the author. Nevertheless, the fact that Thomson adopted in his private letters the changing habits of punctuation and capitalization which appear in his printed poems suggests that those printed accidentals had in general, at the very least, his passive authorization. Broad features of punctuation and incidence of typographical emphasis in the editions of the 1740s appear to be the culmination of a steady and consistent process of tidying in which Thomson must, at the very least, have acquiesced.

Dimpling along, the breezy-ruffled Lake,
The Forest humming round, the ... Spire,
Th' ethereal Mountain, and the distant Main.
But why so far excursive? when at hand, 485
Along the blushing Borders, damp-bright,
And in yon mingled Wilderness of Flowers,
Fair-handed SPRING unbosoms every Grace
Throws out the Snow-drop, and the Crocus first, 490
The Daisy, Primrose, Violet darkly blue,
Dew-bending Cowslips, and of nameless Dyes
Anemonies, Auriculas a Tribe
Peculiar powder'd with a shining Sand,
Renunculas, and Iris many-hued.
Then comes the Tulip-race, where Beauty plays
Her ... Freaks: from Family diffus'd 496
To Family, as flies the Father-duft,
The varied Colours run; and while they BREAK,
On the charm'd FLORIST'S Eye, ... curious stands, 500
And new-flush'd Glories all ecstatic marks
Nor Hyacinths are wanting, nor Junquils

Of

Thomson's 1743 revisions of *Spring*, 482–501

THE
SEASONS.
BY
JAMES THOMSON.

V^d Gucht Sc.

LONDON:
Printed for A. MILLAR, in the *Strand.* 1746.

Title-page, *The Seasons,* 1746

HIS ROYAL HIGHNESS

FREDERIC

PRINCE OF WALES,

THIS POEM,

CORRECTED AND MADE LESS UNWORTHY
OF HIS PROTECTION

IS,

WITH THE UTMOST GRATITUDE
AND VENERATION,

INSCRIBED,

BY HIS ROYAL HIGHNESS'S
MOST OBEDIENT
AND
MOST DEVOTED SERVANT,

JAMES THOMSON.

THIS POEM *having been published several Years
ago, and considerable Additions made to it lately,
some little Anachronisms have thence arisen,
which it is hoped the Reader will excuse.*

---

title: THE SEASONS *30q 44 45 46* THE SEASONS, A POEM. *300
not in 38 44Wks*

dedication: 44 45 46 not in 30q–38 44Wks

prefatory note: 44–46 not in 30q–38
THIS POEM] THE SEASONS *44Wks*
to it] to them *44Wks*

B

SPRING

The ARGUMENT

The Subject proposed. Inscribed to the Countess of HARTFORD.
*The Season is described as it affects the various Parts of Nature,
ascending from the Lower to the Higher; and mixed with Digressions
arising from the Subject. Its Influence on inanimate Matter, on
Vegetables, on brute Animals, and last on Man; concluding with a
Dissuasive from the wild and irregular Passion of Love, opposed to
That of a pure and happy Kind.*

    COME, gentle SPRING, Etherial Mildness, come,
And from the Bosom of yon dropping Cloud,
While Music wakes around, veil'd in a Shower
Of shadowing Roses, on our Plains descend.

    O HARTFORD, fitted, or to shine in Courts   5
With unaffected Grace, or walk the Plain
With Innocence and Meditation join'd
In soft Assemblage, listen to my Song,
Which thy own Season paints; when Nature all
Is blooming, and benevolent, like thee.   10

---

half title: SPRING.] SPRING. A POEM. *28 300 38*
30q–38 add: Inscrib'd to the RIGHT HONOURABLE the Countess of
Hartford.
28 31 34 have separate title-page with following epigraph:
    Et nunc omnis Ager, nunc omnis parturit Arbos,
    Nunc frondent Silvae, nunc formosissimus Annus. VIRG.
28 adds dedication and advertisement (reprinted in Appendix B below).
The Argument *30q–46 not in 28*
1 *the Countess of* HARTFORD.] *Lady* HARTFORD. *30q–38*
2 *The*] *This 30q–45*
7 *pure and happy Kind.*] *purer and more reasonable kind. 30q–38 purer
and reasonable MS*
1729 reissue of 28 adds a list of Contents, reading as follows:
THE *Subject,* Spring. *Described as a Personage descending on Earth.
Address to Lady* Hartford. *Winter described as a Personage, resigning the*

Dominion of the Year. Spring, *yet unconfirmed.* *The Sun in* Taurus *fixes the Spring Quarter.* *First Effects of the* Spring, *in softening Nature.* *Plowing.* *Sowing and Harrowing.* *The Praise of Agriculture.* *Particularly applied to* Britons. *Effects of the Spring in colouring the Fields, and unfolding the Leaves.* *The Country in Blossom.* *A Blight.* *A Philosophical Account of Insects, producing the Blight.* *A Spring-Shower.* *The Sun breaking out in the Evening after the Rain.* *The Rainbow.* *Herbs produced;* *the Food of Man in the first Ages of the World.* *Then, the Golden Age.* *As described by the Poets.* *The Degeneracy of Mankind from that State.* *On This, the Deluge, and Effects thereof, particularly in shortening the Life of Man.* *Hence, a Vegetable Diet recommended.* *The Cruelty of feeding on Animals.* *Flowers in Prospect.* *The Difficulty of describing that delicate Part of the Season.* *A Wild Flower-Piece.* *A Garden Flower-Piece.* *An Apostrophe to the* Supream Being, *as the Soul of Vegetation.* *Influence of the Spring on Birds; and first of their Singing.* *Their Courtship.* *Building their Nests.* *Brooding, and Care of their Young.* *Arts to secure them.* *Against confining them in Cages, and particularly the Nightingale;* *her Lamentation for her Young.* *Teaching their Young to fly.* *The Eagle trying his at the Sun.* *A Piece of Houshold-Fowl.* *Influence of the Spring on other Animals, the Bull, Horse,* &c. *A Landskip of the Shepherd tending his Flock, with Lambs frisking around him;* *and a Transition in Praise of our present Happy Constitution.* *This various Instinct in Brutes ascribed to the continual, and unbounded Energy of* Divine Providence. *Influence of the Spring on Man, inspiring an universal Benevolence, the Love of Mankind, and of Nature.* *Accounted for from that general Harmony which then attunes the World.* *Effects of the Spring in Woman;* *with a Caution to the Fair Sex.* *Hence a Dissuasive from the feverish, extravagant, and unchastised Passion of Love;* *in an Account of its false Raptures, Pangs, and Jealousies.* *The Whole concludes with the Happiness of a pure, mutual Love, founded on Friendship, conducted with Honour, and confirmed by Children.*

1–54 *28–46*
1 Etherial Mildness] [fair Queen of Seasons *del.*] MS
3–4 [With the glad *Hours*, the *Zephirs*, *Loves*, and *Joys*, Gay-fluttering round thee, on our Plains descend. *del.*] MS
5 O] Oh *28*
9 Which] That *30q–38*

---

1 aetherial Mildness *30q–38*   5 courts, *30q–38*   6 grace; *30q–38*
Plain, *28–38*   7 *Innocence*, *28* ∼ˌ *30q–38*   Meditation *28–38*   9 paints,
28   Nature *30q–38*   10 benevolentˌ *28–38*

AND see where surly WINTER passes off,
Far to the North, and calls his ruffian Blasts:
His Blasts obey, and quit the howling Hill,
The shatter'd Forest, and the ravag'd Vale;
While softer Gales succeed, at whose kind Touch,   15
Dissolving Snows in livid Torrents lost,
The Mountains lift their green Heads to the Sky.

As yet the trembling Year is unconfirm'd,
And WINTER oft at Eve resumes the Breeze,
Chills the pale Morn, and bids his driving Sleets   20
Deform the Day delightless: so that scarce
The Bittern knows his Time, with Bill ingulpht,
To shake the sounding Marsh; or from the Shore
The Plovers when to scatter o'er the Heath,
And sing their wild Notes to the listening Waste.   25

AT last from *Aries* rolls the bounteous Sun,
And the bright *Bull* receives him. Then no more
Th' expansive Atmosphere is cramp'd with Cold;
But, full of Life and vivifying Soul,
Lifts the light Clouds sublime, and spreads them thin,   30
Fleecy, and white, o'er all-surrounding Heaven.

FORTH fly the tepid Airs; and unconfin'd,
Unbinding Earth, the moving Softness strays.
Joyous, th' impatient Husbandman perceives
Relenting Nature, and his lusty Steers   35
Drives from their Stalls, to where the well-us'd Plow
Lies in the Furrow, loosen'd from the Frost.
There, unrefusing to the harness'd Yoke,
They lend their Shoulder, and begin their Toil,
Chear'd by the simple Song and soaring Lark.   40
Meanwhile, incumbent o'er the shining Share,
The Master leans, removes th' obstructing Clay,
Winds the whole Work, and sidelong lays the Glebe.

WHITE, thro' the neighbouring Fields the Sower stalks,
With measur'd Step; and, liberal, throws the Grain   45

Into the faithful Bosom of the Ground.
The Harrow follows harsh, and shuts the Scene.

BE gracious, HEAVEN! for now laborious Man
Has done his Part. Ye fostering Breezes blow!
Ye softening Dews, ye tender Showers, descend!　　　50
And temper All, thou world-reviving Sun,
Into the perfect Year! Nor, ye, who live
In Luxury and Ease, in Pomp and Pride,
Think these lost Themes unworthy of your Ear:
Such Themes as these the *rural* MARO sung　　　55
To wide-imperial *Rome*, in the full Height
Of Elegance and Taste, by *Greece* refin'd.
In antient Times, the sacred Plow employ'd
The Kings, and awful Fathers of Mankind:
And Some, with whom compar'd, your Insect-Tribes　　　60
Are but the Beings of a Summer's Day,

---

16 livid] sudden *28*
22 his] *MS* the *34 38*
24 when] *MS* theirs, *28–38*
46 Ground] Earth *28*
49 Part] Due *28–38*
51 world-reviving] influential *28*
　55–61 *44–46*
55–61 *28–38 as follows:*
　　'Twas such as these the *Rural Maro* sung　　　(*28*, 55)
　　To the full *Roman* Court, in all it's height
　　Of Elegance and Taste. The sacred Plow
　　Employ'd the Kings and Fathers of Mankind,
　　In antient Times. And Some, with whom compar'd
　　You're but the Beings of a Summer's Day,　　　(*28*, 60)

---

12 Blasts; *28–38*　　14 Vale: *28–38*　　19 Winter *44 44Wks*　　21 delight-
less; *28–38*　　22 ingulpht˄ *28–38*　　28 Cold, *28–38*　　29 But˄ *28–38*
Life, *28–38*　　32 unconfin'd˄ *34 38*　　34 Joyous˄ *28–38*　　35 steers,
30q–38　　37 Furrow˄ *28–45*　　40 Song, *28–38*　　41 Mean-while˄
28–38　　Share˄ *28–38*　　43 WHITE˄ *28–45*　　44 neighbring *28*　　45 Step,
28–38　　and˄ liberal˄ *28–38*　　49 Breezes˄ *28*　　50 Showers˄ *28*
52 Nor˄ *44 44Wks*　　Ye˄ *28–44Wks*　　54 Ear. *28–38*　　55 rural *30q–*
44Wks　　59 Kings˄ *44 44Wks*

Have held the Scale of Empire, rul'd the Storm
Of mighty War; then, with victorious Hand,
Disdaining little Delicacies, seiz'd
The Plow, and greatly independant scorn'd　　　　65
All the vile Stores Corruption can bestow.

YE generous BRITONS, venerate the Plow!
And o'er your Hills, and long withdrawing Vales,
Let Autumn spread his Treasures to the Sun,
Luxuriant, and unbounded! As the Sea,　　　　70
Far thro' his azure turbulent Domain,
Your Empire owns, and from a thousand Shores
Wafts all the Pomp of Life into your Ports;
So with superior Boon may your rich Soil,
Exuberant, Nature's better Blessings pour　　　　75
O'er every Land, the naked Nations cloath,
And be th' exhaustless Granary of a World!

NOR only thro' the lenient Air this Change,
Delicious, breathes; the penetrative Sun,
His Force deep-darting to the dark Retreat　　　　80
Of Vegetation, sets the steaming Power
At large, to wander o'er the vernant Earth,
In various Hues; but chiefly thee, gay *Green*!
Thou smiling Nature's universal Robe!
United Light and Shade! where the Sight dwells　　　　85
With growing Strength, and ever-new Delight.

FROM the moist Meadow to the wither'd Hill,
Led by the Breeze, the vivid Verdure runs,
And swells, and deepens, to the cherish'd Eye.
The Hawthorn whitens; and the juicy Groves　　　　90
Put forth their Buds, unfolding by Degrees,
Till the whole leafy Forest stands display'd,
In full Luxuriance, to the sighing Gales;
Where the Deer rustle thro' the twining Brake,
And the Birds sing conceal'd. At once, array'd　　　　95
In all the Colours of the flushing Year,
By Nature's swift and secret-working Hand,
The Garden glows, and fills the liberal Air
With lavish Fragrance; while the promis'd Fruit

Lies yet a little Embryo, unperceiv'd,   100
Within its crimson Folds. Now from the Town
Buried in Smoke, and Sleep, and noisom Damps,
Oft let me wander o'er the dewy Fields,
Where Freshness breathes, and dash the trembling Drops
From the bent Bush, as thro' the verdant Maze   105
Of Sweet-briar Hedges I pursue my Walk;
Or taste the Smell of Dairy; or ascend
Some Eminence, AUGUSTA, in thy Plains,
And see the Country, far-diffus'd around,
One boundless Blush, one white-empurpled Shower   110
Of mingled Blossoms; where the raptur'd Eye
Hurries from Joy to Joy, and, hid beneath
The fair Profusion, yellow Autumn spies.

62–86 *28–46*
62 Empire, rul'd the Storm] *MS* Justice, shook the Launce *28–38*
63 victorious] descending *28–38*
64 Disdaining] Unus'd to *28–38*
65–6 independant scorn'd / All the vile Stores Corruption can bestow.]
independant liv'd. *28–38*
67 venerate] cultivate *28–38*
71 Domain] Extent *28–38*
77 a World] the World *28*
78 NOR thro' the lenient Air alone, this Change *28–38*
82 vernant] verdant *31–38*
    87–113 *WEP 28–46*
87 wither'd] brown-brow'd *WEP 28–38*
94 Where] While *WEP 28–38*
104 trembling] lucid *WEP 28–38*
105 verdant] fuming *WEP 28–38*
110 white-empurpled] snow-empurpled *WEP 28*
111 raptur'd] busy *WEP*
112 Hurries] Travels *WEP 28–38*

---

63 War, then∧ *28–38*   67 *Britons*∧ *28*   69 *Autumn 28–38*   70 un-
bounded. *28–38*   71 azure, *28–38*   73 Ports, *28*   76 Land;
28   77 World. *28–38*   78 Change∧ *28–38*   79 Delicious∧ *28–38*
82 Earth∧ *28 30q*   83 Hues, *28–38*   84 *Nature's 28–38*   86 Delight!
28–38   89 deepens∧ *WEP 28–38*   92 display'd∧ *28*   93 Gales, *28*
95 once∧ *WEP 28–38*   97 *Nature's 28–38*   swift, *WEP*   100 yet, *45*
101 Town, *WEP 44–45*   106 Walk: *WEP*   109 Country∧ *WEP 28–*
38   around∧ *28–38*   112 and∧ *38*   113 *Autumn 28–38*

If, brush'd from *Russian* Wilds, a cutting Gale
Rise not, and scatter from his humid Wings   115
The clammy Mildew; or, dry-blowing, breathe
Untimely Frost; before whose baleful Blast
The full-blown Spring thro' all her Foliage shrinks,
Joyless, and dead, a wide-dejected Waste.
For oft, engender'd by the hazy North,   120
Myriads on Myriads, Insect-Armies waft
Keen in the poison'd Breeze; and wasteful eat,
Thro' Buds and Bark, into the blacken'd Core,
Their eager Way. A feeble Race! yet oft
The sacred Sons of Vengence! on whose Course   125
Corrosive Famine waits, and kills the Year.
To check this Plague the skilful Farmer Chaff,
And blazing Straw, before his Orchard burns;
Till, all involv'd in Smoke, the latent Foe
From every Cranny suffocated falls: 130
Or scatters o'er the Blooms the pungent Dust
Of Pepper, fatal to the frosty Tribe:
Or, when th' envenom'd Leaf begins to curl,
With sprinkled Water drowns them in their Nest:
Nor, while they pick them up with busy Bill,   135
The little trooping Birds unwisely scares.

114–23 *28–46*
115 humid] foggy *28–38*
116 clammy] bitter *28–38*
119 Into a smutty, wide-dejected Waste. *28–38*
123 into the blacken'd Core,] even to the Heart of Oak *28*
124–36 *44–46*
124–36 *28–38 as follows:*
> Their eager Way. A feeble Race! scarce seen,
> Save to the prying Eye; yet Famine waits
> On their corrosive Course, and starves the Year.
> Sometimes o'er Cities as they steer their Flight,   *(28,* 125*)*
> Where rising Vapour melts their Wings away,
> Gaz'd by th' astonish'd Crowd, the horrid Shower
> Descends. And hence the skillful Farmer Chaff
> And blazing Straw before his Orchard burns,
> Till all involv'd in Smoak the latent Foe   *(28,* 130*)*

From every Cranny suffocated falls;
Or Onions steaming hot beneath his Trees
Exposes, fatal to the frosty Tribe:
Nor, from their friendly Task, the busy Bill
Of little trooping Birds instinctive scares.   (*28*, 135)

(123) to] by *30q–38*
(124) starves] kills *30q–38*

136+ *28–38 have the following thirty-three lines (transferred, with
revisions, to Su. 44; see OET Su. 287–317):*

THESE are not idle Philosophic Dreams;
Full Nature swarms with Life. Th' unfaithful Fen
In putrid Steams emits the living Cloud
Of Pestilence. Thro' subterranean Cells,
Where searching Sun-Beams never found a Way,   (*28*, 140)
Earth animated heaves. The flowery Leaf
Wants not it's soft Inhabitants. The Stone,
Hard as it is, in every winding Pore
Holds Multitudes. But chief the Forest-Boughs,
Which dance unnumber'd to th' inspiring Breeze,   (*28*, 145)
The downy Orchard, and the melting Pulp
Of mellow Fruit the nameless Nations feed
Of evanescent Insects. Where the Pool
Stands mantled o'er with Green, invisible,
Amid the floating Verdure Millions stray.   (*28*, 150)
Each Liquid too, whether of acid Taste,
Milky, or strong, with various Forms abounds.
Nor is the lucid Stream, nor the pure Air,
Tho' one transparent Vacancy they seem,
Devoid of theirs. Even Animals subsist   (*28*, 155)
On Animals, in infinite Descent;
And all so fine adjusted, that the Loss
Of the least Species would disturb the whole.
Stranger than this th' inspective Glass confirms,
And to the Curious gives th' amazing Scenes   (*28*, 160)

(138) living] livid *30q–38*
(152) Milky, or strong] Potent, or mild *30q–38*
(136–60) *del. MS*

---

114 IF∧ *28–45*   Wilds∧ *28–45*   116 Mildew, or∧ *28–38*   blowing∧ *28–38*
117 Blast, *28–45*   118 *Spring 28–38*   120 oft∧ *28–38*   122 eat∧ *28–*
38   123 Buds, *28–44Wks*   (*28*, 128) chaff, *30q–38*   (129) burns;
30q–38   (130) Till, *30q–38*   smoak, *30q–38*   (132) onions, *30q–38*
hot, *30q–38*   (*28*, 136) dreams, *30q–38*   (137) NATURE *30q–38*
(159) confirms∧ *31 34 38*

BE patient, Swains; these cruel-seeming Winds
Blow not in vain. Far hence they keep, repress'd,
Those deepening Clouds on Clouds, surcharg'd with Rain,
That o'er the vast *Atlantic* hither borne,   140
In endless Train, would quench the Summer-Blaze,
And, chearless, drown the crude unripen'd Year.

THE North-East spends his Rage, and now, shut up
Within his iron Caves, th' effusive South
Warms the wide Air, and o'er the Void of Heaven   145
Breathes the big Clouds with vernal Showers distent.
At first a dusky Wreath they seem to rise,
Scarce staining Ether; but by fast Degrees,
In Heaps on Heaps, the doubling Vapour sails
Along the loaded Sky, and, mingling deep,   150
Sits on th' Horizon round a settled Gloom.
Not such as wintry Storms on Mortals shed,
Oppressing Life, but lovely, gentle, kind,
And full of every Hope and every Joy,
The Wish of Nature. Gradual, sinks the Breeze,   155
Into a perfect Calm; that not a Breath
Is heard to quiver thro' the closing Woods,
Or rustling turn the many-twinkling Leaves
Of Aspin tall. Th' uncurling Floods, diffus'd
In glassy Breadth, seem thro' delusive Lapse   160
Forgetful of their Course. 'Tis Silence all,
And pleasing Expectation. Herds and Flocks
Drop the dry Sprig, and mute-imploring eye
The falling Verdure. Hush'd in short Suspense,
The plumy People streak their Wings with Oil,   165
To throw the lucid Moisture trickling off;
And wait th' approaching Sign to strike, at once,
Into the general Choir. Even Mountains, Vales,
And Forests seem, impatient, to demand
The promis'd Sweetness. Man superior walks   170
Amid the glad Creation, musing Praise,
And looking lively Gratitude. At last,
The Clouds consign their Treasures to the Fields,
And, softly shaking on the dimpled Pool

Prelusive Drops, let all their Moisture flow,   175
In large Effusion o'er the freshen'd World.
The stealing Shower is scarce to patter heard,
By such as wander thro' the Forest-Walks,
Beneath th' umbrageous Multitude of Leaves.
But who can hold the Shade, while Heaven descends   180
In universal Bounty, shedding Herbs,
And Fruits, and Flowers, on Nature's ample Lap?
Swift Fancy fir'd anticipates their Growth;
And, while the milky Nutriment distills,
Beholds the kindling Country colour round.   185

136+ *28–38 continues as follows:*
        Of lessning Life; by *Wisdom* kindly hid
        From Eye, and Ear of Man: for if at once
        The Worlds in Worlds enclos'd were push'd to Light,
        Seen by his sharpen'd Eye, and by his Ear
        Intensely bended Heard, from the choice Cate,   (*28,* 165)
        The freshest Viands, and the brightest Wines,
        He'd turn abhorrent, and in Dead of Night,
        When Silence sleeps o'er all, be stun'd with Noise.
See OET Su. 287–317 *apparatus for MS variants.*
   137–42 *44–46   not in 28–38*
   143–271 *28–46*
150 deep,] *MS* thick *28–38*
166 *not in 28–38*
169 impatient,] expansive *28–38*
174 dimpled] dimply *28–44Wks*
177 'Tis scarce to patter heard, the stealing Shower, *28–38*
180 can] would *28*
181 Bounty] beauty *300*
183 Imagination fir'd prevents their Growth, *28–38*
184 milky] verdant *28–38*

---

(161) lessening *30q–38*   Wisdom *MS*   143 now˄ *28–44Wks*   150 and,]
MS ~˄ *28–46*   deep,] *MS* ~˄ *44–46*   152 shed˄ *28*   154 Hope,
28–38   155 Gradual˄ *28–44Wks*   Breeze˄ *28–38*   164 Suspense˄ *28*
167 strike˄ *28–38*   once˄ *28–38*   168 Ev'n *28*   169 seem˄ *28*
169a expansive, *30q–38*   172 last˄ *28–38*   175 flow˄ *28*   176 World.]
MS ~; *31 34 38*   180 *Heaven 28–38*   descends, *30q 300*   182 *Nature's*
28–38   184 And˄ *28–38*

THUS all day long the full-distended Clouds
Indulge their genial Stores, and well-shower'd Earth
Is deep enrich'd with vegetable Life;
Till, in the western Sky, the downward Sun
Looks out, effulgent, from amid the Flush   190
Of broken Clouds, gay-shifting to his Beam.
The rapid Radiance instantaneous strikes
Th' illumin'd Mountain, thro' the Forest streams,
Shakes on the Floods, and in a yellow Mist,
Far smoking o'er th' interminable Plain,   195
In twinkling Myriads lights the dewy Gems.
Moist, bright, and green, the Landskip laughs around.
Full swell the Woods; their every Musick wakes,
Mix'd in wild Concert with the warbling Brooks
Increas'd, the distant Bleatings of the Hills,   200
The hollow Lows responsive from the Vales,
Whence blending all the sweeten'd Zephyr springs.
Meantime refracted from yon eastern Cloud,
Bestriding Earth, the grand ethereal Bow
Shoots up immense; and every Hue unfolds,   205
In fair Proportion, running from the Red,
To where the Violet fades into the Sky.
Here, awful NEWTON, the dissolving Clouds
Form, fronting on the Sun, thy showery Prism;
And to the sage-instructed Eye unfold   210
The various Twine of Light, by thee disclos'd
From the white mingling Maze. Not so the Swain,
He wondering views the bright Enchantment bend,
Delightful, o'er the radiant Fields, and runs
To catch the falling Glory; but amaz'd   215
Beholds th' amusive Arch before him fly,
Then vanish quite away. Still Night succeeds,
A soften'd Shade, and saturated Earth
Awaits the Morning-Beam, to give to Light,
Rais'd thro' ten thousand different Plastic Tubes,   220
The balmy Treasures of the former Day.

THEN spring the living Herbs, profusely wild,
O'er all the deep-green Earth, beyond the Power
Of Botanist to number up their Tribes:

Whether he steals along the lonely Dale,   225
In silent Search; or thro' the Forest, rank
With what the dull Incurious Weeds account,
Bursts his blind Way; or climbs the Mountain-Rock,
Fir'd by the nodding Verdure of its Brow.
With such a liberal Hand has Nature flung   230
Their Seeds abroad, blown them about in Winds,
Innumerous mix'd them with the nursing Mold,
The moistening Current, and prolifick Rain.

But who their Virtues can declare? Who pierce
With Vision pure, into these secret Stores   235
Of Health, and Life, and Joy? The Food of Man,
While yet he liv'd in Innocence, and told
A Length of golden Years, unflesh'd in Blood,
A Stranger to the savage Arts of Life,
Death, Rapine, Carnage, Surfeit, and Disease,   240
The Lord, and not the Tyrant of the World.

---

190 Looks out, effulgent,] Looks out illustrious *28–38* Breaks forth, effulgent, *MS*   amid] *MS* amidst *31 34 38*
199 Concert] Consort *28–38*
200 the distant] *MS* th'unnumber'd *28–38*
208 awful] mighty *28–44Wks*
209 Are, as they scatter round, thy numerous Prism, *28–38* Form, as they scatter round, thy showery Prism; *44 44Wks*
210 Untwisting to the Philosophic Eye *28–44Wks*   sage-instructed] well-instructed *45*
211–12 disclos'd / From] *MS* pursu'd / Thro' *28–38*
212 the white] all the *28*
219–21   Awaits the Morning-Beam, to give again,
            Transmuted soon by Nature's Chymistry,
            The blooming Blessings of the former Day.   *28–38*
223 green] *MS* green'd *38*
235 Vision pure] holy Eye *28*
236 Of Health, and Life] Of Life, and Health *28–38*

---

187 showr'd *28*   193 Mountain,] *MS* ~ₐ *31 34 38*   205 immense! *28–38*   206 Proportionₐ *38 45 46*   210a Untwisting, *44 44Wks*   Eye, *44 44Wks*   215 Glory, *28*   218 Shade; *28 30q 300*   222 wildₐ *28 30q*   224 *Botanist 28–38*   Tribes; *28–38*   225 Dale,] *MS* ~ₐ *28–38*   230 *Nature 28–38*   234 declare? who *28*   pierce, *44–45*   235 pureₐ *30q–38*   236 Manₐ *28–45*

THE first fresh Dawn then wak'd the gladden'd Race
Of uncorrupted Man, nor blush'd to see
The Sluggard sleep beneath its sacred Beam.
For their light Slumbers gently fum'd away;   245
And up they rose as vigorous as the Sun,
Or to the Culture of the willing Glebe,
Or to the chearful Tendance of the Flock.
Meantime the Song went round; and Dance and Sport,
Wisdom and friendly Talk, successive stole   250
Their Hours away. While in the rosy Vale
Love breath'd his infant Sighs, from Anguish free,
And full replete with Bliss; save the sweet Pain,
That, inly thrilling, but exalts it more.
Nor yet injurious Act, nor surly Deed,   255
Was known among these happy Sons of HEAVEN;
For Reason and Benevolence were Law.
Harmonious Nature too look'd smiling on.
Clear shone the Skies, cool'd with eternal Gales,
And balmy Spirit all. The youthful Sun   260
Shot his best Rays, and still the gracious Clouds
Drop'd Fatness down; as, o'er the swelling Mead,
The Herds and Flocks, commixing, play'd secure.
This when, emergent from the gloomy Wood,
The glaring Lion saw, his horrid Heart   265
Was meeken'd, and he join'd his sullen Joy.
For Music held the whole in perfect Peace:
Soft sigh'd the Flute; the tender Voice was heard,
Warbling the vary'd Heart; the Woodlands round
Apply'd their Quire; and Winds and Waters flow'd   270
In Consonance. Such were those Prime of Days.

---

242 THEN the glad Morning wak'd the gladden'd Race *28–38*
243 Man] Men *28–38*
244 its] her *28–38*
253–4 Fragrant with Bliss, and only wept for Joy. *28* Replete with bliss,
and only wept for joy. *30q–38*
259 Clear] *MS* Clean *28–38*
264 This] Which *28–38*

269 vary'd] *MS* joyous *28–38*
271 those] *MS* these *28–38*
271+ *28–38 have the following twenty-eight lines (not in 44–46):*

THIS to the *Poets* gave the golden Age;
When, as they sung in Allegoric Phraze,
The Sailor-Pine had not the Nations yet
In Commerce mix'd; for every Country teem'd
With every Thing. Spontaneous Harvests wav'd   (*28*, 300)
Still in a Sea of yellow Plenty round.
The Forest was the Vineyard, where untaught
To climb, unprun'd, and wild, the juicy Grape
Burst into Floods of Wine. The knotted Oak
Shook from his Boughs the long transparent Streams (*28*, 305)
Of Honey, creeping thro' the matted Grass.
Th' uncultivated Thorn a ruddy Shower
Of Fruitage shed, on such as sat below,
In blooming Ease, and from brown Labour free,
Save what the copious Gathering, grateful, gave.   (*28*, 310)
The Rivers foam'd with Nectar; or diffuse,
Silent, and soft, the milky Maze devolv'd.
Nor had the spongy, full-expanded Fleece
Yet drunk the *Tyrian* Die. The stately Ram
Shone thro' the Mead, in native Purple clad,   (*28*, 315)
Or milder Saffron; and the dancing Lamb
The vivid Crimson to the Sun disclos'd.
Nothing had Power to hurt; the savage Soul,
Yet untransfus'd into the Tyger's Heart,
Burn'd not his Bowels, nor his gamesome Paw   (*28*, 320)
Drove on the fleecy Partners of his Play:
While from the flowery Brake the Serpent roll'd
His fairer Spires, and play'd his pointless Tongue.

(297) Allegoric] elevated *30q–38*   boldly-figur'd *MS*
(311) diffuse] calm-spread *MS*

---

245 away, *28–38*   249 Dance, *28–38*   Sportₐ *46*   250 Wisdomₐ] *MS* ∼,
28–34 ∼; *38*   Talk,] *MS* ∼ₐ *28–38*   successive, *MS 44–45*   255 Deed,]
MS ∼ₐ *28–38*   256 Heaven *28–44Wks*   261 Rays; *28–38*   262 as,]
MS ∼ₐ *28–38*   Mead,] *MS* ∼ₐ *28–38*   263 Flocks, commixing,] *MS*
∼ₐ ∼ₐ *28–38*   268 heardₐ *28*   270 quire, *300*   271 Consonance.—
28   (*28*, 300) wav'd, *30q–38*   (310) grateful,] *MS* ∼ₐ *31 34 38*
(313) spongyₐ *MS*   fleece, *30q–38*   (318) hurt;] *MS* ∼ₐ *34 38*

But now those white unblemish'd Minutes, whence
The fabling Poets took their golden Age,
Are found no more amid these iron Times,
These Dregs of Life! Now the distemper'd Mind   275
Has lost that Concord of harmonious Powers,
Which forms the Soul of Happiness; and all
Is off the Poise within: the Passions all
Have burst their Bounds; and Reason half extinct,
Or impotent, or else approving, sees   280
The foul Disorder. Senseless, and deform'd,
Convulsive Anger storms at large; or pale,
And silent, settles into fell Revenge.
Base Envy withers at another's Joy,
And hates that Excellence it cannot reach.   285
Desponding Fear, of feeble Fancies full,
Weak, and unmanly, loosens every Power.
Even Love itself is Bitterness of Soul,
A pensive Anguish pining at the Heart:
Or, sunk to sordid Interest, feels no more   290
That noble Wish, that never-cloy'd Desire,
Which, selfish Joy disdaining, seeks, alone,
To bless the dearer Object of its Flame.
Hope sickens with Extravagance; and Grief,
Of Life impatient, into Madness swells;   295
Or in dead Silence wastes the weeping Hours.
These, and a thousand mix'd Emotions more,
From ever-changing Views of Good and Ill,
Form'd infinitely various, vex the Mind
With endless Storm. Whence, deeply rankling, grows   300
The partial Thought, a listless Unconcern,
Cold, and averting from our Neighbour's Good;
Then dark Disgust, and Hatred, winding Wiles,
Coward Deceit, and ruffian Violence.
At last, extinct each social Feeling, fell   305
And joyless Inhumanity pervades,
And petrifies the Heart. Nature disturb'd
Is deem'd, vindictive, to have chang'd her Course.

272–3 *44–46*

272–3 *28–38 as follows:*

   BUT now what-e'er those gaudy Fables meant,

   And the white Minutes that they shadow'd out, (*28*, 325)

  (324) those] these *30q–38*

  (325) white] blest *MS* that] which *30q–38*

 274–80 *28–46*

274 these] those *30q–38*

275 These] Those *30q–38* Now the distemper'd Mind] *MS* in which the Human Mind *28–38* [in which the jarring Mind *del.*] *MS*

276 *MS* Has lost that Harmony ineffable, *28–38*

277 Which forms the Soul of Happiness;] [The Soul of Peace and Happiness! *del.*] That forms the Soul of Happiness; *MS*

 281–93 *44–46*

285 And hates whate'er is excellent and good. *44 44Wks*

291 noble] restless *44 44Wks* never-cloy'd] infinite *44 44Wks*

292 seeks] seek *44 44Wks*

 281–93 *28–38 as follows:*

   The foul Disorder. Anger storms at large,

   Without an equal Cause; and fell Revenge

   Supports the falling Rage. Close Envy bites (*28*, 335)

   With venom'd Tooth; while weak, unmanly Fear,

   Full of frail Fancies, loosens every Power.

   Even Love itself is Bitterness of Soul,

   A pleasing Anguish pining at the Heart.

 294–302 *28–46*

297 mix'd] new *28*

298–300 From ever-changing . . . endless Storm.] That from their Mixture spring, distract the Mind / With endless Tumult. *28*

300 Whence, deeply rankling, grows] Whence resulting rise *28* Whence, inly-rankling, grows *30q–45*

301 partial] selfish *28–38* Unconcern] *MS* Inconcern *28–38*

 303–8 *MS 44–46*

306 joyless] *MS* [loveless *del.*] *MS* pervades] *MS* [corrodes *del.*] *MS*

307 petrifies] *MS* [gangrenes all *del.*] *MS* Nature disturb'd] Even Nature's self *MS*

---

278 within; *28–38* (*28*, 335) bites, *MS* 295 swells, *28 MS*

HENCE, in old dusky Time, a Deluge came:
When the deep-cleft disparting Orb, that arch'd   310
The central Waters round, impetuous rush'd,
With universal Burst, into the Gulph,
And o'er the high-pil'd Hills of fractur'd Earth
Wide-dash'd the Waves, in Undulation vast;
Till, from the Center to the streaming Clouds,   315
A shoreless Ocean tumbled round the Globe.

THE Seasons since have, with severer Sway,
Oppress'd a broken World: the Winter keen
Shook forth his Waste of Snows; and Summer shot
His pestilential Heats. Great Spring, before,   320
Green'd all the Year; and Fruits and Blossoms blush'd,
In social Sweetness, on the self-same Bough.
Pure was the temperate Air; an even Calm
Perpetual reign'd, save what the Zephyrs bland
Breath'd o'er the blue Expanse: for then nor Storms   325
Were taught to blow, nor Hurricanes to rage;
Sound slept the Waters; no sulphureous Glooms
Swell'd in the Sky, and sent the Lightning forth;
While sickly Damps, and cold autumnal Fogs,
Hung not, relaxing, on the Springs of Life.   330
But now, of turbid Elements the Sport,
From Clear to Cloudy tost, from Hot to Cold,
And Dry to Moist, with inward-eating Change,
Our drooping Days are dwindled down to Nought,
Their Period finish'd ere 'tis well begun.   335

303–8 *28–38 as follows:*

    Then dark Disgust, and Malice, winding Wiles,
    Sneaking Deceit, and Coward Villany:
    At last unruly Hatred, lewd Reproach,   (*28*, 350)
    Convulsive Wrath, and thoughtless Fury quick
    To every evil Deed. Even Nature's self
    Is deem'd vindictive, to have chang'd her Course.

  (350) unruly] deep-rooted *30q–38*
  (352) to every evil Deed] To deeds of vilest aim *30q–38*
309–13 *44–46*

309–13 *28–38 as follows:*

HENCE in old Time, they say, a Deluge came;
When the dry-crumbling Orb of Earth, which arch'd (*28*, 355)
Th' imprison'd Deep around, impetuous rush'd,
With Ruin inconceivable, at once
Into the Gulph, and o'er the highest Hills

(355) dry-crumbling] disparting *30q–38*   which] that *30q–38*
(358) highest] high-pil'd *MS*
then (355–8) *del. MS and redrafted as follows:*
When the deep-[chapt *del.* parcht *del.* chapt *del.*] cleft disparting
    Orb, that arch'd
The rarefy'd Abyss, whose searching Steams
Expansive sought a Vent, impetuous rush'd
With universal Lapse, into the Gulph,
And o'er the high-pil'd Hills of fractur'd Earth
then T. writes or thus *and redrafts MS to read as OET* 310–13, *except as*
follows:
312 Burst] Lapse *MS*
313 high-pil'd] *MS* new-form'd *MS*
    314–30 *28–46*
317–18 since have, with severer Sway, / Oppress'd a broken World:]
since, as hoar *Tradition* tells, / Have kept their constant Chace; *28–
44Wks.*
319 Shook forth] Pour'd out *28–38*   and] *MS* The *38*
323 Pure] *MS* Clear *28–38*
330 Hung not, relaxing,] Sat not pernicious *28–38* Oppressive, sat not
44 44Wks
    331–5 *MS 44–46*
333 Dry to Moist] Moist to Dry *MS*
    331–5 *28–38 as follows:*

But now from clear to cloudy, moist to dry,   (*28*, 376)
And hot to cold, in restless Change revolv'd,
Our drooping Days are dwindled down to nought,
The fleeting Shadow of a Winter's Sun.

(*28*, 351) fury, *30q–38*   (353) deem'd, *30q–38*   309 came:] *MS*
314 vast;] *MS* ~: *28–38*   315 Till∧ *28*   Clouds∧ *28*   317 *Seasons*
28–38   317a Tradition *44 44Wks*   318a Chace: *MS 44 44Wks*
318 *Winter 28–38*   319 Snows, *28*   *Summer 28–38*   320 Heats. Great]
MS ~: great *28 30q* ~;~ *31–38*   *Spring*∧ before∧ *28–38*   321 blush'd∧
28–38   322 Sweetness∧ *28–38*   325 Expanse:] *MS* ~; *28–38*
327 Waters;] *MS* ~: *28–31 34 38*   328 forth: *28–38 MS*   329 Fogs∧
28   (*28*, 376) now, *30q–38*

AND yet the wholesome Herb neglected dies;
Tho' with the pure exhilarating Soul
Of Nutriment and Health, and vital Powers,
Beyond the Search of Art, 'tis copious blest.
For, with hot Ravine fir'd, ensanguin'd Man   340
Is now become the Lion of the Plain,
And worse. The Wolf, who from the nightly Fold
Fierce-drags the bleating Prey, ne'er drunk her Milk,
Nor wore her warming Fleece: nor has the Steer,
At whose strong Chest the deadly Tyger hangs,   345
E'er plow'd for him. They too are temper'd high,
With Hunger stung, and wild Necessity,
Nor lodges Pity in their shaggy Breast.
But *Man*, whom Nature form'd of milder Clay,
With every kind Emotion in his Heart,   350
And taught alone to weep; while from her Lap
She pours ten thousand Delicacies, Herbs,
And Fruits, as numerous as the Drops of Rain
Or Beams that gave them Birth: shall he, fair Form!
Who wears sweet Smiles, and looks erect on Heaven,   355
E'er stoop to mingle with the prowling Herd,
And dip his Tongue in Gore? The Beast of Prey,
Blood-stain'd, deserves to bleed: but you, ye Flocks,
What have you done; ye peaceful People, What,
To merit Death? You, who have given us Milk   360
In luscious Streams, and lent us your own Coat
Against the Winter's Cold? And the plain Ox,
That harmless, honest, guileless Animal,
In What has he offended? He, whose Toil,
Patient and ever-ready, clothes the Land   365
With all the Pomp of Harvest; shall he bleed,
And struggling groan beneath the cruel Hands
Even of the Clowns he feeds? And That, perhaps,
To swell the Riot of th' autumnal Feast,
Won by his Labour? This the feeling Heart   370

336–9 *44–46*
338–9 and vital Powers, / Beyond the Search of Art, 'tis copious blest.]
salubrious, blest, / And deeply stor'd with wondrous vital Powers. *44*
44Wks

336–9 *28–38 as follows:*

> AND yet the wholesome Herb neglected dies   (*28*, 380)
> In lone Obscurity, unpriz'd for Food,
> Altho' the pure, exhilerating Soul
> Of Nutriment, and Health, salubrious breathes,
> By *Heaven* infus'd, along it's secret Tubes.

340–56 *WEP PS 28–46*
347 With] By *WEP PS*
348 Breast] *MS* Breasts *WEP PS 28–38*
349+ *WEP and PS have the following (not in 28–46):*

> By Reason lighted into nobler Life,

354 Or] And *WEP PS 28–38*   that] which *WEP PS 28*   gave] give
300

357–8 *44–46*
357–8 *WEP PS 28–38 as follows:*

> And dip his Tongue in Blood? The Beast of Prey,
> 'Tis true, deserves the Fate in which He deals;
> Him from the Thicket let the hardy Youth
> Provoke, and foaming thro' th' awakened Woods   (*28*, 405)
> With every Nerve pursue. But You, ye Flocks,

359–70 *WEP PS 28–46*
359 have you] *MS* have ye *28–38*
362 Cold? And the plain Ox] *MS* Cold; whose Usefulness / In living
only lies. And the plain Ox *28–38*
363 guileless] guiltless *300*
365 Land] Fields *WEP PS 28*
367 struggling] wrestling *WEP PS 28–38*
369 th' autumnal] the gathering *WEP PS 28–38*
370 This] Thus *28–45 not in WEP PS*   the feeling Heart] *not in WEP
PS*

(*28*, 381) food; *30q–38*   (382) pure∧ *MS*   340 For,] *MS* ∼∧ *WEP
PS 38*   341 Lion *WEP PS*   349 Nature *28–38*   353 Fruits∧ *28*
Rain, *28–45*   (*28*, 402) Blood. *WEP PS*   (403) deals. *30q–38*
(404) Him, *30q–38*   thicket, *30q–38*   (405) th'] the *30q–34*   358 stain'd∧
46   359 done? *WEP PS 28–38*   Ye peaceful *30q–38*   What∧ *WEP PS*
362a cold? Whose *30q–38*   lies? *30q–38*   363 honest,] *MS* ∼∧ *38*
365 Patient, *WEP PS 28–300*   ready,] *MS* ∼∧ *31 34 38*   Land∧] *MS* ∼, *38*
366 Harvest. Shall *WEP PS*   368 feeds; and *WEP PS*   That∧ *WEP PS*
28–38 46   perhaps∧ *WEP PS 28–38*   370 Labour. *28*

Would tenderly suggest: but 'tis enough,
In this late Age, adventurous, to have touch'd
Light on the Numbers of the *Samian* Sage.
High HEAVEN forbids the bold presumptuous Strain,
Whose wisest Will has fix'd us in a State　　　　　375
That must not yet to pure Perfection rise.
Besides, who knows, how *rais'd* to higher Life,
From Stage to Stage, the *Vital Scale ascends?*

　　Now when the first foul Torrent of the Brooks,
Swell'd with the vernal Rains, is ebb'd away;　　　380
And, whitening, down their mossy-tinctur'd Stream
Descends the billowy Foam: now is the Time,
While yet the dark-brown Water aids the Guile,
To tempt the Trout. The well-dissembled Fly,
The Rod fine-tapering with elastic Spring,　　　385
Snatch'd from the hoary Steed the floating Line,
And all thy slender watry Stores prepare.
But let not on thy Hook the tortur'd Worm,
Convulsive, twist in agonizing Folds;
Which, by rapacious Hunger swallow'd deep,　　　390
Gives, as you tear it from the bleeding Breast
Of the weak, helpless, uncomplaining Wretch,
Harsh Pain and Horror to the tender Hand.

　　WHEN, with his lively Ray, the potent Sun
Has pierc'd the Streams, and rous'd the finny Race,　　395
Then, issuing chearful, to thy Sport repair;
Chief should the Western Breezes curling play,
And light o'er Ether bear the shadowy Clouds.
High to their Fount, this Day, amid the Hills,
And Woodlands warbling round, trace up the Brooks;　　400
The Next, pursue their rocky-channel'd Maze,
Down to the River, in whose ample Wave
Their little Naiads love to sport at large.
Just in the dubious Point, where with the Pool
Is mix'd the trembling Stream, or where it boils　　405
Around the Stone, or from the hollow'd Bank,
Reverted, plays in undulating Flow,
There throw, nice-judging, the delusive Fly;

And, as you lead it round in artful Curve,
With Eye attentive mark the springing Game.   410
Strait as above the Surface of the Flood
They wanton rise, or urg'd by Hunger leap,
Then fix, with gentle Twitch, the barbed Hook:
Some lightly tossing to the grassy Bank,
And to the shelving Shore, slow-dragging some,   415
With various Hand proportion'd to their Force.
If yet too young, and easily deceiv'd,
A worthless Prey scarce bends your pliant Rod,
Him, piteous of his Youth, and the short Space
He has enjoy'd the vital Light of Heaven,   420
Soft disengage, and back into the Stream
The speckled Infant throw. But should you lure
From his dark Haunt, beneath the tangled Roots
Of pendant Trees, the Monarch of the Brook,
Behoves you then to ply your finest Art.   425
Long time he, following cautious, scans the Fly;
And oft attempts to seize it, but as oft
The dimpled Water speaks his jealous Fear.
At last, while haply o'er the shaded Sun
Passes a Cloud, he desperate takes the Death,   430
With sullen Plunge. At once he darts along,
Deep-struck, and runs out all the length'd Line;
Then seeks the farthest Ooze, the sheltering Weed,

371–6 *28–46*
374 High *Heaven* beside forbids the daring Strain, *28–38* HEAVEN too
forbids the bold presumptuous Strain, *44–45*
376 That] Which *28*
377–8 *46 not in 28–45*
379–466 *44–46 not in 28–38*
380 with] by *44–45*
422 Infant] Captive *44 44Wks*
425 you] thee *44 44Wks*   your] thy *44 44Wks*

---

371 suggest. But *28*   372 adventurous∧ *28–38*   touch'd, *30q–38*
375 State, *28–38*   389 Folds, *44–45*   390 Which∧ *44–45*   deep∧
44–45   392 weak∧ helpless∧ *45 46*   413 Hook; *44–45*   415 Shore∧
44–45   423 Roots, *44–45*   431 once, *44 44Wks*

The cavern'd Bank, his old secure Abode;
And flies aloft, and flounces round the Pool,   435
Indignant of the Guile. With yielding Hand,
That feels him still, yet to his furious Course
Gives way, you, now retiring, following now
Across the Stream, exhaust his idle Rage:
Till floating broad upon his breathless Side,   440
And to his Fate abandon'd, to the Shore
You gaily drag your unresisting Prize.

    THUS pass the temperate Hours: but when the Sun
Shakes from his Noon-day Throne the scattering Clouds,
Even shooting listless Languor thro' the Deeps;   445
Then seek the Bank where flowering Elders croud,
Where scatter'd wild the Lily of the Vale
Its balmy Essence breathes, where Cowslips hang
The dewy Head, where purple Violets lurk,
With all the lowly Children of the Shade: 450
Or lie reclin'd beneath yon spreading Ash,
Hung o'er the Steep; whence, borne on liquid Wing,
The sounding Culver shoots; or where the Hawk,
High, in the beetling Cliff, his Airy builds.
There let the Classic Page thy Fancy lead   455
Thro' rural Scenes; such as the *Mantuan* Swain
Paints in the matchless Harmony of Song.
Or catch thy self the Landskip, gliding swift
Athwart Imagination's vivid Eye:
Or by the vocal Woods and Waters lull'd,   460
And lost in lonely Musing, in a Dream,
Confus'd, of careless Solitude, where mix
Ten thousand wandering Images of Things,
Soothe every Gust of Passion into Peace,
All but the Swellings of the soften'd Heart,   465
That waken, not disturb the tranquil Mind.

    BEHOLD yon breathing Prospect bids the Muse
Throw all her Beauty forth. But who can paint
Like Nature? Can Imagination boast,
Amid its gay Creation, Hues like hers?   470
Or can it mix them with that matchless Skill,

And lose them in each other, as appears
In every Bud that blows? If Fancy then
Unequal fails beneath the pleasing Task;
Ah what shall Language do? Ah where find Words   475
Ting'd with so many Colours; and whose Power,
To Life approaching, may perfume my Lays
With that fine Oil, those aromatic Gales,
That inexhaustive flow continual round?

    YET, tho' successless, will the Toil delight.   480
Come then, ye Virgins, and ye Youths, whose Hearts
Have felt the Raptures of refining Love;
And thou, AMANDA, come, Pride of my Song!
Form'd by the Graces, Loveliness itself!
Come with those downcast Eyes, sedate and sweet,   485
Those Looks demure, that deeply pierce the Soul;
Where with the Light of thoughtful Reason mix'd,
Shines lively Fancy and the feeling Heart:

---

457 the matchless Harmony of Song.] immortal Verse and matchless
Song: *44 44Wks* unequall'd Harmony of Song. *45*
   467–71 *28–46*
467 BEHOLD yon] *MS* But yonder *28–38*
468 forth. But who] *MS* forth, that Daubing all / Will be to what I
gaze; for who *28–38*
470 its] his *28–38*
471 Or can it] And can he *28–38*
471+ *28–38 have the following (not in 44–46):*
And lay them on so delicately sweet,   sweet] fine *30q–38*
   472–82 *28–46*
474 pleasing] lovely *28–38*
478 those] *MS* these *28–38*
479 That] *MS* Which *28–38*
   483–8 *MS 44–46 not in 28–38*

---

439 Rage; *44–45*   458 Landskip‸ *44Wks*   467 BEHOLD, *MS*   468 forth:
but *MS*   469 *Nature 28–38*   *Imagination 28–38*   boast‸ *28*   470 Crea-
tion‸ *28*   475 Words, *MS*   476 Colours? And *28–38*   Power,] *MS*
~‸ *28–38*   479 round. *28*   480 YET‸ *46*   481 then‸ *28*
482 Love, *28* ~: *44–45*   483 Amanda *MS*   487 Reason, *MS 44–45*
488 Heart. *MS*

Oh come! and while the rosy-footed May
Steals blushing on, together let us tread   490
The Morning-Dews, and gather in their Prime
Fresh-blooming Flowers, to grace thy braided Hair,
And thy lov'd Bosom that improves their Sweets.

SEE, where the winding Vale its lavish Stores,
Irriguous, spreads. See, how the Lily drinks   495
The latent Rill, scarce oozing thro' the Grass,
Of Growth luxuriant; or the humid Bank,
In fair Profusion, decks. Long let us walk,
Where the Breeze blows from yon extended Field
Of blossom'd Beans. *Arabia* cannot boast   500
A fuller Gale of Joy than, liberal, thence
Breathes thro' the Sense, and takes the ravish'd Soul.
Nor is the Mead unworthy of thy Foot,
Full of fresh Verdure, and unnumber'd Flowers,
The Negligence of *Nature*, wide, and wild;   505
Where, undisguis'd by mimic *Art*, she spreads
Unbounded Beauty to the roving Eye.
Here their delicious Task the fervent Bees,
In swarming Millions, tend. Around, athwart,
Thro' the soft Air, the busy Nations fly,   510
Cling to the Bud, and, with inserted Tube,
Suck its pure Essence, its ethereal Soul.
And oft, with bolder Wing, they soaring dare
The purple Heath, or where the Wild-thyme grows,
And yellow load them with the luscious Spoil.   515

AT length the finish'd Garden to the View
Its Vistas opens, and its Alleys green.
Snatch'd thro' the verdant Maze, the hurried Eye
Distracted wanders; now the bowery Walk
Of Covert close, where scarce a Speck of Day   520
Falls on the lengthen'd Gloom, protracted, sweeps;
Now meets the bending Sky, the River now,
Dimpling along, the breezy-ruffled Lake,
The Forest darkening round, the glittering Spire,
Th' etherial Mountain, and the distant Main.   525
But why so far excursive? when at Hand,

489–97 *28–46*
490 tread] walk *28–38*
492 grace thy braided] deck the flowing *28* deck the braided *30q–38*
493 And for a Breast which can improve their Sweets. *28* And the white
bosom that improves their sweets. *30q–38*   white] [fair *del.*] full *MS*
494 its] her *28–44Wks*
    498 *44–46*
    498 *28–38 as follows:*

> Profusely climbs. Turgent, in every Pore
> The Gummy Moisture shines, new Lustre lends,
> And feeds the Spirit that diffusive round   (*28*, 455)
> Refreshes all the Dale. Long let us walk,

  499–511 *28–46*
503 Mead unworthy] *MS* Meadow worthless *28–38*   thy] our *28–38*
506 spreads] shows *28*
507 roving] *MS* boundless *28–38*
508 'Tis here that their delicious Task the Bees, *28–38*
510 Thro' the soft Air,] This Way and that *28–38*
    512–13 *MS 44–46*
512 pure] [sweet *del.*] soft *MS*
513 And oft, of [more excursive Wing he *del.*] bolder Wing, he soaring
dares *MS*
    512–13 *28–38 as follows:*

> It's Soul, it's Sweetness, and it's Manna suck.   (*28*, 470)
> The little Chymist thus, all-moving *Heaven*
> Has taught. And oft, of bolder Wing, he dares

  514–31 *28–46*
515 load them] loads him *28–38*
521 sweeps] *MS* darts *28–38*
523 breezy-ruffled] *MS* [Zephir-ruffled *del.* Breeze-discolour'd *del.*] *MS*
524 darkening] *MS* running *28–38*   glittering] *MS* rising *28–38*

---

489 come, *28–38*   *May 28–38 44Wks*   492 Fresh-blooming] *MS* ~ₐ~ *38*
495 spreads: see, *MS*   496 Grass, *MS* ~ₐ *28–38*   497 luxuriant, *28*
Bankₐ *28–38*   (*28*, 454) shines; *30q–38*   500 Beans: *28–34*   Beams:
38 ~. *MS 44–46*   501 thence, *MS*   505 wild, *28*   506 Whereₐ
34 38   510a Wayₐ] *MS* ~, *30q–38*   511 andₐ *34 38*   512 Soul:
MS   (*28*, 470) suck: *MS*   (472) taught: and *30q–38*   514 grows,]
MS ~ₐ *38*   521 protracted,] *MS* ~ₐ *28–46*   522 now,] *MS* ~ₐ *28–*
46   525 Mountainₐ *MS*

Along these blushing Borders, bright with Dew,
And in yon mingled Wilderness of Flowers,
Fair-handed Spring unbosoms every Grace:
Throws out the Snow-drop, and the Crocus first;   530
The Daisy, Primrose, Violet darkly blue,
And Polyanthus of unnumber'd Dyes;
The yellow Wall-Flower, stain'd with iron Brown;
And lavish Stock that scents the Garden round.
From the soft Wing of vernal Breezes shed,   535
Anemonies; Auriculas, enrich'd
With shining Meal o'er all their velvet Leaves;
And full Renunculas, of glowing Red.
Then comes the Tulip-Race, where Beauty plays
Her idle Freaks: from Family diffus'd   540
To Family, as flies the Father Dust,
The varied Colours run; and, while they *break*
On the charm'd Eye, th' exulting Florist marks,
With secret Pride, the Wonders of his Hand.
No gradual Bloom is wanting; from the Bud,   545
First-born of Spring, to Summer's musky Tribes:
Nor Hyacinths, of purest virgin White,
Low-bent, and blushing inward; nor Jonquils,
Of potent Fragrance; nor Narcissus fair,
As o'er the fabled Fountain hanging still;   550
Nor broad Carnations; nor gay-spotted Pinks;
Nor, shower'd from every Bush, the Damask-rose.
Infinite Numbers, Delicacies, Smells,
With Hues on Hues Expression cannot paint,
The Breath of Nature, and her endless Bloom.   555

---

527 these] the *28–45*
527–8 bright with Dew, / And in yon mingled Wilderness of Flowers]
MS dewy-bright, / And in yon mingled Wilderness of Flowers *28–38*
[in that wild, / Or those well-mingled Beds of choicer Flowers *del.*] *MS*
    532–8 *44–46*
    532–8 *28–38 as follows:*

        Soft-bending Cowslips, and of nameless Dies   (*28*, 491)
        Anemonies, Auriculas, a Tribe
        Peculiar powder'd with a shining Sand,
        Renunculas, and Iris many-hued.

(491) Soft-bending] Dew-bending *30q–38*   and of nameless Dies] [by the Zephirs blown *del.*] *MS*

532–8 *MS as follows:*

> [And *del.*] With Polyanthus of unnumber'd Dies;
> The yellow Wall-Flower, [bright *del.*] mark'd with iron Brown,
> And lovely-tinctur'd Stock [that breathes the Spring *del.*] of
>   mild Perfume;
> By the soft Breath of vernal Breezes blown,
> Anemonies; Auriculas, a Tribe,
> Peculiar, powder'd with a shining Sand;
> Renunculas, and Iris many-hued.

539–42 *28–46*
540 idle] *MS* gayest *28–38* [wildest *del.*] *MS*
543–6 *44–46*
543–6 *28–38 as follows:*

> On the charm'd *Florist*'s Eye, he wondering stands,
> And new-flush'd Glories all ecstatic marks.   (*28,* 500)

(499) wondering] curious *30q–38*
543–6 *MS as follows:*

> On the charm'd *Florist's* Eye, with secret Pride,
> He marks the gay Creation of his Hand.
> No gradual Bloom is wanting; from the Bud

The first *Spring* [breathes *del.* knows *del.*] blows, to *Summer's* musky
Tribes:
547–8 *46*
547–8 *28–45 as follows:*

Nor Hyacinths are wanting, nor Junquils	*28–38*
Nor Hyacinths sweet-breathing, nor Jonquils	*MS*
Nor Hyacinths, deep-purpled; nor Jonquils,	*44–45*

549–607 *28–46*
549 fair] *MS* white *28–38*
550 *MS not in 28–38*
551 broad] deep *28* strip'd *30q–38* [full *del.* pounc'd *del.* rich *del.*]
bright *MS*   gay-spotted] enamel'd *28–38* [gay-spotted *del.*] enamell'd
MS
552 Nor,] And *28*

---

529 *Spring 28–38*   Grace:] *MS* ~; *28–38*   530 Crocus, *MS*   first;] *MS*
~, *28–38*   (*28,* 492) auriculas∧ *30q–38*   540 Freaks; *28*   542 and∧
28–45   break *28*   544 Pride∧ *46*   549 Fragrance;] *MS* ~, *28–*
38   fair,] *MS* ~. *46*   551 Carnations, *28–38 MS*   Pinks, *28–38 MS*
552 Nor∧ *30q–38*   showr'd *28*   Bush∧ *28–38*   555 *Nature 28–38*

Hail, Source of Beings! Universal Soul
Of Heaven and Earth! Essential Presence, hail!
To Thee I bend the Knee; to Thee my Thoughts,
Continual, climb; who, with a Master-hand,
Hast the great Whole into Perfection touch'd.   560
By Thee the various vegetative Tribes,
Wrapt in a filmy Net, and clad with Leaves,
Draw the live Ether, and imbibe the Dew.
By Thee dispos'd into congenial Soils,
Stands each attractive Plant, and sucks, and swells   565
The juicy Tide; a twining Mass of Tubes.
At Thy Command the vernal Sun awakes
The torpid Sap, detruded to the Root
By wintry Winds, that now in fluent Dance,
And lively Fermentation, mounting, spreads   570
All this innumerous-colour'd Scene of Things.

        As rising from the vegetable World
My Theme ascends, with equal Wing ascend,
My panting Muse; and hark, how loud the Woods
Invite you forth in all your gayest Trim.   575
Lend me your Song, ye Nightingales! oh pour
The mazy-running Soul of Melody
Into my varied Verse! while I deduce,
From the first Note the hollow Cuckoo sings,
The Symphony of Spring, and touch a Theme   580
Unknown to Fame, *the Passion of the Groves.*

        When first the Soul of Love is sent abroad,
Warm thro' the vital Air, and on the Heart
Harmonious seizes, the gay Troops begin,
In gallant Thought, to plume the painted Wing;   585
And try again the long-forgotten Strain,
At first faint-warbled. But no sooner grows
The soft Infusion prevalent, and wide,
Than, all alive, at once their Joy o'erflows
In Musick unconfin'd. Up-springs the Lark,   590
Shrill-voic'd, and loud, the Messenger of Morn;
Ere yet the Shadows fly, he mounted sings

Amid the dawning Clouds, and from their Haunts
Calls up the tuneful Nations. Every Copse
Deep-tangled, Tree irregular, and Bush   595
Bending with dewy Moisture, o'er the Heads
Of the coy Quiristers that lodge within,
Are prodigal of Harmony. The Thrush
And Wood-lark, o'er the kind contending Throng
Superior heard, run thro' the sweetest Length   600
Of Notes; when listening *Philomela* deigns
To let them joy, and purposes, in Thought
Elate, to make her Night excel their Day.
The Black-bird whistles from the thorny Brake;
The mellow Bullfinch answers from the Grove: 605
Nor are the Linnets, o'er the flowering Furze
Pour'd out profusely, silent. Join'd to These,
Innumerous Songsters, in the freshening Shade
Of new-sprung Leaves, their Modulations mix

---

556 Source of Beings] *MS Mighty Being 28–38*
564 congenial] cogenial *28–34*
572–3   Ascending from the vegetable World
                To higher Life, with equal Wing ascend,   *28–38*
582 When first the Soul of Love] Just as the Spirit of Love *28–38*
583 the Heart] their Hearts *28–38*
585 the painted Wing] their painted Wings *28*
595 Deep-tangled,] Thick-wove, and *28–45*
   608–9 *44–46*
   608–9 *28–38 as follows:*

        Thousands beside, thick as the covering Leaves   *(28, 560)*
        They warble under, or the nitid Hues
        Which speck them o'er, their Modulations mix

     (562) Which] That *30q–38*

---

558 Knee, *28*   Thoughts,] *MS ~ʌ 28–38*   559 Continual,] *MS ~ʌ 28–*
38   climb, *28*   561 Thee, *30q–38*   564 Soilsʌ *28*   *566* Tide,
28   567 thy *44–45*   Command, *28–34*   569 now, *28–34*   Danceʌ *28*
574 harkʌ *38–45*   577 mazy-running] *MS ~ʌ~ 38*   580 *Spring 28–38*
581 the Passion of the Groves *28*   584 beginʌ *28*   585 Thoughtʌ *28*
589 Thanʌ *28*   aliveʌ *28*   595 Bush, *28*   596 Moistureʌ *28*
598 Thrush, *28*   601 Notes, *28*   606 Furze, *28*   607 Theseʌ
31–46

Mellifluous. The Jay, the Rook, the Daw,
And each harsh Pipe, discordant heard alone,
Aid the full Concert: while the Stock-dove breathes
A melancholy Murmur thro' the Whole.

'Tis Love creates their Melody, and all
This Waste of Music is the Voice of Love;　　　　615
That even to Birds, and Beasts, the tender Arts
Of pleasing teaches. Hence the glossy Kind
Try every winning Way inventive Love
Can dictate, and in Courtship to their Mates
Pour forth their little Souls. First, wide around,　　　620
With distant Awe, in airy Rings they rove,
Endeavouring by a thousand Tricks to catch
The cunning, conscious, half-averted Glance
Of their regardless Charmer. Should she seem
Softening the least Approvance to bestow,　　　625
Their Colours burnish, and by Hope inspir'd,
They brisk advance; then, on a sudden struck,
Retire disorder'd; then again approach;
In fond Rotation spread the spotted Wing,
And shiver every Feather with Desire.　　　630

Connubial Leagues agreed, to the deep Woods
They haste away, all as their Fancy leads,
Pleasure, or Food, or secret Safety prompts;
That Nature's *great Command* may be obey'd,
Nor all the sweet Sensations they perceive　　　635
Indulg'd in vain. Some to the Holly-Hedge
Nestling repair, and to the Thicket some;
Some to the rude Protection of the Thorn
Commit their feeble Offspring. The cleft Tree
Offers its kind Concealment to a Few,　　　640
Their Food its Insects, and its Moss their Nests.
Others apart far in the grassy Dale,
Or roughening Waste, their humble Texture weave.
But most in woodland Solitudes delight,
In unfrequented Glooms, or shaggy Banks,　　　645
Steep, and divided by a babbling Brook,
Whose Murmurs soothe them all the live-long Day,

When by kind Duty fix'd. Among the Roots
Of Hazel, pendant o'er the plaintive Stream,
They frame the first Foundation of their Domes;   650

610–13 *28–46*
611 each harsh Pipe, discordant] all these jangling Pipes, when *28*
612 Aid the full Concert] Here aid the Consort *28–38*   Stock-dove]
Wood-Dove *28*
614–18 *PS 28–46*
614 Melody] Gaiety *PS 28–38*
616 That] *MS* Which *PS 28–38*
619–21 *MS 44–46*
619 Mates] Fair *MS*
620 forth] [forth *del.*] out *MS*
621 With distant Awe] Aw'd by Respect *MS*
619–21 *PS 28–38 as follows:*

> Can dictate, and in fluttering Courtship pour   (*28,* 572)
> Their little Souls before Her. Wide around,
> Respectful, first in airy Rings they rove,

622–30 *PS 28–46*
628+ *PS 28–38 have the following (not in 44–46):*
> And throwing out the last Efforts of Love,

631–42 *28–46*
632 all] each *28–38*
633 secret] latent *28*
635 the] these *28*
639 *MS* Resolve to trust their Young. The clefted Tree *28–38*
643–4 *MS 44–46*
643–4 *28–38 as follows:*
> Their humble Texture weave. But most delight   (*28,* 597)

(597) [Weave their low Dwellings. But most [love *del.*] joy to
[haunt *del.* build *del.*] lodge *all del.*] *MS*   Their] [The *del.*] *MS*
645–79 *28–46*
648 When for a Season fix'd. Among the Roots *28–38 MS 44–45* [When
fix'd by Duty. *del.*] [And [ease *del.*] lull their Labours. Dark, among the
Roots *all del.*] *MS*

---

611 Pipe‸ *38–46*   620 First‸ *MS*   (*28,* 574) Respectful‸ *PS*   624 seem,
PS   625 Softening, *PS*   626 inspir'd‸ *PS 28–38*   627 then‸ *PS*
28–38   struck‸ *PS 28–38*   628 approach, *PS 28*   634 Nature's *44–45*
great Command *28–45*   642 Dale,] *MS* ~‸ *28–38*   650 Domes;] *MS*
~, *28–38*

Dry Sprigs of Trees, in artful Fabrick laid,
And bound with Clay together. Now 'tis nought
But restless Hurry thro' the busy Air,
Beat by unnumber'd Wings. The Swallow sweeps
The slimy Pool, to build his hanging House　　　655
Intent. And often, from the careless Back
Of Herds and Flocks, a thousand tugging Bills
Pluck Hair and Wool; and oft, when unobserv'd,
Steal from the Barn a Straw: till soft and warm,
Clean, and compleat, their Habitation grows.　　　660

　　As thus the patient Dam assiduous sits,
Not to be tempted from her tender Task,
Or by sharp Hunger, or by smooth Delight,
Tho' the whole loosen'd Spring around Her blows,
Her sympathizing Lover takes his Stand　　　665
High on th' opponent Bank, and ceaseless sings
The tedious Time away; or else supplies
Her Place a Moment, while she sudden flits
To pick the scanty Meal. Th' appointed Time
With pious Toil fulfill'd, the callow Young,　　　670
Warm'd and expanded into perfect Life,
Their brittle Bondage break, and come to Light,
A helpless Family, demanding Food
With constant Clamour. O what Passions then,
What melting Sentiments of kindly Care,　　　675
On the new Parents seize! Away they fly
Affectionate, and undesiring bear
The most delicious Morsel to their Young,
Which equally distributed, again
The Search begins. Even so a gentle Pair,　　　680
By Fortune sunk, but form'd of generous Mold,
And charm'd with Cares beyond the vulgar Breast,
In some lone Cott amid the distant Woods,
Sustain'd alone by providential HEAVEN,
Oft, as they weeping eye their infant Train,　　　685
Check their own Appetites and give them all.

　　NOR Toil alone they scorn: exalting Love,
By the great FATHER OF THE SPRING inspir'd,

Gives instant Courage to the *fearful* Race,
And to the *simple* Art. With stealthy Wing,   690
Should some rude Foot their woody Haunts molest,
Amid a neighbouring Bush they silent drop,
And whirring thence, as if alarm'd, deceive
Th' unfeeling School-Boy. Hence, around the Head
Of wandering Swain, the white-wing'd Plover wheels   695

---

651 Fabrick] Manner *28–38*
653 restless Hurry] *MS* Hurry Hurry *28–38*
656 *MS* Ingeniously intent. Oft from the Back *28–38*
659 the Barn a] *MS* the Barn the *28–38* a Barn the *MS*
661 As thus] Mean-time *28*
674 O] Oh *28–34*
676 On the new Parents seize] Seize the new Parents' Hearts *28–38*
Seize the new Parents' Heart *MS*
  680–6 *44–46*
682 charm'd] pierc'd *44–45*
  680–6 *28–38 as follows:*

> The Search begins. So pitiful, and poor,
> A gentle Pair on Providential *Heaven*
> Cast, as they weeping eye their clamant Train,   (*28*, 635)
> Check their own Appetites, and give them all.

  (635) Cast] Thrown *MS*
687–95 *44–46*
687 Toil] Pain *44–45*
  687–95 *28–38 as follows:*

> Nor is the Courage of the fearful Kind,
> Nor is their Cunning less, should some rude Foot
> Their Woody Haunts molest; stealthy aside
> Into the Centre of a neighbring Bush   (*28*, 640)
> They drop, and whirring thence alarm'd, deceive
> The rambling School-Boy. Hence around the Head
> Of Traveller, the white-wing'd Plover wheels

---

657 Flocks∧ *28–38*   658 Hair, *28–45*   Wool, *28*   oft∧ *28*   unobserv'd∧
28   659 Straw:] *MS* ∼; *28–38*   soft, *28–38*   670 Young,] *MS* ∼∧
28–38   671 Warm'd∧] *MS* ∼, *28–38*   675 Care,] *MS* ∼∧ *28–*
38   676a hearts? *30q–38*   676 fly, *MS*   687 Love∧ *44–45*
(*28*, 640) neighbouring *30q–38*   (641) thence, *MS*   (642) Hence, *MS*

Her sounding Flight, and then directly on
In long Excursion skims the level Lawn,
To tempt him from her Nest. The Wild-Duck, hence,
O'er the rough Moss, and o'er the trackless Waste
The Heath-Hen flutters, (pious Fraud!) to lead   700
The hot pursuing Spaniel far astray.

BE not the Muse asham'd, here to bemoan
Her Brothers of the Grove, by tyrant Man
Inhuman caught, and in the narrow Cage
From Liberty confin'd, and boundless Air.   705
Dull are the pretty Slaves, their Plumage dull,
Ragged, and all its brightening Lustre lost;
Nor is that sprightly Wildness in their Notes,
Which, clear and vigorous, warbles from the Beech.
Oh then, ye Friends of Love and Love-taught Song,   710
Spare the soft Tribes, this barbarous Art forbear!
If on your Bosom Innocence can win,
Music engage, or Piety persuade.

BUT let not chief the Nightingale lament
Her ruin'd Care, too delicately fram'd   715
To brook the harsh Confinement of the Cage.
Oft when, returning with her loaded Bill,
Th' astonish'd Mother finds a vacant Nest,
By the hard Hand of unrelenting Clowns
Robb'd, to the Ground the vain Provision falls;   720
Her Pinions ruffle, and low-drooping scarce
Can bear the Mourner to the poplar Shade;
Where, all abandon'd to Despair, she sings
Her Sorrows thro' the Night; and, on the Bough,
Sole-sitting, still at every dying Fall   725
Takes up again her lamentable Strain
Of winding Woe; till wide around the Woods
Sigh to her Song, and with her Wail resound.

BUT now the feather'd Youth their former Bounds,
Ardent, disdain; and, weighing oft their Wings,   730
Demand the free Possession of the Sky.
This one glad Office more, and then dissolves

Parental Love at once, now needless grown.
Unlavish *Wisdom* never works in vain.
'Tis on some Evening, sunny, grateful, mild,   735
When nought but Balm is breathing thro' the Woods,
With yellow Lustre bright, that the new Tribes
Visit the spacious Heavens, and look abroad
On Nature's Common, far as they can see,
Or wing, their Range, and Pasture. O'er the Boughs   740
Dancing about, still at the giddy Verge
Their Resolution fails; their Pinions still,

696–708 *28–46*
698 him] *MS* you *28–38*
700 (pious Fraud!)] as if hurt, *28–38*
708 sprightly] luscious *28–38* [sprightly *del.*] luscious *MS*
  709–13 *44–46*
  709–13 *28–38 as follows:*

> That warbles from the Beech. Oh then desist,
> Ye Friends of Harmony! this barbarous Art
> Forbear, if Innocence and Music can
> Win on your Hearts, or Piety perswade.   (*28*, 660)

  709–13 *MS as follows:*

> That warbles from the Beech. [Oh then forbear
> Ye Friends of Harmony this barbarous Art! *del.*]
>   Oh then, ye Friends
> Of Harmony, this barbarous Art forbear!
> If on your Bosoms Innocence can win,
> Music engage, or Piety perswade.

  714–54 *28–46*
719 Hand] Hands *28*
725 Sole-sitting] Sad-sitting *28–38*
728 Sigh to] *MS* Sigh at *28 30q 30o* Sigh with *31 34 38*
729 BUT] AND *28–38*
732 This one] But this *28–38*
733 now] for *28–38*

---

697 Lawn,] *MS* ~∧ *38*   698 Duck,] *MS* ~∧ *28–38*   hence,] *MS* ~∧
28–38   701 hot, *28*   708 Notes∧ *28–38*   717 when∧ *28–38*
722 Shade, *28*   723 Where∧ *28*   Despair∧ *28*   724 Bough∧ *28–45*
727 Woe, *28–45*   729 Bounds∧ *28–38*   730 Ardent∧ *28–38*   disdain,
and∧ *28–38*   733 once; *28–38*   grown, *28–38*   739 *Nature's 28–38*

In loose Libration stretch'd, to trust the Void
Trembling refuse: till down before them fly
The Parent-Guides, and chide, exhort, command,   745
Or push them off. The surging Air receives
The plumy Burden; and their self-taught Wings
Winnow the waving Element. On Ground
Alighted, bolder up again they lead,
Farther and farther on, the lengthening Flight;   750
Till vanish'd every Fear, and every Power
Rouz'd into Life and Action, light in Air
Th' acquitted Parents see their soaring Race,
And once rejoicing never know them more.

HIGH from the Summit of a craggy Cliff,   755
Hung o'er the Deep, such as amazing frowns
On utmost *Kilda's Shore, whose lonely Race
Resign the setting Sun to *Indian* Worlds,
The royal Eagle draws his vigorous Young,
Strong-pounc'd, and ardent with paternal Fire.   760
Now fit to raise a Kingdom of their own,
He drives them from his Fort, the towering Seat,
For Ages, of his Empire; which, in Peace,
Unstain'd he holds, while many a League to Sea
He wings his Course, and preys in distant Isles.   765

SHOULD I my Steps turn to the rural Seat,
Whose lofty Elms, and venerable Oaks,
Invite the Rook, who high amid the Boughs,
In early Spring, his airy City builds,
And ceaseless caws amusive; there, well-pleas'd,   770
I might the various Polity survey
Of the mixt Houshold-Kind. The careful Hen
Calls all her chirping Family around,
Fed, and defended by the fearless Cock,
Whose Breast with Ardour flames, as on he walks,   775
Graceful, and crows Defiance. In the Pond,
The finely-checker'd Duck, before her Train,
Rows garrulous. The stately-sailing Swan

*The farthest of the Western Islands of Scotland.

Gives out his snowy Plumage to the Gale;
And, arching proud his Neck, with oary Feet   780
Bears forward fierce, and guards his Osier-Isle,
Protective of his Young. The Turkey nigh,
Loud-threatning, reddens; while the Peacock spreads
His every-colour'd Glory to the Sun,

---

743 to trust the Void] the void Abrupt *28* the void abrupt *30q–34* the
Void abrupt *38* [? *del.*] the void Abrupt *MS*
752 light in Air] in the Void *28–38*
753 Th' acquitted] *MS* Th' exoner'd *28–38* [The faithful *del.*] *MS*
  755–65 *44–46*
  755–65 *28–38 as follows:*

> HIGH from the Summit of a craggy Cliff,
> Hung o'er the green Sea grudging at it's Base,
> The Royal Eagle draws his Young, resolv'd
> To try them at the Sun. Strong-pounc'd, and bright (*28*, 705)
> As burnish'd Day, they up the blue Sky wind,
> Leaving dull Sight below, and with fixt Gaze
> Drink in their native Noon: The Father-King
> Claps his glad Pinions, and approves the Birth.

766–70 *44–46*
766–70 *28–38 as follows:*

> AND should I wander to the Rural Seat,   (*28*,710)
> Whose aged Oaks, and venerable Gloom
> Invite the noisy Rook, with Pleasure there,

(711) Oaks] Elms *MSLytt*   Gloom] Oaks *MSLytt*
(712) with Pleasure] delighted *MS*
(712)   Invite the Rooks; who high amid the Boughs
>   In early Spring their Airy City build
>   And [ceaseless *del.*] caw with ceaseless Clamour.
>   There well-pleas'd *MSLytt*
771–821 *28–46*
781 forward] onward *28*   guards his Osier-Isle] beats you from the
Bank *28–38*

---

749 Alighted˄ bolder, *28*   lead˄ *28–38*   750 on˄ *28–38*   lengthning
28–45   752 Life, *28–45*   Action,] *MS* ~˄ *38*   754 rejoicing, *28–34*
(*28*, 703) sea, *30q–38*   (705) pounc'd˄ *38*   bright, *MS*   (*28*, 711) Oaks˄
38   gloom, *30q–38*   (712) rook; *30q–38*   775 walks˄ *28–38*
779 Gale, *28–38*   783 reddens; *MS* ~, *38*

And swims in radiant Majesty along.
O'er the whole homely Scene, the cooing Dove
Flies thick in amorous Chace, and wanton rolls
The glancing Eye, and turns the changeful Neck.

WHILE thus the gentle Tenants of the Shade
Indulge their purer Loves, the rougher World   790
Of Brutes, below, rush furious into Flame,
And fierce Desire. Thro' all his lusty Veins
The Bull, deep-scorch'd, the raging Passion feels.
Of Pasture sick, and negligent of Food,
Scarce seen, he wades among the yellow Broom,   795
While o'er his ample Sides the rambling Sprays
Luxuriant shoot; or thro' the mazy Wood
Dejected wanders, nor th' inticing Bud
Crops, tho' it presses on his careless Sense.
And oft, in jealous madning Fancy wrapt,   800
He seeks the Fight; and, idly-butting, feigns
His Rival gor'd in every knotty Trunk.
Him should he meet, the bellowing War begins;
Their Eyes flash Fury; to the hollow'd Earth,
Whence the Sand flies, they mutter bloody Deeds,   805
And groaning deep th' impetuous Battle mix:
While the fair Heifer, balmy-breathing, near,
Stands kindling up their Rage. The trembling Steed,
With this hot Impulse seiz'd in every Nerve,
Nor hears the Rein, nor heeds the sounding Thong;   810
Blows are not felt; but tossing high his Head,
And by the well-known Joy to distant Plains
Attracted strong, all wild he bursts away;
O'er Rocks, and Woods, and craggy Mountains flies;
And, neighing, on the aerial Summit takes   815
Th' exciting Gale; then, steep-descending, cleaves
The headlong Torrents foaming down the Hills,
Even where the Madness of the straiten'd Stream
Turns in black Eddies round: such is the Force
With which his frantick Heart and Sinews swell.   820

NOR undelighted, by the boundless Spring,
Are the broad Monsters of the foaming Deep:

From the deep Ooze and gelid Cavern rous'd,
They flounce and tumble in unwieldy Joy.
Dire were the Strain, and dissonant, to sing   825
The cruel Raptures of the Savage Kind:
How by this Flame their native Wrath sublim'd,
They roam, amid the Fury of their Heart,
The far-resounding Waste in fiercer Bands,

---

785 radiant] floating *28–45*
793 the raging Passion feels] *MS* receives the raging Fire *28–38*
796 ample Sides] brawny Back *28–38*
800–1 And oft . . . seeks the Fight;] For, wrapt in mad Imagination,
he / Roars for the Fight, *28–38*
802 His Rival] A Rival *28–38*
803 Him] *MS* Such *28–38*
806 deep] vast *28–38*
807 balmy-breathing, near,] *MS* redolent, in View *28–38*
810 Thong] Whip *28–38*
816 Th' exciting] Th' informing *28–38*   cleaves] stems *28*
818 Stream] streams *30q–38*
     822–3 *30q–46*
822 foaming] boiling *30q–45*
     822–3 *28 as follows:*

     Are the broad Monsters of the Deep: thro' all
     Their oozy Caves, and gelid Kingdoms rous'd,

824–6 *28–46*
827–9 *44–46*
827–9 *28–38 as follows:*

     How the red Lioness, her Whelps forgot
     Amid the thoughtless Fury of her Heart,   (*28*, 770)
     The lank rapacious Wolf, th' unshapely Bear,
     The spotted Tyger, fellest of the Fell,

---

786 Scene͜ *45*   791 Brutes, *MS* ~͜ *28–38*   below͜ *28*   799 Sense:
28–38   801 and͜ *28–38*   butting͜ *28*   804 Earth, *MS* ~͜ *38*
806 th'] the *30o*   812 joy, *30q–38*   813 wild, *28–34*   814 Rocks͜
45   flies, *28–34*   815 And͜ *28–38*   neighing͜ *28*   816 then,] *MS*
~͜ *28–38*   descending͜ *28*   817 Hills,] *MS* ~͜ *38*   819 Such *28–*
38   820 Heart, *28–38*   821 Nor, *28–38*   undelighted͜ *28–38*   *Spring*
28–38   822 Deep: *MS* ~͜ *38*   823 ooze, *30q–45*   824 flounce,
28–34   826 Kind; *28*   (*28*, 770) heart; *30q–38*   (771) wolf; *30q–*
38   bear; *30q–38*   (772) fell; *30q–38*

And growl their horrid Loves. But this the Theme   830
I sing, enraptur'd, to the BRITISH FAIR,
Forbids, and leads me to the Mountain-brow,
Where sits the Shepherd on the grassy Turf,
Inhaling, healthful, the descending Sun.
Around him feeds his many-bleating Flock,   835
Of various Cadence; and his sportive Lambs,
This way and that convolv'd, in friskful Glee,
Their Frolicks play. And now the sprightly Race
Invites them forth; when swift, the Signal given,
They start away, and sweep the massy Mound   840
That runs around the Hill; the Rampart once
Of iron War, in ancient barbarous Times,
When disunited BRITAIN ever bled,
Lost in eternal Broil: ere yet she grew
To this deep-laid indissoluble State,   845
Where *Wealth* and *Commerce* lift the golden Head;
And, o'er our Labours, *Liberty* and *Law*,
Impartial, watch, the Wonder of a World!

    WHAT is this *mighty Breath*, ye Curious, say,
That, in a powerful Language, felt not heard,   850
Instructs the Fowls of Heaven; and thro' their Breast
These Arts of Love diffuses? What, but GOD?
Inspiring GOD! who boundless Spirit all,
And unremitting Energy, pervades,
Adjusts, sustains, and agitates the Whole.   855
He ceaseless works *alone*, and yet *alone*
Seems not to work; with such Perfection fram'd
Is this complex stupendous Scheme of Things.
But, tho' conceal'd, to every purer Eye
Th' informing Author in his Works appears: 860
Chief, lovely Spring, in thee, and thy soft Scenes,
The SMILING GOD is seen; while Water, Earth,

827-9 *28-38 continue as follows:*

      And all the Terrors of the *Lybian* Swain,
      By this new Flame their Native Wrath sublim'd,
      Roam the resounding Waste in fiercer Bands,   (*28*, 775)

830–60 *28–46*
831 enraptur'd,] transported *28–38*
838 Their little Frolicks play. And now the Race *28–38*
840 massy] circly *28*
846 the] their *28–38*   golden] *MS* [happy *del.*] *MS*
848 Impartial,] *MS* Illustrious *28–38*   a World!] *MS* the World? *38*
850 That] *MS* Which *28–38*   powerful Language, felt not heard]
Language rather felt than heard *28–45*
851 Breast] Breasts *28–38*
853 who] *MS* whose *38*
855 Adjusts, sustains] Subsists, adjusts *28*
857 with such Perfection] so exquisitely *28*
858 stupendous] amazing *28–38*   Scheme] Scene *28*
860 Works] Work *31–45*
  861–4 *44–46*
  861–4 *28–38 as follows:*

> His Grandeur in the Heavens: the Sun, and Moon,
> Whether that fires the Day, or falling this
> Pours out a lucid Softness o'er the Night,
> Are but a Beam from Him. The glittering Stars,   (*28*, 810)
> By the deep Ear of Meditation heard,
> Still in their Midnight Watches sing of Him.
> He nods a Calm. The Tempest blows His Wrath,
> Roots up the Forest, and o'erturns the Main.
> The Thunder is His Voice; and the red Flash   (*28*, 815)
> His speedy Sword of Justice. At His Touch
> The Mountains flame. He takes the solid Earth,
> And rocks the Nations. Nor in these alone,
> In every common Instance *GOD* is seen;

(807) His Grandeur in the Heavens] [The Heavens his Grandeur
speak *del.*] *MS*
(817) takes] *MS* shakes *38*

---

831 Fair *28–45*   831a transported, *30q–38*   835 flock∧ *31 34 38*
837 way∧] *MS* ∼, *30q–38*   that∧] *MS* ∼, *30q–38*   convolv'd,] *MS* ∼∧ *28–*
38   839 swift,] *MS* ∼∧ *34 38*   844 Broil:] *MS* ∼; *28–38*   845 laid∧]
MS ∼, *28–38*   846 Head;] *MS* ∼, *28–38* [∼: *del.*] *MS*   847 And∧
28–38   Labours∧ *28 MS*   *Law,*] *MS* ∼∧ *28–38*   849 Curious, *MS* ∼∧ *38*
852 diffuses? — What? *28*   *GOD!* *28*   854 Energy,] *MS* ∼∧ *34 38*
856 alone *28–45*   alone *28–45*   857 work, *28–38*   858 complex∧
MS ∼, *28–38*   859 But∧ *28–38*   860 appears; *28–38* ∼. *MS*
(*28*, 808) falling, *30q–38*   (814) forest∧ *34*

And Air attest his Bounty; which exalts
The Brute-Creation to this finer Thought,
And annual melts their undesigning Hearts　　　865
Profusely thus in Tenderness and Joy.

　　STILL let my Song a nobler Note assume,
And sing th' infusive Force of Spring on Man;
When Heaven and Earth, as if contending, vye
To raise his Being, and serene his Soul.　　　870
Can he forbear to join the general Smile
Of Nature? Can fierce Passions vex his Breast,
While every Gale is Peace, and every Grove
Is Melody? Hence! from the bounteous Walks
Of flowing Spring, ye sordid Sons of Earth,　　　875
Hard, and unfeeling of Another's Woe,
Or only lavish to yourselves; away!
But come, ye generous Minds, in whose wide Thought,
Of all his Works, CREATIVE BOUNTY burns,
With warmest Beam; and on your open Front,　　　880
And liberal Eye, sits, from his dark Retreat,
Inviting modest Want. Nor, till invok'd,
Can restless Goodness wait; your active Search
Leaves no cold wintry Corner unexplor'd;
Like silent-working HEAVEN, surprizing oft　　　885
The lonely Heart with unexpected Good.
For you the roving Spirit of the Wind
Blows Spring abroad; for you the teaming Clouds
Descend in gladsome Plenty o'er the World;
And the Sun sheds his kindest Rays for you,　　　890
Ye Flower of human Race!—In these green Days,
Reviving Sickness lifts her languid Head;
Life flows afresh; and young-ey'd Health exalts
The whole Creation round. Contentment walks
The sunny Glade, and feels an inward Bliss　　　895
Spring o'er his Mind, beyond the Power of Kings
To purchase. Pure Serenity apace
Induces Thought, and Contemplation still.
By swift Degrees the Love of Nature works,
And warms the Bosom; till at last sublim'd　　　900
To Rapture, and enthusiastic Heat,

861–4 *28–38 continue as follows:*

       And to the Man, who casts his mental Eye   (*28*, 820)
       Abroad, unnotic'd Wonders rise. But chief
       In Thee, Boon *Spring*, and in thy softer Scenes,
       The *Smiling GOD* appears; while Water, Earth,
       And Air attest his Bounty, which instils
       Into the Brutes this temporary Thought,   (*28*, 825)

  (820) casts] [gives *del.*] *MS*
  (821) Abroad, unnotic'd Wonders rise.] [To range abroad, new Wonders rise. *del.*] *MS*
  (807–21) *del. MS*
  (822) But cheif in Thee, Boon *Spring*, and thy kind Scenes, *MS*
  (823) appears] is seen *MS*
  (824) which] that *MS*
865–70 *28–46*
870 raise] chear *MS*   serene] elate *MS*
  871–2 *MS 44–46*
872 his] *MS* [the *del.*] *MS*
  871–2 *28–38 as follows:*

       Can he forbear to smile with *Nature?* Can   (*28*, 832)
       The stormy Passions in his Bosom rowl,

873–903 *28–46*
878 Minds] *MS* Breasts *28–38*
879–80 burns, / With warmest Beam] *MS* most, / Divinely burns *28–38*
882–3 Nor, till invok'd, / Can restless Goodness wait] Nor only fair, / And easy of Approach *28–38*
889 gladsome] buxom *28–38*
890 sheds his kindest Rays] spreads his genial Blaze *28–38*
892 Reviving] Sad-pining *28–38*
896–7 Power of Kings / To purchase. Pure Serenity] Pride of Kings / E'er to bestow. Serenity *28*
899 swift] small *28–38*
900 sublim'd] arriv'd *28–38*

---

(820) Man͏ͅ *38* ~, *MS*   (821) Abroad͏ͅ *34 38*   866 Tenderness, *28–34*   868 *Spring 28–38*   869 vye, *MS*   872 *Nature MS* Breast; *MS*   (*28*, 832) NATURE! *300*   874 Hence, *28–45*   875 *Spring 28–38*   876 unfeeling, *30q 31 34*   877 Yourselves, — *28* away. *28–45* 878 come͏ͅ *300*   879 *Bounty, 28–38*   881 Retreat͏ͅ *28–38*   884 unexplor'd, *28–38* ~: *MS*   888 *Spring 28–38* abroad, *28*   889 World, *28*   891 Race!—] *MS* ~! *28–38*

We feel the present DEITY, and taste
The Joy of GOD to see a happy World!

THESE are the Sacred Feelings of thy Heart,
Thy Heart inform'd by Reason's purer Ray,   905
O LYTTELTON, the Friend! thy Passions thus
And Meditations vary, as at large,
Courting the Muse, thro' HAGLEY-PARK you stray,
Thy *British Tempe*! There along the Dale,
With Woods o'er-hung, and shag'd with mossy Rocks,   910
Whence on each Hand the gushing Waters play,
And down the rough Cascade white-dashing fall,
Or gleam in lengthen'd Vista thro' the Trees,
You silent steal; or sit beneath the Shade
Of solemn Oaks, that tuft the swelling Mounts   915
Thrown graceful round by Nature's careless Hand,
And pensive listen to the various Voice
Of rural Peace: the Herds, the Flocks, the Birds,
The hollow-whispering Breeze, the Plaint of Rills,
That, purling down amid the twisted Roots   920
Which creep around, their dewy Murmurs shake
On the sooth'd Ear. From these abstracted oft,
You wander thro' the Philosophic World;
Where in bright Train continual Wonders rise,
Or to the curious or the pious Eye.   925
And oft, conducted by Historic Truth,
You tread the long Extent of backward Time:
Planning, with warm Benevolence of Mind,
And honest Zeal unwarp'd by Party-Rage,
BRITANNIA'S Weal; how from the venal Gulph   930
To raise her Virtue, and her Arts revive.
Or, turning thence thy View, these graver Thoughts
The Muses charm: while, with sure Taste refin'd,
You draw th' inspiring Breath of antient Song;
Till nobly rises, emulous, thy own.   935
Perhaps thy lov'd LUCINDA shares thy Walk,
With Soul to thine attun'd. Then Nature all
Wears to the Lover's Eye a Look of Love;
And all the Tumult of a guilty World,
Tost by ungenerous Passions, sinks away.   940

The tender Heart is animated Peace;
And as it pours its copious Treasures forth,
In vary'd Converse, softening every Theme,
You, frequent-pausing, turn, and from her Eyes,
Where meeken'd Sense, and amiable Grace,   945
And lively Sweetness dwell, enraptur'd, drink
That nameless Spirit of etherial Joy,
Inimitable Happiness! which Love,
Alone, bestows, and on a *favour'd Few*.
Meantime you gain the Height, from whose fair Brow   950
The bursting Prospect spreads immense around;
And snatch'd o'er Hill and Dale, and Wood and Lawn,
And verdant Field, and darkening Heath between,
And Villages embosom'd soft in Trees,
And spiry Towns by surging Columns mark'd   955
Of houshold Smoak, your Eye excursive roams:
Wide-stretching from the *Hall*, in whose kind Haunt
The *Hospitable Genius* lingers still,
To Where the broken Landskip, by Degrees,
Ascending, roughens into rigid Hills;   960
O'er which the *Cambrian* Mountains, like far Clouds
That skirt the blue Horizon, dusky, rise.

FLUSH'D by the Spirit of the genial Year,
Now from the Virgin's Cheek a fresher Bloom

904–64 *44–46*
905 purer] purest *44–45*
955 surging] dusky *44–45*
956 houshold] rising *44–45*
958 lingers] harbours *44–45*
960 rigid] ridgy *44–45*
962 dusky] doubtful *44–45*
    904–64 *28–38 as follows:*
        'TIS *Harmony*, that World-embracing Power,   (*28*, 865)
        (865) World-embracing] world-attuning *30q–38*

---

903 GOD, *28–34 MS*   God, *38*   World. *28–45*   949 favour'd Few
44–45

Shoots, less and less, the live Carnation round;   965
Her Lips blush deeper Sweets; she breathes of Youth;
The shining Moisture swells into her Eyes,
In brighter Flow; her wishing Bosom heaves,
With Palpitations wild; kind Tumults seize
Her Veins, and all her yielding Soul is Love.   970
From the keen Gaze her Lover turns away,
Full of the dear exstatic Power, and sick
With sighing Languishment. Ah then, ye Fair!
Be greatly cautious of your sliding Hearts:
Dare not th' infectious Sigh; the pleading Look,   975
Down-cast, and low, in meek Submission drest,
But full of Guile. Let not the fervent Tongue,
Prompt to deceive, with Adulation smooth,
Gain on your purpos'd Will. Nor in the Bower,
Where Woodbines flaunt, and Roses shed a Couch,   980
While Evening draws her crimson Curtains round,
Trust your soft Minutes with betraying Man.

   AND let th' aspiring Youth beware of Love,
Of the smooth Glance beware; for 'tis too late,
When on his Heart the Torrent-Softness pours.   985
Then Wisdom prostrate lies, and fading Fame
Dissolves in Air away; while the fond Soul,
Wrapt in gay Visions of unreal Bliss,
Still paints th' illusive Form; the kindling Grace;
Th' inticing Smile; the modest-seeming Eye,   990
Beneath whose beauteous Beams, belying Heaven,
Lurk searchless Cunning, Cruelty, and Death:
And still, false-warbling in his cheated Ear,
Her syren Voice, enchanting, draws him on,
To guileful Shores, and Meads of fatal Joy.   995

   EVEN present, in the very Lap of Love
Inglorious laid; while Musick flows around,
Perfumes, and Oils, and Wine, and wanton Hours;
Amid the Roses fierce Repentance rears
Her snaky Crest: a quick-returning Pang   1000
Shoots thro' the conscious Heart; where Honour still,

904–64 *28–38 continue as follows:*

   By which all Beings are adjusted, each
   To all around, impelling and impell'd
   In endless Circulation, that inspires
   This universal Smile. Thus the glad Skies,
   The wide-rejoycing Earth, the Woods, the Streams, *(28,* 870)
   With every *Life* they hold, down to the Flower
   That paints the lowly Vale, or Insect-Wing
   Wav'd o'er the Shepherd's Slumber, touch the Mind
   To Nature tun'd, with a light-flying Hand,
   Invisible; quick-urging, thro' the Nerves,   *(28,* 875)
   The glittering Spirits, in a Flood of Day.

   HENCE from the Virgin's Cheek, a fresher Bloom

 (876) The glittering] Th' enliven'd *MS*
965–74 *28–46*
974 sliding] [soften'd *del.*] *MS*
 975–7 *MS 44–46*
 975–7 *28–38 as follows:*

   Dare not th' infectious Sigh, the pleading Eye
   In meek Submission drest, deject, and low,
   But full of tempting Guile. Let not the Tongue,

 978–89 *28–46*
979 Will] *MS* Wills *28–38*
981 crimson] crimson'd *28 MS*
984 Of the smooth Glance beware;] And shun th' enchanting Glance, *28*
986 Then Interest sinks to Dirt, and distant Fame *28*
988 Is wrapt in Dreams of Ecstacy, and Bliss; *28–38*
 990–1008 *30q–46*
1000 Pang] *MS* twinge *30q–38*

––––––––––

(28, 867) impelling, *30q–38* impell'd, *30q–38* (870) wide-rejoicing] *MS*
~ʌ~ *38* (873) Mind, *MS* (876) spiritsʌ *30q–38* (877) Cheekʌ
MS 965 Shoots,] *MS* ~ʌ *300 38* 968 heaves,] *MS* ~ʌ *28–38*
974 Hearts:] *MS* ~; *28–38* 975a sigh; *30q–38* eye, *30q–38* 984 lateʌ
28 986 lies; *30q–34* 987 away. While *28* ~: while *30q–38* Soulʌ
28–38 989 Form, *28* Grace, *28* 993 stillʌ *38* 996 present,]
MS ~ʌ *31–38* 998 Hours;] *MS* ~, *30q–38* 1000 quick-returning]
MS ~ʌ~ *38* 1001 stillʌ *300*

And great Design, against th' oppressive Load
Of Luxury, by Fits, impatient heave.

BUT absent, what fantastic Woes, arrous'd,
Rage in each Thought, by restless Musing fed,   1005
Chill the warm Cheek, and blast the Bloom of Life?
Neglected Fortune flies; and sliding swift,
Prone into Ruin, fall his scorn'd Affairs.
'Tis nought but Gloom around. The darken'd Sun
Loses his Light. The rosy-bosom'd Spring   1010
To weeping Fancy pines; and yon bright Arch,
Contracted, bends into a dusky Vault.
All Nature fades extinct; and she alone
Heard, felt, and seen, possesses every Thought,
Fills every Sense, and pants in every Vein.   1015
Books are but formal Dulness, tedious Friends;
And sad amid the social Band he sits,
Lonely, and unattentive. From the Tongue
Th' unfinish'd Period falls: while borne away,
On swelling Thought, his wafted Spirit flies   1020
To the vain Bosom of his distant Fair;
And leaves the Semblance of a Lover, fix'd
In melancholy Site, with Head declin'd,
And love-dejected Eyes. Sudden he starts,
Shook from his tender Trance, and restless runs   1025
To glimmering Shades, and sympathetic Glooms;
Where the dun Umbrage o'er the falling Stream,
Romantic, hangs; there thro' the pensive Dusk
Strays, in heart-thrilling Meditation lost,
Indulging all to Love: or on the Bank   1030
Thrown, amid drooping Lilies, swells the Breeze
With Sighs unceasing, and the Brook with Tears.
Thus in soft Anguish he consumes the Day,
Nor quits his deep Retirement, till the Moon
Peeps thro' the Chambers of the fleecy East,   1035
Enlighten'd by Degrees, and in her Train
Leads on the gentle Hours; then forth he walks,
Beneath the trembling Languish of her Beam,
With soften'd Soul, and wooes the Bird of Eve
To mingle Woes with his: or, while the World   1040

And all the Sons of Care lie hush'd in Sleep,
Associates with the midnight Shadows drear;
And, sighing to the lonely Taper, pours
His idly-tortur'd Heart into the Page,
Meant for the moving Messenger of Love;   1045
Where Rapture burns on Rapture, every Line
With rising Frenzy fir'd. But if on Bed

1004 Woes,] pangs *30q–38* Fears *MS*
  990–1008 *28 as follows:*

> Th' alluring Smile, the full æthereal Eye
> Effusing Heaven; and listens ardent still
> To the small Voice, where Harmony and Wit,   (*28*, 905)
> A modest, melting, mingled Sweetness, flow.
> No sooner is the fair Idea form'd,
> And Contemplation fixes on the Theme,
> Than from his own Creation wild He flies,
> Sick of a Shadow. Absence comes apace,   (*28*, 910)
> And shoots his every Pang into his Breast.

  1009–45 *28–46*
1012 Contracted, bends] Of Heaven, low-bends *28–38*
1018 unattentive] inattentive *28–38*
1021 vain] dear *28*   distant] absent *28*
1038 Beam] *MS* Beams *28–38*
1044 idly-tortur'd] sweetly-tortur'd *28*
  1046–7 *30q–46*
  1046–7 *28 as follows:*

> But ah how faint, how meaningless, and poor
> To what his Passion swells! which bursts the Bounds (*28*, 950)
> Of every Eloquence, and asks for Looks,
> Where Fondness flows on Fondness, Love on Love,
> Entwisting Beams with Her's, and speaking more
> Than ever charm'd, ecstatic Poet sigh'd
> To listening Beauty, bright with conscious Smiles,   (*28*, 955)
> And graceful Vanity. But if on Bed

1002 Design,] *MS* ~ˆ *30q–38*   Load, *MS*   1010 *Spring 28–38*   1011 Archˆ
28–45   1016 Friends, *28–45*   1017 sits; *44–45*   1019 while, *28–*
38   away, *MS* ~ˆ *28–38*   1026 Glooms, *28–38*   1027 Streamˆ *28–38*
1028 Romanticˆ *28–38*   1033 Day; *28*   1040 or,] *MS* ~ˆ *28–46*
Worldˆ] *MS* ~, *28–38*   1041 Careˆ] *MS* ~, *30q–38*   1042 drear, *28*
1044 Pageˆ *28*   1045 Love. *28*

Delirious flung, Sleep from his Pillow flies.
All Night he tosses, nor the balmy Power
In any Posture finds; till the grey Morn   1050
Lifts her pale Lustre on the paler Wretch,
Exanimate by Love: and then perhaps
Exhausted Nature sinks awhile to Rest,
Still interrupted by distracted Dreams,
That o'er the sick Imagination rise,   1055
And in black Colours paint the mimick Scene.
Oft with th' Enchantress of his Soul he talks;
Sometimes in Crouds distress'd; or if retir'd
To secret-winding, flower-enwoven Bowers,
Far from the dull Impertinence of Man,   1060
Just as he, credulous, his endless Cares
Begins to lose in blind oblivious Love,
Snatch'd from her yielded Hand, he knows not how,
Thro' Forests huge, and long untravel'd Heaths
With Desolation brown, he wanders waste,   1065
In Night and Tempest wrapt; or shrinks aghast,
Back, from the bending Precipice; or wades
The turbid Stream below, and strives to reach
The farther Shore; where succourless, and sad,
She with extended Arms his Aid implores,   1070
But strives in vain; borne by th' outragious Flood
To Distance down, he rides the ridgy Wave,
Or whelm'd beneath the boiling Eddy sinks.
These are the charming Agonies of Love,
Whose Misery delights. But thro' the Heart   1075
Should Jealousy its Venom once diffuse,
'Tis then delightful Misery no more,
But Agony unmix'd, incessant Gall,
Corroding every Thought, and blasting all
Love's Paradise. Ye fairy Prospects, then,   1080
Ye Beds of Roses, and ye Bowers of Joy,
Farewel! Ye Gleamings of departed Peace,
Shine out your last! The yellow-tinging Plague
Internal Vision taints, and in a Night
Of livid Gloom Imagination wraps.   1085
Ah then instead of love-enliven'd Cheeks,

Of sunny Features, and of ardent Eyes
With flowing Rapture bright, dark Looks succeed,
Suffus'd, and glaring with untender Fire,
A clouded Aspect, and a burning Cheek,   1090
Where the whole poison'd Soul, malignant, sits,
And frightens Love away. Ten thousand Fears
Invented wild, ten thousand frantic Views
Of horrid Rivals, hanging on the Charms
For which he melts in Fondness, eat him up   1095
With fervent Anguish, and consuming Rage.
In vain Reproaches lend their idle Aid,
Deceitful Pride, and Resolution frail,

1048–73 *28–46*
1053 awhile] *MS* a-while *28* a while *30q–46*
1054 distracted] disorder'd *28*
1057 th' Enchantress] the Charmer *28*
1061 he, credulous, his endless Cares] He kneeling all his former Cares
28 he, credulous, his thousand cares *30q–38*
1062 blind] vast *28*
1063 yielded] *MS* yielding *30o 38*
1070 *MS* His Dearer Life extends her beckoning Arms, *28* Wild as a
Bacchanal she spreads her arms, *30q–38*
1073 + *28–38 have the following three lines (not in 44–46):*

> Then a weak, wailing, lamentable Cry
> Is heard, and all in Tears he wakes, again
> To tread the Circle of revolving Woe.   (*28*, 985)

1074–1160 *28–46*
1078 Gall] Rage *28–38*
1080 Love's Paradise] The Paradise of Love *28*
1082 departed] departing *28–45*
1086 Ah] Ay *28–34*
1088 Rapture] *MS* raptures *31–38*
1090 clouded] cloudy *44–45*
1096 Rage] Pine *28–38* Care *MSLytt*

1059 winding‸ *38–46*   1069 Shore, *28*   1071 vain, *28–38*   (*28*,
984) weak‸ *MS* wailing‸ *34 38*   1080 Prospects,] *MS* ∼‸ *28–38*   then,]
MS ∼‸ *38*   1083 the *38–46*   1086 then, *28*   1092 Fears, *28*
30q

Giving false Peace a Moment. Fancy pours,
Afresh, her Beauties on his busy Thought,   1100
Her first Endearments, twining round the Soul,
With all the Witchcraft of ensnaring Love.
Strait the fierce Storm involves his Mind anew,
Flames thro' the Nerves, and boils along the Veins:
While anxious Doubt distracts the tortur'd Heart;   1105
For even the sad Assurance of his Fears
Were Peace to what he feels. Thus the warm Youth,
Whom Love deludes into his thorny Wilds,
Thro' flowery-tempting Paths, or leads a Life
Of fever'd Rapture, or of cruel Care;   1110
His brightest Aims extinguish'd all, and all
His lively Moments running down to Waste.

But happy they! the happiest of their Kind!
Whom gentler Stars unite, and in one Fate
Their Hearts, their Fortunes, and their Beings blend.   1115
'Tis not the coarser Tie of human Laws,
Unnatural oft, and foreign to the Mind,
That binds their Peace, but Harmony itself,
Attuning all their Passions into Love;
Where Friendship full-exerts her softest Power,   1120
Perfect Esteem enliven'd by Desire
Ineffable, and Sympathy of Soul;
Thought meeting Thought, and Will preventing Will,
With boundless Confidence: for nought but Love
Can answer Love, and render Bliss secure.   1125
Let him, ungenerous, who, alone intent
To bless himself, from sordid Parents buys
The loathing Virgin, in eternal Care,
Well-merited, consume his Nights and Days:
Let barbarous Nations, whose inhuman Love   1130
Is wild Desire, fierce as the Suns they feel;
Let Eastern Tyrants from the Light of Heaven
Seclude their Bosom-slaves, meanly possess'd
Of a meer, lifeless, violated Form:
While Those whom Love cements in holy Faith,   1135
And equal Transport, free as Nature live,

Disdaining Fear. What is the World to them,
Its Pomp, its Pleasure, and its Nonsense all!
Who in each other clasp whatever fair
High Fancy forms, and lavish Hearts can wish;   1140
Something than Beauty dearer, should they look
Or on the Mind, or mind-illumin'd Face,
Truth, Goodness, Honour, Harmony, and Love,
The richest Bounty of indulgent HEAVEN.
Mean-time a smiling Offspring rises round,   1145
And mingles both their Graces. By degrees,
The human Blossom blows; and every Day,
Soft as it rolls along, shews some new Charm,
The Father's Lustre, and the Mother's Bloom.
Then infant Reason grows apace, and calls   1150
For the kind Hand of an assiduous Care.
Delightful Task! to rear the tender Thought,
To teach the young Idea how to shoot,
To pour the fresh Instruction o'er the Mind,
To breathe th' enlivening Spirit, and to fix   1155
The generous Purpose in the glowing Breast.
Oh speak the Joy! ye, whom the sudden Tear
Surprizes often, while you look around,
And nothing strikes your Eye but Sights of Bliss,
All various Nature pressing on the Heart: 1160

1099 Giving a Moment's Ease. Reflection pours, *28–38*
1107 Peace] Heaven *28*
1118 That] Which *28*
1120 her] his *28–38*
1137 Fear. What is] *MS* Fear; for what's *28–38*
1155 enlivening] inspiring *28–38*   to fix] to plant *28–38* [to fix *del.*]
call forth *MS*
1156 in] from *MS*
1157 ye,] You, *28–38* [ye *del.*] you, *MS*

1104 Veins; *28–38*   1107 Youth∧ *45*   1122 Soul, *28–38*   1124 Con-
fidence; *28–38*   1129 Days. *28*   1131 Desire∧ *28*   feel, *28*
1135 cements, *28–34*   1136 Nature, *28–38*   1140 wish, *28–38*
1143 Harmony∧ *28*   1149 lustre∧ *30q*   1151 Care: *28–34*   1157a you,]
MS ∼∧ *30q–38*   1160 Heart, *28–38*

An elegant Sufficiency, Content,
Retirement, rural Quiet, Friendship, Books,
Ease and alternate Labour, useful Life,
Progressive Virtue, and approving HEAVEN.
These are the matchless Joys of virtuous Love;　　1165
And thus their Moments fly. The Seasons thus,
As ceaseless round a jarring World they roll,
Still find them happy; and consenting SPRING
Sheds her own rosy Garland on their Heads:
Till Evening comes at last, serene and mild;　　1170
When after the long vernal Day of Life,
Enamour'd more, as more Remembrance swells
With many a Proof of recollected Love,
Together down they sink in social Sleep;
Together freed, their gentle Spirits fly　　1175
To Scenes where Love and Bliss immortal reign.

1161–5 *MS 44–46*
1163 useful [social *del.*] *MS*
    1161–5 *28–38 as follows:*

> Obedient Fortune, and approving *Heaven*.   (*28*, 1073)
> These are the Blessings of diviner Love;

1166–71 *28–46*
1169 Heads] Head *28–38*
1170 serene and mild] cool, gentle, calm *28–38* pleasing, serene *MS*
    1172–6 *MS 44–46*
    1172–6 *28–38 as follows:*

> Enamour'd more, as Soul approaches Soul,
> Together, down They sink in social Sleep.   (*28*, 1082)

28 adds: THE END.
31 34 add: FINIS.

1164 Virtue‸ *MS*   Heaven *MS*   1165 Love‸ *MS*   1166 fly; the *28*
Seasons 28   1175 fly, *MS*

SUMMER

FROM brightening Fields of Ether fair disclos'd,
Child of the Sun, refulgent SUMMER comes,
In pride of Youth, and felt thro' Nature's Depth:
He comes attended by the sultry *Hours*,
And ever-fanning *Breezes*, on his Way; 5
While, from his ardent Look, the turning SPRING
Averts her blushful Face; and Earth, and Skies,
All-smiling, to his hot Dominion leaves.

HENCE, let me haste into the mid-wood Shade,
Where scarce a Sun-beam wanders thro' the Gloom; 10
And on the dark-green Grass, beside the Brink
Of haunted Stream, that by the Roots of Oak
Rolls o'er the rocky Channel, lie at large,
And sing the Glories of the circling Year.

COME, *Inspiration*! from thy Hermit-Seat, 15
By Mortal seldom found: may Fancy dare,

half title: SUMMER] SUMMER. A POEM. *300 38   no half title in*
   27 35
30q 30p 300 38 add: Inscribed to the RIGHT HONOURABLE Mr.
DODINGTON.
27 30p 35 have separate title-page
27 has the following title-page epigraph:

> Jam clarus Occultum Andromedae Pater
> Ostendit Ignem: Jam Procyon furit
>   Et Stella vesani Leonis,
>   Sole Dies referente siccos.
> Jam Pastor Umbras cum Grege languido,
> Rivumque fessus quaerit, & horridi
>   Dumeta Sylvani: caretque
>   Ripa vagis taciturna Ventis.   HOR.

27 adds a dedication (reprinted in Appendix B below)
   The Argument *30q–46   not in 27*
5 *The Dawn. Sun-rising.*] *Morning. A view of the sun rising. 30q–38*
6 *Summer Insects describ'd. Hay-making. Sheep-shearing.*] *Rural
prospects. Summer insects described. 30q–38*
7 *Groupe of Herds and Flocks.*] *A groupe of flocks and herds. 30q–38*
8–14 *A Cataract . . . Summer Meteors.*] *Transition to the prospect of a
rich well-cultivated country; which introduces a panegyric on* GREAT
BRITAIN. *A digression on foreign summers. Storm of thunder and
lightning. A tale. The storm over; a serene afternoon. Bathing. Sun set.
Evening. 30q–38*
14 *A Comet*] *not in 30q–45*
   1–20 27–46
1–2 FROM brightening . . . Child of the Sun,] FROM Southern Climes,
where unremitting Day / Burns over Head, *27* FROM yonder fields of
aether fair disclos'd, / Child of the Sun! *30q–38*
1 brightening] *MS*
2 refulgent] illustrious *27–38* resplendent *MS*
12 Oak] Oaks, *27*
16 may Fancy dare,] may I presume *27*

Argument 3 SEASONS *30q–38*   2 comes,] *MS* ∼∧ *30p 35 38*   3 Depth:]
MS ∼. *27–38*   4 comes! *27* ∼, *30q–38*   7 Face, *27 30*] Earth∧ *38*
8 smiling,] *MS* ∼∧ *38*   11 And, *27*   12 Stream] *MS* ∼∧ *30p 35*
38 that, *27*   14 Year] *MS* year *30p–38*   15 Seat,] *MS* ∼∧ *30p*
35 38

From thy fix'd serious Eye, and raptur'd Glance
Shot on surrounding Heaven, to steal one Look
Creative of the Poet, every Power
Exalting to an Ecstasy of Soul.   20

AND thou, my youthful Muse's early Friend,
In whom the Human Graces all unite:
Pure Light of Mind, and Tenderness of Heart;
Genius, and Wisdom; the gay social Sense,
By Decency chastis'd; Goodness and Wit,   25
In seldom-meeting Harmony combin'd;
Unblemish'd Honour, and an active Zeal,
For BRITAIN's Glory, Liberty, and Man:
O DODINGTON! attend my rural Song,
Stoop to my Theme, inspirit every Line,   30
And teach me to deserve thy just Applause.

WITH what an awful world-revolving Power,
Were first th' unwieldy Planets launch'd along
Th' illimitable Void! Thus to remain,
Amid the Flux of many thousand Years,   35
That oft has swept the toiling Race of Men,
And all their labour'd Monuments away,
Firm, unremitting, matchless, in their Course;
To the kind-temper'd Change of Night and Day,
And of the Seasons ever stealing round,   40
Minutely faithful: Such TH' ALL-PERFECT HAND,
That pois'd, impels, and rules the steady Whole.

WHEN now no more th' alternate *Twins* are fir'd,
And *Cancer* reddens with the solar Blaze,
Short is the doubtful Empire of the Night;   45
And soon, observant of approaching Day,
The meek-ey'd Morn appears, Mother of Dews,
At first faint-gleaming in the dappled East:
Till far o'er Ether spreads the widening Glow;
And, from before the Lustre of her Face,   50
White break the Clouds away. With quicken'd Step,
Brown Night retires. Young Day pours in apace,
And opens all the lawny Prospect wide.

The dripping Rock, the Mountain's misty Top
Swell on the Sight, and brighten with the Dawn. 55
Blue, thro' the Dusk, the smoking Currents shine;
And from the bladed Field the fearful Hare
Limps, aukward: while along the Forest-glade
The wild Deer trip, and often turning gaze

---

17 Eye] *MS* Muse *27–38*   and] or *MS*   Glance] *MS* eye *30q–38*
  21–31 *30q–46 not in 27*
21 my youthful Muse's early Friend,] the muse's honour! and her
friend! *30q–38*
31 just] *MS* BEST *30q–38*
  32–8 *27–46*
32 an awful] *MS* a perfect, *27–38*
33 th' unwieldy] *MS* [the cumbrous *del.*] *MS*
36 toiling] busy *27–38*
38 Firm, unremitting] *MS* Unresting, changeless *27–38* Firm, unabating
MS
  39–42 *44–46*
41 TH' ALL-PERFECT HAND] the perfect Hand *44–45*
  39–42 *27–38 as follows:*

        To Day, and Night, and the delightful Round   (*27, 28*)
        Of *Seasons*, faithful; not excentric once:
        So pois'd, and perfect, is the vast Machine!

    (28) Day, and Night, and] night and day, with *30q–38*
  43–96 *27–46*
45 the doubtful] th' uncertain *27*
46 approaching] *MS* th' approaching *30o 38*
48 Mildly elucent in the streaky East; *27*
49 Till far o'er aether shoots the trembling glow; *30q–38 not in 27*
51 quicken'd] tardy *27–38*
55 Sight] Eye *27–38*
57 the fearful] th' unhunted *27*

---

17 fix'd, *27*   18 Look, *27–38*   20 Soul! *27*   27 honour; *30q*
28 Liberty∧ *38*   Man:] *MS* ∼; *30q–38*   31a best *30p–38*   32 Power,]
MS ∼∧ *27 30p–45*   32a perfect∧ *30p–38*   36 Men∧] *MS* ∼, *27–38*
(*27, 29*) faithful, *38*   (30) perfect,] *MS* ∼∧ *30q–38*   machine. *30q–38*
45 *Night 27*   46 *Day 27*   47 *Morn 27*   Dews! *27–38*   48 faint∧
46   east; *30q*   51 White, *27*   Step∧ *27*   52 *Night 27*   *Day 27*
54 Rock∧ *46*   56 Blue,] *MS* ∼∧ *30q–38*   Dusk,] *MS* ∼∧ *30p–38*
57 And, *27*   Field, *27*   58 Limps,] *MS* ∼∧ *27–38*   aukward; *30q–38*
while, *27*   Glade, *27*   59 and, *27*   turning, *27*

At early Passenger. Musick awakes,   60
The native Voice of undissembled Joy;
And thick around the woodland Hymns arise.
Rous'd by the Cock, the soon-clad Shepherd leaves
His mossy Cottage, where with *Peace* he dwells;
And from the crouded Fold, in Order, drives   65
His Flock, to taste the Verdure of the Morn.

    FALSELY luxurious, will not Man awake;
And, springing from the Bed of Sloth, enjoy
The cool, the fragrant, and the silent Hour,
To Meditation due, and sacred Song?   70
For is there Aught in Sleep can charm the Wise?
To lie in dead Oblivion, losing Half
The fleeting Moments of too short a Life?
Total extinction of th' enlighten'd Soul;
Or else to feverish Vanity alive,   75
Wilder'd, and tossing thro' distemper'd Dreams?
Who would in such a gloomy State remain,
Longer than Nature craves; when every Muse
And every blooming Pleasure wait without,
To bless the wildly-devious Morning-walk?   80

    BUT yonder comes the powerful King of Day,
Rejoicing in the East. The lessening Cloud,
The kindling Azure, and the Mountain's Brow
Illum'd with fluid Gold, his near Approach
Betoken glad. Lo! now apparent all,   85
Aslant the dew-bright Earth, and colour'd Air,
He looks in boundless Majesty abroad;
And sheds the shining Day, that burnish'd plays
On Rocks, and Hills, and Towers, and wandering Streams,
High-gleaming from afar. Prime Chearer Light!   90
Of all material Beings first, and best!
Efflux divine! Nature's resplendent Robe!
Without whose vesting Beauty all were wrapt
In unessential Gloom; and thou, O Sun!
Soul of surrounding Worlds! in whom best seen   95
Shines out thy Maker! may I sing of thee?

'Tis by thy secret, strong, attractive Force,
As with a Chain indissoluble bound,
Thy System rolls entire: from the far Bourne
Of utmost *Saturn*, wheeling wide his Round   100
Of thirty Years; to *Mercury*, whose Disk
Can scarce be caught by Philosophic Eye,
Lost in the near Effulgence of thy Blaze.

---

61 undissembled] undissembling *27 30q*
68 springing] *MS* starting *27–38*
71 For] *MSLytt* And *27–38*
72–3 losing Half / The fleeting Moments of too short a Life?] lost to all, / Our Natures boast of noble, and divine: *27*
83 Brow] Brim *27-38*
84 Illum'd with fluid Gold] Tipt with aethereal Gold *27–38*
85 glad. Lo!] glad: and *27–38*
94 O] *MS* red *27–38*
95–6 Soul of surrounding Worlds! in whom best seen / Shines out thy Maker!] In whose wide Circle Worlds of Radiance lie, / Exhaustless Brightness! *27–38*
    96+ *27–38 have the following five lines (not in 44–46):*

> Who would the Blessings, first and last, recount,
> That, in a full Effusion, from Thee flow,   (*27, 85*)
> As soon might number, at the Height of Noon,
> The Rays that radiate from thy cloudless Sphere,
> An universal Glory darting round.

    (84) But he who would the Blessings all recount, *MS*
    (87) cloudless] dazzling *MS*
    (88) An] A *30q 30p 35 38*
    (84–8) *del. MS*
97–9 *27–46*
100–3 *44–46*

---

60 awakes∧ *300*   64 cottage∧ *30q*   65 Fold,] *MS* ∼∧ *30p–38*   Order,] *MS* ∼∧ *30p–38*   67 awake;] *MS* ∼, *27 30p–38*   68 And∧ *27*
70 Song?] *MS* ∼! *27* ∼. *30q–38*   74 Soul! *27–38*   76 Dreams. *27*
77 remain∧ *27*   78 craves? *27*   Muse∧] *MS Muse*, *27* Muse, *30q–38*
79 *Pleasure 27*   without,] *MS* ∼∧ *38*   80 walk. *27*   81 *King 27*
87 looks, *27*   Majesty, *27*   88 that, burnish'd, *27*   90 Chearer, *27*
44–45   Light 27   92 Robe, *27*   93 Beauty, *27*   94 Sun, *27–38*
96 Thee! *27–38*   96a brightness, *30q–38*   (*27, 85*) That∧ *30q–38*
effusion∧ *30q–38*   (86) number∧ *30q*   98 Chain, *27 30q*   indissoluble, *27 30q*   99 entire; *27–38*   100 *Saturn*∧ *30p–38*

INFORMER of the planetary Train!
Without whose quickening Glance their cumbrous Orbs   105
Were brute unlovely Mass, inert and dead,
And not as now the green Abodes of Life;
How many Forms of Being wait on thee!
Inhaling Spirit; from th' unfetter'd Mind,
By thee sublim'd, down to the daily Race,   110
The mixing Myriads of thy setting Beam.

THE vegetable World is also thine,
Parent of *Seasons*! who the Pomp precede
That waits thy Throne, as thro' thy vast Domain,
Annual, along the bright Ecliptic-Road,   115
In World-rejoicing State, it moves sublime.
Mean-time th' expecting Nations, circled gay
With all the various Tribes of foodful Earth,
Implore thy Bounty, or send grateful up
A common Hymn: while, round thy beaming Car,   120
High-seen, the *Seasons* lead, in sprightly Dance
Harmonious knit, the rosy-finger'd *Hours*,
The *Zephyrs* floating loose, the timely *Rains*,
Of Bloom etherial the light-footed *Dews*,
And soften'd into Joy the surly *Storms*.   125
These, in successive Turn, with lavish Hand,
Shower every Beauty, every Fragrance shower,
Herbs, Flowers, and Fruits; till, kindling at thy Touch,
From Land to Land is flush'd the vernal Year.

100–3 *27–38 as follows:*

    Of slow-pac'd *Saturn*, to the scarce-seen Disk
    Of *Mercury*, lost in excessive Blaze.

104–6 *44–46*
104–6 *27–38 as follows:*

    INFORMER of the planetary Train!
    Without whose vital, and effectual Glance,   *(27, 95)*
    They'd be but brute, uncomfortable Mass,

  (95) vital] quickening *MS*
  (96) They'd be but] They wou'd be *30p–38*

107–11 *27–46*
109 Spirit;] Gladness! *27–38*
110 down to the daily Race] to that Day-living Race *27–38*
111 setting] evening *27*
   112–29 *44–46*
   112–29 *27–38 as follows:*

   THE vegetable World is also thine,
   Parent of Seasons! from whose rich-stain'd Rays,
   Reflected various, various Colours rise:
   The freshening Mantle of the youthful Year; *(27, 105)*
   The wild Embroidery of the watry Vale;
   With all that chears the Eye, and charms the Heart.

   THE branching Grove thy lusty Product stands,
   To quench the Fury of thy Noon-Career;
   And crowd a Shade for the retreating Swain, *(27, 110)*
   When on his russet Fields You look direct.

 (107) Eye] sense *30q–38*
 (103–8) *MS as follows:*

Parent of *Seasons!* thine the lovely *Spring,*
Thy fairest Offspring. [her each Beauty thine
Her every Grace *del.*] Her each Beauty owes,
Its Birth to Thee; as from thy rich-stain'd Rays,
Reflected various, various Colours rise:
The freshening Mantle of the youthful Year,
The wild Embroidery of the watry Vale,
The Meadow blooming broad, the blossom'd Woods,
And all the flowery Pride of rising May.
 [Summer is chiefly thine; *del.*]
 [The Summer, chief, is thine, his vital Force, *del.*]
 Summer is thine; thine his expanding Force
His [quickening *del.*] vital Vigour, [and *del.*] his prolific Heat,
[Whence swells *del.*]
Whence [teeming *del.*] pregnant Earth swells joyous to thy Ray:
And whence the Grove thy lusty Product stands,

 (109) Diffus'd, and deep, to quench the summer noon; *30q–38*
   the summer noon;] [thy fiery Rage, *del.*] the Dog-Star's
Rage, *MS*

(27, 95) vital⌃ *30p–38* (96) brute⌃ *MS* 107 not, *27* now, *27*
Life, *27* 108 Thee, *27* ~? *30o* ~⌃ *44–45* 109a gladness; *30q–38*
(27, 103) SEASONS *30q–38* (105) Year, *MS* (106) watery *30o 38*
Vale, *MS* (109a) deep; *30p–38* noon, *30p–38*

Nor to the Surface of enliven'd Earth,   130
Graceful with Hills and Dales, and leafy Woods,
Her liberal Tresses, is thy Force confin'd:
But, to the bowel'd Cavern darting deep,
The mineral Kinds confess thy mighty Power.
Effulgent, hence the veiny Marble shines;   135
Hence Labour draws his Tools; hence burnish'd War
Gleams on the Day; the nobler Works of Peace
Hence bless Mankind, and generous Commerce binds
The Round of Nations in a golden Chain.

Th' unfruitful Rock itself impregn'd by thee,   140
In dark Retirement, forms the lucid Stone.
The lively Diamond drinks thy purest Rays,
Collected Light, compact; that polish'd bright,
And all its native Lustre let abroad,
Dares, as it sparkles on the Fair-one's Breast,   145
With vain Ambition emulate her Eyes.
At thee the Ruby lights its deepening Glow,
And with a waving Radiance inward flames.
From thee the Saphire, solid Ether, takes
Its Hue cerulean; and, of evening Tinct,   150
The purple-streaming Amethyst is thine.
With thy own Smile the yellow Topaz burns.
Nor deeper Verdure dyes the Robe of Spring,
When first she gives it to the southern Gale,
Than the green Emerald shows. But, all combin'd,   155

129+ *27–38 have the following thirteen lines (not in 44–46):*

Fruit is thy Bounty too, with Juice replete,
Acid, or mild; and from thy Ray receives
A Flavour pleasing to the Taste of Man.
By Thee concocted, blushes; and by Thee   (*27*, 115)
Fully matur'd, into the verdant Lap
Of *Industry*, the mellow Plenty falls.

Extensive Harvests wave at thy Command,
And the bright Ear, consolidate by Thee,
Bends, unwithholding, to the Reaper's Hand.   (*27*, 120)

Even *Winter* speaks thy Power, whose every Blast,
O'ercast with Tempest, or severely sharp

With breathing Frost, is eloquent of Thee,
And makes us languish for thy vernal Gleams.
(113–20) *MS as follows:*

Acid, or mild; or sweetly-various mixt:
Whatever *Autumn* o'er the Garden showers,
In radiant Heaps; or, in bright Prospect round,
Spreads unwitholding to the Reaper's Hand.

130–9 *44–46*
130–9 *27 as follows:*

Shot to the Bowels of the teeming Earth,
The ripening Oar confesses all thy Flame.

130–9 *30q–38 as follows:*

Shot to the bowels of the teeming earth,
The ripening oar confesses all thy power.
Hence labour draws his tools; hence waving war
Flames on the day; hence busy commerce binds (*30q*, 140)
The round of nations in a golden chain;
And hence the sculptur'd palace, sumptuous, shines
With glittering silver, and refulgent gold.

(139) waving] burnish'd *MSLytt*
(140–1) hence busy commerce binds / The round of
[and busy Commerce hence, / Wide, binds the *del.*] *MS*
(142–3) *del. MS*
140–68 *27–46*
142 *MS not in 27–38*
145–6 *MS* Shines proudly on the Bosoms of the Fair! *27–38*
147 its] his *27–38*
148 *MS* A bleeding Radiance! grateful to the View. *27–38* [And seems
to wave with *del.*] [And inward seems to wave it's radiant Flame. *del.*]
MS
150 Its] His *27–38*

(27, 114) flavour, *30p–38*   (115) concocted˄ *30q–38*   and, *30p–38*
(117) *Industry*˄ *30p–38*   (118) command; *30p–38*   (120) Bends˄ *30q–*
38   unwitholding˄ *30q–38*   (121) power; *30q–38*   Blast˄ *38*   130 *new*
paragraph] *MS* no new paragraph *30p–38*   139 Chain.] *MS*   140 Rock,
itself, *27*   141 *lucid 27*   Stone.] *MS Stone,* 27 stone, *30q* ~; *30p–38*
143 compact! *27 MS* ~, *30o 38*   that, *27*   146a fair. *30q–38*   146 Am-
bition, *MS*   147 *no new paragraph*] *MS new paragraph 27–38*   *Ruby 27*
deepning *30o 38*   148a radiance, *30q–38*   149 *Saphire 27*   Aether! *27*
151 *Amethyst 27*   152 *Topaz 27*   153 *Spring 27 30q*   155 *Emerald*
27   But˄ *30q*

Thick thro' the whitening Opal play thy Beams;
Or, flying several from its Surface, form
A trembling Variance of revolving Hues,
As the Site varies in the Gazer's Hand.

THE very dead Creation, from thy Touch,   160
Assumes a mimic Life. By thee refin'd,
In brighter Mazes, the relucent Stream
Plays o'er the Mead. The Precipice abrupt,
Projecting Horror on the blacken'd Flood,
Softens at thy Return. The Desart joys   165
Wildly, thro' all his melancholy Bounds.
Rude Ruins glitter; and the briny Deep,
Seen from some pointed Promontory's Top,
Far to the blue Horizon's utmost Verge,
Restless, reflects a floating Gleam. But This,   170
And all the much transported Muse can sing,
Are to thy Beauty, Dignity, and Use,
Unequal far, great delegated Source,
Of Light, and Life, and Grace, and Joy below!

How shall I then attempt to sing of HIM,   175
Who, LIGHT HIMSELF, in uncreated Light
Invested deep, dwells awfully retir'd
From mortal Eye, or Angel's purer Ken;
Whose single Smile has, from the first of Time,
Fill'd, overflowing, all those Lamps of Heaven, 180
That beam for ever thro' the boundless Sky:
But, should he hide his Face, th' astonish'd Sun,
And all th' extinguish'd Stars, would loosening reel
Wide from their Spheres, and Chaos come again.

AND yet was every faultering Tongue of Man,   185
ALMIGHTY FATHER! silent in thy Praise;
Thy Works themselves would raise a general Voice,
Even in the Depth of solitary Woods,
By human Foot untrod, proclaim thy Power,
And to the Quire celestial THEE resound,   190
Th' eternal Cause, Support, and End of all!

To me be Nature's Volume broad-display'd;
And to peruse its all-instructing Page,

Or, haply catching Inspiration thence,
Some easy Passage, raptur'd, to translate,   195
My sole Delight; as thro' the falling Glooms
Pensive I stray, or with the rising Dawn
On Fancy's Eagle-wing excursive soar.

---

157 its] his *27 30q*
159 varies] changes *27*
162 In brighter Mazes,] *MS* In brisker Measures, *27–38* [With living
Lustre *del.*] *MS*
163 Plays o'er] Frisks o'er *27–38* [Shines o'er *del.*] Plays thro' *MS*
  169–70 *MS 44–46*
170 floating] waving *MS*   This] these *MS*
  169–70 *27–38 as follows:*

> Reflects, from every fluctuating Wave,
> A Glance, extensive as the Day. But these,   (*27*, 155)

  171–86 *27–46*
174 Of Light, and Life] Of Life, and Light *27 30q*
180 those] these *27*
181 the boundless] th' immeasur'd *27*
182 But] And *MS*
183 And] With *MS*   reel] start *44–45*
186 FATHER] POET *27–38* MAKER *44–45*
  187–91 *44–46*
  187–91 *27–38 as follows:*

> Thy matchless Works, in each exalted Line,
> And all the full, harmonic Universe,
> Would tuneful, or expressive, Thee attest,
> The Cause, the Glory, and the End of All!   (*27*, 175)

  (174) tuneful] vocal *30q–38*
  192–204 *27–46*
192 broad-display'd] wide, display'd *27–38*
193 its all-instructing] the broad, illumin'd *27–38*
197 stray] muse *27–38*   Dawn] Day, *27–38*

---

156 Thick, *27*   Opal, *27*   157 flying, several, *27*   (*27*, 155) glance‸
30q–38   172 Dignity‸ *27*   173 great, *27*   175 Him *27–38*
176 uncreated Light, *27*   182 But‸ *27 30q*   183 would, loosening, *27*
reel, *27 30q–38*   184 Wide, *27*   185 yet, *27 35*   186 Praise, *27*
(*27*, 172) works‸ *30q–38*   (173) full‸ *30q–38*   192 *Nature's 27 30q*
Volume, *27*   192a wide‸ *30q–38*   193a broad‸ *30q–38*   194 Or‸
27 30q   196 Glooms, *27*   197 Pensive, *27*   or, *27*   197a day‸
30p–38   198 *Fancy's 27*   Wing, excursive, *27*

Now, flaming up the Heavens, the potent Sun
Melts into limpid Air the high-rais'd Clouds,   200
And morning Fogs, that hover'd round the Hills
In party-colour'd Bands; till wide unveil'd
The Face of Nature shines, from where Earth seems,
Far-stretch'd around, to meet the bending Sphere.

HALF in a Blush of clustering Roses lost,   205
Dew-dropping *Coolness* to the Shade retires;
There, on the verdant Turf, or flowery Bed,
By gelid Founts and careless Rills to muse:
While tyrant *Heat*, dispreading thro' the Sky,
With rapid Sway, his burning Influence darts   210
On Man, and Beast, and Herb, and tepid Stream.

WHO can unpitying see the flowery Race,
Shed by the Morn, their new-flush'd Bloom resign,
Before the parching Beam? So fade the Fair,
When Fevers revel thro' their azure Veins.   215
But one, the lofty Follower of the Sun,
Sad when he sets, shuts up her yellow Leaves,
Drooping all Night; and, when he warm returns,
Points her enamour'd Bosom to his Ray.

HOME, from his morning Task, the Swain retreats;   220
His Flock before him stepping to the Fold:
While the full-udder'd Mother lows around
The chearful Cottage, then expecting Food,
The Food of Innocence, and Health! The Daw,
The Rook and Magpie, to the grey-grown Oaks   225
(That the calm Village in their verdant Arms,
Sheltering, embrace) direct their lazy Flight;
Where on the mingling Boughs they sit embower'd,
All the hot Noon, till cooler Hours arise.
Faint, underneath, the houshold Fowls convene;   230
And, in a Corner of the buzzing Shade,
The House-Dog, with the vacant Greyhound, lies,
Out-stretch'd, and sleepy. In his Slumbers one
Attacks the nightly Thief, and one exults
O'er Hill and Dale; till waken'd by the Wasp,   235

They starting snap. Nor shall the Muse disdain
To let the little noisy Summer-race
Live in her Lay, and flutter thro' her Song,
Not mean tho' simple: to the Sun ally'd,
From him they draw their animating Fire.   240

    WAK'D by his warmer Ray, the reptile Young
Come wing'd abroad; by the light Air upborn,

---

199 Now,] *MS* FIERCE, *27–38*   potent] *MS* peircing *27–38*
200 Melts into limpid Air] Attenuates to Air *27*
201 Fogs,] Mists *27–45*   round] o'er *44Wks*
202 wide] all *27–38*
   205–11 *44–46*
   205–11 *27–38 as follows:*

       HALF in a Blush of clustering Roses lost,
       Dew-dropping *Coolness* to the Shade retires;   (*27*, 190)
       And Tyrant *Heat*, dispreading thro' the Sky,
       By sharp Degrees, his burning Influence rains
       On Man, and Beast, and Herb, and tepid Stream.

   (192) sharp] swift *MS*
In MS T. deletes (189–93), *then writes* This Paragraph to be restored.
   212–44 *27–46*
214 the parching] th' unbating *27–38*
214–15 And [flagging *del.*] withering fade before the fervid Beam? *MS*
216 the lofty Follower of the Sun] *the Follower of the Sun,* They say
27–38
218 Drooping] *MS* Weeping *27–38*
230 houshold] homely *27–38*
232 the vacant] *MS* th' employless *27–38*
236 starting] *MS* bootless *27–38*
240 they draw their animating Fire] their high Descent, direct, They
draw *27–38*

199a FIERCE︿ FLAMING *30q* ~-~ *30p–38*   201a mists, *30p–45*   201 Hills,
27 30q   202 till, *27*   unveil'd, *27*   203 seems︿ *27*   206 *Coolness*
MS   207 There︿ *44–45*   209 *Heat MS*   (*27*, 190) Coolness *30q–*
38   (191) Heat *30q–38*   212 can, unpitying, *27*   214 Beam! *27*
30q   so *30q*   216a the follower of the sun *30q–38*   217 Sad, *27*
sets︿ *30p 35*   218 and︿ *27 30q*   He, warm, *27*   220 retreats, *27*
221 Fold; *27*   223 Cottage︿ *27–38*   225 Rook, *27 30q*   Oaks, *27*
226 ︿That *27*   Village, *27–38*   227 embrace, *27*   228 Where, *27*
Boughs, *27*   232 grey-hound︿ *300 38*   233 sleepy: in *27 30q*
235 till, *30p–38*   237 little, *27*   239 mean, *30q–38*   simple; *27–38*
242 abroad, *38*

Lighter, and full of Soul. From every Chink,
And secret Corner, where they slept away
The wintry Storms; or rising from their Tombs,   245
To higher Life; by Myriads, forth at once,
Swarming they pour; of all the vary'd Hues
Their Beauty-beaming Parent can disclose.
Ten thousand Forms! Ten thousand different Tribes!
People the Blaze. To sunny Waters some   250
By fatal Instinct fly; where on the Pool
They, sportive, wheel; or, sailing down the Stream,
Are snatch'd immediate by the quick-eyed Trout,
Or darting Salmon. Thro' the green-wood Glade
Some love to stray; there lodg'd, amus'd and fed,   255
In the fresh Leaf. Luxurious, others make
The Meads their Choice, and visit every Flower,
And every latent Herb: for the sweet Task,
To propagate their Kinds, and where to wrap,
In what soft Beds, their Young yet undisclos'd,   260
Employs their tender Care. Some to the House,
The Fold, and Dairy, hungry, bend their Flight;
Sip round the Pail, or taste the curdling Cheese:
Oft, inadvertent, from the milky Stream
They meet their Fate; or, weltering in the Bowl,   265
With powerless Wings around them wrapt, expire.

But chief to heedless Flies the Window proves
A constant Death; where, gloomily retir'd,
The villain Spider lives, cunning, and fierce,
Mixture abhorr'd! Amid a mangled Heap   270
Of Carcasses, in eager Watch he sits,
O'erlooking all his waving Snares around.
Near the dire Cell the dreadless Wanderer oft
Passes, as oft the Ruffian shows his Front.
The Prey at last ensnar'd, he dreadful darts,   275
With rapid Glide, along the leaning Line;
And, fixing in the Wretch his cruel Fangs,
Strikes backward grimly pleas'd: the fluttering Wing,
And shriller Sound declare extreme Distress,
And ask the helping hospitable Hand.   280

Resounds the living Surface of the Ground:
Nor undelightful is the ceaseless Hum,
To him who muses thro' the Woods at Noon;

---

243 Soul] Life *27–38*
  245–8 *44–46*
  245–8 *27–38 as follows:*

> The wintry Glooms, by Myriads, all at once,
> Swarming, they pour: green, speckled, yellow, grey,
> Black, azure, brown; more than th' assisted Eye
> Of poring *Virtuoso* can discern.   (*27*, 230)

  (228–9) green, speckled . . . azure, brown; *del.MS*
  249–57 *27–46*
249 Forms] Hues *MS*
253 quick-eyed] *MS* springing *27–38*
254 Or darting Salmon.] *MS* Often beguil'd. *27–38* [And springing
Salmon. *del.*] *MS*
254–5 Thro' the greenwood Glade / Some love to] *MS* Some thro' the
green-Wood Glade / Delight to *27–38*
  258–61 *44–46*
  258–61 *27–38 as follows:*

> And every latent Herb; but careful still   (*27*, 240)
> To shun the Mazes of the sounding Bee,
> As o'er the Blooms He sweeps. Some to the House,

  262–86 *27–46*
264 from] *MS* by *27–38*   milky] boiling *27–38*
265 They meet their Fate] *MS* They're pierc'd to Death *27 30q* Are
pierc'd to death *30p–38*
272 O'erlooking] Surveying *27*
273 Near the dire Cell] *MS* Within an Inch *27–38*
277 Wretch] *MS* Fly *27–38*
278 Strikes] Strides *27–38*
281 Resounds] Ecchoes *27–38*   Ground:] Earth; *27*
282 ceaseless Hum,] humming Sound *27*

---

243 Lighter‸ *44Wks*   (*27*, 228) Swarming‸ *30o 38*   (230) Virtuoso
30q–38   251 fly: *MS*   where, *27*   Pool, *27*   252 down‸] *MS* ～, *38*
253 snatch'd, immediate, *27*   255 amus'd, *27–30p 35*   263 Cheese; *44Wks*
265 or‸ *30q 45*   267 chief, *27*   269 Villain *27*   271 Watch, *27*
274 Front, *46*   275 He, dreadful, *27*   278 backward, *27*   280 help-
ing, *27–35*   281 Ground:] *MS* ～; *30q–38*   283 muses, *27*   Woods, *27*

Or drowsy Shepherd, as he lies reclin'd,
With half-shut Eyes, beneath the floating Shade   285
Of Willows grey, close-crouding o'er the Brook.

GRADUAL, from These what numerous Kinds descend,
Evading even the microscopic Eye!
Full Nature swarms with Life; one wondrous Mass
Of Animals, or Atoms organiz'd,   290
Waiting the *vital Breath*, when PARENT-HEAVEN
Shall bid his Spirit blow. The hoary Fen,
In putrid Steams, emits the living Cloud
Of Pestilence. Thro' subterranean Cells,
Where searching Sun-Beams scarce can find a Way,   295
Earth animated heaves. The flowery Leaf
Wants not its soft Inhabitants. Secure,
Within its winding Citadel, the Stone
Holds Multitudes. But chief the Forest-Boughs,
That dance unnumber'd to the playful Breeze,   300
The downy Orchard, and the melting Pulp
Of mellow Fruit, the nameless Nations feed
Of evanescent Insects. Where the Pool
Stands mantled o'er with Green, invisible,
Amid the floating Verdure Millions stray.   305
Each Liquid too, whether it pierces, sooths,
Inflames, refreshes, or exalts the Taste,
With various Forms abounds. Nor is the Stream
Of purest Crystal, nor the lucid Air,
Tho' one transparent Vacancy it seems,   310
Void of their unseen People. These, conceal'd
By the kind Art of forming HEAVEN, escape
The grosser Eye of Man: for, if the Worlds
In Worlds inclos'd should on his Senses burst,
From Cates ambrosial, and the nectar'd Bowl,   315
He would abhorrent turn; and in dead Night,
When Silence sleeps o'er all, be stun'd with Noise.

---

284 drowsy] [slumbering *del.*] *MS*
  287–317 *Su.44–46   not in Su.27–38*
A roughly corresponding passage on animalculae appeared in Sp.28–38. It

*is printed consecutively in the apparatus to OET Sp. 136+, but variants
of that text (as well as of MS) are also recorded below.*

287–92 *MS Su.44–46*

287 GRADUAL] Downward *MS*

289 Mass] *MS* [Heap *del.*] *MS*

287–92 *Sp.28–38 as follows:*

> THESE are not idle Philosophic Dreams;　　(*Sp.28*, 136)
> Full Nature swarms with Life. Th' unfaithful Fen

293–6 *Sp.28–38 MS Su.44–46*

293 Steams] *MS* Streams *44Wks*　　living] *MS* livid *Sp.30q–38*

295 scarce can find] *MS* never found *Sp.28–38*

297–9 *MS Su.44–46*

297–9 *Sp.28–38 as follows:*

> Wants not it's soft Inhabitants. The Stone,　　(*Sp.28*, 142)
> Hard as it is, in every winding Pore
> Holds Multitudes. But chief the Forest-Boughs,

300–5 *Sp.28–38 MS Su.44–46*

300 That] *MS* Which *Sp.28–38*　　the playful] th'inspiring *Sp.28–38*

306–17 *Su.44–46*

306–17 *Sp.28–38 as follows:*

> Each Liquid too, whether of acid Taste,
> Milky, or strong, with various Forms abounds.
> Nor is the lucid Stream, nor the pure Air,
> Tho' one transparent Vacancy they seem,
> Devoid of theirs. Even Animals subsist　　(*Sp.28*, 155)
> On Animals, in infinite Descent;

(151) Taste] Point *MS*

(152) Milky, or strong] Potent, or mild *Sp.30q–38*

(152–6) *MS as follows:*

Or oily [Globule *del.*] smooth, whether severe & harsh,
Or rais'd to racy [Flaf *del.*] Flavour, [bright *del.*] quick & high,
Wth various Forms abounds, [whence is deriv'd *del.*]
[Perhaps, their various Taste. *del.*] whence is, perhaps
Deriv'd their various Taste. Nor is the Stream
Of purest Chrystal, nor the limpid Air,
Tho' one transparent Vacancy it seems
Devoid of Life. Even Animals subsist
On Animals, in infinite Descent.

---

288 Eye. *MS*　　291 vital Breath *MS 44–45*　　(*Sp.28*, 136) dreams,
30q–38　　(137) NATURE *30q–38*　　302 Fruitˏ *MS*　　304 green *46*
308 Stream, *45*

LET no presuming impious Railer tax
CREATIVE WISDOM, as if Aught was form'd
In vain, or not for admirable Ends.   320
Shall little haughty Ignorance pronounce
His Works unwise, of which the smallest Part
Exceeds the narrow Vision of her Mind?
As if upon a full-proportion'd Dome,
On swelling Columns heav'd, the Pride of Art!   325
A Critic-Fly, whose feeble Ray scarce spreads
An Inch around, with blind Presumption bold,
Should dare to tax the Structure of the Whole.
And lives the Man, whose universal Eye
Has swept at once th' unbounded Scheme of Things;   330
Mark'd their Dependance so, and firm Accord,
As with unfaultering Accent to conclude
That *This* availeth nought? Has any seen
The mighty Chain of Beings, lessening down
From INFINITE PERFECTION to the Brink   335
Of dreary *Nothing*, desolate Abyss!
From which astonish'd Thought, recoiling, turns?
Till then alone let zealous Praise ascend,
And Hymns of holy Wonder, to that POWER,
Whose Wisdom shines as lovely on our Minds,   340
As on our smiling Eyes his Servant-Sun.

THICK in yon Stream of Light, a thousand Ways,
Upward, and downward, thwarting, and convolv'd,
The quivering Nations sport; till, Tempest-wing'd,
Fierce Winter sweeps them from the Face of Day.   345
Even so luxurious Men, unheeding, pass
An idle Summer-Life in Fortune's Shine,

306-17 *Sp. 28-38 continue as follows:*

And all so fine adjusted, that the Loss
Of the least Species would disturb the whole.
Stranger than this th' inspective Glass confirms,
And to the Curious gives th'amazing Scenes   (*Sp.28*, 160)
Of lessning Life; by *Wisdom* kindly hid
From Eye, and Ear of Man: for if at once
The Worlds in Worlds enclos'd were push'd to Light,

Seen by his sharpen'd Eye, and by his Ear
Intensely bended Heard, from the choice Cate,   (*Sp.28*, 165)
The freshest Viands, and the brightest Wines,
He'd turn abhorrent, and in Dead of Night,
When Silence sleeps o'er all, be stun'd with Noise.

(157–60) *MS as follows:*
  These, more & more, th'Inspective Glass discerns,
  As more it's finer Curve collects the Rays,
  And to the Curious gives th'amusing Scenes.
    (167) He would abhorrent turn, and in dead Night, *MS*
318–23 *27–46*
323 her] his *27–38*
  324–8 *44–46*
  324–8 *27–38 as follows:*

        So on the Concave of a sounding Dome,
        On swelling Columns heav'd, the Pride of Art!   (*27*, 275)
        Wanders a critic Fly; his feeble Ray
        Extends an Inch around; yet, blindly bold,
        He dares dislike the Structure of the Whole.

    (274) So] Thus *30q–38*   sounding] lofty *MS*
    (277) Extends] Scarce spread *MS*
329–36 *27–46*
330 Scheme] *MS* Scene *38*
  337 *44–46*
  337 *27–38 as follows:*

        Recoiling giddy Thought: or with sharp Glance,
        Such as remotely wafting Spirits use,
        Survey'd the Glories of the little World?   (*27*, 289)

    (289) Survey'd] Beheld *30q–38*
    (287–9) *del.MS*
  338–47 *27–46*
339 holy] heavenly *27–38*
343 Upward,] Upwards *27–38*   downward] downwards *27–38*
344 Nations] Kingdoms *27–38*
344–5 till, Tempest-wing'd, / Fierce Winter] with Tempest-Wing, /
Till *Winter 27–38*

(*Sp.28*, 159) confirms˄ *31 34 38*   (161) lessening *30q–38*   Wisdom *MS*
318 presuming, *27*   319 Creative Wisdom *30p–45*   321 little, *27–38*
Ignorance 27   322 unwise; *27–38*   which, *27*   323 Mind! *27*
(*27*, 277) around, yet˄ *30q–38*   bold˄ *30q–38*   330 swept, *27*   once, *27*
332 As, *27*   Accent, *27*   334 down, *MS*   335 infinite *27*   Perfec-
tion˄ *27*   PERFECTION, *MS*   338 then, alone, *27*   342 THICK, *27–300*
38–45   345 Day: *27*   347 idle, *27*   Life, *27 38*

A Season's Glitter! Thus they flutter on
From Toy to Toy, from Vanity to Vice;
Till, blown away by Death, Oblivion comes   350
Behind, and strikes them from the Book of Life.

    Now swarms the Village o'er the jovial Mead:
The rustic Youth, brown with meridian Toil,
Healthful, and strong; full as the Summer-Rose
Blown by prevailing Suns, the ruddy Maid,   355
Half naked, swelling on the Sight, and all
Her kindled Graces burning o'er her Cheek.
Even stooping Age is here; and Infant-Hands
Trail the long Rake, or, with the fragrant Load
O'ercharg'd, amid the kind Oppression roll.   360
Wide flies the tedded Grain; all in a Row
Advancing broad, or wheeling round the Field,
They spread the breathing Harvest to the Sun,
That throws refreshful round a rural Smell:
Or, as they rake the green-appearing Ground,   365
And drive the dusky Wave along the Mead,
The russet Hay-cock rises thick behind,
In order gay. While heard from Dale to Dale,
Waking the Breeze, resounds the blended Voice
Of happy Labour, Love, and social Glee.   370

    Or rushing thence, in one diffusive Band,
They drive the troubled Flocks, by many a Dog
Compell'd, to where the mazy-running Brook
Forms a deep Pool: This Bank abrupt and high,
And That fair-spreading in a pebbled Shore.   375
Urg'd to the giddy Brink, much is the Toil,
The Clamour much of Men, and Boys, and Dogs,
Ere the soft fearful People to the Flood
Commit their woolly Sides. And oft the Swain,
On some impatient seizing, hurls them in: 380
Embolden'd then, nor hesitating more,
Fast, fast, they plunge amid the flashing Wave,
And panting labour to the farther Shore.
Repeated This, till deep the well-wash'd Fleece
Has drunk the Flood, and from his lively Haunt   385

The Trout is banish'd by the sordid Stream;
Heavy, and dripping, to the breezy Brow
Slow-move the harmless Race: where, as they spread
Their swelling Treasures to the sunny Ray,
Inly disturb'd, and wondering what this wild   390
Outrageous Tumult means, their loud Complaints
The Country fill; and, toss'd from Rock to Rock,
Incessant Bleatings run around the Hills.
At last, of snowy White, the gather'd Flocks
Are in the wattled Pen innumerous press'd,   395
Head above Head; and, rang'd in lusty Rows,
The Shepherds sit, and whet the sounding Shears.
The Housewife waits to roll her fleecy Stores,
With all her gay-drest Maids attending round.
One, chief, in gracious Dignity inthron'd,   400
Shines o'er the Rest, the pastoral Queen, and rays
Her Smiles, sweet-beaming, on her Shepherd-King;
While the glad Circle round them yield their Souls
To festive Mirth, and Wit that knows no Gall.

348–9 *44–46*
348–9 *27–38 as follows:*

    A Season's Glitter! In soft-circling Robes,   (*27, 300*)
    Which the hard Hand of Industry has wrought,
    The human *Insects* glow; by *Hunger* fed,
    And chear'd by toiling *Thirst*, They rowl about
    From Toy to Trifle, Vanity to Vice;

350–1 *27–46*
352–70 *30q–46   not in 27*
355 ruddy] blooming *30q–38*
360 kind] soft *30q–38*
363 breathing] tawny *30q–38*
364 throws] *MS* casts *30q–38*
367 The russet Hay-cock rises] *MS* Rises the russet hay-cock *30q–38*
   371–431 *44–46 not in 27–38*
377 Dogs] Dog *44Wks*

(*27, 301*) INDUSTRY *30q–38*   (*302*) insects *30q–38*   350 Till‸ *27–38*
Death, Oblivion 27   351 *Life 27*   352 mead; *30q–38*   359 or, *MS*
∼‸ *30q–38*   363 Sun, *MS* ∼‸ *38*   365 Or‸ *300 38*   green-appearing]
MS ∼‸∼ *38*   374 this *44 45 46*   377 much, *44–45*   394 Flocks,
44Wks

Meantime, their joyous Task goes on apace:　　　405
Some mingling stir the melted Tar, and Some,
Deep on the new-shorn Vagrant's heaving Side,
To stamp his Master's Cipher ready stand;
Others th' unwilling Wether drag along,
And, glorying in his Might, the sturdy Boy　　　410
Holds by the twisted Horns th' indignant Ram.
Behold where bound, and of its Robe bereft,
By needy Man, that all-depending Lord,
How meek, how patient, the mild Creature lies!
What Softness in its melancholy Face,　　　415
What dumb complaining Innocence appears!
Fear not, ye gentle Tribes, 'tis not the Knife
Of horrid Slaughter that is o'er you wav'd;
No, 'tis the tender Swain's well-guided Shears,
Who having now, to pay his annual Care,　　　420
Borrow'd your Fleece, to you a cumbrous Load,
Will send you bounding to your Hills again.

　　A simple Scene! yet hence BRITANNIA sees
Her solid Grandeur rise: hence she commands
Th' exalted Stores of every brighter Clime,　　　425
The Treasures of the Sun without his Rage:
Hence, fervent all, with Culture, Toil, and Arts,
Wide glows her Land: her dreadful Thunder hence
Rides o'er the Waves sublime, and now, even now,
Impending hangs o'er *Gallia's* humbled Coast,　　　430
Hence rules the circling Deep, and awes the World.

　　'TIS raging Noon; and, vertical, the Sun
Darts on the Head direct his forceful Rays.
O'er Heaven and Earth, far as the ranging Eye
Can sweep, a dazling Deluge reigns; and all　　　435
From Pole to Pole is undistinguish'd Blaze.
In vain the Sight, dejected to the Ground,
Stoops for Relief; thence hot ascending Steams
And keen Reflection pain. Deep to the Root
Of Vegetation parch'd, the cleaving Fields　　　440
And slippery Lawn an arid Hue disclose,
Blast Fancy's Blooms, and wither even the Soul.

Echo no more returns the chearful Sound
Of sharpening Scythe: the Mower sinking heaps
O'er him the humid Hay, with Flowers perfum'd;   445
And scarce a chirping Grass-hopper is heard
Thro' the dumb Mead. Distressful Nature pants.
The very Streams look languid from afar;
Or, thro' th' unshelter'd Glade, impatient, seem
To hurl into the Covert of the Grove.   450

432–42 *44–46*
432–42 *27–38 as follows:*

      'Tis raging Noon; and, vertical, the Sun
Shoots, thro' th' expanding Air, a torrid Gleam.
O'er Heaven, and Earth, far, as the darted Eye
Can pierce, a dazzling Deluge reigns; and all,   *(27, 310)*
From Pole to Pole, is undistinguish'd Blaze.
Down to the dusty Earth the Sight, o'er-power'd,
Stoops for Relief; but thence ascending Steams,
And keen Reflection pain. Burnt to the Heart
Are the refreshless Fields; their arid Hue   *(27, 315)*
Adds a new Fever to the sickening Soul:
And, o'er their slippery Surface, wary, treads
The Foot of thirsty Pilgrim, often dipt
In a cross Rill, presenting to his Wish
A living Draught, He feels before He drinks!   *(27, 320)*

  (310) pierce] sweep *MS*
  (317) o'er] on *MS*
  (318 20) *MS as follows:*

      The thirsty Pilgrim; who, to firm his Step,
      Dips in the passing Rill his dusty Foot.

  443–7 *27–46*
443 Echo no more returns] No more the Woods return *27*   chearful]
sandy *27–38*
445 humid] tedded *27* [breathing *del.*] *MS*
447 the dumb] all the *27*
  448–50 *44–46*

---

432 Noon: *44Wks*   (27, 307) and,] *MS* ∼∧ *30o 38*   (308) Shoots∧
30q–38   air∧ *30q–38*   (309) heaven∧ *30q–38*   far∧ *30q–38*   (310) all,]
MS ∼∧ *30q–38*   (311) Pole to Pole,] *MS* ∼∧ *30q–38*   (312) sight∧
30o 38   (317) And∧ *30q–38* surface∧ wary∧ *30q–38*   (320) draught:
30q–38   444 scythe; *30q–38*   Mower, sinking, *27 35*

ALL-CONQUERING Heat, oh intermit thy Wrath!
And on my throbbing Temples potent thus
Beam not so fierce! Incessant still you flow,
And still another fervent Flood succeeds,
Pour'd on the Head profuse. In vain I sigh,   455
And restless turn, and look around for Night;
Night is far off; and hotter Hours approach.
Thrice happy he! who on the sunless Side
Of a romantic Mountain, forest-crown'd,
Beneath the whole collected Shade reclines: 460
Or in the gelid Caverns, woodbine-wrought,
And fresh bedew'd with ever-spouting Streams,
Sits coolly calm; while all the World without,
Unsatisfy'd, and sick, tosses in Noon.
Emblem instructive of the virtuous Man,   465
Who keeps his temper'd Mind serene, and pure,
And every Passion aptly harmoniz'd,
Amid a jarring World with Vice inflam'd.

WELCOME, ye Shades! ye bowery Thickets, hail!
Ye lofty Pines! ye venerable Oaks!   470
Ye Ashes wild, resounding o'er the Steep!
Delicious is your Shelter to the Soul,
As to the hunted Hart the sallying Spring,
Or Stream full-flowing, that his swelling Sides
Laves, as he floats along the herbag'd Brink.   475
Cool, thro' the Nerves, your pleasing Comfort glides;
The Heart beats glad; the fresh-expanded Eye
And Ear resume their Watch; the Sinews knit;
And Life shoots swift thro' all the lighten'd Limbs.

AROUND th' adjoining Brook, that purls along   480
The vocal Grove, now fretting o'er a Rock,
Now scarcely moving thro' a reedy Pool,
Now starting to a sudden Stream, and now
Gently diffus'd into a limpid Plain;

448-50 *27-38 as follows:*

        The Desart singes; and the stubborn Rock,
        Split to the Centre, sweats at every Pore.

The very Streams look languid from afar;
Or, thro' the fervid Glade, impetuous, hurl
Into the Shelter of the crackling Grove.　　(27, 330)

(326) singes] reddens *30q–38*
(329) fervid] [sultry *del.*] *MS*
(329–30) impetuous, hurl . . . crackling Grove.] impatient, seem /
To Hurl into the Shelter of the Grove. *MS*
　451–7 *27–46*
451 ALL-CONQUERING] PREVAILING *27*
452 throbbing] aking *27*
453 fierce!] hard!—*27–38*
455 sigh] groan *27*
　457+ *27–38 have the following seven lines (not in 44–46):*

Who shall endure!—The too resplendent Scene
Already darkens on the dizzy Eye;
And double Objects dance: unreal Sounds　　(27, 340)
Sing round the Ears: a Weight of sultry Dew
Hangs, deathful, on the Limbs: shiver the Nerves:
The supple Sinews sink; and on the Heart,
Misgiving, *Horror* lays his heavy Hand.

(338) shall] can *30q–38*
(339) Eye;] sight, *30q–38*
(341) round the Ears:] deep around; *30q–38*
　458–505 *27–46*
458 who] that *30q–45*
467 every Passion] all his Passions *27–38*
468 Amid] Amidst *27*
471 Ye] With *27*
476 Cool] Cold *27–38*　　Comfort glides] Comforts glide *27*
477–8 the fresh-expanded Eye / And Ear resume] the misty Eyes
refulge: / The Ears resume *27*
479 all the lighten'd Limbs] every active Limb *27* every lighten'd limb
30q–38
480 AROUND] ALL in *27–38*　　purls] shrills *27–38*

(27, 329) Or‸ *MS*　　impetuous‸ *30q–38*　　　　452 Temples, potent, *27*
453a hard! *30q–38*　　　　453 Incessant, *27*　　incessant‸ *30q*　　flow; *27*
455 profuse — *27*　　456 And, restless, *27*　　457 off, *MS*　　(27, 338) en-
dure! *30q–38* ∼? *MS*　　The] *MS* the *30p–38*　　(340) dance; *30q–
38*　　(342) Hangs‸ deathful‸ *30q–38*　　limbs; *30q–38*　　nerves; *30q–38*
(344) horror *30q–38*　　458 who, *27*　　468 world, *30q–38*　　469 Thickets‸
27　　474 full-flowing] *MS* ∼‸∼ *38*　　476a Cold,] *MS* ∼‸ *30q–38*
477 glad: *27*　　eye, *30q–38*　　478 Watch: *27*　　484 Plain, *27*

A various Groupe the Herds and Flocks compose,   485
Rural Confusion! On the grassy Bank
Some ruminating lie; while others stand
Half in the Flood, and often bending sip
The circling Surface. In the Middle droops
The strong laborious Ox, of honest Front,   490
Which incompos'd he shakes; and from his Sides
The troublous Insects lashes with his Tail,
Returning still. Amid his Subjects safe,
Slumbers the Monarch-Swain; his careless Arm
Thrown round his Head, on downy Moss sustain'd;   495
Here laid his Scrip, with wholesome Viands fill'd:
There, listening every Noise, his watchful Dog.

   Light fly his Slumbers, if perchance a Flight
Of angry Gad-Flies fasten on the Herd;
That startling scatters from the shallow Brook,   500
In search of lavish Stream. Tossing the Foam,
They scorn the Keeper's Voice, and scowr the Plain,
Thro' all the bright Severity of Noon;
While, from their labouring Breasts, a hollow Moan,
Proceeding, runs low-bellowing round the Hills.   505

   Oft in this Season too the Horse, provok'd,
While his big Sinews full of Spirits swell,
Trembling with Vigour, in the Heat of Blood,
Springs the high Fence; and, o'er the Field effus'd,
Darts on the gloomy Flood, with stedfast Eye,   510
And Heart estrang'd to Fear: his nervous Chest,
Luxuriant, and erect, the Seat of Strength!
Bears down th' opposing Stream: quenchless his Thirst;
He takes the River at redoubled Draughts;
And with wide Nostrils, snorting, skims the Wave.   515

   Still let me pierce into the midnight Depth
Of yonder Grove, of wildest largest Growth:
That, forming high in Air a woodland Quire,
Nods o'er the Mount beneath. At every Step,
Solemn, and slow, the Shadows blacker fall,   520
And all is awful listening Gloom around.

THESE are the Haunts of Meditation, These
The Scenes where antient Bards th' inspiring Breath,
Extatic, felt; and, from this World retir'd,
Convers'd with Angels, and immortal Forms,   525
On gracious Errands bent: to save the Fall
Of Virtue struggling on the Brink of Vice;
In waking Whispers, and repeated Dreams,
To hint pure Thought, and warn the favour'd Soul
For future Trials fated to prepare;   530
To prompt the Poet, who devoted gives
His Muse to better Themes; to sooth the Pangs

---

492 troublous] busy *27*
493–5 Amid his . . . Moss sustain'd;] *MS as follows:*

> Stretch'd on [his *del.*] the grassy Bed,
> To Guilt and Care unknown, slumbers the Swain:
> Around his Head, on downy Moss sustain'd,
> His loosen'd Arm in careless Manner thrown;

497 *MS* And there his Sceptre-Crook, and watchful Dog. *27–38*
499 Gad-Flies] Hornets *27–38*
  506–15 *LH 27–46*
508 Trembling with Vigour] With Ardor trembling *MS*
510 stedfast] steady *LH 27–38*
512–13 Luxuriant . . . opposing Stream] The Seat of Strength! bears down th' opposing Stream, / Luxuriant, and arrect *LH*
  516–55 *27–46*
518 forming high in Air a woodland Quire] high embowering in the middle Air *27–38*
521 listening] silent *27–38*
526 gracious] heavenly *27–38*   Errands] Errand *MS*

---

485 compose; *30q–38*   488 and, *27*   bending, *27*   490 strong, *27*
491 Which, incompos'd, *27*   495 Head‸ *27–38*   496 fill'd; *27–45*
498 LIGHT, *27*   499 Herd, *27*   500 That, startling, *27*   503 Noon: *45*   504 While‸ *44Wks*   Moan,] *MS* ~‸ *27–44 45 46*   506 Season, too,‸ *LH* Horse‸ *27–38*   507 Sinews, *LH 27–38*   Spirits, *LH 27–38*   509 and‸ *LH 30p–38*   511 Fear; *LH*   513 Thirst, *LH 27–38*   514 River, *LH* Draughts, *LH*   515 And, *LH 27*   snorting, *MS 30o 38*   516 wildest, *27–38*   Growth; *27–45*   521 awful‸] *MS* ~, *27–38*   524 Extatic,] *MS* ~‸ *30q–38*   felt, *35*   and,] *MS* ~‸ *30o–38*   525 Angels‸ *MS*
526 bent — To *27*   527 Vertue, *27 MS*   529 Soul‸] *MS* ~, *27–38*
530 Tryals, fated, *27*   531 who, devoted, *27*

Of dying Worth, and from the Patriot's Breast,
(Backward to mingle in detested War,
But foremost when engag'd) to turn the Death;   535
And numberless such Offices of Love,
Daily, and nightly, zealous to perform.

    SHOOK sudden from the Bosom of the Sky,
A thousand Shapes or glide athwart the Dusk,
Or stalk majestic on. Deep-rous'd, I feel   540
A sacred Terror, a severe Delight,
Creep thro' my mortal Frame; and thus, methinks,
A Voice, than Human more, th' abstracted Ear
Of Fancy strikes. "Be not of us afraid,
"Poor kindred Man! thy Fellow-creatures, we   545
"From the same PARENT-POWER our Beings drew,
"The same our Lord, and Laws, and great Pursuit.
"Once some of us, like thee, thro' stormy Life,
"Toil'd, Tempest-beaten, ere we could attain
"This holy Calm, this Harmony of Mind,   550
"Where Purity and Peace immingle Charms.
"Then fear not us; but with responsive Song,
"Amid these dim Recesses, undisturb'd
"By noisy Folly and discordant Vice,
"Of Nature sing with us, and Nature's GOD.   555
"Here frequent, at the Visionary Hour,
"When musing Midnight reigns or silent Noon,
"Angelic Harps are in full Concert heard,
"And Voices chaunting from the Wood-crown'd Hill,
"The deepening Dale, or inmost silvan Glade: 560
"A Privilege bestow'd by us, alone,
"On Contemplation, or the hallow'd Ear
"Of Poet, swelling to seraphic Strain."

    AND art thou, *STANLEY, of that sacred Band?
Alas, for us too soon!—Tho' rais'd above   565
The Reach of human Pain, above the Flight
Of human Joy; yet, with a mingled Ray
Of sadly-pleas'd Remembrance, must thou feel

*A Young Lady, well known to the Author, who died at the Age of Eighteen, in
the Year 1738.

A Mother's Love, a Mother's tender Woe:
Who seeks Thee still, in many a former Scene;   570
Seeks thy fair Form, thy lovely-beaming Eyes,
Thy pleasing Converse, by gay lively Sense
Inspir'd: where moral Wisdom mildly shone,
Without the Toil of Art; and Virtue glow'd,
In all her Smiles, without forbidding Pride.   575
But, O thou best of Parents! wipe thy Tears;
Or rather to PARENTAL NATURE pay

---

533 Worth;] *MS* Saints; *27–38*
538 Sky] Air *27*
540 on. Deep-rous'd] on: harrow'd *27* on. Arrous'd *30q–38*
541 a severe] and severe *27–45*
543–4 A Voice . . . Fancy strikes.] Those hollow Accents, floating on my
Ear, / Pronounce, distinct— *27* Those accents murmur'd in th' abs-
tracted ear, / Pronounce distinct. *30q–38*
546 PARENT-POWER] bounteous POWER *27*
552 not us] *MS* us not *30q–38*   responsive] commutual *27*
553 Amid] Oft, in *27–38*
    556–61 *44–46*
    556–61 *27–38 as follows:*
            "And, frequent, at the middle Waste of Night,
            "Or, all Day long, in Desarts *still*, are heard,
            "Now here, now there, now wheeling in mid-Sky, (*27*, 445)
            "Around, or underneath, aerial Sounds,
            "Sent from angelic Harps, and Voices join'd;
            "A Happiness bestow'd by Us, alone,

    (443–4) And, frequent . . . all Day long,] Here frequent at the
    solemn midnight Hour, / Or silent Depth of Noon *MS*
    562–3 *27–46*
    564–84 *44–46   not in 27–38*

---

533 and, *27*   breast‸ *300*   534 ‸Backward *27*   535 engag'd, *27*
Death 27   537 zealous, *27*   538 SHOOK, sudden, *27*   539 Shapes,
27   540 stalk, majestic, *27*   540a Arrous'd‸ *38*   543a Accents,
MS   545 Poor, *27*   Man, *27–38* ~; *MS 44–45*   547 LORD *30q–38*
MS   Pursuit.] *MS* ~! *27*   548 Once, *27*   Life‸ *27*   552 but, *27*
553a Oft‸ *30q–38*   554 Folly‸] *MS Folly, 27* folly, *30q–45*   *Vice 27*
555 GOD — *27*   (*27*, 443) And‸ frequent‸ *30q–38*   (444) Or‸ *30q–38*
still, *30q–35*: ~‸ *38*   (446) Around‸ *300*   (447) Harps‸ *MS*   join'd.
30q–38   562 *Contemplation 27*   563 *Poet 27*   573 Inspir'd; *44–45*
574 Art, *44–45*

The Tears of grateful Joy, who for a while
Lent thee this younger Self, this opening Bloom
Of thy enlighten'd Mind and gentle Worth.   580
Believe the Muse: the wintry Blast of Death
Kills not the Buds of Virtue; no, they spread,
Beneath the heavenly Beam of brighter Suns,
Thro' endless Ages, into higher Powers.

    THUS up the Mount, in airy Vision rapt,   585
I stray, regardless whither; till the Sound
Of a near Fall of Water every Sense
Wakes from the Charm of Thought: swift-shrinking back,
I check my Steps, and view the broken Scene.

    SMOOTH to the shelving Brink a copious Flood   590
Rolls fair, and placid; where collected all,
In one impetuous Torrent, down the Steep
It thundering shoots, and shakes the Country round.
At first, an azure Sheet, it rushes broad;
Then whitening by Degrees, as prone it falls,   595
And from the loud-resounding Rocks below
Dash'd in a Cloud of Foam, it sends aloft
A hoary Mist, and forms a ceaseless Shower.
Nor can the tortur'd Wave here find Repose:
But, raging still amid the shaggy Rocks,   600
Now flashes o'er the scatter'd Fragments, now
Aslant the hollow'd Channel rapid darts;
And falling fast from gradual Slope to Slope,
With wild infracted Course, and lessen'd Roar,
It gains a safer Bed, and steals, at last,   605
Along the Mazes of the quiet Vale.

    INVITED from the Cliff, to whose dark Brow
He clings, the steep-ascending Eagle soars,

585–9 *27–46*
585 in airy Vision rapt,] in visionary Muse *27–38*
586 Sound] Stun *27–38*
589 I check my Steps] I stand aghast *27–38*

590–3 *44–46*
590–3 *27 as follows:*

> LIKE one who flows in Joy, when, all at once,
> Misfortune hurls Him down the Hill of Life,
> Smooth, to the giddy Brink a lucid Stream
> Rolls, unsuspecting, till, surpris'd, 'tis thrown,
> In loose Meanders, thro' the trackless Air;   (*27*, 460)

590–3 *30q–38 as follows:*

> SMOOTH to the shaggy brink a spreading flood
> Rolls fair, and placid; till collected all,
> In one big glut, as sinks the shelving ground,
> Th' impetuous torrent, tumbling down the steep, (*30q*, 495)
> Thunders, and shakes th' astonished country round.

594–606 *44–46*
603 Slope to Slope] Steep to Steep *44–45*
594–606 *27–38 as follows:*

> Now a blue watry Sheet, anon, dispers'd,
> A hoary Mist, then, gather'd in again,
> A darted Stream, aslant the hollow Rock,
> This Way, and that tormented, dashing thick,
> From Steep to Steep, with wild, infracted Course, (*27*, 465)
> And, restless, roaring to the humble Vale.

607 *44–46*
607 *27–38 as follows:*

> WITH the rough Prospect tir'd, I turn my Eyes
> Where, in long *Visto*, the soft-murmuring Main
> Darts a green Lustre, trembling, thro' the Trees;
> Or to yon Silver-streaming Threads of Light,   (*27*, 470)
> A showery Beauty beaming thro' the Boughs.
> Invited from the Rock, to whose dark Cliff

(467) Eyes] gaze, *30q–38*
(468) *Visto*] vista *30q–38*
(468–9) [To where the River, as it various winds / It's **mazy**
Current, gleams amid the Trees; *del.*] *MS*
(471) Beauty] radiance, *30q–38*
(467–71) *del. MS*

---

585 Mount,] *MS* ~∧ *38*   585a muse, *30q–38*   588 Swift, shrinking *27*
(*30q*, 492) flood, *38*   (493) fair∧ *30p–38*   (496) Thunders,. *30p 35*
(*27*, 461) sheet; *30q–38*   anon∧ *30q–38*   (462) mist; then∧ *30q–38*
(463) stream∧ *30q–38*   (464) tormented; *30q–38*   (466) And∧ restless∧
30q–38   (469) trembling∧ *30q–38*

With upward Pinions thro' the Flood of Day;
And, giving full his Bosom to the Blaze,   610
Gains on the Sun; while all the tuneful Race,
Smit by afflictive Noon, disorder'd droop,
Deep in the Thicket; or, from Bower to Bower
Responsive, force an interrupted Strain.
The Stock-Dove only thro' the Forest cooes,   615
Mournfully hoarse; oft ceasing from his Plaint,
Short Interval of weary Woe! again
The sad Idea of his murder'd Mate,
Struck from his Side by savage Fowler's Guile,
Across his Fancy comes; and then resounds   620
A louder Song of Sorrow thro' the Grove.

    BESIDE the dewy Border let me sit,
All in the Freshness of the humid Air;
There on that hollow'd Rock, grotesque and wild,
An ample Chair Moss-lin'd, and over Head   625
By flowering Umbrage shaded; where the Bee
Strays diligent, and with th' extracted Balm
Of fragrant Woodbine loads his little Thigh.

    Now, while I taste the Sweetness of the Shade,
While Nature lies around deep-lull'd in Noon,   630
Now come, bold *Fancy*, spread a daring Flight,
And view the Wonders of the *torrid Zone*:
Climes unrelenting! with whose Rage compar'd,
Yon Blaze is feeble, and yon Skies are cool.

    SEE, how at once the bright-effulgent Sun,   635
Rising direct, swift chases from the Sky
The short-liv'd Twilight; and with ardent Blaze
Looks gayly fierce o'er all the dazzling Air:
He mounts his Throne; but kind before him sends,
Issuing from out the Portals of the Morn,   640
The *general Breeze*, to mitigate his Fire,
And breathe Refreshment on a fainting World.

**Which blows constantly between the Tropics from the East, or the collateral
Points, the North-East and South-East: caused by the Pressure of the rarefied Air
on That before it, according to the diurnal Motion of the Sun from East to West.*

608–28 *27–46*

609 the Flood of Day] *MS* th' attractive Gleam *27–38*

611 tuneful] feathery *27–38*

612 Smit] *MS* Smote *27–38*   by] with *30q–38*

615 The Wood-Dove, only, in the Centre, coos, *27*

624 *MS* There, on that Rock, by *Nature's* Chissel carv'd, *27–38*

626 With weaving Umbrage hung; thro' which the Bee *27*

627 Balm] Sweet *27–38*

628 Of fragrant Woodbine] Of Honey-Suckle, *27–38*

628+ *In Su.27 here follows a passage praising Britain and British worthies (Su.27, 494–609 in Appendix A), part of which is expanded and transferred to Au.30q–38, 801–44 (see OET Au. 862–909 and apparatus), and part of which is expanded in Su.30q–38, 530–670, then further expanded and transferred to a later position in Su.44–46: see the apparatus to OET Su. 1438–1619.*

After praise of Britain and British worthies Su.27–38 continue with a tropical excursion, reprinted in the following apparatus and corresponding at some points with OET Su.629–1102. In MS T. deleted all the 38 text of this tropical excursion down to the line corresponding with OET 958.

629–68 *44–46*

628+ *27–38 as follows:*

> Thus far, transported by my Country's Love,   (*27*, 610)
> Nobly digressive from my Theme, I've aim'd
> To sing her Praises, in ambitious Verse;
> While, slightly to recount, I simply meant,
> The various Summer-Horrors, which infest
> Kingdoms that scorch below severer Suns: (*27*, 615)

(610) far, transported] [I, enraptur'd *del.*] *MS*

(611) I've aim'd] [have dar'd *del.*] *MS*

(613–14) *MS as follows (then all deleted):*

> But other Prospects now, appalling, rise;
> [And the fierce *torrid Summer* spreads to view *del.*]
> And dire to view the *torrid Summer* spreads

(615) scorch below] [parch below *del.*] *MS* [parch beneath *del.*]
MSLytt

---

609 Pinions, *27*   613 Deep, *27*   to Bower, *27*   617 again, *27*

624a There͙ *30q–38*   rock͙ *30p–38*   carv'd͙ *35*   625 Chair, *27–38*

627 Strays, diligent; and, *27*   628a honey-suckle͙ *30q–38*   (*27*, 610) far͙

30q–38   (612) praises͙ *30q–38*   Verse: *MS*   635 *no new paragraph*

44–45

Great are the Scenes, with dreadful Beauty crown'd
And barbarous Wealth, that see, each circling Year,
Returning Suns and *double Seasons pass: 645
Rocks rich in Gems, and Mountains big with Mines,
That on the high Equator ridgy rise,
Whence many a bursting Stream auriferous plays:
Majestic Woods, of every vigorous Green,
Stage above Stage, high-waving o'er the Hills;   650
Or to the far Horizon wide diffus'd,
A boundless deep Immensity of Shade.
Here lofty Trees, to ancient Song unknown,
The noble Sons of potent Heat and Floods
Prone-rushing from the Clouds, rear high to Heaven   655
Their thorny Stems, and broad around them throw
Meridian Gloom. Here, in eternal Prime,
Unnumber'd Fruits, of keen delicious Taste
And vital Spirit, drink amid the Cliffs,
And burning Sands that bank the shrubby Vales,   660
Redoubled Day, yet in their rugged Coats
A friendly Juice to cool its Rage contain.

BEAR me, *Pomona*! to thy Citron-Groves;
To where the Lemon and the piercing Lime,
With the deep Orange, glowing thro' the Green,   665
Their lighter Glories blend. Lay me reclin'd
Beneath the spreading Tamarind that shakes,
Fann'd by the Breeze, its Fever-cooling Fruit.
Deep in the Night the massy Locust sheds,
Quench my hot Limbs; or lead me thro' the Maze,   670
Embowering endless, of the *Indian* Fig;
Or thrown at gayer Ease, on some fair Brow,
Let me behold, by breezy Murmurs cool'd,
Broad o'er my Head the verdant Cedar wave,
And high Palmetos lift their graceful Shade.   675
O stretch'd amid these Orchards of the Sun,
Give me to drain the Cocoa's milky Bowl,
And from the Palm to draw its freshening Wine!

**In all Places between the Tropics, the Sun, as he passes and repasses in his
annual Motion, is twice a-year perpendicular, which produces this Effect.*

More bounteous far than all the frantic Juice
Which *Bacchus* pours. Nor, on its slender Twigs   680
Low-bending, be the full Pomegranate scorn'd;
Nor, creeping thro' the Woods, the gelid Race
Of Berries. Oft in humble Station dwells
Unboastful Worth, above fastidious Pomp.

628+ *27–38 continue as follows:*

      Kingdoms, on which, direct, the Flood of Day,
      Oppressive, falls, and gives the gloomy Hue,
      And Feature gross; or worse, to ruthless Deeds,
      Wan Jealousy, red Rage, and fell Revenge,
      Their hasty Spirits prompts. Ill-fated Race!   (27, 620)
      Altho' the Treasures of the Sun be theirs,
      Rocks rich in Gems, and Mountains big with Mines,
      Whence, over Sands of Gold, the *Niger* rolls
      His amber Wave; while on his balmy Banks,
      Or in the Spicy, *Abyssinian* Vales,   (27, 625)
      The Citron, Orange, and Pomegranate drink
      Intolerable Day, yet, in their Coats,
      A cooling Juice contain. Peaceful, beneath,
      Leans the huge Elephant, and, in his Shade,
      A Multitude of beauteous Creatures play;   (27, 630)
      And Birds, of bolder Note, rejoice around.

(619) Wan] [Wild *del.*] *MS*   red] [blind *del.*] *MS*
(620) Spirits] spirit *30q–38*
(626) [Unnumber'd Fruits of keen refreshful Taste, / Pome-
granates, Citrons, & Ananas drink *del.*] *MS*
(628) [A gelid Juice to cool it's Rage contain. / Peaceful, meantime,
amid the mighty Woods, *del.*] *MS*
 669–75 *46 only   not in 27–45*
 676–897 *44–46   not in 27–38*
676 O] Or, *44–45*
677 Give me to] O let me *44–45*
678 *not in 44–45*

(27, 616) *no new paragraph 30o 38*   Kingdoms∧ *30q–38*   direct, *MS* ∼∧
38   day∧ *30q–38*   (617) Oppressive∧ *30q–38*   (622) mines; *30q–35*
(625) spicy∧ *30q–38*   (626) pomegranate, *30q–38*   (627) Day; *MS*
yet∧ *30q–38*   coats∧ *30q–38*   (628) Peaceful∧ *30q–38*   (629) elephant;
and∧ *30q–38*   shade∧ *30q–38*   (630) play, *30q–38*   (631) birds∧ *30q–*
38   note∧ *30q–38*   668 Fruit; *44–45*   680 pours! *44–45*

Witness, thou best Anana, thou the Pride   685
Of vegetable Life, beyond whate'er
The Poets imag'd in the golden Age:
Quick, let me strip thee of thy tufty Coat,
Spread thy ambrosial Stores, and feast with *Jove*!

 FROM These the Prospect varies. Plains immense   690
Lie stretch'd below, interminable Meads,
And vast Savannahs, where the wandering Eye,
Unfixt, is in a verdant Ocean lost.
Another *Flora* there of bolder Hues,
And richer Sweets, beyond our Garden's Pride,   695
Plays o'er the Fields, and showers with sudden Hand
Exuberant Spring: for oft these Valleys shift
Their green-embroider'd Robe to fiery Brown,
And swift to Green again, as scorching Suns,
Or streaming Dews and torrent Rains, prevail.   700
Along these lonely Regions, where retir'd,
From little Scenes of Art, great *Nature* dwells
In awful Solitude, and Nought is seen
But the wild Herds that own no Master's Stall,
Prodigious Rivers roll their fatning Seas: 705
On whose luxuriant Herbage, half-conceal'd,
Like a fallen Cedar, far diffus'd his Train,
Cas'd in green Scales, the Crocodile extends.
The Flood disparts: behold! in plaited Mail,
*Behemoth rears his Head. Glanc'd from his Side,   710
The darted Steel in idle Shivers flies:
He fearless walks the Plain, or seeks the Hills;
Where, as he crops his vary'd Fare, the Herds,
In widening Circle round, forget their Food,
And at the harmless Stranger wondering gaze.   715

 PEACEFUL, beneath primeval Trees, that cast
Their ample Shade o'er *Niger's* yellow Stream,
And where the *Ganges* rolls his sacred Wave;
Or mid the Central Depth of blackning Woods,
High-rais'd in solemn Theater around,   720

The Hippopotamus, or River-Horse.

Leans the huge Elephant: wisest of Brutes!
O truly wise! with gentle Might endow'd,
Tho' powerful, not destructive! Here he sees
Revolving Ages sweep the changeful Earth,
And Empires rise and fall; regardless he   725
Of what the never-resting Race of Men
Project: thrice happy! could he scape their Guile,
Who mine, from cruel Avarice, his Steps;
Or with his towry Grandeur swell their State,
The Pride of Kings! or else his Strength pervert,   730
And bid him rage amid the mortal Fray,
Astonish'd at the Madness of Mankind.

   WIDE o'er the winding Umbrage of the Floods,
Like vivid Blossoms glowing from afar,
Thick-swarm the brighter Birds. For Nature's Hand,   735
That with a sportive Vanity has deck'd
The plumy Nations, there her gayest Hues
Profusely pours. *But, if she bids them shine,
Array'd in all the beauteous Beams of Day,
Yet frugal still, she humbles them in Song.   740
Nor envy we the gaudy Robes they lent
Proud *Montezuma's* Realm, whose Legions cast
A boundless Radiance waving on the Sun,
While Philomel is ours, while in our Shades,
Thro' the soft Silence of the listening Night,   745
The sober-suited Songstress trills her Lay.

   BUT come, my *Muse*, the Desart-Barrier burst,
A wild Expanse of lifeless Sand and Sky:
And, swifter than the toiling Caravan,
Shoot o'er the Vale of *Sennar*; ardent climb   750
The *Nubian* Mountains, and the secret Bounds

---

* *In all the Regions of the torrid Zone, the Birds, tho' more beautiful in their Plumage, are observed to be less melodious than ours.*

---

688 tufty] spiny *44–45*

---

691 Meads‸ *45*   707 fall'n *44–45*

Of jealous *Abyssinia* boldly pierce.
Thou art no Ruffian, who beneath the Mask
Of social Commerce com'st to rob their Wealth;
No *holy Fury* Thou, blaspheming HEAVEN,   755
With consecrated Steel to stab their Peace,
And thro' the Land, yet red from Civil Wounds,
To spread the purple Tyranny of *Rome*.
Thou, like the harmless Bee, may'st freely range,
From Mead to Mead bright with exalted Flowers,   760
From Jasmine Grove to Grove, may'st wander gay,
Thro' Palmy Shades and Aromatic Woods,
That grace the Plains, invest the peopled Hills,
And up the more than Alpine Mountains wave.
There on the breezy Summit, spreading fair,   765
For many a League; or on stupendous Rocks,
That from the Sun-redoubling Valley lift,
Cool to the middle Air, their lawny Tops;
Where Palaces, and Fanes, and Villas rise;
And Gardens smile around, and cultur'd Fields;   770
And Fountains gush; and careless Herds and Flocks
Securely stray; a World within itself,
Disdaining all Assault: there let me draw
Etherial Soul, there drink reviving Gales,
Profusely breathing from the spicy Groves,   775
And Vales of Fragrance; there at distance hear
The roaring Floods, and Cataracts, that sweep
From disembowel'd Earth the virgin Gold;
And o'er the vary'd Landskip, restless, rove,
Fervent with Life of every fairer Kind: 780
A Land of Wonders! which the Sun still eyes
With Ray direct, as of the lovely Realm
Inamour'd, and delighting there to dwell.

    How chang'd the Scene! In blazing Height of Noon,
The Sun, oppress'd, is plung'd in thickest Gloom.   785
Still Horror reigns, a dreary Twilight round,
Of struggling Night and Day malignant mix'd.
For to the hot Equator crouding fast,
Where, highly rarefy'd, the yielding Air

Admits their Stream, incessant Vapours roll,   790
Amazing Clouds on Clouds continual heap'd;

628+ *27–38 continue as follows:*

    AND oft amid their aromatic Groves,
    Touch'd by the Torch of Noon, the gummy Bark,
    Smouldering, begins to roll the dusky Wreath.
    Instant, so swift the ruddy Ruin spreads,   (*27*, 635)
    A Cloud of Incense shadows all the Land;
    And, o'er a thousand, thundering Trees, at once,
    Riots, with lawless Rage, the running Blaze:
    But chiefly, if fomenting Winds assist,
    And, doubling, blend the circulating Waves   (*27*, 640)
    Of Flame tempestuous, or, directly on,
    Far-streaming, drives Them thro' the Forest's Length.

(639) if] should *30q–38*
(642) drives] drive *30q–38*

    BUT other Views await—where Heaven above,
    Glows like an Arch of Brass; and all below,
    The Earth a Mass of rusty Iron lies,   (*27*, 645)
    Of Fruits, and Flowers, and every Verdure spoilt,
    Barren, and bare, a joyless, weary Waste,
    Thin-cottag'd, and, in Time of trying Need,
    Abandon'd by the vanish'd Brook, like One
    Of fading Fortune by his treacherous Friend.   (*27*, 650)

(645) The brown-burnt earth a mass of iron lies; *30q–38*

    SUCH are thy horrid Desarts, *Barca*, such,
    Zaara, thy hot, interminable Sands,
    Continuous, rising often with the Blast,
    Till the Sun sees no more; and unknit Earth,
    Shook by the South into the darken'd Air,   (*27*, 655)
    Falls, in new, hilly Kingdoms, o'er the Waste.

(652) interminable] inhospitable *30q–38*

---

767 That, *44–45*   768 Cool, *44–45*   (*27*, 634) Smould'ring *300 38*
(637) And˄ *300 38*   trees˄ *30q–38*   (638) Riots˄ *30q–38*   rage˄ *30q–38*
(639) chiefly˄ *30q–38*   (640) And˄ doubling˄ *30q–38*   (641) tem-
pestuous; or˄ *30q–38*   (*27*, 643) await; *30q–38*   above˄ *30q–38*
(646) spoilt; *30q–38*   (647) waste; *30q–38*   (648) cottag'd; and˄ *30q–*
38   (649) brook; *30q–38*   (*27*, 651) BARCA; *30q–38*   such˄ *35*
38   (652) hot˄ *30q–38*   sands; *30q–38*   (653) Continuous˄ *30q–38*
(656) Falls˄ *30q–38*   new˄ *30q–38*   kingdoms˄ *30q–38*

Or whirl'd tempestuous by the gusty Wind,
Or silent borne along, heavy, and slow,
With the big Stores of steaming Oceans charg'd.
Meantime, amid these upper Seas, condens'd   795
Around the cold aërial Mountain's Brow,
And by conflicting Winds together dash'd,
The Thunder holds his black tremendous Throne,
From Cloud to Cloud the rending Lightnings rage;
Till, in the furious elemental War   800
Dissolv'd, the whole precipitated Mass
Unbroken Floods and solid Torrents pours.

 THE Treasures These, hid from the bounded Search
Of ancient Knowledge; whence, with annual Pomp,
Rich King of Floods! o'erflows the swelling *Nile*.   805
From his two Springs, in *Gojam's* sunny Realm,
Pure-welling out, he thro' the lucid Lake
Of fair *Dambea* rolls his Infant-Stream.
There, by the Naiads nurs'd, he sports away
His playful Youth, amid the fragrant Isles,   810
That with unfading Verdure smile around.
Ambitious, thence the manly River breaks;
And gathering many a Flood, and copious fed
With all the mellow'd Treasures of the Sky,
Winds in progressive Majesty along: 815
Thro' splendid Kingdoms now devolves his Maze,
Now wanders wild o'er solitary Tracts
Of Life-deserted Sand; till, glad to quit
The joyless Desart, down the *Nubian* Rocks
From thundering Steep to Steep, he pours his Urn,   820
And *Egypt* joys beneath the spreading Wave.

 HIS Brother *Niger* too, and all the Floods
In which the full-form'd Maids of *Afric* lave
Their jetty Limbs; and all that from the Tract
Of woody Mountains stretch'd thro' gorgeous *Ind*   825
Fall on *Cormandel's* Coast, or *Malabar*;
From **Menam's* orient Stream, that nightly shines

---

*The River that runs thro' Siam; *on whose Banks a vast Multitude of those
Insects called* Fire-Flies *make a beautiful Appearance in the Night.*

With Insect-Lamps, to where Aurora sheds
On *Indus'* smiling Banks the rosy Shower:
All, at this bounteous Season, ope their Urns,   830
And pour untoiling Harvest o'er the Land.

   Nor less thy World, Columbus, drinks, refresh'd,
The lavish Moisture of the melting Year.
Wide o'er his Isles, the branching *Oronoque*
Rolls a brown Deluge; and the Native drives   835

628+ *30q–38 continue as follows (not in 27):*

    Hence late expos'd (if distant fame says true)
    A smother'd city from the sandy wave
    Emergent rose; with olive-fields around,   *(30q, 720)*
    Fresh woods, reclining herds, and silent flocks,
    Amusing all, and incorrupted seen.
    For by the nitrous penetrating salts,
    Mix'd copious with the sand, pierc'd, and preserv'd,
    Each object hardens gradual into stone,   *(30q, 725)*
    Its posture fixes, and its colour keeps.
    The statue-folk, within, unnumber'd crowd
    The streets, in various attitudes surpriz'd
    By sudden fate, and live on every face
    The passions caught, beyond the sculptor's art.   *(30q, 730)*
    Here leaning soft, the marble-lovers stand,
    Delighted even in death; and each for each
    Feeling alone, with that expressive look,
    Which perfect Nature only knows to give.
    And there the father agonizing bends   *(30q, 735)*
    Fond o'er his weeping wife, and infant train
    Aghast, and trembling, tho' they know not why.
    The stiffen'd vulgar stretch their arms to heaven,
    With horror staring; while in council deep
    Assembled full, the hoary-headed sires   *(30q, 740)*
    Sit sadly-thoughtful of the public fate.
    As when old Rome, beneath the raging Gaul,
    Sunk her proud turrets, resolute on death,
    Around the Forum sat the grey divan
    Of Senators, majestic, motionless,   *(30q, 745)*
    With ivory-staves, and in their awful robes
    Dress'd like the falling fathers of mankind;
    Amaz'd, and shivering, from the solemn sight
    The red barbarians shrunk, and deem'd them Gods.

To dwell aloft on Life-sufficing Trees,
At once his Dome, his Robe, his Food, and Arms.
Swell'd by a thousand Streams, impetuous hurl'd
From all the roaring *Andes*, huge descends
The mighty *Orellana. Scarce the Muse   840
Dares stretch her Wing o'er this enormous Mass
Of rushing Water, scarce she dares attempt
The Sea-like *Plata*; to whose dread Expanse,
Continuous Depth, and wondrous Length of Course,
Our Floods are Rills. With unabated Force,   845
In silent Dignity they sweep along,
And traverse Realms unknown, and blooming Wilds,
And fruitful Desarts, Worlds of Solitude,
Where the Sun smiles and Seasons teem in vain,
Unseen, and unenjoy'd. Forsaking These,   850
O'er peopled Plains they fair-diffusive flow,
And many a Nation feed, and circle safe,
In their soft Bosom, many a happy Isle;
The Seat of blameless *Pan*, yet undisturb'd
By christian Crimes and *Europe's* cruel Sons.   855
Thus pouring on they proudly seek the Deep,
Whose vanquish'd Tide, recoiling from the Shock,
Yields to this liquid Weight of half the Globe;
And Ocean trembles for his green Domain.

    But what avails this wondrous Waste of Wealth?   860
This gay Profusion of luxurious Bliss?
This Pomp of Nature? what their balmy Meads,
Their powerful Herbs, and *Ceres* void of Pain?
By vagrant Birds dispers'd, and wafting Winds,
What their unplanted Fruits? What the cool Draughts,   865
Th' ambrosial Food, rich Gums, and spicy Health,
Their Forests yield? Their toiling Insects what,
Their silky Pride, and vegetable Robes?
Ah! what avail their fatal Treasures, hid
Deep in the Bowels of the pitying Earth,   870
Golconda's Gems, and sad *Potosi's* Mines;
Where dwelt the gentlest Children of the Sun?

           **The River of the Amazons.*

What all that *Afric's* golden Rivers rowl,
Her odorous Woods, and shining Ivory Stores?
Ill-fated Race! the softening Arts of Peace,   875
Whate'er the humanizing Muses teach;
The godlike Wisdom of the temper'd Breast;
Progressive Truth, the patient Force of Thought;
Investigation calm, whose silent Powers
Command the World; the LIGHT that leads to HEAVEN;   880
Kind equal Rule, the Government of Laws,
And all-protecting FREEDOM, which alone
Sustains the Name and Dignity of Man:
These are not theirs. The Parent-Sun himself
Seems o'er this World of Slaves to tyrannize;   885
And, with oppressive Ray, the roseat Bloom
Of Beauty blasting, gives the gloomy Hue,
And Feature gross: or worse, to ruthless Deeds,
Mad Jealousy, blind Rage, and fell Revenge,
Their fervid Spirit fires. Love dwells not there,   890
The soft Regards, the Tenderness of Life,
The Heart-shed Tear, th' ineffable Delight
Of sweet Humanity: These court the Beam
Of milder Climes; in selfish fierce Desire,

628+ *27 38 continue as follows:*

    'TIS here, that *Thirst* has fix'd his dry Domain,
    And walks his wide, malignant Round, in search
    Of Pilgrim lost; or, on the *Merchant's Tomb,
    Triumphant, sits, who, for a single Cruise   (*27*, 660)
    Of unavailing Water paid so dear:
    Nor could the Gold his hard Associate save.

   * *In the Desert of* Araoan, *are two Tombs with Inscriptions on Them,*
importing that the Persons there interr'd were a rich Merchant, and a poor
Carrier, who both died of Thirst; and that the Former had given to the Latter
Ten Thousand Ducats for one Cruise of Water.

676–897 *44–46   not in 27–38*
863 Herbs] Herds *44Wks*
865 What their] With their *45*

---

849 smiles, *45*   855 Crimes, *45*   (*27*, 657) here˄ *30q–38*   domain;
30q–38   (659) or˄ *30q–38*   tomb˄ *30q–38*   (659n.) Araoan˄ *30q–38*
(660) Triumphant˄ *30q–38*   who˄ *30q–38*

And the wild Fury of voluptuous Sense,   895
There lost. The very Brute-Creation there
This Rage partakes, and burns with horrid Fire.

 Lo! the green Serpent, from his dark Abode,
Which even Imagination fears to tread,
At Noon forth-issuing, gathers up his Train   900
In Orbs immense, then, darting out anew,
Seeks the refreshing Fount; by which diffus'd,
He throws his Folds: and while, with threatning Tongue,
And deathful Jaws erect, the Monster curls
His flaming Crest, all other Thirst, appall'd,   905
Or shivering flies, or check'd at Distance stands,
Nor dares approach. But still more direful He,
The small close-lurking Minister of Fate,
Whose high-concocted Venom thro' the Veins
A rapid Lightning darts, arresting swift   910
The vital Current. Form'd to humble Man,
This Child of vengeful Nature! There, sublim'd
To fearless Lust of Blood, the Savage Race
Roam, licens'd by the shading Hour of Guilt,
And foul Misdeed, when the pure Day has shut   915
His sacred Eye. The Tyger darting fierce,
Impetuous on the Prey his Glance has doom'd.
The lively-shining Leopard, speckled o'er
With many a Spot, the Beauty of the Waste;
And, scorning all the taming Arts of Man,   920
The keen Hyena, fellest of the Fell.
These, rushing from th' inhospitable Woods
Of *Mauritania*, or the tufted Isles,
That verdant rise amid the *Lybian* Wild,
Innumerous glare around their shaggy King,   925
Majestic, stalking o'er the printed Sand;
And, with imperious and repeated Roars,
Demand their fated Food. The fearful Flocks
Croud near the guardian Swain; the nobler Herds,
Where round their lordly Bull, in rural Ease,   930
They ruminating lie, with Horror hear
The coming Rage. Th' awaken'd Village starts;
And to her fluttering Breast the Mother strains

Her thoughtless Infant. From the *Pyrate's* Den,
Or stern *Morocco's* tyrant Fang escap'd,   935
The Wretch half-wishes for his Bonds again:
While, Uproar all, the Wilderness resounds,
From *Atlas* Eastward to the frighted *Nile*.

UNHAPPY he! who from the first of Joys,
Society, cut off, is left alone   940

898–938 *44–46*
936 Bonds] Bounds *44Wks*
898–938 *27–38 as follows:*

HERE the green Serpent gathers up his Train,
In Orbs immense, then darting out anew,
Progressive, rattles thro' the wither'd Brake;   (27, 665)
And lolling, frightful, guards the scanty Fount,
If Fount there be: or, of diminish'd Size,
But mighty Mischief, on th'unguarded Swain
Steals, full of Rancour. Here the savage Race
Roam, licens'd by the shading Hour of Blood,   (27, 670)
And foul Misdeed, when the pure Day has shut
His sacred Eye. The rabid Tyger, then,
The fiery Panther, and the whisker'd Pard,
Bespeckl'd fair, the Beauty of the Waste,
In dire Divan, surround their *shaggy King*,   (27, 675)
Majestic, stalking o'er the burning Sand,
With planted Step; while an obsequious Crowd,
Of grinning Forms, at humble Distance wait.
These, all together join'd, from darksome Caves,
Where, o'er gnaw'd Bones, They slumber'd out the Day,
By supreme Hunger smit, and Thirst intense,   (27, 681)
At once, their mingling Voices raise to Heaven;
And, with imperious, and repeated Roars,
Demanding Food, the Wilderness resounds,
From *Atlas* eastward to the frighted *Nile*.   (27, 685)

(27, 663) Train˄ *38*   (664) immense; *30q–38*   anew˄ *300*   (666) And,
lolling˄ *30q–38*   (667) or˄ *30q–38*   (672) tyger˄ *30q–38*   (674) (Be-
speckled *30q–38*   waste) *30q–38*   (677) crowd˄ *30q–38*   (678) forms˄
30q–38   (679) These˄ *30q–38*   join'd˄ *30q–38*   (680) Where˄ *30q–38*
bones˄ *30q–38*   (682) once˄ *30q–38*   HEAVEN *30q–38*   (683) imperious˄
30q–38   roars˄ *300*   939 who, *27*   940 alone, *27*

Amid this World of Death. Day after Day,
Sad on the jutting Eminence he sits,
And views the Main that ever toils below;
Still fondly forming in the farthest Verge,
Where the round Ether mixes with the Wave,   945
Ships, dim-discovered, dropping from the Clouds.
At Evening, to the setting Sun he turns
A mournful Eye, and down his dying Heart
Sinks helpless; while the wonted Roar is up,
And Hiss continual thro' the tedious Night.   950
Yet here, even here, into these black Abodes
Of Monsters, unappall'd, from stooping *Rome*,
And guilty *Caesar*, LIBERTY retir'd,
Her CATO following thro' *Numidian* Wilds:
Disdainful of *Campania's* gentle Plains,   955
And all the green Delights *Ausonia* pours;
When for them she must bend the servile Knee,
And fawning take the splendid Robber's Boon.

    NOR stop the Terrors of these Regions here.
Commission'd Demons oft, Angels of Wrath,   960
Let loose the raging Elements. Breath'd hot,
From all the boundless Furnace of the Sky,
And the wide glittering Waste of burning Sand,
A suffocating Wind the Pilgrim smites
With instant Death. Patient of Thirst and Toil,   965
Son of the Desert! even the Camel feels,
Shot thro' his wither'd Heart, the fiery Blast.
Or from the black-red Ether, bursting broad,
Sallies the sudden Whirlwind. Strait the Sands,
Commov'd around, in gathering Eddies play: 970
Nearer and nearer still they darkening come;
Till with the general all-involving Storm
Swept up, the whole continuous Wilds arise;
And by their noonday Fount dejected thrown,
Or sunk at Night in sad disastrous Sleep,   975
Beneath descending Hills, the Caravan
Is buried deep. In *Cairo's* crouded Streets,
Th' impatient Merchant, wondering, waits in vain,
And *Mecca* saddens at the long Delay.

Bᴜᴛ chief at Sea, whose every flexile Wave 980
Obeys the Blast, th' aërial Tumult swells.
In the dread Ocean, undulating wide,
Beneath the radiant Line that girts the Globe,
The circling *Typhon, whirl'd from Point to Point,
Exhausting all the Rage of all the Sky, 985
And dire *Ecnephia reign. Amid the Heavens,
Falsely serene, deep in a cloudy †Speck
Compress'd, the mighty Tempest brooding dwells.
Of no Regard, save to the skilful Eye,
Fiery and foul, the small Prognostic hangs 990
Aloft, or on the Promontory's Brow
Musters its Force. A faint deceitful Calm,
A fluttering Gale, the Demon sends before,
To tempt the spreading Sail. Then down at once,
Precipitant, descends a mingled Mass 995
Of roaring Winds, and Flame, and rushing Floods.
In wild Amazement fix'd the Sailor stands.

*Typhon *and* Ecnephia, *Terms for particular Storms or Hurricanes known only between the Tropics.*
†*Called by Sailors the* Ox-eye, *being in Appearance at first no bigger.*

939–58 *27–46*
941 Day after Day] Ceaseless, He sits *27–38*
942 jutting] rocky *27*
942–3 he sits, / And views the Main] and views / The rowling Main, *27–38*
945 round] blue *27*
948 mournful] watry *27*
951 these] those *300*
953 guilty] haughty *27–38*
954 Her Cᴀᴛᴏ following] With *Cato* leading *27–38*
955 gentle] fertile *27–38*
956 *Ausonia* pours;] of *Italy,* *27–38*
958 splendid Robber's Boon] Blessings once her own *27–38*
959–1051 *44–46   not in 27–38*

941a Ceaseless˄ *30q–38*   942 Sad, *27*   Eminence, *27–38*   944 forming, *27*   946 Clouds, *46*   948 Heart, *300*   949 Sinks, *27*   950 Hiss, continual, *27*   951 *new paragraph 27–38*   956a Iᴛᴀʟʏ; *30q–38*
957 When, *27*   Them, *27*   958 And, fawning, *27*

Art is too slow. By rapid Fate oppress'd,
His broad-wing'd Vessel drinks the whelming Tide,
Hid in the Bosom of the black Abyss.   1000
With such mad Seas the daring *GAMA fought,
For many a Day, and many a dreadful Night,
Incessant, lab'ring round the *stormy Cape*;
By bold Ambition led, and bolder Thirst
Of Gold. For then from antient Gloom emerg'd   1005
The rising World of Trade: the *Genius*, then,
Of Navigation, that, in hopeless Sloth,
Had slumber'd on the vast Atlantic Deep,
For idle Ages, starting, heard at last
The †LUSITANIAN PRINCE; who, HEAV'N-inspired,   1010
To Love of useful Glory rous'd Mankind,
And in unbounded Commerce mix'd the World.

    INCREASING still the Terrors of these Storms,
His Jaws horrific arm'd with threefold Fate,
Here dwells the direful Shark. Lur'd by the Scent   1015
Of steaming Crouds, of rank Disease, and Death,
Behold! he rushing cuts the briny Flood,
Swift as the Gale can bear the Ship along;
And, from the Partners of that cruel Trade,
Which spoils unhappy *Guinea* of her Sons,   1020
Demands his share of Prey, demands themselves.
The stormy Fates descend: one Death involves
Tyrants and Slaves; when strait, their mangled Limbs
Crashing at once, he dyes the purple Seas
With Gore, and riots in the vengeful Meal.   1025

    WHEN o'er this World, by Equinoctial Rains
Flooded immense, looks out the joyless Sun,
And draws the copious Steam: from swampy Fens,
Where Putrefaction into Life ferments,
And breathes destructive Myriads; or from Woods,   1030

---

* VASCO DE GAMA, *the first who sailed round* Africa, *by the* Cape of Good-Hope,
to the East-Indies.
    †DON HENRY, *third Son to* John *the first, King of* Portugal. *His strong Genius
to the Discovery of new Countries was the chief Source of all the modern Improve-
ments in Navigation.*

Impenetrable Shades, Recesses foul,
In Vapours rank and blue Corruption wrapt,
Whose gloomy Horrors yet no desperate Foot
Has ever dar'd to pierce; then, wasteful, forth
Walks the dire *Power* of pestilent Disease.   1035
A thousand hideous Fiends her Course attend,
Sick Nature blasting, and to heartless Woe,
And feeble Desolation, casting down
The towering Hopes and all the Pride of Man.
Such as, of late, at *Carthagena* quench'd   1040
The BRITISH Fire. You, gallant VERNON, saw
The miserable Scene; you, pitying, saw,
To Infant-Weakness sunk the Warrior's Arm;
Saw the deep-racking Pang, the ghastly Form,
The Lip pale-quivering, and the beamless Eye   1045
No more with Ardor bright: you heard the Groans
Of agonizing Ships, from Shore to Shore;
Heard, nightly plung'd amid the sullen Waves,
The frequent Corse; while on each other fix'd,
In sad Presage, the blank Assistants seem'd,   1050
Silent, to ask, whom Fate would next demand.

  WHAT need I mention those inclement Skies,
Where, frequent o'er the sickening City, Plague,
The fiercest Child of NEMESIS DIVINE,
Descends? *From *Ethiopia's* poison'd Woods,   1055
From stifled *Cairo's* Filth, and fetid Fields
With Locust-Armies putrefying heap'd,

These are the Causes supposed to be the first Origin of the Plague, *in* DOCTOR
MEAD'S *elegant Book on that Subject.*

---

999 His] The *44–45*
1001 footnote *who*] *that 44Wks*
1010 footnote *the chief Source*] *the Source 44–45*
    1052–4 *27–46*
1054 Child *MSLytt*] Son *27–38*

1003 stormy Cape *44–45*   1034 pierce, *44–45*   1042 saw∧ *44–45*
1053 Where∧ *30q–38*   frequent, *27–38*   *Plague 27–38*   1054 *divine! 27*

This great Destroyer sprung. Her awful Rage
The Brutes escape. Man is her destin'd Prey,
Intemperate Man! and, o'er his guilty Domes,   1060
She draws a close incumbent Cloud of Death;
Uninterrupted by the living Winds,
Forbid to blow a wholesome Breeze; and stain'd
With many a Mixture by the Sun, suffus'd,
Of angry Aspect. Princely Wisdom, then,   1065
Dejects his watchful Eye; and from the Hand
Of feeble Justice, ineffectual, drop
The Sword and Balance: mute the Voice of Joy,
And hush'd the Clamour of the busy World.
Empty the Streets, with uncouth Verdure clad;   1070
Into the worst of Desarts sudden turn'd
The chearful Haunt of Men: unless escap'd
From the doom'd House, where matchless Horror reigns,
Shut up by barbarous Fear, the smitten Wretch,
With Frenzy wild, breaks loose; and, loud to Heaven   1075
Screaming, the dreadful Policy arraigns,
Inhuman, and unwise. The sullen Door,
Yet uninfected, on its cautious Hinge
Fearing to turn, abhors Society.
Dependants, Friends, Relations, Love himself,   1080
Savag'd by Woe, forget the tender Tie,
The sweet Engagement of the feeling Heart.
But vain their selfish Care: the circling Sky,
The wide enlivening Air is full of Fate;
And, struck by Turns, in solitary Pangs   1085
They fall, unblest, untended, and unmourn'd.
Thus o'er the prostrate City black Despair
Extends her raven Wing; while, to compleat
The Scene of Desolation, stretch'd around,
The grim Guards stand, denying all Retreat,   1090
And give the flying Wretch a better Death.

     MUCH yet remains unsung: the Rage intense
Of brazen-vaulted Skies, of iron Fields,
Where Drought and Famine starve the blasted Year:
Fir'd by the Torch of Noon to tenfold Rage,   1095
Th' infuriate Hill that shoots the pillar'd Flame;

1055–60 *44–46*   *not in 27–38*
1061–70 *27–46*
1061 She draws] Collects *27–38*   Cloud] Night *27–38*
1067 feeble] drooping *27–38*   drop] falls *27–38*
1069 Clamour] Murmur *30q–38*
1071–91 *44–46*
1071–91 *27–38 as follows:*

> And rang'd, at open Noon, by Beasts of Prey,
> And Birds of bloody Beak: while, all Night long,   (*27*, 720)
> In spotted Troops, the recent Ghosts complain,
> Demanding but the covering Grave. Mean time,
> Lock'd is the deaf Door to Distress; even Friends,
> And Relatives, endear'd for many a Year,
> Savag'd by Woe, forget the social Tye,   (*27*, 725)
> The blest Engagement of the yearning Heart;
> And sick, in Solitude, successive, die,
> Untended, and unmourn'd. And, to compleat
> The Scene of Desolation, wide around,
> Denying all Retreat, the grim Guards stand,   (*27*, 730)
> To give the flying Wretch a better Death.

(720–3) *30q–38 as follows:*

> And birds of bloody beak. The sullen door
> No visit knows, nor hears the wailing voice
> Of fervent Want. Even soul-attracted friends,

(726) blest] close *30q–38*   yearning] kindred *30q–38*
(728) And,] While *30q–38*
(731) To] And *30q–38*
1092–1102 *44–46*
1092–1102 *27–38 as follows:*

> MUCH of the Force of foreign *Summers* still,
> Of growling Hills, that shoot the pillar'd Flame,
> Of Earthquake, and pale Famine, could I sing;
> But equal Scenes of Horror call Me Home.   (*27*, 735)

(734) *in MS beside* Earthquake *T. writes* described.

1061 close, *27–38*   Death, *27*   1063 Breeze, *27*   1064 Mixture, *27–38*
Sun‸ *27–38*   1065 aspect? *30q–38*   *Wisdom*, *27*   ∼‸ *30q–38*   then‸ *30q–*
38   1067 *Justice 27–38*   1068 Sword, *27–38*   Balance. Mute *27–38*
Joy; *27–38*   1070 clad, *27–38*   (*27*, 719) rang'd‸ *30q–38*   noon‸ *30q–*
38   (724) relatives‸ *30q–38*   (727) And, sick‸ *30q–38*   successive‸
30q–38   (*27*, 733) hills‸ *30q–38*

And, rous'd within the subterranean World,
Th' expanding Earthquake, that resistless shakes
Aspiring Cities from their solid Base,
And buries Mountains in the flaming Gulph.   1100
But 'tis enough; return, my vagrant Muse:
A nearer Scene of Horror calls thee home.

    BEHOLD, slow-settling o'er the lurid Grove
Unusual Darkness broods; and growing gains
The full Possession of the Sky, surcharg'd   1105
With wrathful Vapour, from the secret Beds,
Where sleep the mineral Generations, drawn.
Thence Niter, Sulphur, and the fiery Spume
Of fat Bitumen, steaming on the Day,
With various-tinctur'd Trains of latent Flame,   1110
Pollute the Sky, and in yon baleful Cloud,
A reddening Gloom, a Magazine of Fate,
Ferment; till, by the Touch etherial rous'd,
The Dash of Clouds, or irritating War
Of fighting Winds, while all is calm below,   1115
They furious spring. A boding Silence reigns,
Dread thro' the dun Expanse; save the dull Sound
That from the Mountain, previous to the Storm,
Rolls o'er the muttering Earth, disturbs the Flood,
And shakes the Forest-Leaf without a Breath.   1120
Prone, to the lowest Vale, th' aërial Tribes
Descend: the Tempest-loving Raven scarce
Dares wing the dubious Dusk. In rueful Gaze
The Cattle stand, and on the scouling Heavens
Cast a deploring Eye; by Man forsook,   1125
Who to the crouded Cottage hies him fast,
Or seeks the Shelter of the downward Cave.

    'TIS listening Fear, and dumb Amazement all:
When to the startled Eye the sudden Glance
Appears far South, eruptive thro' the Cloud;   1130
And following slower, in Explosion vast,
The Thunder raises his tremendous Voice.
At first, heard solemn o'er the Verge of Heaven,
The Tempest growls; but as it nearer comes,
And rolls its awful Burden on the Wind,   1135

The Lightnings flash a larger Curve, and more
The Noise astounds: till over Head a Sheet
Of livid Flame discloses wide, then shuts

1103–7 *27–46*
1103 BEHOLD] FOR now *27–38*
1104 growing] spreading *MSLytt*
1105 full Possession] whole Possession *27* broad possession *30q–38* wide
Dominion *MSLytt*   Sky] Air *27*
1106 secret Beds] damp Abrupt *27–38* [cavern'd Earth *del.*] dark Abyss
MSLytt

    1108–16 *44–46*
    1108–16 *27–38 as follows:*

> Thence Nitre, Sulphur, Vitriol, on the Day
> Stream, and fermenting in yon baleful Cloud,
> Extensive o'er the World, a reddening Gloom!
> In dreadful Promptitude to spring, await
> The high Command. A boding Silence reigns   (*27*, 745)

   (742) Stream] Steam *30q–38*
   (743) That o'er the World extends a Reddening Gloom, *MSLytt*
    1117–27 *27–46*
1117 Dread thro'] Thro' all *27*
1118 That] Which *MS*
1119 muttering] trembling *27–38*
1120 shakes] *MSLytt* stirs *27–38*

    1128–35 *44–46*
    1128–35 *27–38 as follows:*

> 'TIS dumb Amaze, and listening Terror all;
> When, to the quicker Eye, the livid Glance
> Appears, far South, emissive thro' the Cloud;
> And, by the powerful Breath of GOD inflate,   (*27*, 760)
> The Thunder raises his tremendous Voice,
> At first low-muttering; but, at each Approach,

   (758) When darting from the Cloud the livid Glance *MSLytt*
   (761) his] it's *MS*
    1136–43 *27–46*
1138 livid] various *27–38*

1103 settling, *27–38*   Grove, *27–38*   1104 and, growing, *27*   1106 Vapour⌃
MSLytt   (*27*, 743) world⌃ *30q–38*   1117 Expanse, *27–38*   Sound,
27–45   1118 That, *27*   1125 Eye, *27*   (*27*, 758) When⌃ *30q–*
38   eye⌃ *30q–38*   (759) Appears⌃ *30q–38*   (761) voice; *30q–38*
(762) but⌃ *30q–38*   1137 till, *27*   Head, *27*

And opens wider, shuts and opens still
Expansive, wrapping Ether in a Blaze.   1140
Follows the loosen'd aggravated Roar,
Enlarging, deepening, mingling, Peal on Peal
Crush'd horrible, convulsing Heaven and Earth.

    DOWN comes a Deluge of sonorous Hail,
Or prone-descending Rain. Wide-rent, the Clouds,   1145
Pour a whole Flood; and yet, its Flame unquench'd,
Th' unconquerable Lightning struggles thro',
Ragged and fierce, or in red whirling Balls,
And fires the Mountains with redoubled Rage.
Black from the Stroke, above, the smouldring Pine   1150
Stands a sad shatter'd Trunk; and, stretch'd below,
A lifeless Groupe the blasted Cattle lie:
Here the soft Flocks, with that same harmless Look
They wore alive, and ruminating still
In Fancy's Eye; and there the frowning Bull,   1155
And Ox half-rais'd. Struck on the castled Cliff,
The venerable Tower and spiry Fane
Resign their aged Pride. The gloomy Woods
Start at the Flash, and from their deep Recess,
Wide-flaming out, their trembling Inmates shake.   1160
Amid *Carnarvon's* Mountains rages loud
The repercussive Roar: with mighty Crush,
Into the flashing Deep, from the rude Rocks
Of *Penmannaur* heap'd hideous to the Sky,
Tumble the smitten Cliffs; and *Snowden's* Peak,   1165
Dissolving, instant yields his wintry Load.

1144–9 *44–46*
1144–9 *27–38 as follows:*

    DOWN comes a Deluge of sonorous Hail,
    In the white, heavenly Magazines congeal'd;
    And often fatal to th'unshelter'd Head
    Of Man, or rougher Beast. The sluicy Rain,
    In one unbroken Flood, descends; and yet   (*27*, 775)
    Th' unconquerable Lightning struggles thro',
    Ragged, and fierce, or in red whirling Balls,
    And strikes the Shepherd, as He, shuddering, sits,

Presaging Ruin, in the rocky Clift.
His inmost Marrow feels the gliding Flame;   (*27*, 780)
He dies—and, like a Statue grim'd with Age,
His live, dejected Posture still remains;
His Russet sing'd, and rent his hanging Hat;
Against his Crook his sooty Cheek reclin'd;
While, whining at his Feet, his half-stun'd Dog,   (*27*, 785)
Importunately kind, and fearful, pats
On his insensate Master, for Relief.

(774–5) The sluicy Rain . . . and yet] Wide-rent, the clouds / Pour a whole flood; and yet, its rage unquench'd, *30q–38*

(776) unconquerable] inconquerable *30q–38*

(779) in] mid *30q–38*

1150–1 *44–46*

1150–1 *27–38 as follows:*

> BLACK, from the Stroak, above, the Mountain-Pine,
> A leaning, shatter'd Trunk, stands scath'd to Heaven,
> The Talk of future Ages! and, below,   (*27*, 790)

(789–90) Stands [scath'd to Heaven; *del.*] a wild shatter'd Trunk; and stretch'd, below, *MS*

1152–5 *27–46*

1156–68 *44–46*

1156–68 *27–38 as follows:*

> And Ox half-rais'd. A little farther, burns   (*27*, 795)
> The guiltless Cottage; and the haughty Dome
> Stoops to the Base. Th'uprooted Forrest flies
> Aloft in Air, or, flaming out, displays
> The savage Haunts, by Day unpierc'd before.
> Scar'd is the Mountains Brow; and, from the Cliff, (*27*, 800)
> Tumbles the smitten Rock. The Desart shakes,
> And gleams, and grumbles, through his deepest Dens.

(795) farther] further *30p–38*

(797–8) Th' uprooted Forrest flies / Aloft in Air,] In one immediate flash, / The forest falls; *30q–38*

(799) by Day unpierc'd] unpierc'd by day *30q–38*

1141 loosen'd, *27–45*   1143 Heaven, *27*   (*27*, 774a) rent∧ *30p–38*
(778) he∧ shuddering∧ *30q–38*   (781) dies; *30q–38*   (782) live∧ *30q–*
38   (787) master∧ *30q–38*   1150 *new paragraph 27–38*   above∧ *44Wks*
(*27*, 788) BLACK∧ *30q–38*   Pine∧ *MS*   (789) leaning∧ *30q–38*   (790) ages;
30q–38   1152 lie. *27*   1153 Here, *27*   Look, *27–35*   1154 still,
27–38   1155 *Fancy's 27*   there, *27*   (*27*, 800) and∧ *30q–38*   cliff∧
30q–38

Far-seen, the Heights of heathy *Cheviot* blaze,
And *Thulè* bellows thro' her utmost Isles.

GUILT hears appall'd, with deeply troubled Thought;
And yet not always on the guilty Head   1170
Descends the fated Flash. Young CELADON
And his AMELIA were a matchless Pair,
With equal Virtue form'd, and equal Grace,
The same, distinguish'd by their Sex alone:
Hers the mild Lustre of the blooming Morn,   1175
And his the Radiance of the risen Day.

THEY lov'd. But such their guileless Passion was,
As in the Dawn of Time inform'd the Heart
Of Innocence, and undissembling Truth.
'Twas Friendship heighten'd by the mutual Wish,   1180
Th' enchanting Hope, and sympathetic Glow,
Beam'd from the mutual Eye. Devoting all
To Love, each was to each a dearer Self;
Supremely happy in th' awaken'd Power
Of giving Joy. Alone, amid the Shades,   1185
Still in harmonious Intercourse they liv'd
The rural Day, and talk'd the flowing Heart,
Or sigh'd, and look'd unutterable Things.

So pass'd their Life, a clear united Stream,
By Care unruffled; till, in evil Hour,   1190
The Tempest caught them on the tender Walk,
Heedless how far, and where its Mazes stray'd,
While, with each other blest, creative Love
Still bade eternal *Eden* smile around.
Heavy with instant Fate her Bosom heav'd   1195
Unwonted Sighs, and stealing oft a Look
Of the big Gloom on CELADON her Eye
Fell tearful, wetting her disorder'd Cheek.
In vain assuring Love, and Confidence
In HEAVEN repress'd her Fear; it grew, and shook   1200
Her Frame near Dissolution. He perceiv'd
Th' unequal Conflict, and as Angels look
On dying Saints, his Eyes Compassion shed,

With Love illumin'd high. "Fear not, he said,
"Sweet Innocence! thou Stranger to Offence,   1205
"And inward Storm! HE, who yon Skies involves
"In Frowns of Darkness, ever smiles on thee,
"With kind Regard. O'er thee the secret Shaft
"That wastes at Midnight, or th' undreaded Hour
"Of Noon, flies harmless: and that very Voice,   1210

1168+ 27 *adds here twenty-four lines not in 30q–46. See Appendix A,*
Summer 803–26.

  1169 *30q–46 not in 27*
hears appall'd] dubious hears *30q–38*
  1170–1222 *27–46*
1171 Descends the fated] Falls the devoted *27–38*
1172 were a matchless Pair,] an unrival'd Twain! *27* were a matchless
twain; *30q–38*
1175 the blooming] th'unfolding *27*
1176 And his the] His the full *MSLytt*
1178 inform'd] alarm'd *27–38*
1180 mutual] [charming *del.*] nameless *MS*
1181–2 Glow, / Beam'd from the mutual Eye] Glow, / Struck from the
charmful Eye *27–38* [Throb *del.*] Shake / Of mutual Hearts high-tun'd
MS
1186 harmonious] angelic *27*
1189 So] THUS *27–38*   pass'd] flow'd *MS*
1192–5 Heedless how far. Her Breast, presageful, heav'd *27–38.* Regard-
less whither. Touch'd by Fate, she heav'd *MS*
1198 her disorder'd] all her glowing *27*
1204 With Love illumin'd high.] Mingl'd with matchless Love.— *27*
1205 Sweet] Fair *27–38*
1206 yon Skies involves] enwraps yon Skies *27*
1208 kind] full *27–38*
1210 harmless] hurtless *27–38*

1170 *new paragraph 27*   1171 *Celadon, 27*   1172 *Amelia, 27*   1174 alone;
27   1177 lov'd — but *27*   1178 As, *27*   Time, *27*   1179 Innocence]
MS Innocence *27–38*   Truth] *MS Truth 27–38*   1180 Friendship, *27–30p*
35   1183 Self! *27*   1185 Joy! *27*   1186 Still, *27*   Intercourse, *27*
1188 Things! *27*   1189 clear, *27*   1190 till˄ *30q–38*   hour˄ *30q–38*
1192a Breast, presageful,] *MS* ˜˄˜˄ *30q–38*   1196 Sighs; and, *MS*
1197 Gloom, *27–38*   1200 Heaven˄ *27–38* ˜, *MS*   grew, *MS* ˜˄ *38*
1202 and, *27*   1208 Shaft, *MS*   1210a hurtless; *30q–38*

"Which thunders Terror thro' the guilty Heart,
"With Tongues of Seraphs whispers Peace to thine.
" 'Tis Safety to be near thee sure, and thus
"To clasp Perfection!" From his void Embrace,
(Mysterious Heaven!) that moment, to the Ground,   1215
A blacken'd Corse, was struck the beauteous Maid.
But who can paint the Lover, as he stood,
Pierc'd by severe Amazement, hating Life,
Speechless, and fix'd in all the Death of Woe!
So, faint Resemblance, on the Marble-Tomb,   1220
The well-dissembled Mourner stooping stands,
For ever silent, and for ever sad.

   As from the Face of Heaven the shatter'd Clouds
Tumultuous rove, th' interminable Sky
Sublimer swells, and o'er the World expands   1225
A purer Azure. Nature, from the Storm,
Shines out afresh; and thro' the lighten'd Air
A higher Luster and a clearer Calm,
Diffusive, tremble; while, as if in Sign
Of Danger past, a glittering Robe of Joy,   1230
Set off abundant by the yellow Ray,
Invests the Fields, yet dropping from Distress.

   'Tis Beauty all, and grateful Song around,
Join'd to the Low of Kine, and numerous Bleat
Of Flocks thick-nibbling thro' the clover'd Vale.   1235
And shall the Hymn be marr'd by thankless Man,
Most-favour'd; who with Voice articulate
Should lead the Chorus of this lower World?
Shall he, so soon forgetful of the Hand
That hush'd the Thunder, and serenes the Sky,   1240
Extinguish'd feel that Spark the Tempest wak'd,
That Sense of Powers exceeding far his own,
Ere yet his feeble Heart has lost its Fears?

1211 guilty] Sinner's *27* conscious *30q–38*
1215–16 to the Ground, / A blacken'd Corse, was struck] *MS* in a
Heap / Of pallid Ashes, fell *27–38*
1218 Pierc'd] *MS* Struck *27–38*

1222+ *27 adds here eleven lines not in 30q–46. See Appendix A,*
Summer 877–87

1223–7 *30q–46*

1224 Sky] blue *30q–38*

1225–6 Sublimer swells . . . A purer Azure.] Delightful swells into the
general arch, / That copes the nations. *30q–38*

1223–7 *27 as follows:*

> As from the Face of Heaven, each shatter'd Cloud,
> Tumultuous, roves, th'unfathomable Blue,
> That constant Joy to every finer Eye,   (*27, 890*)
> That Rapture! swells into the general Arch,
> Which copes the Nations.—On the lilly'd Bank,
> Where a Brook quivers, often, careless, thrown,
> Up the wide Scene I've gaz'd whole Hours away,
> With growing Wonder, while the Sun declin'd,   (*27, 895*)
> As now, forth-breaking from the blotting Storm,
> Nature shines out; and, thro' the lighten'd Air,

1228–38 *27–46*

1229 while] and *27*

1230 Robe] Face *27*

1231 yellow] level *27–38*

1232 Fields, yet dropping] Earth, yet weeping *27*

1239–43 *44–46*

1239–43 *27–38 as follows:*

> Shall He, so soon, forgetful of the past,
> After the Tempest, puff his transient Vows,   (*27, 910*)
> And a new Dance of Vanity begin,
> Scarce ere the Pant forsakes his feeble Heart!

(909) past,] hand/That hush'd the thunder, and expands the sky,
30q–38

(910) transient] idle *30q–38*

(912) Scarce ere] Ere yet *MS*   forsakes his] forsake the *30p–38*

1214 Perfection!— *27*   1215 ₐMysterious Heaven!ₐ *27*   1216a ashesₐ
30q–38   1220 Resemblance! *27*   Tombₐ *27*   1221 Mourner, stoop-
ing, *27*   1225a Delightful, *MS*   1226 Natureₐ *30q–38*   stormₐ *30q–
38*   1227 and, *27 MS*   Air, *27 MS*   (*27, 896*) ∼. *27*   (897) *new
paragraph 27*   1228 Lustreₐ] *MS* ∼, *27 300 38*   1229 tremble: *MS*
1231 off, abundant, *27*   1237 favour'd, *27*   who, *27*   articulate, *27*
1238 World! *27*   (*27, 909*) soonₐ *30q–38*   (910) tempestₐ *30q–38*
vows; *30q*   (912) heart? *30q–38*

CHEAR'D by the milder Beam, the sprightly Youth
Speeds to the well-known Pool, whose crystal Depth   1245
A sandy Bottom shews. A while he stands
Gazing th' inverted Landskip, half afraid
To meditate the blue Profound below;
Then plunges headlong down the circling Flood.
His ebon Tresses, and his rosy Cheek   1250
Instant emerge; and thro' th' obedient Wave,
At each short Breathing by his Lip repell'd,
With Arms and Legs according well, he makes,
As Humour leads, an easy-winding Path;
While, from his polish'd Sides, a dewy Light   1255
Effuses on the pleas'd Spectators round.

   THIS is the purest Exercise of Health,
The kind Refresher of the Summer-Heats;
Nor, when cold Winter keens the brightening Flood,
Would I weak-shivering linger on the Brink.   1260
Thus Life redoubles, and is oft preserv'd,
By the bold Swimmer, in the swift Illapse
Of Accident disastrous. Hence the Limbs
Knit into Force; and the same *Roman* Arm,
That rose victorious o'er the conquer'd Earth,   1265
First learn'd, while tender, to subdue the Wave.
Even, from the Body's Purity, the Mind
Receives a secret sympathetic Aid.

   CLOSE in the Covert of an Hazel Copse,
Where winded into pleasing Solitudes   1270
Runs out the rambling Dale, young DAMON sat,
Pensive, and pierc'd with Love's delightful Pangs.
There to the Stream that down the distant Rocks
Hoarse-murmuring fell, and plaintive Breeze that play'd
Among the bending Willows, falsely he   1275
Of MUSIDORA's Cruelty complain'd.
She felt his Flame; but deep within her Breast,
In bashful Coyness, or in maiden Pride,
The soft Return conceal'd; save when it stole
In side-long Glances from her downcast Eye,   1280
Or from her swelling Soul in stifled Sighs.

Touch'd by the Scene, no Stranger to his Vows,
He fram'd a melting Lay, to try her Heart;
And, if an infant Passion struggled there,
To call that Passion forth. Thrice happy Swain!   1285
A lucky Chance, that oft decides the Fate
Of mighty Monarchs, then decided thine.
For lo! conducted by the laughing Loves,
This cool Retreat his MUSIDORA sought:
Warm in her Cheek the sultry Season glow'd;   1290
And, robe'd in loose Array, she came to bathe
Her fervent Limbs in the refreshing Stream.
What shall he do? In sweet Confusion lost,
And dubious Flutterings, he a while remain'd.
A pure ingenuous Elegance of Soul,   1295
A delicate Refinement, known to Few,
Perplex'd his Breast, and urg'd him to retire.
But Love forbade. Ye Prudes in Virtue, say,
Say, ye severest, what would you have done?

1244–56 *27–46*
1244 milder] setting *27–38*
1248+ *27 has the following (not in 30q–46):*

        Till disenchanted by the ruffling Gale,

1249 Then] He *27* circling] closing *27*
1251 th'obedient] the glassy *27* the flexile *30q–38*
1255 polish'd] snowy *27* dewy] humid *27*
1257–68 *The twelve corresponding lines in 30q–38 follow the Damon
episode; i.e. their position corresponds to OET 1370+.*
   1257–68 *27–46*
1257 of] for *38*
1258 kind] great *27*
1259 *MS* Nor, when, the Brook pellucid, Winter keens, *27–38*
1264 the] that *27*
1265 That rose] Which stretch'd, *27*
1268 Strictly ally'd, receives a secret Aid. *27*
   1269–1370 *44–46*

1251 and, *27*   1252 Breathing, *27*   1253 Arms, *27*   Legs, *27*
1254 Path: *27*   1259 Nor∧ *30q–38 MS*   1260 I, *27*   shivering, *27*
1261 preserv'd∧ *27–38*   1265 victorious, *27*   1266 Wave.] *MS* ∼, *38*
1267 Even,] *MS* ∼∧ *30q–38*   Purity,] *MS* ∼∧ *30q–38*   1268 secret∧]
MS ∼, *30q–38*

Meantime, this fairer Nymph than ever blest   1300
Arcadian Stream, with timid Eye around
The Banks surveying, strip'd her beauteous Limbs,
To taste the lucid Coolness of the Flood.
Ah then! not *Paris* on the piny Top
Of *Ida* panted stronger, when aside   1305
The Rival-Goddesses the Veil divine
Cast unconfin'd, and gave him all their Charms,
Than, DAMON, thou; as from the snowy Leg,
And slender Foot, th' inverted Silk she drew;
As the soft Touch dissolv'd the virgin Zone;   1310
And, thro' the parting Robe, th' alternate Breast,
With Youth wild-throbbing, on thy lawless Gaze
In full Luxuriance rose. But, desperate Youth,
How durst thou risque the Soul-distracting View;
As from her naked Limbs, of glowing White,   1315
Harmonious swell'd by Nature's finest Hand,
In Folds loose-floating fell the fainter Lawn;

1304 piny] shady *44–45*
  1269–1370 *30q–38 as follows (not in 27):*

          'Twas then beneath a secret-waving shade,   (*30q*, 980)
          Where winded into lovely solitudes
          Runs out the rambling dale, that DAMON sat,
          Thoughtful, and fix'd in philosophic muse:
          DAMON, who still amid the savage woods,
          And lonely lawns, the force of beauty scorn'd,   (*30q*, 985)
          Firm, and to false philosophy devote.
          The brook ran babbling by; and sighing weak,
          The breeze among the bending willows play'd:
          When SACHARISSA to the cool retreat,
          With AMORET, and MUSIDORA stole.   (*30q*, 990)
          Warm in their cheek the sultry season glow'd;
          And, rob'd in loose array, they came to bathe
          Their fervent limbs in the refreshing stream.
          Tall, and majestic, SACHARISSA rose,
          Superior treading, as on IDA's top   (*30q*, 995)
          (So GRECIAN bards in wanton fable sung)
          High-shone the sister and the wife of JOVE.
          Another PALLAS MUSIDORA seem'd,

Meek-ey'd, sedate, and gaining every look
A surer conquest of the sliding heart.　　　　　(*30q*, 1000)
While, like the Cyprian goddess, Amoret,
Delicious dress'd in rosy-dimpled smiles,
And all one softness, melted on the sense.
Nor Paris panted stronger, when aside
The rival-goddesses the veil divine　　　　　(*30q*, 1005)
Cast unconfin'd, and gave him all their charms,
Than, Damon, thou; the stoick now no more,
But man deep-felt, as from the snowy leg,
And slender foot, th' inverted silk they drew;
As the soft touch dissolv'd the virgin-zone;　　　　　(*30q*, 1010)
And, thro' the parting robe, th' alternate breast,
With youth wild-throbbing, on thy lawless gaze
Luxuriant rose. Yet more enamour'd still,
When from their naked limbs, of glowing white,
In folds loose-floating fell the fainter lawn;　　　　　(*30q* 1015)
And fair expos'd they stood, shrunk from themselves;
With fancy blushing; at the doubtful breeze
Arrous'd, and starting, like the fearful fawn.
*So stands the statue that enchants the world,
Her full proportions such, and bashful so　　　　　(*30q*, 1020)
Bends ineffectual from the roving eye.
Then to the flood they rush'd; the plunging fair
The parted flood with closing waves receiv'd;
And, every beauty softening, every grace
Flushing afresh, a mellow lustre shed:　　　　　(*30q*, 1025)
As shines the lily thro' the crystal mild;
Or as the rose amid the morning-dew
Puts on a warmer glow. In various play,
While thus they wanton'd; now beneath the wave,
But ill conceal'd; and now with streaming locks　　　　　(*30q*, 1030)
That half-embrac'd them in a humid veil,
Rising again; the latent Damon drew
Such draughts of love and beauty to the soul,
As put his harsh philosophy to flight,
The joyless search of long-deluded years;　　　　　(*30q*, 1035)
And Musidora fixing in his heart,
Inform'd, and humaniz'd him into man.

* *The* Venus *of* Medicis.

———

(*30q*, 980) shade∧ *300*　　　　(982) dale∧ *35*　　　　(1014) limbs∧ *30p–38*
(1016) themselves, *300*

And fair-expos'd she stood, shrunk from herself,
With Fancy blushing, at the doubtful Breeze
Alarm'd, and starting like the fearful Fawn?   1320
Then to the Flood she rush'd; the parted Flood
Its lovely Guest with closing Waves receiv'd;
And every Beauty softening, every Grace
Flushing anew, a mellow Luster shed:
As shines the Lily thro' the Crystal mild;   1325
Or as the Rose amid the Morning Dew,
Fresh from *Aurora's* Hand, more sweetly glows.
While thus she wanton'd, now beneath the Wave
But ill-conceal'd; and now with streaming Locks,
That half embrac'd Her in a humid Veil,   1330
Rising again, the latent DAMON drew
Such madning Draughts of Beauty to the Soul,
As for a while o'erwhelm'd his raptur'd Thought
With Luxury too-daring. Check'd, at last,
By Love's respectful Modesty, he deem'd   1335
The Theft profane, if Aught profane to Love
Can e'er be deem'd, and, struggling from the Shade,
With headlong Hurry fled: but first these Lines,
Trac'd by his ready Pencil, on the Bank
With trembling Hand he threw. "Bathe on, my Fair,   1340
"Yet unbeheld save by the sacred Eye
"Of faithful Love. I go to guard thy Haunt,
"To keep from thy Recess each vagrant Foot,
"And each licentious Eye." With wild Surprize,
As if to Marble struck, devoid of Sense,   1345
A stupid Moment motionless she stood:
So stands the *Statue that enchants the World,
So bending tries to veil the matchless Boast,
The mingled Beauties of exulting *Greece*.
Recovering, swift she flew to find those Robes   1350
Which blissful *Eden* knew not; and, array'd
In careless Haste, th' alarming Paper snatch'd.
But, when her DAMON's well-known Hand she saw,
Her Terrors vanish'd, and a softer Train
Of mixt Emotions, hard to be describ'd,   1355

The Venus of Medici.

Her sudden Bosom seiz'd: Shame void of Guilt,
The charming Blush of Innocence, Esteem
And Admiration of her Lover's Flame,
By Modesty exalted. Even a Sense
Of self-approving Beauty stole across   1360
Her busy Thought. At length, a tender Calm
Hush'd by Degrees the Tumult of her Soul;
And on the spreading Beech, that o'er the Stream
Incumbent hung, she with the silvan Pen
Of rural Lovers this Confession carv'd,   1365
Which soon her DAMON kiss'd with weeping Joy.
"Dear Youth! sole Judge of what these Verses mean,
"By Fortune too much favour'd, but by Love,
"Alas! not favour'd less, be still as now
"Discreet: the Time may come you need not fly."   1370

    THE Sun has lost his Rage: his downward Orb
Shoots nothing now but animating Warmth,
And vital Lustre; that, with various Ray,
Lights up the Clouds, those beauteous Robes of Heaven,
Incessant roll'd into romantic Shapes,   1375
The Dream of waking Fancy! Broad below,
Cover'd with ripening Fruits, and swelling fast
Into the perfect Year, the pregnant Earth
And all her Tribes rejoice. Now the soft Hour
Of Walking comes: for him who lonely loves   1380
To seek the distant Hills, and there converse
With Nature; there to harmonize his Heart,
And in pathetic Song to breathe around
The Harmony to others. Social Friends,
Attun'd to happy Unison of Soul;   1385
To whose exalting Eye a fairer World,
Of which the Vulgar never had a Glimpse,

1370+ *In 30q–38 here follow twelve lines corresponding to OET* 1257–
68 (*q.v. for variants*).
    1371–1437 *44–46   not in 27–38*

1321 rush'd: *45*   1326 Rose, *44–45*   Dew∧ *44–45*   1329 Locks∧
44Wks   1337 deem'd; *44–45*   1338 Lines∧ *44Wks*   1339 Bank,
46

Displays its Charms; whose Minds are richly fraught
With Philosophic Stores, superior Light;
And in whose Breast, enthusiastic, burns   1390
Virtue, the Sons of Interest deem Romance;
Now call'd abroad enjoy the falling Day:
Now to the verdant *Portico* of Woods,
To Nature's vast *Lyceum*, forth they walk;
By that kind *School* where no proud Master reigns,   1395
The full free Converse of the friendly Heart,
Improving and improv'd. Now from the World,
Sacred to sweet Retirement, Lovers steal,
And pour their Souls in Transport, which the SIRE
Of Love approving hears, and *calls it good*.   1400
Which Way, AMANDA, shall we bend our Course?
The Choice perplexes. Wherefore should we chuse?
All is the same with Thee. Say, shall we wind
Along the Streams? or walk the smiling Mead?
Or court the Forest-Glades? or wander wild   1405
Among the waving Harvests? or ascend,
While radiant Summer opens all its Pride,
Thy Hill, delightful **Shene*? Here let us sweep
The boundless Landskip: now the raptur'd Eye,
Exulting swift, to huge AUGUSTA send,   1410
Now to the †*Sister-Hills* that skirt her Plain,
To lofty *Harrow* now, and now to where
Majestic *Windsor* lifts his Princely Brow.
In lovely Contrast to this glorious View,
Calmly magnificent, then will we turn   1415
To where the silver THAMES first rural grows.
There let the feasted Eye unweary'd stray:
Luxurious, there, rove thro' the pendant Woods
That nodding hang o'er HARRINGTON'S Retreat;
And, stooping thence to *Ham's* embowering Walks,   1420
Beneath whose Shades, in spotless Peace retir'd,
With HER the pleasing Partner of his Heart,
The worthy QUEENSB'RY yet laments his GAY,
And polish'd CORNBURY wooes the willing Muse,

*The old Name of Richmond, *signifying in Saxon* Shining, *or* Splendor.
†Highgate *and* Hamstead.

Slow let us trace the matchless VALE OF THAMES;   1425
Fair-winding up to where the Muses haunt
In *Twit'nam's* Bowers, and for their POPE implore
The healing God; to royal *Hampton's* Pile,
To *Clermont's* terrass'd Height, and *Esher's* Groves,
Where in the sweetest Solitude, embrac'd   1430
By the soft Windings of the silent *Mole*,
From Courts and Senates PELHAM finds Repose.
Inchanting Vale! beyond whate'er the Muse
Has of *Achaia* or *Hesperia* sung!
O Vale of Bliss! O softly-swelling Hills!   1435
On which the *Power of Cultivation* lies,
And joys to see the Wonders of his Toil.

    HEAVENS! what a goodly Prospect spreads around,
Of Hills, and Dales, and Woods, and Lawns, and Spires,
And glittering Towns, and gilded Streams, till all   1440
The stretching Landskip into Smoke decays!
Happy BRITANNIA! where the QUEEN OF ARTS,
Inspiring Vigor, LIBERTY abroad
Walks, unconfin'd, even to thy farthest Cotts,
And scatters Plenty with unsparing Hand.   1445

    RICH is thy Soil, and merciful thy Clime;
Thy Streams unfailing in the Summer's Drought;

1438–1619 *In 27–38 lines praising Britain and British worthies (variants
of which are recorded below in the apparatus to OET 1438–1619) precede
the tropical excursion (reprinted in the apparatus to OET 629–1102). See
the note at 628+ on p. 91.*
    1438–78 *27–46*
1438 HEAVENS!] AND *27–38* See *MS* goodly Prospect spreads] pleasing
Prospect lies *27* various prospect lies *30q–38*
1439 Dales] Vales *27–38*
1440 glittering Towns] Towns betwixt *27–38*
1444 *MS.* Walks thro' the Land of Heroes, unconfin'd, *27–38*
1446 Clime] Skies *27–38*

1438 around! *27–38*   1439 Spires‸ *27 30q*   1440 Streams! *27* ~;
30q–38   1441 decays. *27–38*   1442 *new paragraph 27–38*   Queen of
Arts *27–38*   1443 LIBERTY, *27*   abroad‸] *MS* ~, *27 38*   1444a un-
confin'd‸ *30q–35*   1447 Drought: *27*

Unmatch'd thy Guardian-Oaks; thy Valleys float
With golden Waves: and on thy Mountains Flocks
Bleat numberless; while, roving round their Sides,   1450
Bellow the blackening Herds in lusty Droves.
Beneath, thy Meadows glow, and rise unquell'd
Against the Mower's Scythe. On every hand,
Thy Villas shine. Thy Country teems with Wealth;
And Property assures it to the Swain,   1455
Pleas'd, and unweary'd, in his guarded Toil.

    FULL are thy Cities with the Sons of Art;
And Trade and Joy, in every busy Street,
Mingling are heard: even Drudgery himself,
As at the Car he sweats, or dusty hews   1460
The Palace-Stone, looks gay. Thy crouded Ports,
Where rising Masts an endless Prospect yield,
With Labour burn, and echo to the Shouts
Of hurry'd Sailor, as he hearty waves
His last Adieu, and loosening every Sheet,   1465
Resigns the spreading Vessel to the Wind.

    BOLD, firm, and graceful, are thy generous Youth,
By Hardship sinew'd, and by Danger fir'd,
Scattering the Nations where they go; and first
Or in the listed Plain, or stormy Seas.   1470
Mild are thy Glories too, as o'er the Plans
Of thriving Peace thy thoughtful Sires preside;
In Genius, and substantial Learning, high;
For every Virtue, every Worth, renown'd;
Sincere, plain-hearted, hospitable, kind;   1475
Yet like the mustering Thunder when provok'd,
The Dread of Tyrants, and the sole Resource
Of those that under grim Oppression groan.

    THY SONS OF GLORY many! ALFRED thine,
In whom the Splendor of heroic War,   1480
And more heroic Peace, when govern'd well,
Combine; whose hallow'd Name the Virtues saint,
And *his own* Muses love, the best of *Kings*.
With him thy EDWARDS and thy HENRYS shine,

Names dear to Fame; the First who deep impress'd   1485
On haughty *Gaul* the Terror of thy Arms,
That awes her Genius still. In *Statesmen* Thou,
And *Patriots*, fertile. Thine a steady MORE,
Who, with a generous tho' mistaken Zeal,
Withstood a brutal Tyrant's useful Rage,   1490
Like CATO firm, like ARISTIDES just,
Like rigid CINCINNATUS nobly poor,
A dauntless Soul erect, who smil'd on Death.
Frugal, and wise, a WALSINGHAM is thine;
A DRAKE, who made thee Mistress of the Deep,   1495
And bore thy Name in Thunder round the World.
Then flam'd thy Spirit high: but who can speak
The numerous Worthies of the MAIDEN REIGN?

1452 glow] *MSLytt* flame *27–38*
1456 guarded] certain *27–38*
1470 in] on *27*   stormy] wintry *27–45*
1471 Plans] Arts *27*
1477 Dread] Scourge *27*
1478 Of those that] *MS* Of such as *27–38*
    1479–93 *44–46*
    1479–93 *27 as follows:*

        HENCE may'st Thou boast a *Bacon*, and a *More*;   *(27, 535)*
        Nor cease to vie Them with the noblest Names
        Of ancient Times, or Patriot, or Sage.

    1479–93 *30q–38 as follows:*

        THY sons of glory many! thine a MORE,   *(30q, 571)*
        As CATO firm, as ARISTIDES just,
        Like rigid CINCINNATUS nobly poor,
        A dauntless soul, erect, who smil'd on death.

    1494–1510 *30q–46*   *not in 27*

1448 Oaks: *27*   1449 Waves; *27–38*   1450 Bleat, *27–38*   number-less: *27*   1451 Herds, *27*   1452 unquell'd, *27–38*   1454 *Villas 27*   1455 *Property 27–38*   1457 ART *30q*   1458 Trade, *27–38* 1459 Mingling, *27*   *Drudgery, 27* ~∧ *30q–38*   1460 or, dusty, *27* 1461 Stone∧ *38*   1464 He, hearty, *27*   1465 and, *27*   1469 first, *27–38*   1473 Learning∧ *27–38*   1474 Worth∧ *27–38 45*   renown'd, *27–38*   1475 kind, *27*   1476 provok'd; *27–38*   1494 Frugal∧ *300 38*   1497 high; *30q–38*   1498 reign *30q–38*

In RALEIGH mark their every Glory mix'd,
RALEIGH, the Scourge of *Spain*! whose Breast with all   1500
The Sage, the Patriot, and the Hero burn'd.
Nor sunk his Vigour, when a Coward-Reign
The Warrior fetter'd, and at last resign'd,
To glut the Vengeance of a vanquish'd Foe.
Then, active still and unrestrain'd, his Mind   1505
Explor'd the vast Extent of Ages past,
And with his Prison-Hours enrich'd the World;
Yet found no Times, in all the long Research,
So glorious, or so base, as Those he prov'd,
In which he conquer'd, and in which he bled.   1510
Nor can the Muse the gallant SIDNEY pass,
The Plume of War! with early Laurels crown'd,
The Lover's Myrtle, and the Poet's Bay.
A HAMPDEN too is thine, illustrious Land,
Wise, strenuous, firm, of unsubmitting Soul,   1515
Who stem'd the Torrent of a downward Age
To Slavery prone, and bade thee rise again,
In all thy native Pomp of Freedom bold.
Bright, at his Call, thy Age of *Men* effulg'd,
Of Men on whom late Time a kindling Eye   1520
Shall turn, and Tyrants tremble while they read.
Bring every sweetest Flower, and let me strew
The Grave where RUSSEL lies; whose temper'd Blood,
With calmest Chearfulness for Thee resign'd,
Stain'd the sad Annals of a giddy Reign,   1525
Aiming at lawless Power, tho' meanly sunk
In loose inglorious Luxury. With him
His Friend, the *BRITISH CASSIUS, fearless bled;
Of high determin'd Spirit, roughly brave,
By antient Learning to th' enlighten'd Love   1530
Of antient Freedom warm'd. Fair thy Renown
In awful *Sages* and in noble *Bards*;
Soon as the Light of dawning Science spread
Her orient Ray, and wak'd the Muses' Song.
Thine is a BACON, hapless in his Choice;   1535
Unfit to stand the civil Storm of State,

            *ALGERNON SIDNEY.

1505–6] *MS* Then deep thro' fate his mind retorted saw, *30q–38*
   1511–18 *MS 44–46*
1511 SIDNEY] *MS adds footnote* SIR PHILIP SIDNEY
1515 *not in MS*
1518 Pomp] Pride *MS*
   1511–18 *30q–38 as follows (not in 27):*

> A HAMBDEN thine, of unsubmitting soul;
> Who stem'd the torrent of a downward age,
> To slavery prone; and bad thee rise again,
> In all thy native pomp of FREEDOM fierce.
> Nor can the muse the gallant SIDNEY pass,   (*30q*, 595)
> The plume of war! with every laurel crown'd,
> The lover's myrtle, and the poet's bay.

   1519–24 *MS 44–46*   *not in 27*
1519 Bright,] [Rous'd *del.*] Wide *MS*
1524+ *MS as follows:*

> [And later Sidney's to thy [sacred Rights *del.*] pleaded Cause
> And well-defended Rights a constant Friend, *all del.*]
> [And *LATER SIDNEY, thine, vow'd to the Cause
> Of LIBERTY her rough determin'd Friend, *all del.*]
> And thine, thou BRITISH BRUTUS, to the Love
> Of warm enlighten'd LIBERTY sublim'd,
> *ALGERNON SIDNEY

   1519–24 *30q–38 as follows (not in 27):*

> Nor him of later name, firm to the cause
> Of LIBERTY, her rough determin'd friend,
> The BRITISH BRUTUS; whose united blood   (*30q*, 600)
> With RUSSEL, thine, thou patriot wise, and calm,

   1525–6 *30q–46*   *not in 27*
1527–50 *44–46*
1527–50 *30q–38 as follows (not in 27):*

> In loose inglorious sloth. High thy renown
> In SAGES too, far as the sacred light   (*30q*, 605)
> Of science spreads, and wakes the muses' song.
> Thine is a BACON form'd of happy mold,
> When NATURE smil'd, deep, comprehensive, clear,
> Exact, and elegant; in one rich soul,
> PLATO, the STAGYRITE, and TULLY join'd.   (*30q*, 610)

1505 unrestrain'dˏ *44Wks*   1518 FREEDOM *MS*   1519 effulg'd; *MS*
1521 *Tyrants MS*   1523 Blood,] *MS* ∼ˏ *44–46*   (*30q*, 601) With, *MS*
1525 Reign,] *MS* ∼; *30q–44 45 46* ∼: *44Wks*   (*30q*, 607) BACON, *300 38*
1535 Choice, *44–45*

And thro' the smooth Barbarity of Courts,
With firm but pliant Virtue, forward still
To urge his Course. Him for the studious Shade
Kind Nature form'd, deep, comprehensive, clear,   1540
Exact, and elegant; in one rich Soul,
PLATO, the STAGYRITE, and TULLY join'd.
The great Deliverer he! who from the Gloom
Of cloister'd Monks, and Jargon-teaching Schools,
Led forth the true Philosophy, there long   1545
Held in the magic Chain of Words and Forms,
And Definitions void: he led Her forth,
Daughter of HEAVEN! that, slow-ascending still,
Investigating sure the Chain of Things,
With radiant Finger points to HEAVEN again.   1550
The generous *ASHLEY thine, the Friend of Man;
Who scann'd his Nature with a Brother's Eye,
His Weakness prompt to shade, to raise his Aim,
To touch the finer Movements of the Mind,
And with the *moral Beauty* charm the Heart.   1555
Why need I name thy BOYLE, whose pious Search
Amid the dark Recesses of his Works,
The great CREATOR sought? And why thy LOCKE,
Who made the whole internal World his own?
Let NEWTON, *pure Intelligence*, whom GOD   1560
To Mortals lent, to trace his boundless Works
From Laws sublimely simple, speak thy Fame
In all Philosophy. For lofty Sense,
Creative Fancy, and Inspection keen
Thro' the deep Windings of the human Heart,   1565
Is not wild SHAKESPEAR thine and Nature's Boast?
Is not each great, each amiable Muse
Of Classic Ages in thy MILTON met?
A Genius universal as his Theme,
Astonishing as Chaos, as the Bloom   1570
Of blowing Eden fair, as Heaven sublime.

*ANTHONY ASHLEY COOPER, *Earl of* Shaftesbury.

1551-5 *30q–46*   *not in 27*

1556–9 *44–46*
1556–9 27 *as follows:*

> And for the Strength, and Elegance of Truth,
> A *Barrow*, and a *Tillotson* are thine:
> A *Locke*, inspective into human Minds,   (*27*, 540)
> And all *th' unnotic'd World* that passes there.
> Nor be thy *Boyle* forgot; who, while He liv'd,
> Seraphic, sought TH' ETERNAL thro' his Works,
> By sure Experience led; and, when He dy'd,
> Still bid his *Bounty* argue for his GOD,   (*27*, 545)
> Worthy of Riches He!—But what needs more—

1556–9 *30q–38 as follows:*

> What need I name thy BOYLE, whose pious search (*30q*, 616)
> Still sought the great CREATOR in his works,
> By sure experience led? and why thy LOCKE,
> Who made the whole internal world his own?

1560–71 *MSLytt 44–46*
1560 GOD] Heavn *MSLytt*
1561 *MSLytt* [Lent to Mankind *del.*] To Mortals lent its boundless
Works to trace *MSLytt*   its] *MSLytt* his *MS*
1568 Classic] Elder *MSLytt*
1569 universal] *MS* vast, and boundless *MSLytt*
1571 blowing] blissfull *MSLytt*
1560–71 *27–38 as follows:*

> Let comprehensive *Newton* speak thy Fame,
> In all Philosophy. For solemn Song
> Is not wild *Shakespear* Nature's Boast, and thine!
> And every greatly amiable *Muse*   (*27*, 550)
> Of elder Ages in thy *Milton* met!
> His was the Treasure of Two Thousand Years,
> Seldom indulg'd to Man, a God-like Mind,
> Unlimited, and various, as his Theme;
> Astonishing as *Chaos*; as the Bloom   (*27*, 555)
> Of blowing *Eden* fair; soft as the Talk
> Of our *grand Parents*, and as *Heaven* sublime.

1548 that∧ *46*   1555 moral Beauty *44–45*   (*30q*, 618) And *30p–38*
1560 Newton, *MSLytt*   pure Intelligence∧ *MSLytt*   1560a HEAVN *MS*
1565 Heart! *MSLytt*   1566 Shakespeare thine, *MSLytt*   Boast! *MSLytt*
1567 great,] *MSLytt* ∼∧ *44–45*   (*27*, 548) song, *30q–38*   (549) thine?
30q–38   (550) muse *30q–38*   (551) met? *30q–38*   (553) man;
30q–38   (554) THEME *30q–38*

Nor shall my Verse that elder Bard forget,
The gentle SPENSER, Fancy's pleasing Son;
Who, like a copious River, pour'd his Song
O'er all the Mazes of enchanted Ground: 1575
Nor Thee, his antient Master, laughing Sage,
CHAUCER, whose native Manners-painting Verse,
Well-moraliz'd, shines thro' the Gothic Cloud
Of Time and Language o'er thy Genius thrown.

  MAY my Song soften, as thy DAUGHTERS I,   1580
BRITANNIA, hail! for Beauty is their own,
The feeling Heart, Simplicity of Life,
And Elegance, and Taste: the faultless Form,
Shap'd by the Hand of Harmony; the Cheek,
Where the live Crimson, thro' the native White   1585
Soft-shooting, o'er the Face diffuses Bloom,
And every nameless Grace; the parted Lip,
Like the red Rose-bud moist with Morning-Dew,
Breathing Delight; and, under flowing Jet,
Or sunny Ringlets, or of circling Brown,   1590
The Neck slight-shaded, and the swelling Breast;
The Look resistless, piercing to the Soul,
And by the Soul inform'd, when drest in Love
She sits high-smiling in the conscious Eye.

  ISLAND of Bliss! amid the subject Seas,   1595
That thunder round thy rocky Coasts, set up,
At once the Wonder, Terror, and Delight,
Of distant Nations; whose remotest Shore
Can soon be shaken by thy Naval Arm,
Not to be shook thy self, but all Assaults   1600
Baffling, like thy hoar Cliffs the loud Sea-Wave.

  O THOU! by whose almighty *Nod* the Scale
Of Empire rises, or alternate falls,
Send forth the saving VIRTUES round the Land,
In bright Patrol: white *Peace*, and social *Love*;   1605
The tender-looking *Charity*, intent
On gentle Deeds, and shedding Tears thro' Smiles;

Undaunted *Truth,* and *Dignity* of Mind;
Courage compos'd, and keen; sound *Temperance,*
Healthful in Heart and Look; clear *Chastity*   1610
With Blushes reddening as she moves along,
Disorder'd at the deep Regard she draws;
Rough *Industry*; *Activity* untir'd,
With copious Life inform'd, and all awake:
While, in the radiant Front, superior shines   1615
That first paternal Virtue, *public Zeal,*
Who throws o'er all an equal wide Survey,
And, ever musing on the common Weal,
Still labours glorious with some great Design.

1572–9 *MS 44–46   not in 27–38*
1572 that elder Bard forget] *MS* [forget that elder Bard *del.*] *MS*
1573 pleasing] *MS* [gaudy *del.*] *MS*
1576 Thee] *MSLytt* Him *MS*
1576+ [The pure well *del.*] *MS*
1577 Verse] *MS* [Song *del.*] *MS*
1579 Time] *MSLytt* [Life *del.*] *MS*   thy] his *MS*
    1579+ *27 adds here thirteen lines on Scotland (not in Su.30q–46) which
were transferred to Au.30q and there expanded. See Appendix A, Summer
558–70 for the original version and OET Au. 862–909 for later versions.*
    1580–1619 *27–46*
1582 *not in 27*
1590 circling] lovely *MSLytt*
1594 high-smiling] sweet-smiling, *27*   conscious] lovely *27*
1617 throws] *MS* casts *27–38*
1619 great] brave *27–38*
    1619+ *In 27–38 praise of Britain and British worthies is followed by
the tropical excursion reprinted in the apparatus to OET 629–1102. See
the note at 628+.*

1573 SPENCER *46*   Son, *MS*   1580 soften∧ as, *27–38*   Daughters, *27–
38* ∼∧ *MS*   I,] *MS* ∼∧ *38*   1582 Heart∧ *35*   1584 *Harmony:* 27
∼; *30q–38*   Cheek∧ *38*   1585 White, *27*   1586 shooting,] *MS* ∼∧
38   1587 Grace: *27*   1588 bud∧] *MS* ∼, *30q–38*   1591 Breast:
27   1593 when, *27–30p 35 38*   Love, *27–38*   1594 sits, *27*   high-
smiling] *MS* ∼∧∼ *30q–38*   1597 Delight∧ *27*   1599 arm; *30q–38*
1602 THOU, *27*   Nod, *27* Nod∧ *MS*   1605 Patrol:] *MS* ∼; *38*
1610 *Chastity,* 27–38   1615 While∧ *46*   superior, *27*   1616 first, *27*
1617 equal∧ *MS* ∼, *27–38*   1618 And, *MS* ∼∧ *27–38*   1619 labours,
glorious, *27*

Low walks the Sun, and broadens by Degrees,   1620
Just o'er the Verge of Day. The shifting Clouds
Assembled gay, a richly-gorgeous Train,
In all their Pomp attend his setting Throne.
Air, Earth and Ocean smile immense. And now,
As if his weary Chariot sought the Bowers   1625
Of *Amphitritè*, and her tending Nymphs,
(So *Grecian* Fable sung) he dips his Orb;
Now half-immers'd; and now a golden Curve
Gives one bright Glance, then total disappears.

For ever running an enchanted Round,   1630
Passes the Day, deceitful, vain, and void;
As fleets the Vision o'er the formful Brain,
This Moment hurrying wild th' impassion'd Soul,
The next in nothing lost. 'Tis so to him,
The Dreamer of this Earth, an idle Blank: 1635
A Sight of Horror to the cruel Wretch,
Who all day long in sordid Pleasure roll'd,
Himself an useless Load, has squander'd vile,
Upon his scoundrel Train, what might have chear'd
A drooping Family of modest Worth.   1640
But to the generous still-improving Mind,
That gives the hopeless Heart to sing for Joy,
Diffusing kind Beneficence around,
Boastless, as now descends the silent Dew;
To him the long Review of order'd Life   1645
Is inward Rapture, only to be felt.

Confess'd from yonder slow-extinguish'd Clouds,
All Ether softening, sober *Evening* takes
Her wonted Station in the middle Air;

1620–9 *44–46*
1620–9 *27–38 as follows:*

    Low walks the Sun, and broadens by degrees,
    Just o'er the Verge of Day. The rising Clouds,   (*27*, 940)
    That shift, perpetual, in his vivid Train,
    Their dewy Mirrors, numberless, oppos'd,
    Unfold the hidden Riches of his Ray,

And chase a Change of Colours round the Sky.
'Tis all one Blush from East to West! and now,   (27, 945)
Behind the dusky Earth, He dips his Orb,
Now half immers'd, and now a golden Curve
Gives one faint Glimmer, and then disappears.

(942) dewy] watry *30q–38*
1630–6 *27–46*
1630–1 FOR ever . . . Day, deceitful] PASSES the Day illusive *27*
1631 vain, and void;] and perplext, *27* tedious, void; *30q–38*
1633 wild] all *27–38*
1635 an idle] a chearless *27–38*
1636 the cruel] th' ungodly *27*
1637–41 *44–46*
1637–41 *27 as follows:*

> The Hard, the Lewd, the Cruel, and the False,   (27, 955)
> Who, all Day long, have made the Widow weep,
> And snatch'd the Morsel from her Orphan's Mouth,
> To give their Dogs: but to th' harmonious Mind,

1637–41 *30q–38 as follows:*

> Who, rowling in inhuman pleasure deep,
> The whole day long has made the widow pine;
> And snatch'd the morsel from her orphan's mouth,
> To give his dogs. But to the tuneful mind,   (*30q*, 1070)

1637–41 *MS as follows:*

> Who rather than [his selfish Joys retrench *del.*]
>   retrench his selfish Joys,
> His gross inhuman Luxuries, will leave
> The lonely Widow desolate to pine,
> And give his Dogs the Morsel that [had made *del.*]
>   woud make
> Her Orphans glad. But to the tuneful Mind,

1642–57 *27–46*
1642 That gives] Who makes *27–38*
1648 All Ether softening] The Sky begreying *27* All ether sadening *30q–38*

1628 immers'd: *44Wks*   (27, 941) shift⌃ perpetual⌃ *30q–38*   (943) Ray,]
MS ∼; *30q–38*   (945) West! And *MS*   (946) orb; *30q–38*   (947) im-
mers'd; *30q–38*   1634 lost; 'tis *27*   1635 Blank! *27*   1636 Horror!
27   wretch; *30q–38*   (*30q*, 1068) pine, *MS*   1643 around⌃ *27*
1644 Dew, *27*   1645 Him, *27*   1646 felt! *27*   1647 CONFESS'D,
27   1648a sadd'ning *300 38*   1649 Air, *27*

A thousand *Shadows* at her Beck. First *This*   1650
She sends on Earth; then *That* of deeper Dye
Steals soft behind; and then a *Deeper* still,
In Circle following Circle, gathers round,
To close the Face of Things. A fresher Gale
Begins to wave the Wood, and stir the Stream,   1655
Sweeping with shadowy Gust the Fields of Corn;
While the Quail clamours for his running Mate.
Wide o'er the thistly Lawn, as swells the Breeze,
A whitening Shower of vegetable Down
Amusive floats. The kind impartial Care   1660
Of Nature nought disdains: thoughtful to feed
Her lowest Sons, and clothe the coming Year,
From Field to Field the feather'd Seeds she wings.

His folded Flock secure, the Shepherd home
Hies, merry-hearted; and by Turns relieves   1665
The ruddy Milk-Maid of her brimming Pail;
The Beauty whom perhaps his witless Heart,
Unknowing what the Joy-mixt Anguish means,
Sincerely loves, by that best Language shewn
Of cordial Glances, and obliging Deeds.   1670
Onward they pass, o'er many a panting Height,
And Valley sunk, and unfrequented; where
At Fall of Eve the Fairy People throng,
In various Game, and Revelry to pass
The Summer-Night, as Village-Stories tell.   1675
But far about they wander from the Grave
Of him, whom his ungentle Fortune urg'd
Against his own sad Breast to lift the Hand
Of impious Violence. The lonely Tower
Is also shun'd; whose mournful Chambers hold,   1680
So night-struck Fancy dreams, the yelling Ghost.

Among the crooked Lanes, on every Hedge,
The Glow-Worm lights his Gem; and, thro' the Dark,

1653 In Circle following Circle] In well-adjusted Circles *27*
1654 A fresher Gale] Th' expected Breeze *27* A fresher breeze *30q–38*

1658–63 *44–46   not in 30q–38*
1658–63 *27 as follows:*

>   WILD-WAFTING o'er the Lawn, the thistly Down   *(27, 975)*
> Plays in the fickle Air, now seems to fall,
> And now, high-soaring over Head, an Arch,
> Amusive, forms, then slanting down eludes
> The Grasp of idle Swain. But should the *West*
> A little swell the Breeze, the woolly Shower,   *(27, 980)*
> Blown, in a white Confusion, thro' the Dusk,
> Falls o'er the Face unfelt, and, settling slow,
> Mantles the Twilight Plain. And yet even here,
> As thro' all Nature, in her lowest Forms,
> A fine Contrivance lies, to wing the Seed,   *(27, 985)*
> By this light Plumage, into distant Vales.

  1664–77 *27–46*
1669 Sincerely loves, by that best] Loves fond, by that sincerest *27*
Loves fond, by the sincerest *30q–38*
1675 The] A *27*
1677 urg'd] forc'd, *27*
    1678–81 *44–46*
    1678–81 *27–38 as follows:*

> Against Himself, to lift the hated Hand
> Of Violence; by Man cast out from Life,
> And, after Death, to which They drove his Hope
> Into the broad Way side. The ruin'd Tower
> Is also shun'd, whose unblest Chambers hold,   *(27, 1005)*
> Nightly, sole Habitant, the yelling *Ghost.*

  (1002) Man] men *30q–38*
  (1005) unblest] hoary *30q–38*
  (1006) So night-struck fancy dreams, the yelling ghost. *30q–38*
  1681+ *27 adds here fourteen lines on wildfire (not in Su.30q–46) which
were revised and transferred to Au.30q. See Appendix A, Summer
1007–20 for the original version and OET Au. 1151–64 for later versions.*
  1682–92 *27–46*
1683 Gem] Lamp *27–38*

1656 Corn, *27*   1665 hearted, *27*   1666 Pail, *27*   1667 *The
Beauty, 27* The Beauty, *30q–38*   1669 Language, shown, *27*   1672 un-
frequented, *27*   where, *27*   1673 Eve, *27*   *the Fairy People 27*
(27, 1001) himself˄ *30q–38*   (1003) And˄ *30q–38*   hope, *30q–38*
(1005) shun'd; *30q–38*   1683a lamp; *30q–38*

A moving Radiance twinkles. *Evening* yields
The World to *Night*; not in her Winter-Robe   1685
Of massy Stygian Woof, but loose array'd
In Mantle dun. A faint erroneous Ray,
Glanc'd from th' imperfect Surfaces of Things,
Flings half an Image on the straining Eye;
While wavering Woods, and Villages, and Streams,   1690
And Rocks, and Mountain-tops, that long retain'd
Th' ascending Gleam, are all one swimming Scene,
Uncertain if beheld. Sudden to Heaven
Thence weary Vision turns; where, leading soft
The silent Hours of Love, with purest Ray   1695
Sweet *Venus* shines; and from her genial Rise,
When Day-Light sickens till it springs afresh,
Unrival'd reigns, the fairest Lamp of Night.
As thus th' Effulgence tremulous I drink,
With cherish'd Gaze, the lambent Lightnings shoot   1700
Across the Sky; or horizontal dart,
In wondrous Shapes: by fearful murmuring Crouds
Portentous deem'd. Amid the radiant Orbs,
That more than deck, that animate the Sky,
The Life-infusing Suns of other Worlds;   1705
Lo! from the dread Immensity of Space
Returning, with accelerated Course,
The rushing Comet to the Sun descends;
And as he sinks below the shading Earth,
With awful Train projected o'er the Heavens,   1710
The guilty Nations tremble. But, above
Those superstitious Horrors that enslave
The fond sequacious Herd, to mystic Faith
And blind Amazement prone, th' enlighten'd Few,
Whose Godlike Minds Philosophy exalts,   1715
The glorious Stranger hail. They feel a Joy
Divinely great; they in their Powers exult,
That wondrous Force of Thought, which mounting spurns
This dusky Spot, and measures all the Sky;
While, from his far Excursion thro' the Wilds   1720
Of barren Ether, faithful to his Time,
They see the blazing Wonder rise anew,
In seeming Terror clad, but kindly bent

To work the Will of all-sustaining LOVE:
From his huge vapoury Train perhaps to shake   1725
Reviving Moisture on the numerous Orbs,
Thro' which his long Ellipsis winds; perhaps
To lend new Fuel to declining Suns,
To light up Worlds, and feed th' eternal Fire.

1684-5 A moving Radiance . . . World to *Night*] Twinkles a moving
Gem. On *Evening's* Heel,/ *Night* follows fast *27–38*
1687 faint erroneous Ray] few erroneous Rays *27*
1689 Flings] Fling *27*
  1693-8 *44–46*
  1693-8 *27–38 as follows:*

> Doubtful if seen; whence posting *Vision* turns
> To Heaven, where *Venus*, in the starry Front,
> Shines eminent, and from her genial Rise,
> When Day-Light sickens, till it springs afresh,   (*27*, 1035)
> Sheds Influence on Earth, to Love, and Life,
> And every Form of Vegetation kind.

  (1032) posting] sudden *30q–38*
1699-1729 *44–46*
1699-1729 *27–38 as follows:*

> As thus, *th'Effulgence* tremulous, I drink,
> With fix'd Peruse, the lambent Lightnings shoot
> A-cross the Sky, or, horizontal, dart   (*27*, 1040)
> O'er half the Nations, in a Minute's Space,
> Conglob'd, or long. Astonishment succeeds,
> And Silence, ere the various Talk begins.

  (1039) fix'd] glad *30q–38*
  (1043) begins] begin *30q–38*
  1729 + *27* adds here thirty-two lines on meteors (*not in Su. 30q–46*) which
were revised and transferred to Au.30q.
See Appendix A, Summer 1044–75 for the original version and OET Au.
1108–37 *for later versions.*

1685 Robe, *27*   1686 massy, *27*   array'd, *27*   1689 Eye. *27–*
38   (*27*, 1032) seen: *30q–38*   (1033) heaven; *30q–38*   *Venus*‸ *30o 38*
(1034) eminent; *30q–38*   (*27*, 1038) thus‸ th' effulgence tremulous‸ *30q–*
38   (1040) sky; or‸ horizontal‸ *30q–38*

WITH Thee, serene PHILOSOPHY, with Thee,   1730
And thy bright Garland, let me crown my Song!
Effusive Source of Evidence, and Truth!
A Luster shedding o'er th' ennobled Mind,
Stronger than Summer-Noon; and pure as That,
Whose mild Vibrations sooth the parted Soul,   1735
New to the Dawning of celestial Day.
Hence thro' her nourish'd Powers, enlarged by thee,
She springs aloft, with elevated Pride,
Above the tangling Mass of low Desires,
That bind the fluttering Croud; and, Angel-wing'd,   1740
The Heights of Science and of Virtue gains,
Where All is calm and clear; with Nature round,
Or in the starry Regions, or th' Abyss,
To Reason's and to Fancy's Eye display'd:
The *First* up-tracing, from the dreary Void,   1745
The Chain of Causes and Effects to HIM,
The World-producing ESSENCE, who alone
Possesses Being; while the *Last* receives
The whole Magnificence of Heaven and Earth,
And every Beauty, delicate or bold,   1750
Obvious or more remote, with livelier Sense,
Diffusive painted on the rapid Mind.

TUTOR'D by thee, hence POETRY exalts
Her Voice to Ages; and informs the Page
With Music, Image, Sentiment, and Thought,   1755
Never to die! the Treasure of Mankind,
Their highest Honour, and their truest Joy!

WITHOUT thee what were unenlighten'd Man?
A Savage roaming thro' the Woods and Wilds,
In quest of Prey; and with th' unfashion'd Fur   1760
Rough-clad; devoid of every finer Art,
And Elegance of Life. Nor Happiness
Domestic, mix'd of Tenderness and Care,
Nor moral Excellence, nor social Bliss,
Nor guardian Law were his; nor various Skill   1765
To turn the Furrow, or to guide the Tool
Mechanic; nor the Heaven-conducted Prow

Of Navigation bold, that fearless braves
The burning Line or dares the wintry Pole,
Mother severe of infinite Delights!   1770

1729+ *30q–38 have the following five lines (not in 27 44–46):*

    THE vulgar stare; amazement is their joy,   (*30q*, 1130)
    And mystic faith, a fond sequacious herd!
    But scrutinous PHILOSOPHY looks deep,
    With piercing eye, into the latent cause;
    Nor can she swallow what she does not see.

1730–64 *27–46*
1731 bright Garland] high Praises *27–38*
1735 Which gently vibrates on the Eye of Saint, *27*
1738–9   She, soaring, spurns, with elevated Pride,
    The tangling Mass of Cares, and low Desires,   *27–38*
1742 clear;] bright! *27*
1745 the dreary Void] *the vast Inane 27–38*
1747 The World-producing ESSENCE, who] WHO, absolutely, in
HIMSELF, *27* Who, all-sustaining, in himself, *30q–38*
1752 A World swift-painted, on th' attentive Mind! *27–38*
1758 unenlighten'd] unassisted *27–38*
1761 finer] honest *27–38*
1762 Nor Happiness] Nor Home, nor Joy *27–38*
  1765–70 *44–46*
  1765–70 *27–38 as follows:*

    Nor Law were his; nor Property, nor Swain   (*27*, 1111)
    To turn the Furrow, nor mechanic Hand
    Harden'd to Toil, nor Servant prompt, nor *Trade*
    Mother severe of infinite Delights!

   (1113) Servant prompt,] sailor bold; *30q–38*

1730 *no new paragraph 30q–38*   Thee, *27*   PHILOSOPHY! *27–45*   *Thee!*
27   1734 Noon, *27*   1737 Hence, *27*   *Thee, 27*   1738a She⌄ soar-
ing⌄ *30q–38*   1740 Crowd, *27*   1741 Science, *27–38*   1742 calm,
27   round⌄ *27–45*   1744 *Reason's, 27* Reason's, *30q–38*   *Fancy's 27*
display'd; *27*   1745 up-tracing⌄ *30q–38*   1745a the vast inane *30q–38*
1746 Causes, *27*   1747 alone, *27*   1748 *Being 27–38*   1749 Heaven,
27   1752a painted⌄ *30q–38*   Mind. *30q–38*   1753 *Thee 27*   1754 Ages,
27   1756 Mankind! *46*   1758 *Thee, 27*   Man! *27*   1760 Prey,
27 ~: *44Wks* Furr, *27*   1761 clad, *27*   (*27*, 1111) property; *30q–*
38 swain, *30q 30p 35 38*   (1112) furrow; *30q–38*   hand, *30q–30o 38*
(1113) toil; *30q–38*   trade, *30q–38*

Nothing, save Rapine, Indolence, and Guile,
And Woes on Woes, a still-revolving Train!
Whose horrid Circle had made human Life
Than Non-existence worse: but, taught by Thee,
Ours are the Plans of Policy, and Peace; 1775
To live like Brothers, and conjunctive all
Embelish Life. While thus laborious Crouds
Ply the tough Oar, PHILOSOPHY directs
The ruling Helm; or like the liberal Breath
Of potent Heaven, invisible, the Sail 1780
Swells out, and bears th' inferior World along.

NOR to this evanescent Speck of Earth
Poorly confin'd, the radiant Tracts on high
Are her exalted Range; intent to gaze
Creation thro'; and, from that full Complex 1785
Of never-ending Wonders, to conceive
Of the SOLE BEING right, who *spoke the Word*,
And Nature mov'd compleat. With inward View,
Thence on th' ideal Kingdom swift she turns
Her Eye; and instant, at her powerful Glance, 1790
Th' obedient Phantoms vanish or appear;
Compound, divide, and into Order shift,
Each to his Rank, from plain Perception up
To the fair Forms of Fancy's fleeting Train;
To Reason then, deducing Truth from Truth; 1795
And Notion quite abstract; where first begins
The World of Spirits, Action all, and Life
Unfetter'd, and unmix'd. But here the Cloud,
So wills ETERNAL PROVIDENCE, sits deep.
Enough for us to know that this dark State, 1800
In wayward Passions lost, and vain Pursuits,
This Infancy of Being, cannot prove
The final Issue of the Works of GOD,
By boundless LOVE and perfect WISDOM form'd,
And ever rising with the rising Mind. 1805

1771–1805 *27–46*
1772–3 And Woes on Woes, to render human Life *27*
1775 Plans] Arts *27*
1779 The ruling Helm] Star-led, the Helm *27–38*
1780 potent] urgent *27–38*   Sail] Sails *27–38*
1783 the] those *27*
1785 full Complex] *round Complex 27*
1786 ending] ceasing *27*
1788 mov'd compleat. With inward View] circled.With inflected View
27
1790 powerful] virtual *27–38*
1791 or] and *27*
1794 *not in 27–38*
1795 *not in 27–45*
1796 And] To *27–38*
1798 Unfetter'd] Immediate *27–38*
1800 to know] we know *27–44Wks*
1804 By *Love*, and *Wisdom*, inexpressive, form'd, *27–38*
    27 30p 35 add: The END.

1771 Nothing∧ *27*   1774 worse. But∧ *27–38*   *Thee*∧ *27* thee∧ *30q–45*
1775 policy∧ *300 38*   Peace, *27*   1776 and, conjunctive, *27*   1778 directs,
27–38   1780 invisible∧ *38*   1780a Sails, *38*   1782 NOR, *27*   Earth,
27   1784 *her 27*   intent, *27*   1785 thro', *27*   1787 THE *27–38*
WHO *27*   spoke the *27–38*   Word,— *27* word, *30q–38*   1789 Thence,
27   *th' Ideal Kingdom, 27*   swift, *27*   1791 vanish, *27*   appear, *27*
1794 Train, *44–45*   1797 *The World of Spirits 27*   1798 unmix'd —
but *27*   1800 know, *27*   1802 Being! *27*   1803 GOD; *30q–38*
1804a LOVE∧ *30q–38*   WISDOM∧ inexpressive∧ *30q–38*

AUTUMN

The ARGUMENT

The Subject propos'd. Address to Mr. ONSLOW. A Prospect of the Fields ready for Harvest. Reflexions in praise of Industry rais'd by that View. Reaping. A Tale relative to it. A Harvest Storm. Shooting and Hunting, their Barbarity. A ludicrous Account of Fox-hunting. A View of an Orchard. Wall-Fruit. A Vineyard. A 5
Description of Fogs, frequent in the latter part of Autumn: *whence a Digression, enquiring into the Rise of Fountains and Rivers. Birds of Season considered, that now shift their Habitation. The prodigious Number of them that cover the northern and western Isles of* SCOTLAND. *Hence a View of the Country. A Prospect of the* 10
discoloured, fading Woods. After a gentle dusky Day, Moon-light. Autumnal Meteors. Morning: to which succeeds a calm, pure, Sun-shiny Day, such as usually shuts up the Season. The Harvest being gathered in, the Country dissolv'd in Joy. The whole concludes with a Panegyric on a Philosophical Country Life. 15

 CROWN'D with the Sickle, and the wheaten Sheaf,
While AUTUMN, nodding o'er the yellow Plain,
Comes jovial on; the *Doric* Reed once more,
Well pleas'd, I tune. Whate'er the wintry Frost
Nitrous prepar'd; the various-blossom'd Spring   5
Put in white Promise forth; and Summer-Suns
Concocted strong, rush boundless now to View,
Full, perfect all, and swell my glorious Theme.

 ONSLOW! the Muse, ambitious of thy Name,
To grace, inspire, and dignify her Song,   10
Would from the *Public Voice* thy gentle Ear
A while engage. Thy noble Cares she knows,
The Patriot-Virtues that distend thy Thought,
Spread on thy Front, and in thy Bosom glow;

While listening Senates hang upon thy Tongue,   15
Devolving thro' the Maze of Eloquence
A Rowl of Periods, sweeter than her Song.
But she too pants for public Virtue, she,
Tho' weak of Power yet strong in ardent Will,
Whene'er her Country rushes on her Heart,   20
Assumes a bolder Note, and fondly tries
To mix the Patriot's with the Poet's Flame.

    WHEN the bright *Virgin* gives the beauteous Days,
And *Libra* weighs in equal Scales the Year;
From Heaven's high Cope the fierce Effulgence shook   25
Of parting Summer, a serener Blue,
With golden Light enliven'd wide invests
The happy World. Attemper'd Suns arise,
Sweet-beam'd, and shedding oft thro' lucid Clouds
A pleasing Calm; while broad, and brown, below,   30
Extensive Harvests hang the heavy Head.
Rich, silent, deep, they stand; for not a Gale
Rolls its light Billows o'er the bending Plain;

---

half-title: AUTUMN.] AUTUMN. A POEM. *30o 38*
30q–38 add: Inscribed to the RIGHT HONOURABLE *ARTHUR ONSLOW*, Esq; SPEAKER of the HOUSE OF COMMONS.
30p has separate title-page
The Argument *30q–46*
1 *Address*] *Address'd 30o–46*
2–3 *Reflexions . . . rais'd by that View.*] *not in 30q–38*
3 *A Tale relative to it.*] *A tale 30q–38*
13 *Sun-shiny*] *MS* sun-shine *30q–38*
   1–117 *30q–46*
14 Bosom] *MS* conduct *30q–38*
27 enliven'd] *MS* irradiate, *30q–38*
31 Extensive] *MS* Unbounded *30q–38*

Argument 1 Address'd *30o–46*   6 AUTUMN *30q–38*   7 *fountains,* *30q 30p*   3 doric *30q–30o*   4 wintry] *MS* WINTRY *30q–38*   5 Spring] *MS* SPRING *30q–38*   6 Summer-Suns] *MS* SUMMER-SUNS *30q–38*   19 power, *30q–38*   26 SUMMER *30q–38*   30 below‸ *46*

A Calm of Plenty! till the ruffled Air
Falls from its Poise, and gives the Breeze to blow.   35
Rent is the fleecy Mantle of the Sky;
The Clouds fly different; and the sudden Sun
By Fits effulgent gilds th' illumin'd Field,
And black by Fits the Shadows sweep along.
A gayly-checker'd Heart-expanding View,   40
Far as the circling Eye can shoot around,
Unbounded tossing in a Flood of Corn.

THESE are thy Blessings, INDUSTRY! rough Power!
Whom Labour still attends, and Sweat, and Pain;
Yet the kind Source of every gentle Art,   45
And all the soft Civility of Life:
Raiser of Human Kind! by Nature cast,
Naked, and helpless, out amid the Woods,
And Wilds, to rude inclement Elements;
With various Seeds of Art deep in the Mind   50
Implanted, and profusely pour'd around
Materials infinite; but idle all.
Still unexerted, in th' unconscious Breast,
Slept the lethargic Powers; Corruption still,
Voracious, swallow'd what the liberal Hand   55
Of Bounty scatter'd o'er the savage Year:
And still the sad Barbarian, roving, mix'd
With Beasts of Prey; or for his Acorn-Meal
Fought the fierce tusky Boar; a shivering Wretch!
Aghast, and comfortless, when the bleak North,   60
With Winter charg'd, let the mix'd Tempest fly,
Hail, Rain, and Snow, and bitter-breathing Frost:
Then to the Shelter of the Hut he fled;
And the wild Season, sordid, pin'd away.
For Home he had not; Home is the Resort   65
Of Love, of Joy, of Peace and Plenty, where,
Supporting and supported, polish'd Friends,
And dear Relations mingle into Bliss.
But this the rugged Savage never felt,
Even desolate in Crouds; and thus his Days   70
Roll'd heavy, dark, and unenjoy'd along;
A Waste of Time! till INDUSTRY approach'd,

And rous'd him from his miserable Sloth:
His Faculties unfolded; pointed out,
Where lavish Nature the directing Hand   75
Of Art demanded; shew'd him how to raise
His feeble Force by the mechanic Powers,
To dig the Mineral from the vaulted Earth,
On what to turn the piercing Rage of Fire,
On what the Torrent, and the gather'd Blast;   80
Gave the tall antient Forest to his Ax;
Taught him to chip the Wood, and hew the Stone,
Till by Degrees the finish'd Fabric rose;
Tore from his Limbs the Blood-polluted Fur,
And wrapt them in the woolly Vestment warm,   85
Or bright in glossy Silk, and flowing Lawn;
With wholesome Viands fill'd his Table, pour'd
The generous Glass around, inspir'd to wake
The Life-refining Soul of decent Wit:
Nor stopp'd at barren bare Necessity;   90
But still advancing bolder, led him on,
To Pomp, to Pleasure, Elegance, and Grace;
And, breathing high Ambition thro' his Soul,
Set Science, Wisdom, Glory, in his View,
And bad him be the *Lord* of All below.   95

---

40 Heart-expanding] *MS* wide-extended *30q–38* [Heart-delighting *del.*]
MSLytt
42 *MS* Convolv'd, and tossing in a flood of corn. *30q–38* [O'er waving
golden Seas of Ripend Corn. *del.*] *MSLytt*
50 Seeds of Art deep in the Mind] *MS* powers of deep efficiency *30q–38*
60 bleak] *MSLytt* red *30q–38*
91+ By hardy patience, and experience slow, *30q–38 del. MS, not in*
44–46

---

40 checker'd, *30q–38*   42 Unbounded, *MS*   43 blessings˄ *30q 30p*
47 Nature *30q–38 MS*   56 Bounty] *MS* Bounty *30q–38*   year. *30q–38*
59 boar: *30q–38*   62 frost. *30q–38*   63 fled˄ *MS*   66 Peace,] *MS*
˜, *30q–38*   70 Days, *45*   73 Sloth:] *MS* ˜ *30q–38*   74 unfolded:
44Wks   75 Nature *30q–38*   76 Art *30q–38*   88 inspir'd, *30q–38*
90 barren, *30q–38*   Necessity, *45*   93 And˄ *30q–38*   94 glory˄ *30q–*
300   95 Lord *MS*

THEN gathering Men their natural Powers combin'd,
And form'd a *Public*; to the general Good
Submitting, aiming, and conducting All.
For This the *Patriot-Council* met, the full,
The free, and fairly represented *Whole*;   100
For This they plann'd the holy Guardian-Laws,
Distinguish'd Orders, animated Arts,
And with joint Force *Oppression* chaining, set
Imperial Justice at the Helm; yet still
To them accountable: nor slavish dream'd   105
That toiling Millions must resign their Weal,
And all the Honey of their Search, to such
As for themselves alone themselves have rais'd.

HENCE every Form of cultivated Life
In Order set, protected, and inspir'd,   110
Into Perfection wrought. Uniting All,
Society grew numerous, high, polite,
And happy. Nurse of Art! the City rear'd
In beauteous Pride her Tower-encircled Head;
And, stretching Street on Street, by Thousands drew,   115
From twining woody Haunts, or the tough Yew
To Bows strong-straining, her aspiring Sons.

THEN Commerce brought into the public Walk
The busy Merchant; the big Ware-house built;
Rais'd the strong Crane; choak'd up the loaded Street   120
With foreign Plenty; and thy Stream, O THAMES,
Large, gentle, deep, majestic, King of Floods!
Chose for his grand Resort. On either Hand,
Like a long wintry Forest, Groves of Masts
Shot up their Spires; the bellying Sheet between   125
Possess'd the breezy Void; the sooty Hulk
Steer'd sluggish on; the splendid Barge along
Row'd, regular, to Harmony; around,
The Boat, light-skimming, stretch'd its oary Wings;
While deep the various Voice of fervent Toil   130
From Bank to Bank increas'd; whence ribb'd with Oak,
To bear the BRITISH THUNDER, black, and bold,
The roaring Vessel rush'd into the Main.

THEN too the pillar'd Dome, magnific, heav'd
Its ample Roof; and Luxury within   135
Pour'd out her glittering Stores: the Canvas smooth,
With glowing Life protuberant, to the View
Embodied rose; the Statue seem'd to breathe,
And soften into Flesh, beneath the Touch
Of forming Art, Imagination-flush'd.   140

ALL is the Gift of INDUSTRY; whate'er
Exalts, embellishes, and renders Life
Delightful. Pensive Winter chear'd by him

---

101 they plann'd] devis'd *30q–38*
111 wrought] rose *MSLytt*
113–14 the City rear'd . . . encircled Head] *MSLytt* the city rose
30q–38
115 drew] *MS* led *30q–38*
116 or] and *30q 30p*
115–17 *del. MSLytt; restored by T.*
117+ *30q–38 as follows (not in 44–46):*

> 'Twas nought but labour, the whole dusky groupe
> Of clustering houses, and of mingling men,
> Restless design, and execution strong.   (*30q*, 120)
> In every street the sounding hammer ply'd
> His massy task; while the corrosive file,
> In flying touches, form'd the fine machine.

(118–23) *del. MSLytt*
(121–3) *del. MS*
118–83 *30q–46*
121 thy Stream, O THAMES] *MS* on thee, thou THAMES *30q–38* thy
[banks *del.*] streams, O *Thames MSLytt*
122+ Than whom no river heaves a fuller tide, *30q–45, del. then*
restored in MS not in 46
123 Chose] *MSLytt* Seiz'd *30q–38*
135 Its] *MS* His *30q–38*

---

96 combin'd‸ *45*   113 Art; *MS* ~, *MSLytt*   115 And,] *MS* ~‸
30q–38   on Street,] *MS* ~‸ *30q–38*   drew‸ *44Wks*   117 Sons: *MS*
118 Commerce] *MS* COMMERCE *30q–38*   Walk, *MS*   121 Plenty, *46*
132 thunder *30q–38*   135 Luxury] *MS* LUXURY *30q–38*   136 Stores:
the] *MS* ~. The *30q–38*   138 rose; the] *MS* ~. The *30q–38*   140 Im-
agination‸ *44Wks–46*   143 WINTER *30q–38*

Sits at the social Fire, and happy hears
Th' excluded Tempest idly rave along;   145
His harden'd Fingers deck the gaudy Spring;
Without him Summer were an arid Waste;
Nor to th' autumnal Months could thus transmit
Those full, mature, immeasureable Stores,
That, waving round, recal my wandering Song.   150

    Soon as the Morning trembles o'er the Sky,
And, unperceiv'd, unfolds the spreading Day;
Before the ripen'd Field the Reapers stand,
In fair Array; each by the Lass he loves,
To bear the rougher Part, and mitigate   155
By nameless gentle Offices her Toil.
At once they stoop and swell the lusty Sheaves;
While thro' their chearful Band the rural Talk,
The rural Scandal and the rural Jest
Fly harmless, to deceive the tedious Time,   160
And steal unfelt the sultry Hours away.
Behind the Master walks, builds up the Shocks;
And, conscious, glancing oft on every Side
His sated Eye, feels his Heart heave with Joy.
The Gleaners spread around, and here and there,   165
Spike after Spike, their sparing Harvest pick.
Be not too narrow, Husbandmen! but fling
From the full Sheaf, with charitable Stealth,
The liberal Handful. Think, oh grateful think!
How good the God of Harvest is to you;   170
Who pours Abundance o'er your flowing Fields;
While these unhappy Partners of your Kind
Wide-hover round you, like the Fowls of Heaven,
And ask their humble Dole. The various Turns
Of Fortune ponder; that your Sons may want   175
What now, with hard Reluctance, faint, ye give.

    The lovely young Lavinia once had Friends;
And Fortune smil'd, deceitful, on her Birth.
For in her helpless Years depriv'd of all,
Of every Stay, save Innocence and Heaven,   180
She with her widow'd Mother, feeble, old,

And poor, liv'd in a Cottage, far retir'd
Among the Windings of a woody Vale;
By Solitude and deep surrounding Shades,
But more by bashful Modesty, conceal'd.   185
Together thus they shunn'd the cruel Scorn
Which Virtue, sunk to Poverty, would meet
From giddy Fashion and low-minded Pride:
Almost on Nature's common Bounty fed,
Like the gay Birds that sung them to Repose,   190
Content, and careless of to-morrow's Fare.
Her Form was fresher than the Morning-Rose,
When the Dew wets its Leaves; unstain'd, and pure,
As is the Lily, or the Mountain Snow.

---

149 Those] *MSLytt* These *30q–38*
158 While thro' their chearful Band] *MSLytt* While, bandied round and round, *30q–38*   their] [the *del.*] *MSLytt*
159–60 *del. by Lyttelton, restored by T.* [With hearty Mirth deceive the tedious Time /And Rural Jests smooth all the [Sense of Pain *del.*] painful Task *all del.*] *MSLytt, del. by T.*
160 harmless] *MS* hearty *30q–38*
161 steal unfelt] *MSLytt* chearly steal *30q–38*
163 on every Side] *MS* this way and that *30q–38*
181–2 old, / And poor] poor, / And old *MS*
182 far retir'd] *MS* lost far up *30q–38*
183 Among] *MSLytt* Amid *30q–38*
    184–7 *MSLytt 44–46*
187 would meet] *MSLytt MS* [still meets *del.*] *MS*
188 *MS 44–46* [From the base Pride of the malignant World *del.*] *MSLytt*
    184–8 *30q–38 as follows:*

        Safe from the cruel, blasting arts of man;

    189–202 *30q–46*

---

145 along. *30q–38*   146 SPRING. *30q–38*   147 SUMMER *30q–38*
148 AUTUMNAL *30q–38*   157 stoop, *30q–38*   158 Talk˄ *44–45*
159 Scandal˄] *MS* ~, *30q–38*   163 And˄ *45*   170 harvest *30q–38*
180 Heaven, *MS*   184 Solitude, *MSLytt*   185 Modesty˄ *MSLytt*
187 Which, *MS*   189 Nature's *MS* NATURE'S *30q–38*

The modest Virtues mingled in her Eyes,   195
Still on the Ground dejected, darting all
Their humid Beams into the blooming Flowers:
Or when the mournful Tale her Mother told,
Of what her faithless Fortune promis'd once,
Thrill'd in her Thought, they, like the dewy Star   200
Of Evening, shone in Tears. A native Grace
Sat fair-proportion'd on her polish'd Limbs,
Veil'd in a simple Robe, their best Attire,
Beyond the Pomp of Dress; for Loveliness
Needs not the foreign Aid of Ornament,   205
But is when unadorn'd adorn'd the most.
Thoughtless of Beauty, she was Beauty's Self,
Recluse amid the close-embowering Woods.
As in the hollow Breast of *Appenine*,
Beneath the Shelter of encircling Hills,   210
A Myrtle rises, far from human Eye,
And breathes its balmy Fragrance o'er the Wild;
So flourish'd blooming, and unseen by All,
The sweet LAVINIA; till, at length, compell'd
By strong Necessity's supreme Command,   215
With smiling Patience in her Looks, she went
To glean PALEMON's Fields. The Pride of Swains
PALEMON was, the Generous, and the Rich,
Who led the rural Life in all its Joy,
And Elegance, such as *Arcadian* Song   220
Transmits from antient uncorrupted Times;
When tyrant Custom had not shackled Man,
But free to follow Nature was the Mode.
He then, his Fancy with autumnal Scenes
Amusing, chanc'd beside his Reaper-Train   225
To walk, when poor LAVINIA drew his Eye;
Unconscious of her Power, and turning quick
With unaffected Blushes from his Gaze:
He saw her charming, but he saw not Half
The Charms her down-cast Modesty conceal'd.   230
That very Moment Love and chaste Desire
Sprung in his Bosom, to himself unknown;
For still the World prevail'd, and its dread Laugh,
Which scarce the firm Philosopher can scorn,

Should his Heart own a Gleaner in the Field: 235
And thus in secret to his Soul he sigh'd.

"WHAT Pity! that so delicate a Form,
"By Beauty kindled, where enlivening Sense,
"And more than vulgar Goodness seem to dwell,

---

196 dejected,] deject, and *30q 30p*
198 mournful Tale] *MSLytt* stories that *30q–38* Stories which *MS*
199 promis'd] *MS* flatter'd *30q–38*
  203–17 *MSLytt 44–46*
204+ [Than if adorn'd in all the Pride of Dress *del.*] *MSLytt*
206 *MS not in MSLytt*
208 close-embowering] *MSLytt* [deep-embow'ring *del.*] *MSLytt*
211 Eye] Eyes *MSLytt*
  203–17 *30q–38 as follows:*

      Veil'd in a simple robe; for loveliness
      Needs not the foreign aid of ornament,
      But is when unadorn'd adorn'd the most.
      Thoughtless of beauty, she was Beauty's self,
      Recluse among the woods; if city-dames   (*30q*, 210)
      Will deign their faith. And thus she went compell'd
      By strong necessity, with as serene,
      And pleas'd a look as patience can put on,
      To glean PALEMON's fields. The pride of swains

  203–17 *MSLytt at first as follows:*

      [Veil'd in a simple Robe, [*? del.*] their best Attire.
      Compell'd by strong Necessity, she went
      To glean etc. *all del.*]

  218–37 *30q–46*
221 uncorrupted] *MS* incorrupted *30q–38*
223 But] *MS* And *30q–38*
  238–9 *MSLytt 44–46*
238 enlivening] *MSLytt* [exalted *del.*] *MSLytt*
  238–9 *30q–38 as follows:*

      By beauty kindled, and harmonious shap'd,   (*30q*, 235)
      Where sense sincere, and goodness seem to dwell,

---

200 Thought‸ *MSLytt*   209 Appenine, *MSLytt Appenine‸ 44Wks*
214 Lavinia, *MSLytt* LAVINIA: *44–45*   till‸ *MSLytt 45*   (*30q*, 208) un-
adorn'd, *30o 38*   218 Rich; *MS*   221 antient‸] *MS* ～, *30q–38*
228 gaze. *30q 30p MS* ～, *30o 38*   233 laugh‸ *30p 30o*

"Should be devoted to the rude Embrace　　　　　240
"Of some indecent Clown? She looks, methinks,
"Of old ACASTO's Line; and to my Mind
"Recalls that Patron of my happy Life,
"From whom my liberal Fortune took its Rise;
"Now to the Dust gone down; his Houses, Lands,　　　245
"And once fair-spreading Family dissolv'd.
" 'Tis said that in some lone obscure Retreat,
"Urg'd by Remembrance sad, and decent Pride,
"Far from those Scenes which knew their better Days,
"His aged Widow and his Daughter live,　　　　　250
"Whom yet my fruitless Search could never find.
"Romantic Wish, would this the Daughter were!"

WHEN, strict enquiring, from herself he found
She was the same, the Daughter of his Friend,
Of bountiful ACASTO; who can speak　　　　　255
The mingled Passions that surpriz'd his Heart,
And thro' his Nerves in shivering Transport ran?
Then blaz'd his smother'd Flame, avow'd, and bold;
And as he view'd Her, ardent, o'er and o'er,
Love, Gratitude, and Pity wept at once.　　　　　260
Confus'd, and frighten'd at his sudden Tears,
Her rising Beauties flush'd a higher Bloom,
As thus PALEMON, passionate, and just,
Pour'd out the pious Rapture of his Soul.

"AND art thou then ACASTO's dear Remains?　　　265
"She, whom my restless Gratitude has sought,
"So long in vain? Oh yes! the very same,
"The soften'd Image of my noble Friend,
"Alive, his every Feature, every Look,
"More elegantly touch'd. Sweeter than Spring!　　　270
"Thou sole surviving Blossom from the Root,
"That nourish'd up my Fortune, say, ah where,
"In what sequester'd Desart, hast thou drawn
"The kindest Aspect of delighted Heaven?
"Into such Beauty spread, and blown so fair;　　　275
"Tho' Poverty's cold Wind, and crushing Rain,
"Beat keen, and heavy, on thy tender Years?

"O let me now, into a richer Soil,
"Transplant thee safe! where vernal Suns, and Showers,
"Diffuse their warmest, largest Influence;   280
"And of my Garden be the Pride, and Joy!
"It ill befits thee, oh it ills befits
"Acasto's Daughter, his, whose open Stores,
"Tho' vast, were little to his ampler Heart,
"The Father of a Country, thus to pick   285
"The very Refuse of those Harvest-Fields,
"Which from his bounteous Friendship I enjoy.
"Then throw that shameful Pittance from thy Hand,
"But ill apply'd to such a rugged Task;
"The Fields, the Master, All, my Fair, are thine;   290
"If to the various Blessings which thy House
"Has on me lavish'd, thou wilt add that Bliss,
"That dearest Bliss, the Power of blessing Thee!"

240–89 *30q–46*
242 Line] blood *MSLytt*
247 *MS* I've heard that, in some waste obscure retreat, *30q–38* ['Tis rumour'd that in some obscure Retreat, *del.*] *MS* lone] *MS* [waste *del.*] *MS*
255 Of] *MS* The *30q–38*
256 mingled] *MS* mingling *30q–38* Passions] *MS* passion *30q–38*
259 he view'd Her, ardent,] *MS* he run her, ardent, *30q–38* [he, ardent, ey'd her *del.*] *MS*
263 As] And *45*
270 Sweeter] *MS* Fairer *30q–38*
273 sequester'd] *MSLytt* unsmiling *30q–38*
275 fair;] *MS* white? *30q–38*
287 *MSLytt* His bounty taught to gain, and right enjoy. *30q–38*
   290–3 *MSLytt 44–46*
292 Has on me lavish'd] *MS* [Has shower'd upon me *del. by T.*] *MSLytt* Has lavish'd on me *44Wks* wilt add that Bliss] *MSLytt* that Bliss wilt add *MSLytt*
293 dearest] *MSLytt* [sweetest *del.*] *MSLytt*

---

241 Clown?] *MS* ! *38* methinks‸ *44Wks 45* 250 live,] *MS* ~; *30q–38*
266 sought‸ *30q–38* 267 oh *30q* 275 spread? *30q–38* fair? *MS*
277 years. *30q–38* 279 Suns‸ *MS* Showers‸ *MS* 280 warmest‸
MS 283 his‸ *46* 291 If, *MSLytt*

Here ceas'd the Youth: yet still his speaking Eye
Express'd the sacred Triumph of his Soul,   295
With conscious Virtue, Gratitude, and Love,
Above the vulgar Joy divinely rais'd.
Nor waited he Reply. Won by the Charm
Of Goodness irresistible, and all
In sweet Disorder lost, she blush'd Consent.   300
The News immediate to her Mother brought,
While, pierc'd with anxious Thought, she pin'd away
The lonely Moments for Lavinia's Fate;
Amaz'd, and scarce believing what she heard,
Joy seiz'd her wither'd Veins, and one bright Gleam   305
Of setting Life shone on her Evening-Hours:
Not less enraptur'd than the happy Pair;
Who flourish'd long in tender Bliss, and rear'd
A numerous Offspring, lovely like themselves,
And good, the Grace of all the Country round.   310

Defeating oft the Labours of the Year,
The sultry South collects a potent Blast.
At first, the Groves are scarcely seen to stir
Their trembling Tops; and a still Murmur runs
Along the soft-inclining Fields of Corn: 315
But as th' aërial Tempest fuller swells,
And in one mighty Stream, invisible,
Immense, the whole excited Atmosphere,
Impetuous rushes o'er the sounding World;
Strain'd to the Root, the stooping Forest pours   320
A rustling Shower of yet untimely Leaves.
High-beat, the circling Mountains eddy in,
From the bare Wild, the dissipated Storm,
And send it in a Torrent down the Vale.
Expos'd, and naked, to its utmost Rage,   325
Thro' all the Sea of Harvest rolling round,
The billowy Plain floats wide; nor can evade,
Tho' pliant to the Blast, its seizing Force;
Or whirl'd in Air, or into vacant Chaff
Shook waste. And sometimes too a Burst of Rain,   330
Swept from the black Horizon, broad, descends
In one continuous Flood. Still over head

The mingling Tempest weaves its Gloom, and still
The Deluge deepens; till the Fields around
Lie sunk, and flatted, in the sordid Wave.   335
Sudden, the Ditches swell; the Meadows swim.
Red, from the Hills, innumerable Streams
Tumultuous roar; and high above its Banks
The River lift; before whose rushing Tide,
Herds, Flocks, and Harvests, Cottages, and Swains,   340
Roll mingled down; all that the Winds had spar'd,
In one wild Moment ruin'd, the big Hopes,
And well-earn'd Treasures of the painful Year.
Fled to some Eminence, the Husbandman,
Helpless beholds the miserable Wreck   345
Driving along; his drowning Ox at once
Descending, with his Labours scatter'd round,
He sees; and instant o'er his shivering Thought
Comes Winter unprovided, and a Train
Of clamant Children dear. Ye Masters, then,   350
Be mindful of the rough laborious Hand,
That sinks you soft in Elegance and Ease;
Be mindful of those Limbs in Russet clad,
Whose Toil to yours is Warmth, and graceful Pride;

290–3 *30q–38 as follows:*

> With harvest shining all these fields are thine;
> And, if my wishes may presume so far,
> Their master too, who then indeed were blest,
> To make the daughter of ACASTO so.   (*30q, 290*)

294–371 *30q–46*
308 tender Bliss] mutual bliss *30q–38* tender Peace *MSLytt*
327 The billowy Plain floats wide] The billowy plain boils wide *30q–38*
Wide shakes the billowy Plain *MSLytt* Wide floats the billowy Plain *MS*
333 The mingling Tempest weaves its Gloom] *MS* The glomerating
tempest grows *30q–38*
339 rushing Tide] *MSLytt* weighty rush *30q–38* [Rushing Foam *del.*]
MSLytt

---

302 While‸ *44–45*   315 corn. *30q–38*   316 swells; *30q–38*   319 world:
300   322 in‸ *44Wks*   336 swim, *44Wks*   350 then‸ *30q–38*
352 elegance, *30q–38*   353 limbs, *30q–45*   clad‸ *44Wks*

And oh be mindful of that sparing Board,   355
Which covers yours with Luxury profuse,
Makes your Glass sparkle, and your Sense rejoice!
Nor cruelly demand what the deep Rains,
And all-involving Winds have swept away.

HERE the rude Clamour of the Sportsman's Joy,   360
The Gun fast-thundering, and the winded Horn,
Would tempt the Muse to sing the *rural Game*:
How, in his Mid-career, the Spaniel struck,
Stiff, by the tainted Gale, with open Nose,
Outstretch'd, and finely sensible, *draws* full,   365
Fearful, and cautious, on the latent Prey;
As in the Sun the circling Covey bask
Their varied Plumes, and watchful every Way
Thro' the rough Stubble turn the secret Eye.
Caught in the meshy Snare, in vain they beat   370
Their idle Wings, intangled more and more:
Nor on the Surges of the boundless Air,
Tho' borne triumphant, are they safe; the Gun,
Glanc'd just, and sudden, from the Fowler's Eye,
O'ertakes their sounding Pinions; and again,   375
Immediate, brings them from the towering Wing,
Dead to the Ground; or drives them wide-dispers'd,
Wounded, and wheeling various, down the Wind.

THESE are not Subjects for the peaceful Muse,
Nor will she stain with such her spotless Song;   380
Then most delighted, when she social sees
The whole mix'd Animal-Creation round
Alive, and happy. 'Tis not Joy to Her,
This falsely chearful barbarous Game of Death;
This Rage of Pleasure, which the restless Youth   385
Awakes, impatient, with the gleaming Morn;
When Beasts of Prey retire, that all Night long,
Urg'd by Necessity, had rang'd the Dark,
As if their conscious Ravage shun'd the Light,
Asham'd. Not so the steady Tyrant Man,   390
Who with the thoughtless Insolence of Power
Inflam'd, beyond the most infuriate Wrath

Of the worst Monster that e'er roam'd the Waste,
For Sport alone pursues the cruel Chace,
Amid the Beamings of the gentle Days.   395
Upbraid, ye ravening Tribes, our wanton Rage,
For Hunger kindles you, and lawless Want;
But lavish fed, in Nature's Bounty roll'd,
To joy at Anguish, and delight in Blood,
Is what your horrid Bosoms never knew.   400

---

355 oh] O *30q*
361 fast-thundering] thick-thundering *30q–38*
362 sing the] *MS* sing a *300 38*
368 and watchful] *MS* watchful, and *30q–38*
369 turn] *MS* turn'd *30q–38*
370 in vain they beat] they vainly beat *MSLytt*
371 idle] *MS* useless *30q–38*
371+ *MSLytt as follows:*

> [Sad Captives never more to taste the Joys
> Of Liberty without redemption lost. *del.*]
> [Unhappy Captives whom from instant Death
> No Ransom shall redeem, nor Pity save *del.*]

372–447 *30q–46*
377 wide-] else *30q–38* [far *del.*] wide *MS*
379 not] no *MS*
380 with such her spotless Song] her spotless theme with such *30q–38*
[with such her spotless Theme *del.*] *MS*
381 social] *MS* smiling *30q–38*
388 rang'd] *MS* roam'd *30q–38*
392 Wrath] *MS* rage *30q–38*
393 roam'd] *MS* howl'd *30q–38* [trod *del.*] *MSLytt*
394 pursues] *MSLytt* takes up *30q–38*   Chace] *MSLytt* tract *30q–38*
396 Upbraid us not, ye wolves! ye tygers fell! *30q–38* [Upbraid Man-
kind, ye Wolves! ye Tygers fell! *del. by T.*] *MSLytt* Ye ravening
Tribes, upbraid our wanton Rage! *MS 44–45*
399 joy at] laugh at *30q–38* joy in *MS*   delight] *MS* rejoice *30q–38*

---

359 away! *MS*   362 GAME. *30q–38*   365 *draws*] *MS* draws *30q–38*
368 and, *MS*   374 Eye˅ *46*   384 chearful, *30q–38*   388 dark;
30q 30p   394 alone, *30q*   396 Rage˅ *44–45*

Poor is the Triumph o'er the timid Hare!
Scar'd from the Corn, and now to some lone Seat
Retir'd: the rushy Fen; the ragged Furze,
Stretch'd o'er the stony Heath; the Stubble chapt;
The thistly Lawn; the thick entangled Broom;   405
Of the same friendly Hue, the wither'd Fern;
The fallow Ground laid open to the Sun,
Concoctive; and the nodding sandy Bank,
Hung o'er the Mazes of the Mountain-Brook.
Vain is her best Precaution; tho' she sits   410
Conceal'd, with folded Ears; unsleeping Eyes,
By Nature rais'd to take th' Horizon in;
And Head couch'd close betwixt her hairy Feet,
In Act to spring away. The scented Dew
Betrays her early Labyrinth; and deep,   415
In scatter'd sullen Openings, far behind,
With every Breeze she hears the coming Storm.
But nearer, and more frequent, as it loads
The sighing Gale, she springs amaz'd, and all
The savage Soul of Game is up at once: 420
The Pack full-opening, various; the shrill Horn,
Resounded from the Hills; the neighing Steed,
Wild for the Chace; and the loud Hunter's Shout;
O'er a weak, harmless, flying Creature, all
Mix'd in mad Tumult, and discordant Joy.   425

    The Stag too, singled from the Herd, where long
He rang'd the branching Monarch of the Shades,
Before the Tempest drives. At first, in Speed
He, sprightly, puts his Faith; and, rous'd by Fear,
Gives all his swift aërial Soul to flight.   430
Against the Breeze he darts, that Way the more
To leave the lessening murderous Cry behind.
Deception short! tho' fleeter than the Winds
Blown o'er the keen-air'd Mountain by the North,
He bursts the Thickets, glances thro' the Glades,   435
And plunges deep into the wildest Wood.
If slow, yet sure, adhesive to the Track
Hot-steaming, up behind him come again
    Th' inhuman Rout, and from the shady Depth

Expel him, circling thro' his every Shift.   440
He sweeps the Forest oft; and sobbing sees
The Glades, mild-opening to the golden Day;
Where, in kind Contest, with his butting Friends
He wont to struggle, or his Loves enjoy.
Oft in the full-descending Flood he tries   445
To lose the Scent, and lave his burning Sides;
Oft seeks the Herd; the watchful Herd, alarm'd,
With selfish Care avoid a Brother's Woe.
What shall he do? His once so vivid Nerves,
So full of buoyant Spirit, now no more   450
Inspire the Course; but fainting breathless Toil,
Sick, seizes on his Heart: he stands at Bay;
And puts his last weak Refuge in Despair.
The big round Tears run down his dappled Face;
He groans in Anguish; while the growling Pack,   455

---

402 Scar'd] *MS* Shook *30q–38*
427 rang'd] reign'd *30q*
429 rous'd by Fear] fear-arrous'd *30q–45*
437 Track] tract *30q–300*
438 come] comes *30q–45*
440 Expel] Expels *44Wks*
444 wont] *MS* went *30q–38*
  448 *MS 44–46*
a] their *MS*
  448 *30q–38 have:*

> With quick consent, avoid th' infectious maze.

449 *30q–46*
450–1 *MSLytt 44–46*
450 buoyant] *MSLytt* [active *del.*] *MSLytt*
  450–1 *30q–38 as follows:*

> So full of buoyant soul, inspire no more
> The fainting course; but wrenching, breathless toil,

---

404 Heath: *38–45*   405 thick, intangled *30q–38* ∼-∼ *44Wks*   406 Fern:
44 45   416 scatter'd, *30q–38*   428 first∧ *30q–38 44Wks*   speed, *30q–*
38 44Wks   430 swift∧] *MS* ∼, *30q–38*   432 lessening, *30q–38*
443 Contest∧ *MS* Friends, *MS*   447 watchful herd∧ *30p–38*   448 Care,
MS   451 Course, *MSLytt*   453 last, *30q*

G

Blood-happy, hang at his fair jutting Chest,
And mark his beauteous chequer'd Sides with Gore.

OF this enough. But if the silvan Youth
Whose fervent Blood boils into Violence,
Must have the Chace; behold, despising Flight,   460
The rous'd-up Lion, resolute, and slow,
Advancing full on the protended Spear,
And Coward-Band, that circling wheel aloof.
Slunk from the Cavern, and the troubled Wood,
See the grim Wolf; on him his shaggy Foe   465
Vindictive fix, and let the Ruffian die:
Or, growling horrid, as the brindled Boar
Grins fell Destruction, to the Monster's Heart
Let the Dart lighten from the nervous Arm.

THESE BRITAIN knows not; give, ye BRITONS, then   470
Your sportive Fury, pityless, to pour
Loose on the nightly Robber of the Fold:
Him, from his craggy winding Haunts unearth'd,
Let all the Thunder of the Chace pursue.
Throw the broad Ditch behind you; o'er the Hedge   475
High bound, resistless; nor the deep Morass
Refuse, but thro' the shaking Wilderness
Pick your nice Way; into the perilous Flood
Bear fearless, of the raging Instinct full;
And as you ride the Torrent, to the Banks   480
Your Triumph sound sonorous, running round,
From Rock to Rock, in circling Echo tost:
Then scale the Mountains to their woody Tops;
Rush down the dangerous Steep; and o'er the Lawn,
In Fancy swallowing up the Space between,   485
Pour all your Speed into the rapid Game.
For happy he! who tops the wheeling Chace;
Has every Maze evolv'd, and every Guile
Disclos'd; who knows the Merits of the Pack;
Who saw the Villain seiz'd, and dying hard,   490
Without Complaint, tho' by an hundred Mouths
Relentless torn: O glorious he, beyond
His daring Peers! when the retreating Horn

Calls them to ghostly Halls of grey Renown,
With woodland Honours grac'd; the Fox's Fur,   495
Depending decent from the Roof; and spread
Round the drear Walls, with antick Figures fierce,
The Stag's large Front: he then is loudest heard,
When the Night staggers with severer Toils,
With Feats *Thessalian* Centaurs never knew,   500
And their repeated Wonders shake the Dome.

452–69 *30q–46*
466 And let the Ruffian die] *MS* for murder is his trade *30q–38* and let
the Murderer Die *MSLytt*
467 Or] *MSLytt* And *30q–38*
468 fell] *MSLytt* near *30q–38*
  470-2 *30q–46*
472 nightly Robber of the Fold:] *MS* sly destroyer of the flock. *30q–38*
  470-2 *MSLytt as follows:*

> [These Britain knows not; pour, ye Britons, then
> Your sportive Fury, on the Wily Fox
> [The sly Destroyer of your harmless Flock. *del.*]
> The nightly Robber of the sleeping Fold. *all del.*]

Wily] *MSLytt* [Prowling *del.*] *MS*
  473–91 *30q–46*
479 Bear] [Hurl *del.*] *MS*
483 scale] *MS* snatch *30q–38* [climb *del.*] *MSLytt*   to] *MSLytt* by
30q–38
  492–3 *44–46*
  492–3 *30q–38 as follows:*

> At once tore, merciless. Thrice happy he!
> At hour of dusk, while the retreating horn   (*30q*, 490)

  (489) [Relentless, torn at once. Thrice happy he! *del.*] *MSLytt*
  Torn unrelenting: happy, Glorious, he! *MS*
  (490) while] when *MS*
  494–521 *30q–46*
499 Toils,] toil; *300*
500 *not in 30q–38*

---

456 fair, *30q–38*   457 beauteous, *30q*   458 youth, *30q*   466a *Mur-
derer MS*   470a BRITONS *MS*   476 High-bound *30q–46*   482 tost;
30q–45   486 Game, *44–46*   499 Toils; *30q 30p 38* ∼ₐ *MS*

BUT first the fuel'd Chimney blazes wide;
The Tankards foam; and the strong Table groans
Beneath the smoking Sirloin, stretch'd immense
From Side to Side; in which, with desperate Knife,   505
They deep Incision make, and talk the while
Of ENGLAND's Glory, ne'er to be defac'd,
While hence they borrow Vigour: or amain
Into the Pasty plung'd, at Intervals,
If Stomach keen can Intervals allow,   510
Relating all the Glories of the Chace.
Then sated *Hunger* bids his Brother *Thirst*
Produce the mighty Bowl; the mighty Bowl,
Swell'd high with fiery Juice, steams liberal round
A potent Gale, delicious as the Breath   515
Of *Maia*, to the love-sick Shepherdess,
On Violets diffus'd, while soft she hears
Her panting Shepherd stealing to her Arms.
Nor wanting is the brown October, drawn
Mature and perfect, from his dark Retreat   520
Of thirty Years; and now his honest Front
Flames in the Light refulgent, not afraid
Even with the Vineyard's best Produce to vie.
To cheat the thirsty Moments, *Whist* a while
Walks his grave Round, beneath a Cloud of Smoak,   525
Wreath'd fragrant from the Pipe; or the quick Dice,
In Thunder leaping from the Box, awake
The sounding Gammon: while Romp-loving Miss
Is haul'd about, in Gallantry robust.

AT last these puling Idlenesses laid   530
Aside, frequent and full, the dry Divan
Close in firm Circle; and set, ardent, in
For serious Drinking. Nor Evasion sly,
Nor sober Shift, is to the puking Wretch
Indulg'd apart; but earnest, brimming Bowls   535
Lave every Soul, the Table floating round,
And Pavement, faithless to the fuddled Foot.
Thus as they swim in mutual Swill, the Talk,
Vociferous at once from twenty Tongues,
Reels fast from Theme to Theme; from Horses, Hounds,   540

To Church or Mistress, Politicks or Ghost,
In endless Mazes, intricate, perplex'd.
Mean-time, with sudden Interruption, loud,
Th' impatient Catch bursts from the joyous Heart:
That Moment touch'd is each congenial Soul; 545
And, opening in a full-mouth'd *Cry* of Joy,
The Laugh, the Slap, the jocund Curse goes round;
While from their Slumbers shook, the kennel'd Hounds
Mix in the Music of the Day again.
As when the Tempest, that has vex'd the Deep 550

---

505 in] *MS* on *30q–38*   desperate Knife] fell intent *30q–38*
509 plung'd] plung *MS*
511 all the Glories of the Chace] *MS* how it ran, and how it fell *30q–38*
   Glories] [Wonders *del.*] *MS*
515 delicious] *MS* reviving *30q–38*
516 Of Love-inspiring May to the sick Maid *MS*   Maia] [*Flora del.*]
MS
   522–5 *44–46*
524 *Whist*] Whisk *44–45*
525 grave] dull *44–45*
   522–5 *30q–38 as follows:*

> Flames in the light refulgent, not asham'd
> To vie it with the vineyard's best produce.
> Perhaps a while, amusive, thoughtful Whisk   (*30q*, 520)
> Walks gentle round, beneath a cloud of smoak,

   (518) not] *MS* nor *30p–38*
   (521) gentle round] his dull Round *MS*
   526–56 *30q–46*
535 apart] *MSLytt* askew *30q–38* ascance *MS*
539 Vociferous at once from] *MSLytt* Vociferate at once by *30q–38*
545 each congenial] every kindred *30q–45*
547 goes] go *44Wks*

---

512 Hunger *30q 30p*   Thirst *30q 30p*   515 delicious, *44Wks*   519 drawn,
30q–38 44Wks   520 Mature∧] *MS* ~, *30q–38*   526 Wreath'd∧
fragrant∧] *MS* ~, ~, *30q–38 44Wks*   531 frequent∧] *MS* ~, *30q–38*
534 Shift,] *MS* ~∧ *30q–38*   535 earnest∧ *MS*   541 church, *30q–38*
politicks, *30q–38*   544 heart. *30q–38* ~; *44Wks*   548 While, *30q–38*

The dark Night long, with fainter Murmurs falls:
So gradual sinks their Mirth. Their feeble Tongues,
Unable to take up the cumbrous Word,
Lie quite dissolv'd. Before their maudlin Eyes,
Seen dim and blue, the double Tapers dance,   555
Like the Sun wading thro' the misty Sky.
Then, sliding soft, they drop. Confus'd above,
Glasses and Bottles, Pipes and Gazetteers,
As if the Table even itself was drunk,
Lie a wet broken Scene; and wide, below,   560
Is heap'd the social Slaughter; where astride
The *lubber Power* in filthy Triumph sits,
Slumbrous, inclining still from Side to Side,
And steeps them drench'd in potent Sleep till Morn.
Perhaps some Doctor, of tremendous Paunch,   565
Awful and deep, a black Abyss of Drink,
Out-lives them all; and from his bury'd Flock
Retiring, full of Rumination sad,
Laments the Weakness of these latter Times.

But if the rougher Sex by this fierce Sport   570
Is hurry'd wild, let not such horrid Joy
E'er stain the Bosom of the BRITISH FAIR.
Far be the Spirit of the Chace from them!
Uncomely Courage, unbeseeming Skill,
To spring the Fence, to rein the prancing Steed,   575
The Cap, the Whip, the masculine Attire,
In which they roughen to the Sense, and all
The winning Softness of their Sex is lost.
In them 'tis graceful to dissolve at Woe;
With every Motion, every Word, to wave   580
Quick o'er the kindling Cheek the ready Blush;
And from the smallest Violence to shrink,
Unequal, then the loveliest in their Fears;
And by this silent Adulation, soft,
To their Protection more engaging Man.   585
O may their Eyes no miserable Sight,
Save weeping Lovers, see! a nobler Game,
Thro' Love's enchanting Wiles pursu'd, yet fled,
In Chace ambiguous. May their tender Limbs

Float in the loose Simplicity of Dress! 590
And, fashion'd all to Harmony, alone
Know they to seize the captivated Soul,
In Rapture warbled from Love-breathing Lips;
To teach the Lute to languish; with smooth Step,
Disclosing Motion in its every Charm, 595
To swim along, and swell the mazy Dance;
To train the Foliage o'er the snowy Lawn;
To guide the Pencil, turn the tuneful Page;

---

551 with fainter Murmur falls:] falls murmuring towards morn; *30q–38*
falls murmuring at Morn; *MS*
552 So gradual sinks their Mirth] *MSLytt* So their mirth gradual sinks
30q–38
554 maudlin] [foggy *del.*] *MS*
  557–64 *44–46*
  557–64 *30q–38 as follows:*

> Then, sliding sweet, they drop. O'erturn'd above
> Lies the wet, broken scene; and stretch'd below,
> Each way, the drunken slaughter; where astride (*30q, 555*)
> The lubber Power himself triumphant sits,
> Slumbrous, inclining still from side to side,
> And steeps them, silent all, in sleep till morn.

  (553) sweet] soft *MS*   O'erturn'd] Confus'd, *MS*
565–9 *44–46 not in 30q–38*
570–8 *30q–46*
570 fierce] *MSLytt* red *30q–38*
571 Is] Are *30q–45*
572 Bosom] bosoms *30q*
578+ *30q–38 as follows (not in 44–46):*

> Made up of blushes, tenderness, and fears,

  fears] Fear *MS*
579–606 *30q–46*
593 Love-breathing Lips] *MS* the radiant lip *30q–38*
598 guide] *MSLytt* play *30q–38*   the tuneful] *MS* th'instructive
30q–38

---

551 long∧ *44–45*   555 dim, *30q–45*   (*30q, 553) above, MS*   (554) wet∧
MS   (556) *lubber Power MS*   561 Slaughter: *44–46*   583 Fears∧
44–45   587 see! A *MS*   591 And∧ *30q–38*   alone, *30q–38*
593 Love∧ *46*

To lend new Flavour to the fruitful Year,
And heighten Nature's Dainties; in their Race   600
To rear their Graces into second Life;
To give Society its highest Taste;
Well-order'd Home Man's best Delight to make;
And by submissive Wisdom, modest Skill,
With every gentle Care-eluding Art,   605
To raise the Virtues, animate the Bliss,
Even charm the Pains to something more than Joy,
And sweeten all the Toils of human Life:
This be the female Dignity, and Praise.

    Ye Swains now hasten to the Hazel-Bank;   610
Where, down yon Dale, the wildly-winding Brook
Falls hoarse from Steep to Steep. In close Array,
Fit for the Thickets and the tangling Shrub,
Ye Virgins, come. For you their latest Song
The Woodlands raise; the clustering Nuts for you   615
The Lover finds amid the secret Shade;
And, where they burnish on the topmost Bough,
With active Vigour crushes down the Tree;
Or shakes them ripe from the resigning Husk,
A glossy Shower, and of an ardent Brown,   620
As are the Ringlets of Melinda's Hair:
Melinda form'd with every Grace compleat,
Yet These neglecting, above Beauty wise,
And far transcending such a vulgar Praise.

    Hence from the busy Joy-resounding Fields,   625
In chearful Error, let us tread the Maze
Of Autumn, unconfin'd; and taste, reviv'd,
The Breath of Orchard big with bending Fruit.
Obedient to the Breeze and beating Ray,
From the deep-loaded Bough a mellow Shower,   630
Incessant melts away. The juicy Pear
Lies, in a soft Profusion, scatter'd round.
A various Sweetness swells the gentle Race;
By Nature's all-refining Hand prepar'd,
Of temper'd Sun, and Water, Earth, and Air,   635
In ever-changing Composition mixt.

Such, falling frequent thro' the chiller Night,
The fragrant Stores, the wide-projected Heaps
Of Apples, which the lusty-handed Year,
Innumerous, o'er the blushing Orchard shakes.   640
A various Spirit, fresh, delicious, keen,
Dwells in their gelid Pores; and, active, points
The piercing Cyder for the thirsty Tongue:
Thy *Native* Theme, and boon Inspirer too,
PHILLIPS, *Pomona*'s Bard, the second thou   645
Who nobly durst, in Rhyme-unfetter'd Verse,
With BRITISH Freedom sing the BRITISH Song;
How, from *Silurian* Vats, high-sparkling Wines
Foam in transparent Floods; some strong, to cheer

---

599 lend] *MS* give *30q–38*
605 gentle] kinder, *30q–38*   Care-eluding] care-elusive *30q–38* [Soul-
endearing *del.* Soul-enjoying *del.*] Love-securing *MS*
606 Virtues] *MS* glory *30q–38*   Bliss] *MS* joys *30q–38*
   607 *MS 44–46 not in 30q–38*
Pains] Cares *MS*
   608–33 *30q–46*
609 Praise] Fame *MS*
615 clustering Nuts] cluster'd nut *30q–38*
617 And] *MS* Or *30q–38*
627 taste, reviv'd,] *MSLytt* vital taste *30q–38* [taste refreshd *del.*]
MSLytt
631 melts] [drops *del.*] *MSLytt*
633+ *30q–45 as follows (not in 46):*
            In species different, but in kind the same,
   634–66 *30q–46*
637–8 So fares it with those wide-projected heaps *30q–38* Such, nightly
shook, the wide-projected Heaps *MS*
645 PHILLIPS, *Pomona*'s Bard] PHILLIPS, facetious bard *30q–38* Plain
PHILLIPS, careless Bard *MS*

---

603 *best MS*   608 Life:] *MS* ~; *30q–38*   609 Dignity‸ *MS*
610 swains, *30q–38*   612 Array,] *MS* ~‸ *30p–38*   613 Thickets‸]
MS ~, *30q–45*   615 clustring *44–45*   625 busy‸] *MS* ~, *30q–*
38   627 AUTUMN *30q–38 MS*   629 breeze, *30q–45*   633 race, *30q*
633+ *Species MS*   *Kind MS*   634 Nature's] *MS* NATURE'S *30q–38*
640 shakes: *MS*   642 active‸ *46*   644 *Native] MS* native *30q–38*
645 *second MS*   647 SONG *MS*

The wintry Revels of the labouring Hind;   650
And tasteful some, to cool the Summer-Hours.

   IN this glad Season, while his sweetest Beams
The Sun sheds equal o'er the meeken'd Day;
Oh lose me in the green delightful Walks
Of, DODINGTON! thy Seat, serene and plain;   655
Where simple Nature reigns; and every View,
Diffusive, spreads the pure *Dorsetian* Downs,
In boundless Prospect, yonder shagg'd with Wood,
Here rich with Harvest, and there white with Flocks.
Mean time the Grandeur of thy lofty Dome,   660
Far-splendid, seizes on the ravish'd Eye.
New Beauties rise with each revolving Day;
New Columns swell; and still the fresh Spring finds
New Plants to quicken, and new Groves to green.
Full of thy Genius all! the Muses' Seat;   665
Where in the secret Bower, and winding Walk,
For virtuous YOUNG and Thee they twine the Bay.
Here wandering oft, fir'd with the restless Thirst
Of thy Applause, I solitary court
Th' inspiring Breeze; and meditate the Book   670
Of Nature, ever open, aiming thence,
Warm from the Heart, to learn the moral Song.
And, as I steal along the sunny Wall,
Where Autumn basks, with Fruit empurpled deep,
My pleasing Theme continual prompts my Thought: 675
Presents the downy Peach; the shining Plumb,
With a fine blueish Mist of Animals
Clouded; the ruddy Nectarine; and dark,
Beneath his ample Leaf, the luscious Fig.
The Vine too here her curling Tendrils shoots;   680
Hangs out her Clusters, glowing to the South;
And scarcely wishes for a warmer Sky.

   TURN we a Moment Fancy's rapid Flight
To vigorous Soils, and Climes of fair Extent;
Where, by the potent Sun elated high,   685
The Vineyard swells refulgent on the Day;
Spreads o'er the Vale; or up the Mountain climbs,

Profuse; and drinks amid the sunny Rocks,
From Cliff to Cliff increas'd, the heighten'd Blaze.
Low bend the weighty Boughs. The Clusters clear, 690
Half thro' the Foliage seen, or ardent flame,
Or shine transparent; while Perfection breathes
White o'er the turgent Film the living Dew.
As thus they brighten with exalted Juice,
Touch'd into Flavour by the mingling Ray; 695
The rural Youth and Virgins o'er the Field,
Each fond for each to cull th' autumnal Prime,
Exulting rove, and speak the Vintage nigh.
Then comes the crushing Swain; the Country floats,
And foams unbounded with the mashy Flood; 700
That by Degrees fermented, and refined,
Round the rais'd Nations pours the Cup of Joy:

---

652 sweetest] *MS* last, best *30q–38*
654 green delightful] green, majestic *30q–38* once-delightful *MS*
655 plain] fair *MS*
664 Plants] plans *30q*
   667–9 *44–46*
   667–9 *30q–38 as follows:*

        They twine the bay for thee. Here oft alone,
        Fir'd by the thirst of thy applause, I court

   670–713 *30q–46*
672 Warm from the Heart] Heart-taught like thine *30q–38* Heart-taught
like thee *MS*
675 My theme still urges in my vagrant thought; *30q–38* My Theme still
urges on my vagrant Thought; *MS* My urgent Theme recalls my
vagrant Thought; *MS*
676 shining] purple *30q–38*
681 glowing] *MSLytt* swelling *30q–38*
682 scarcely] [hardly *del.*] *MS*
686 swells] *MSLytt* heaves *30q–38*
690 weighty] *MS* gravid *30q–38*

---

655 serene, *30q–38*   plain! *300*   658 wood; *30q–38*   659 harvest;
30q–38   666 walk⌃ *30q–38*   671 Nature] *MS* NATURE *30q–38*   open;
30q–38   673 along⌃] *MS* ~, *30q–38*   674 AUTUMN *30q–38 MS*
deep⌃ *44–45*   675 thought; *30q–45*   683 FANCY'S *30q–38*   686 Day:
44Wks   702 Joy, *38*

The Claret smooth, red as the Lip we press,
In sparkling Fancy, while we drain the Bowl;
The mellow-tasted Burgundy; and quick,   705
As is the Wit it gives, the gay Champaign.

  Now, by the cool declining Year condens'd,
Descend the copious Exhalations, check'd
As up the middle Sky unseen they stole,
And roll the doubling Fogs around the Hill.   710
No more the Mountain, horrid, vast, sublime,
Who pours a Sweep of Rivers from his Sides,
And high between contending Kingdoms rears
The rocky long Division, fills the View
With great Variety; but in a Night   715
Of gathering Vapour, from the baffled Sense,
Sinks dark and dreary. Thence expanding far,
The huge Dusk, gradual, swallows up the Plain.
Vanish the Woods. The dim-seen River seems
Sullen, and slow, to rowl the misty Wave.   720
Even in the Height of Noon opprest, the Sun
Sheds weak, and blunt, his wide-refracted Ray;
Whence glaring oft, with many a broaden'd Orb,
He frights the Nations. Indistinct on Earth,
Seen thro' the turbid Air, beyond the Life,   725
Objects appear; and, wilder'd, o'er the Waste
The Shepherd stalks gigantic. Till at last
Wreath'd dun around, in deeper Circles still
Successive closing, sits the general Fog
Unbounded o'er the World; and, mingling thick,   730
A formless grey Confusion covers all.
As when of old (so sung the HEBREW BARD)
Light, uncollected, thro' the Chaos urg'd
Its Infant Way; nor Order yet had drawn
His lovely Train from out the dubious Gloom.   735

  THESE roving Mists, that constant now begin
To smoak along the hilly Country, These,
With weighty Rains, and melted Alpine Snows,
The Mountain-Cisterns fill, those ample Stores
Of Water, scoop'd among the hollow Rocks;   740

Whence gush the Streams, the ceaseless Fountains play,
And their unfailing Wealth the Rivers draw.

---

703 red] *MS* deep *30q–38*
706 gay] bright *30q–38*
706+ *MSLytt adds marginal note:* Here bring in the Verses on Stowe.
713 high between] deep betwixt *30q–38*   rears] lays *30q–38*
  714–15 *MSLytt 44–46*
714 View] *MSLytt* [Eye *del.*] *MSLytt*
715 great] Grand *MSLytt*
  714–15 *30q–38 as follows:*

> The rocky, long division; while aloft,
> His piny top is, lessening, lost in air:
> No more his thousand prospects fill the view
> With great variety; but in a night   *(30q, 705)*

  (702–3) while aloft, . . . lost in air] *MSLytt as follows:*

> [views the Realms *del.*] [views, beneath,
> Their ample Circuit from his piny Top
> Or stands the awfull Object of their Gaze *all del.*]

  716 *30q–46*
  717 *MSLytt 44–46*
dark and dreary] *MSLytt* [undistinguished *del.*] *MSLytt* far]
MSLytt [wide *del.* broad *del.*] *MSLytt*
  717 *30q–38 as follows:*

> Sink dark, and total. Nor alone immerst;

  718–42 *30q–46*
728 dun] close *30q–38*
729 closing] floating *30q–38* gathering *MS*
735 His lovely Train from out] His endless train forth from *30q–38*
738 weighty] mighty *30q–38*   and melted Alpine Snows] *MS* the
skill'd in nature say *30q–38* some Skill'd in Nature say *MS* [and Alpine
Loads of Snow *del.*] *MS*
739 ample Stores] *MS* grand reserves *30q–38*
740 Rocks] *MS* Rock *44Wks*
742 Wealth] stores *30q–38 MS*

---

707 Now‸ *30q–38*   cool, *30q–38*   712 sides; *30q–38*   717 dreary.
Thence] *MSLytt* ∼; thence *MSLytt*   722 wide‸ *46*   723 oft,] *MS*
∼‸ *30q–38*   Orb,] *MS* ∼‸ *30q–38*   726 waste, *30p–38*   730 and‸
30q–38   731 formless, *30q–38*   732 bard *30q–38*   740 Water‸
MS

Some Sages say, that, where the numerous Wave
For ever lashes the resounding Shore,
Drill'd thro' the sandy *Stratum*, every Way,   745
The Waters with the sandy *Stratum* rise;
Amid whose Angles infinitely strain'd,
They joyful leave their jaggy Salts behind,
And clear and sweeten, as they soak along.
Nor stops the restless Fluid, mounting still,   750
Tho' oft amidst th' irriguous Vale it springs;
But to the Mountain courted by the Sand,
That leads it darkling on in faithful Maze,
Far from the Parent-Main, it boils again
Fresh into Day; and all the glittering Hill   755
Is bright with spouting Rills. But hence this vain
Amusive Dream! Why should the Waters love
To take so far a Journey to the Hills,
When the sweet Valleys offer to their Toil
Inviting Quiet, and a nearer Bed?   760
Or if, by blind Ambition led astray,
They must aspire; why should they sudden stop
Among the broken Mountain's rushy Dells,
And, ere they gain its highest Peak, desert

---

742 + *30q–38 as follows (not in 44–46):*

> But is this equal to the vast effect?
> Is thus the VOLGA fill'd? the rapid RHINE?
> The broad EUPHRATES? all th' unnumber'd floods,   (*30q*, 735)
> That large refresh the fair-divided earth;
> And, in the rage of summer, never cease
> To send a thundering torrent to the main?
>
> WHAT tho' the sun draws from the steaming deep
> More than the rivers pour? How much again,   (*30q*, 740)
> O'er the vext surge, in bitter-driving showers,
> Frequent returns, let the wet sailor say:
> And on the thirsty down, far from the burst
> Of springs, how much, to their reviving fields,
> And feeding flocks, let lonely shepherds sing.   (*30q*, 745)
> But sure 'tis no weak, variable cause,
> That keeps at once ten thousand thousand floods,
> Wide-wandering o'er the world, so fresh, and clear,
> For ever flowing, and for ever full.

(738) a thundering torrent] their [chrystal *del.*] ample Tribute
MSLytt
(746) But sure 'tis no weak,] ['Tis, sure, no weak, nor *del.*]
MSLytt   But] [For *del.*] *MS*
743 *44–46*
743 *MS as follows:*

> Some Sages doubt: they [scarce can This believe *del.*]
>   scarcely This can deem
> A Cause sufficient for the vast Effect;
> And thus, amusive, search another Source
> Amid the secret [Caverns *del.*] Chambers of the Globe.
> They teach, that, where th'innumerable Wave,

743 *30q–38 as follows:*

> And thus some sages, deep-exploring, teach: (*30q*, 750)
>   That, where the hoarse, innumerable wave,

744–55 *30q–46*
744 For ever] Eternal, *30q–38*
745 Drill'd] Suck'd *30q–38*
748 They leave each saline particle behind, *30q–38* They joyful leave
their drossy Salts behind, *MS*
750 mounting still,] rising still; *MS*
751 Tho' here and there in lowly plains it springs, *30q–38 del. MS* Tho'
oft amid th' irriguous Vale it springs; *44–45*
756–72 *44–46*
756–72 *30q–38 as follows:*

> Is bright with spouting rills. The vital stream
> Hence, in its subterranean passage, gains,   (*30q*, 765)
> From the wash'd mineral, that restoring power,
> And salutary virtue, which anew
> Strings every nerve, calls up the kindling soul
> Into the healthful cheek, and joyous eye:
> And whence, the royal maid, AMELIA blooms   (*30q*, 770)
> With new-flush'd graces; yet reserv'd to bless,
> Beyond a crown, some happy prince; and shine,
> In all her mother's matchless virtues drest,
> The CAROLINA of another land.

(768) calls up] and calls *MS*
(770–4) *del. MS*

---

744 Shore, *MS*] ~; *30q–38*   749 clear, *30q–38*   757 why *44–46*
(*30q*, 769) Eye. *MS*

Th' attractive Sand that charm'd their Course so long?   765
Besides, the hard agglomerating Salts
The Spoil of Ages, would impervious choak
Their secret Channels; or, by slow Degrees,
High as the Hills protrude the swelling Vales:
Old Ocean too, suck'd thro' the porous Globe,   770
Had long ere now forsook his horrid Bed,
And brought *Deucalion's* watry Times again.

    SAY then, where lurk the vast eternal Springs,
That, like CREATING NATURE, lie conceal'd
From mortal Eye, yet with their lavish Stores   775
Refresh the Globe, and all its joyous Tribes?
O thou pervading *Genius*, given to Man,
To trace the Secrets of the dark Abyss,
O lay the Mountains bare! and wide display
Their hidden Structure to th' astonish'd View!   780
Strip from the branching *Alps* their piny Load,
The huge Incumbrance of horrific Woods
From *Asian Taurus*, from *Imaüs* stretch'd
Athwart the roving *Tartar's* sullen Bounds!
Give opening *Hemus* to my searching Eye,   785
And high **Olympus* pouring many a Stream!
O from the sounding Summits of the North,
The *Dofrine Hills*, thro' *Scandinavia* roll'd
To farthest *Lapland* and the frozen Main;
From lofty *Caucasus*, far-seen by Those   790
Who in the *Caspian* and black *Euxine* toil;
From cold *Riphean Rocks*, which the wild *Russ*
Believes the †*stony Girdle* of the World;
And all the dreadful Mountains, wrapt in Storm,
Whence wide *Siberia* draws her lonely Floods;   795
O sweep th' eternal Snows! Hung o'er the Deep,
That ever works beneath his sounding Base,
Bid *Atlas*, propping Heaven, as Poets feign,
His subterranean Wonders spread! unveil
The miny Caverns, blazing on the Day,   800

---

*The Mountain called by that Name in the lesser Asia.
    †*The* Moscovites *call the* Riphean *Mountains* Weliki Camenypoys, *that is*, the
great stony Girdle; *because they suppose them to encompass the whole Earth.*

Of *Abyssinia's* Cloud-compelling Cliffs,
And of the bending **Mountains of the Moon*!
O'ertopping all these Giant-Sons of Earth,
Let the dire *Andes*, from the radiant Line
Stretch'd to the stormy Seas that thunder round   805
The southern Pole, their hideous Deeps unfold!
Amazing Scene! Behold! the Glooms disclose.
I see the Rivers in their infant Beds!
Deep deep I hear them, lab'ring to get free!
I see the leaning *Strata*, artful rang'd;   810
The gaping Fissures to receive the Rains,
The melting Snows, and ever-dripping Fogs.
Strow'd bibulous above I see the Sands,
The pebbly Gravel next, the Layers then
Of mingled Moulds, of more retentive Earths,   815
The guttur'd Rocks and mazy-running Clefts;
That, while the stealing Moisture they transmit,
Retard its Motion, and forbid its Waste.
Beneath th' incessant weeping of these Drains,
I see the rocky Siphons stretch'd immense,   820
The mighty Reservoirs, of harden'd Chalk,
Or stiff compacted Clay, capacious form'd.
O'erflowing thence, the congregated Stores,
The crystal Treasures of the liquid World,
Thro' the stirr'd Sands a bubbling Passage burst;   825
And welling out, around the middle Steep,
Or from the Bottoms of the bosom'd Hills,
In pure Effusion flow. United, thus,
Th' exhaling Sun, the Vapour-burden'd Air,
The gelid Mountains, that to Rain condens'd   830
These Vapours in continual Current draw,
And send them, o'er the fair-divided Earth,
In bounteous Rivers to the Deep again,
A social Commerce hold, and firm support
The full-adjusted Harmony of Things.   835

*A Range of Mountains in Africa, *that surround almost all* Monomotapa.

773–835 *44–46   not in 30q–38*

---

807 disclose, *46*

WHEN Autumn scatters his departing Gleams,
Warn'd of approaching Winter, gather'd, play
The Swallow-People; and toss'd wide around,
O'er the calm Sky, in Convolution swift,
The feather'd Eddy floats: rejoicing once,   840
Ere to their wintry Slumbers they retire;
In Clusters clung, beneath the mouldring Bank,
And where, unpierc'd by Frost, the Cavern sweats.
Or rather into warmer Climes convey'd,
With other kindred Birds of Season, there   845
They twitter chearful, till the vernal Months
Invite them welcome back: for, thronging, now
Innumerous Wings are in Commotion all.

WHERE the *Rhine* loses his majestic Force
In *Belgian* Plains, won from the raging Deep,   850
By Diligence amazing, and the strong
Unconquerable Hand of Liberty,
The Stork-Assembly meets; for many a Day,
Consulting deep, and various, ere they take
Their arduous Voyage thro' the liquid Sky.   855
And now their Rout design'd, their Leaders chose,
Their Tribes adjusted, clean'd their vigorous Wings;
And many a Circle, many a short Essay,
Wheel'd round and round, in Congregation full,
The figur'd Flight ascends; and, riding high   860
Th' aërial Billows, mixes with the Clouds.

OR where the *Northern* Ocean, in vast Whirls,
Boils round the naked melancholy Isles
Of farthest *Thulè*, and th' *Atlantic* Surge
Pours in among the stormy *Hebrides*;   865
Who can recount what Transmigrations there
Are annual made? What Nations come and go?
And how the living Clouds on Clouds arise?
Infinite Wings! till all the Plume-dark Air,
And rude resounding Shore are one wild Cry.   870

HERE the plain harmless Native his small Flock,
And Herd diminutive of many Hues,

Tends on the little Island's verdant Swell,
The Shepherd's sea-girt Reign; or, to the Rocks
Dire-clinging, gathers his ovarious Food;   875
Or sweeps the fishy Shore; or treasures up
The Plumage, rising full, to form the Bed
Of Luxury. And here a while the Muse,
High-hovering o'er the broad cerulean Scene,
Sees CALEDONIA, in romantic View: 880
Her airy Mountains, from the waving Main,
Invested with a keen diffusive Sky,
Breathing the Soul acute; her Forests huge,
Incult, robust, and tall, by Nature's Hand
Planted of old; her azure Lakes between,   885
Pour'd out extensive, and of watry Wealth
Full; winding deep, and green, her fertile Vales;
With many a cool translucent brimming Flood
Wash'd lovely, from the *Tweed* (pure *Parent-Stream*,
Whose pastoral Banks first heard my *Doric* Reed,   890
With, silvan *Jed*, thy tributary Brook)
To where the North-inflated Tempest foams

pastoral [margin annotation]

836–61 *30q–46*
836 WHEN] WHILE *30q–38*
839–40 *MS* [O'er the calm Sky, the feather'd Eddy floats,
      In rapid Convolution. Thus they joy *all del.*] *MS*

843 And where the cavern sweats, as sages dream. *30q–38*
846 vernal] vernant *30q*
855 arduous] *MSLytt* plumy *30q–38*
  862–909 *30q–46*
870 rude] white *30q–38*
881 waving] gelid *30q–38*
890–1 *not in 30q–38*
890 heard] wak'd *44–45*

---

836 AUTUMN *30q–38*   840 floats: rejoicing] *MS* ~. Rejoycing *30q–38*
842 mouldering *30q–30o*   843a dream: *MS*   847 back; *44Wks*
850 Deep,] *MS* ~ₐ *30q–38*   851 strong ₐ] *MS* ~, *30q–38*   852 LIBERTY
30q–38   858 Essay,] *MS* ~ₐ *30q–38*   862 Ocean,] *MS* ~ₐ *38*
863 naked ₐ] *MS* ~, *30q–38*   864 the *Atlantic 44Wks*   867 what *30q*
871 plain ₐ] *MS* ~, *30q–38*   882 keen ₐ] *MS* ~, *30q–38*   884 NATURE'S
30q–38   888 cool ₐ translucent ₐ] *MS* ~, ~, *30q–38*   889 TWEED,
pure *30q–38*   *Parent-Stream,*] *MS* parent-stream, *30q–38*

O'er *Orca*'s or *Betubium*'s highest Peak.
Nurse of a People, in Misfortune's School
Train'd up to hardy Deeds; soon visited   895
By *Learning*, when before the *Gothic* Rage
She took her western Flight. A manly Race,
Of unsubmitting Spirit, wise, and brave,
Who still thro' bleeding Ages struggled hard,
(As well unhappy WALLACE can attest,   900
Great Patriot-Heroe! ill-requited Chief!)
To hold a generous undiminish'd State;
Too much in vain! Hence of unequal Bounds
Impatient, and by tempting Glory borne
O'er every Land, for every Land their Life   905
Has flow'd profuse, their piercing Genius plan'd,
And swell'd the Pomp of Peace their faithful Toil,
As from their own clear North, in radiant Streams,
Bright over *Europe* bursts the *Boreal Morn*.

OH is there not some Patriot, in whose Power   910
That best, that godlike Luxury is plac'd,
Of blessing Thousands, Thousands yet unborn,
Thro' late Posterity? some, large of Soul,
To chear dejected Industry? to give
A double Harvest to the pining Swain?   915
And teach the labouring Hand the Sweets of Toil?
How, by the finest Art, the native Robe
To weave; how, white as Hyperborean Snow,
To form the lucid Lawn; with venturous Oar,
How to dash wide the Billow; nor look on,   920
Shamefully passive, while *Batavian* Fleets
Defraud us of the glittering finny Swarms,
That heave our Friths, and croud upon our Shores;
How all-enlivening Trade to rouse, and wing
The prosperous Sail, from every growing Port,   925
Uninjur'd, round the sea-incircled Globe;
And thus, in Soul united as in Name,
Bid BRITAIN reign the Mistress of the Deep.

YES, there are such. And full on thee, ARGYLE,
Her Hope, her Stay, her Darling, and her Boast,   930
From her first Patriots and her Heroes sprung,

Thy fond imploring Country turns her Eye;
In thee, with all a Mother's Triumph, sees
Her every Virtue every Grace combin'd,
Her Genius, Wisdom, her engaging Turn,   935
Her Pride of Honour, and her Courage try'd,
Calm, and intrepid, in the very Throat
Of sulphurous War, on *Tenier*'s dreadful Field.
Nor less the Palm of Peace inwreathes thy Brow:

---

893 *Orca's* or] ORCA, or *30q–38 Orca's* and *MS*
897 manly] generous *30q–38*
900–1 *not in 30q–38*
902 generous] hapless, *30q–38* free and *MS*
903 unequal] ignoble *30q–38*
   862–909 *Cf. the following in Su.27 (not in later editions of Su.):*

      AND should I northward turn my filial Eye,
      Beyond the *Tweed*, pure Parent-Stream! to where
      The hyperborean Ocean, furious, foams   (*Su.27*, 560)
      O'er *Orca*, or *Betubium*'s highest Peak,
      Rapt, I might sing thy *Caledonian* Sons,
      A gallant, warlike, unsubmitting Race!
      Nor less in *Learning* vers'd, *soon* as He took
      Before the Gothic Rage his Western Flight;   (565)
      Wise in the Council, at the Banquet gay:
      The Pride of Honour burning in their Breasts,
      And Glory, not to their own Realms confin'd,
      But into foreign Countries shooting far,
      As over *Europe* bursts the *Boreal Morn*.   (570)
   910–37 *30q–46*
921 passive] careless *MSLytt*
926 Uninjur'd] *MSLytt* Unchalleng'd *30q–38*
927–8   And thus united BRITAIN BRITAIN make
        Intire, th' imperial MISTRESS of the deep.   *30q 30p*
929 *MS adds the following footnote:* [The late Duke of Argyle *del.* John
Duke of Argyle and Greenwich, who died *del.*]
935 engaging] politest *30q–38*
   938–9 *44–46*
939 *MS* [Mix'd with thy Laurels the deep Olive twines: *del.*] *MS*

---

897 Race,] *MS* ~ₐ *30p–38*   898 brave; *MS*   907 Toil. *30q–46*
911 best ₐ *46*   913 soul! *30q–38*   922 glittering, *30q–38*   927 *Soul*
MS   *Name MS*   931 patriots, *30q–38*   932 fond, *30q–38* eye:
30q–45   934 virtue, *30q–45*   938 Field.] *MS* ~, *30q–38*

For, powerful as thy Sword, from thy rich Tongue   940
Persuasion flows, and wins the high Debate;
While mix'd in thee combine the Charm of Youth,
The Force of Manhood, and the Depth of Age.
Thee, FORBES, too, whom every Worth attends,
As Truth sincere, as weeping Friendship kind,   945
Thee, truly generous, and in Silence great,
Thy Country feels thro' her reviving Arts,
Plan'd by thy Wisdom, by thy Soul inform'd;
And seldom has she felt a Friend like thee.

    BUT see the fading many-colour'd Woods,   950
Shade deepening over Shade, the Country round
Imbrown; a crouded Umbrage, dusk, and dun,
Of every Hue, from wan declining Green
To sooty Dark. These now the lonesome Muse,
Low-whispering, lead into their leaf-strown Walks,   955
And give the Season in its latest View.

    MEAN-TIME, light-shadowing all, a sober Calm
Fleeces unbounded Ether; whose least Wave
Stands tremulous, uncertain where to turn
The gentle Current: while illumin'd wide,   960
The dewy-skirted Clouds imbibe the Sun,
And thro' their lucid Veil his soften'd Force
Shed o'er the peaceful World. Then is the Time,
For Those whom Wisdom and whom Nature charm,
To steal themselves from the degenerate Croud,   965
And soar above this little Scene of Things;
To tread low-thoughted Vice beneath their Feet;

938–9 *30q–38 as follows:*
        Of sulphurous war, on TENIER's dreadful field,
        While thick around the deadly tempest flew.
        And when the trumpet, kindling war no more,   (*30q, 875*)
        Pours not the flaming squadrons o'er the field;
        But, fruitful of fair deeds, and mutual faith,
        Kind peace unites the jarring world again;
        Let the deep olive thro' thy laurels twine.

  (874–9) *del. MS*

940–9 *30q–46*
949 a Friend] *MS* the friend *30q–38*
A description of autumnal melancholy corresponding in part to OET Au.
950–1036, 1082–102 *first appeared in Wi.26f–28. The 26f text of the*
complete passage is reprinted in Appendix A, Winter 17–111. Later
variants are recorded in the apparatus to Au. below.
950–63 *Au.30q–46*
962 *MS* And thro' their uvid pores his temper'd force *30q–38*   their]
MS [the *del.*] *MS*
950–63 *Wi.26f–28 as follows:*

> Thee too, Inspirer of the toiling Swain!
> Fair Autumn, yellow rob'd! I'll sing of thee,
> Of thy last, temper'd, Days, and sunny Calms;
> When all the golden *Hours* are on the Wing,   *(26f, 20)*
> Attending thy Retreat, and round thy Wain,
> Slow-rolling, onward to the Southern Sky.
>
> Behold! the well-pois'd *Hornet*, hovering, hangs,
> With quivering Pinions, in the genial Blaze;
> Flys off, in airy Circles: then returns,   *(26f, 25)*
> And hums, and dances to the beating Ray.
> Nor shall the Man, that, musing, walks alone,
> And, heedless, strays within his radiant Lists,
> Go unchastis'd away.—Sometimes, a Fleece
> Of Clouds, wide-scattering, with a lucid Veil,   *(26f, 30)*
> Soft, shadow o'er th' unruffled Face of Heaven;
> And, thro' their dewy Sluices, shed the Sun,
> With temper'd Influence down. Then is the Time,

(19) temper'd] equal *260 28*   sunny] clouded *260 28*
(23) Behold!] Mark, how *260 28*   (27) that] who *28*
(31) Soft] Light *260 28*

———

(*30q*, 875) Trumpet,] *MS* ~ʌ *38*   (877) Deedsʌ] *MS* ~, *30q–38*
941 Debate;] *MS* ~: *30q–38*   950 fading, *30q 30p*   953 wanʌ] *MS*
~, *30q–38*   956 Season *30q–38*   (*26f*, 19) lastʌ *28*   (19a) equalʌ
28   (22) rollingʌ *28*   (23) *Hornet*ʌ hovering, *260* Hornetʌ ~ʌ *28*
(25) offʌ *28*   Circles, *28*   (26) Ray; *260* ~: *28*   (27) Manʌ *28*
musingʌ *28*   (27a) whoʌ *28*   (28) Andʌ heedlessʌ *28*   (29) away
— *260* ~. *28*   Sometimesʌ *260 28*   (30) Cloudsʌ *28*   (31a) Lightʌ
28   (32) Andʌ *260 28*   Sluicesʌ *28*   (33) Timeʌ *260 28*   964 those,
Wi.26f–260   Wisdom,ʌ] *MS* Wisdom, *Wi.26f–28* Wisdom, *Au.30q–38*
966 *little Wi.26f 260*   Things: *Wi.26f 260*   967 *Vice Wi.26f–28*   Feet:
Wi.26f 260

To soothe the throbbing Passions into Peace;
And wooe lone *Quiet* in her silent Walks.

THUS solitary, and in pensive Guise,   970
Oft let me wander o'er the russet Mead,
And thro' the sadden'd Grove, where scarce is heard
One dying Strain, to chear the Woodman's Toil.
Haply some widow'd Songster pours his Plaint,
Far, in faint Warblings, thro' the tawny Copse.   975
While congregated Thrushes, Linnets, Larks,
And each wild Throat, whose artless Strains so late
Swell'd all the Music of the swarming Shades,
Robb'd of their tuneful Souls, now shivering sit
On the dead Tree, a dull-despondent Flock!   980
With not a Brightness waving o'er their Plumes,
And Nought save chattering Discord in their Note.
O let not, aim'd from some inhuman Eye,
The Gun the Music of the coming Year
Destroy; and harmless, unsuspecting Harm,   985
Lay the weak Tribes, a miserable Prey,
In mingled Murder, fluttering on the Ground!

THE pale descending Year, yet pleasing still,
A gentler Mood inspires; for now the Leaf
Incessant rustles from the mournful Grove,   990
Oft startling such as, studious, walk below,
And slowly circles thro' the waving Air.
But should a quicker Breeze amid the Boughs
Sob, o'er the Sky the leafy Deluge streams;
Till choak'd, and matted with the dreary Shower,   995
The Forest-Walks, at every rising Gale,
Roll wide the wither'd Waste, and whistle bleak.
Fled is the blasted Verdure of the Fields;
And, shrunk into their Beds, the flowery Race
Their sunny Robes resign. Even what remain'd   1000
Of bolder Fruits falls from the naked Tree;
And Woods, Fields, Gardens, Orchards, all around
The desolated Prospect thrills the Soul.

964-74 *Wi.26f-28 Au.3oq-46*
968 To lay their Passions in a gentle Calm, *26f*
970 THUS] Now, *26f-28*
972 And] Or *26f-28*   sadden'd] pining *26f-28*
974 Sad *Philomel*, perchance, pours forth her Plaint, *26f*
  975-1003 *Au.3oq-46*
982 save chattering] but joyless *MSLytt*
991 startling] *MS* starting *3oq-38*
994 Deluge] ruin *3oq-38*
1001 Fruits] fruit *3oq*
  975-1003 *Wi.26f-28 as follows:*

> Far, thro' the withering Copse. Mean while, the Leaves, (*26f*, 45)
> That, late, the Forest clad with lively Green,
> Nipt by the drizzly Night, and Sallow-hu'd,
> Fall, wavering, thro' the Air; or shower amain,
> Urg'd by the Breeze, that sobs amid the Boughs.
> Then list'ning *Hares* forsake the rusling Woods,   (*26f*, 50)
> And, starting at the frequent Noise, escape
> To the rough Stubble, and the rushy Fen.
> Then *Woodcocks*, o'er the fluctuating Main,
> That glimmers to the Glimpses of the Moon,
> Stretch their long Voyage to the woodland Glade: (*26f*, 55)
> Where, wheeling with uncertain Flight, they mock
> The nimble *Fowler*'s Aim.—Now *Nature* droops;
> Languish the living Herbs, with pale Decay:
> And all the *various Family* of Flowers
> Their sunny Robes resign. The falling Fruits,   (*26f*, 60)
> Thro' the still Night, forsake the Parent-Bough,
> That, in the first, grey, Glances of the Dawn,
> Looks wild, and wonders at the wintry Waste.

(47) drizzly] grizzly *28*
(54) That] Which *28*

---

968 Peace, *Wi.260*   969 *Quiet, Wi.26f 260* ~ₐ *Wi.28 Au.3oq-38*   *Walks*
Wi.26f 260   970a Nowₐ *Wi.28*   971 Oft, *Wi.26f*   972 Grove;
Wi.26f-28 Au.3oq   973 *Woodman's Wi.26f-28*   974 Haply, *Wi.260*
Plaint,] *MS* ~ₐ *Au.3oq-38*   979 Souls,] *MS* ~ₐ *38*   980 dull-] *MS*
~, *3oq-38* ~ₐ *44-46*   986 Prey,] *MS* ~! *3oq-38*   987 Ground!] *MS*
~. *3oq-38*   988 paleₐ] *MS* ~, *3oq-38*   989 Leaf, *MS*   990 In-
cessant, *MS*   Grove. *46*   (*26f*, 45) Mean whileₐ *260 28*   (46) Thatₐ
lateₐ *28*   (48) Fallₐ wavfeatngₐ *260 28*   (49) Breezeₐ *28*   (51) Andₐ
28   Noiseₐ *28*   (53) Woodcocksₐ *28* Main; *28*   (55) Glade; *28*
(57) Fowler's *28*   (58) Herbsₐ *28*   Decay; *28*   (62) Thatₐ *28*   firstₐ
greyₐ *28*   Dawnₐ *28*

HE comes! he comes! in every Breeze the POWER
Of PHILOSOPHIC MELANCHOLY comes!   1005
His near Approach the sudden-starting Tear,
The glowing Cheek, the mild dejected Air,
The soften'd Feature, and the beating Heart,
Pierc'd deep with many a virtuous Pang, declare.
O'er all the Soul his sacred Influence breathes;   1010
Inflames Imagination; thro' the Breast
Infuses every Tenderness; and far
Beyond dim Earth exalts the swelling Thought.
Ten thousand thousand fleet Ideas, such
As never mingled with the vulgar Dream,   1015
Croud fast into the Mind's creative Eye.
As fast the correspondent Passions rise,
As varied, and as high: Devotion rais'd
To Rapture, and divine Astonishment;
The Love of Nature unconfin'd, and, chief,   1020
Of human Race; the large ambitious Wish,
To make them blest; the Sigh for suffering Worth,
Lost in Obscurity; the noble Scorn,
Of Tyrant-Pride; the fearless great Resolve;
The Wonder which the dying Patriot draws,   1025
Inspiring Glory thro' remotest Time;
Th' awaken'd Throb for Virtue, and for Fame;
The Sympathies of Love, and Friendship dear;
With all the *social Offspring of the Heart.*

OH bear me then to vast embowering Shades!   1030
To twilight Groves, and visionary Vales!
To weeping Grottoes, and prophetic Glooms!
Where Angel-Forms athwart the solemn Dusk,
Tremendous sweep, or seem to sweep along;
And Voices more than human, thro' the Void   1035
Deep-sounding, seize th' enthusiastic Ear.

1004–13 *Au.30q–46*
1009 virtuous] *MS* secret *30q–38*
1010+ In all the bosom triumphs, all the nerves; *30q–38 del. MS
not in 44–46*

1011 Breast] *MS* sense *30q–38*
    1004–13 *Wi.26f–28 as follows:*

> THE *Year*, yet pleasing, but declining fast,
> Soft, o'er the secret Soul, in gentle Gales,   (*26f*, 65)
> A Philosophic Melancholly breathes,
> And bears the swelling Thought aloft to Heaven.

1014–29 *Au.30q–46*
1015 vulgar] *MS* Vulgar's *30q–38*
1021 human Race] *MS* humankind *30q–38*
1023–4 the noble Scorn,/Of Tyrant-Pride] th' indignant scorn/Of mighty pride *30q–38* the [virtuous *del.*] poignant Scorn,/The [strong *del.*] sweet Disdain, mix'd with sublime Humility,/Of [worldly *del.*] tyrant Pride *MS*
1025 which] *MS* that *30q–38*
1027 awaken'd Throb] *MS* arrousing pant *30q–38*
    1014–29 *Wi.26f–28 as follows:*

> Then forming *Fancy* rouses to conceive,
> What never mingled with the Vulgar's Dream:
> Then wake the tender *Pang*, the pitying *Tear*,   (*26f*, 70)
> The *Sigh* for suffering Worth, the *Wish* prefer'd
> For Humankind, the *Joy* to see them bless'd,
> And all the *Social Off-spring* of the Heart!

1030–2 *Wi.26f–28 Au.30q–46*
1030 vast] high, *26f–28*
1032 prophetic Glooms] to hoary Caves *26f*
    1033–6 *Au.30q–46*
    1033–6 *Wi.26f–28 as follows:*

> Where Angel-Forms are seen, and Voices heard,   (*26f*, 77)
> Sigh'd in low Whispers, that abstract the Soul,
> From outward Sense, far into Worlds remote.

    (78) that] which *28*
1036+ *MS as follows (indicating that the verses on Stowe are to be taken in; cf.* 706+):
> Or is this Gloom too much? Then &c.
> —— thy veteran Skill.

(*26f*, 64) Year∧ *28*   (65) Soft∧ *28*   Soul∧ *28*   1018 high; *300*
1019 Astonishment;] *MS* ~. *30q–38*   1020 and∧ chief∧ *30q–38*   1021 large∧
MS ~, *30q–38*   1024 fearless∧] *MS* ~, *30q–38*   1029 social offspring
of the heart. *30q–38*   (*26f*, 69) *Vulgar's 260*   Dream. *28*   1030 vast∧]
MS ~, *Au.30q–38*   embowering, *Wi.26f*   (*26f*, 78) Soul∧ *28*

Or is this Gloom too much? Then lead, ye Powers,
That o'er the Garden and the rural Seat
Preside, which shining thro' the chearful Land
In countless Numbers blest BRITANNIA sees;   1040
O lead me to the wide-extended Walks,
The fair Majestic Paradise of STOWE!
Not *Persian Cyrus* on *Iönia's* Shore,
E'er saw such silvan Scenes; such various Art
By Genius fir'd, such ardent Genius tam'd   1045
By cool judicious Art; that, in the strife,
All-beauteous Nature fears to be outdone.
And there, O PIT, thy Country's early Boast,
There let me sit beneath the shelter'd Slopes,
Or in that *Temple where, in future Times,   1050
Thou well shalt merit a distinguish'd Name;
And, with thy Converse blest, catch the last Smiles
Of Autumn beaming o'er the yellow Woods.
While there with Thee th' inchanted Round I walk,
The regulated Wild, gay Fancy then   1055
Will tread in Thought the Groves of *Attic Land*;
Will from thy standard Taste refine her own,
Correct her Pencil to the purest Truth
Of Nature, or, the unimpassion'd Shades
Forsaking, raise it to the human Mind.   1060
O if hereafter she, with *juster* Hand,
Shall draw the Tragic Scene, instruct Her thou,
To mark the vary'd Movements of the Heart,
What every decent Character requires,
And every Passion speaks: O thro' her Strain   1065
Breathe thy pathetic Eloquence! that moulds
Th' attentive Senate, charms, persuades, exalts,
Of honest Zeal th' indignant Lightning throws,
And shakes Corruption on her venal Throne.
While thus we talk, and thro' *Elysian Vales*   1070
Delighted rove, perhaps a Sigh escapes:
What pity, COBHAM, thou thy verdant Files
Of order'd Trees shouldst here inglorious range,
Instead of Squadrons flaming o'er the Field,

The Temple of Virtue in Stowe-Gardens.

And long-embattled Hosts! when the proud Foe   1075
The faithless vain Disturber of Mankind,
Insulting *Gaul*, has rous'd the World to War;
When keen, once more, within their Bounds to press
Those polish'd Robbers, those ambitious Slaves,
The BRITISH YOUTH would hail thy wise Command,   1080
Thy temper'd Ardor and thy veteran Skill.

THE Western Sun withdraws the shorten'd Day;
And humid Evening, gliding o'er the Sky,
In her chill Progress, to the Ground condens'd
The Vapours throws. Where creeping Waters ooze,   1085

1037–81 *44–46   not in 30q–38*
1082 *MS 44–46*
1082 *30q–38 as follows:*

   AND now the western sun withdraws the day;
 AND] But *MS*
1083–90 *30q–46*
1085 Th' ascending vapour throws. Where waters ooze, *30q–38* [Throws
the damp Vapour where still Waters ooze *del.*] The [Vapour throws
del.] Vapours throw. Where creeping Waters ooze, *MS*
 1082–90 *Wi.26f–28 as follows:*

  Now, when the Western Sun withdraws the Day,   (*26f, 80*)
  And humid *Evening*, gliding o'er the Sky,
  In her chill Progress, checks the straggling Beams,
  And robs them of their gather'd, vapoury, Prey,
  Where Marshes stagnate, and where Rivers wind,
  Cluster the rolling *Fogs*, and swim along   (*26f, 85*)
  The dusky-mantled Lawn: then slow descend,
  Once more to mingle with their *Watry Friends*.
  The vivid Stars shine out, in radiant Files;
  And boundless *Ether* glows, till the fair Moon
  Shows her broad Visage, in the crimson'd East;   (*26f, 90*)

 (83) And their moist *Captives* frees; where waters ooze, *260 28*
 (88) radiant] brightening *260 28*

1043 *Cyrus, 44–45* 1075 When *44–46* 1088 moon, *30q* (*26f, 80*) Now˄
28 (81) Sky˄ *28*   (83a) Captives *28*   (85) Fogs *28*   (86) Lawn;
28   (87) Watry Friends *28*   (89) glows; *28*

Where Marshes stagnate, and where Rivers wind,
Cluster the rolling Fogs, and swim along
The dusky-mantled Lawn. Mean-while the Moon
Full-orb'd, and breaking thro' the scatter'd Clouds,
Shews her broad Visage in the crimson'd East.   1090
Turn'd to the Sun direct, her spotted Disk,
Where Mountains rise, umbrageous Dales descend,
And Caverns deep, as optic Tube descries,
A smaller Earth, gives all his Blaze again,
Void of its Flame, and sheds a softer Day.   1095
Now thro' the passing Cloud she seems to stoop,
Now up the pure Cerulean rides sublime.
Wide the pale Deluge floats, and streaming mild
O'er the sky'd Mountain to the shadowy Vale,
While Rocks and Floods reflect the quivering Gleam,   1100
The whole Air whitens with a boundless Tide
Of silver Radiance, trembling round the World.

     BUT when half-blotted from the Sky her Light,
Fainting, permits the starry Fires to burn,
With keener Luster thro' the Depth of Heaven;   1105
Or quite extinct her deaden'd Orb appears,
And scarce appears, of sickly beamless White;
Oft in this Season, silent from the North
A Blaze of Meteors shoots: ensweeping first
The lower Skies, they all at once converge   1110
High to the Crown of Heaven, and all at once
Relapsing quick as quickly reascend,

1091–5 Au.30q–46   not in Wi.26f–28
1093 And Caverns deep] And oceans roll 30q–45
1094 smaller] lesser 30q–38   his] its 44Wks
  1096–1102 Au.30q–46
  1096–1102 Wi.26f–28 as follows:

        Now, stooping, seems to kiss the passing Cloud:
        Now, o'er the pure *Cerulean*, rides sublime.
        Wide the pale Deluge floats, with silver Waves,
        O'er the sky'd Mountain, to the low-laid Vale;
        From the white Rocks, with dim Reflexion, gleams, (26f, 95)
        And faintly glitters thro' its waving Shades.

ALL Night, abundant Dews, unnoted, fall,
And, at Return of Morning, silver o'er
The Face of Mother-Earth; from every Branch
Depending, tremble the translucent Gems,   (*26f*, 100)
And, quivering, seem to fall away, yet cling,
And sparkle in the Sun, whose rising Eye,
With Fogs bedim'd, portends a beauteous Day.

Now, giddy Youth, whom headlong Passions fire,
Rouse the wild Game, and stain the guiltless Grove,
With Violence, and Death; yet call it Sport,   (*26f*, 106)
To scatter Ruin thro' the Realms of *Love*,
And *Peace*, that thinks no Ill: But These, the *Muse*,
Whose Charity, unlimited, extends
As wide as *Nature* works, disdains to sing,   (*26f*, 110)
Returning to her nobler Theme in view—

(98) That, lighted by the *Morning's* Ray, impearl *260 28*
(101) quivering] twinkling *260 28*
(102) Eye] Orb *28*
(104) giddy] roving *260 28*
(108) that] who *28*
1103–7 *30q–46*

An account of meteors, corresponding in part to OET Au. 1108–37,
appeared in Su.27. See Appendix A, Summer 1044–75 *for the original
version. Later variants are recorded in the apparatus to Au. below.*
1108–27 *Su.27 Au.30q–46*
1108 Oft in this Season, silent] That Instant, flashing, noiseless, *Su.27*
1109 A Blaze of Meteors shoots:] A thousand Meteors stream, *Su.27*
1110 they] then, *Su.27 Au.30q–38*

1092 ‸Where] *MS* (∼ *30q–38*   1093 descries,] *MS* ∼) *30q–38*
1094 earth‸ *30p–38*   1098 floats; *30q–38*   1100 Rocks‸] *MS* ∼,
30q–38   (*26f*, 91) Now‸ stooping‸ *28*   Cloud; *28*   (92) Now‸ *28*
Cerulean‸ *28*   (93) Wide, *260*   floats‸ *28*   (94) Mountain‸ *28*
(95) Rocks‸ *28*   Reflection‸ *28*   (97) Night‸ *28*   Dews‸ unnoted‸
28   (98a) Morning's *28*   (99) Earth. From *28*   (101) And‸ *28*
(101a) twinkling‸ *28*   (102) Sun; *28*   (104) Now‸ *28*   (105) Grove‸
28   (108) Peace‸ *260*   Ill. *28*   these‸ *28*   (109) Charity‸ unlimited‸
28   (111) view, *260 28*   1103 BUT‸ when, *30q 30p* ∼, ∼‸ *300 38*
sky, *30q–38*   1106 extinct, *30q–38*   1107 sickly‸] *MS* ∼, *30q–38*
white: *30q–38*   1108 North, *Su.27*   1109 shoots, *Au.30q–38*
1110 once, *Su.27*   1110a then‸ *Au.30q–38*   1111 and, *Su.27*   once,
Su.27   1112 quick‸] *MS* ∼, *Su.27 Au.30q–38*

And mix, and thwart, extinguish, and renew,
All Ether coursing in a Maze of Light.

From Look to Look, contagious thro' the Croud,   1115
The Pannic runs, and into wondrous Shapes
Th' Appearance throws: Armies in meet Array,
Throng'd with aërial Spears, and Steeds of Fire;
Till the long Lines of full-extended War
In bleeding Fight commixt, the sanguine Flood   1120
Rolls a broad Slaughter o'er the Plains of Heaven.
As thus they scan the visionary Scene,
On all Sides swells the superstitious Din,
Incontinent; and busy Frenzy talks
Of Blood and Battle; Cities over-turn'd,   1125
And late at Night in swallowing Earthquake sunk,
Or hideous wrapt in fierce ascending Flame;
Of sallow Famine, Inundation, Storm;
Of Pestilence, and every great Distress;
Empires subvers'd, when ruling Fate has struck   1130
Th' unalterable Hour: even Nature's self
Is deem'd to totter on the Brink of Time.
Not so the Man of philosophic Eye,
And Inspect sage; the waving Brightness he
Curious surveys, inquisitive to know   1135
The Causes, and Materials, yet unfix'd,
Of this Appearance beautiful, and new.

Now black, and deep, the Night begins to fall,
A Shade immense. Sunk in the quenching Gloom,
Magnificent and vast, are Heaven and Earth.   1140
Order confounded lies; all Beauty void;
Distinction lost; and gay Variety
One universal Blot: such the fair Power
Of Light, to kindle and create the Whole.
Drear is the State of the benighted Wretch,   1145
Who then, bewilder'd, wanders thro' the Dark,
Full of pale Fancies, and Chimeras huge;
Nor visited by one directive Ray,
From Cottage streaming, or from airy Hall.
Perhaps impatient as he stumbles on,   1150

Struck from the Root of slimy Rushes, blue,
The Wild-fire scatters round, or gather'd trails
A Length of Flame deceitful o'er the Moss;
Whither decoy'd by the fantastick Blaze,
Now lost and now renew'd, he sinks absorpt,   1155
Rider and Horse, amid the miry Gulph:
While still, from Day to Day, his pining Wife,

1115 Look to Look] Eye to Eye *Su.27*
1118 Throng'd] *MS* Throng *Su.27 Au.30q–38*
1122 As the mad People scan the fancy'd Scene, *Su.27*
1124 Frenzy] Fancy *MS*
1127 Or painted hideous with ascending Flame; *Su.27 Au.30q–38* Or
[hideous wrapt in all-consuming *del.*] blazing dreadfull [in *del.*] with
consuming Flame *MSLytt*
   1128 *Au.30q–46*
   1128 *Su.27 as follows:*

> Of Blights, that blacken the white-bosom'd *Spring*,
> And Tempest, shaking *Autumn* into Chaff,   (*Su.27*, 1065)
> Till *Famine*, empty-handed, starves the Year;

   1129–37 *Su.27 Au.30q–46*
   1138–50 *30q–46*
1139 A solid shade, immense. Sunk in the gloom *30q–38* A Shade
immense. [Sunk *del.*] Wrapt in the quenching Gloom, *MS*
An account of wildfire, corresponding in part to OET Au. 1151–64,
appeared in Su.27. See Appendix A, Summer 1007–20 *for the original
version. Later variants are recorded in the apparatus to Au. below.*
   1151–3 *Su.27 Au.30q–46*
1151 Root] Roots *Su.27*
   1154–9 *30q–46*
1155 lost] *MS* sunk *30q–38*   he sinks] *MS* he's quite *30q–38*
1156 amid] into *30q–38*

1115 to Look,] *MS* ⁓ₐ *38*   contagious, *Su.27*   1116 *Pannic Su.27 Au.30q–*
38   1119 Till, *Su.27*   1122 *new paragraph Su.27*   1124 Inconti-
nent, *Su.27*   Frenzy *Su.27*   1125 Blood, *Su.27*   1126 And, *Su.27*
Au.30q–38   Night, *Su.27 Au.30q–38*   1129 Distress, *Su.27*   1130 *Fate*
Su.27   1131 *Nature's Self Su.27*   1133 *new paragraph Su.27*
Philosophic Su.27   1134 sage, *Su.27*   the waving Brightness, *Su.27*
1140 Magnificent, *30q–38*   1144 kindle, *30q–38*   1151 *new paragraph*
Su.27   1152 Wildₐ *46*   or, gather'd, *Su.27*   1153 Flame, deceitful,
Su.27   Moss, *Su.27*   1156 Horse,] *MS* ⁓ₐ *30p–38*

H

And plaintive Children his Return await,
In wild Conjecture lost. At other Times,
Sent by the *better Genius* of the Night,   1160
Innoxious, gleaming on the Horse's Mane,
The Meteor sits; and shews the narrow Path,
That winding leads thro' Pits of Death, or else
Instructs him how to take the dangerous Ford.

THE lengthen'd Night elaps'd, the Morning shines   1165
Serene, in all her dewy Beauty bright,
Unfolding fair the last Autumnal Day.
And now the mounting Sun dispels the Fog;
The rigid Hoar-Frost melts before his Beam;
And hung on every Spray, on every Blade   1170
Of Grass, the myriad Dew-Drops twinkle round.

AH see where robb'd, and murder'd, in that Pit,
Lies the still heaving Hive! at Evening snatch'd,
Beneath the Cloud of Guilt-concealing Night,
And fix'd o'er Sulphur: while, not dreaming Ill,   1175
The happy People, in their waxen Cells,
Sat tending public Cares, and planning Schemes
Of Temperance, for Winter poor; rejoic'd
To mark, full-flowing round, their copious Stores.
Sudden the dark oppressive Steam ascends;   1180
And, us'd to milder Scents, the tender Race,
By Thousands, tumbles from their honey'd Domes,
Convolv'd, and agonizing in the Dust.
And was it then for This you roam'd the Spring,
Intent from Flower to Flower? for This you toil'd   1185
Ceaseless the burning Summer-Heats away?
For This in Autumn search'd the blooming Waste,
Nor lost one sunny Gleam? for this sad Fate?
O Man! tyrannic Lord! how long, how long,
Shall prostrate Nature groan beneath your Rage,   1190
Awaiting Renovation? When oblig'd,
Must you destroy? Of their ambrosial Food
Can you not borrow; and, in just Return,
Afford them Shelter from the wintry Winds;
Or, as the sharp Year pinches, with their Own   1195

Again regale them on some smiling Day?
See where the stony Bottom of their Town
Looks desolate, and wild; with here and there
A helpless Number, who the ruin'd State
Survive, lamenting weak, cast out to Death.   1200
Thus a proud City, populous and rich,
Full of the Works of Peace, and high in Joy,
At Theater or Feast, or sunk in Sleep,
(As late, *Palermo*, was thy Fate) is seiz'd
By some dread Earthquake, and convulsive hurl'd,   1205
Sheer from the black Foundation, stench-involv'd,
Into a Gulph of blue sulphureous Flame.

1154–9 *Su.27 as follows:*

    Whither, entangled in the Maze of Night,   (*Su.27*, 1010)
    While the *damp Desart* breathes his Fogs around,
    The Traveller, decoy'd, is quite absorpt,
    Rider and Horse, into the miry Gulph,
    Leaving his Wife, and Family involv'd
    In sorrowful Conjecture. Other Times,   (*Su.27*, 1015)

1160–4 *Su.27 Au.30q–46*
1160 *better Genius*] quick-ey'd *Angel Su.27*
1161 gleaming on the] on th' unstartling *Su.27*
1164 Instructs] Directs *Su.27*
    1165–1373 *30q–46*
1175 fix'd] whelm'd *30q–38*   not dreaming] *MSLytt* undreaming
30q–38
1182 tumbles] tumble *30p–38*
1184 you] *MS* ye *30q–38*
1185 you] *MS* ye *30q–38*
1187 Waste] Heath *MS*
1191 When] Still *MSLytt*
1197 See where] *MSLytt* Hard by, *30q–38*
1206 Sheer] Ev'n *MSLytt*

1160 better Genius *30q–38*   1162 *Meteor* sits, *Su.27*   1163 That,
winding, *Su.27*   1167 AUTUMNAL *30q–38*   1169 Beam;] *MS* ~,
30q–38   1172 see! *MS*   1173 hive; *30q–38*   1179 full˄ *46*
1180 dark, *30q–38*   1187 *Autumn 30p–38*   1191 when *44–46*
1193 borrow? *30q–38*   and,] *MS* ~˄ *30q–38*   1201 populous, *30q 30p*
1203 theatre, *30q–38*   1204 PALERMO! *300*   1207 blue˄] *MS* ~, *30q–
38*

HENCE every harsher Sight! for now the Day,
O'er Heaven and Earth diffus'd, grows warm, and high,
Infinite Splendor! wide investing All.   1210
How still the Breeze! save what the filmy Threads
Of Dew evaporate brushes from the Plain.
How clear the cloudless Sky! how deeply ting'd
With a peculiar Blue! th' ethereal Arch
How swell'd immense! amid whose Azure thron'd   1215
The radiant Sun how gay! how calm below
The gilded Earth! the Harvest-Treasures all
Now gather'd in, beyond the Rage of Storms,
Sure to the Swain; the circling Fence shut up;
And instant Winter's utmost Rage defy'd.   1220
While, loose to festive Joy, the Country round
Laughs with the loud Sincerity of Mirth,
Shook to the Wind their Cares. The Toil-strung Youth
By the quick Sense of Music taught alone,
Leaps wildly graceful in the lively Dance.   1225
Her every Charm abroad, the Village-Toast,
Young, buxom, warm, in native Beauty rich,
Darts not-unmeaning Looks; and, where her Eye
Points an approving Smile, with double Force,
The Cudgel rattles, and the Wrestler twines.   1230
Age too shines out; and, garrulous, recounts
The Feats of Youth. Thus they rejoice; nor think
That, with to-morrow's Sun, their annual Toil
Begins again the never-ceasing Round.

Oh knew he but his Happiness, of Men   1235
The happiest he! who far from public Rage,
Deep in the Vale, with a *choice Few* retir'd,
Drinks the pure Pleasures of the RURAL LIFE.
What tho' the Dome be wanting, whose proud Gate,
Each Morning, vomits out the sneaking Croud   1240
Of Flatterers false, and in their Turn abus'd?
Vile Intercourse! What tho' the glittering Robe,
Of every Hue reflected Light can give,
Or floating loose, or stiff with mazy Gold,
The Pride and Gaze of Fools! oppress him not?   1245
What tho', from utmost Land and Sea purvey'd,

For him each rarer tributary Life
Bleeds not, and his insatiate Table heaps
With Luxury, and Death? What tho' his Bowl
Flames not with costly Juice; nor sunk in Beds,   1250
Oft of gay Care, he tosses out the Night,
Or melts the thoughtless Hours in idle State?
What tho' he knows not those fantastic Joys,
That still amuse the Wanton, still deceive;
A Face of Pleasure, but a Heart of Pain;   1255
Their hollow Moments undelighted all?
Sure Peace is his; a solid Life, estrang'd
To Disappointment, and fallacious Hope:
Rich in Content, in Nature's Bounty rich,
In Herbs and Fruits; whatever greens the Spring,   1260
When Heaven descends in Showers; or bends the Bough,
When Summer reddens, and when Autumn beams;
Or in the Wintry Glebe whatever lies
Conceal'd, and fattens with the richest Sap:
These are not wanting; nor the milky Drove,   1265

1220 Winter's utmost Rage defy'd] *MSLytt* Winter bid to do his worst
30q–38
1223 Care shook away. The toil-invigorate youth, *30q–38*
1224 Not needing the melodious impulse much, *30q–38 del. MS*
1230 Wrestler twines] *MSLytt* struggle twists *30q–38*
1234 the] it's *MS*
1249–50 Bowl/Flames not with costly Juice] wine/Flows not from
brighter gems *30q–38*
1252 Or melts the thoughtless Hours] Or, thoughtless, sleeps at best
30q–38
1253 he knows not] depriv'd of *30q–38*   those] these *30q 30p 38*

1215 azure *30q–46*   1221 While‸ *30q–38*   1223 Youth‸] *MS* ~, *30q–38*   1225 Leaps, *30q*   graceful, *30q 30p*   1237 choice few *30q–38*
1239 gate‸ *30q 30p*   1240 Morning,] *MS* ~‸ *30q–38*   1241 abus'd,
30q–38 ~: *MS*   1242 What] *MS* what *38*   1245 Pride‸] *MS* ~, *30q*
30p 38   not. *30q–38*   1246 tho'‸ *30q–38*   land, *30q–38*   sea, *30q–38*
1247 rarer‸] *MS* ~, *30q–38*   1249 death. *30q–38*   1251 night; *30q–*
38   1252 state. *30q–38*   1256 all. *30q–38*   1258 hope; *30q–38*
1260 Herbs‸] *MS* ~, *30q–38*   Spring, *30q–38*   1261 Heaven] *MS* heav'n
30p–38   Showers] *MS* show'rs *30p–38*   1262 Summer *30q–38*   Autumn
30q–38   1263 Wintry *30q–38*   1264 Sap:] *MS* ~; *30q–38*

Luxuriant, spread o'er all the lowing Vale;
Nor bleating Mountains; nor the Chide of Streams,
And Hum of Bees, inviting Sleep sincere
Into the guiltless Breast, beneath the Shade,
Or thrown at large amid the fragrant Hay;   1270
Nor Aught besides of Prospect, Grove, or Song,
Dim Grottoes, gleaming Lakes, and Fountain clear.
Here too dwells simple Truth; plain Innocence;
Unsully'd Beauty; sound unbroken Youth,
Patient of Labour, with a Little pleas'd;   1275
Health ever-blooming; unambitious Toil;
Calm Contemplation, and poetic Ease.

   LET others brave the Flood in Quest of Gain,
And beat, for joyless Months, the gloomy Wave.
Let such as deem it Glory to destroy   1280
Rush into Blood, the Sack of Cities seek;
Unpierc'd, exulting in the Widow's Wail,
The Virgin's Shriek, and Infant's trembling Cry.
Let some, far-distant from their native Soil,
Urg'd or by Want or harden'd Avarice,   1285
Find other Lands beneath another Sun.
Let This thro' Cities work his eager Way,
By legal Outrage, and establish'd Guile,
The social Sense extinct; and That ferment
Mad into Tumult the seditious Herd,   1290
Or melt them down to Slavery. Let These
Insnare the Wretched in the Toils of Law,
Fomenting Discord, and perplexing Right,
An iron Race! and Those of fairer Front,
But equal Inhumanity, in Courts,   1295
Delusive Pomp, and dark Cabals, delight;
Wreathe the deep Bow, diffuse the lying Smile,
And tread the weary Labyrinth of State.
While He, from all the stormy Passions free
That restless Men involve, hears, and but hears,   1300
At Distance safe, the Human Tempest roar,
Wrapt close in conscious Peace. The Fall of Kings,
The Rage of Nations, and the Crush of States,

Move not the Man, who, from the World escap'd,
In still Retreats, and flowery Solitudes,   1305
To Nature's Voice attends, from Month to Month,
And Day to Day, thro' the revolving Year;
Admiring, sees Her in her every Shape;
Feels all her sweet Emotions at his Heart;
Takes what she liberal gives, nor thinks of more.   1310
He, when young Spring protrudes the bursting Gems,
Marks the first Bud, and sucks the healthful Gale
Into his freshen'd Soul; her genial Hours
He full enjoys; and not a Beauty blows,
And not an opening Blossom breathes in vain.   1315
In Summer he, beneath the living Shade,
Such as o'er frigid *Tempè* wont to wave,
Or *Hemus* cool, reads what the Muse, of These
Perhaps, has in immortal Numbers sung;
Or what she dictates writes; and, oft an Eye   1320
Shot round, rejoices in the vigorous Year.
When Autumn's yellow Luster gilds the World,
And tempts the sickled Swain into the Field,
Seiz'd by the general Joy, his Heart distends
With gentle Throws; and, thro' the tepid Gleams   1325

1271 besides] beside *30q–38*
1273 dwells] *MS* lives *30q–38*
1287 eager] *MSLytt* ardent *30q–38*
1296 And slippery pomp delight, in dark cabals; *30q–38*
1306–7 Month to Month,/And Day to Day] day to day,/And month to
month *30q-38*
1309 sweet] fine *30q–38* [kind *del.*] *MS*
1314 full] *MS* quite *30q–38*
1317 o'er] *MS* from *30q–38*   wave] *MS* fall *30q–38*

1270 hay: *30q–45*   1274 sound, *30q–300*   1278 flood, *30q–45*
1280 such, *MS*   destroy, *30q–38*   1281 blood; *30q–38*   1284 some∧
30q–38   1285 Urg'd∧] *MS* ∼, *30q–38*   want, *30q–38*   1299 free,
30q–38   1303 Nations∧ *MS*   states∧ *30q–38*   1304 who∧ *300 45*
1305 Retreats∧ *MS*   1306 NATURE'S *30q–38*   1307 YEAR; *30q–38*
∼: *MS*   1308 Shape;] *MS* ∼: *30p–38*   1311 SPRING *30q–38*
1316 SUMMER *30q–38*   1322 AUTUMN'S *30q–38*   1325 and,] *MS* ∼∧
30q–38

Deep-musing, then he *best* exerts his Song.
Even Winter wild to him is full of Bliss.
The mighty Tempest, and the hoary Waste,
Abrupt, and deep, stretch'd o'er the bury'd Earth,
Awake to solemn Thought. At Night the Skies,   1330
Disclos'd, and kindled, by refining Frost,
Pour every Luster on th' exalted Eye.
A Friend a Book the stealing Hours secure,
And mark them down for Wisdom. With swift Wing,
O'er Land and Sea Imagination roams;   1335
Or Truth, divinely breaking on his Mind,
Elates his Being, and unfolds his Powers;
Or in his Breast Heroic Virtue burns.
The Touch of Kindred too and Love he feels;
The modest Eye, whose Beams on His alone   1340
Extatic shine; the little strong Embrace
Of prattling Children, twin'd around his Neck,
And emulous to please him, calling forth
The fond parental Soul. Nor Purpose gay,
Amusement, Dance, or Song, he sternly scorns;   1345
For Happiness and true Philosophy
Are of the social still, and smiling Kind.
This is the Life which those who fret in Guilt,
And guilty Cities, never knew; the Life,
Led by primeval Ages, uncorrupt,   1350
When Angels dwelt, and GOD himself, with Man!

　　OH NATURE! all-sufficient! over all!
Inrich me with the Knowledge of thy Works!
Snatch me to Heaven; thy rolling Wonders there,
World beyond World, in infinite Extent,   1355
Profusely scatter'd o'er the blue Immense,
Shew me; their Motions, Periods, and their Laws,
Give me to scan; thro' the disclosing Deep
Light my blind Way: the mineral *Strata* there;
Thrust, blooming, thence the vegetable World;   1360
O'er that the rising System, more complex,
Of Animals; and higher still, the Mind,
The vary'd Scene of quick-compounded Thought,
And where the mixing Passions endless shift;

These ever open to my ravish'd Eye: 1365
A Search, the Flight of Time can ne'er exhaust!
But if to that unequal; if the Blood,
In sluggish Streams about my Heart, forbid
That *best* Ambition; under closing Shades,
Inglorious, lay me by the lowly Brook,   1370
And whisper to my Dreams. From THEE begin,
Dwell all on THEE, with THEE conclude my Song;
And let me never never stray from THEE!

1326 he] *MS* the *30q–38*
1332 exalted] astonish'd *30q–38*
1339 of Kindred too and Love] *MS* of love, and kindred too *30q–38*
1347 Still are, and have been of the smiling kind. *30q–38*
1350 uncorrupt] *MS* incorrupt *30q–38*
1351 When GOD himself, and ANGELS dwelt with men! *30q–38* When Angels dwelt, and GOD himself, with Men! *MS*
1356 blue Immense] void immense *30q–300* void Immense *38–45*
1361 O'er that the] *MS* O'er that *30p* Over that *38*
1368 forbid] forbids *30q–38*
30p adds. The END.

1326 *best*] *MS* best *30q–38*   1327 WINTER *30q–38*   1333 Friend˄]
MS ~, *30q–38*   Book˄] *MS* ~, *30q–38*   1335 land, *30q–38*   sea, *30q–38*   1339 too, *MS*   Love, *MS*   feels, *30q–38* ~: *MS*   1339a Kindred, *MS*   1341 little, *30q–38*   1346 Happiness˄] *MS* ~, *30q–38*
1347a been, *MS*   1349 Life˄ *MS*   1358 scan. Thro' *MS*   1364 shift:
MS   1365 eye; *30q–38*   1369 best *30q–38*   1372 Song, *MS*
1373 never˄ never˄] *MS* ~, ~˄ *30q–38*

WINTER

    SEE, WINTER comes, to rule the vary'd Year,
Sullen, and sad, with all his rising Train;
Vapours, and *Clouds*, and *Storms*. Be these my Theme,
These, that exalt the Soul to solemn Thought,
And heavenly Musing. Welcome, kindred Glooms!   5
Cogenial Horrors, hail! With frequent Foot,
Pleas'd have I, in my chearful Morn of Life,
When nurs'd by careless Solitude I liv'd,
And sung of Nature with unceasing Joy,
Pleas'd have I wander'd thro' your rough Domain;   10
Trod the pure Virgin-Snows, myself as pure;
Heard the Winds roar, and the big Torrent burst;
Or seen the deep fermenting Tempest brew'd,
In the grim Evening-Sky. Thus pass'd the Time,
Till thro' the lucid Chambers of the South   15
Look'd out the joyous SPRING, look'd out and smil'd.

---

half title: WINTER.] WINTER, A POEM. *300 38*   *no half title in*
26f–28 34
30q 30p 300 add: Inscribed to the RIGHT HONOURABLE the LORD
WILMINGTON.

26f–28 30p 34 have separate title-page
26f–28 have title-page epigraphs as follows:
——————————————————————*Rapidus Sol*
Nondum Hyemem contingit Equis. Jam praeterit aestas. VIRG.
—— *Glacialis* HYEMS *canos hirsuta Capillos.* OVID.   *26f*
——— *Horrida cano*
BRUMA *Gelu.* ——— *260*
——— *Horrida cano*
BRUMA *Gelu.* —— *Virg.*   *28*
26f–28 add a dedication (reprinted in Appendix B below).
260 adds preface and commendatory poems (reprinted in Appendix B below).

The Argument   30q–46   not in 26f–28
1 *the Earl of*] Lord *30q–45*
2 *Course*] order *30q–38*
4–6 *among them; . . .* Apennines.] *among them. A short digression into* RUSSIA. *The wolves in* ITALY. *30q–38*
7–8 *A View of Winter*] Its effects *30q–38*
9 *moral*] philosophical *30q–38*

   1–16 *26f–46*

6 Cogenial] Wish'd, wintry, *26f–28*
10 Domain] Domains *26f–28*
14 grim] red, *26f–38* pale *MS*
15 lucid] opening *26f–28*
   16+ *26f–28 add here ninety-five lines (not in Wi.30q–46) which were revised and transferred to Au.30q.*
See Appendix A, Winter 17–111 *for the original version, and OET Au.* 950–1036 *and* 1082–1102 *for later versions.*

————————

Argument 2 WINTER *30q–38*   6 *described, 30q–38*   8 *polar circle 30q–38*   1 SEE! *26f 260* ∼ˏ *28–38*   comesˏ *28*   2 sad; *26f 260 MS* Train, *26f–38*   3 *Storms: 26f 260*   4 Theseˏ *28*   5 Welcomeˏ *26f–28*   6 hail!— *26f–28*   with *30p–46*   6a wint'ryˏ *28*   7 Pleas'd, *26f 260*   8 When, *26f 260*   Solitude, *26f 260* ∼ˏ *28–38*   10 Pleas'd, *26f 260*   11 pure, virgin, Snows, *26f* ∼ˏ∼ˏ∼, *260 28*   my selfˏ *26f 28 30q* ∼, *260*   as pure: *26f–28*   12 burst: *26f 260* ∼, *28*   13 deepˏ] *MS* ∼, *26f–38*   fermenting, *26f*   brew'd,] *MS* ∼ˏ *28–38*   14 evening, Sky. — *26f 260* Evening-sky.— *28*   14a redˏ *28–38*   15 Till, *26f 260* South, *26f 260*   16 outˏ and] *MS* ∼, ∼ *26f–45*

To Thee, the Patron of *this first* Essay,
The Muse, O WILMINGTON! renews her Song.
Since has she rounded the revolving Year:
Skim'd the gay Spring; on Eagle-Pinions borne,   20
Attempted thro' the Summer-Blaze to rise;
Then swept o'er Autumn with the shadowy Gale;
And now among the Wintry Clouds again,
Roll'd in the doubling Storm, she tries to soar;
To swell her Note with all the rushing Winds;   25
To suit her sounding Cadence to the Floods;
As is her Theme, her Numbers wildly great:
Thrice happy! could she fill thy judging Ear
With bold Description, and with manly Thought.
Nor art thou skill'd in awful Schemes alone,   30
And how to make a mighty People thrive:
But equal Goodness, sound Integrity,
A firm unshaken uncorrupted Soul
Amid a sliding Age, and burning strong,
Not vainly blazing, for thy Country's Weal,   35
A steady Spirit regularly free;
These, each exalting each, the Statesman light
Into the Patriot; These, the publick Hope
And Eye to thee converting, bid the Muse
Record what Envy dares not Flattery call.   40

Now when the chearless Empire of the Sky
To *Capricorn* the *Centaur-Archer* yields,
And fierce *Aquarius* stains th' inverted Year;
Hung o'er the farthest Verge of Heaven, the Sun
Scarce spreads o'er Ether the dejected Day.   45
Faint are his Gleams, and ineffectual shoot
His struggling Rays, in horizontal Lines,
Thro' the thick Air; as cloath'd in cloudy Storm,
Weak, wan, and broad, he skirts the Southern Sky;
And, soon-descending, to the long dark Night,   50
Wide-shading All, the prostrate World resigns.
Nor is the Night unwish'd; while vital Heat,
Light, Life, and Joy, the dubious Day forsake.
Mean-time, in sable Cincture, Shadows vast,
Deep-ting'd and damp, and congregated Clouds,   55

And all the vapoury Turbulence of Heaven
Involve the Face of Things. Thus Winter falls,
A heavy Gloom oppressive o'er the World,
Thro' Nature shedding Influence malign,
And rouses up the Seeds of dark Disease.　　　　60
The Soul of Man dies in him, loathing Life,
And black with more than melancholy Views.
The Cattle droop; and o'er the furrow'd Land,
Fresh from the Plow, the dun discolour'd Flocks,
Untended spreading, crop the wholesome Root.　　65
Along the Woods, along the moorish Fens,
Sighs the sad *Genius* of the coming Storm;
And up among the loose disjointed Cliffs,
And fractur'd Mountains wild, the brawling Brook

17–71 *30q–46   not in 26f–28*
17 *this first*] her first *30q–34* MS *44–45* our first *38*
30 *MSLytt   30q–38 as follows:*

> For thee the Graces smooth; thy softer thoughts　　(*30q*, 30)
> The Muses tune; nor art thou skill'd alone
> In awful schemes, the management of states,

　　(30) Graces] [Muses *del.*] *MSLytt*
38 These] *MSLytt* and *30q–38*
41–2 WHEN SCORPIO gives to CAPRICORN the sway, *30q–38*
43 fierce] sad *MS*　　stains] *MS* fouls *30q–38*
44 Hung o'er the farthest] Retiring to the *30q–38*
48 as cloath'd in cloudy Storm] as at dull distance seen *30q–38*
60 up] all *30q–38*
62–3 And black . . . The Cattle droop] *MS* And black with horrid views. The cattle droop/The conscious head *30q–38*
64 Fresh] Red *30q–38* Brown *MS*
69 Brook] Brooks, *MS*

---

19 Year:] *MS* YEAR: *30q–300* ∼; *34 38*　　　　20 Spring] *MS* SPRING *30q–38*
21 Summer] *MS* SUMMER *30q–38*　　　　22 Autumn] *MS* AUTUMN *30q–38*
23 Wintry] *MS* WINTRY *30q–38*　　27 great. *MS* ∼: *30q–38*　　30a tune.
Nor *MS*　　　　32 Goodness,] *MS* ∼; *30q–38*　　Integrity,] *MS* ∼; *30q–38*
33 firm∧ unshaken∧] *MS* ∼, ∼, *30q–38*　　Soul∧] *MS* ∼, *30q–38*　　34 Age,]
MS ∼; *30q–38*　　　　35 blazing∧ *44–46*　　　　36 spirit, *30q–38*　　free, *MS*
43 *Aquarius, 44–46*　　　　46 gleams; *30q*　　53 Life∧ *MS*　　Joy,] *MS* ∼∧
30q–38　　55 ting'd∧] *MS* ∼, *30q–38*　　56 Heaven, *MS*　　57 WINTER
30q–38　　67 genius *30q–38*　　68 loose∧] *MS* ∼, *30q–38*　　69 brook,
30q–38

And Cave, presageful, send a hollow Moan,   70
Resounding long in listening Fancy's Ear.

THEN comes the Father of the Tempest forth,
Wrapt in black Glooms. First joyless Rains obscure
Drive thro' the mingling Skies with Vapour foul;
Dash on the Mountain's Brow, and shake the Woods,   75
That grumbling wave below. Th' unsightly Plain
Lies a brown Deluge; as the low-bent Clouds
Pour Flood on Flood, yet unexhausted still
Combine, and deepening into Night shut up
The Day's fair Face. The Wanderers of Heaven,   80
Each to his Home, retire; save Those that love
To take their Pastime in the troubled Air,
Or skimming flutter round the dimply Pool.
The Cattle from th' untasted Fields return,
And ask, with meaning Lowe, their wonted Stalls,   85
Or ruminate in the contiguous Shade.
Thither the houshold feathery People croud,
The crested Cock, with all his female Train,
Pensive, and dripping; while the Cottage-Hind
Hangs o'er th' enlivening Blaze, and taleful there   90
Recounts his simple Frolick: much he talks,
And much he laughs, nor recks the Storm that blows
Without, and rattles on his humble Roof.

WIDE o'er the Brim, with many a Torrent swell'd,
And the mix'd Ruin of its Banks o'erspread,   95
At last the rous'd-up River pours along:
Resistless, roaring, dreadful, down it comes,
From the rude Mountain, and the mossy Wild,
Tumbling thro' Rocks abrupt, and sounding far;
Then o'er the sanded Valley floating spreads,   100
Calm, sluggish, silent; till again constrain'd,
Between two meeting Hills it bursts a Way,
Where Rocks and Woods o'erhang the turbid Stream;
There gathering triple Force, rapid, and deep,
It boils, and wheels, and foams, and thunders' thro'.   105

NATURE! great Parent! whose unceasing Hand
Rolls round the Seasons of the changeful Year,

How mighty, how majestic, are thy Works!
With what a pleasing Dread they swell the Soul!
That sees astonish'd! and astonish'd sings!   110
Ye too, ye Winds! that now begin to blow,
With boisterous Sweep, I raise my Voice to you.
Where are your Stores, ye powerful Beings! say,

72–117 *26f–46*
72 FOR, see! where *Winter* comes, himself, confest, *26f* WINTER! who
rides along the darken'd Air, *26o 28*
73 Striding the gloomy Blast. First Rains obscure *26f–38* [Striding the
Blast. First joyless Rains obscure *del.*] *MS*
74 Vapour foul] *MS* Tempest foul *26f–28* vapour vile *30q–38*
75 Dash] Beat *26f–28*
76 That] Which *28*   grumbling] sounding, *26f–28*   Th'unsightly]
The dreary *26f*
77–8 Lies overwhelm'd, and lost. The bellying Clouds *26f–28*
80 Face. The Wanderers] [Circle. Struck, the Fowls *del.*] *MS*
83 Or] And *26f*   Pool] Flood *26f–28*
89 dripping; while] *MSLytt* wet. Mean while, *26f–38* Hind] *MSLytt*
Swain *26f–38*
92 that] which *28*
94–6 AT last, the muddy Deluge pours along, *26f–28*
95 Ruin] ruins *30q–38*
98 rude] chapt *26f–38* cleft *MS*
102 Between] Betwixt *26f–38*   a Way] *MS* away *26o 34 38*
106 unceasing] *MS* directing *26f–28* continual *30q–38*
111 Ye too] You too *26f–28*
113 powerful] *MS* viewless *26f–28* subtile *30q–38*

---

74 Skies, *26f–30o MS*   75 Woods∧ *45*   76 That, *26f*   76a sound-
ing∧ *28*   79 Night, *26f 26o*   83 Or, *26o*   skimming, *26f 26o*
84 Cattle, *26f 26o*   Fields, *26f 26o*   85 ask∧ *28*   Low∧ *28*   Stalls; *26f*
26o   86 Shade: *26f 26o*   87 Thither, *26f 26o*   houshold∧] *MS* ~,
26f–38   feathery, *26f 26o*   89 Dripping, *MSLytt*   89a Mean while∧
28–38   90 and, taleful, there, *26f 26o*   96 along:] *MS* ~, *26f–38*
96a last∧ *28*   97 roaring, dreadful,] *MS* ~; ~∧ *26f–38*   comes,] *MS*
~∧ *26f–38*   98 Mountain∧ *MS*   99 far: *26f–30o*   100 Valley,
floating, *26f 26o*   101 till, *MS*   102 Hills, *26f 26o*   103 Rocks,
26f–38   Woods, *26o*   Stream. *26f 26o*   108 mighty! *26f 26o*   majestick∧
26f–38   109 Soul, *26f 26o*   110 sees, *26f 26o*   and, *26f 26o*
111 *Winds! 26f 26o*   113 *Beings! 26f 26o*

Where your aërial Magazines reserv'd,
To swell the brooding Terrors of the Storm?   115
In what far-distant Region of the Sky,
Hush'd in deep Silence, sleep you when 'tis calm?

WHEN from the palid Sky the Sun descends,
With many a Spot, that o'er his glaring Orb
Uncertain wanders, stain'd; red fiery Streaks   120
Begin to flush around. The reeling Clouds
Stagger with dizzy Poise, as doubting yet
Which Master to obey: while rising slow,
Blank, in the leaden-colour'd East, the Moon
Wears a wan Circle round her blunted Horns.   125
Seen thro' the turbid fluctuating Air,
The Stars obtuse emit a shivering Ray;
Or frequent seem to shoot athwart the Gloom,
And long behind them trail the whitening Blaze.
Snatch'd in short Eddies, plays the wither'd Leaf;   130
And on the Flood the dancing Feather floats.
With broaden'd Nostrils to the Sky upturn'd,
The conscious Heifer snuffs the stormy Gale.
Even as the Matron, at her nightly Task,
With pensive Labour draws the flaxen Thread,   135
The wasted Taper and the crackling Flame
Foretel the Blast. But chief the plumy Race,
The Tenants of the Sky, its Changes speak.
Retiring from the Downs, where all Day long
They pick'd their scanty Fare, a blackening Train   140
Of clamorous Rooks thick-urge their weary Flight,
And seek the closing Shelter of the Grove.
Assiduous, in his Bower, the wailing Owl
Plies his sad Song. The Cormorant on high
Wheels from the Deep, and screams along the Land.   145
Loud shrieks the soaring Hern; and with wild Wing
The circling Sea-Fowl cleave the flaky Clouds.
Ocean, unequal press'd, with broken Tide
And blind Commotion heaves; while from the Shore,
Eat into Caverns by the restless Wave,   150
And Forest-rustling Mountain, comes a Voice,
That solemn-sounding bids the World prepare.

Then issues forth the Storm with sudden Burst,
And hurls the whole precipitated Air,
Down, in a Torrent. On the passive Main   155
Descends th' etherial Force, and with strong Gust

---

115 Against the Day of Tempest perilous? *26f–38*
116 In what untravel'd Country of the Air, *26f–28*
117 deep] still *26f–28* dead *30q–45*
    118–20 *44–46*
    118–20 *26f–38 as follows:*

           Late, in the louring Sky, red, fiery, Streaks   (*26f*, 155)

    121–5 *26f–46*
121 around.] *MS* about; *26f–38*
122 Poise] Aim *26f–28*
124 Blank] Sad *26f*
125 wan] bleak *26f*   blunted Horns] sully'd Orb *26f–38* blunted Orb
MS
    126–49 *44–46*   not in *26f–28*
    126–49 *30q–38 as follows:*

           The stars obtuse emit a shivering ray;   (*30q*, 125)
           Snatch'd in short eddies plays the fluttering straw;
           Loud shrieks the soaring hern; and, skreaming wild,
           The circling sea-fowl rise; while from the shore,

    (125) obtuse emit] faint-gleaming shed *MS*   shivering] [quiver-
ing *del.*] *MS*
    150–2 *30q–46*   not in *26f–28*
150 Eat] [Ate *del.*] *MS*
    153–5 *44–46*
    154–5 *MS*
    153–5 *26f–38 as follows:*

           Then issues forth the Storm, with loud Control, (*26f*, 161)
           And the thin Fabrick of the pillar'd Air
           O'erturns, at once. Prone, on th' uncertain Main,

    (161) loud] mad *260–38*
    (163) O'erturns, at once. Prone, on] [Hurls into Ruins. On *del.*] *MS*
th'uncertain] the passive *260–38*

---

115 Storm. *44–45*   117 you, *26f 260*   (*26f*, 155) Late,] *MS* ~ˍ *30q–*
38   Skyˍ redˍ fieryˍ *28* ~, ~, ~ˍ *30q–38* ~, ~ˍ ~ˍ *MS*   121 the *26f–*
38   123 rising, *26f–28*   124 Blank,] *MS* ~ˍ *300–38*   141 thickˍ
urge *46*   (*26f*, 163) O'erturnsˍ *28–38*

Turns from its Bottom the discolour'd Deep.
Thro' the black Night that sits immense around,
Lash'd into Foam, the fierce conflicting Brine
Seems o'er a thousand raging Waves to burn;　　　160
Meantime the Mountain-Billows, to the Clouds
In dreadful Tumult swell'd, Surge above Surge,
Burst into Chaos with tremendous Roar,
And anchor'd Navies from their Stations drive,
Wild as the Winds across the howling Waste　　　165
Of mighty Waters: now th' inflated Wave
Straining they scale, and now impetuous shoot
Into the secret Chambers of the Deep,
The wintry *Baltick* thundering o'er their Head.
Emerging thence again, before the Breath　　　170
Of full-exerted Heaven they wing their Course,
And dart on distant Coasts; if some sharp Rock,
Or Shoal insidious break not their Career,
And in loose Fragments fling them floating round.

　　NOR less at Land the loosen'd Tempest reigns.　　　175
The Mountain thunders; and its sturdy Sons

156–7 *28–46*
157 its] *MS* the *28–38*
　156–7 *26f as follows:*

　　Descends th' Etherial Force, and plows its Waves,
　　With dreadful Rift: from the mid-Deep, appears,　(*26f,* 165)
　　Surge after Surge, the rising, wat'ry, War.

　156–7 *260 as follows:*

　　Descends th' Etherial Force, and plows its Waves,
　　In frightful Furrows: From the brawling deep;　(*260,* 165)
　　Heav'd to the Clouds, the watry *Tumult* comes.

　158–63 *44–46　not in 26f 260*
158 *MSLytt*
160 *MS*
　158–63 *28–38 as follows:*

　　Thro' the loud Night, which harrows up the Waves,
　　Lasht into Foam, the fierce conflicting Brine
　　Seems as it sparkles all around to burn.
　　Mean time whole Oceans heaving to the Clouds,

And in broad Billows rowling gather'd Seas,   (*28*, 170)
Surge over surge, burst in a general Roar,

(166) which harrows up the Waves] that bids the waves arise *30q–38*
(169–70)   Mean-time, o'er all the rough tempestuous Flood
                    tremendous
     The Billows swell'd, amazing, to the Clouds, *MS*

  164–74 *28–46* *not in 26f 260*
165 across] athwart *28–38*
166 th' inflated] the hilly *28–38*
167 Straining] Labring *28*
169 wintry] *MSLytt* full-blown *28–38*   Head] Heads *28 44–45*
171 full-exerted] *MSLytt* all-exerted *28–38*
172 Coasts] coast *300*
173 Shoal] *MS* sand *28–38*   insidious] *MSLytt* dire-lurking, *MS*
  break] snap *28*
  174+ *26f 260 add the following (not in 28–46):*

    Whitening, the angry Billows rowl immense,
    And roar their Terrors, thro' the shuddering Soul
    Of feeble Man, amidst their Fury caught,
    And, dash'd upon his Fate: Then, o'er the Cliff,   (*26f*, 170)
    Where dwells the *Sea-Mew*, unconfin'd, they fly,
    And, hurrying, swallow up the steril Shore.

  (167–8)   Rumbling, the Wind-swoln Billows, rowl, immense,
             And, on the evanish'd Vessel, bursting fierce,
             Their Terrors thunder, thro' the prostrate Soul   *260*

  174+ *28–38 add the following (not in 26f 260 44–46):*

    Nor raging here alone unrein'd at Sea,
    To Land the Tempest bears; and o'er the Cliff,
    Where screams the Sea-Mew, foaming unconfin'd, (*28*, 185)
    Feirce swallows up the long-resounding Shore.

  (183–6) *del. MS*
175 *MS 44–46* *not in 26f–38*
176–82 *26f–46*
176 The Mountain thunders; and its] The Mountain growls; and all its
26f–38 [The Mountain thunders, and its *del.*] [Now growls *del.*] Bellows
the Mountain; and his *MS* The Mountain groans and all his *MSLytt*

---

158 Night, *MSLytt*   159 fierce.] *MS* ~, *30q–38*   (*28*, 168) Seems,
30q–38   sparkles, *30q–38*   (169) oceans, *30q–38*   166 Waters: now]
MS ~. Now *28–38*   172 Coasts: *28*   176 *Sons 26f 260*

Stoop to the Bottom of the Rocks they shade.
Lone on the midnight Steep, and all aghast,
The dark way-faring Stranger breathless toils,
And, often falling, climbs against the Blast.   180
Low waves the rooted Forest, vex'd, and sheds
What of its tarnish'd Honours yet remain;
Dash'd down, and scatter'd, by the tearing Wind's
Assiduous Fury, its gigantic Limbs.
Thus struggling thro' the dissipated Grove,   185
The whirling Tempest raves along the Plain;
And on the Cottage thatch'd, or lordly Roof,
Keen-fastening, shakes them to the solid Base.
Sleep frighted flies; and round the rocking Dome,
For Entrance eager, howls the savage Blast.   190
Then too, they say, thro' all the burthen'd Air,
Long Groans are heard, shrill Sounds, and distant Sighs,
That, utter'd by the Demon of the Night,
Warn the devoted Wretch of Woe and Death.

    HUGE Uproar lords it wide. The Clouds commix'd   195
With Stars swift-gliding sweep along the Sky.
All Nature reels. Till Nature's KING, who oft
Amid tempestuous Darkness dwells alone,
And on the Wings of the careering Wind
Walks dreadfully serene, commands a Calm;   200
Then straight Air Sea and Earth are hush'd at once.

    As yet 'tis Midnight deep. The weary Clouds,
Slow-meeting, mingle into solid Gloom.
Now, while the drowsy World lies lost in Sleep,
Let me associate with the serious *Night*,   205
And *Contemplation* her sedate Compeer;
Let me shake off th' intrusive Cares of Day,
And lay the meddling Senses all aside.

    WHERE now, ye lying Vanities of Life!
Ye ever-tempting ever-cheating Train!   210
Where are you now? and what is your Amount?
Vexation, Disappointment, and Remorse.

Sad, sickening Thought! and yet deluded Man,
A Scene of crude disjointed Visions past,

---

178 on] to *44Wks*   the midnight Steep] *MS* its Midnight-Side
26f–38
180 And, often . . . Blast.] And climbs against the Blast —— *26f 260*
182 tarnish'd] leafy *26f–28* remain] remains *26f 260* remain'd *28MS*
   183–4 *30q–46 not in 26f–28*
   185–96 *26f–46*
187 Roof] Dome *26f–28*
189–90   *Sleep*, frighted, flies; the hollow Chimney howls,
     The Windows rattle, and the Hinges creak.   *26f–28*
193 utter'd] murmur'd *26f 260*
195 HUGE] Wild *26f*
   197–201 *260–46*
201 Then] And, *260 28*   Air Sea and Earth] Earth, Sea, and Air,
260–28 [Earth Air and Sea *del.* Earth Sea and Air *del.*] Air Earth and
Sea *MS*
   197–201 *26f as follows:*

     All Nature reels. —— But hark! the *Almighty* speaks:
     Instant, the chidden Storm begins to pant,
     And dies, at once, into a noiseless Calm.   (*26f*, 194)

   202–31 *26f–46*
202 Midnight deep. The] *MS* Midnight's Reign; the *26f 260* Midnight
waste. The *28–38*
205 serious] low-brow'd *26f–28*
209 WHERE] AND *26f–38*
210 Ye] You *26f–28*
214 crude] wild, *26f*

---

177 shade: *26f 260*   178 Lone, *26f 260*   179 dark∧] *MS* ~, *26f–38*
way-faring, *Stranger*, breathless, *26f 260*   181 Low, *26f 260*   185 Thus,
26f 260   187 And, *26f 260*   189a *Sleep*∧ 28   frighted∧ 28   191 *new
paragraph 26f–28*   THEN, *26f 260*   Air,] *MS* ~∧ *28–38*   193 *Demon
26f–28*   194 *Wretch 26f 260*   Woe, *26f–34*   Death! *26f 260*   195 *no
new paragraph 26f–260*   Uproar] *MS* Uproar *260–38*   wide: the *26f 260*
Clouds, *MS*   commixt, *26f 260*   196 Stars, *26f 260*   gliding, *26f 260
MS*   197 reels. — *26f–28*   oft, *260*   198 dwells, *260*   199 And,
260   201 strait, *260*   air, *30q–38 45*   sea, *30q–38*   hush'd, *260*
202 yet, *26f 260*   203 Gloom: *26f 260*   206 *Contemplation, 26f 260*
209 now∧ *28*   *Vanities 26f–28*   210 tempting∧] *MS* ~, *26f–38 45*
212 Remorse: *28*   213 sickening, *26f 260*   And *30q*   yet, *26f 260*
214 crude, *260 28*   disjointed, *26f 260*

And broken Slumbers, rises still resolv'd,   215
With new-flush'd Hopes, to run the giddy Round.

   FATHER of Light and Life! thou GOOD SUPREME!
O teach me what is good! teach me THYSELF!
Save me from Folly, Vanity, and Vice,
From every low Pursuit! and feed my Soul   220
With Knowledge, conscious Peace, and Virtue pure,
Sacred, substantial, never-fading Bliss!

   THE keener Tempests come: and fuming dun
From all the livid East, or piercing North,
Thick Clouds ascend; in whose capacious Womb   225
A vapoury Deluge lies, to Snow congeal'd.
Heavy they roll their fleecy World along;
And the Sky saddens with the gather'd Storm.
Thro' the hush'd Air the whitening Shower descends,
At first thin-wavering; till at last the Flakes   230
Fall broad, and wide, and fast, dimming the Day,
With a continual Flow. The cherish'd Fields
Put on their Winter-Robe, of purest White.
'Tis Brightness all; save where the new Snow melts,
Along the mazy Current. Low, the Woods   235
Bow their hoar Head; and, ere the languid Sun
Faint from the West emits his Evening Ray,
Earth's universal Face, deep-hid, and chill,
Is one wild dazzling Waste, that buries wide
The Works of Man. Drooping, the Labourer-Ox   240
Stands cover'd o'er with Snow, and then demands
The Fruit of all his Toil. The Fowls of Heaven,
Tam'd by the cruel Season, croud around
The winnowing Store, and claim the little Boon
Which PROVIDENCE assigns them. One alone,   245
The Red-Breast, sacred to the houshold Gods,
Wisely regardful of th' embroiling Sky,

---

216 the] your *26f–28*
223–4 Lo! from the livid East, or piercing North, *26f* Dun, from the
livid East, or piercing North, *260 28*
228 the gather'd] th' impending *26f–28*

232–8 *30q–46*
232 With a continual flow. Sudden the fields *30q–38* With Flow con-
tinual. Swift, the cherish'd Fields *MS*
235 mazy Current. Low, the Woods] mazy stream. The leafless woods
30q–38
236 Head] heads *30q–38*
   232–8 *26f as follows:*

> With a continual Flow. See! sudden, hoar'd
> The Woods beneath the stainless Burden bow,   *(26f, 225)*
> Blackning, along the mazy Stream it melts;
> Earth's universal Face, deep-hid, and chill,

   232–8 *26o 28 as follows:*

> With a continual Flow. Blackening, they melt,
> Along the mazy Stream. The leafless Woods
> Bow their hoar' Heads. And ere the languid Sun,
> Faint, from the West, emit his evening Ray,   *(26o, 230)*
> Earth's universal Face, deep-hid, and chill,

   (227) Flow. Blackening, they melt,] Flow; and blackening melt *28*
239–40 *MS 44–46*
239 buries wide] [covers all *del.*] buries deep *MS*
240 Man] Men *MS*
   239–40 *26f–28 as follows:*

>   Is all one, dazzling, Waste. The Labourer-Ox

   239–40 *30q–38 as follows:*

>   Is one wild, dazzling waste. The labourer-ox

   241–4 *26f–46*
241–2 demands/The Fruit of all his Toil. The Fowls] [demands,/With
meaning Lowe, the Fruit of all his Toil,/Well earn'd *del.*] [demands/
His well-earn'd Stall. Meantime the Fowls *del.*] *MS*
   245–56 *26o 28 30p–46*
245–6 *MS* That *Providence* allows. The *Red-Breast*, sole, *26o 28 30p–38*

---

215 rises, *26f 26o*   216 Hopes,] *MS* ~∧ *30q–38*   217 Light, *26f–38*
Thou *26f–28*   GOOD SUPREME] *MS* Good supreme *30q–38*   218 O! *26f*
26o   THYSELF] *MS* thy self *26f–30q* thyself *30p–38*   219 Vanity∧ *26f–*
28   220 Soul, *26f 26o*   223 come; *30o*   225 ascend, *26f–28*
Womb, *26f 26o*   226 congeal'd: *26f 26o*   227 Heavy, *26f 26o*
229 Air∧] *MS* ~, *26f 26o 30o 38*   230 first, *26f 26o*   till, at last, *26f 26o*
231 Day∧ *28*   236a heads. And, *30q–38* ~; and, *MS*   *(26o, 229)* Heads.
And, *28*   Sun∧ *28*   (230) Faint∧ *28*   West∧ *28*   *(231)* Face∧ *28*
239a one∧ dazzling∧ *28*   240a *Labourer-Ox 26o*   244 Boon, *26f*
245 Providence *30p–38*   246a Red-Breast∧ *28 30p–38*

In joyless Fields, and thorny Thickets, leaves
His shivering Mates, and pays to trusted Man
His annual Visit. Half-afraid, he first   250
Against the Window beats; then, brisk, alights
On the warm Hearth; then, hopping o'er the Floor,
Eyes all the smiling Family askance,
And pecks, and starts, and wonders where he is:
Till more familiar grown, the Table-Crumbs   255
Attract his slender Feet. The foodless Wilds
Pour forth their brown Inhabitants. The Hare,
Tho' timorous of Heart, and hard beset
By Death in various Forms, dark Snares, and Dogs,
And more unpitying Men, the Garden seeks,   260
Urg'd on by fearless Want. The bleating Kind
Eye the bleak Heaven, and next the glistening Earth,
With Looks of dumb Despair; then, sad-dispers'd,
Dig for the wither'd Herb thro' Heaps of Snow.

    Now, Shepherds, to your helpless Charge be kind,   265
Baffle the raging Year, and fill their Pens
With Food at Will; lodge them below the Storm,
And watch them strict: for from the bellowing East,
In this dire Season, oft the Whirlwind's Wing
Sweeps up the Burthen of whole wintry Plains   270
In one wide Waft, and o'er the hapless Flocks,
Hid in the Hollow of two neighbouring Hills,
The billowy Tempest whelms; till, upward urg'd,
The Valley to a shining Mountain swells,
Tipt with a Wreath, high-curling in the Sky.   275

    As thus the Snows arise; and foul, and fierce,
All Winter drives along the darken'd Air;
In his own loose-revolving Fields, the Swain
Disaster'd stands; sees other Hills ascend,
Of unknown joyless Brow; and other Scenes,   280
Of horrid Prospect, shag the trackless Plain:
Nor finds the River, nor the Forest, hid
Beneath the formless Wild; but wanders on
From Hill to Dale, still more and more astray;
Impatient flouncing thro' the drifted Heaps,   285

Stung with the Thoughts of Home; the Thoughts of Home
Rush on his Nerves, and call their Vigour forth
In many a vain Attempt. How sinks his Soul!
What black Despair, what Horror fills his Heart!

249–51 *MS*
249–50 His shivering Fellows, and to *trusted* Man
    His annual Visit pays: New to the Dome, *260 28 30p–38*
252 then] and *260 28 30p–38* [then *del.*] *MS*
 245–56 *26f as follows:*

   That *Providence* allows. The foodless Wilds

 245–56 *30q as follows:*

   That *Providence* allows. The Red-breast sole,
   Wisely regardful of th' embroiling sky,
   In joyless fields, and thorny thickets, leaves
   His shivering fellows, and to trusted man
   His annual visit pays. The foodless wilds   (*30q*, 230)
 257–64 *26f–46*
262 Heaven] Heavens *26f–28*
 265–75 *26f–46*
267 Food at Will:] plenteous Food. *MSLytt* Storm] Blast *26f*
271 wide Waft] fierce Blast *26f 260* the hapless] th' unhappy *26f–28*
272 Hid] Lodg'd *26f*
273 upward] upwards *26f–38*
275 That curls its Wreaths amid the freezing Sky *26f 260* Which curls
its Wreaths amid the freezing Sky *28*
 276–375 *30q–46 not in 26f–28*
283 formless Wild] white abrupt *30q–38*
288 Attempt] effort *30q–38*

---

248 Thickets⌃ *28* 249a trusted *30p–38* 250a pays. *28 30p–38* Dome⌃
28 30p–38 251 beats;] *MS* ∼, *28 30p–38* then, brisk,] *MS* ∼⌃ ∼⌃ *28*
30p–38 252 Hearth;] *MS* ∼, *28 30p–38* Floor,] *MS* ∼⌃ *28 30p–38*
252a and,] *MS* ∼⌃ *28 30p–38* 253 Family⌃] *MS Family,* *260* ∼⌃ *28*
30p–38 254 starts⌃ *28* is:] *MS* ∼; *28 30p–38* 255 Till, *260*
28 30p 300 257 *Inhabitants;* the *26f 260* ∼. The *28* *Hare 260 28*
259 Death, *26f 260* 261 *fearless 26f* 262 next, *26f 260* 263 then⌃
sad, dispers'd, *26f–38* 264 Herb, *26f 260* 265 Now⌃ *260 28* *Shep-*
herds, *26f 260* Shepherds⌃ *28* kind; *26f 260* 267 Food, *26f 260* will:
26f 260 268 strict; *26f 260* 270 Plains, *MS* 273 till⌃ *28–38*
278 Fields⌃ *MS* Swain, *MS* 279 Disaster'd, *MS* stands;] *MS* ∼,
38 ascend,] *MS* ∼⌃ *30q–38* 284 astray: *30q–45*

When for the dusky Spot, which Fancy feign'd   290
His tufted Cottage rising thro' the Snow,
He meets the Roughness of the middle Waste,
Far from the Track, and blest Abode of Man;
While round him Night resistless closes fast,
And every Tempest, howling o'er his Head,   295
Renders the savage Wilderness more wild.
Then throng the busy Shapes into his Mind,
Of cover'd Pits, unfathomably deep,
A dire Descent! beyond the Power of Frost;
Of faithless Bogs; of Precipices huge,   300
Smooth'd up with Snow; and, what is Land unknown,
What Water, of the still unfrozen Spring,
In the loose Marsh or solitary Lake,
Where the fresh Fountain from the Bottom boils.
These check his fearful Steps; and down he sinks   305
Beneath the Shelter of the shapeless Drift,
Thinking o'er all the Bitterness of Death,
Mix'd with the tender Anguish Nature shoots
Thro' the wrung Bosom of the dying Man,
His Wife, his Children, and his Friends unseen.   310
In vain for him th' officious Wife prepares
The Fire fair-blazing, and the Vestment warm;
In vain his little Children, peeping out
Into the mingling Storm, demand their Sire,
With Tears of artless Innocence. Alas!   315
Nor Wife, nor Children, more shall he behold,
Nor Friends, nor sacred Home. On every Nerve
The deadly Winter seizes; shuts up Sense;
And, o'er his inmost Vitals creeping cold,
Lays him along the Snows, a stiffen'd Corse,   320
Stretch'd out, and bleaching in the northern Blast.

    Ah little think the gay licentious Proud,
Whom Pleasure, Power, and Affluence surround;
They, who their thoughtless Hours in giddy Mirth,
And wanton, often cruel, Riot waste;   325
Ah little think they, while they dance along,
How many feel, this very Moment, Death
And all the sad Variety of Pain.

How many sink in the devouring Flood,
Or more devouring Flame. How many bleed,   330
By shameful Variance betwixt Man and Man.
How many pine in Want, and Dungeon Glooms;
Shut from the common Air, and common Use
Of their own Limbs. How many drink the Cup
Of baleful Grief, or eat the bitter Bread   335
Of Misery. Sore pierc'd by wintry Winds,
How many shrink into the sordid Hut
Of chearless Poverty. How many shake
With all the fiercer Tortures of the Mind,
Unbounded Passion, Madness, Guilt, Remorse;   340
Whence tumbled headlong from the Height of Life,
They furnish Matter for the Tragic Muse.
Even in the Vale, where Wisdom loves to dwell,
With Friendship, Peace, and Contemplation join'd,
How many, rack'd with honest Passions, droop   345
In deep retir'd Distress. How many stand
Around the Death-bed of their dearest Friends,
And point the parting Anguish. Thought fond Man
Of These, and all the thousand nameless Ills,
That one incessant Struggle render Life,   350
One Scene of Toil, of Suffering, and of Fate,
Vice in his high Career would stand appall'd,
And heedless rambling Impulse learn to think;
The conscious Heart of Charity would warm,

---

290 which] *MS* that *30q–38*
293 Track] tract *30q–38*
302 Spring] *MSLytt* eye *30q–38*
314 Storm] *MSLytt* rack *30q–38*
319 inmost] stronger *30q–38*
321 Stretch'd out] *MSLytt* Unstretch'd *30q–38*
347+ Like wailing pensive ghosts awaiting theirs, *30q–38 del. MS*
348 Anguish. Thought fond] pang. Thought but fond *30q–38*
351 Suffering] anguish *30q–38*

---

293 man: *30q–45*   299 frost, *30q–46*   303 marsh, *30q–38*   316 child-
ren‸ *30q–38*   317 nerve, *30q–34*   327 feel,] *MS* ~‸ *30q–38*   death,
300   328 Pain! *44–45*   347+ Ghosts, *MS*

And her wide Wish Benevolence dilate;   355
The social Tear would rise, the social Sigh;
And into clear Perfection, gradual Bliss,
Refining still, the social Passions work.

AND here can I forget the generous *Band,
Who, touch'd with human Woe, redressive search'd   360
Into the Horrors of the gloomy Jail?
Unpity'd, and unheard, where Misery moans;
Where Sickness pines; where Thirst and Hunger burn,
And poor Misfortune feels the Lash of Vice.
While in the Land of Liberty, the Land   365
Whose every Street and public Meeting glow
With open Freedom, little Tyrants rag'd:
Snatch'd the lean Morsel from the starving Mouth;
Tore from cold wintry Limbs the tatter'd Weed;
Even robb'd them of the last of Comforts, Sleep;   370
The free-born BRITON to the Dungeon chain'd,
Or, as the Lust of Cruelty prevail'd,
At pleasure mark'd him with inglorious Stripes;
And crush'd out Lives, by secret barbarous Ways,
That for their Country would have toil'd, or bled.   375
O great Design! if executed well,
With patient Care, and Wisdom-temper'd Zeal.
Ye Sons of Mercy! yet resume the Search;
Drag forth the legal Monsters into Light,
Wrench from their Hands Oppression's iron Rod,   380
And bid the Cruel feel the Pains they give.
Much still untouch'd remains; in this rank Age,
Much is the Patriot's weeding Hand requir'd.
The Toils of Law, (what dark insidious Men
Have cumbrous added to perplex the Truth,   385
And lengthen simple Justice into Trade)
How glorious were the Day! that saw These broke,
And every Man within the Reach of Right.

The Jail-Committee, in the Year 1729.

---

355 her] *MS* his *30q–38*
359 AND] But *MS*   Band] few *30q–38*

359 *footnote not in 30q–38*
360 search'd] sought *30q–38*
366 glow] *MS* glows *30q–38*
369 Weed] *MS* robe *30q–38*
374 secret barbarous] various nameless *30q–38*
   376–81 *44–46   not in 26f–28*

  376–81 *30q–38 as follows:*

> Hail patriot-band! who, scorning secret scorn,
> When Justice, and when Mercy led the way,
> Drag'd the detected monsters into light,
> Wrench'd from their hand Oppression's iron rod,
> And bad the cruel feel the pains they gave.   (*30q,* 355)
> Yet stop not here, let all the land rejoice,
> And make the blessing unconfin'd, as great.

  382–8 *30q–46   not in 26f–28*
387 How] Oh *30q–38*
  388+ *260 28 as follows (cf. OET Wi.* 895–7, 827–33):

> In *Russia's* wide, immeasurable, Moors,
> Where WINTER keeps his unrejoicing Court,
> And in his airy *Hall,* the loud Misrule
> Of driving *Tempest* is for ever heard: (*260,* 270)
> Seen, by the wilder'd Traveller, who roams,
> Guideless, the Yew-clad, stony, Wastes, the *Bear,*
> Rough *Tenant* of these Shades! shaggy with Ice,
> And dangling Snow, stalks thro' the Woods, forlorn.
> Slow-pac'd, and sowrer, as the Storms increase,   (*260,* 275)
> He makes his Bed beneath th' inclement Wreath,
> And scorning the Complainings of Distress,
> Hardens his Heart against assailing *Want.*

  388+ *30q–38 as follows (cf. OET Wi.* 895–7, 827–33):

> YET more outragious is the season still,   (*30q,* 365)
> A deeper horror, in SIBERIAN wilds;
> Where WINTER keeps his unrejoicing court,
> And in his airy hall the loud misrule
> Of driving tempest is for ever heard.
> There thro' the ragged woods absorpt in snow,   (*30q,* 370)

---

362 moans! *300*   366 Street∧] *MS* ∼, *30q–38*   369 cold∧] *MS* ∼
30q–38   (*30q,* 352) Justice∧ *MS*   (*260,* 271) Seen∧ *28*   (272) clad∧
stony∧ *28*   (273) Tenant *28*   (274) Woods∧ *28*   (275) sowrer∧ *28*

By wintry Famine rous'd, from all the Tract
Of horrid Mountains which the shining *Alps*,   390
And wavy *Appenines*, and *Pyrenees*,
Branch out stupendous into distant Lands;
Cruel as Death, and hungry as the Grave!
Burning for Blood! bony, and ghaunt, and grim!
Assembling Wolves in raging Troops descend;   395
And, pouring o'er the Country, bear along,
Keen as the North-Wind sweeps the glossy Snow.
All is their Prize. They fasten on the Steed,
Press him to Earth, and pierce his mighty Heart.
Nor can the Bull his awful Front defend,   400
Or shake the murdering Savages away.
Rapacious, at the Mother's Throat they fly,
And tear the screaming Infant from her Breast.
The godlike Face of Man avails him nought.
Even Beauty, Force divine! at whose bright Glance   405
The generous Lion stands in soften'd Gaze,
Here bleeds, a hapless undistinguish'd Prey.
But if, appriz'd of the severe Attack,
The Country be shut up, lur'd by the Scent,
On Church-Yards drear (inhuman to relate!)   410
The disappointed Prowlers fall, and dig
The shrouded Body from the Grave; o'er which,
Mix'd with foul Shades, and frighted Ghosts, they howl.

Among those hilly Regions, where embrac'd
In peaceful Vales the happy *Grisons* dwell;   415
Oft, rushing sudden from the loaded Cliffs,
Mountains of Snow their gathering Terrors roll.
From Steep to Steep, loud-thundering, down they come,
A wintry Waste in dire Commotion all;
And Herds, and Flocks, and Travellers, and Swains,   420
And sometimes whole Brigades of marching Troops,
Or Hamlets sleeping in the Dead of Night,
Are deep beneath the smothering Ruin whelm'd.

Now, all amid the Rigours of the Year,
In the wild Depth of Winter, while without   425
The ceaseless Winds blow Ice, be my Retreat,

388+ *30q–38 continue as follows:*

> Sole tenant of these shades, the shaggy bear,
> With dangling ice all horrid, stalks forlorn;
> Slow-pac'd, and sowrer as the storms increase,
> He makes his bed beneath the drifted snow;
> And, scorning the complainings of distress,   *(30q, 375)*
> Hardens his heart against assailing want.
> While tempted vigorous o'er the marble waste,
> On sleds reclin'd, the furry Russian sits;
> And, by his rain-deer drawn, behind him throws
> A shining kingdom in a winter's day.   *(30q, 380)*

(377–80) *del. MS*
389–92 *44–46   not in 26f*
389–92 *260–38 as follows:*

> Or from the cloudy *Alps*, and *Appenine*,
> Capt with grey Mists, and everlasting Snows,   *(260, 280)*
> Where Nature in stupendous Ruin lyes;
> And from the leaning Rock, on either Side,
> Gush out those Streams that *classic* Song renowns:

(279) Or] Now, *MSLytt*
(280) Capt with] Wrapt in *MS*
(283) that] which *28 MS*
393–413 *260–46   not in 26f*
395 raging] torrent *260–38*

396 And spread wide-wasting *Desolation* round.
Nought may their Course withstand. They bear along, *260 28*

412 Grave;] *MS* Tomb, *260–38*
414–23 *44–46   not in 26f–38*
424–6 *26f–46*
426 Ice] *260–46* keen *26f 260 press variant*

(*30q, 373*) pac'd∧ *30p–38*   (377) Waste,] *MS* ∼∧ *38*   (379) And,] *MS*
∼∧ *38*   (*260, 280*) snows; *30q–38*   (281) lies, *28–38*   (282) Rock∧
28   Side∧ *28*   (283) classic *28–38*   renowns, *28*   393 Death! *260*
28   395 Wolves, *260*   Troops, *260*   descend, *260 28*   396a Desola-
tion *28*   397 Keen, *260*   398 *Steed 260*   400 *Bull 260*   402 *Mother's*
260   fly∧ *34*   404 *God-like 260*   *Man 260*   405 *Beauty, Force*
Divine! 260   Glance *260*   406 *Lyon 260*   407 hapless, *260–38*   un-
distinguish'd, *260*   409 *Country 260*   up; *260*   410 *Church-Yards 260*
411 *Prowlers 260*   412 *Body 260*   which∧ *28*   412a Tomb, *28* ∼;
30q–38   413 *Shades 260*   *Ghosts, 260* Ghosts∧ *28*   425 *Winter 260–*
38   426 Retreat∧ *26f 260*

Between the groaning Forest and the Shore,
Beat by the boundless Multitude of Waves,
A rural, shelter'd, solitary, Scene;
Where ruddy Fire and beaming Tapers join,   430
To chear the Gloom. There studious let me sit,
And hold high Converse with the MIGHTY DEAD;
Sages of antient Time, as Gods rever'd,
As Gods beneficent, who blest Mankind
With Arts, and Arms, and humaniz'd a World.   435
Rous'd at th'inspiring Thought, I throw aside
The long-liv'd Volume; and, deep-musing, hail
The sacred Shades, that slowly-rising pass
Before my wondering Eyes. First SOCRATES,
Who firmly good in a corrupted State,   440
Against the Rage of Tyrants *single* stood,
Invincible! calm Reason's holy Law,
That *Voice* of GOD within th' attentive Mind,
Obeying, fearless, or in Life, or Death:
Great Moral Teacher! *Wisest of Mankind*!   445
SOLON the next, who built his Common-Weal
On Equity's wide Base; by *tender* Laws
A lively People curbing, yet undamp'd
Preserving still that quick peculiar Fire,
Whence in the laurel'd Field of finer Arts,   450
And of bold Freedom, they unequal'd shone,
The Pride of smiling GREECE, and Human-kind.
LYCURGUS then, who bow'd beneath the Force
Of strictest Discipline, *severely wise*,
All human Passions. Following Him, I see,   455
As at *Thermopylae* he glorious fell,
The firm *DEVOTED CHIEF, who prov'd by Deeds
The hardest Lesson which the *other* taught.
Then ARISTIDES lifts his honest Front;
Spotless of Heart, to whom th' unflattering Voice   460
Of Freedom gave the noblest Name of *Just*;
In pure majestic Poverty rever'd;
Who, even his Glory to his Country's Weal
Submitting, swell'd a haughty †*Rival's* Fame.

*LEONIDAS.   †THEMISTOCLES.

Rear'd by his Care, of softer Ray, appears 465
Cimon sweet-soul'd; whose Genius, rising strong,
Shook off the Load of young Debauch; abroad
The Scourge of *Persian* Pride, at home the Friend
Of every Worth and every splendid Art;
Modest, and simple, in the Pomp of Wealth. 470
Then the last Worthies of declining Greece,
Late-call'd to Glory, in *unequal* Times,
Pensive, appear. The fair *Corinthian* Boast,
Timoleon, temper'd happy, mild, and firm,
Who wept the *Brother* while the *Tyrant* bled. 475
And, equal to the best, the *Theban Pair,
Whose Virtues, in *heroic Concord* join'd,
Their Country rais'd to Freedom, Empire, Fame.
He too, with whom *Athenian* Honour sunk,
And left a Mass of sordid Lees behind, 480

*Pelopidas, *and* Epaminondas.

427–8 *28–46   not in 26f 260*
428 the] a *28–45*
429–39 *26f–46*
431 To chase the cheerless Gloom: there let me sit *26f–38*
440–5 *MSLytt 44–46*
442 calm] pure *MSLytt*   holy] sacred *MSLytt*
443 th' attentive] the spotless *MSLytt*
440–5 *26f–28 as follows:*

       Truth's early Champion, Martyr for his God: (*26f, 267*)

440–5 *30q–38 as follows:*

       Whose simple question to the folded heart
       Stole unperceiv'd, and from the maze of thought
       Evolv'd the secret truth—a god-like man!   (*30q, 425*)

446–526 *44–46*

---

427 Shore‸ *28 44Wks*   430 Fire, *26f–28*   join‸ *26f–28*   431a Gloom.
There *28–38*   432 mighty Dead, *26f–28* ~·~; *30q–38*   433 *Sages*
26f 260   434 Mankind, *26f*   436 Thought‸— *26f 260* ~,— *28*
437 Volume, *26f–28*   and‸ *260 28*   musing‸ *28*   438 *Shades 26f–28*
that, *26f*   rising, *26f 260* ~.— *28–38*   First, *26f*
260   440 State‸ *MSLytt*   441 single *MSLytt*   443 of God MSLytt*
444 Obeying‸ fearless‸ *MSLytt*   (*26f, 267*) God. *28*

PHOCION the *Good*; in public Life severe,
To Virtue still inexorably firm;
But when, beneath his low illustrious Roof,
Sweet Peace and happy Wisdom smooth'd his Brow,
Not Friendship softer was, nor Love more kind.   485
And He, the *last* of old LYCURGUS' Sons,
The generous Victim to that vain Attempt,
To save a rotten State, AGIS, who saw
Even SPARTA's self to servile Avarice sunk.
The two *Achaian* Heroes close the Train.   490
ARATUS, who a while relum'd the Soul
Of fondly lingering Liberty in GREECE:
And He her Darling as her latest Hope,
The *gallant* PHILOPEMON; who to Arms
Turn'd the luxurious Pomp he could not cure;   495
Or toiling in his Farm, a simple Swain;
Or, bold and skilful, thundering in the Field.

OF rougher Front, a mighty People come!
A Race of Heroes! in those virtuous Times
Which knew no Stain, save that with partial Flame   500
Their *dearest* Country they *too fondly* lov'd.

446–526 *26f–38 as follows:*

    Solon, the next, who built his Commonweal,
    On Equity's firm Base: *Lycurgus*, then,
    Severely good, and him of rugged *Rome*,   (*26f*, 270)
    Numa, who soften'd *her* rapacious *Sons*.
    Cimon sweet-soul'd, and *Aristides* just.
    Unconquer'd *Cato*, virtuous in Extreme;
    With that attemper'd Heroe, mild, and firm,
    Who wept the Brother, while the Tyrant bled.   (*26f*, 275)
    Scipio, the humane Warriour, gently brave,
    Fair Learning's Friend; who early sought the Shade,
    To dwell, with *Innocence*, and *Truth*, retir'd.
    And, equal to the best, the *Theban*, *He*
    Who, *single*, rais'd his Country into Fame.   (*26f*, 280)

(268) Commonweal,] common-wealth *300*
(269) firm] wide *30q–38*
(273) *placed after* (274–5) *in 260–38*
(274) Heroe] *26f–38 add footnote: Timoleon.*

(277-8)   Who soon the race of spotless glory ran,
             And, warm in youth, to the poetic shade,
             With friendship, and philosophy, retir'd.   *30q–38*

(279) *He*] twain, *30q–38*
(279a) twain] *30q–38 add footnote:* PELOPIDAS, *and* EPAMINONDAS.
(280) his] their *30q–38*
446–526 *MSLytt as follows* (*cf. OET* 446–9, 453–5, 503, 511, 517–20,
523–6, 466, 475–8):

> *Solon* the next, who built his Common-weal
> On Equity's wide Base by gentle Laws
> A lively People curbing, yet unquenchd
> Preserving still their native, generous Fire.
> Lycurgus then, who bow'd beneath the Force
> Of strictest Discipline, severely [Good *del.*] Wise,
> All human Passions — Next, the Light of Rome,
> Numa, who softend her rapacious Sons.
> Fabricius Scorner of all-conquering Gold.
> Scipio the *gentle* Chief, humanely Brave;
> Who soon the Race of spotless Glory ran,
> And warm in Youth, to the Poetick Shade
> With Friendship, and Philosophy retird.
> Unconquerd Cato, Virtuous in Extreme.
> Thou, too, unhappy Brutus, kind of Heart
> Whose steady Arm, by awfull Virtue urg'd,
> Lifted the *Roman* Steel against thy *Friend.*
> And They, the Boast of Greece, [while *del.*]
>   when Greece was Free,
> Cimon sweet sould, and Aristides just
> With that attemperd Hero, mild, and firm
> Who wept the Brother while the Tyrant bled
> And equal to the Best the Theban[, He
> Who single rais'd his Country into Fame. *del.*] [Pair
> Who gave their Country Liberty and Fame. *del.*] Pair
> Whose Virtues, in Heroick Concord join'd,
> Their Country raisd to Freedom, Empire, Fame.

---

492 GREECE; *44Wks*   (*26f,* 268) *Solon*ᴧ *28–38*   Commonweal ᴧ *260–38*
(269) Base. *28–38*   *Lycurgus*ᴧ *28–38*   (270) good; *260–38*   (271) her
28–38   Sons *28–38*   (272) *Cimon, 260*   just; *260–38*   (273) Extreme:
260 ∼. *28–38*   (275) *Brother*ᴧ *260 28* brother ᴧ *30q–38*   *Tyrant 260 28*
bled: *260*   (276) brave; *30q–38*   (277) Friend, *28*   (278) dwell ᴧ
28   Innocence *28*   Truth *28*   retir'd: *260*   (279) THEBAN ᴧ *30q–38*
He *28*   (280) Who ᴧ *28*   single, *28* ∼ᴧ *30q–38*

Her *better Founder* first, the Light of Rome,
Numa, who soften'd her rapacious Sons.
Servius the *King*, who laid the solid Base
On which o'er Earth the *vast Republic* spread.   505
Then the great Consuls venerable rise.
The *Public Father who the *Private* quell'd,
As on the dread Tribunal sternly sad.
He, whom his thankless Country *could not* lose,
Camillus, only vengeful to her Foes.   510
Fabricius, Scorner of all-conquering Gold;
And Cincinnatus, awful from the Plow.
Thy †willing Victim, *Carthage*, bursting loose
From all that pleading Nature could oppose,
From a whole City's Tears, by rigid Faith   515
Imperious call'd, and Honour's dire Command.
Scipio, the *gentle Chief*, humanely brave,
Who soon the Race of spotless Glory ran,
And, warm in Youth, to the *Poetic Shade*
With *Friendship* and *Philosophy* retir'd.   520
Tully, whose powerful Eloquence a while
Restrain'd the *rapid* Fate of rushing Rome.
Unconquer'd Cato, virtuous in *Extreme*.
And Thou, unhappy Brutus, kind of Heart,
Whose steady Arm, by awful Virtue urg'd,   525
Lifted the *Roman Steel* against thy *Friend*.
Thousands, besides, the Tribute of a Verse
Demand; but who can count the Stars of Heaven?
Who sing their Influence on this lower World?

    Behold, who yonder comes! in sober State,   530
Fair, mild, and strong, as is a vernal Sun:
'Tis *Phoebus*' self, or else the *Mantuan Swain*!
Great Homer too appears, of daring Wing,
Parent of Song! and *equal* by his Side,
The British Muse; join'd Hand in Hand they walk,   535
Darkling, full up the middle Steep to Fame.
Nor absent are those Shades, whose skilful Touch
Pathetic drew th' impassion'd Heart, and charm'd

---

*Marcus Junius Brutus.   †Regulus.

Transported *Athens* with the MORAL SCENE:
Nor Those who, tuneful, wak'd th' enchanting LYRE.   540

FIRST of your Kind! Society divine!
Still visit thus my Nights, for you reserv'd,
And mount my soaring Soul to Thoughts like yours.

---

527 *MSLytt 44–46*
527 *26f–38 as follows:*

    Thousands behind, the Boast of *Greece* and *Rome*, (*26f*, 281)
    Whom *Vertue* owns, the Tribute of a Verse

528–9 *26f–46*
529 Who] Or *MSLytt*
  530–2 *30q–46*
530 BEHOLD] But see *30q–38*
  530–2 *26f–28 as follows:*

    But see who yonder comes! nor comes alone,   (*26f*, 285)
    With *sober* State, and of *majestic* Mien,
    The Sister-Muses in his Train — 'Tis He!
    Maro! the best of Poets, and of Men!

  (288) *Maro!* the Glory of the Poet's Art! *26o 28*
533–6 *26f–46*
536 *Darkling*, nor miss their Way to Fame's Ascent. *26f–28*
  537–40 *MS 44–46   not in 26f–28*
537 Touch] Hand *MS 44–45*
538 drew] *MS* [trace *del.*] *MS*
540 wak'd] wake *MS*   LYRE] *MS* [String *del.*] *MS*
  537–40 *30q–38 as follows:*

    Nor absent are those tuneful shades, I ween,   (*30q*, 451)
    Taught by the Graces, whose inchanting touch
    Shakes every passion from the various string;
    Nor those, who solemnize the moral scene.

  541–9 *26f–46*
541 SOCIETY divine! immortal Minds! *26f–28*
543 Thoughts] Deeds *26f–38*

(*26f*, 282) Virtue *30q–38*   528 Demand, but *26f* ∼: But *26o*   530 *new paragraph*] *MS no new paragraph 26f–38*   (*26f*, 286) sober *28*   majestic *28*   532 swain *30q–38*   533 *daring* Wing! *26f 26o*   534 Parent *28–38* and, *26f 26o*   equal, *26f 26o* equal∧ *28–38*   535 muse *30q–38*   in Hand, *26f 26o*   536a Darkling *28*   539 moral Scene *MS*   540 Lyre *MS*   542 you *26f 26o*

Silence, thou lonely Power! the Door be thine;
See on the hallow'd Hour that none intrude,   545
Save a few chosen Friends, who sometimes deign
To bless my humble Roof, with Sense refin'd,
Learning digested well, exalted Faith,
Unstudy'd Wit, and Humour ever gay.
Or from the Muses' Hill will POPE descend,   550
To raise the sacred Hour, to bid it smile,
And with the social Spirit warm the Heart:
For tho' not sweeter his own HOMER sings,
Yet is his Life the more endearing Song.

    WHERE art Thou, HAMMOND? Thou the darling Pride,   555
The Friend and Lover of the tuneful Throng!
Ah why, dear Youth, in all the blooming Prime
Of vernal Genius, where disclosing fast
Each active Worth each manly Virtue lay,
Why wert thou ravish'd from our Hope so soon?   560
What now avails that noble Thirst of Fame,
Which stung thy fervent Breast? That treasur'd Store
Of Knowledge, early gain'd? That eager Zeal
To serve thy Country, glowing in the Band
Of YOUTHFUL PATRIOTS, who sustain her Name?   565
What now, alas! that Life-diffusing Charm
Of sprightly Wit? That Rapture for the Muse,
That Heart of Friendship, and that Soul of Joy,
Which bade with softest Light thy Virtues smile?
Ah! only shew'd, to check our fond Pursuits,   570
And teach our humbled Hopes that Life is vain!

    THUS in some deep Retirement would I pass,
The Winter-Glooms, with Friends of pliant Soul,
Or blithe, or solemn, as the Theme inspir'd:
With them would search, if Nature's boundless Frame   575
Was call'd, late-rising, from the Void of Night,
Or sprung *eternal* from th' ETERNAL MIND;
Its Life, its Laws, its Progress, and its End.
Hence larger Prospects of the beauteous Whole
Would, gradual, open on our opening Minds;   580
And each diffusive Harmony unite,

In full Perfection, to th' astonish'd Eye.
Then would we try to scan the *moral World*,
Which, tho' to us it seems embroil'd, moves on
In higher Order; fitted, and impell'd, 585
By WISDOM'S finest Hand, and issuing all
In *general Good*. The sage Historic Muse
Should next conduct us thro' the Deeps of Time:
Shew us how Empire grew, declin'd, and fell,
In scatter'd States; what makes the Nations smile, 590
Improves their Soil, and gives them double Suns;
And why they pine beneath the brightest Skies,
In Nature's richest Lap. As thus we talk'd,
Our Hearts would burn within us, would inhale

546–7 Save a few chosen . . . humble Roof] Save *Lycidas*, the Friend
26f–38 Save a few chosen Friends, that sometimes deign/To bless my
humble [Cell *del.*] Roof *MS*
546 who] that *MS 44–45*
547 Roof] *MS* [Cell *del.*] *MS*
550–4 *30q–46   not in 26f–28*
551 bid] *MS* make *30q–38*
   555–71 *44–46   not in 26f–38*
   572–608 *30q–46   not in 26f–28*
573 pliant Soul] various turn *30q–38*
574 blithe] gay *MS*
575–6 if Nature's . . . Void of Night] *MSLytt* if this unbounded frame/
Of nature rose from unproductive night *30q–38*
577 MIND;] CAUSE, *30q–38*
578 Life] springs *30q–45*
583 Then] *MS* Thence *30q–38*   try to scan] plunge into *30q–38* [dive
into *del.*] *MS* [search into *del.*] *MSLytt* [try to scan *del.*] try to grasp *MS*
584 *MS* Which, tho' more seemingly perplex'd, moves on *30q–38*
[Which tho' it spreads *del.*] *MS*
587 In universal good. Historic truth *30q–38*
589 Shew] Point *30q–38*   declin'd] *MSLytt* revolv'd *30q–38*

---

544 *Silence! 26f 260* ~ₐ *28*   Silence, *30q–38*   *Power 26f 260*   thine: *26f 260*
545 See, *26f 260*   Hour, *26f 260*   546a *Lycidas*ₐ *28–38*   572 passₐ
30q–38   576 rising,] *MSLytt* ~ₐ *44–46*   577 sprung *eternal*] *MS-
Lytt* sprung eternal *30q–38*   MIND, *44–45*   578 progressₐ *30q 30p 34*
580 Would, gradual,] *MS* ~ₐ~ₐ *30q–38*   583 moral world; *30q–38* ~~ₐ
MS   586 Wisdom's *30q–38*   587 general Good *44–45*

That Portion of Divinity, that Ray
Of purest Heaven, which lights the public Soul
Of Patriots, and of Heroes. But if doom'd,
In powerless humble Fortune, to repress
These ardent Risings of the kindling Soul;
Then, even superior to Ambition, we   600
Would learn the private Virtues; how to glide
Thro' Shades and Plains, along the smoothest Stream
Of rural Life: or snatch'd away by Hope,
Thro' the dim Spaces of Futurity,
With earnest Eye anticipate those Scenes   605
Of Happiness, and Wonder; where the Mind,
In endless Growth and infinite Ascent,
Rises from State to State, and World to World.
But when with These the serious Thought is foil'd,
We, shifting for Relief, would play the Shapes   610
Of frolic Fancy; and incessant form
Those rapid Pictures, that assembled Train
Of fleet Ideas, never join'd before,
Whence lively *Wit* excites to gay Surprize;
Or Folly-painting *Humour*, grave himself,   615
Calls Laughter forth, deep-shaking every Nerve.

MEAN-TIME the Village rouzes up the Fire;
While well attested, and as well believ'd,
Heard solemn, goes the Goblin-Story round;
Till superstitious Horror creeps o'er all.   620
Or, frequent in the sounding Hall, they wake
The rural Gambol. Rustic Mirth goes round:
The simple Joke that takes the Shepherd's Heart,
Easily pleas'd; the long loud Laugh, sincere;
The Kiss, snatch'd hasty from the sidelong Maid,   625
On purpose guardless, or pretending Sleep;
The Leap, the Slap, the Haul; and, shook to Notes
Of native Music, the respondent Dance.
Thus jocund fleets with them the Winter-Night.

THE City swarms intense. The public Haunt,   630
Full of each Theme, and warm with mixt Discourse,
Hums indistinct. The Sons of Riot flow

Down the loose Stream of false inchanted Joy,
To swift Destruction. On the rankled Soul
The gaming Fury falls; and in one Gulph   635
Of total Ruin, Honour, Virtue, Peace,
Friends, Families, and Fortune, headlong sink.
Up-springs the Dance along the lighted Dome,
Mix'd, and evolv'd, a thousand sprightly Ways.
The glittering Court effuses every Pomp;   640

---

596 public Soul] glorious flame *30q–38*
　609–16 *44–46　not in 26f–28*
　609–16 *30q–38 as follows:*

      And when with these the serious soul is foil'd,　(*30q, 505*)
      We, shifting for relief, would play the shapes
      Of frolic fancy; and incessant form
      Unnumber'd pictures, fleeting o'er the brain,
      Yet rapid still renew'd, and pour'd immense
      Into the mind, unbounded without space:　(*30q, 510*)
      The great, the new, the beautiful; or mix'd,
      Burlesque, and odd, the risible and gay;
      Whence vivid Wit, and Humour, droll of face,
      Call laughter forth, deep-shaking every nerve.

   (505–14) *del. MS*
616+ *MS and MSLytt as follows (indicating that here should follow, in
turn, lines corresponding to OET* 555–71, 656–90, 630–52 *and* 617–29)*:*
[Here the Verses on Hammond & Ld Chesterfield Q.] *MS Lytt, del. by T.*
         [the fair impartial Laugh.
     But from the Town, the rude untuneful
       [Haunt *del.*] Range
     Of prowling Men, return, my rural Muse,
     To where the Village rouzes up the Fire;
     While well attested, &c *all del.*] *MS*
　617–29 *30q–46　not in 26f–28*
　629+ *MS as follows (cf. OET* 691a)*:*
     CLEAR Frost succeeds; &c/rowls the mighty Flood.

　630–52 *30q–46　not in 26f–28*
638 Up-springs] Rises *30q–38*

---

597 doom'd⌃ *300*　　　607 Ascent,] *MS* ⌃ *38–45*　　　619 round, *MS*
621 *new paragraph 30q–38*　　　622 round; *46*　　　626 sleep: *300 38–46*
630 swarms, *MS*　　　637 fortune⌃ *30q–38*

The Circle deepens: beam'd from gaudy Robes,
Tapers, and sparkling Gems, and radiant Eyes,
A soft Effulgence o'er the Palace waves:
While, a gay Insect in *his* Summer-shine,
The Fop, light-fluttering, spreads his mealy Wings.   645

DREAD o'er the Scene, the Ghost of HAMLET stalks;
OTHELLO rages; poor MONIMIA mourns;
And BELVIDERA pours her Soul in Love.
Terror alarms the Breast; the comely Tear
Steals o'er the Cheek: or else the COMIC MUSE   650
Holds to the World a Picture of itself,
And raises sly the fair impartial Laugh.
Sometimes she lifts her Strain, and paints the Scenes
Of beauteous Life; whate'er can deck Mankind,
Or charm the Heart, in generous *BEVIL shew'd.   655

O THOU, whose Wisdom, solid yet refin'd,
Whose Patriot-Virtues, and consummate Skill
To touch the finer Springs that move the World,
Join'd to whate'er the *Graces* can bestow,
And all *Apollo's* animating Fire,   660
Give Thee, with pleasing Dignity, to shine
At once the Guardian, Ornament, and Joy,
Of polish'd Life; permit the *Rural Muse*,
O CHESTERFIELD, to grace with Thee her Song!
Ere to the Shades again she humbly flies,   665
Indulge her fond Ambition, in thy Train,
(For every Muse has in thy Train a Place)
To mark thy various full-accomplish'd Mind:
To mark that Spirit, which, with *British Scorn*,
Rejects th' Allurements of corrupted Power;   670
That elegant Politeness, which excels,
Even in the Judgment of presumptuous *France*,
The boasted Manners of her shining Court;
That Wit, the vivid Energy of Sense,
The Truth of Nature, which, with *Attic* Point,   675
And kind well-temper'd Satire, smoothly keen,

A Character in the CONSCIOUS LOVERS, *written by Sir* RICHARD STEELE.

Steals through the Soul, and without Pain corrects.
Or, rising thence with yet a brighter Flame,
O let me hail thee on some glorious Day,
When to the listening Senate, ardent, croud   680
BRITANNIA'S Sons to hear her pleaded Cause.
Then drest by Thee, more amiably fair,
Truth the soft Robe of mild Persuasion wears:
Thou to assenting Reason giv'st again
Her own enlighten'd Thoughts; call'd from the Heart,   685
Th' obedient Passions on thy Voice attend;
And even reluctant Party feels a while
Thy gracious Power: as thro' the vary'd Maze
Of Eloquence, now smooth, now quick, now strong,
Profound and clear, you roll the copious Flood.   690

To thy lov'd Haunt return, my happy Muse:
For now, behold, the joyous Winter-Days,
Frosty, succeed; and thro' the blue Serene,
For Sight too fine, th' etherial Nitre flies;
Killing infectious Damps, and the spent Air   695

641–2 MS The circle deepens; rain'd from radiant eyes, *30q–38*
641 beam'd] MS [rain'd *del.*] MS
644 a gay Insect in *his*] thick as insects in the *30q–38*
649 Assenting terror shakes; the silent tear *30q–38* Deep-thrilling
Terror shakes; the comely Tear MS *44–45*
650 o'er] down MS
651 a Picture] the picture *30q–38*
  652+ MS and MSLytt *as follows* (*indicating that here should follow, in
turn, lines corresponding to OET 551–71, 656–90, and 617–29*):
[Here the Verses upon Hammond, & Ld Chesterfield] *MS Lytt del. by T.*
        But from the Town, the rude &c
        fleets with them the Winter-Night *MS*
[Quaere, Does not there want a better Connection here.] *MS Lytt, del.
by T.*
  653–90 *44–46   not in 26f–38*
  691–759 *30q–46*
691–3 CLEAR frost succeeds; and thro' the blue serene, *30q–38*

---

646 DREAD, MS   scene‸ *30q–34* MS   651 itself‸ *300*   671 excels‸
44–45   694 flies: *30q–38*

Storing afresh with elemental Life.
Close crouds the shining Atmosphere; and binds
Our strengthen'd Bodies in its cold Embrace,
Constringent; feeds, and animates our Blood;
Refines our Spirits, thro' the new-strung Nerves,   700
In swifter Sallies darting to the Brain;
Where sits the Soul, intense, collected, cool,
Bright as the Skies, and as the Season keen.
All Nature feels the renovating Force
Of Winter, only to the thoughtless Eye   705
In Ruin seen. The Frost-concocted Glebe
Draws in abundant vegetable Soul,
And gathers Vigour for the coming Year.
A stronger Glow sits on the lively Cheek
Of ruddy Fire: and luculent along   710
The purer Rivers flow; their sullen Deeps,
Transparent, open to the Shepherd's Gaze,
And murmur hoarser at the fixing Frost.

    WHAT art thou, Frost? and whence are thy keen Stores
Deriv'd, thou secret all-invading Power,   715
Whom even th' illusive Fluid cannot fly?
Is not thy potent Energy, unseen,
Myriads of little Salts, or hook'd, or shap'd
Like double Wedges, and diffus'd immense
Thro' Water, Earth, and Ether? Hence at Eve,   720
Steam'd eager from the red Horizon round,
With the fierce Rage of Winter deep suffus'd,
An icy Gale, oft shifting, o'er the Pool
Breathes a blue Film, and in its mid Career
Arrests the bickering Stream. The loosen'd Ice,   725
Let down the Flood, and half dissolv'd by Day,
Rustles no more; but to the sedgy Bank
Fast grows, or gathers round the pointed Stone,
A crystal Pavement, by the Breath of Heaven
Cemented firm; till, seiz'd from Shore to Shore,   730
The whole imprison'd River growls below.
Loud rings the frozen Earth, and hard reflects
A double Noise; while, at his evening Watch,
The village Dog deters the nightly Thief;

The Heifer lows; the distant Water-fall 735
Swells in the Breeze; and, with the hasty Tread
Of Traveller, the hollow-sounding Plain
Shakes from afar. The full ethereal Round,
Infinite Worlds disclosing to the View,
Shines out intensely keen; and, all one Cope 740
Of starry Glitter, glows from Pole to Pole.
From Pole to Pole the rigid Influence falls,
Thro' the still Night, incessant, heavy, strong,
And seizes Nature fast. It freezes on;
Till Morn, late-rising o'er the drooping World, 745
Lifts her pale Eye unjoyous. Then appears
The various Labour of the silent Night:
Prone from the dripping Eave, and dumb Cascade,
Whose idle Torrents only seem to roar,
The pendant Icicle; the Frost-Work fair, 750
Where transient Hues, and fancy'd Figures rise;
Wide-spouted o'er the Hill, the frozen Brook,
A livid Tract, cold-gleaming on the Morn;
The Forest bent beneath the plumy Wave;
And by the Frost refin'd the whiter Snow, 755
Incrusted hard, and sounding to the Tread
Of early Shepherd, as he pensive seeks
His pining Flock, or from the Mountain-top,
Pleas'd with the slippery Surface, swift descends.

---

706 *MS* In desolation seen. The vacant glebe *30q–38*
712 Transparent] Amazing *30q–38* Delightful *MS*
714 are] art *44*
722 fierce] still *30q–38*
731 imprison'd] *MS* detruded *30q–38*
737 hollow-sounding] many-sounding *30q–38* [shrill-resounding *del.*]
shrilly-sounding *MS*
751+ The liquid kingdom all to solid turn'd; *30q–38 not in 44–46*
752 Hill] *MS* brow *30q–38*

---

705 Winter] *MS* WINTER *30q–38*   720 earth∧ *30q–34*   722 Winter]
MS WINTER *30q–38*   730 till,] *MS* ∼∧ *30q–38*

On blithsome Frolicks bent, the youthful Swains,   760
While every Work of Man is laid at rest,
Fond o'er the River croud, in various Sport
And Revelry dissolv'd; where mixing glad,
Happiest of all the Train! the raptur'd Boy
Lashes the whirling Top. Or, where the *Rhine*   765
Branch'd out in many a long Canal extends,
From every Province swarming, void of Care,

691–759 *26f–28 as follows:*

      Clear Frost succeeds, and thro' the blew Serene,
    For Sight too fine, th' Ætherial Nitre flies,
    To bake the Glebe, and bind the slip'ry Flood.
    This of the wintry Season is the Prime;
    Pure are the Days, and lustrous are the Nights,   *(26f,* 305*)*
    Brighten'd with starry Worlds, till then unseen.
    Mean while, the Orient, darkly red, breathes forth
    An Icy Gale, that, in its mid Career,
    Arrests the bickering Stream. The nightly Sky,
    And all her glowing Constellations pour   *(26f,* 310*)*
    Their rigid Influence down: It freezes on
    Till Morn, late-rising, o'er the drooping World,
    Lifts her pale Eye, unjoyous: then appears
    The various Labour of the silent Night,
    The pendant Isicle, the Frost-Work fair,   *(26f,* 315*)*
    Where thousand Figures rise, the crusted Snow,
    Tho' white, made whiter, by the fining North.

  (306) Brighten'd] Radiant *260 28*
  (316) thousand] fancy'd *260 28*
  (317+) And Gem-besprinkled in the Mid-Day Beam *260 28 not in*
  26f
760–1 *26f–46*
762–78 *44–46*
762–78 *26f–28 as follows* (*cf.* OET 789–93)*:*

    Rush o'er the watry Plains, and, shuddering, view *(26f,* 320*)*
    The fearful Deeps below: or with the Gun,
    And faithful Spaniel, range the ravag'd Fields,
    And, adding to the Ruins of the Year,
    Distress the Feathery, or the Footed *Game.*

762–78 *30q–38 as follows:*

    Fond o'er the river rush, and shuddering view   *(30q,* 620*)*
    The doubtful deeps below. Or where the lake

And long canal the cerule plain extend,
The city pours her thousands, swarming all,
From every quarter: and, with him who slides;
Or skating sweeps, swift as the winds, along,　　　(*30q*, 625)
In circling poise; or else disorder'd falls,
His feet, illuded, sprawling to the sky,
While the laugh rages round; from end to end,
Encreasing still, resounds the crowded scene.

(620–9) *del. MS*

762–78 *MS as follows:*

Fond o'er the River croud, in various Sport
And [Jollity *del.*] Revelry dissolv'd; [while *del.* and *del.*] where mixing
　glad,
Even with his Master, Partner of his Play,
Happiest of all the Train! the raptur'd Boy
Lashes the whirling Top. Or, where the Rhine
Branch'd out in many a long Canal extends,
From every Province swarming, void of Care,
[Batavia pours her Thousands, swarming *del.*]
The rous'd Batavians rush; [with those who skate *del.*] and as they [skate
　del.] sweep [wide *del.*]
On sounding skates a thousand different Ways
In circling Poise, swift as the Winds, along,
[Is only then a *del.*]
Gay only then, [is all a Scene of Joy *del.*] are madden'd all with Joy.
[Then to their gelid King the northern Courts *del.*]
The northern Courts, a long the harden'd Snow,
Pour a new Pomp. [On rapid sleds reclin'd *del.*] Hung o'er the rapid
　sled,
Their vigorous youth in kind Contention wheel
The long-resounding Course. Meantime around,
Their charms exalted by the [pointing *del.*] healthful year,
[Kindling the manly strife *del.*] Kindling the Strife, fair Scandinavia's
　dames
And Russia's buxom daughters glowing shine.

(26f, 302) fine∧ 28　　　(304) *Prime; 260*　　　(307) Mean while∧ 28
(311) down. 28　　on, 260 28　　　(312) rising∧ 28　　　(313) unjoyous. 28
Then 260 28　　　(314) Night; 260 28　　　(315) Isicle; 28　　　(316) rise;
260 28　　　(317) white∧ 28　　whiter∧ 28　　　760 *no new paragraph 26f*
(26f, 320) and∧ shuddering∧ 28　　　(321) Or, 260　　　(322) Fields; 260 28
(323) And∧ 28　　　(324) Game 28

Batavia rushes forth; and as they sweep,
On sounding Skates, a thousand different Ways,
In circling Poise, swift as the Winds, along,   770
The *then gay* Land is madden'd all to Joy.
Nor less the northern Courts, wide o'er the Snow,
Pour a new Pomp. Eager, on rapid Sleds,
Their vigorous Youth in bold Contention wheel
The long-resounding Course. Mean-time, to raise   775
The manly Strife, with highly-blooming Charms,
Flush'd by the Season, *Scandinavia's* Dames,
Or *Russia's* buxom Daughters glow around.

    PURE, quick, and sportful, is the wholesome Day;
But soon elaps'd. The horizontal Sun,   780
Broad o'er the South, hangs at his utmost Noon;
And, ineffectual, strikes the gelid Cliff.
His azure Gloss the Mountain still maintains,
Nor feels the feeble Touch. Perhaps the Vale
Relents a while to the reflected Ray;   785
Or from the Forest falls the cluster'd Snow,
Myriads of Gems, that in the waving Gleam
Gay-twinkle as they scatter. Thick around
Thunders the Sport of Those, who with the Gun,
And Dog impatient bounding at the Shot,   790
Worse than the Season, desolate the Fields;
And, adding to the Ruins of the Year,
Distress the footed or the feather'd Game.

    BUT what is This? Our infant Winter sinks,
Divested of his Grandeur, should our Eye   795
Astonish'd shoot into the *Frigid Zone*;
Where, for relentless Months, continual Night,
Holds o'er the glittering Waste her starry Reign.

    THERE, thro' the Prison of unbounded Wilds,
Barr'd by the Hand of Nature from Escape,   800
Wide-roams the *Russian* Exile. Nought around
Strikes his sad Eye, but Desarts lost in Snow;
And heavy-loaded Groves; and solid Floods,
That stretch, athwart the solitary Vast,

Their icy Horrors to the frozen Main;   805
And chearless Towns far-distant, never bless'd,
Save when its annual Course the Caravan
Bends to the golden Coast of rich *Cathay,
With News of Human-kind. Yet there Life glows;
Yet cherish'd there, beneath the shining Waste,   810
The furry Nations harbour: tipt with Jet,
Fair Ermines, spotless as the Snows they press;
Sables, of glossy Black; and dark-embrown'd,
Or beauteous freakt with many a mingled Hue,
Thousands besides, the costly Pride of Courts.   815
There, warm together press'd, the trooping Deer
Sleep on the new-fallen Snows; and, scarce his Head
Rais'd o'er the heapy Wreath, the branching Elk
Lies slumbering sullen in the white Abyss.
The ruthless Hunter wants nor Dogs nor Toils,   820
Nor with the Dread of sounding Bows he drives

The old Name for China.

779–93 *30q–46   not in 26f–28*
783 The mountain still his azure gloss maintains, *30q–38*
787–8 that in the waving Gleam . . . Thick around] *MS* that, by the
breeze diffus'd,/Gay-twinkle thro' the gleam. Heard thick around,
30q–38
794–8 *44–46   not in 26f–28*
794–8 *30q–38 as follows (cf. OET 890):*

> BUT what is this? these infant tempests what?   (*30q*, 645)
> The mockery of WINTER: should our eye
> Astonish'd shoot into the frozen zone;
> Where more than half the joyless year is night;
> And, failing gradual, life at last goes out.

(645   *d l. MS*
798+ *MS as follows (indicating that here should follow lines correspond-
ing to OET 799–886):*

> [—— their blooming Daugters Woe. *del.*]

799–819 *44–46   not in 26f–38*
808 footnote for] of *44Wks*
820–1 *46   not in 26f–38*

---

789 who, *30q 30p 34*   793 footed, *30q–38*   817 new∧ *46*

The fearful-flying Race; with ponderous Clubs,
As weak against the Mountain-Heaps they push
Their beating Breast in vain, and piteous bray,
He lays them quivering on th' ensanguin'd Snows,   825
And with loud Shouts rejoicing bears them home.
There thro' the piny Forest half-absorpt,
Rough Tenant of these Shades, the shapeless Bear,
With dangling Ice all horrid, stalks forlorn;
Slow-pac'd, and sourer as the Storms increase,   830
He makes his Bed beneath th' inclement Drift,
And, with stern Patience, scorning weak Complaint,
Hardens his Heart against assailing Want.

    WIDE o'er the spacious Regions of the North,
That see *Boötes* urge his tardy Wain,   835
A boisterous Race, by frosty *Caurus pierc'd,
Who little Pleasure know and fear no Pain,
Prolific swarm. They once relum'd the Flame
Of lost Mankind in polish'd Slavery sunk,
Drove martial †Horde on Horde, with dreadful Sweep   840
Resistless rushing o'er th' enfeebled South,
And gave the vanquish'd World another Form.
Not such the Sons of *Lapland*: wisely They
Despise th' insensate barbarous Trade of War;
They ask no more than simple Nature gives,   845
They love their Mountains and enjoy their Storms.
No false Desires, no Pride-created Wants,
Disturb the peaceful Current of their Time;
And thro' the restless ever-tortur'd Maze
Of Pleasure, or Ambition, bid it rage.   850
Their Rain-Deer form their Riches. These their Tents,
Their Robes, their Beds, and all their homely Wealth
Supply, their wholesome Fare, and chearful Cups.
Obsequious at their Call, the docile Tribe
Yield to the Sled their Necks, and whirl them swift   855
O'er Hill and Dale, heap'd into one Expanse
Of marbled Snow, or far as Eye can sweep
With a blue Crust of Ice unbounded glaz'd.

---

  * *The North-West Wind.*   † *The wandering* Scythian-Clans.

By dancing Meteors then, that ceaseless shake
A waving Blaze refracted o'er the Heavens, 860
And vivid Moons, and Stars that keener play
With doubled Lustre from the radiant Waste,
Even in the Depth of *Polar Night*, they find
A wondrous Day: enough to light the Chace,
Or guide their daring Steps to *Finland*-Fairs. 865
Wish'd Spring returns; and from the hazy South,
While dim Aurora slowly moves before,
The welcome Sun, just verging up at first,
By small Degrees extends the swelling Curve;
Till seen at last for gay rejoicing Months, 870
Still round and round, his spiral Course he winds,
And as he nearly dips his flaming Orb,
Wheels up again, and reascends the Sky.
In that glad Season, from the Lakes and Floods,

820–1 *44–45 as follows:*

> Nor Dogs, nor Toils, he wants; nor with the Dread
> Of sounding Bows the ruthless Hunter drives

822–6 *44–46   not in 26f–38*
827–33 *44–46   not in 26f*
In Wi.260–38 the bear is introduced before the Alpine and Appenine wolves. Versions of the passage describing the bear are printed consecutively in the apparatus to OET Wi. 388+, but variants are also recorded below.

827–8 Seen, by the wilder'd Traveller, who roams,
  Guideless, the Yew-clad, stony, Wastes, the *Bear, 260 28*
  There thro' the ragged woods absorpt in snow,
  Sole tenant of these shades, the shaggy bear, *30q–38*

829 Rough *Tenant* of these Shades! shaggy with Ice,
  And dangling Snow, stalks thro' the Woods, forlorn. *260 28*

831 th' inclement Drift,] th' inclement Wreath, *260 28* the drifted snow; *30q–38*
832 And scorning the Complainings of Distress, *260–38*
  834–86 *44–46   not in 26f–38*
848 Time] Days *44–45*

827a Seen‸ *28*   828a clad‸ stony‸ *28*   832a And, *30q–38*   833 Want. *260 28*   837 know, *45*   846 Mountains, *45*   868 Sun‸ *45*   871 round‸ his *45*

Where pure **Niemi's* fairy Mountains rise,   875
And fring'd with Roses †*Tenglio* rolls his Stream,
They draw the copious Fry. With These, at Eve,
They chearful-loaded to their Tents repair;
Where, all Day long in useful Cares employ'd,
Their kind unblemish'd Wives the Fire prepare.   880
Thrice happy Race! by Poverty secur'd
From legal Plunder and rapacious Power:
In whom fell Interest never yet has sown
The Seeds of Vice; whose spotless Swains ne'er knew
Injurious Deed, nor, blasted by the Breath   885
Of faithless Love, their blooming Daughters Woe.

    STILL pressing on, beyond *Tornéa's* Lake,
And *Hecla* flaming thro' a Waste of Snow,
And farthest *Greenland*, to the Pole itself,
Where failing gradual Life at length goes out,   890
The Muse expands her solitary Flight;
And, hovering o'er the wild stupendous Scene,
Beholds new Seas beneath ‡another Sky.
Thron'd in his Palace of cerulean Ice,
Here WINTER holds his unrejoicing Court;   895
And thro' his airy Hall the loud Misrule
Of driving Tempest is for ever heard:
Here the grim Tyrant meditates his Wrath;
Here arms his Winds with all-subduing Frost;
Moulds his fierce Hail, and treasures up his Snows,   900
With which he now oppresses half the Globe.

    THENCE winding eastward to the *Tartar's* Coast,
She sweeps the howling Margin of the Main;

---

*M. de Maupertuis, *in his Book on* the Figure of the Earth, *after having
described the beautiful Lake and Mountain of* Niemi *in* Lapland, *says*—"*From
this Height we had Occasion several times to see those Vapours rise from the Lake
which the People of the Country call* Haltios, *and which they deem to be the guardian
Spirits of the Mountains. We had been frighted with Stories of Bears that haunted
this Place, but saw none. It seem'd rather a Place of Resort for* Fairies *and* Genii
than Bears."

  †*The same Author observes*—"*I was surprized to see upon the Banks of this
River,* (the Tenglio) *Roses of as lively a Red as any that are in our Gardens.*"

  ‡*The other Hemisphere.*

Where undissolving, from the First of Time,
Snows swell on Snows amazing to the Sky;   905
And icy Mountains high on Mountains pil'd,
Seem to the shivering Sailor from afar,
Shapeless and white, an Atmosphere of Clouds.
Projected huge, and horrid, o'er the Surge,
Alps frown on Alps; or rushing hideous down,   910
As if old Chaos was again return'd,

887–94 *MS 44–46 not in 26f–38*
887–91 *MS   MS first draft as follows:*

[Still farther on, even to the Pole itself,
Where failing gradual Life at [last *del.*] Length goes out,
The Muse, sole Creature there alive, expands
A [dare *del.*] fearless Wing
The Muse [expands *del.*] directs her solitary [Wing *del.*] Flight *all del.*]

891 expands] directs *MS*
892 stupendous] *MS* [tremendous *del.*] *MS*
893 footnote *not in MS*
894 Thron'd] *MS* [High *del.*] *MS*   his] a *MS*   cerulean] *MS*
[eternal *del.*] *MS*
   895–7 *MS 44–46 not in 26f*
*In Wi.260–38 lines on Winter's court appear before the description of the
bear. Versions of these lines are printed consecutively in the apparatus to
OET Wi. 388+, but variants are also recorded below.*
895 Here] *MS* Where *260–38*   holds] *MS* keeps *260–38*
896 thro'] *MS* in *260–38*
   898–903 *MS 44–46 not in 26f–38*
899 arms] wings *MS*
901 Globe] *MS* [World *del.*] *MS*
902 winding] *MS* [curving *del.*] *MS*
903 the howling] *MS* [along the *del.*] *MS*
   904–11 *30q–46 not in 26f–28*
904 Where] *MS* There *30q–38*
906 high] *MS* there, *30q–38*
909 Surge] main *30q–38* Deep *MS*

---

885 nor∧ *45*   887 Tornea's *MS*   888 Hecla *MS*   889 Greenland
MS   895 Winter *MS*   Court, *260–38*   896 *Hall, 260*   897 heard,
28 ∼. *30q–38*   906 icy Mountains, *44–45*   908 Shapeless∧] *MS* ∼,
30q–38   910 Alps . . . Alps] *MS* ALPS . . . ALPS *300 38*

Wide-rend the Deep, and shake the solid Pole.
Ocean itself no longer can resist
The binding Fury; but, in all its Rage
Of Tempest taken by the boundless Frost,   915
Is many a Fathom to the Bottom chain'd,
And bid to roar no more: a bleak Expanse,
Shagg'd o'er with wavy Rocks, chearless, and void
Of every Life, that from the dreary Months
Flies conscious southward. Miserable they!   920
Who, here entangled in the gathering Ice,
Take their last Look of the descending Sun;
While, full of Death, and fierce with tenfold Frost,
The long long Night, incumbent o'er their Heads,
Falls horrible. Such was the *BRITON's Fate,   925
As with *first* Prow, (What have not BRITONS dar'd!)
He for the Passage sought, attempted since
So much in vain, and seeming to be shut
By jealous Nature with eternal Bars.
In these fell Regions, in *Arzina* caught,   930
And to the stony Deep his idle Ship
Immediate seal'd, he with his hapless Crew,
Each full-exerted at his several Task,
Froze into Statues; to the Cordage glued
The Sailor, and the Pilot to the Helm.   935

    HARD by these Shores, where scarce his freezing Stream
Rolls the wild *Oby*, live the Last of Men;
And, half-enliven'd by the distant Sun,
That rears and ripens Man, as well as Plants,
Here Human Nature wears its rudest Form.   940
Deep from the piercing Season sunk in Caves,
Here by dull Fires, and with unjoyous Chear,
They waste the tedious Gloom. Immers'd in Furs,
Doze the gross Race. Nor sprightly Jest, nor Song,
Nor Tenderness they know; nor Aught of Life,   945
Beyond the kindred Bears that stalk without.
Till Morn at length, her Roses drooping all,

* *Sir* HUGH WILLOUGHBY, *sent by* QUEEN ELIZABETH *to discover the North-East Passage.*

Sheds a long Twilight brightening o'er their Fields,
And calls the quiver'd Savage to the Chace.

WHAT cannot active Government perform, 950
New-moulding Man? Wide-stretching from these Shores,
A People savage from remotest Time,
A huge neglected Empire ONE VAST MIND,
By HEAVEN inspir'd, from Gothic Darkness call'd.

912–13 *44–46   not in 26f–28*
912–13 *30q–38 as follows:*

> Shake the firm pole, and make an ocean boil.
> Whence heap'd abrupt along the howling shore,
> And into various shapes (as fancy leans)   *(30q, 660)*
> Work'd by the wave, the crystal pillars heave,
> Swells the blue portico, the gothic dome
> Shoots fretted up; and birds, and beasts, and men,
> Rise into mimic life, and sink by turns.
> The restless deep itself cannot resist   *(30q, 665)*

  (659–64) *del. MS*
 914–46 *30q–46   not in 26f–28*
924 Heads] head *30q–38*
925 footnote *sent*] *sent out 30q*
936 these Shores] this Coast *MS*
936–7 where scarce . . . Last of Men] the last of mankind live *30q–38*
where wedg'd within the Main/Lies icy *Oby*, live the last of Men *MS*
936a mankind] Mortals *MS*
938 half-] scarce *30q–38*
940 wears its rudest Form] just begins to dawn *30q–38*
943 waste] *MSLytt* wear *30q–38*
944 Doze] Ly *30q–38* Sleep *MS*
 947–8 *MS 44–46   not in 26f–28*
 947–8 *30q–38 as follows:*

> Till long-expected morning looks at length   *(30q, 698)*
> Faint on their fields (where WINTER reigns alone)

949 *30q–46   not in 26f–28*
950–87 *44–46   not in 26f–38*

(30q, 660) Shapes, *MS*   leans, *MS*   *(662)* GOTHIC *30o 38*   914 but,]
MS ~∧ *30o–38*   923 Frost,] *MS* ~∧ *38*   926 first *30q–38*   933 full-]
MS ~∧ *30q–46*   939 ∧That] *MS* (~ *30q–38*   Plants,] *MS* ~) *30q–38*

Immortal PETER! First of Monarchs! He   955
His stubborn Country tam'd, her Rocks, her Fens,
Her Floods, her Seas, her ill-submitting Sons;
And while the fierce *Barbarian* he subdu'd,
To more exalted Soul he raised the *Man*.
Ye Shades of antient Heroes, ye who toil'd   960
Thro' long successive Ages to build up
A lab'ring Plan of State, behold at once
The Wonder done! behold the matchless Prince!
Who left his native Throne, where reign'd till then
A mighty Shadow of unreal Power;   965
Who greatly spurn'd the slothful Pomp of Courts;
And roaming every Land, in every Port,
His Scepter laid aside, with glorious Hand
Unweary'd plying the mechanic Tool,
Gather'd the Seeds of Trade, of useful Arts,   970
Of Civil Wisdom, and of Martial Skill.
Charg'd with the Stores of *Europe* home he goes!
Then Cities rise amid th' illumin'd Waste;
O'er joyless Deserts smiles the rural Reign;
Far-distant Flood to Flood is social join'd;   975
Th' astonish'd *Euxine* hears the *Baltic* roar;
Proud Navies ride on Seas that never foam'd
With daring Keel before; and Armies stretch
Each Way their dazzling Files, repressing here
The frantic *Alexander* of the North,   980
And awing there stern *Othman's* shrinking Sons.
Sloth flies the Land, and *Ignorance*, and *Vice*,
Of old Dishonour proud: it glows around,
Taught by the ROYAL HAND that rous'd the Whole,
One Scene of Arts, of Arms, of rising Trade: 985
For what his Wisdom plann'd, and Power enforc'd,
More potent still, his great *Example* shew'd.

MUTTERING, the Winds at Eve, with blunted Point,
Blow hollow-blustering from the South. Subdu'd,
The Frost resolves into a trickling Thaw.   990
Spotted the Mountains shine; loose Sleet descends,
And floods the Country round. The Rivers swell,
Of Bonds impatient. Sudden from the Hills,

O'er Rocks and Woods, in broad brown Cataracts,
A thousand snow-fed Torrents shoot at once; 995
And, where they rush, the wide-resounding Plain
Is left one slimy Waste. Those sullen Seas,
That wash th' ungenial Pole, will rest no more
Beneath the Shackles of the mighty North;
But, rousing all their Waves, resistless heave— 1000
And hark! the lengthening Roar continuous runs
Athwart the rifted Deep: at once it bursts,
And piles a thousand Mountains to the Clouds.
Ill fares the Bark with trembling Wretches charg'd,
That, tost amid the floating Fragments, moors 1005
Beneath the Shelter of an icy Isle,
While Night o'erwhelms the Sea, and Horror looks

988–92 *26f–46*
988 BUT hark! the nightly Winds, with hollow Voice *26f* MUTTERING,
the Winds, at Eve, with hoarser Voice, *260–38*
989–90 Blow hollow blustering . . . The Frost] Blow, blustering, from
the South:—the Frost subdu'd,/Gradual, *26f–38*
990 trickling] weeping *26f*
   993–7 *260–46*
993 Of Bonds impatient. Sudden] Impatient for the Day. Broke *260–38*
   993–7 *26f as follows:*

      Impatient for the Day. — Those sullen Seas,

   998–1012 *26f–46*
998 That] Which *28*
1002 Deep:] Main; *26f–38*
1004 with trembling Wretches charg'd] the Wretches' last Resort *26f*
260 the Wretch's last Resort *28–38*
1005 tost] lost *26f–38*

988a Winds∧ *28–38*   Eve∧ *28*   Voice∧ *28–38*   989a Blow∧ *28–38* bluster-
ing∧ *28–38*   South. The *28–38*   990 resolves, *260*   991 Spotted,
26f 260   shine: *26f 260*   Loose *260*   992 round: *26f 260*   the Rivers
26f   994 broad, *260 28*   995 thousand, *260 28*   fed, *260*   shoot,
260   998 more, *26f*   999 North, *28*   1000 heave,— *26f 260* ∼;
— *28*   1001 hark!— *26f 260*   Roar, continuous, *26f 260*   1002 once,
26f 260   1002a Main: *28–38*   1003 Clouds! *26f–28*   1004 Bark,
26f–38   1006 Isle; *26f 260*   1007 *Horror 260 28*

More horrible. Can human Force endure
Th' assembled Mischiefs that besiege them round?
Heart-gnawing Hunger, fainting Weariness,   1010
The Roar of Winds and Waves, the Crush of Ice,
Now ceasing, now renew'd with louder Rage,
And in dire Echoes bellowing round the Main.
More to embroil the Deep, Leviathan
And his unwieldy Train, in dreadful Sport,   1015
Tempest the loosen'd Brine, while thro' the Gloom,
Far, from the bleak inhospitable Shore,
Loading the Winds, is heard the hungry Howl
Of famish'd Monsters, there awaiting Wrecks.
Yet PROVIDENCE, that *ever-waking Eye*,   1020
Looks down with Pity on the feeble Toil
Of Mortals lost to Hope, and lights them safe,
Thro' all this dreary Labyrinth of Fate.

'TIS done!—Dread WINTER spreads his latest Glooms,
And reigns tremendous o'er the conquer'd Year.   1025
How dead the vegetable Kingdom lies!
How dumb the tuneful! Horror wide extends
His desolate Domain. Behold, fond Man!
See here thy pictur'd Life; pass some few Years,
Thy flowering Spring, thy Summer's ardent Strength,   1030
Thy sober Autumn fading into Age,
And pale concluding Winter comes at last,
And shuts the Scene. Ah! whither now are fled,
Those Dreams of Greatness? those unsolid Hopes
Of Happiness? those Longings after Fame?   1035
Those restless Cares? those busy bustling Days?
Those gay-spent, festive Nights? those veering Thoughts,
Lost between Good and Ill, that shar'd thy Life?
All now are vanish'd! VIRTUE sole survives,
Immortal, never-failing Friend of Man,   1040
His Guide to Happiness on high.—And see!
'Tis come, the glorious Morn! the second Birth
Of Heaven, and Earth! Awakening Nature hears

1008 Force] Hearts *26f 260*
1010 Heart-gnawing] Unlist'ning *26f 260*

1013 *30q–46*
1013 *26f–28 as follows:*

> And bellowing round the Main: Nations remote,
> Shook from their Midnight-Slumbers, deem they hear
> Portentous Thunder, in the troubled Sky.   (*26f*, 348)

(348) troubled] gelid *260 28*
1014–43 *26f–46*
1015 dreadful] horrid *26f–38*
1017 bleak] dire, *26f–28*   inhospitable] unhospitable *26f 260*
1018–19 Loading the Winds, is heard the hungry Howl/Of] The Lyon's
Rage, the Wolf's sad Howl is heard,/And *26f* At once, is heard th' united,
hungry, Howl,/Of *260*
1019 famish'd Monsters, there awaiting Wrecks] all the fell Society of
Night *26f–28*
1021 feeble] fruitless *26f–38*
1024 spreads his latest Glooms] has subdu'd the Year *26f–38*
1025 conquer'd Year.] desart Plains! *26f–38*
1028 desolate Domain. Behold] solitary Empire—Now *26f–28* solitary
empire. Here *30q–38* melancholy Empire. Here *44–45*
1029 See here] Behold *26f–45*
1030 Summer's ardent] short-liv'd SUMMER's *26f–28*

1032–3   And pale, concluding, WINTER shuts thy Scene,
              And shrouds *Thee* in the Grave. — Where now,
                 are fled *26f–28*

1037 gay-spent, festive Nights] Nights of secret Guilt *26f 260*
1038 Lost between] Flutt'ring 'twixt *26f 260*
1040 never-failing Friend of Man] Mankind's never-failing Friend
26f–38

1009 *Mischiefs, 26f* ∼∧ *260 28*   round: *26f–38*   1010 *Hunger 26f–28*
Weariness 26f–28   1010a Unlistening *260*   1011 *Roar 26f–28*   Winds,
26f 260   *Crush 26f–28*   1012 Now, *26f 260*   now, renew'd, *26f 260*
1013a Main. *28*   Thunder∧ *260 28*   1014 Leviathan, *26f 28–38 Leviathan,*
260   1016 Brine; *26f–34*   while, *26f 260*   1017 Far∧ *28*   1020 Yet,
26f 260   *ever-waking*] MS ever-waking *26f–38*   Eye] MS Eye *30q–38*
1021 down, *26f 260*   Pity, *26f 260*   1022 Mortals, *26f–28*   lights *26f 260*
1024 dread *30q–45*   1025 reigns, tremendous, *26f 260*   1025a Plains.
28–38   1027 *Horror 26f–28*   1028a Empire. *28*   1028 *Man 26f*
260   1029 Life: *26f 260*   Pass *260*   1030 flow'ring *26f* SPRING,
26f–38 MS   SUMMER's *26f–38 MS*   1031 AUTUMN *26f–38 MS*
1032 pale, *26f–28*   concluding, *26f* WINTER *26f–38 MS*   1033a Thee
28   Grave. *28*   where *26f*   1034 greatness! *300 45*   1036 busy,
26f–28   1038 Good, *26f 260*   1039 All, now, *26f 260*   *Vertue,* sole,
26f 260   1041 high — and *26f 260* ∼. And *28*   1042 *Morn 26f 260*
1043 Heaven∧ *300*   — awakening *Nature 26f 260*

The *new-creating Word*, and starts to Life,
In every heighten'd Form, from Pain and Death 1045
For ever free. *The great eternal Scheme*
Involving All, and in a *perfect Whole*
Uniting, as the Prospect wider spreads,
To Reason's Eye refin'd clears up apace.
Ye vainly wise! ye blind Presumptuous! now, 1050
Confounded in the Dust, adore that POWER,
And WISDOM oft arraign'd: see now the Cause,
Why unassuming Worth in secret liv'd,
And dy'd, neglected: why the good Man's Share
In Life was Gall and Bitterness of Soul: 1055
Why the lone Widow, and her Orphans pin'd,
In starving Solitude; while Luxury,
In Palaces, lay straining her low Thought,
To form unreal Wants: why Heaven-born Truth,
And Moderation fair, wore the red Marks 1060
Of Superstition's Scourge: why licens'd Pain,
That cruel Spoiler, that embosom'd Foe,
Imbitter'd all our Bliss. Ye good Distrest!
Ye noble Few! who here unbending stand
Beneath Life's Pressure, yet bear up a While, 1065
And what your bounded View, which only saw
A little Part, deem'd *Evil* is no more:
The Storms of WINTRY TIME will quickly pass,
And one unbounded SPRING encircle All.

THE END

1044–55 *30q–46*
1050 Presumptuous] *MS* presuming *30q–38*
1044–55 *26f–28 as follows:*

> Th' Almighty Trumpet's Voice, and starts to Life,
> Renew'd, unfading. Now, th' Eternal *Scheme*,   (*26f*, 380)

That Dark Perplexity, that Mystic Maze,
Which Sight cou'd never trace, nor Heart conceive,
To *Reason*'s Eye, refin'd, clears up apace.
Angels, and Men, astonish'd, pause—and dread
To travel thro' the Depths of Providence,　　*(26f, 385)*
Untry'd, unbounded. Ye vain *Learned!* see,
And, prostrate in the Dust, adore that *Power*,
And *Goodness*, oft arraign'd. See now the Cause,
Why conscious *Worth*, oppress'd, in secret long
Mourn'd, unregarded: Why the *Good Man*'s Share *(26f, 390)*
In Life, was Gall, and Bitterness of Soul:

　1056–64 *26f–46*
1058 straining] prompting *26f–38*　　her] *MS* his *30q–38*
1059 Truth] *Faith 26f–28*
1060 Moderation fair,] *Charity*, prime Grace! *26f–28*
1061 Superstition's] *Persecution's 26f–28*
1064 who] that, *26f 260*
　1065–9 *30q–46*
1065 yet bear up a While] yet a little while *30q–45*
1066–7 And what you reckon evil is no more; *30q–38*
　1065–9 *26f–28 as follows:*

　　　Beneath Life's Pressures—yet a little while,
　　　And all your Woes are past. *Time* swiftly fleets,
　　　And wish'd *Eternity*, approaching, brings
　　　Life undecaying, Love without Allay,
　　　Pure flowing Joy, and Happiness sincere.　　*(26f, 405)*

THE END] *not in 30q 300 38*

—————

1044 *new-creating Word*] *MS* new-creating word *30q–38*　　　1046 The great
eternal *30q–38*　　*Scheme, 44–45* Scheme, *30q–38*　　　1047 perfect whole *30q–38*
1055 gall, *30q–38*　　　(*26f*, 380) Nowʌ *28*　　Scheme *28*　　　(383) Reason's
28　　Eyeʌ refin'dʌ *28*　　　(384) pause, *28*　　　(386) Learned, *28*
(387) Andʌ *28*　　Dustʌ *28*　　　(389) long, *260*　　　(390) unregarded;
28　　(391) Lifeʌ *28*　　1056 *Widow 26f–28*　　Orphans, *26f 260* ~ʌ
28　　1057 *Luxury 26f–28*　　　1058 Thoughtʌ *260 28*　　　1059 Why
260　　1060 red *26f 260*　　marks, *300*　　　1061 Why *260 28*　　*Pain 26f–*
28　　　1062 *Spoiler 26f 260*　　*Foe 26f 260*　　　1063 *Distrest 26f 260*
1064 *Few 26f 260*　　　1064 here, unbending, *26f 260*　　　1064a thatʌ *260*
(*26f*, 401) Pressures, *28*　　　(402) Time *28*　　　(403) Eternity *28*

A

HYMN

THESE, as they change, ALMIGHTY FATHER, these,
Are but the *varied* GOD. The rolling Year
Is full of Thee. Forth in the pleasing Spring
THY Beauty walks, THY Tenderness and Love.
Wide-flush the Fields; the softening Air is Balm;   5
Echo the Mountains round; the Forest smiles;
And every Sense, and every Heart is Joy.
Then comes THY Glory in the Summer-Months,
With Light and Heat refulgent. Then THY Sun
Shoots full Perfection thro' the swelling Year: 10
And oft THY Voice in dreadful Thunder speaks;
And oft at Dawn, deep Noon, or falling Eve,
By Brooks and Groves, in hollow-whispering Gales.
THY Bounty shines in Autumn unconfin'd,
And spreads a common Feast for all that lives.   15
In Winter awful THOU! with Clouds and Storms
Around THEE thrown, Tempest o'er Tempest roll'd,
Majestic Darkness! on the Whirlwind's Wing,
Riding sublime, THOU bidst the World adore,
And humblest Nature with THY northern Blast.   20

MYSTERIOUS Round! what Skill, what Force divine,
Deep-felt, in These appear! a simple Train,
Yet so delightful mix'd, with such kind Art,
Such Beauty and Beneficence combin'd;
Shade, unperceiv'd, so softening into Shade;   25
And all so forming an harmonious Whole;
That, as they still succeed, they ravish still.
But wandering oft, with brute unconscious Gaze,
Man marks not THEE, marks not the mighty Hand,
That, ever-busy, wheels the silent Spheres;   30
Works in the secret Deep; shoots, steaming, thence

The fair Profusion that o'erspreads the Spring:
Flings from the Sun direct the flaming Day;
Feeds every Creature; hurls the Tempest forth;
And, as on Earth this grateful Change revolves,   35
With Transport touches all the Springs of Life.

---

head-title:

A HYMN.] A HYMN On the SEASONS. *30p 300 38*
  1–13 *30q–46*
6 Forest smiles] forests live *30q–38*
9 refulgent. Then] severe. Prone, then *30q–38*
11 dreadful] awful *30q–38*
  14–15 *44–46*   *30q–38 as follows:*

> A yellow-floating pomp, thy *Bounty* shines
> In AUTUMN unconfin'd. Thrown from thy lap, (*30q*, 15)
> Profuse o'er nature, falls the lucid shower
> Of beamy fruits; and, in a radiant stream,
> Into the stores of steril WINTER pours.

  16–74 *30q–46*
16 awful] *dreadful 30q–38*
18 Majestic Darkness] Horrible blackness *30q–38*
19 adore] be low *30q–38*
23 delightful] harmonious *30q–38*
23–4 with such kind … Beneficence combin'd;] *MS* so fitly join'd,/One
following one in such inchanting sort, *30q–38*
26 an harmonious] such a perfect *30q–38*
28 wandering] *MS* wondering *300–38*
29 not THEE] THEE not *30q–38*

---

1 FATHER! *30q–38*   2 Year] *MS* YEAR *30q–38*   3 Spring] *MS* SPRING
30q–38   4 Thy *30q–38*   *Beauty 30q*   thy *30q–38*   *Tenderness 30q*
Love 30q   7 Heart, *44–5*   8 thy *30q–38*   *Glory 30q*   Summer] *MS*
SUMMER *30q–38*   9 light, *30q–38*   heat, *30q–38*   thy *30q–38*   10 year.
30q–45   11 thy *30q–38*   (*30q*, 14) Bounty *30p–38*   (15) Autumn
MS   (18) Winter *MS*   16 Winter] *MS* WINTER *30q–38*   Thou *MS*
16a dreadful *30p–38*   17 Thee *MS*   18 On *30q–38*   19 Thou
MS   20 thy *30q–38*   22 A *30q*   25 Shade;] *MS* ∼, *30q–38*
26 Whole;] *MS* ∼, *30q–38*   27 That,] *MS* ∼∧ *34 38*   29 Thee *MS*
31 Thence *44–46*   32 Spring; *MS* SPRING; *30q–38*   33 flaming Day]
MS FLAMING DAY *30q–38*   34 Feeds] *MS* FEEDS *30q–38*   Tempest] *MS*
TEMPEST *30q–38*   35 And∧ *300*

Nature, attend! join every living Soul,
Beneath the spacious Temple of the Sky,
In Adoration join; and, ardent, raise
One general Song! To Him, ye vocal Gales,   40
Breathe soft, whose Spirit in your Freshness breathes:
Oh talk of Him in solitary Glooms!
Where, o'er the Rock, the scarcely-waving Pine
Fills the brown Shade with a religious Awe.
And ye, whose bolder Note is heard afar,   45
Who shake th' astonish'd World, lift high to Heaven
Th' impetuous Song, and say from whom you rage.
His Praise, ye Brooks, attune, ye trembling Rills;
And let me catch it as I muse along.
Ye headlong Torrents, rapid, and profound;   50
Ye softer Floods, that lead the humid Maze
Along the Vale; and thou, majestic Main,
A secret World of Wonders in thyself,
Sound his stupendous Praise; whose greater Voice
Or bids you roar, or bids your Roarings fall.   55
Soft-roll your Incense, Herbs, and Fruits, and Flowers,
In mingled Clouds to Him; whose Sun exalts,
Whose Breath perfumes you, and whose Pencil paints.
Ye Forests bend, ye Harvests wave, to Him;
Breathe your still Song into the Reaper's Heart,   60
As home he goes beneath the joyous Moon.
Ye that keep watch in Heaven, as Earth asleep
Unconscious lies, effuse your mildest Beams,
Ye Constellations, while your Angels strike,
Amid the spangled Sky, the silver Lyre.   65
Great Source of Day! best Image here below
Of thy Creator, ever pouring wide,
From World to World, the vital Ocean round,
On Nature write with every Beam his Praise.
The Thunder rolls: be hush'd the prostrate World;   70
While Cloud to Cloud returns the solemn Hymn.
Bleat out afresh, ye Hills; ye mossy Rocks,
Retain the Sound: the broad responsive Low,
Ye Valleys, raise; for the Great Shepherd reigns;
And his *unsuffering* Kingdom yet will come.   75
Ye Woodlands all, awake: a boundless Song

Burst from the Groves; and when the restless Day,
Expiring, lays the warbling World asleep,
Sweetest of Birds! sweet Philomela, charm
The listening Shades, and teach the Night HIS Praise.   80
Ye chief, for whom the whole Creation smiles;
At once the Head, the Heart, and Tongue of all,
Crown the great Hymn! in swarming Cities vast,

---

40 An universal HYMN! To HIM, ye gales, *30q–38*   Song] *MS*
41 in your Freshness breathes:] *MS* teaches you to breathe. *30q–38*
44 Shade] void *30q–38*
54 stupendous] tremendous *30q–38*
56 Soft-roll] Roll up *30q–38*
57 exalts] elates *30q–38*
58 Breath] hand *30q–38*
59 bend] bow *MS*
61 Homeward, rejoycing with the joyous moon. *30q–38*
67 pouring] darting *30q–38*
71 solemn] dreadful *30q–38*
   75 *MS 44–46*
unsuffering] mild bloodless *MS*   will] shall *MS*
   75 *30q–38 as follows:*

          And yet again the golden age returns.
          Wildest of creatures, be not silent here;
          But, hymning horrid, let the desert roar.   (*30q*, 80)

   76–9 *30q–46*
76 boundless] general *30q–38*
   80 *44–46   30q–38 as follows:*

          The listening shades; and thro' the midnight hour,   (*30q*, 85)
          Trilling, prolong the wildly-luscious note;
          That night, as well as day, may vouch his praise.

   81–106 *30q–46*
82 Tongue] *MS* mouth *30q–38*

---

37 attend!] *MS* ~; *30q–38*   40 Him *MS*   40a to *30p–38*   41 soft,]
MS ~; *30q–38*   spirit *30q–38*   42 Him *MS*   45 Whose *44–46*
48 His *30q–38*   53 thyself˰ *30p*   54 his *30q–38*   57 Him *MS*
58 paints.] *MS* ~˰ *30p 34* ~, *30o 38–45 MS*   59 forests, *30q–38*   bend,] *MS*
~; *30q–38*   harvests, wave˰ *30q–38*   HIM: *30q–38* Him: *MS*   69 his
30q–38   79 Philomela] *MS philomela 30p–38*   83 Hymn] *MS* HYMN
30q–38   In *30q MS*

Assembled Men, to the deep Organ join
The long-resounding Voice, oft breaking clear,   85
At solemn Pauses, thro' the swelling Base;
And, as each mingling Flame increases each,
In one united Ardor rise to Heaven.
Or if you rather chuse the rural Shade,
And find a Fane in every sacred Grove;   90
There let the Shepherd's Flute, the Virgin's Lay,
The prompting Seraph, and the Poet's Lyre,
Still sing the GOD OF SEASONS, as they roll.
For me, when I forget the darling Theme;
Whether the Blossom blows, the Summer-Ray   95
Russets the Plain, *inspiring* Autumn gleams,
Or Winter rises in the blackening East;
Be my Tongue mute, may Fancy paint no more,
And, dead to Joy, forget my Heart to beat!

SHOULD Fate command me to the farthest Verge   100
Of the green Earth, to distant barbarous Climes,
Rivers unknown to Song; where first the Sun
Gilds *Indian* Mountains, or his setting Beam
Flames on th' *Atlantic* Isles; 'tis Nought to me:
Since GOD is ever present, ever felt,   105
In the void Waste as in the City full;
And where HE vital spreads there must be Joy.
When even at last the solemn Hour shall come,
And wing my mystic Flight to future Worlds,
I chearful will obey, there, with new Powers,   110
Will rising Wonders sing: I cannot go
Where UNIVERSAL LOVE not smiles around,
Sustaining all yon Orbs and all their Sons,
From *seeming Evil* still educing *Good*,
And *Better* thence again, and *Better* still,   115
In infinite Progression. —— But I lose
Myself in HIM, in LIGHT INEFFABLE!
Come then, expressive Silence, muse HIS Praise.

THE END

84 Assembled] Concourse of *30q–38*
87 Flame] *MS* frame *30q–38*
90 And] To *30q–38*
91 Lay] chaunt *30q–38*
96 *inspiring*] *MS* delicious *30q–38*
97 blackening] reddening *30q–38*
101 distant] *MS* hostile *30q–38*
104 'tis Nought to me:] *MS as follows:*

> [or even, at last,
> Winging
> Thro' the dark Gulph, to other future Worlds;
> I chearful will obey; 'tis Nought to me; *all del.*]

107–13 *MS 44–46*
108 the solemn] *MS* [it's awful *del.*] *MS*   Hour shall come] Mandate comes *MS*
109 wing my mystic Flight] my dark Flight I wing *MS*
110–11 *MS* [I chearful will obey. I cannot go *del.*] *MS*
110 there, with new] *MS* [with rising *del.*] *MS*
112 Where UNIVERSAL GOODNESS does not reign, *MS*
113 Sustaining] *MS* [Sustain'd *del.*] *MS*
107–13 *30q–38 as follows:*

> Rolls the same kindred SEASONS round the world,
> In all apparent, wise, and good in all;   (*30q,* 115)
> Since HE sustains, and animates the whole;

114–18 *30q–46*
114 educing] *MS* educes *30q–38*
THE END *not in 38 44 Wks*

---

85 oft˄] *MS* oft- *30q–46*   93 God of Seasons *MS*   94 theme, *30q–46*
95 Blossom blows] *MS* BLOSSOM BLOWS *30q–38*   Summer-Ray] *MS* SUMMER-RAY *30q–38*   96 Autumn] *MS* AUTUMN *30q–38*   gleams; *30q–46*
97 Winter] *MS* WINTER *30q–38*   99 beat! *MS* ∼. *30q–38*   104 me; *30q–45*   106 waste, *30q–38*   107 He *MS*   110 there˄ *MS* There, *44–46*   Powers˄ *MS*   114 *seeming Evil*] *MS* seeming evil *30q–38*   Good] *MS* good *30q–38*   115 *Better . . . Better*] *MS* better . . . better *30q–38*   117 LIGHT INEFFABLE] *MS* Light ineffable *30q–38*   118 his *30q–38*

APPENDIX A

WINTER. A POEM. folio 1726

SEE! WINTER comes, to rule the varied Year,
Sullen, and sad; with all his rising Train,
Vapours, and *Clouds*, and *Storms*: Be these my Theme,
These, that exalt the Soul to solemn Thought,
And heavenly Musing. Welcome kindred Glooms!   5
Wish'd, wint'ry, Horrors, hail!—With frequent Foot,
Pleas'd, have I, in my cheerful Morn of Life,
When, nurs'd by careless *Solitude*, I liv'd,
And sung of Nature with unceasing Joy,
Pleas'd, have I wander'd thro' your rough Domains;   10
Trod the pure, virgin, Snows, my self as pure:
Heard the Winds roar, and the big Torrent burst:
Or seen the deep, fermenting, Tempest brew'd,
In the red, evening, Sky.—Thus pass'd the Time,
Till, thro' the opening Chambers of the South,   15
Look'd out the joyous *Spring*, look'd out, and smil'd.

THEE too, Inspirer of the toiling Swain!
Fair AUTUMN, yellow rob'd! I'll sing of thee,
Of thy last, temper'd, Days, and sunny Calms;
When all the golden *Hours* are on the Wing,   20
Attending thy Retreat, and round thy Wain,
Slow-rolling, onward to the Southern Sky.

BEHOLD! the well-pois'd *Hornet*, hovering, hangs,
With quivering Pinions, in the genial Blaze;
Flys off, in airy Circles: then returns,   25
And hums, and dances to the beating Ray:
Nor shall the Man, that, musing, walks alone,
And, heedless, strays within his radiant Lists,
Go unchastis'd away.—Sometimes, a Fleece
Of Clouds, wide-scattering, with a lucid Veil,   30

1–16 Cf. *OET* 1–16.
  There are anticipations of these opening lines in T.'s letter to Cranstoun, late
September 1725. See Introduction, pp. xxxv–xxxvi
  17–111 Cf. *OET Au.* 950–1036, 1082–1102.

Spring

Summer

Autumn

Winter

Soft, shadow o'er th' unruffled Face of Heaven;
And, thro' their dewy Sluices, shed the Sun,
With temper'd Influence down. Then is the Time,
For those, whom *Wisdom*, and whom *Nature* charm,
To steal themselves from the degenerate Croud,   35
And soar above this *little* Scene of Things:
To tread low-thoughted *Vice* beneath their Feet:
To lay their Passions in a gentle Calm,
And woo lone *Quiet*, in her silent *Walks*.

  Now, solitary, and in pensive Guise,   40
Oft, let me wander o'er the russet Mead,
Or thro' the pining Grove; where scarce is heard
One dying Strain, to chear the *Woodman*'s Toil:
Sad *Philomel*, perchance, pours forth her Plaint,
Far, thro' the withering Copse. Mean while, the Leaves, 45
That, late, the Forest clad with lively Green,
Nipt by the drizzly Night, and Sallow-hu'd,
Fall, wavering, thro' the Air; or shower amain,
Urg'd by the Breeze, that sobs amid the Boughs.
Then list'ning *Hares* forsake the rusling Woods,   50
And, starting at the frequent Noise, escape
To the rough Stubble, and the rushy Fen.
Then *Woodcocks*, o'er the fluctuating Main,
That glimmers to the Glimpses of the Moon,
Stretch their long Voyage to the woodland Glade: 55
Where, wheeling with uncertain Flight, they mock
The nimble *Fowler*'s Aim.—Now *Nature* droops;
Languish the living Herbs, with pale Decay:
And all the *various Family* of Flowers
Their sunny Robes resign. The falling Fruits,   60
Thro' the still Night, forsake the Parent-Bough,
That, in the first, grey, Glances of the Dawn,
Looks wild, and wonders at the wintry Waste.

  THE *Year*, yet pleasing, but declining fast,
Soft, o'er the secret Soul, in gentle Gales,   65
A Philosophic Melancholly breathes,
And bears the swelling Thought aloft to Heaven.
Then forming *Fancy* rouses to conceive,
What never mingled with the Vulgar's Dream:
Then wake the tender *Pang*, the pitying *Tear*,   70
The *Sigh* for suffering Worth, the *Wish* prefer'd

For Humankind, the *Joy* to see them bless'd,
And all the *Social Off-spring* of the Heart!

Oh! bear me then to high, embowering, Shades;
To twilight Groves, and visionary Vales;   75
To weeping Grottos, and to hoary Caves;
Where Angel-Forms are seen, and Voices heard,
Sigh'd in low Whispers, that abstract the Soul,
From outward Sense, far into Worlds remote.

Now, when the Western Sun withdraws the Day,   80
And humid *Evening*, gliding o'er the Sky,
In her chill Progress, checks the straggling Beams,
And robs them of their gather'd, vapoury, Prey,
Where Marshes stagnate, and where Rivers wind,
Cluster the rolling *Fogs*, and swim along   85
The dusky-mantled Lawn: then slow descend,
Once more to mingle with their *Watry Friends*.
The vivid Stars shine out, in radiant Files;
And boundless *Ether* glows; till the fair Moon
Shows her broad Visage, in the crimson'd East;   90
Now, stooping, seems to kiss the passing Cloud:
Now, o'er the pure *Cerulean*, rides sublime.
Wide the pale Deluge floats, with silver Waves,
O'er the sky'd Mountain, to the low-laid Vale;
From the white Rocks, with dim Reflexion, gleams,   95
And faintly glitters thro' the waving Shades.

All Night, abundant Dews, unnoted, fall,
And, at Return of Morning, silver o'er
The Face of Mother-Earth; from every Branch
Depending, tremble the translucent Gems,   100
And, quivering, seem to fall away, yet cling,
And sparkle in the Sun, whose rising Eye,
With Fogs bedim'd, portends a beauteous Day.

Now, giddy Youth, whom headlong Passions fire,
Rouse the wild Game, and stain the guiltless Grove,   105
With Violence, and Death; yet call it Sport,
To scatter Ruin thro' the Realms of *Love*,
And *Peace*, that thinks no Ill: But These, the *Muse*,
Whose Charity, unlimited, extends
As wide as *Nature* works, disdains to sing,   110
Returning to her nobler Theme in view—

For, see! where *Winter* comes, himself, confest,
Striding the gloomy Blast. First Rains obscure
Drive thro' the mingling Skies, with Tempest foul;
Beat on the Mountain's Brow, and shake the Woods,   115
That, sounding, wave below. The dreary Plain
Lies overwhelm'd, and lost. The bellying Clouds
Combine, and deepening into Night, shut up
The Day's fair Face. The Wanderers of Heaven,
Each to his Home, retire; save those that love   120
To take their Pastime in the troubled Air,
And, skimming, flutter round the dimply Flood.
The Cattle, from th' untasted Fields, return,
And ask, with meaning Low, their wonted Stalls;
Or ruminate in the contiguous Shade: 125
Thither, the houshold, feathery, People croud,
The crested Cock, with all his female Train,
Pensive, and wet. Mean while, the Cottage-Swain
Hangs o'er th' enlivening Blaze, and, taleful, there,
Recounts his simple Frolic: Much he talks,   130
And much he laughs, nor recks the Storm that blows
Without, and rattles on his humble Roof.

At last, the muddy Deluge pours along,
Resistless, roaring; dreadful down it comes
From the chapt Mountain, and the mossy Wild,   135
Tumbling thro' Rocks abrupt, and sounding far:
Then o'er the sanded Valley, floating, spreads,
Calm, sluggish, silent; till again constrain'd,
Betwixt two meeting Hills, it bursts a Way,
Where Rocks, and Woods o'erhang the turbid Stream.   140
There gathering triple Force, rapid, and deep,
It boils, and wheels, and foams, and thunders thro'.

Nature! great Parent! whose directing Hand
Rolls round the Seasons of the changeful Year,
How mighty! how majestick are thy Works!   145
With what a pleasing Dread they swell the Soul,
That sees, astonish'd! and, astonish'd sings!
You too, ye *Winds!* that now begin to blow,
With boisterous Sweep, I raise my Voice to you.
Where are your Stores, ye viewless *Beings!* say?   150
Where your aerial Magazines reserv'd,

112–252 Cf. *OET* 72–275.

Against the Day of Tempest perilous?
In what untravel'd Country of the Air,
Hush'd in still Silence, sleep you, when 'tis calm?

LATE, in the louring Sky, red, fiery, Streaks   155
Begin to flush about; the reeling Clouds
Stagger with dizzy Aim, as doubting yet
Which Master to obey: while rising, slow,
Sad, in the Leaden-colour'd East, the Moon
Wears a bleak Circle round her sully'd Orb.   160
Then issues forth the Storm, with loud Control,
And the thin Fabrick of the pillar'd Air
O'erturns, at once. Prone, on th' uncertain Main,
Descends th' Etherial Force, and plows its Waves,
With dreadful Rift: from the mid-Deep, appears,   165
Surge after Surge, the rising, wat'ry, War.
Whitening, the angry Billows rowl immense,
And roar their Terrors, thro' the shuddering Soul
Of feeble Man, amidst their Fury caught,
And, dash'd upon his Fate: Then, o'er the Cliff,   170
Where dwells the *Sea-Mew*, unconfin'd, they fly,
And, hurrying, swallow up the steril Shore.

THE Mountain growls; and all its sturdy *Sons*
Stoop to the Bottom of the Rocks they shade:
Lone, on its Midnight-Side, and all aghast,   175
The dark, way-faring, *Stranger*, breathless, toils,
And climbs against the Blast—
Low, waves the rooted Forest, vex'd, and sheds
What of its leafy Honours yet remains.
Thus, struggling thro' the dissipated Grove,   180
The whirling Tempest raves along the Plain;
And, on the Cottage thacht, or lordly Dome,
Keen-fastening, shakes 'em to the solid Base.
Sleep, frighted, flies; the hollow Chimney howls,
The Windows rattle, and the Hinges creak.   185

THEN, too, they say, thro' all the burthen'd Air,
Long Groans are heard, shrill Sounds, and distant Sighs,
That, murmur'd by the *Demon* of the Night,
Warn the devoted *Wretch* of Woe, and Death!
Wild Uproar lords it wide: the Clouds commixt,   190
With Stars, swift-gliding, sweep along the Sky.
All Nature reels.—But hark! the *Almighty* speaks:

Instant, the chidden Storm begins to pant,
And dies, at once, into a noiseless Calm.

As yet, 'tis Midnight's Reign; the weary Clouds,   195
Slow-meeting, mingle into solid Gloom:
Now, while the drousy World lies lost in Sleep,
Let me associate with the low-brow'd *Night*,
And *Contemplation*, her sedate Compeer;
Let me shake off th' intrusive Cares of Day,   200
And lay the medling Senses all aside.

AND now, ye lying *Vanities* of Life!
You ever-tempting, ever-cheating Train!
Where are you now? and what is your Amount?
Vexation, Disappointment, and Remorse.   205
Sad, sickening, Thought! and yet, deluded Man,
A Scene of wild, disjointed, Visions past,
And broken Slumbers, rises, still resolv'd,
With new-flush'd Hopes, to run your giddy Round.

FATHER of Light, and Life! Thou *Good Supreme!*   210
O! teach me what is Good! teach me thy self!
Save me from Folly, Vanity and Vice,
From every low Pursuit! and feed my Soul,
With Knowledge, conscious Peace, and Vertue pure,
Sacred, substantial, never-fading Bliss!   215

Lo! from the livid East, or piercing North,
Thick Clouds ascend, in whose capacious Womb,
A vapoury Deluge lies, to Snow congeal'd:
Heavy, they roll their fleecy World along;
And the Sky saddens with th' impending Storm.   220
Thro' the hush'd Air, the whitening Shower descends,
At first, thin-wavering; till, at last, the Flakes
Fall broad, and wide, and fast, dimming the Day,
With a continual Flow. See! sudden, hoar'd,
The Woods beneath the stainless Burden bow,   225
Blackning, along the mazy Stream it melts;
Earth's universal Face, deep-hid, and chill,
Is all one, dazzling, Waste. The Labourer-Ox
Stands cover'd o'er with Snow, and then demands
The Fruit of all his Toil. The Fowls of Heaven,   230
Tam'd by the cruel Season, croud around

The winnowing Store, and claim the little Boon,
That *Providence* allows. The foodless Wilds
Pour forth their brown *Inhabitants*; the Hare,
Tho' timorous of Heart, and hard beset   235
By Death, in various Forms, dark Snares, and Dogs,
And more unpitying Men, the Garden seeks,
Urg'd on by *fearless* Want. The bleating Kind
Eye the bleak Heavens, and next, the glistening Earth,
With Looks of dumb Despair; then sad, dispers'd,   240
Dig, for the wither'd Herb, thro' Heaps of Snow.

Now, *Shepherds*, to your helpless Charge be kind;
Baffle the raging Year, and fill their Penns
With Food, at will: lodge them below the Blast,
And watch them strict; for from the bellowing East,   245
In this dire Season, oft the Whirlwind's Wing
Sweeps up the Burthen of whole wintry Plains,
In one fierce Blast, and o'er th' unhappy Flocks,
Lodg'd in the Hollow of two neighbouring Hills,
The billowy Tempest whelms; till, upwards urg'd,   250
The Valley to a shining Mountain swells,
That curls its Wreaths amid the freezing Sky.

Now, all amid the Rigours of the Year,
In the wild Depth of Winter, while without
The ceaseless Winds blow keen, be my Retreat   255
A rural, shelter'd, solitary, Scene;
Where ruddy Fire, and beaming Tapers join
To chase the chearless Gloom: there let me sit,
And hold high Converse with the mighty Dead,
Sages of ancient Time, as Gods rever'd,   260
As Gods beneficent, who blest Mankind,
With Arts, and Arms, and humaniz'd a World.
Rous'd at th' inspiring Thought—I throw aside
The long-liv'd Volume, and, deep-musing, hail
The sacred *Shades*, that, slowly-rising, pass   265
Before my wondering Eyes—First, *Socrates*,
Truth's early Champion, Martyr for his God:
Solon, the next, who built his Commonweal,
On Equity's firm Base: *Lycurgus*, then,
Severely good: and him of rugged *Rome*,   270
Numa, who soften'd *her* rapacious *Sons*.

253–300 Cf. *OET* 424–549.

Cimon sweet-soul'd, and *Aristides* just.
Unconquer'd *Cato*, virtuous in Extreme;
With that attemper'd *Heroe, mild, and firm,
Who wept the Brother, while the Tyrant bled.   275
Scipio, the humane Warriour, gently brave,
Fair Learning's Friend, who early sought the Shade,
To dwell, with *Innocence*, and *Truth*, retir'd.
And, equal to the best, the *Theban, He*
Who, *single*, rais'd his Country into Fame.   280
Thousands behind, the Boast of *Greece* and *Rome*,
Whom *Vertue* owns, the Tribute of a Verse
Demand, but who can count the Stars of Heaven?
Who sing their Influence on this lower World?
But see who yonder comes! nor comes alone,   285
With *sober* State, and of *majestic* Mien,
The Sister-Muses in his Train—'Tis He!
Maro! the best of Poets, and of Men!
Great *Homer* too appears, of *daring* Wing!
Parent of Song! and, *equal*, by this Side,   290
The *British Muse*, join'd Hand in Hand, they walk,
Darkling, nor miss their Way to Fame's Ascent.

   SOCIETY divine! Immortal Minds!
Still visit thus my Nights, for *you* reserv'd,
And mount my soaring Soul to Deeds like yours.   295
Silence! thou lonely *Power!* the Door be thine:
See, on the hallow'd Hour, that none intrude,
Save *Lycidas*, the Friend, with Sense refin'd,
Learning digested well, exalted Faith,
Unstudy'd Wit, and Humour ever gay.   300

   CLEAR Frost succeeds, and thro' the blew Serene,
For Sight too fine, th' Ætherial Nitre flies,
To bake the Glebe, and bind the slip'ry Flood.
This of the wintry Season is the Prime;
Pure are the Days, and lustrous are the Nights,   305
Brighten'd with starry Worlds, till then unseen.
Mean while, the Orient, darkly red, breathes forth
An Icy Gale, that, in its mid Career,
Arrests the bickering Stream. The nightly Sky,
And all her glowing Constellations pour   310

Timoleon.
301–24 Cf. *OET* 691–778.

Their rigid Influence down: It freezes on
Till Morn, late-rising, o'er the drooping World,
Lifts her pale Eye, unjoyous: then appears
The various Labour of the silent Night,
The pendant Isicle, the Frost-Work fair,   315
Where thousand Figures rise, the crusted Snow,
Tho' white, made whiter, by the fining North.
On blithsome Frolics bent, the youthful Swains,
While every Work of Man is laid at Rest,
Rush o'er the watry Plains, and, shuddering, view   320
The fearful Deeps below: or with the Gun,
And faithful Spaniel, range the ravag'd Fields,
And, adding to the Ruins of the Year,
Distress the Feathery, or the Footed *Game*.

        But hark! the nightly Winds, with hollow Voice,   325
Blow, blustering, from the South—the Frost subdu'd,
Gradual, resolves into a weeping Thaw.
Spotted, the Mountains shine: loose Sleet descends,
And floods the Country round: the Rivers swell,
Impatient for the Day.—Those sullen Seas,   330
That wash th' ungenial Pole, will rest no more,
Beneath the Shackles of the mighty North;
But, rousing all their Waves, resistless heave,—
And hark!—the length'ning Roar, continuous, runs
Athwart the rifted Main; at once, it bursts,   335
And piles a thousand Mountains to the Clouds!
Ill fares the Bark, the Wretches' last Resort,
That, lost amid the floating Fragments, moors
Beneath the Shelter of an Icy Isle;
While Night o'erwhelms the Sea, and Horror looks   340
More horrible. Can human Hearts endure
Th' assembled *Mischiefs*, that besiege them round:
Unlist'ning *Hunger*, fainting *Weariness*,
The *Roar* of Winds, and Waves, the *Crush* of Ice,
Now, ceasing, now, renew'd, with louder Rage,   345
And bellowing round the Main: Nations remote,
Shook from their Midnight-Slumbers, deem they hear
Portentous Thunder, in the troubled Sky.
More to embroil the Deep, Leviathan,
And his unweildy Train, in horrid Sport,   350
Tempest the loosen'd Brine; while, thro' the Gloom,

325–405 Cf. *OET* 988–1069.

Far, from the dire, unhospitable Shore,
The Lyon's Rage, the Wolf's sad Howl is heard,
And all the fell Society of Night.
Yet, *Providence*, that ever-waking *Eye*   355
Looks down, with Pity, on the fruitless Toil
Of Mortals, lost to Hope, and *lights* them safe,
Thro' all this dreary Labyrinth of Fate.

'TIS done!—Dread WINTER has subdu'd the Year,
And reigns, tremenduous, o'er the desart Plains!   360
How dead the Vegetable Kingdom lies!
How dumb the Tuneful! *Horror* wide extends
His solitary Empire.—Now, fond *Man!*
Behold thy pictur'd Life: pass some few Years,
Thy flow'ring SPRING, thy short-liv'd SUMMER's Strength,   365
Thy sober AUTUMN, fading into Age,
And pale, concluding, WINTER shuts thy Scene,
And shrouds *Thee* in the Grave—Where now, are fled
Those Dreams of Greatness? those unsolid Hopes
Of Happiness? those Longings after Fame?   370
Those restless Cares? those busy, bustling Days?
Those Nights of secret Guilt? those veering Thoughts,
Flutt'ring 'twixt Good, and Ill, that shar'd thy Life?
All, now, are vanish'd! *Vertue*, sole, survives,
Immortal, Mankind's never-failing Friend,   375
His Guide to Happiness on high—and see!
'Tis come, the Glorious *Morn!* the second Birth
Of Heaven, and Earth!—awakening *Nature* hears
Th' Almighty Trumpet's Voice, and starts to Life,
Renew'd, unfading. Now, th' Eternal *Scheme*,   380
That Dark Perplexity, that Mystic Maze,
Which Sight cou'd never trace, nor Heart conceive,
To *Reason*'s Eye, refin'd, clears up apace.
Angels, and Men, astonish'd, pause—and dread
To travel thro' the Depths of Providence,   385
Untry'd, unbounded. Ye vain *Learned!* see,
And, prostrate in the Dust, adore that *Power*,
And *Goodness*, oft arraign'd. See now the Cause,
Why conscious *Worth*, oppress'd, in secret long
Mourn'd, unregarded: Why the *Good Man*'s Share   390
In Life, was Gall, and Bitterness of Soul:
Why the lone *Widow*, and her *Orphans*, pin'd,
In starving Solitude; while *Luxury*,
In Palaces, lay prompting her low Thought,

To form unreal Wants: why Heaven-born *Faith*,   395
And *Charity*, prime Grace! wore the *red* Marks
Of *Persecution*'s Scourge: why licens'd *Pain*,
That cruel *Spoiler*, that embosom'd *Foe*,
Imbitter'd all our Bliss. Ye Good *Distrest!*
Ye Noble *Few!* that, here, unbending, stand   400
Beneath Life's Pressures—yet a little while,
And all your Woes are past. *Time* swiftly fleets,
And wish'd *Eternity*, approaching, brings
Life undecaying, Love without Allay,
Pure flowing Joy, and Happiness sincere.   405

The END.

SUMMER. A POEM. 1727

FROM Southern Climes, where unremitting Day
Burns over Head, illustrious SUMMER comes,
In Pride of Youth, and felt thro' Nature's Depth.
He comes! attended by the sultry *Hours*,
And ever-fanning *Breezes*, on his Way;   5
While, from his ardent Look, the turning SPRING
Averts her blushful Face, and Earth, and Skies,
All-smiling, to his hot Dominion leaves.

   HENCE, let me haste into the mid-wood Shade,
Where scarce a Sun-Beam wanders thro' the Gloom;   10
And, on the dark-green Grass, beside the Brink
Of haunted Stream, that, by the Roots of Oaks,
Rowls o'er the rocky Channel, lie at large,
And sing the Glories of the circling Year.

   COME, INSPIRATION! from thy Hermit-Seat,   15
By Mortal seldom found: may I presume
From thy fix'd, serious Muse, and raptur'd Glance
Shot on surrounding Heaven, to steal one Look,
Creative of the Poet, every Power
Exalting to an Extasy of Soul!   20

   WITH what a perfect, World-revolving Power
Were first th' unweildy Planets launch'd along

1–20 Cf. *OET* 1–20.   21–267 Cf. *OET* 32–286.

Th' illimitable Void! thus to remain,
Amid the Flux of many thousand Years,
That oft has swept the busy Race of Men,   25
And all their labour'd Monuments away,
Unresting, changeless, matchless, in their Course;
To Day, and Night, and the delightful Round
Of *Seasons*, faithful; not excentric once:
So pois'd, and perfect, is the vast Machine!   30

WHEN now no more th' alternate *Twins* are fir'd,
And *Cancer* reddens with the Solar Blaze,
Short is th' uncertain Empire of the *Night*;
And soon, observant of approaching *Day*,
The meek-ey'd *Morn* appears, Mother of Dews!   35
Mildly elucent in the streaky East;
And, from before the Lustre of her Face,
White, break the Clouds away. With tardy Step
Brown *Night* retires. Young *Day* pours in a-pace,
And opens all the lawny Prospect wide.   40
The dripping Rock, the Mountain's misty Top
Swell on the Eye, and brighten with the Dawn.
Blue, thro' the Dusk, the smoaking Currents shine;
And, from the bladed Field, th' unhunted Hare
Limps aukward: while, along the Forest-Glade,   45
The wild Deer trip, and, often turning, gaze
At early Passenger. Musick awakes,
The native Voice of undissembling Joy;
And thick around the wood-land Hymns arise.
Rous'd by the Cock, the soon-clad Shepherd leaves   50
His mossy Cottage, where with *Peace* he dwells;
And from the crowded Fold, in Order, drives
His Flock, to taste the Verdure of the Morn.

FALSLY luxurious, will not Man awake,
And starting from the Bed of Sloth, enjoy   55
The cool, the fragrant, and the silent Hour,
To Meditation due, and sacred Song!
And is there ought in Sleep can charm the Wise!
To lie in dead Oblivion, lost to all,
Our Natures boast of noble, and divine: 60
Total Extinction of th' enlighten'd Soul!
Or else to feaverish Vanity alive,
Wilder'd, and tossing thro' distemper'd Dreams.

Who would in such a gloomy State remain
Longer than Nature craves? When every *Muse*,   65
And every blooming *Pleasure* wait without,
To bless the wildly-devious morning Walk.

But yonder comes the powerful *King* of Day,
Rejoicing in the East. The lessening Cloud,
The kindling Azure, and the Mountain's Brim   70
Tipt with æthereal Gold, his near Approach
Betoken glad: and now apparent all,
Aslant the Dew-bright Earth, and colour'd Air,
He looks, in boundless Majesty, abroad;
And sheds the shining Day, that, burnish'd, plays   75
On Rocks, and Hills, and Towers, and wandering Streams,
High-gleaming from afar. Prime Chearer, *Light!*
Of all material Beings first, and best!
Efflux divine! Nature's resplendent Robe,
Without whose vesting Beauty, all were wrapt   80
In unessential Gloom; and Thou, red Sun,
In whose wide Circle Worlds of Radiance lie,
Exhaustless Brightness! may I sing of Thee!

Who would the Blessings, first and last, recount,
That, in a full Effusion, from Thee flow,   85
As soon might number, at the Height of Noon,
The Rays that radiate from thy cloudless Sphere,
An universal Glory darting round.

'Tis by thy secret, strong, attractive Force,
As with a Chain, indissoluble, bound,   90
Thy System rolls entire; from the far Bourn
Of slow-pac'd *Saturn*, to the scarce-seen Disk
Of *Mercury*, lost in excessive Blaze.

Informer of the planetary Train!
Without whose vital, and effectual Glance,   95
They'd be but brute, uncomfortable Mass,
And not, as now, the green Abodes of Life,
How many Forms of Being wait on Thee,
Inhaling Gladness! from th'unfetter'd Mind,
By Thee sublim'd, to that Day-living Race,   100
The mixing Myriads of thy evening Beam.

The vegetable World is also thine,
Parent of Seasons! from whose rich-stain'd Rays,

Reflected various, various Colours rise:
The freshening Mantle of the youthful Year; 105
The wild Embroidery of the watry Vale;
With all that chears the Eye, and charms the Heart.

THE branching Grove thy lusty Product stands,
To quench the Fury of thy Noon-Career;
And crowd a Shade for the retreating Swain, 110
When on his russet Fields You look direct.

FRUIT is thy Bounty too, with Juice replete,
Acid, or mild; and from thy Ray receives
A Flavour pleasing to the Taste of Man.
By Thee concocted, blushes; and by Thee 115
Fully matur'd, into the verdant Lap
Of *Industry*, the mellow Plenty falls.

EXTENSIVE Harvests wave at thy Command,
And the bright Ear, consolidate by Thee,
Bends, unwitholding, to the Reaper's Hand. 120

EVEN *Winter* speaks thy Power, whose every Blast,
O'ercast with Tempest, or severely sharp
With breathing Frost, is eloquent of Thee,
And makes us languish for thy vernal Gleams.

SHOT to the Bowels of the teeming Earth, 125
The ripening Oar confesses all thy Flame.

TH'UNFRUITFUL Rock, itself, impregn'd by Thee,
In dark Retirement, forms the *lucid Stone*,
Collected Light, compact! that, polish'd bright,
And all its native Lustre let abroad, 130
Shines proudly on the Bosoms of the Fair!

AT Thee the *Ruby* lights his deepening Glow,
A bleeding Radiance! grateful to the View.
From Thee the *Saphire*, solid Æther! takes
His Hue cerulean; and, of evening Tinct, 135
The Purple-streaming *Amethyst* is thine.
With thy own Smile the Yellow *Topaz* burns.
Nor deeper Verdure dies the Robe of *Spring*,
When first she gives it to the Southern Gale,

Than the green *Emerald* shows. But, all combin'd,   140
Thick, thro' the whitening *Opal*, play thy Beams;
Or, flying, several, from his Surface, form
A trembling Variance of revolving Hues,
As the Site changes in the Gazer's Hand.

THE very dead Creation, from thy Touch,   145
Assumes a mimic Life. By Thee refin'd,
In brisker Measures, the relucent Stream
Frisks o'er the Mead. The Precipice abrupt,
Projecting Horror on the blacken'd Flood,
Softens at thy Return. The Desart joys   150
Wildly, thro' all his melancholy Bounds.
Rude Ruins glitter; and the briny Deep,
Seen from some pointed Promontory's Top,
Reflects, from every fluctuating Wave,
A Glance, extensive as the Day. But these,   155
And all the much transported Muse can sing,
Are to thy Beauty, Dignity and Use,
Unequal far, great, delegated Source,
Of Life, and Light, and Grace, and Joy below!

How shall I then attempt to sing of Him,   160
Who, LIGHT HIMSELF, in uncreated Light,
Invested deep, dwells awfully retir'd
From Mortal Eye, or Angel's purer Ken;
Whose single Smile has, from the First of Time,
Fill'd, over-flowing, all these Lamps of Heaven,   165
That Beam for ever thro' th' immeasur'd Sky:
But should He hide his Face, th' astonished Sun,
And all th' extinguish'd Stars, would, loosening, reel,
Wide, from their Spheres, and Chaos come again.

AND yet, was every faultering Tongue of Man,   170
ALMIGHTY POET! silent in thy Praise,
Thy matchless Works, in each exalted Line,
And all the full, harmonic Universe,
Would tuneful, or expressive, Thee attest,
The Cause, the Glory, and the End of All!   175

To Me be *Nature*'s Volume, wide, display'd;
And to peruse the broad, illumin'd Page,
Or haply catching Inspiration thence,

Some easy Passage, raptur'd, to translate,
My sole Delight; as thro' the falling Glooms,   180
Pensive, I muse, or, with the rising Day,
On *Fancy*'s Eagle-Wing, excursive, soar.

FIERCE, flaming up the Heavens, the peircing Sun
Attenuates to Air the high-rais'd Clouds,
And Morning Mists that hover'd round the Hills,   185
In Party-colour'd Bands; till, all unveil'd,
The Face of Nature shines, from where Earth seems
Far-stretch'd around, to meet the bending Sphere.

HALF in a Blush of clustering Roses lost,
Dew-dropping *Coolness* to the Shade retires;   190
And Tyrant *Heat*, dispreading thro' the Sky,
By sharp Degrees, his burning Influence rains
On Man, and Beast, and Herb, and tepid Stream.

WHO can, unpitying, see the flowery Race,
Shed by the Morn, their new-flush'd Bloom resign,   195
Before th' unbating Beam! So fade the Fair,
When Fevers revel thro' their azure Veins.
But One, *the Follower of the Sun*, They say,
Sad, when he sets, shuts up her yellow Leaves,
Weeping all Night; and when He, warm, returns,   200
Points her enamour'd Bosom to his Ray.

HOME, from his Morning Task, the Swain retreats,
His Flock before Him stepping to the Fold;
While the full-udder'd Mother lows around
The chearful Cottage then expecting Food,   205
The Food of Innocence, and Health! The Daw,
The Rook, and Magpie, to the grey-grown Oaks,
That the calm Village, in their verdant Arms,
Sheltering, embrace, direct their lazy Flight;
Where, on the mingling Boughs, they sit embower'd,   210
All the hot Noon, till cooler Hours arise.
Faint, underneath, the homely Fowls convene;
And, in a Corner of the buzzing Shade,
The House-Dog, with th'employless Grey-Hound, lies,
Outstretch'd, and sleepy: in his Slumbers One   215
Attacks the nightly Thief, and One exults
O'er Hill and Dale; till waken'd by the Wasp,

They bootless snap. Nor shall the Muse disdain
To let the little, noisy Summer-Race
Live in her Lay, and flutter thro' her Song,   220
Not mean tho' simple; to the Sun ally'd,
From Him their high Descent, direct, They draw.

WAK'D by his warmer Ray, the reptile Young
Come wing'd abroad; by the light Air upborn,
Lighter, and full of Life. From every Chink,   225
And secret Corner, where they slept away
The wintry Glooms, by Myriads, all at once,
Swarming, they pour: green, speckled, yellow, grey,
Black, azure, brown; more than th'assisted Eye
Of poring *Virtuoso* can discern.   230
Ten thousand Forms! Ten thousand different Tribes!
People the Blaze. To sunny Waters some
By fatal instinct fly; where, on the Pool,
They, sportive, wheel; or, sailing down the Stream,
Are snatch'd, immediate, by the springing Trout,   235
Often beguil'd. Some thro' the green-Wood Glade
Delight to stray; there lodg'd, amus'd, and fed,
In the fresh Leaf. Luxurious, others make
The Meads their Choice, and visit every Flower,
And every latent Herb; but careful still   240
To shun the Mazes of the sounding Bee,
As o'er the Blooms He sweeps. Some to the House,
The Fold, and Dairy, hungry, bend their Flight;
Sip round the Pail, or taste the curdling Cheese:
Oft, inadvertent, by the boiling Stream   245
They're pierc'd to Death; or, weltering in the Bowl,
With powerless Wings around them wrapt, expire.

BUT chief, to heedless Flies the Window proves
A constant Death; where, gloomily retir'd,
The Villain Spider lives, cunning, and fierce,   250
Mixture abhorr'd! Amid a mangled Heap
Of Carcasses, in eager Watch, He sits,
Surveying all his waving Snares around.
Within an Inch the dreadless Wanderer oft
Passes, as oft the Ruffian shows his Front.   255
The Prey at last ensnar'd, He, dreadful, darts,
With rapid Glide, along the leaning Line;
And, fixing in the Fly his cruel Fangs,

Strides backward, grimly pleas'd: the fluttering Wing,
And shriller Sound declare extream Distress,   260
And ask the helping, hospitable Hand.

    Ecchoes the living Surface of the Earth;
Nor undelightful is the humming Sound
To Him who muses, thro' the Woods, at Noon;
Or drowsy Shepherd, as He lies reclin'd,   265
With half-shut Eyes, beneath the floating Shade
Of Willows grey, close-crowding o'er the Brook.

    LET no presuming, impious Railer tax
CREATIVE WISDOM, as if ought was form'd
In vain, or not for admirable Ends.   270
Shall little, haughty *Ignorance* pronounce
His Works unwise; of which, the smallest Part
Exceeds the narrow Vision of his Mind!
So on the Concave of a sounding Dome,
On swelling Columns heav'd, the Pride of Art!   275
Wanders a critic Fly; his feeble Ray
Extends an Inch around; yet, blindly bold,
He dares dislike the Structure of the Whole.
And lives the Man, whose universal Eye
Has swept, at once, th' unbounded Scheme of Things;   280
Mark'd their Dependance so, and firm Accord,
As, with unfaultering Accent, to conclude
That *this* availeth nought? Has any seen
The mighty Chain of Beings, lessening down
From infinite Perfection to the Brink   285
Of dreary *Nothing*, desolate Abyss!
Recoiling giddy Thought: or with sharp Glance,
Such as remotely wafting Spirits use,
Survey'd the Glories of the litte World?
Till then, alone, let zealous Praise ascend,   290
And Hymns of heavenly Wonder, to that POWER,
Whose Wisdom shines as lovely on our Minds,
As on our smiling Eyes his Servant-Sun.

    THICK, in yon Stream of Light, a Thousand Ways,
Upwards and downwards, thwarting, and convolv'd,   295
The quivering Kingdoms sport; with Tempest-Wing,
Till *Winter* sweeps them from the Face of Day:

268–306 Cf. *OET* 318–51.

Even so luxurious Men, unheeding, pass
An idle, Summer Life, in Fortune's Shine,
A Season's Glitter! In soft-circling Robes,   300
Which the hard Hand of Industry has wrought,
The human *Insects* glow; by *Hunger* fed,
And chear'd by toiling *Thirst*, They rowl about
From Toy to Trifle, Vanity to Vice;
Till blown away by *Death*, *Oblivion* comes   305
Behind, and strikes Them from the Book of *Life*.

  'TIS raging Noon; and, vertical, the Sun
Shoots, thro' th' expanding Air, a torrid Gleam.
O'er Heaven, and Earth, far, as the darted Eye
Can pierce, a dazzling Deluge reigns; and all,   310
From Pole to Pole, is undistinguish'd Blaze.
Down to the dusty Earth the Sight, o'er-power'd,
Stoops for Relief; but thence ascending Steams,
And keen Reflection pain. Burnt to the Heart
Are the refreshless Fields; their arid Hue   315
Adds a new Fever to the sickening Soul:
And, o'er their slippery Surface, wary, treads
The Foot of thirsty Pilgrim, often dipt
In a cross Rill, presenting to his Wish
A living Draught, He feels before He drinks!   320
No more the Woods return the sandy Sound
Of sharpening Sithe: the Mower, sinking, heaps
O'er Him the tedded Hay, with Flowers perfum'd;
And scarce a chirping Grashopper is heard
Thro' all the Mead. Distressful Nature pants.   325
The Desart singes; and the stubborn Rock,
Split to the Centre, sweats at every Pore.
The very Streams look languid from afar;
Or, thro' the fervid Glade, impetuous, hurl
Into the Shelter of the crackling Grove.   330

  PREVAILING Heat! oh intermit thy Wrath!
And on my aking Temples, potent, thus
Beam not so hard!—Incessant, still You flow;
And still another fervent Flood succeeds,
Pour'd on the Head profuse—In vain I groan,   335
And, restless, turn, and look around for Night;
Night is far off; and hotter Hours approach.

307–450 Cf. *OET* 432–563.

Who shall endure!—The too resplendent Scene
Already darkens on the dizzy Eye;
And double Objects dance: unreal Sounds   340
Sing round the Ears: a Weight of sultry Dew
Hangs, deathful, on the Limbs: shiver the Nerves:
The supple Sinews sink; and on the Heart,
Misgiving, *Horror* lays his heavy Hand.
Thrice happy He! who, on the Sunless Side   345
Of a romantic Mountain, Forrest-crown'd,
Beneath the whole collected Shade reclines:
Or in the gelid Caverns, Woodbine-wrought,
And fresh bedew'd with ever-spouting Streams,
Sits cooly calm; while all the World without,   350
Unsatisfy'd, and sick, tosses in Noon.
Emblem instructive of the virtuous Man,
Who keeps his temper'd Mind serene, and pure,
And all his Passions aptly harmoniz'd,
Amidst a jarring World with Vice inflam'd.   355

    WELCOME, ye Shades! ye bowery Thickets hail!
Ye lofty Pines! ye venerable Oaks!
With Ashes wild, resounding o'er the Steep!
Delicious is your Shelter to the Soul,
As to the hunted Hart the sallying Spring,   360
Or Stream full-flowing, that his swelling Sides
Laves, as He floats along the Herbag'd Brink.
Cold, thro' the Nerves, your pleasing Comforts glide;
The Heart beats glad: the misty Eyes refulge:
The Ears resume their Watch: the Sinews knit;   365
And Life shoots swift thro' every active Limb.

    ALL in th' adjoining Brook, that shrills along
The vocal Grove, now fretting o'er a Rock,
Now scarcely moving thro' a reedy Pool,
Now starting to a sudden Stream, and now   370
Gently diffus'd into a limpid Plain,
A various Groupe the Herds and Flocks compose,
Rural Confusion! On the grassy Bank
Some ruminating lie; while Others stand
Half in the Flood, and, often bending, sip   375
The circling Surface. In the Middle droops
The strong, laborious Ox, of honest Front,
Which, incompos'd, He shakes; and from his Sides

The busy Insects lashes with his Tail,
Returning still. Amid his Subjects safe,   380
Slumbers the Monarch-Swain; his careless Arm
Thrown round his Head on downy Moss sustain'd;
Here laid his Scrip, with wholesome Viands fill'd;
And there his Sceptre-Crook, and watchful Dog.

LIGHT, fly his Slumbers, if perchance a Flight   385
Of angry Hornets fasten on the Herd,
That, startling, scatters from the shallow Brook,
In search of lavish Stream. Tossing the Foam,
They scorn the Keeper's Voice, and scour the Plain,
Thro' all the bright Severity of Noon;   390
While, from their labouring Breasts, a hollow Moan
Proceeding, runs low-bellowing round the Hills.

OFT in this Season too the Horse provok'd,
While his big Sinews, full of Spirits, swell,
Trembling with Vigour, in the Heat of Blood,   395
Springs the high Fence; and, o'er the Field effus'd,
Darts on the gloomy Flood, with steady Eye,
And Heart estrang'd to Fear: his nervous Chest,
Luxuriant, and erect, the Seat of Strength!
Bears down th'opposing Stream: quenchless his Thirst,   400
He takes the River at redoubled Draughts;
And, with wide Nostrils, snorting, skims the Wave.

STILL let me pierce into the midnight Depth
Of yonder Grove, of wildest, largest Growth;
That, high embowering in the middle Air,   405
Nods o'er the Mount beneath. At every Step,
Solemn, and slow, the Shadows blacker fall,
And all is awful, silent Gloom around.

THESE are the Haunts of Meditation, these
The Scenes where antient Bards th'inspiring Breath,   410
Extatic, felt; and, from this World retir'd,
Convers'd with Angels, and immortal Forms,
On heavenly Errands bent——To save the Fall
Of Vertue, struggling on the Brink of Vice;
In waking Whispers, and repeated Dreams,   415
To hint pure Thought, and warn the favour'd Soul,
For future Tryals, fated, to prepare;
To prompt the Poet, who, devoted, gives

His Muse to better Themes; to sooth the Pangs
Of dying Saints; and, from the Patriot's Breast, 420
Backward to mingle in detested War,
But foremost when engag'd, to turn the *Death*;
And numberless such Offices of Love,
Daily, and nightly, zealous, to perform.

 SHOOK, sudden, from the Bosom of the Air, 425
A thousand Shapes, or glide athwart the Dusk,
Or stalk, majestic, on: harrow'd, I feel
A sacred Terror, and severe Delight,
Creep thro' my mortal Frame; and thus, methinks,
Those hollow Accents, floating on my Ear, 430
Pronounce, distinct—"Be not of Us afraid,
"Poor, kindred Man, thy fellow Creatures, We
"From the same bounteous POWER our Beings drew,
"The same our Lord, and Laws, and great Pursuit!
"Once, some of Us, like Thee, thro' stormy Life 435
"Toil'd, Tempest-beaten, ere We could attain
"This holy Calm, this Harmony of Mind,
"Where Purity and Peace immingle Charms.
"Then fear not Us; but, with commutual Song,
"Oft, in these dim Recesses, undisturb'd 440
"By noisy *Folly*, and discordant *Vice*,
"Of Nature sing with Us, and Nature's GOD—
"And, frequent, at the middle Waste of Night,
"Or, all Day long, in Desarts *still*, are heard,
"Now here, now there, now wheeling in mid-Sky, 445
"Around, or underneath, aerial Sounds,
"Sent from angelic Harps, and Voices join'd;
"A Happiness bestow'd by Us, alone,
"On *Contemplation*, or the hallow'd Ear
"Of *Poet*, swelling to seraphic Strain. 450

 THUS up the Mount, in visionary Muse
I stray, regardless whither; till the Stun
Of a near Fall of Water every Sense
Wakes from the Charm of Thought: Swift, shrinking back,
I stand aghast, and view the broken Scene. 455

 LIKE one who flows in Joy, when, all at once,
Misfortune hurls Him down the Hill of Life,

451–93 Cf. *OET* 585–628.

Smooth, to the giddy Brink a lucid Stream
Rolls, unsuspecting, till, surpris'd, 'tis thrown,
In loose Meanders, thro' the trackless Air;   460
Now a blue watry Sheet, anon, dispers'd,
A hoary Mist, then, gather'd in again,
A darted Stream, aslant the hollow Rock,
This Way, and that tormented, dashing thick,
From Steep to Steep, with wild, infracted Course,   465
And, restless, roaring to the humble Vale.

WITH the rough Prospect tir'd, I turn my Eyes
Where, in long *Visto*, the soft-murmuring Main
Darts a green Lustre, trembling, thro' the Trees;
Or to yon Silver-streaming Threads of Light,   470
A showery Beauty beaming thro' the Boughs.
Invited from the Rock, to whose dark Cliff
He clings, the steep-ascending Eagle soars,
With upward Pinions, thro' th'attractive Gleam;
And, giving full his Bosom to the Blaze,   475
Gains on the Sun; while all the feathery Race,
Smote by afflictive Noon, disorder'd droop,
Deep, in the Thicket; or, from Bower to Bower,
Responsive, force an interrupted Strain.
The Wood-Dove, only, in the Centre, coos,   480
Mournfully hoarse; oft ceasing from his Plaint,
Short Interval of weary Woe! again,
The sad Idea of his murder'd Mate,
Struck from his Side by savage Fowler's Guile,
Across his Fancy comes; and then resounds   485
A louder Song of Sorrow thro' the Grove.

BESIDE the dewy Border let Me sit,
All in the Freshness of the humid Air;
There, on that Rock, by *Nature's* Chissel carv'd,
An ample Chair, moss-lin'd, and over Head   490
With weaving Umbrage hung; thro' which the Bee
Strays, diligent; and, with th'extracted Sweet
Of Honey-Suckle, loads his little Thigh.

AND what a pleasing Prospect lies around!
Of Hills, and Vales, and Woods, and Lawns, and Spires 495
And Towns betwixt, and gilded Streams! till all
The stretching Landskip into Smoak decays.

494–557 Cf. *OET* 1438–1579.

HAPPY BRITANNIA! where the Queen of Arts,
Inspiring Vigour, LIBERTY, abroad,
Walks thro' the Land of Heroes, unconfin'd,   500
And scatters Plenty with unsparing Hand.

  RICH is thy Soil, and merciful thy Skies;
Thy Streams unfailing in the Summer's Drought:
Unmatch'd thy Guardian-Oaks: thy Vallies float
With golden Waves; and on thy Mountains Flocks   505
Bleat, numberless: while, roving round their Sides,
Bellow the blackening Herds, in lusty Droves.
Beneath, thy Meadows flame, and rise unquell'd,
Against the Mower's Sythe. On every Hand,
Thy *Villas* shine. Thy Country teems with Wealth;   510
And *Property* assures it to the Swain,
Pleas'd, and unweary'd, in his certain Toil.

  FULL are thy Cities with the Sons of Art;
And Trade, and Joy, in every busy Street,
Mingling, are heard: even *Drudgery*, Himself,   515
As at the Car He sweats, or, dusty, hews
The Palace-Stone, looks gay. Thy crowded Ports,
Where rising Masts an endless Prospect yield,
With Labour burn, and eccho to the Shouts
Of hurry'd Sailor, as He, hearty, waves   520
His last Adieu, and, loosening every Sheet,
Resigns the spreading Vessel to the Wind.

  BOLD, firm, and graceful, are thy generous Youth,
By Hardship sinew'd, and by Danger fir'd,
Scattering the Nations where They go; and first,   525
Or on the listed Plain, or wintry Seas.
Mild are thy Glories too, as o'er the Arts
Of thriving Peace thy thoughtful Sires preside;
In Genius, and substantial Learning high;
For every Vertue, every Worth renown'd,   530
Sincere, plain-hearted, hospitable, kind,
Yet like the mustering Thunder when provok'd;
The Scourge of Tyrants, and the sole Resource
Of such as under grim Oppression groan.

  HENCE may'st Thou boast a *Bacon*, and a *More*;   535
Nor cease to vie Them with the noblest Names

Of ancient Times, or Patriot, or Sage.
And for the Strength, and Elegance of Truth,
A *Barrow*, and a *Tillotson* are thine:
A *Locke*, inspective into human Minds,   540
And all *th' unnotic'd World* that passes there.
Nor be thy *Boyle* forgot; who, while He liv'd,
Seraphic, sought TH' ETERNAL thro' his Works,
By sure Experience led; and, when He dy'd,
Still bid his *Bounty* argue for his GOD,   545
Worthy of Riches He!—But what needs more—
Let comprehensive *Newton* speak thy Fame,
In all Philosophy. For solemn Song
Is not wild *Shakespear* Nature's Boast, and thine!
And every greatly amiable *Muse*   550
Of elder Ages in thy *Milton* met!
His was the Treasure of Two Thousand Years,
Seldom indulg'd to Man, a God-like Mind,
Unlimited, and various, as his Theme;
Astonishing as *Chaos*; as the Bloom   555
Of blowing *Eden* fair; soft as the Talk
Of our *grand Parents*, and as *Heaven* sublime.

   AND should I northward turn my filial Eye,
Beyond the *Tweed*, pure Parent-Stream! to where
The hyperborean Ocean, furious, foams   560
O'er *Orca*, or *Betubium*'s highest Peak,
Rapt, I might sing thy *Caledonian* Sons,
A gallant, warlike, unsubmitting Race!
Nor less in *Learning* vers'd, *soon* as He took
Before the Gothic Rage his Western Flight;   565
Wise in the Council, at the Banquet gay:
The Pride of Honour burning in their Breasts,
And Glory, not to their own Realms confin'd,
But into foreign Countries shooting far,
As over *Europe* bursts the *Boreal Morn*.   570

   May my Song soften as, thy Daughters, I,
BRITANNIA, hail! for Beauty is their own,
And Elegance, and Taste: the faultless Form,
Shap'd by the Hand of *Harmony*: the Cheek,
Where the live Crimson, thro' the native White,   575
Soft-shooting, o'er the Face diffuses Bloom,

558-70 Cf. *OET Au.* 862-909.   571-609 Cf. *OET* 1580-1619.

And every nameless Grace: the parted Lip,
Like the red Rose-Bud moist with morning Dew,
Breathing Delight; and, under flowing Jet,
Or sunny Ringlets, or of circling Brown,   580
The Neck slight-shaded, and the swelling Breast:
The Look resistless, piercing to the Soul,
And by the Soul inform'd, when, drest in Love,
She sits, sweet-smiling, in the lovely Eye.

ISLAND of Bliss! amid the Subject Seas,   585
That thunder round thy rocky Coasts, set up,
At once the Wonder, Terror, and Delight
Of distant Nations; whose remotest Shore
Can soon be shaken by thy naval Arm,
Not to be shook Thy self, but all Assaults   590
Baffling, like thy hoar Cliffs the loud Sea-Wave.

O THOU, by whose almighty *Nod*, the Scale
Of Empire rises, or alternate falls,
Send forth the saving VERTUES round the Land,
In bright Patrol: white *Peace*, and social *Love*;   595
The tender-looking *Charity*, intent
On gentle Deeds, and shedding Tears thro' Smiles;
Undaunted *Truth*, and *Dignity* of Mind;
Courage compos'd, and keen; sound *Temperance*,
Healthful in Heart and Look; clear *Chastity*,   600
With Blushes reddening as she moves along,
Disorder'd at the deep Regard she draws;
Rough *Industry*; *Activity* untir'd,
With copious Life inform'd, and all awake:
While, in the radiant Front, superiour, shines   605
That first, paternal Vertue, *public Zeal*,
Who casts o'er all an equal, wide Survey,
And ever musing on the Common Weal,
Still labours, glorious, with some brave Design.

THUS far, transported by my Country's Love,   610
Nobly digressive from my Theme, I've aim'd
To sing her Praises, in ambitious Verse;
While, slightly to recount, I simply meant,
The various Summer-Horrors, which infest
Kingdoms that scorch below severer Suns: 615

KINGDOMS, on which, direct, the Flood of Day,
Oppressive, falls, and gives the gloomy Hue,
And Feature gross; or worse, to ruthless Deeds,
Wan Jealousy, red Rage, and fell Revenge,
Their hasty Spirits prompts. Ill-fated Race!   620
Altho' the Treasures of the Sun be theirs,
Rocks rich in Gems, and Mountains big with Mines,
Whence, over Sands of Gold, the *Niger* rolls
His amber Wave; while on his balmy Banks,
Or in the Spicy, *Abyssinian* Vales,   625
The Citron, Orange, and Pomegranate drink
Intolerable Day, yet, in their Coats,
A cooling Juice contain. Peaceful, beneath,
Leans the huge Elephant, and, in his Shade,
A Multitude of beauteous Creatures play;   630
And Birds, of bolder Note, rejoice around.

AND oft amid their aromatic Groves,
Touch'd by the Torch of Noon, the gummy Bark,
Smouldering, begins to roll the dusky Wreath.
Instant, so swift the ruddy Ruin spreads,   635
A Cloud of Incense shadows all the Land;
And, o'er a thousand, thundering Trees, at once,
Riots, with lawless Rage, the running Blaze:
But chiefly, if fomenting Winds assist,
And, doubling, blend the circulating Waves   640
Of Flame tempestuous, or, directly on,
Far-streaming, drives Them thro' the Forest's Length.

BUT other Views await—where Heaven above,
Glows like an Arch of Brass; and all below,
The Earth a Mass of rusty Iron lies,   645
Of Fruits, and Flowers, and every Verdure spoilt,
Barren, and bare, a joyless, weary Waste,
Thin-cottag'd, and, in Time of trying Need,
Abandon'd by the vanish'd Brook, like One
Of fading Fortune by his treacherous Friend.   650

SUCH are thy horrid Desarts, *Barca*, such,
Zaara, thy hot, interminable Sands,
Continuous, rising often with the Blast,
Till the Sun sees no more; and unknit Earth,
Shook by the South into the darken'd Air,   655
Falls, in new, hilly Kingdoms, o'er the Waste.

'Tis here, that *Thirst* has fix'd his dry Domain,
And walks his wide, malignant Round, in search
Of Pilgrim lost; or, on the *Merchant's Tomb,
Triumphant, sits, who, for a single Cruise   660
Of unavailing Water paid so dear:
Nor could the Gold his hard Associate save.

Here the green Serpent gathers up his Train,
In Orbs immense, then darting out anew,
Progressive, rattles thro' the wither'd Brake;   665
And lolling, frightful, guards the scanty Fount,
If Fount there be: or, of diminish'd Size,
But mighty Mischief, on th'unguarded Swain
Steals, full of Rancour. Here the savage Race
Roam, licens'd by the shading Hour of Blood,   670
And foul Misdeed, when the pure Day has shut
His sacred Eye. The rabid Tyger, then,
The fiery Panther, and the whisker'd Pard,
Bespeckl'd fair, the Beauty of the Waste,
In dire Divan, surround their *shaggy King*,   675
Majestic, stalking o'er the burning Sand,
With planted Step; while an obsequious Crowd,
Of grinning Forms, at humble Distance wait.
These, all together join'd, from darksome Caves,
Where, o'er gnaw'd Bones, They slumber'd out the Day, 680
By supreme Hunger smit, and Thirst intense,
At once, their mingling Voices raise to Heaven;
And, with imperious, and repeated Roars,
Demanding Food, the Wilderness resounds,
From *Atlas* eastward to the frighted *Nile*.   685

Unhappy He! who, from the first of Joys,
Society, cut off, is left alone,
Amid this World of Death. Ceaseless, He sits,
Sad, on the rocky Eminence, and views
The rowling Main, that ever toils below;   690
Still fondly forming, in the farthest Verge,
Where the blue Æther mixes with the Wave,

* *In the Desert of* Araoan, *are two Tombs with Inscriptions on Them, importing that the Persons there interr'd were a rich Merchant, and a poor Carrier, who both died of Thirst; and that the Former had given to the Latter Ten Thousand Ducats for one Cruise of Water.*

663–705 Cf. *OET* 898–958.

Ships, dim-discover'd, dropping from the Clouds.
At Evening, to the setting Sun He turns
A watry Eye, and down his dying Heart   695
Sinks, helpless; while the wonted Roar is up,
And Hiss, continual, thro' the tedious Night.

Yet here, even here, into these black Abodes
Of Monsters, unappall'd, from stooping *Rome*,
And haughty *Cæsar*, *Liberty* retir'd,   700
With *Cato* leading thro' *Numidian* Wilds:
Disdainful of *Campania*'s fertile Plains,
And all the green Delights of *Italy*,
When, for Them, she must bend the servile Knee,
And, fawning, take the Blessings once her own.   705

WHAT need I mention those inclement Skies,
Where, frequent, o'er the sickening City, *Plague*,
The fiercest Son of *Nemesis divine!*
Collects a close, incumbent Night of Death,
Uninterrupted by the living Winds,   710
Forbid to blow a wholesome Breeze, and stain'd
With many a Mixture, by the Sun suffus'd,
Of angry Aspect. Princely *Wisdom*, then,
Dejects his watchful Eye; and from the Hand
Of drooping *Justice*, ineffectual, falls   715
The Sword, and Ballance. Mute the Voice of Joy;
And hush'd the Clamour of the busy World.
Empty the Streets, with uncouth Verdure clad,
And rang'd, at open Noon, by Beasts of Prey,
And Birds of bloody Beak: while, all Night long,   720
In spotted Troops, the recent Ghosts complain,
Demanding but the covering Grave. Mean time,
Lock'd is the deaf Door to Distress; even Friends,
And Relatives, endear'd for many a Year,
Savag'd by Woe, forget the social Tye,   725
The blest Engagement of the yearning Heart;
And sick, in Solitude, successive, die,
Untended, and unmourn'd. And, to compleat
The Scene of Desolation, wide around,
Denying all Retreat, the grim Guards stand,   730
To give the flying Wretch a better Death.

706–802 Cf. *OET* 1052–1168.

MUCH of the Force of foreign *Summers* still,
Of growling Hills, that shoot the pillar'd Flame,
Of Earthquake, and pale Famine, could I sing;
But equal Scenes of Horror call Me Home.   735

FOR now, slow-settling, o'er the lurid Grove,
Unusual Darkness broods; and, growing, gains
The whole Possession of the Air, surcharg'd
With wrathful Vapour, from the damp Abrupt,
Where sleep the mineral Generations, drawn.   740
Thence Nitre, Sulphur, Vitriol, on the Day
Stream, and fermenting in yon baleful Cloud,
Extensive o'er the World, a reddening Gloom!
In dreadful Promptitude to spring, await
The high Command. A boding Silence reigns   745
Thro' all the dun Expanse, save the dull Sound,
That, from the Mountain, previous to the Storm.
Rowls o'er the trembling Earth, disturbs the Flood,
And stirs the Forrest-Leaf without a Breath.
Prone, to the lowest Vale, th' aerial Tribes   750
Descend: the Tempest-loving Raven scarce
Dares wing the dubious Dusk. In rueful Gaze
The Cattle stand, and on the scowling Heavens
Cast a deploring Eye, by Man forsook,
Who to the crowded Cottage hies Him fast,   755
Or seeks the Shelter of the downward Cave.

'TIS dumb Amaze, and listening Terror all;
When, to the quicker Eye, the livid Glance
Appears, far South, emissive thro' the Cloud;
And, by the powerful Breath of GOD inflate,   760
The Thunder raises his tremendous Voice,
At first low-muttering; but, at each Approach,
The Lightnings flash a larger Curve, and more
The Noise astounds: till, over Head, a Sheet
Of various Flame discloses wide, then shuts   765
And opens wider, shuts and opens still
Expansive, wrapping Æther in a Blaze.
Follows the loosen'd, aggravated Roar,
Enlarging, deepening, mingling, Peal on Peal
Crush'd horrible, convulsing Heaven, and Earth.   770

DOWN comes a Deluge of sonorous Hail,
In the white, heavenly Magazines congeal'd;

And often fatal to th'unshelter'd Head
Of Man, or rougher Beast. The sluicy Rain,
In one unbroken Flood, descends; and yet   775
Th' unconquerable Lightning struggles thro',
Ragged, and fierce, or in red whirling Balls,
And strikes the Shepherd, as He, shuddering, sits,
Presaging Ruin, in the rocky Clift.
His inmost Marrow feels the gliding Flame;   780
He dies—and, like a Statue grim'd with Age,
His live, dejected Posture still remains;
His Russet sing'd, and rent his hanging Hat;
Against his Crook his sooty Cheek reclin'd;
While, whining at his Feet, his half-stun'd Dog,   785
Importunately kind, and fearful, pats
On his insensate Master, for Relief.

   BLACK, from the Stroak, above, the Mountain-Pine,
A leaning, shatter'd Trunk, stands scath'd to Heaven,
The Talk of future Ages! and, below,   790
A lifeless Groupe the blasted Cattle lie.
Here, the soft Flocks, with that same harmless Look,
They wore alive, and ruminating still,
In *Fancy*'s Eye; and there, the frowning Bull,
And Ox half-rais'd. A little farther, burns   795
The guiltless Cottage; and the haughty Dome
Stoops to the Base. Th'uprooted Forrest flies
Aloft in Air, or, flaming out, displays
The savage Haunts, by Day unpierc'd before.
Scar'd is the Mountains Brow; and, from the Cliff,   800
Tumbles the smitten Rock. The Desart shakes,
And gleams, and grumbles, through his deepest Dens.

   Now swells the Triumph of the Virtuous Man;
And this outrageous, elemental Fray,
To Him, a dread Magnificence appears,   805
The Glory of that POWER He calls his *Friend*,
Sole honourable Name!—But Woe to Him,
Who, of infuriate Malice, and confirm'd
In Vice long-practis'd, is a Foe to Man
His Brother, and at Variance with his GOD.   810
He thinks the Tempest weaves around his Head;
Loudens the Roar to Him, and in his Eye
The bluest Vengeance glares. Th'Oppressor, who,

Unpitying, heard the Wailings of *Distress*,
Gall'd by his Scourge, now shrinks at other Sounds.   815
Hid are the *Neroes* of the Earth—in vain,
Like Children hid in Sport. Chief, in the Breast
Of solitary Atheist, Wildness reigns,
Licentious; vanish'd every quaint Conceit,
And impious Jest, with which He us'd to pelt   820
Superiour Reason; Anguish in his Look,
And Supplication lifts his Hand. He'd pray;
If his hard Heart would flow. At last He runs,
Precipitant, and entering just the Cave,
The Messenger of Justice, glancing, comes,   825
With swifter Sweep, behind, and trips his Heel.

    AND yet not always on the guilty Head
Falls the devoted Flash. Young *Celadon*,
And his *Amelia*, an unrival'd Twain!
With equal Vertue form'd, and equal Grace,   830
The same, distinguish'd by their Sex alone;
Hers the mild Lustre of th'unfolding Morn,
And his the Radiance of the risen Day.

    THEY lov'd—but such their guileless Passion was,
As, in the Dawn of Time, alarm'd the Heart   835
Of *Innocence*, and undissembling *Truth*.
'Twas Friendship, heighten'd by the mutual Wish,
Th'enchanting Hope, and sympathetic Glow,
Struck from the charmful Eye. Devoting all
To Love, Each was to Each a dearer Self!   840
Supremely happy in th'awaken'd Power
Of giving Joy! Alone, amid the Shades,
Still, in angelic Intercourse, They liv'd
The rural Day, and talk'd the flowing Heart,
Or sigh'd, and look'd unutterable Things!   845

    THUS pass'd their Life, a clear, united Stream,
By Care unruffled; till, in evil Hour,
The Tempest caught Them on the tender Walk,
Heedless how far. Her Breast, presageful, heav'd
Unwonted Sighs, and stealing oft a Look   850
Of the big Gloom, on *Celadon* her Eye
Fell tearful, wetting all her glowing Cheek.

827–76 Cf. *OET* 1169–1222.

In vain assuring Love, and Confidence
In Heaven repress'd her Fear; it grew, and shook
Her Frame near Dissolution. He perceiv'd   855
Th' unequal Conflict, and, as Angels look
On dying Saints, his Eyes Compassion shed,
Mingl'd with matchless Love.—"Fear not, He said,
"Fair Innocence! thou Stranger to Offence,
"And inward Storm! HE, who enwraps yon Skies   860
"In Frowns of Darkness, ever smiles on Thee,
"With full Regard. O'er Thee the secret Shaft
"That wastes at Midnight, or th' undreaded Hour
"Of Noon, flies hurtless: and that very Voice,
"Which thunders Terror thro' the Sinner's Heart,   865
"With Tongues of Seraphs whispers Peace to thine.
" 'Tis Safety to be near Thee sure, and thus
"To clasp Perfection!—From his void Embrace,
Mysterious Heaven! that Moment, in a Heap
Of pallid Ashes, fell the beauteous Maid.   870
But who can paint the Lover, as He stood,
Struck by severe Amazement, hating Life,
Speechless, and fixt in all the Death of Woe!
So, faint Resemblance! on the Marble-Tomb
The well-dissembl'd Mourner, stooping, stands,   875
For ever silent, and for ever sad.

HEARD indistinct, the far-off Thunder peals,
From suffering Earth, commission'd o'er the Main,
Where the black Tempest, pressing on the Pool,
Heaves the dead Billows to the bursting Clouds.   880
Dire is the Fate of Those, who, reeling high,
From Wave to Wave, even at the very Source
Of Lightning, feel th'undissipated Flame;
Or, should They in a watry Vale escape,
If, on their Heads, the forceful *Spout* descends,   885
And drives the dizzy Vessel down the Deep,
Till in the oozy Bottom stuck, profound.

As from the Face of Heaven, each shatter'd Cloud,
Tumultuous, roves, th'unfathomable Blue,
That constant Joy to every finer Eye,   890
That Rapture! swells into the general Arch,
Which copes the Nations.— On the lilly'd Bank,

888–938 Cf. *OET* 1223–68.

Where a Brook quivers, often, careless, thrown,
Up the wide Scene I've gaz'd whole Hours away,
With growing Wonder, while the Sun declin'd,   895
As now, forth-breaking from the blotting Storm,
Nature shines out; and, thro' the lighten'd Air,
A higher Lustre, and a clearer Calm,
Diffusive, tremble; and, as if in sign
Of Danger past, a glittering Face of Joy,   900
Set off, abundant, by the level Ray,
Invests the Earth, yet weeping from Distress.

   'Tis Beauty all, and grateful Song around,
Join'd to the Low of Kine, and numerous Bleat
Of Flocks thick-nibbling thro' the clover'd Vale.   905
And shall the Hymn be marr'd by thankless Man,
Most-favour'd, who, with Voice articulate,
Should lead the Chorus of this lower World!
Shall He, so soon, forgetful of the past,
After the Tempest, puff his transient Vows,   910
And a new Dance of Vanity begin,
Scarce ere the Pant forsakes his feeble Heart!

   CHEAR'D by the setting Beam, the sprightly Youth
Speeds to the well-known Pool, whose chrystal Depth
A sandy Bottom shows. A-while He stands,   915
Gazing th'inverted Landskip, half afraid
To meditate the blue Profound below;
Till disenchanted by the ruffling Gale,
He plunges headlong down the closing Flood.
His ebon Tresses, and his rosy Cheek   920
Instant emerge; and, thro' the glassy Wave,
At each short Breathing, by his Lip repell'd,
With Arms, and Legs, according well, He makes,
As Humour leads, an easy-winding Path:
While, from his snowy Sides, a humid Light   925
Effuses on the pleas'd Spectators round.

   THIS is the purest Exercise of Health,
The great Refresher of the Summer-Heats;
Nor, when, the Brook pellucid, Winter keens,
Would I, weak-shivering, linger on the Brink.   930
Thus Life redoubles, and is oft preserv'd
By the bold Swimmer, in the swift Illapse

Of Accident disastrous. Hence the Limbs
Knit into Force; and that same *Roman* Arm,
Which stretch'd, victorious, o'er the conquer'd Earth,   935
First learn'd, while tender, to subdue the Wave.
Even, from the Body's Purity, the Mind,
Strictly ally'd, receives a secret Aid.

    Low walks the Sun, and broadens by degrees,
Just o'er the Verge of Day. The rising Clouds,   940
That shift, perpetual, in his vivid Train,
Their dewy Mirrors, numberless, oppos'd,
Unfold the hidden Riches of his Ray,
And chase a Change of Colours round the Sky.
'Tis all one Blush from East to West! and now,   945
Behind the dusky Earth, He dips his Orb,
Now half immers'd, and now a golden Curve
Gives one faint Glimmer, and then disappears.

    Passes the Day illusive, and perplext,
As fleets the Vision o'er the formful Brain,   950
This Moment hurrying all th'impassion'd Soul,
The next in Nothing lost; 'tis so to Him,
The Dreamer of this Earth, a chearless Blank!
A Sight of Horror! to th'ungodly Wretch,
The Hard, the Lewd, the Cruel, and the False,   955
Who, all Day long, have made the Widow weep,
And snatch'd the Morsel from her Orphan's Mouth,
To give their Dogs: but to th'harmonious Mind,
Who makes the hopeless Heart to sing for Joy,
Diffusing kind Beneficence around   960
Boastless, as now descends the silent Dew,
To Him, the long Review of order'd Life
Is inward Rapture, only to be felt!

    Confess'd, from yonder slow-extinguish'd Clouds,
The Sky begreying, sober *Evening* takes   965
Her wonted Station in the middle Air,
A thousand *Shadows* at her Beck. First *This*
She sends on Earth; then *That* of deeper Die
Steals soft behind; and then a *Deeper* still,
In well-adjusted Circles, gathers round,   970
To close the Face of Things. Th'expected Breeze

939–1006 Cf. *OET* 1620–81.

Begins to wave the Wood, and stir the Stream,
Sweeping with shadowy Gust the Fields of Corn,
While the Quail clamours for his running Mate.

WILD-WAFTING o'er the Lawn, the thistly Down   975
Plays in the fickle Air, now seems to fall,
And now, high-soaring over Head, an Arch,
Amusive, forms, then slanting down eludes
The Grasp of idle Swain. But should the *West*
A little swell the Breeze, the woolly Shower,   980
Blown, in a white Confusion, thro' the Dusk,
Falls o'er the Face unfelt, and, settling slow,
Mantles the Twilight Plain. And yet even here,
As thro' all Nature, in her lowest Forms,
A fine Contrivance lies, to wing the Seed,   985
By this light Plumage, into distant Vales.

HIS folded Flock secure, the Shepherd Home
Hies, merry-hearted, and by turns relieves
The ruddy Milk-Maid of her brimming Pail,
The Beauty, whom perhaps his witless Heart,   990
Unknowing what the Joy-mixt Anguish means,
Loves fond, by that sincerest Language, shown,
Of cordial Glances, and obliging Deeds.
Onward They pass, o'er many a panting Height,
And Valley sunk, and unfrequented, where,   995
At Fall of Eve, *the Fairy People* throng,
In various Game, and Revelry to pass
A Summer-Night, as village Stories tell.
But far about They wander from the Grave
Of Him, whom his ungentle Fortune forc'd,   1000
Against Himself, to lift the hated Hand
Of Violence; by Man cast out from Life,
And, after Death, to which They drove his Hope
Into the broad Way side. The ruin'd Tower
Is also shun'd, whose unblest Chambers hold,   1005
Nightly, sole Habitant, the yelling *Ghost*.

STRUCK from the Roots of slimy Rushes, blue,
The Wild-Fire scatters round, or, gather'd, trails
A Length of Flame, deceitful, o'er the *Moss*,
Whither, entangled in the Maze of Night,   1010

1007–20 Cf. *OET Au.* 1151–64.

While the *damp Desart* breathes his Fogs around,
The Traveller, decoy'd, is quite absorpt,
Rider and Horse, into the miry Gulph,
Leaving his Wife, and Family involv'd
In sorrowful Conjecture. Other Times,   1015
Sent by the quick-ey'd *Angel* of the Night,
Innoxious, on th'unstartling Horses Mane,
The *Meteor* sits, and shows the narrow Path,
That, winding, leads thro' Pits of Death, or else
Directs Him how to take the dangerous Ford.   1020

AMONG the crooked Lanes, on every Hedge,
The Glow-worm lights his Lamp, and, thro' the Dark,
Twinkles a moving Gem. On *Evening*'s Heel,
Night follows fast; not in her Winter-Robe,
Of massy, stygian Woof, but loose array'd,   1025
In Mantle dun. A few erroneous Rays,
Glanc'd from th' imperfect Surfaces of Things,
Fling half an Image on the straining Eye.
While wavering Woods, and Villages, and Streams,
And Rocks, and Mountain-Tops, that long retain'd   1030
Th' ascending Gleam, are all one swimming Scene,
Doubtful if seen; whence posting *Vision* turns
To Heaven, where *Venus*, in the starry Front,
Shines eminent, and from her genial Rise,
When Day-Light sickens, till it springs afresh,   1035
Sheds Influence on Earth, to Love, and Life,
And every Form of Vegetation kind.
As thus, *th'Effulgence* tremulous, I drink,
With fix'd Peruse, the lambent Lightnings shoot
A-cross the Sky, or, horizontal, dart   1040
O'er half the Nations, in a Minute's Space,
Conglob'd, or long. Astonishment succeeds,
And Silence, ere the various Talk begins.

THAT Instant, flashing, noiseless, from the North,
A thousand Meteors stream, ensweeping first   1045
The lower Skies, then, all at once, converge
High to the Crown of Heaven, and, all at once,
Relapsing quick, as quickly reascend,
And mix, and thwart, extinguish, and renew,
All Æther coursing in a Maze of Light.   1050

1021–43 Cf. *OET* 1682–1729.   1044–75 Cf. *OET Au.* 1108–37.

FROM Eye to Eye, contagious, thro' the Crowd,
The *Pannic* runs, and into wonderous Shapes
Th'Appearance throws: Armies in meet Array,
Throng with aerial Spears, and Steeds of Fire;
Till, the long Lines of full-extended War   1055
In bleeding Fight commixt, the sanguine Flood
Rowls a broad Slaughter o'er the Plains of Heaven.

    As the mad People scan the fancy'd Scene,
On all Sides swells the superstitious Din,
Incontinent, and busy *Frenzy* talks   1060
Of Blood, and Battle; Cities over-turn'd,
And, late at Night, in swallowing Earthquake sunk,
Or painted hideous with ascending Flame;
Of Blights, that blacken the white-bosom'd *Spring*,
And Tempest, shaking *Autumn* into Chaff,   1065
Till *Famine*, empty-handed, starves the Year;
Of Pestilence, and every great Distress,
Empires subvers'd, when ruling *Fate* has struck
Th'unalterable Hour: even *Nature's Self*
Is deem'd to totter on the Brink of Time.   1070

    NOT so the Man of *Philosophic* Eye,
And Inspect sage, *the waving Brightness*, He,
Curious surveys, inquisitive to know
The Causes, and Materials, yet unfix'd,
Of this Appearance beautiful, and new.   1075

    WITH *Thee*, serene PHILOSOPHY! with *Thee*!
And thy high Praises, let me crown my Song!
Effusive Source of Evidence, and Truth!
A Lustre shedding o'er th'ennobl'd Mind,
Stronger than Summer-Noon, and pure as that,   1080
Which gently vibrates on the Eye of Saint,
New to the Dawning of cœlestial Day.
Hence, thro' her nourish'd Powers, enlarg'd by *Thee*,
She, soaring, spurns, with elevated Pride,
The tangling Mass of Cares, and low Desires,   1085
That bind the fluttering Crowd, and, Angel-wing'd,
The Heights of Science, and of Vertue gains,
Where all is calm, and bright! with Nature round
Or in the starry Regions, or th'Abyss,

1076–1146 Cf. *OET* 1730–1805.

To *Reason*'s, and to *Fancy*'s Eye display'd;   1090
The *First* up-tracing, from *the vast Inane*,
The Chain of Causes, and Effects to HIM,
WHO, absolutely, in HIMSELF, alone,
Possesses *Being*; while the *Last* receives
The whole Magnificence of Heaven, and Earth,   1095
And every Beauty, delicate or bold,
Obvious or more remote, with livelier Sense,
A World swift-painted, on th'attentive Mind!

    TUTOR'D by *Thee*, hence POETRY exalts
Her Voice to Ages, and informs the Page   1100
With Music, Image, Sentiment, and Thought,
Never to die! the Treasure of Mankind,
Their highest Honour, and their truest Joy!

    WITHOUT *Thee*, what were unassisted Man!
A Savage roaming thro' the Woods and Wilds,   1105
In Quest of Prey, and with th'unfashion'd Furr,
Rough-clad, devoid of every honest Art,
And Elegance of Life. Nor Home, nor Joy
Domestick, mix'd of Tenderness and Care,
Nor moral Excellence, nor social Bliss,   1110
Nor Law were his; nor Property, nor Swain
To turn the Furrow, nor mechanic Hand
Harden'd to Toil, nor Servant prompt, nor *Trade*
Mother severe of infinite Delights!
Nothing save Rapine, Indolence, and Guile,   1115
And Woes on Woes, to render human Life
Than Non-Existence worse. But taught by *Thee*
Ours are the Arts of Policy, and Peace,
To live like Brothers, and, conjunctive, all
Embellish Life. While thus laborious Crowds   1120
Ply the tough Oar, PHILOSOPHY directs,
Star-led, the Helm; or like the liberal Breath
Of urgent Heaven, invisible, the Sails
Swells out, and bears th'inferior World along.

    NOR, to this evanescent Speck of Earth,   1125
Poorly confin'd, those radiant Tracts on high
Are *her* exalted Range; intent, to gaze
Creation thro', and, from that *round Complex*
Of never-ceasing Wonders, to conceive
Of THE SOLE BEING right, WHO spoke the Word,—   1130

And Nature circled. With inflected View,
Thence, on *th'Ideal Kingdom*, swift, she turns
Her Eye; and instant, at her virtual Glance,
Th'obedient Phantoms vanish, and appear,
Compound, divide, and into Order shift,   1135
Each to his Rank, from plain Perception up
To Notion quite abstract; where first begins
The World of Spirits, Action all, and Life
Immediate, and unmix'd—but here the Cloud,
So wills ETERNAL PROVIDENCE, sits deep.   1140
Enough for Us we know, that this dark State,
In wayward Passions lost, and vain Pursuits,
This Infancy of Being! cannot prove
The final Issue of the Works of GOD,
By *Love*, and *Wisdom*, inexpressive, form'd,   1145
And ever rising with the rising Mind.

THE END

APPENDIX B

Sp. 28 dedication

To the Right Honourable the
Countess of HERTFORD.

MADAM,

I HAVE always observed that, in Addresses of this Nature, the general
Taste of the World demands ingenious Turns of Wit, and disguised
artful Periods, instead of an open Sincerity of Sentiment flowing in
a plain Expression. From what secret Impatience of the justest Praise,
5 when bestowed on Others, this often proceeds, rather than a pretended
Delicacy, is beyond my Purpose here to enquire. But as nothing is more
foreign to the Disposition of a Soul sincerely pleased with the Con-
templation of what is beautiful, and excellent, than Wit and Turn;
I have too much Respect for your Ladyship's Character, either to touch
10 it in that gay, trifling Manner, or venture on a particular Detail of those
truly amiable Qualities of which it is composed. A Mind exalted, pure,
and elegant, a Heart overflowing with Humanity, and the whole Train
of Virtues thence derived, that give a pleasing Spirit to Conversation,
an engaging Simplicity to the Manners, and form the Life to Harmony,
15 are rather to be felt, and silently admired, than expressed. I have
attempted, in the following Poem, to paint some of the most tender
Beauties, and delicate Appearances of Nature; how much in vain,
your Ladyship's Taste will, I am afraid, but too soon discover: Yet
would it still be a much easier Task to find Expression for all that Variety
20 of Colour, Form, and Fragrance, which enrich the Season I describe,
than to speak the many nameless Graces, and Native Riches of a Mind
capable so much at once to relish Solitude, and adorn Society. To whom
then could these Sheets be more properly inscribed than to You,
MADAM, whose Influence in the World can give them the Protection they
25 want, while your fine Imagination, and intimate Acquaintance with
Rural Nature, will recommend them with the greatest Advantage to
your favourable Notice? Happy! if I have hit any of those Images, and
correspondent Sentiments, your calm Evening Walks, in the most
delightful Retirement, have oft inspired. I could add too, that as this
30 Poem grew up under your Encouragement, it has therefore a natural
Claim to your Patronage. Should You read it with Approbation, it's

Musick shall not droop; and should it have the good Fortune to deserve your Smiles, it's Roses shall not wither. But, where the Subject is so tempting, lest I begin my Poem before the Dedication is ended, I here break short, and beg Leave to subscribe my self, with the highest 35 Respect,

MADAM,

Your most Obedient,

Humble Servant,

JAMES THOMSON.

Sp 28 advertisement

THAT *the following Poem appears at present in Publick, is not any way in Prejudice of the Proposals I lately Published for Printing the* FOUR SEASONS, &c. *by Subscription, but at the Solicitation of some of my Friends who had seen it in Manuscript, and the better to carry on a Work I stand engaged to finish. For* Subscription *is now at its last Gasp, and the* 5 *World seems to have got the better of that many-headed Monster. However, those Gentlemen and Ladies who have been, or may hereafter be so good as to honour me with their Names, shall have the Book next Winter according to my Proposals: And if it should, in any Degree, be judged worthy their Encouragement, I have my best Reward.* 10

Su.27 dedication

To the Right Honourable

Mr. DODINGTON

One of the Lords of HIS MAJESTY's Treasury, &c.

SIR

IT is not my Purpose, in this Address, to run into the common Tract of Dedicators, and attempt a Panegyric which would prove *ungrateful* to You, too *arduous* for Me, and *superfluous* with Regard to the World. To You it would prove *ungrateful*, since there is a certain generous Delicacy in Men of the most distinguished Merit, disposing Them to 5 avoid those Praises They so powerfully attract. And when I consider that a *Character*, in which the VERTUES, the GRACES, and the MUSES join their Influence, as much exceeds the Expression of the most elegant and judicious Pen, as the finish'd *Beauty* does the Representation of the Pencil, I have the best Reasons for declining such an *arduous* 10 Undertaking. As, indeed, it would be *superfluous* in it self; for what

Reader need to be told of those great Abilities in the Management of public Affairs, and those amiable Accomplishments in private Life, which You so eminently possess. The general Voice is loud in the Praise
15 of so many Vertues, tho' Posterity alone will do Them Justice. But may You, SIR, live long to illustrate your own Fame by your own Actions, and by them be transmitted to future Times as the BRITISH MÆCENAS!

YOUR Example has recommended POETRY, with the greatest Grace, to the Admiration of Those, who are engag'd in the highest and most
20 active Scenes of Life: and this, tho' confessedly the least considerable of those exalted Qualities that dignify your Character, must be particularly pleasing to *One*, whose only Hope of being introduced to your Regard is thro' the Recommendation of an ART in which You are a Master.—But I forget what I have been declaring above, and must
25 therefore turn my Eyes to the following Sheets. I am not ignorant that, when offered to your Perusal, they are put into the Hands of one of the finest, and consequently the most indulgent Judges of the Age: but as there is no Mediocrity in POETRY, so there should be no Limits to its Ambition.—I venture directly on the Tryal of my Fame.—If what I
30 here present You has any Merit to gain your Approbation, I am not afraid of its Success; and if it fails of your Notice, I give it up to its just Fate. This Advantage at least I secure to myself, an Occasion of thus publickly declaring that I am, with the profoundest Veneration,

SIR,

Your most devoted,

humble Servant,

JAMES THOMSON.

Wi.26f–28 dedication

TO

The RIGHT HONOURABLE
Sir *SPENCER COMPTON.*

SIR

THE Author of the following POEM begs Leave to inscribe this his first Performance to your Name, and Patronage. Unknown Himself, and only introduced by the *Muse*, He yet ventures to approach You, with a modest Chearfulness: for, whoever attempts to excel in
5 any Generous Art, tho' he comes alone, and unregarded by the World, may hope for your Notice, and Esteem. Happy! if I can, in any Degree,

merit this Good Fortune: as every Ornament, and Grace of Polite
Learning is yours, your single Approbation will be my Fame.

I DARE not indulge my Heart, by dwelling on your *Public* Character;
on that exalted Honour, and Integrity which distinguish You, in that 10
August Assembly, where You preside; that unshaken Loyalty to your
Sovereign; that disinterested Concern for his *Peogle*, which shine out,
united, in all your Behaviour, and finish the *Patriot*. I am conscious of
my Want of Strength, and Skill for so delicate an Undertaking: And
yet, as the Shepherd, in his Cottage, may feel and acknowledge the 15
Influence of the Sun with as lively a Gratitude, as the Great Man, in
his Palace, *even I* may be allowed to publish *my Sense* of those Blessings,
which, from so many powerful Vertues, are derived to the Nation they
adorn.

I conclude with saying, that your fine Discernment and Humanity, 20
in your *Private* Capacity, are so conspicuous, that, if this Address is
not received with some Indulgence, it will be a severe Conviction, that
what I have written has not the least Share of Merit.

I am,

With the profoundest Respect,

SIR,

Your most devoted,

and most faithful,

Humble Servant,

James Thomson.

260 preface

I AM neither ignorant, nor concern'd, how much One may suffer
in the Opinion of several Persons of great Gravity, and Character,
by the Study, and Pursuit, of POETRY.

Altho' there may seem to be some Appearance of Reason for the
present Contempt of it, as managed by the most part of our modern 5
Writers, yet that any Man should, seriously, declare against that DIVINE
ART is, really, amazing. It is declaring against the most charming Power
of Imagination, the most exalting Force of Thought, the most affecting
Touch of Sentiment; in a Word, against the very Soul of all Learning,
and Politeness. It is affronting the universal Taste of Mankind, and 10
declaring against what has charmed the listening World from *Moses*
down to *Milton*. In fine, it is, even, declaring against the sublimest
Passages of the inspired Writings themselves, and what seems to be the
peculiar Language of Heaven.

15 The Truth of the Case is this: These weak-sighted Gentlemen cannot bear the strong Light of POETRY, and the finer, and more amusing, Scene of Things it displays; but must Those, therefore, whom Heaven has blessed with the discerning Eye shut it, to keep them Company?

20 It is pleasant enough, however, to observe, frequently, in these Enemies of POETRY, an aukward Imitation of it. They sometimes, have their little Brightnesses, when the opening Glooms will permit. Nay, I have seen their Heaviness, on some Occasions, deign to turn friskish, and witty, in which they make just such another Figure as *Æsop's Ass*, 25 when he began to fawn. To compleat the Absurdity, They would, even, in their Efforts against POETRY, fain be poetical; like those Gentlemen that reason with a great deal of Zeal, and Severity, against Reason.

That there are frequent, and notorious, Abuses of POETRY is as true as that the best Things are most liable to that Misfortune; but is there 30 no End of that clamorous Argument against the Use of Things from the Abuse of them? And yet, I hope, that no Man, who has the least Sense of Shame in Him, will fall into it after the present, sulphureous, Attacker of the Stage.

To insist no further on this Head, let POETRY, once more, be restored 35 to her antient Truth, and Purity; let Her be inspired from Heaven, and, in Return, her Incense ascend thither; let Her exchange Her low, venal, trifling, Subjects for such as are fair, useful, and magnificent; and, let Her execute these so as, at once, to please, instruct, surprize, and astonish: and then, of Necessity, the most inveterate Ignorance, and 40 Prejudice, shall be struck Dumb; and POETS, yet, become the Delight and Wonder, of Mankind.

But this happy Period is not to be expected, till some long-wished, illustrious Man, of equal Power, and Beneficence, rise on the wintry World of Letters: One of a genuine, and unbounded, Greatness, and 45 Generosity, of Mind; who, far, above all the Pomp, and Pride, of Fortune, scorns the little addressful, Flatterer; peirces thro' the disguised, designing, Villain; discountenances all the reigning Fopperies of a tasteless Age: and who, stretching his Views into late Futurity, has the true Interest of Virtue, Learning, and Mankind, intirely, at Heart— 50 A Character so nobly desirable! that to an honest Heart, it is, almost, incredible so few should have the Ambition to deserve it.

Nothing can have a better Influence towards the Revival of POETRY than the chusing of great, and serious, Subjects; such as, at once, amuse the Fancy, enlighten the Head, and warm the Heart. These give a 55 Weight, and Dignity, to the Poem: Nor is the Pleasure, I should say Rapture, both the Writer, and the Reader, feels, unwarranted by

Reason, or followed by repentant Disgust. To be able to write on a dry,
barren, Theme, is looked upon, by some, as the Sign of a happy,
fruitful, Genius—fruitful indeed!—like one of the pendant Gardens in
Cheapside, water'd, every Morning, by the Hand of the *Alderman*, 60
Himself. And what are we commonly entertain'd with, on these
Occasions, save forced, unaffecting, Fancies; little, glittering Pretti-
nesses; mixed Turns of Wit, and Expression; which are as widely
different from Native POETRY, as Buffoonery is from the Perfection
of human Thinking? A Genius fired with the Charms of Truth, and 65
Nature, is tuned to a sublimer Pitch, and scorns to associate with such
Subjects.

I cannot more emphatically recommend this *Poetical Ambition* than
by the four following Lines from Mr. *Hill's Poem*, called, *The Judgment
Day*, which is so singular an Instance of it. 70

> *For* Me, *suffice it to have taught my Muse,*
> *The* tuneful Triflings *of her Tribe to shun;*
> *And rais'd her Warmth such* Heavenly Themes *to chuse,*
> *As, in past Ages, the best Garlands won.*

I know no Subject more elevating, more amusing; more ready to 75
awake the poetical Enthusiasm, the philosophical Reflection, and the
moral Sentiment, than the *Works of Nature*. Where can we meet with
such Variety, such Beauty, such Magnificence? All that enlarges, and
transports, the Soul? What more inspiring than a calm, wide, Survey of
Them? In every Dress *Nature* is greatly charming! whether she puts 80
on the Crimson Robes of the *Morning!* the strong Effulgence of *Noon!*
the sober Suit of the *Evening!* or the deep Sables of *Blackness*, and
Tempest! How gay looks the *Spring!* how glorious the *Summer!* how
pleasing the *Autumn!* and how venerable the *Winter!*—But there is no
thinking of these Things without breaking out into POETRY; which is, 85
by the bye, a plain, and undeniable, Argument of their superior Excel-
lence.

For this Reason the best, both Antient, and Modern, POETS have been
passionately fond of Retirement, and Solitude. The wild romantic
Country was their Delight. And they seem never to have been more 90
happy, than when lost in unfrequented Fields, far from the little, busy,
World, they were at Leisure, to meditate, and sing the *Works of Nature*.

The Book of *Job*, that noble, and antient, *Poem*, which, even, strikes
so forcibly thro' a mangling Translation, is crowned with a Description
of the grand *Works of Nature*; and that, too, from the Mouth of their 95
ALMIGHTY AUTHOR.

It was this Devotion to the *Works of Nature* that, in his *Georgicks*,
inspired the *rural Virgil* to write so inimitably; and who can forbear

joining with him in this Declaration of his, which has been the Rapture
100 of Ages.

> *Me vero primum dulces ante omnia Musae,*
> *Quarum Sacra fero ingenti percussus Amore,*
> *Accipiant; Coelique Vias et Sidera monstrent,*
> *Defectus solis varios, Lunaeque labores:*
> 105 *Unde tremor Terris: qua vi Maria alta tumescant*
> *Obicibus ruptis rursusque in seipsa residant:*
> *Quid tantum Oceano properent se tinguere soles*
> *Hyberni: vel quae tardis Mora Noctibus obstet.*
> *Sin, has ne possim Naturae accedere Partis,*
> 110 *Frigidus obstiterit circum Praecordia sanguis;*
> *Rura mihi et rigui placeant in vallibus amnes,*
> *Flumina amem silvasque inglorius.*

Which may be Englished thus.

> *Me may the* Muses, *my supreme Delight!*
> 115 *Whose* Priest *I am, smit with immense Desire,*
> *Snatch to their Care; the* Starry Tracts *disclose,*
> *The* Sun's *Distress, the Labours of the* Moon:
> *Whence the* Earth *quakes: and by what Force the* Deeps
> *Heave at the Rocks, then on Themselves reflow:*
> 120 *Why* Winter-Suns *to plunge in Ocean speed:*
> *And what retards the lazy* Summer-Night.
> *But, least I should those mystic-Truths attain,*
> *If the cold Current freezes round my Heart,*
> *The* Country *Me, the brooky* Vales *may please*
> 125 *Mid Woods, and Streams,* unknown.—

I cannot put an End to this *Preface,* without taking the Freedom to
offer my most sincere, and grateful, Acknowledgements to all those
Gentlemen who have given my first Performance so favourable a
Reception.

130   It is with the best Pleasure, and a rising Ambition, that I reflect on
the Honour Mr. *Hill* has done me, in recommending my Poem to the
World, after a manner so peculiar to Himself; than whom, none
approves, and obliges, with a nobler, and more unreserving, Promptitude of Soul. His Favours are the very smiles of Humanity; graceful,
135 and easy; flowing from, and to, the Heart. This agreeable Train of
Thought awakens naturally in my Mind all the other Parts of his great,
and amiable, Character, which I know not well how to quit, and yet
dare not here pursue.

127 offer] pay *260 press variant*
128–9 so favourable a Reception] so favourable Reception; particularly, that
honourable Person, under whose auspicious Name I have met with an Encouragement more answerable to his Generosity, than my Merit *260 press variant*
so favourable Reception *260 press variant*

Every Reader, who has a Heart to be moved, must feel the most gentle Power of POETRY, in the Lines, with which *Mira* has graced my 140 Poem.

It perhaps, might be reckoned Vanity, in me, to say how richly I value the Approbation of a *Gentleman* of Mr. *Malloch*'s fine, and exact Taste, so justly dear, and valuable, to all those that have the Happiness of knowing Him; and who, to say no more of Him, will abundantly 145 make good, to the World, the early Promise, his admired Piece of *William and Margaret* has given.

I only wish my Description of the various Appearance of *Nature* in *Winter*, and, as I purpose, in the other *Seasons*, may have the good Fortune, to give the Reader some of that true Pleasure, which They, in 150 their agreeable Succession, are, always, sure to inspire into my Heart.

260 commendatory poems

[Note. Lines 5–10 of the first poem were printed, from T's letter to Hill of 24 May 1726, in *A Collection of Letters to the late Aaron Hill*, 1751, pp. 60–2. The whole poem appears in *The Works of the late Aaron Hill*, 1753, iii, 77–9. Substantive variants are recorded below as '*51*' and '*53*'. Variants in accidentals are not recorded.]

To Mr. THOMSON,

Doubtful to what Patron he should address his Poem, *call'd,* WINTER

SOme Peers, perhaps, have Skill to judge, 'tis true:
Yet no mean Prospect bounds the *Muse's* View.
Firm in your native Strength, thus nobly shewn,
Slight such delusive Props, and stand alone.
Fruitless Dependance oft has found too late,   5
That Greatness rarely dwells among the Great.
Patrons are *Nature*'s Nobles, not the *State*'s,
And *Wit*'s, a Title no Broad Seal creates:
Even *Kings*, from whose high Source all Honours flow,
Are poor in Power, when they would *Souls* bestow.   10

[*title*] *To Mr.* JAMES THOMPSON; *on his asking my Advice, to what* Patron *he should address his* Poem *called* WINTER. *53*   1 perhaps, have] have noble *53*   2 mean] poor *53*   3 nobly] greatly *53*   5 Smile at your vanish'd Hope—convinc'd, too late, *51* Fruitless dependance, oft has prov'd, too late, *53*   6 rarely dwells among] dwells not, always, with *51 53*
9 Kings, from whose Bounty Wealth's chief Currents flow, *51*

Heedless of Fortune, then look down on State,
Balanc'd, within, by Reason's conscious Weight:
Divinely proud of independant Will,
Prince of your Passions, live their Sovereign still.
He who stoops, safe beneath a Patron's Shade,   15
Shines like the Moon, but by another's Aid:
Free Truth shou'd, open, and unbyas'd steer,
Strong, as Heaven's Heat, and as its Brightness clear.

O, swell not then, the Bosoms of the *Vain*,
With false Conceit that you Protection gain: 20
Poets, like you, their own Protectors stand,
Plac'd above Aid from Pride's inferior Hand.
Time, that devours the *Lord*'s unlasting Name,
Shall lend Her soundless Depth, to float your Fame.

On Verse like yours no Smiles, from Power, expect,   25
Born with a Worth that doom'd you to Neglect:—
Yet, wou'd your Wit, be nois'd, reflect no more;
Let the smooth Veil of Flattery silk you o'er:
Aptly attach'd, the Courts soft Climate try,
Learn your Pen's Duty from your Patron's Eye.   30
Ductile of Soul, each pliant Purpose wind,
And tracing Interest close, leave Doubt behind;
Then shall your Name strike loud, the Publick Ear;
For through Good-fortune, Virtue's self shines clear.

But, in defiance of our Taste, to charm!   35
And Fancy's Force with Judgement's Caution arm!
Disturb, with busy Thought, so lull'd an Age!
And plant strong Meanings o'er the peaceful Page!
Impregnate Sound, with Sense! teach Nature Art!
And warm even WINTER, till it thaws the Heart!   40
How cou'd you thus, your Country's Rules transgress,
Yet think of *Patrons*, and presume Success?

                                                    A. HILL.

11–14 *and* 15–18 *are transposed in* 53   12 Reason's] *merit's 53*
14 Passions] wishes 53   their] a 53   16 another's] a *borrow'd* 53
17 *Truth* should, unbiass'd, free, and open, steer, 53   20 that you] you
their 53   23 the] a 53   27 nois'd] prais'd 53   32 tracing] follow-
ing 53

To Mr. THOMSON,

On his Blooming WINTER

OH gaudy *Summer*, veil thy blushing Head,
  Dull is thy Sun, and all thy Beauties dead:
From thy short Nights, and noisy, mirthful, Day,
My kindling Thoughts, disdainful, turn away.

   Majestic *Winter* with his Floods appears,   5
And o'er the World his awful Terrors rears;
From *North* to *South*, his Train dispreading, slow,
Blue *Frost*, bleak *Rain*, and fleecy-footed *Snow*.

   In Thee, sad *Winter*, I a Kindred find,
Far more related to poor human Kind;   10
To Thee my gently-drooping Head I bend,
Thy *Sigh* my *Sister*, and thy *Tear* my *Friend:*
On Thee I *muse*, and in thy hastening Sun,
See Life expiring e'er 'tis well begun.

   Thy sickening Ray, and venerable Gloom,   15
Show Life's last Scene, the solitary Tomb;
But thou art safe, so shaded by the Bays,
Immortal in the noblest *Poet*'s Praise;
From Time and Death, He will thy Beauties save;
Oh may such Numbers weep o'er *Mira*'s Grave!   20
Secure, and glorious, would her Ashes lie,
Till *Nature* fade—and all the *Seasons* die.

MIRA.

To Mr. THOMSON,

On his publishing the Second Edition *af his* Poem, *call'd,* WINTER

CHarm'd, and instructed, by thy powerful Song,
  I have, unjust, with-held my Thanks too long:
This Debt of Gratitude, at length, receive,
Warmly sincere, 'tis all thy *Friend* can give.

Thy Worth new lights the Poet's darken'd Name,   5
And shews it, blazing, in the brightest Fame.
Thro' all thy various *Winter*, full are found
Magnificence of Thought, and Pomp of Sound,
Clear Depth of Sense, Expression's hightening Grace,
And *Goodness*, eminent in Power, and Place!   10
For this, the *Wise*, the Knowing *Few*, commend
With zealous Joy—for Thou art *Vertue*'s Friend:
Even *Age*, and *Truth* severe, in reading Thee,
That Heaven inspires the *Muse*, convinc'd, agree.

Thus I dare sing of Merit, faintly known,   15
Friendless—supported by its self alone:
For *Those*, whose *aided Will* could lift thee high,
In Fortune, *see* not with *Discernment's Eye*.
Nor Place, nor Power, bestows the *Sight* refin'd;
And Wealth enlarges not the narrow Mind.   20

How couldst thou think of *such*, and write so well?
Or hope Reward, by daring to excell?
Unskilful of the Age! untaught to gain,
Those Favours, which the fawning *Base* obtain!
A thousand, shameful, Arts, to thee unknown,   25
Falshood, and *Flattery*, must be first thy own.
If thy lov'd *Country* lingers in thy Breast,
Thou must drive out th' unprofitable *Guest*:
Extinguish each bright Aim, that kindles there,
And center in thy self thy every Care.   30

But hence that Vileness—pleas'd to charm Mankind,
Cast each low Thought of Interest far behind:
Neglected into noble Scorn—away
From that worn Path, where vulgar Poets stray:
Inglorious Herd! profuse of venal Lays!   35
And by the *Pride* despis'd, they stoop to praise!
Thou, careless of the Statesman's Smile, or Frown,
Tread that strait Way, that leads to fair Renown.
By *Vertue* guided, and by *Glory* fir'd,
And, by reluctant *Envy*, slow admir'd,   40
Dare to do well; and in thy boundless Mind,
Embrace the general Welfare of thy *Kind*:
Enrich them with the Treasures of thy Thought,
What Heaven approves, and what the *Muse* has taught.

Where thy *Power* fails, unable to go on, 45
Ambitious, greatly *will* the Good undone.
So shall thy Name, thro' Ages, brightening shine,
And distant Praise, from *Worth* unborn, be thine:
So shalt thou, happy! merit Heaven's Regard,
And find a glorious, tho' a late Reward. 50

D. MALLOCH.

APPENDIX C

SUBSTANTIVE VARIANTS IN EDITIONS EDITED BY LYTTELTON AND MURDOCH, 1750–62.

See Introduction, pp. lxxiv–lxxix, and Key to the Critical Apparatus, pp. xiii–xiv.

Before h.t. to Spring Lytt adds the following:

Preface to the Seasons,

In this Edition, conformably to the intention and will of the Author, some Expressions in the Seasons which have justly been thought [by good Judges *del.*] too harsh, or obscure, or not strictly grammatical, have been corrected, some Lines transposed, and a few others left out. The Hymn, which was printed at the end of the Seasons in some of the last Editions, is likewise omitted; because it appears to good Judges that all the Matter and Thoughts in that Hymn are much better exprest in the Seasons themselves.

SPRING

Argument *and mixed*] *not in 52dd–62d*   39 Shoulder] shoulders *Lytt*
60 Insect-] gaudy *Lytt*   63 victorious] unwearied *62q 62d*   65 scorn'd]
liv'd. *58–62d* [*as 28–38*]   66 *not in 58–62d* [*as 28–38*]   113 spies: *58–62d*
before 114 Now every Bud expanding bursts to life *Lytt*   121 waft] warp
58–62d ride *Lytt*   126 Destruction waits unseen and Famine dire. *Lytt*
143 and now,] he now *52dd–62d* and sleeps *Lytt*   144 Caves,] cave, *52dd–*
62d ~: *Lytt*   146 Breathes the big Clouds distent with vernal show'rs.
Lytt   148 but] then *Lytt*   fast] swift *58–62d Lytt*   150 mingling
deep] wide diffused *Lytt*   158 many-] ever *Lytt*   164 The teeming
Clouds; while hushd in short Suspense, *Lytt*   185 kindling] various *Lytt*
colour] brightning *Lytt*   198 Full swell the Woods;] The Woods exult:
Lytt   199–202 *del. Lytt*   201 The] And *58–62d*   203 Meantime]
And see! *Lytt*   206 running from] deepning to *Lytt*   212 Swain,]
boy; *58–62d*   243 From beds of leaves or Moss; nor griev'd to see *Lytt*
245 Their temperate slumbers lightly fumed away; *Lytt*   250 stole] shar'd
Lytt   251 Their Hours away]Their blissfull hours *Lytt*   252 infant]
tender *Lytt* free. *Lytt*   Then 249–54 *del. Lytt*   256 these] those *58–*
62d   262 swelling] verdant *Lytt*   263 commixing] promiscuous *Lytt*
272 Minutes] manners *58–62d*   264–74 *del. Lytt*   Then 249–74 *shortened
by Lytt as follows:*

> On every Hill, beneath each spreading Shade
> The Swains and Husbandmen rejoicing hymn
> Their bounteous God. Then festive Dance and Sport
> Kind Deeds, and friendly Talk successive shar'd
> Their blisfull hours: while in the rosy Vale

> Love breath'd his tender Sighs from Anguish free
> And free from Guilt. Such were those prime of Days.
> But now those pure unblemish'd Manners, whence
> The mystick Poets took their golden Age
> Are rarely found amid these iron Times,

277 the Soul of] its genuine *Lytt*   288+ From Wisdom and from Happiness divorced; *Lytt*   289 pensive Anguish] fond Distraction, *Lytt*   309 HENCE, on the guilty World a deluge came: *Lytt*   318 a broken World] afflicted Man *Lytt*   320 Great] Mild *Lytt*   327 No Clouds impregnate with sulphureous Glooms *Lytt*   329 While] No *Lytt*   and] nor *Lytt* 330 Hung on the Springs of Life and clogd their Tone. *Lytt*   358 you,] ah! *Lytt*

360–1   To merit Death? You, who, each Year, resign
               To undefended Man your own attire   *Lytt*

370 This] Thus *52dd–62d [as 28–45]*   377–8 *not in 58–62d [as 28–45]* 422 Infant] captive *58–62d Lytt [as 44 44Wks]*   441 *del. Lytt*   442 gaily drag] drag to land *Lytt*   445 *del. Lytt*   452 liquid] rapid *Lytt* 458–9 *del. Lytt*   461 a Dream] the dream *58–62d*   461–3 *del. Lytt* 464 Soothe] Soothd *Lytt*   467 breathing Prospect] blooming Landskip *Lytt* 468 It's various beauties trace. But who can paint *Lytt*   471 matchless] wondrous *Lytt*   479 Which bounteous Nature breathes continual round. *Lytt*   486 Those] These *52dd–57*   500 Beans] beams *52dd [as 46]* 502 Revives with Fragrance mild the gladdend Soul. *Lytt*   513 And] But soaring dare] soar, to seek *Lytt*   515 And loaded with the luscious spoil return. *Lytt*   518–26 *del. Lytt*   551 broad] streakd *Lytt*   553–5 *del. Lytt*   556 BEINGS] BEING *52dd–62d*   599 kind] gay *Lytt*   602 To let them triumph; but designs, in thought *Lytt*   688 *del. Lytt*   after 701 *Lytt inserts 849–66 with variants, see below*   747 The] Its *62q 62d* 770 amusive *del. Lytt*   786 the whole homely] all the lively *Lytt* 787 thick] quick *Lytt*   821 boundless] wanton *Lytt*   835 Around him feeds dispers'd his bleating flock, *Lytt*   837 *del. Lytt*

838–40   Their frolicks play. Behold in sprightly Race
               At once they start, and sweep the massy mound   *Lytt*

846 the golden Head] their golden heads *58–62d*

844–8   Torn with perpetual Broils: but now o'er all
               The bllisful Isle sweet Concord, Peace, and Love
               Walk hand in hand, and, each returning Year
               Crown the fair Forehead of the gentle May.   *Lytt*

849 Curious] sages *58–62d*   849–66 *transferred by Lytt to 701+, with following variants:*   849 Curious, say] Sages, tell   852 Arts of Love] sentiments   853 *del.*   854 And] Whose   867 Song] Muse *Lytt* 868 Man. *Lytt*   870 Soul, *Lytt*   874 bounteous] flowery *Lytt* 875 flowing] bounteous *Lytt*   879 CREATIVE BOUNTY burns] the Maker's Bounty glows *Lytt*   882–3 Inviting modest Want.   Your active Search *Lytt*   888 teaming] pregnant *Lytt*   891 Ye] The *Lytt*   899 By swift Degrees] With gradual force *Lytt*   908 you stray,] thou strayest; *52dd–62d*   948 Inimitable] Unutterable *58–62d Lytt*   955–6 And spiry Towns, your Eye excursive roams: *Lytt*   971–3 From the keen . . . sighing Languishment. *del. Lytt*   984 smooth] sweet *Lytt*   1018 the Tongue] his tongue *58–62d Lytt*

1020–4   To the vain bosom of his distant Fair
                His wafted spirit flies. Sudden he starts, *Lytt*

1071–5   He wakes appalld: but waking still he dreams,
                With idle fears disturbd and vain Desires.
                Wild Passion's Slave, bereft of Reason's Aid,
                Yet even his Pains delight. But thro' the heart *Lytt*

1074 *new paragraph 58–62d*   1078 But] 'Tis *Lytt*   1088 flowing]
glowing *Lytt*   1099 Peace] ease *Lytt*   1107 Peace] ease *58–62d*
1126–7 alone intent/To bless himself] intent to bless/Himself alone *Lytt*

1129   Well-merited, and all the racking Doubts
                Of Jealousy, consume his nights and days: *Lytt*

1138 and its Nonsense all!] all it's vain Delights, *Lytt*   1140 and] or *Lytt*
1143 Harmony] Sympathy *Lytt*   Love! *Lytt*   1144 *del. Lytt*   1168 and
consenting] still the genial *Lytt*   1170 Till age at last steals on, serene and
mild; *Lytt*   1172 swells] glows *Lytt*

SUMMER

38 matchless,] constant, *Lytt*   57 And] See! *Lytt*   71 For] Say, *Lytt*
81 powerful] glorious *Lytt*   *Lytt comments* 'Powerful *at his rising* does not
seem quite proper.'   107 Abodes] abode, *52dd*   109 th'unfetter'd
Mind,] the Mind of Man, *Lytt*   117–25 *del. Lytt*

128–9   Herbs, Flowers, and Fruits; while round thy beaming Car
               The Zephyrs downy-wing'd, the timely Rains,
               Of bloom ethereal the light-footed Dews,
               Attend, and aid thy fertilizing Ray.   *Lytt*

130–3 *del. Lytt*   134 Power, *Lytt*   134+ Ev'n to the secret Cavern
darting deep. *Lytt*   143–6 And star-like sparkles with collected Light. *Lytt*
Lytt inserts 147–8 after 152.   153 deeper] brighter *Lytt*   161–5 Assumes
a mimic Life. The Desart joys *Lytt*   176–8 *del. Lytt*   185–91 *del.*
Lytt   192 broad-] wide *Lytt* [*as 27–38*]   208–9 By gelid Founts to
muse, while Tyrant Heat, *Lytt*   210 rapid] cruel *Lytt*   231 And
at th' extremest border of the shade *Lytt*   278 Strikes] Stalks *Lytt*
303 evanescent] undistinguishd *Lytt*   421 Borrow'd] Received *Lytt*
451 Wrath!] rage *Lytt*   469 Ye groves high-arched! ye bowery thickets,
hail! *Lytt*   473 sallying] chrystal *Lytt*   532 better] moral *Lytt*
533 and] or *Lytt*   540 rous'd] awed *Lytt*   551 *del. Lytt*   624 on]
in *52pd–62d*   645 footnote *perpendicular*] vertical *58–62d*   669 *Lytt*
notes 'The Locust Tree is one of the largest and most shady Trees in the Indies.'
672 Brow] Mount *Lytt*   701 *new paragraph 58–62d*   737 plumy]
featherd *Lytt*   741 lent] gave *Lytt*

742–3   Proud *Montezuma's* realm, whose plumed Troops
               With various Splendour glitterd o'er the Field;   *Lytt*

790 roll˄ *Lytt*   812 manly] full-grown *Lytt*

813–14   And gathering many a flood, and swell'd with all
               The copious treasures of the humid sky,   *Lytt*

912 *Lytt expands as follows:*
               This Child of vengeful Nature! Various tribes
               Of these infest the Woodland Paths, or glide
               Athwart the sandy Plains. There also fired
               By the strong influence of the torrid Clime

959 these] those *52dd–57*   968 broad,] forth *Lytt*   984 footnote
Terms for] names of 52dd–62d   1010 HEAV'N-inspir'd] truly great
Lytt   1030–1 Woods,/Impenetrable Shades] Shades,/Impenetrably deep
Lytt   1096 Th'infuriate] the burning *Lytt*   1096 + Or pours forth torrent
Streams of Liquid Fire. *Lytt*   1154–5 They wore alive; and there the
frowning Bull, *Lytt*   1175 blooming] opening *Lytt*   1192 and] or *Lytt*
1193–4 *del. Lytt*   1195 Heavy with] Presaging *58–62d*   1206 He *52pd*
58–62d   1226–7 A purer azure. Thro' the lighten'd air *58–62d Lytt*

1229–32   Diffusive, shine: a glittering robe of joy,
                 Invests the fields, and Nature smiles around.   *Lytt*

1232 Invest the fields; and nature smiles reviv'd. *58–62d*   1242–3 *del. Lytt*
1338 Retired unseen by her: but first these lines, *Lytt*   1341 sacred Eye]
tender Glance *Lytt*   1348–9 So bending tries to veil its naked charms.
Lytt   1356 Her sudden] At once her *Lytt*   1398 To sweet retirement
happy lovers steal, *Lytt*   1427–8 *58–62d add the following footnote:* In his
last sickness.   1427–8 and for their POPE implore/The healing God; *del.*
Lytt   1435 softly-] sweetly- *52dd*   1446 merciful] temperate *Lytt*
1448 float] wave *Lytt*   1449 Waves: and] Harvests: *Lytt*   1451 blacken-
ing] well-fed *Lytt*   1469 Despising Death in every Form, and first *Lytt*
1470 in] on *52dd–62d [as 27]*   1479 Illustrious are thy Princes: ALFRED
first *Lytt*   1481 And peacefull Wisdom, more heroic still, *Lytt*

1483–4   And *Muses* venerate: *the best of Kings!*
                Then bright thy EDWARDS and thy HENRYS shine,   *Lytt*

1487   That awes her Genius still. Nor less renownd
              For wisest Policy and manly Strength
              Of Mind thy *Virgin Queen.* In *Statesmen* thou   *Lytt*

1535–40 First Bacon rose, deep, comprehensive, clear, *Lytt*   1549 *del. Lytt*
1551–63 *Lytt expands as follows:*

              By him instructed Boyle with pious search
              Amid the dark recesses of his works,
              The great Creator sought, and Knowledge fix'd
              On sure Experiment, not Systems vain.
              Thine too, Britannia, thine sagacious Locke,
              Who taught the Human Mind itself to know,
              It's Powers unfolded and it's limits markt,
              With cautious Modesty supremely wise:
              And Newton, pure Intelligence, whom God
              To Mortals lent, to trace his boundless Works
              From Laws sublimely simple. Lo! to These
              In every Land th' admiring Sages bend
              And Them their Masters own! nor far behind
              The generous Ashley stands, the friend of Man;

              etc. as 1552–5. *Then:*
              How sweet the Concert of thy various Bards
              Poetick Island! Hark! they strike the Lyre,
              Harmonious Dryden, Waller, Denham, Rowe,
              Gay, Prior, and judicious Addison:
              But see! with perfect Art the Hand of Pope
              Now tunes the strings! around the Graces dance,
              And Wisdom's sober Ear approves the Song.
              Of all thy numerous Wits, Britannia, This

The most correct! But nobler Fame belongs
To Genius more sublime. For lofty sense,

1571 blowing] smiling *Lytt*   1572 Verse] Lays *Lytt*   1573 The
gentle] Inventive *Lytt*   1577 native] lively *Lytt*

1578–9   Sharp with keen Satire, strong with nervous Sense
            And moral Truth, shines through the darkening cloud
            Of Gothic Barbarism around him thrown.   *Lytt*

1598 Shore] shores *52dd–62d*   1601 like] as *52dd–62d*   1605 white]
mild *Lytt*   1645 him] such *Lytt*   *Then* 1630–46 *del. Lytt*   1671 pant-
ing Height] steep ascent *Lytt*   1693 Sudden to Heaven] To heav'ns high
cope *Lytt*   1698–1710 *Lytt expands as follows:*

            Unrival'd reigns. Now, when the whole-some Nights
            Are free from noxious Damps, serene and mild;
            Forth let me walk, and view each glittering Star
            That decks with gentle Light th' unclouded Sky.
            Nor burn these heavn'ly Lamps for Man alone.
            To various Systems of dependant Orbs
            Bright Day, and animating Heat they give.
            The Life-infusing Suns of other Worlds.
            Struck at the Sight with pious Awe my Soul
            Adores the great Creator's Pow'r, and feels
            How small a Portion of his Works contains
            Th' aspiring Sons of Man, and bounds their Pride
            In narrow Limits. On th' effulgent Scene,
            While fix'd I gaze, the lambent Lightnings shoot
            Across the Sky; or horizontal dart,
            In wondrous Shapes: by fearful murmuring Crouds
            Portentous deemd. But greater still their Dread
            If from the void Immensity of Space
            Returning, with accelerated Course,
            The rushing Comet to the Sun descends;
            Then as he blazes in the Front of Night,
            With awfull Train projected o'er the Heavens,

1706 dread] dead *52pd–62q*   1713 mystic] groundless *Lytt*   1720 While]
When *Lytt*   1722 They see him come, and thro' the Planets roll *Lytt*
1726 the numerous] th' exhausted *Lytt*   1728–32 *Lytt expands as follows:*

            To yield new Fuel to the wasted Sun,
            Relume his Beams and feed his sinking Fire.
               By Thee, Divine Philosophy, by Thee
            Conducted, with serene Delight I range
            O'er Nature's Works, through all the varied Year.
            Taught by thy Precepts Poetry exalts
            Her Voice, and animates th' instructive Lay
            With moral Sentiment and Thought sublime.
            Hail bounteous source of Evidence, and Truth!

1737–8 Rais'd by thy pow'rfull Aid she springs aloft *Lytt*   1740 fluttering]
groveling *Lytt*   1741 gains. *Lytt*   1742–57 *del. Lytt*   1763 mix'd]
form'd *Lytt*

1777–8   Sustain the publick Weal. While labouring Crowds
            Ply the tough oar, thy guardian Power directs   *Lytt*

1782 Speck] Spot *Lytt*   1783 Poorly confin'd, the] Art thou confin'd.
The *Lytt*   1784 Are thy exalted range: tis thine to gaze *Lytt*   1789 she
turns] thou turn'st *Lytt*   1790 Her] Thine *Lytt*   her] thy *Lytt*   1795 *del.*
Lytt

AUTUMN

Argument *Address*] *Address'd 52dd 58–62d [as 46]   A ludicrous Account of Fox-hunting*] *not in 52dd–57*   1 Crown'd] Graced *Lytt*   6 white] sweet
Lytt   19 of] in *Lytt*   34 Till, with an instant Change, the ruffled Air
Lytt   91 bolder] higher *Lytt*   93 high] great *Lytt*   115–17 *del.*
Lytt [cf OET 115–17a]   133 roaring] Warrior *Lytt*   159 Scandal]
Courtship *Lytt*   166 sparing] scanty *58–62d*   188 Fashion] passion
52dd–62d   205 Ornament. *Lytt*   206 *del. Lytt [cf OET* 206a]
267 yes] heav'ns *58–62d*   269 Feature, every Look] look, his every feature,
58–62d   282 It ill] Ill it *52pd–62d*   298 Nor waited he reply.] The
maid astonished heard *Lytt*   301 The joyfull Tydings to her Mother came,
Lytt   336 *del. Lytt*

350   Of children dear, in vain from him their Food
        With piteous cries demanding. Landlords, then,   *Lytt*

353–7 *del. Lytt*

360–3   Soon as the gathered Harvest clears the Fields
        Hark! the rude Clamour of the Sportsman's Joy,
        The Gun fast-thundering, and the winded Horn,
        Drive from her rural Haunts affrighted Peace.
        See, in his Mid-career, the Spaniel struck,   *Lytt*

438 steaming] streaming *50*   482 Echo] echos *52dd–62d*   tost:] ∼. *50–7*
∼; *58–62d*   483–569 *not in 50–7*   525 grave] dull *58–62d [as 44–45]*
545 each congenial] every kindred *58–62d [as 30q–38]*   591 *del. Lytt*

599–600   With Sentiment refined and quick to judge
        Each Work of Wit or Fancy; in their Race   *Lytt*

604 Skill] Love *Lytt*   607 *not in 50–62d [as 30q–38]*   623 wise. *Lytt*
624 *del. Lytt*   631 melts] falls *Lytt*   *then* 629–32 *del. Lytt*

636+   Obedient to the Breeze a mellow Shower
        Of juicy Pears from the deep-loaded Bough
        Incessant falls; and scattered wide around
        Or piled in fragrant Heaps beneath their Trees
        The ripend Apples lie: Profusion gay!   *Lytt*

637–40 *del. Lytt*   641 various] vinous *Lytt*

671–4   Of Nature over open. Here, while charm'd
        I steal, at Noon, along the sunny Wall
        To climes, where cherish'd by the potent Sun   *Lytt*

673 And] Here *52dd–62d*   677–8 The ruddy fragrant nectarine; and dark
50–62d

686–7   The Vineyard cloaths each gently-rising Hill
        Or steep ascends the Mountain's sultry Side.   *Lytt*

695 *del. Lytt*   700 unbounded] redundant *Lytt*   705 The light, high-flavour'd Burgundy, and brisk *Lytt*   706 gay] bright *Lytt [as 30q–38]*
728 Wreath'd dun around] O'er all the Land *Lytt*   730 *del. Lytt*   731 A]

And *Lytt*   734 Infant] struggling *Lytt*   741 *del. Lytt*   742 And]
Whence *Lytt*   783 from] and *Lytt*   786 footnote *not in 50–62d*
877 Plumage, rising full] downy plumage, soft *Lytt*   903 unequal] their
narrow *Lytt*   921 passive] indolent *Lytt*   *Batavian*] foreign *Lytt*
922 Defraud] Deprive *Lytt*   949 felt] known *50–62d*   951–2 *del. Lytt*

954   To sooty dark the shaded Country round
           Imbrown! These now the pensive, lonesome Muse,   *Lytt*

955 lead] call *Lytt*   Walks] paths *Lytt*   970 pensive] sober *Lytt*
977 artless] joyfull *Lytt*   980 dull] full *52pd 58 62q*   despondent] de-
sponding *Lytt*

985–7   Destroy nor lay the miserable Tribes,
          Harmless and unsuspecting Harm in Blood
          Weak-fluttering on the Ground! think cruel man,
          Through all the balmy, blisfull days of Spring
          How sweet they sung, and stop thy murderous Hand.   *Lytt*

993–4   But should a quicker breeze disturb the boughs
          A leafy Deluge covers all the Ground,   *Lytt*

997 Waste,] Heaps *Lytt*   1000 sunny] silken *Lytt*   1001 bolder] stronger
50–62d   1038 Garden] gardens *Lytt*   Seat] seats *Lytt*   1042 *50–62d*
add the following footnote: The Seat of the Lord Viscount Cobham.   1061 O]
Or *52dd–62d*   1069 venal] golden *Lytt*   1088 Mean-while] Mean-
time *Lytt*

1093–5   And Caverns deep, again restores his Light
         Void of it's Flame, and sheds a softer Day.   *Lytt*

1094 all] us *58–62d*   1098–1100 *del. Lytt*

1101–2   All Aether whitens with a boundless Tide
         Of silver Radiance, mild; while Rocks and Floods
         And waving Seas reflect the quivering Gleam.   *Lytt*

1106 quite] near *58–62d*   1112 quickly] swiftly *Lytt*

1113–14   Then mix, and thwart, with Streams of various Dies
         Now white and now with glowing Crimson stain'd.   *Lytt*

1123–4 Affrighted Superstition wildly talks *Lytt*

1134–7   The waving brightness he with curious thought
         Surveys, inquisitive to learn the Cause
         And yet unknown Materials which produce
         This beautifull Appearance, rarely seen
         In Britain's Clime, but to the Northern Skies
         Familiar; where it chears the tedious Length
         Of Night, and constant gilds the glowing Pole.   *Lytt*

1140–4   Are Heav'n and Earth. Order confounded lies,
         Distinction blotted out, and Beauty lost.   *Lytt*

1147 huge:] dire, *Lytt*

1177–9   Sat tending public Cares, and joy'd to mark
         Full-flowing round, their copious wintry stores.   *Lytt*

1221 While, loose to] Disposed in *Lytt*   1223 Shook to the Wind their
Cares] Forgetting every Care *Lytt*   1226 Her every Charm abroad] Drest
in her best Attire *Lytt*   1238 Drinks] Tastes *Lytt*   1246 Land and Sea]
Lands and Seas *Lytt*

1250–3   Flames not with costly Juice of foreign Grapes:
                   Nor knows he those fantastic idle Joys   *Lytt*

1256 *del. Lytt*   1257–8 estrang'd/To] secure/From *Lytt*   1263–4
del. Lytt

1266–7   Sweet breathing, spread o'er all the fertile Vale.
                   Nor bleating Flocks that graze the level Down
                   Of verdant Mountain; nor the Purl of Streams.   *Lytt*

1282 Unpierc'd,] Unmoved *Lytt*   1352 Oh NATURE! Handmaid of Celestial
Pow'r! *Lytt*   1356 blue Immense] Void immense *Lytt*

WINTER

5 kindred] awfull *Lytt*   6 *del. Lytt*   7 Oft, in the chearful Morning
of my Life, *Lytt*   17 *this*] her 58–62d her *Lytt*   30 awful Schemes]
Arts of State *Lytt*   31 *del. Lytt*   37 light] raise *Lytt*   43 fierce]
moist *Lytt*   45 spreads o'er] spreads thro' *62q 62d*   110 *del. Lytt*
117 you] ye *58–62d Lytt*   127 shivering] shivered *58–62d* quivering *Lytt*
[*cf. OET* 126–49a]   151 Mountain] mountains *62q*   175 *del. Lytt*
182 remain] remains *Lytt*

183–4   Nor safe the mightiest Trees: the tearing Wind
                   Breaks down and scatters their gigantic Limbs
                   Or prostrate throws to Earth their aged Trunks. *Lytt*

186 whirling] loosen'd *Lytt*   190 savage] furious *Lytt*   195 HUGE]
Wild *Lytt*

213–16 *Lytt expands as follows:*
                   Sad, sickening Thought! of all your idle Joys
                   Scarce on the soberd Mind one Trace remains.
                   So, when our Reason sleeps, with airy Wings
                   Fleets the false Vision o'er the formfull brain,
                   This moment, hurrying wide th' impassion'd Soul
                   The next in nothing lost. Yet still with Hopes
                   New-flush'd, and fresh Desires, deluded Man
                   Again prepares to run the giddy Round.

223 come] rise *62q 62d*   229 whitening] silent *Lytt*   273 till, upward
urg'd,] while foul and fierce *Lytt*   274–6 *del. Lytt*   278 Caught by
the Storm on some lone Heath, the Swain *Lytt*   293 *del. Lytt*

299–302   A dire Descent! of Precipices huge,
                   Smooth'd up with Snow; of faithless Bogs beyond
                   The Power of Frost; of still unfrozen Springs,   *Lytt*

304 *del. Lytt*   310 Who leaves his Friends, his Family, unseen. *Lytt*
351 *del. Lytt*   354 conscious] [generous *del.*] tender *Lytt*   359 AND
here can I] Nor shall my Muse *Lytt*   369 wintry] shivering *Lytt*

373–6   At pleasure mark'd him with inglorious Stripes.
                   To curb this barbarous Insolence arose
                   With honest Zeal the British Senators.
                   O great design! if executed well!   *Lytt*

377 *del. Lytt*   378+ With patient care, and temperate wisdom calm: *Lytt*
379 forth the legal] the Detected *Lytt*   389–413 *Lytt transfers to* 423+,
with following variants: 389–92 Then, from the cloud-topt Alps or Appenines,

395 Assembled   396–7 *del.*   399 Press] Drag   414 embrac'd] en-
closed *Lytt*   419 *del. Lytt*   447 *tender*] gentle *Lytt*   458 the *other*]
his Master *Lytt*   472 *unequal*] unfriendly *Lytt*   *Lytt comments: unequal
is obscure.*   474 temper'd happy,] happy temper! *58–62d* temper'd justly,
Lytt

499–500   A race of Heroes who, for Ages, knew
               No stain of Vice, save that with partial Flame   *Lytt*

502–3   Good NUMA first appears, the Light of Rome
               Whose Wisdom softend her rapacious Sons
               And gentle Virtue taught, and fixd the Yoke
               Of mild Religion on the stubborn Mind.
               Him follows, glorying in his People's Love
               SERVIUS, the *King*, who laid the solid Base   *Lytt*

519   And, warm in Youth, from all the Pride of Power
               Triumphant and supreme, to private Shade   *Lytt*

522 Sustaind the Freedom of corrupted Rome. *Lytt*   541 your Kind] Man-
kind *Lytt*   570 shew'd] shew'n *Lytt*   573 Soul,] Minds *Lytt*   588 the
Deeps of] remotest *Lytt*   590 scatter'd] various *Lytt*   596 public Soul]
noble Fire *Lytt*

619–22   The goblin Tale goes round; till solemn Fear
               And superstitious Horror creeps o'er all.
               Or in the chearfull Hall convened they sport
               With their gay Landlord. Rustick mirth resounds;   *Lytt*

630 The City swarms intense.] The crowded city swarms. *Lytt*   632 flow]
float *Lytt*   638–43 *Lytt transfers to* 655+, *see below.*   643 waves. *Lytt*
644–5 *del. Lytt*

646   FROM Scenes like these avert thy purer Eyes
               Celestial Muse, and view the British Stage.
               Lo! there the Ghost of Hamlet dreadful stalks;   *Lytt*

649 comely] virtuous *Lytt*   651 itself. *Lytt*   652 *del. Lytt*   655 shew'd.]
shewn. *Lytt*   655 footnote *del. Lytt*

655+ *Lytt expands as follows:*
               Then the gay Ball invites the youthful Train:
               Upsprings the Dance *etc., as 638–43*

709–13 *del. Lytt*   754 Wave] Show'r *Lytt*

762–8   Seek the glazed River and the Marbled Lake.
               From every Province, where the Belgick Rhine
               Branch'd out in many a long Canal extends,
               The glad Batavians swarm: and as they sweep,   *Lytt*

779 quick] sharp *Lytt*

793 +   Now let me stand on Cheviot's highest Peak
               Or Skidda's Summit, and beneath me stretch'd
               Behold the vast extent of dazzling Snow
               Deep-covering every Dale, and Hill, and Plain.   *Lytt*

794 infant] feeble *Lytt*   798 glittering Waste] shaded Earth *Lytt*   804 Vast.]
Waste *Lytt*   808 footnote *del. Lytt*   837 know] taste *Lytt*   854 Tribe]
Beasts *Lytt*   857 marbled] hardend *Lytt*   861 And vivid Stars that
gild the cloudless Skies *Lytt*   862 radiant Waste] glossy waste *58–62d* glossy

Snows *Lytt*   875 footnote *Occasion*] *opportunity 62q 62d*   878 *Lytt*
comments: I wish this was alterd, chearful-loaded is not English. "They chear-
full to their shady Tents repair" would be better.   883 Interest] Avarice
893 footnote *del. Lytt*

954–5   Self-taught inspired, and called from Gothic Night.
               Illustrious PETER: First of Monarchs! He   *Lytt*

974 Smiles the rural Reign] rural Plenty smiles *Lytt*   981 shrinking] war-
like *Lytt*   984 *del. Lytt*   985+ All by the mighty Master's Soul
informed: *Lytt*   1028 His] Her *Lytt*

HYMN

2 the *varied* GOD.] thy varying Power. *Lytt*   *Then Lytt deletes the entire Hymn.*
107 spreads] breathes *58–62d*

*The last of the 'Poems on Several Occasions' printed at the end of volume ii in the
demy-duodecimo editions of Thomson's Works edited by Lyttelton and published by
Millar in 1752 and 1757 is the following adaptation of lines omitted from 50–57,
(i.e. OET Au. 483–569):*

THE

RETURN from the Fox-CHACE*.

A BURLESQUE POEM, in the Manner of
Mr. *Philips.*

THE fox is kill'd—Dogs, steeds, and men return
   In weary triumph. Foremost rides *the Squire,*
And leads to ghostly halls of grey renown
With woodland honours grac'd, the fox's fur
Descending decent from the roof, and spread   5
O'er the drear walls with antic figures fierce
The stag's large front. Hark! the sonorous horn
Their near approach proclaims: the joyous troop
Mix their loud hollows, till the crazy dome
Beneath their uproar shakes—Not nore disturb'd   10
Were *Oeta's* caverns, or old *Pelion's* dens,
When, with disorder'd mirth, to midnight bowls,
Thessalian Centaurs from the chace return'd.
Behold! the fuel'd chimney blazes wide;
The tankards foam, and the strong table groans   15
Beneath the vast Sirloin, *Britannia's* boast,
In which, with desperate knife, her hardy sons

* The greater part of these verses were formerly inserted in Mr. *Thomson's*
AUTUMN; but being of a different character and stile from the rest, and rather
belonging to the Mock Heroick, or Burlesque way of writing, it has been judged
proper to leave them out *there* in the present edition, and insert them *here,* by
themselves.

M

Make deep incision, and exulting talk
Of *England*'s glory, ne'er to be defac'd,
While hence they borrow vigour; or amain   20
Into the pasty plung'd, at intervals,
(If stomach keen can intervals allow)
Relate at large the wonders of the day:
He then is loudest heard who topt the chace,
Who every maze evolv'd, and every guile   25
Disclos'd; who knows the merits of the pack;
Who saw the villain seized, and dying hard
Without complaint, tho' by an hundred mouths
Relentless torn: O glorious he beyond
His daring peers! oft have his fractur'd bones   30
And dislocated joints his virtue shewn,
And generous ardour for heroic deeds:
Before him now, to recompense his toils,
The chine immense, or goodly pudding smoaks.
Then sated Hunger bids his brother Thirst   35
Produce the mighty bowl; the mighty bowl,
Swell'd high with fiery juice, steams liberal round
A potent gale, delicious as the breath
Of *Maia*, to the love-sick shepherdess,
On violets diffus'd, while soft she hears   40
Her panting shepherd stealing to her arms.
Nor wanting is the brown October, drawn
Mature and perfect, from its dark retreat
Of thirty years: the *British* nectar now
Flames in the light refulgent, not afraid   45
Even with the vineyard's noblest boast to vie.
Then thoughtful *Whist*, beneath a cloud of smoke,
Wreath'd fragrant from the pipe, each graver head
A while composes: but the jollier train
Of youthful sportsmen beat the brick-pav'd hall   50
With vigorous dancing to the shrill-voic'd pipe
And sounding tabor; or romp-loving miss
Is haul'd about, in gallantry robust.

followed by OET Au. 530–69, *with no substantive variants.*

APPENDIX D

LIST OF EMENDATIONS

SPRING

150 and,] *MS* ~∧ *28–46*   deep,] *MS* ~∧ *44–46*   206 Proportion,]
28–34 44 44Wks ~∧ *38 45 46*   249 Sport,] *28–45* ~ ∧*46*   358 stain'd,]
44–45 ~∧ *46*   368 That,] *44–45* ~∧ *28–38 46*   392 weak, helpless,]
44 44Wks ~∧ ~∧ *45 46*   480 YET,] *28–45* ~∧ *46*   500 Beans.] Beams.
44–46   521 protracted,] *MS* ~∧ *28–46*   522 now,] *MS* ~∧ *28–46*
544 Pride,] *44–45* ~∧ *46*   549 fair,] *MS 44–45* ~. *46*   607 These,
28 30q ~∧ *31–46*   611 Pipe,] *30q–34* ~∧ *38–46*   1040 or,] *MS* ~∧
28–46   1053 awhile] *MS* a-while *28* a while *30q–46*   1059 winding,]
28–34 ~∧ *38–46*   1083 The] *28–34* the *38–46*

SUMMER

48 faint-] *30q–45* ~∧ *46*   54 Rock,] *27–45* ~∧ *46*   274 Front.]
27–45 ~, *46*   304 Green] *Sp. 28 MS Su.44–45* green *Sp.30q–38 Su.46*
374 This] *44Wks* this *44 45 46*   504 Moan,] *MS 44Wks* ~∧ *27–44 45 46*
946 Clouds.] *27–45* ~, *46*   1339 Bank∧] *44–45* ~, *46*   1523 Blood,]
MS ~∧ *44–46*   1525 Reign,] *MS* ~; *30q–44 45 46* ~: *44Wks*   1548 that,]
44–45 ~∧ *46*   1573 SPENSER] *44–45* SPENCER *46*   1615 While,] *27–45*
~∧ *46*   1756 Mankind,] *27–45* ~! *46*

AUTUMN

Argument *Address*] *30q 30p* Address'd *300–46*   30 below,] *30q–45* ~∧ *46*
121 Plenty;] *30q–45* ~, *46*   140 Imagination-] *30q–44* ~∧ *44Wks–46*
258 smother'd∧] *30q–45* ~- *46*   283 his,] *30q–45* ~∧ *46*   374 Eye,]
30q–45 ~∧ *46*   476 High∧] ~- *30q–46*   486 Game.] *30q–38* ~, *44–*
46   561 Slaughter;] *30q–38* ~: *44–46*   593 Love-] *MS 44–45* ~∧ *46*
642 active,] *30q–45* ~∧ *46*   722 wide-]*30q–45* ~∧ *46*   757 Why]
why *44–46*   761 Or] *44–45* Of *46*   807 disclose.] *44–45* ~, *46*
891 Brook] *44–45* Book *46*   907 Toil,] ~. *30q–46*   911 best,] *30q–45*
~∧ *46*   980 dull-] *MS* ~, *30q–38* ~ ∧*44–46*   990 Grove,] *30q–45* ~. *46*
1075 when] When *44–46*   1152 Wild-] *30q–45* ~∧ *46*   1179 full-]
30q–45 ~∧ *46*   1191 When] *30q–38* when *44–46*

WINTER

6 With] *26f–30q* with *30p–46*   35 blazing,] *30q–38* ~∧ *44–46*   43 *Aqua-*
rius∧] *30q–38* ~, *44–46*   299 Frost;] ~, *30q–46*   576 rising,] *MSLytt*
~∧ *44–46*   622 round:] *30q–45* ~; *46*   626 Sleep;] *30q 30p 34* ~:
300 38–46   650 Steals] *30q–45* Steels *46*   817 new-] *44–45* ~∧ *46*
933 full-] *MS* ~∧ *30q–46*   1033a Where] *260 28* where *26f*

HYMN

20 THY] thy *30q–38* THY *44–46*   31 thence] *30q–38* Thence *44–46*
45 whose] *30q–38* Whose *44–46*   85 oft˄] *MS* ~- *30q–46*   94 Theme;]
~, *30q–46*   96 gleams,] ~; *30q–46*   110 there] *MS* There *44–46*

APPENDIX A: EMENDATIONS TO WINTER

5 Musing] musing *26f*   26 Ray:] ~. *26f*   86 dusky-mantled]
dusky˄mantled *26f*   89 glows;] ~, *26f*   124 meaning Low] Meaning
low *26f*   270 good:] ~, *26f*   277 Friend,] ~; *26f*   293 SOCIETY]
Society *26f*   368 Where] where *26f*

EMENDATIONS TO SUMMER

896 Storm,] ~. *27*   897 *no new paragraph*] *new paragraph 27*   1033 *no
new paragraph*] *new paragraph 27*

APPENDIX B

Wi.26f–28 dedication
4 for] *28* For *26f 260*   12 *Sovereign;*] *28* ~, *26f 260*

Wi.260 preface
19 Company?] ~. *260*   36 let] Let *260*

COMMENTARY

SPRING

(*28, epigraph*) Virgil, *Eclogues* iii. 56–7: Even now every field, every tree is budding; now the woods are green, and the year is at its fairest.

1–4 Spring is the only female of T.'s four personified seasons and is associated with the generative power of nature; cf. Lucretius i. 6–9, v. 737–40.

4 shadowing: prefiguring the roses which will bloom later.

5 Frances Thynne (1699–1754), Countess of Hertford, shone in court as Lady of the Bedchamber to Princess, later Queen, Caroline; she asserted her love of rural retirement in her own poems; and she displayed her benevolence by interceding early in 1728 for the life of T.'s friend Richard Savage, condemned to death as a murderer. See Helen Sard Hughes, *The Gentle Hartford* (New York, 1940). T. was recommended to the Countess after publication of *Winter* in 1726. He enjoyed her patronage and friendship until his death, and probably wrote part of *Spring* as her guest at Marlborough Castle, Wiltshire. The story in Johnson's *Life* of T. about the poet's offending the Countess is untrue. (cf. p. xliii Like Pope, T. often pays tribute to his many friends among writers and their patrons; cf. *Sp.* 906, *Su.* 29, 1419–32, *Au.* 9, 655, 667, 929, 944, 1048, 1072, *Wi.* 18, 550, 555, 664.

11–17 Personifications of such natural phenomena as blasts, gales, and mountains complement a traditional mythological personification (11) to convey the notion of an animated world. T. employs such a combination frequently; cf. *Sp.* 1–4, *Su.* 1–8, 46–53, *Au.* 1–3, *Wi.* 1–3, 66–73, etc.

13 howling: dreary; cf. Deut 32: 10.

18 unconfirm'd: 'Not fortified by resolution; not strengthened; raw; weak' (Johnson).

22–3 'The common people are of the opinion that this bird thrusts its bill into a reed, that serves as a pipe for swelling the note above its natural pitch; while others, and in this number we find Thomson the poet, imagine that the bittern puts its head under water, and then violently blowing produces its boomings.' (Goldsmith, *History of the Earth and Animated Nature* (1774), Book VI, chap. vi.) In fact the bittern makes its call in the air after the usual way with birds. The 'Time' (22) is the breeding season.

25 In spring plovers fly inland from the shore in order to breed.

26 Aries: the Ram, the first sign of the zodiac, into which the sun is said to enter at the vernal equinox on 20 or 21 March (*c.* 9 March in the unreformed calendar of T.'s day). The zodiac is a belt of the heavens extending about 8 degrees on each side of the ecliptic, i.e. the apparent course of the sun as viewed from earth. This belt was divided by ancient astronomers into twelve equal arcs counted from the vernal equinox in the order of the sun's progress through them. Each arc, or sign of the zodiac, was named after a constellation whose apparent position in ancient times lay within it; but, as a result of the precession of the equinoxes (a slow, progressive, easterly movement of the two points where the ecliptic crosses the earth's equator), zodiacal signs did not correspond with constellations in T.'s day; nor do they in ours. Consequently the allusions at *Sp.* 26–7, *Su.* 43–4, *Au.* 23–4, and *Wi.* 41–3 are more literary than astronomical.

27 Bull: Taurus, the second sign of the zodiac, into which the sun enters about 21 April; cf. Virgil, *Georgics* i. 217–8.

28 cramp'd: compressed, because cold air is denser than warm; cf. *Wi.* 709–10 n.

30 sublime: high; cf. *PL* vii. 421.

32–77 See Introduction p. xxvi. Lines 32–43 consciously echo *Georgics* ii. 330–1, i. 44–6, 63–5, 98, ('glebe' meaning 'clod', as here, or 'land' (cf. *Sp.* 247) is a word with Virgilian associations); but the patriotic expansion into praise of trade at 48–77 is typical of T.'s age. On the mercantilist muse see Bonamy Dobrée, 'The Theme of Patriotism in the Poetry of the Early Eighteenth Century', *Proceedings of the British Academy* xxxv (1949), 49–65. From the Middle Ages Britain had been an exporter of wool or woollen cloth, but during the half-century to 1765 she exported large quantities of grain too.

41 incumbent: leaning; cf. *PL* i. 226; *Su.* 1061, 1364, *Wi.* 924.

42 obstructing: adhering to the mould-board of the plough, so preventing the clean throw of a furrow.

43 Winds: turns (at the end of a furrow).

44 White: explained from the custom of using a bed-sheet as seed-hopper; or alternatively from the lime with which seeds were coated as a guard against pests and which would blow on to the sower in windy weather; see *Notes and Queries* 3 Oct. 1868, p. 319, and 14 Nov. 1868, p. 470.

46 faithful: cf. Virgil, *Georgics* ii. 460, *iustissima tellus*, which repays the husbandman.

55 rural Maro: Virgil as author of the *Georgics*; cf. *Sp.* 456, *Wi.* 532.

60 Some: e.g. Cincinnatus, Philopoemen, Regulus, and Fabricius; cf. *Su.* 1492, *Wi.* 494, 511–13. For men as summer-insects cf. *Su.* 342–51, *Wi.* 644–5.

66 In adding a reference to 'Corruption' in *44* T. was, no doubt, glancing at politicians of his own day.

79–89 Cf. *Sp.* 184–5, 218–21, 561–71, *Au.* 694. These passages upon the flow of sap in, and the colouring of, plants draw upon Stephen Hales, *Vegetable Staticks* (1727), and upon a letter by Alexander Stuart in

Richard Bradley, *New Improvements of Planting and Gardening* (1717–18). Hales described the process by which water was absorbed at the roots and, quickly or slowly according to temperature, was raised by capillary action within the plant, and was transpired from the leaves. Stuart speculated that movement of liquid produced variety of colour in vegetation. Thomson uses the verbs 'distil' (184) and 'ferment' (570) to describe the processes referred to by Hales and Stuart. See *Background*, pp. 54–8. For the scientific theory that green, the central colour of the spectrum, strengthened and cherished (89) the sight see Addison, *Spectator* 387 (the relevant passage of which is quoted in *Background*, pp. 57–8), and cf. T.'s *Poem to Newton* 105.

81 steaming Power: sap.

82 vernant: 'Flourishing as in the spring' (Johnson); cf. *PL* x. 679.

84 'Smiling . . . a common word in eighteenth century pastoral, may be considered the equivalent of *laetus* [joyous, abundant, etc.] which Virgil constantly applied to crops.' (G. Tillotson, *Augustan Studies* (1961), p. 37). In T. the word often has devotional overtones, as implying or directly referring to the beneficent activities of God: 'Providence has imprinted so many smiles on Nature, that it is impossible for a mind which is not sunk in more gross and sensual delights to take a survey of them without several secret sensations of pleasure.' (Addison, *Spectator* 393). Cf. *Sp.* 258, 862, 871, *Su.* 179, *Wi.* 16, *Hymn* 6, 81, 112 and n.

102 André Deslandes, in his *Nouveau Voyage d'Angleterre* (1717), noted that London was blanketed under clouds so dense that the sun was never visible, and the air was so thick with coal-smoke that he could hardly draw his breath. The first notable protest against atmospheric pollution in London had been John Evelyn's *Fumifugium* (1661). Cf. *PL* ix. 445–51.

107 taste: '*To tast*; i.e. to smell in the North.' (John Ray, *North Country Words* (1674)).

108 Augusta: the title conferred on Roman London in the fourth century, and frequently employed by T.'s contemporaries when referring to the city; cf. Pope, *Windsor Forest* 377; Gay, *Trivia* ii. 145. The 'Eminence' might be Richmond Hill.

110 white-empurpled: Lat. *purpureus* was used of any bright colour; cf. *Au.* 674 (of fruit), Virgil, *Eclogues* v. 38 (of narcissus), Horace, *Odes* IV. i. 10 (of swans).

111–13 Thomson frequently makes the point that the 'eyes' of fancy and reason see far more of Nature's beauty, order and harmony than the physical eye can. Cf. *Sp.* 183–5, 495–6, *Su.* 1730–52, *Au.* 777–835, 1016, *Wi.* 705–6, 1046–9, etc. John Scott objected to the use of 'eye' at *Sp.* 111–13: 'He who sees trees in bloom, must naturally suppose that they will bear fruit, and his imagination may behold them fraught with it; but his *eye* may look in vain among the blossoms to *spy* the poetical person *autumn*.' (*Critical Essays* (1785), pp. 297–8.) A modern reader may be

interested to note Scott's assumption that autumn is personified; cf.
Goldsmith's comment on *Su.* 1435–7 at p. xxx above. Murdoch alters the
full stop (found in all earlier editions) to a semi-colon but does not change
the paragraphing; Lyttelton adds after 113 a line of his own composition
in order to make 114–19 grammatical; see Appendix C.

114–36   Easterly winds in Spring might cause blight either by carrying
insects or their eggs, or by producing the correct temperature to hatch
eggs laid on plants in the previous year. The account of the causes and
cures of blights here and the details of *Sp.28*, 122–35 come from Richard
Bradley, *New Improvements of Planting and Gardening* (1717–18), with
hints from John Philips, *Cyder* (1708), i. 421–45. See *Background*, pp. 45–
8, where relevant passages are quoted. For insects from the east as sons of
vengeance cf. Exod. 10: 13.

121   **waft**: intransitive; cf. *PL* ii. 1042. Murdoch (see Appendix C)
emends to 'warp', emphasizing T.'s echo of *PL* i. 340–1.

129   Cf. *PL* i. 236–7.

132   **frosty Tribe**: biting insects. Throughout *The Seasons* peri-
phrasis is used to define some particular characteristic of the natural object
being described, and/or to indicate that object's place in some system or
order. It is a device analagous to the terms of classification employed by
seventeenth- and eighteenth-century scientists. See John Arthos, *The
Language of Natural Description in Eighteenth Century Poetry* (Ann Arbor,
1949). T.'s periphrases often anthropomorphize the object. Examples of
periphrasis include *Wi.* 793, 811, 822 (animals); *Sp.* 510, *Au.* 1176, 1181
(bees); 1265 (cattle); 633 (fruit); *Sp.* 546 (flowers); 395, 422, 424, *Au.* 922
(fish); *Su.* 237, 344 (insects); 378, 388, 417, *Wi.* 261 (sheep). There is
a large group of periphrases for birds: most are anthropomorphic in
suggestion, e.g. *Sp.* 584, 594, 597, 711, 729, 753, 789, *Su.* 737, 1121, *Wi.*
80, 87, 88, 137, 138, 249, *Hymn* 78, *Cas. Ind.* 1. x; but some are not, e.g.
Sp. 617, 689, 747, *Au.* 840, *Wi.* 793.

143–4   Cf. Virgil, *Aeneid* i. 52–4.

146   **distent**: swollen, Lat. *distentus*.

148   **Ether**: not the 'Air' of *Sp.* 145 but the lighter, more tenuous fluid
medium by which light is transmitted. In T. it also refers to the upper sky
since—according to Lucretius v. 498–533, and Newton, Query 18, added
to the second English edition of his *Opticks* (1717–18)—the ether was
expanded through all the heavens. Cf. *Sp.* 398, 563 and n., *Su.* 1–2,
Au. 957–63, 1213–14, *Wi.* 44–9, 692–7.

159   **uncurling**: without ripples.

160   **thro delusive Lapse**: because their falling cannot be detected;
cf. *PL* viii. 263.

164   **falling Verdure**: A double prolepsis since the rain has not yet
begun to fall or the grass to turn green as a result of its falling; or perhaps
'verdure' is 'freshness', cf. Shakespeare, *Two Gent.* 1. i. 49.

183–5 This anticipation is conveyed by the periphrases for rain at *Sp.* 164, 170, 173, 181–2, and 187; cf. *Sp.* 111–13 n. On sap ('milky Nutriment' 184, 'verdant Nutriment' in *28*) and colour in plants see *Sp.* 79–89 n. 'Fancy' replaces in *44* its synonym 'Imagination'; cf. *Sp.* 459 n.

189–205 Turner attached conflated extracts from these verses to the catalogue entry for his *Buttermere Lake, with part of Cromackwater, Cumberland, a Shower* (exh. 1798, now in the Tate Gallery).

196 Gems: Lat. *gemma* signifies both bud and jewel (cf. Virgil, *Georgics* ii. 335), but here the buds do sparkle like gems with sunlight reflected from raindrops.

203–12 The account of the rainbow is from Newton's *Opticks* (1704). Cf. T.'s *Poem to Newton* (1727), 96–124. T., like Wordsworth (*Prelude*, 1850, iii. 63), was impressed above all by Newton's mind; cf. *Su.* 1560–3. For Keats it was the pre-Newtonian rainbow that was 'awful' (*Lamia* ii. 231).

216 amusive: deceitful, illusive (*OED*, citing 216); 'That which has the power of amusing' (Johnson, citing 216).

220 Plastic Tubes: sap vessels; cf. *Sp.* 79–89 n.

227 With plants which dull and incurious people reckon to be weeds.

229 Cf. Milton, *Comus* 38.

245 fum'd: 'To fume. To pass away in vapours' (Johnson, citing 242–5). However, T. may have in mind Milton's belief that fumes rise from the stomach to the brain, and that diet therefore affects sleep; cf. *PL* ix. 1049-51, v. 3-5.

247 willing Glebe: cf. *volentia rura* (Virgil, *Georgics* ii. 500).

262 Fatness: 'Fertility; fruitfulness' (Johnson); cf. Ps. 65: 11.

266 meeken'd: 'This word I have found no where else' (Johnson, citing 265–6); cf. *Sp.* 945, *Au.* 653.

266 sullen Joy: deep-toned roar; cf. *Au.* 416, Milton, *Il Penseroso* 76.

273 golden Age. According to many ancient poets the period when Saturn ruled an innocently happy world was the Golden Age; it was followed by the progressively more vicious Silver, Bronze, and Iron Ages —in which last those poets and ourselves have had the misfortune to be born. The immediate sources for T.'s description at *Sp.* 242–74, and for the further passage omitted in *44* (see *Sp.* 271+ a), are Ovid, *Metamorphoses* i. 89–112, Virgil, *Eclogues* iv, with Dryden's translation, and Isa. 11: 6–8, with Pope's *Messiah*. *Sp.* 242–6 owe a hint to *PL* v. 1–7.

275–308 Cf. Ovid, *Metamorphoses* i. 127–50 and *PL* ix. 1121–89.

305 On 'social feeling' see *Sp.* 878–903 n.

309–22 It was thought that the antediluvian world was a smooth, regular spheroid with its axis perpendicular to the ecliptic so that the sun was always directly overhead at the earth's equator and perpetual spring reigned. Earth and water were separated from one another so that water was inside the spheroid and earth at the surface; thus there were no mountains or seas. The Flood occurred when the surface of the earth (the 'disparting Orb') was suddenly fractured and fell into the great subterranean abyss ('the central Waters'), throwing up a deluge that engulfed and wrecked the earth (henceforth a rough 'broken World'); at the same time, by the tilting of the earth's axis, the ecliptic became oblique and alternation of the seasons began. T.'s source for this theory is Thomas Burnet, *Sacra Telluris Theoria* (1681–9), trans. *The Theory of the Earth* (1684–9), the relevant passages of which are quoted in *Background* pp. 97–104. Variants in *MS* (309–13a) allude to Burnet's theory that the fracture of the earth's surface was caused when water in the central abyss was 'rarefied' into steam by the sun's heat, and expanded. T. names Burnet and refers to his theory in *Liberty* iv. 283–4. According to ancient poets, the alternation of the seasons began in the Silver Age under the reign of Zeus; cf. Ovid, *Metamorphoses* i. 116–24. Milton attributed the change of seasons to the Fall (*PL* x. 651–707); T., at 317–22, echoes *PL* x. 651–6 and iv. 147–8.

321 Green'd: 'To green. To make green. A low word' (Johnson, citing 320–2); cf. *Au.* 664, 1260.

327–8 Cf. *Su.* 1092–116 n.

329–35 According to Thomas Burnet, the 'unequal action' of the atmosphere and constant changes of weather resulting from alternation of the seasons weaken 'the Springs and Fibres in the Organs of the Body', and, 'though the change is not sensible immediately in these parts, yet after many repeated impressions every year, by unequal heat and cold, driness and moisture, contracting and relaxing the Fibres, their tone at length is in a great measure destroy'd or brought to a manifest debility; and the great Springs failing, the lesser that depend upon them fail in proportion, and all the symptoms of decay and old age follow.' (*Theory of the Earth* (1684), Book II, chaps iii, iv.) Descartes's mechanistic conception of the body as an intricate system of reflexes comparable to the works of a clock (in *Traité de l'homme* and *La Description du corps humain*) was accepted by many English thinkers; cf., e.g., Shaftesbury, *An Essay on the Freedom of Wit and Humour* (1709), Part III, sect. iii, in *Characteristicks* (1714), i. 115–16.

336–78 The passage on vegetarianism (336–73) is based on Ovid, *Metamorphoses* xv. 75–142, and perhaps is influenced by the well-known *Essay on Health and Long Life* (1724) in which the physician George Cheyne had commended a more vegetarian diet to the carnivorous and scurvied English gentry. The '*Samian* Sage' of 373 (i.e. Pythagoras, the Greek philosopher born at Samos *c*.580 BC) had advocated vegetarianism in accordance with his doctrine of the transmigration of souls between brute and man. T.'s conclusion (374–8) suggests that man's diet and his spiritual ascent are related to one another (cf. *PL* v. 469–500), and perhaps implies that the slaughter of brutes may be to their benefit by releasing their souls for admission into higher forms of life. Cf. T.'s lines on Pythagoras in *Liberty* iii (1735):

He taught that Life's indissoluble Flame,
From Brute to Man, and Man to Brute again,
For ever shifting, runs th' Eternal round;
Thence try'd against the blood-polluted Meal,
And Limbs yet quivering with some kindred Soul,
To turn the human Heart. Delightful Truth!
Had he beheld the living Chain ascend,
And form a rising not a circling Whole.
                    (iii. 63–70, corrected from 1738 *errata*.)

Such a notion accords with T.'s interpretation of the idea of the great chain of being (cf. *Su.* 334 n.) in evolutionary terms, so that each being (brute, man, and angel) can step upwards for ever in the vital scale. Cf. *Su.* 1796–1805 and n., *Wi.* 603–8 and n., *Hymn* 114–18.

379–442   The description of fishing is practical and didactic in the manner of the sporting georgic (cf. Gay, *Rural Sports* i. 121–270), but is, perhaps, also an ironic comment on vegetarianism and 'pure Perfection' (376). T.'s 'Of a Country Life' (*Edinburgh Miscellany*, 1720) describes, at lines 53–66, fishing for trout and pike in the River Tweed.

381   mossy-tinctur'd: suggesting that the stream runs through a peat-bog; cf. 'dark-brown' (383).

386   Fishing lines were made of twisted horse-hair. Izaac Walton recommended 'right, sound, clear, glass-colour hair' (*Compleat Angler*, chap. xxi).

388–93   Possibly mock-sentimental, as T.'s concern shifts from worm to fish ('uncomplaining wretch') and then, more realistically, to the angler's hand; but in fishing for trout the fly is a less cruel bait than the worm, for, whereas the worm is swallowed, the fly fastens in the fish's mouth in cartilage which is almost insensitive to pain. Cf. John Gay, *Rural Sports* i. 265–70, and Byron's note to *Don Juan* xiii. cvi.

393   Horror: 'a sense of shuddering or shrinking' (Johnson).

395   finny Race: on periphrases see *Sp.* 132 n.

403   Naiads: fish (mock heroic; lit. water-nymphs).

424   Monarch: 'the salmon is accounted the king of fresh-water fish' (Walton, *Compleat Angler*, chap. vii), but T.'s description of the haunt suggests that he may be referring to the adult trout.

446   Elders: not the common elder but the red elder found in Scotland and north-eastern England which, like the other plants mentioned in *Sp.* 447–9, flowers in Spring.

452   liquid: bright; cf. *Au.* 855. See Arthos, pp. 237–47.

453   sounding: perhaps 'diving' (since the pigeon is flying out from trees on a high river-bank) rather than 'noisy'; cf. *Sp.* 696.

456   Mantuan Swain: Virgil as author of the *Eclogues*; cf. *Sp.* 55, *Wi.* 532.

459 'Imagination' and 'Fancy' (455) are synonymous; cf. *Sp.* 183a, 469, and 473. Both words signify the power to form images in the mind: 'by the pleasures of the imagination or fancy (which I shall use promiscuously) I here mean such as arise from visible objects, either when we have them actually in our view, or when we call up their ideas into our minds' (Addison, *Spectator* 411).

478   Oil: the volatile oil which gives scent to plants.

483 Amanda is Elizabeth Young who had refused T.'s proposal of marriage in 1743 (see *Letters* pp. 146–61, 164–71, 175–7, 182–4).

484   Graces: see *Wi.* 659 n.

495   Irriguous: irrigating; cf. *PL* iv. 255, Virgil, *Georgics* iv. 32. Cf. *Au.* 751.

495   Lily: lent-lily or daffodil.

500–2 Sailors reported smelling the spices of Arabia far out to sea; cf. *PL* iv. 159–63.

505–7 Cf. *PL* v. 294–7.

506   mimic Art: landscape gardening.

518–25 The hurried eye sweeps the bowery walk and meets the bending sky and meets the river, etc.

528–71 See Introduction pp. xxxi–xxxii

529   unbosoms: takes from concealment in the earth.

530–54 Hints for this flower passage are in Shakespeare, *Winter's Tale* IV. iv. 73–129 and Milton, *Lycidas* 142–51.

534   lavish: of perfume.

537   Meal: powder.

541   Father Dust: pollen; 'Male-Dust' according to Bradley (see *Sp.* 114–36 n.).

542   break: burst into colour.

545   gradual: of all different dates of growth.

546   musky Tribes: scented flowers. On periphrases see *Sp.* 132 n.

550   fabled Fountain: Narcissus, in Greek mythology, fell in love with his own reflection in a pool, and was turned into a flower; cf. Ovid, *Metamorphoses* iii. 341–510.

553   Delicacies: Adam's word to sum up the sensuous delights of Paradise (*PL* viii. 526); cf. *Sp.* 352.

556–71 T. connects the universal diffusion of divine power with the penetrative force of the sun and its effect upon vegetation. For the rhapsodic manner cf. *Wi.* 106–17 and n.; for the science cf. *Sp.* 79–89 and n.

557   Essential Presence: God as absolute being.

562   filmy Net: system of sap vessels.

563 The ether (cf. *Sp.* 148 n.) was thought to contain an acid which formed salt-petre or nitre (cf. *Wi.* 694 n.), which supported vegetable life. 'The ancient philosophers supposed the ether to be igneous, and by its kind influence upon the air to be the cause of all vegetation' (Pope, *Iliad* i. 514 n.); cf. Lucretius v. 458–9, where *aether ignifer* refers to ether as combining the primal elements of air and fire. 'For the Air is full of Acid and Sulphureous Particles which, constantly forming in the Air, are doubtless very serviceable in promoting the Work of Vegetation; when being imbibed by the Leaves, they may not improbably be the Materials out of which the more subtle and refined Principles of Vegetables are formed.' (Stephen Hales, *Vegetable Staticks* (1727).)

565 **attractive:** drawing moisture from the earth.

568 **detruded:** 'To detrude. To force into a lower place' (Johnson, citing 567–9); cf. Virgil, *Aeneid* vii. 773, and *Wi.* 731 a.

577 **mazy:** the adjective has Miltonic associations (*PL* iv. 239, ix. 161, and cf. *Sp.* 797, *Su.* 373); but *Sp.* 577 also echoes Milton's use of the noun in *L'Allegro* 142: 'The melting voice through mazes running'.

578 **deduce:** 'lay down in regular order, so as that the following shall naturally rise from the foregoing' (Johnson, citing 576–80); cf. Virgil, *Aeneid* x. 618.

580–1 A theme not entirely unknown to fame; cf. Addison's Latin verses in *Spectator* 412.

584 **gay Troops:** birds; cf. 'tuneful Nations' (594), 'coy Quiristers' (597) where periphrasis emphasizes the attribute under discussion. On periphrases see *Sp.* 132 n.

585 **gallant:** 'Inclined to courtship' (Johnson, citing 582–5).

588 **soft Infusion:** what is poured in, i.e. love. Cf. *Sp.* 868, *PL* viii. 474.

599 **kind:** both 'according to their species' and 'affectionately'.

601 **Philomela:** in Greek mythology, the Athenian king's daughter who was raped, mutilated, and changed into a nightingale; cf. Ovid, *Metamorphoses* vi. 438–674. T., like many poets, mistakenly believes that the hen-nightingale sings; cf. *Su.* 743–6, *Hymn* 79–80, *Au.* 974 a (*Wi. 26 f*, 44).

607 **Pour'd out:** the linnets themselves are poured out because they fly in large flocks; their song too is poured out.

608–9a (*28*, 561) **nitid:** 'Bright, shining; lustrous' (Johnson).

615 **Waste:** profusion; cf. Pope, *Odyssey* vi. 356.

617 **glossy Kind:** T. employs this periphrasis because he is going on to show the importance of glossy plumage for mating.

625 **Approvance:** 'Approbation: a word not much used' (Johnson, citing 624–7).

650 **Domes:** houses, Lat. *domus* (used of birds' nests in Virgil, *Georgics* ii. 209); cf. *Su.* 1060, *Au.* 660, 1182.

682 charm'd with Cares: cf. 'pierc'd in *44* where the meaning is clear. The emendation to 'charm'd' in *46* introduces a new meaning—'enchanted by the objects of solicitude (i.e. children)'—but does not entirely destroy the earlier meaning—'afflicted with anxieties'.

696 sounding: diving (the lapwing's flight is highly erratic when it is trying to decoy predators away from its nest); cf. *Sp.* 453.

697 Excursion: running out; cf. Virgil, *Georgics* iv. 194.

697 Lawn: stretch of untilled ground; cf. *Au.* 405.

700 Heath-Hen: black grouse.

702–3 A belief that the poet was borne aloft on the wings of Pegasus had developed early into the notion of a winged poet (see Mary Lascelles, 'The Rider on the Winged Horse' in *Notions and Facts* (Oxford, 1972), pp. 1–28), so a coincidence of wings and song could easily suggest the parallel indicated in *Sp.* 702–3; but I have found no precedent in mythology for calling birds brothers of the Muse. In *Cas. Ind.* II. xxxiii, xxxiv, the nightingale is sister of a Druid-bard Philomelus ('lover of music'), perhaps in a distorted echo of the relationship between two sisters, Philomela and Procne, in Ovid, *Metamorphoses* vi. 438–674 (cf. *Sp.* 601). The Muses were often represented as winged (cf. *Wi.* 18–23) and Ovid described an attempt to imprison them, *Metamorphoses* v. 274–88.

714–28 Cf. Virgil, *Georgics* iv. 511–15.

715 ruin'd Care: lost offspring.

725 dying Fall: cf. Shakespeare, *Twelfth Night* I. i. 4.

729 feather'd Youth: fledglings. T.'s account (729–54) 'for all its evidence of a close and indeed brilliant observation, is almost equally an account of members of a human family.' (G. Tillotson, 'Gray's Ode on the Spring' in *Augustan Studies* (1961), pp. 214–15.)

730 weighing oft their Wings: balancing themselves.

743 Libration: 'The state of being balanced' (Johnson, citing 742–4).

748 winnow: 'beat as with wings' (Johnson); cf. *PL* v. 270. The 'waving' of the air is a result of winnowing.

755–65 Behind the first version of this passage (*28*, 702–9) lies Pliny's statement that the sea-eagle or osprey rejects any of its young who cannot gaze directly at the sun (*Natural History* x. 10; cf. Lucan, *Pharsalia* ix. 902–6). Pliny also declares that the parent-birds of most kinds of eagle drive their adult young far away, so that they cannot compete over hunting-grounds; but T.'s probable source for the revised passage in *44* is Martin Martin, *A Description of the Western Islands of Scotland* (1703): 'I saw a couple of Eagles [on a small island east of Lewis]: the Natives told me, that these Eagles would never suffer any of their kind to live there but themselves, and that they drove away their young ones as soon as they were able to fly. And they told me likewise, that those Eagles are so careful of the place of their abode, that they never yet killed any Sheep or Lamb in the Island, tho' the Bones of Lambs, of Fawns, and Wild-Fowls, are frequently found in and about their Nests; so that they make their Purchase in the opposite Islands, the nearest of which is a League distant.' (Second edition (1716), p. 26.) St. Kilda, the most westerly inhabited isle of the Outer Hebrides was known to T. through the famous description in Martin Martin, *A Late Voyage to St. Kilda* (1698).

755–65a (28, 703) **grudging**: murmuring.

760 pounc'd: 'Furnished with claws or talons' (Johnson, citing 759–60).

778–81 Cf. *PL* vii. 438–40, esp. 'oary Feet'.

789–830 Cf. Virgil, *Georgics* iii. 212–54. T. uses the same styles as Virgil—mock love-elegiac for the bull, and heroic for the horse and for the fierce creatures in *28* (769–73), deleted from *44* (cf. 827–9a).

797 mazy: see *Sp.* 577 n.

810 hears: obeys; cf. Prior, *Carmen Seculare*, 225–6, 'The fiery Pegasus disdains / To mind the Rider's voice or hear the Reins.'

816a (*28*, 758) **informing Gale**: cf. Virgil, *Georgics* iii. 251, *notas auras*. T. deleted 'informing' in *44*, perhaps because the word is repeated in graver context soon afterwards at *Sp.* 860.

826 Kind: the prime sense here is 'species', but perhaps this does not exclude the meaning 'kind ones', i.e. ones who yield sexually; cf. Dryden's reference to sexually aroused women crying out 'in the fury of their kindness' (*Essay of Dramatick Poesy* in *Essays*, ed. W. P. Ker (1900) i. 54.) Cf. *Sp.* 969.

830–2 T.'s theme of gentle love and his respect for his audience of British women forbid him to sing any longer this dire and discordant song of sexual violence. There is perhaps a hint of self-parody in T.'s genteel self-censorship.

840 massy Mound: Milton invariably uses the old form 'massy', rather than 'massive'. The 'Mound' T. has in mind may be the Early Iron Age fort on Southdean Law above the village where he lived until he was twelve. In dating it to 'ancient barbarous Times' (842) he might seem to be better informed than most antiquarians of his day, who usually attributed all such earthworks to the Romans, but probably—in view of the fact that many border skirmishes (including the Battle of Otterburn) were fought on the road through Southdean—T. is thinking generally of the entire period before an 'indissoluble State' (845) was created by the Act of Union. In 840–8 T.'s view expands characteristically from a simple rural scene to a vision of national greatness; cf. *Sp.* 32–77, *Su.* 352–431, etc.

849–55 Cf. *Cas. Ind.* II. xlvii. 5–9.

853–60 See *Hymn* 107 n.

860 informing: 'To inform. To animate; to actuate by vital powers' (Johnson). *Sp.* 859–60, cf. Shaftesbury, *The Moralists, A Rhapsody* (1709): 'All Nature's Wonders serve to excite and perfect this Idea of their Author.' (*Characteristicks* (1714) ii. 370.) Cf. *Su.* 185–96 and n.

861–4a (*28*, 810–12) Cf. *Hymn* 59–65, *Poem to Newton* 42, and *Liberty* iii. 44. The source may be Addison's restatement of the Pythagorean and Platonic belief that there is a music of the heavenly spheres inaudible to the body's ear:

> What tho', in solemn Silence, all
> Move round the dark terrestrial Ball?
> What tho' nor real Voice nor Sound
> Amidst their radiant Orbs be found?
> In Reason's Ear they all rejoice.　　　　(*Spectator* 465)

(*28*, 813–8) Cf. Ps. 18: 7–14, 97: 2–6. The deletion of *28*, 807–21 suggests that in *44* T. wished to place less emphasis upon the OT conception of Jehovah (though this conception remains strong in *Wi.*), and more upon an enlightened, rational notion of the unobtrusive and infallible operation of Divine Law; cf. deletions at *Su.* 1128–35a and *Su.* 1168+.

862 On the smiling God see *Sp.* 84 n.

864 **finer Thought:** love.

865 **undesigning:** actuated by instinct.

868 **infusive:** 'Having the power of infusion, or being infused. A word not authorised' (Johnson, citing 867–8). *OED* defines as 'having the quality or power of infusing' and has no citation earlier than T.

870 **serene:** make calm; cf. Virgil, *Aeneid* iv. 477.

875 **Sons of Earth:** oppressors who have no thought of Heaven; cf. Ps. 10: 18.

878–903 God's creative bounty (879) is diffused in the form of human charity, and man, in practising charity, enjoys a God-like pleasure (902–3). 'Social love . . . the just and free Exercise of which . . . renders one amiable, and divine . . . . Humanity is the very Smile and Consummation of Virtue; 'tis the Image of that fair Perfection of the Supreme Being, which, while he was infinitely happy in himself, mov'd him to create a World of Beings to make them so.' (T. to Aaron Hill, 1726, *Letters*, p. 26.) 'Charity is the imitation and copy of that immense love, which is the fountain of all being and all good; which made all things, which preserveth the world, which sustaineth every creature: nothing advanceth us so near to a resemblance of him, who is essential love and goodness'. (Isaac Barrow, Sermon xxviii, 'Motives and Arguments to Charity' in *Theological Works* (Oxford, 1830), ii. 83.) Barrow and Tillotson (whose sermons express similar notions) are in T.'s list of worthies in *Su.27* (see *Su.* 1556–9a). Social love or social feeling—so agreeable to its possessor—is a frequent theme in T.; cf. *Sp.* 305, *Su.* 1641–6, *Au.* 1006–29, *Wi.* 348–58, *Sophonisba* v. ii. 149–55, *Liberty* iii. 103–15, v. 221–61, *Cas. Ind.* I. xv. T. always claims that social love is a distinct, heaven-inspired emotion and not, as some moralists claimed (e.g. Pope, *Essay on Man* iii. 318), a rational extension of self-love.

891 **green Days:** Spring.

893 **young-ey'd**: cf. Shakespeare, *Merchant of Venice* v. i. 62.

904–64a (*28*, 865–76) Objects of sense, when charged with the philosopher-poet's projected emotions ('glad Skies', 'wide-rejoycing Earth'), have an active power to touch his educated mind and refined sensibility, and stimulate his animal 'Spirits' (i.e. the thin liquid in the hollow tubes of the nerves which is the immediate instrument of all motion and sensation, cf. Locke, *Essay Concerning Human Understanding*, Book II, chap. viii), so that he feels a warmth and light ('Flood of Day') which is, perhaps, to be identified with the warm beam of enlightened 'Creative Bounty' referred to a little earlier (879–80). The intellectual and moral conception of harmony is apparently felt with bodily senses in a way anticipating Wordsworth. This passage was retained, with some corrections, in the interleaved volume but deleted in *44*, perhaps because T. could not otherwise manage a transition to the new material on Hagley (904–62) but more probably because Lyttelton had persuaded T. to cut out any hint of a causal relationship between physiology and faith.

(*28*, 869) **universal Smile**: both man's godlike benevolence (902–3) and the smile of a natural world (see *Sp.* 84 n.), created by and responsive to a smiling God (862).

906 George, Lord Lyttelton (1709–73), was friend and patron of T., Pope, Fielding, and other writers. Of his courting the muse (908, 932–5) Johnson said that his poems 'have nothing to be despised, and little to be admired' (*Lives of the Poets*). Lyttelton also wrote extensively on English history and on contemporary politics (926–31). A resolute opponent of Walpole, he entered the government after Walpole's fall in 1742, and became in 1744 a Lord of the Treasury. Cf. *Cas. Ind.* I. lxv–lxvi.

908 Hagley Park was Lyttelton's abruptly-contoured estate in Worcestershire, where in the 1740s was created one of the most admired landscape gardens of the eighteenth century. T. first visited Hagley in 1743 (cf. *Letters* p. 165).

909 **Tempe**: the beautiful vale in Thessaly celebrated by classical poets.

909–22 Parallels between these lines and T.'s letter of 29 Aug. 1743 are pointed out in H. E. Hamilton, 'James Thomson recollects Hagley Park', *Modern Language Notes* lxii (1947), 194–7. Cf. *Cas. Ind.* I. iii. 6–v.2.

910 **shag'd**: made rough, cf. Milton, *Comus* 428 and *Wi.* 281, 918.

915 **tuft**: 'To tuft. To adorn with a tuft; a doubtful word, not authorised by any competent writer' (Johnson, citing 914–16); cf. Sylvester's trans. of *Du Bartas* (1598), II. i. 11, and see *Su.* 688 n.

936 **Lucinda**: Lucy Fortescue, married to Lyttelton 1742; her death in 1747 prompted Lyttelton's celebrated *Monody*.

950–62 This landscape is likened to the work of Claude Lorrain in Elizabeth Manwaring, *Italian Landscape in Eighteenth-Century England* (1925), p. 104, and in John Barrell, *The Idea of Landscape and the Sense of*

Place, 1730–1840 (Cambridge, 1972), pp. 14–20; but to that of Carracci in Jeffry Spencer, *Heroic Nature* (Evanston, 1973), pp. 272–4.

954   Cf. Milton, *L'Allegro* 78, whence perhaps 'tuft' at *Sp.* 915.

965   **live Carnation:** pinkness.

969   Cf. the Dryden reference at *Sp.* 826 n.

989   **illusive:** 'Deceiving by false show' (Johnson, citing 987–9); cf. *Wi.* 716.

991   **belying:** counterfeiting.

992   **searchless:** resisting investigation, inscrutable.

994   **syren:** the Sirens in Greek mythology were beautiful women (or half-woman monsters) who lured men to destruction by their enchanting song; cf. Homer, *Odyssey* xii. 39–200.

996–1003   Cf. Lucretius, iv. 1133–6. I have found no model for the personification of repentance as snaky-crested; perhaps T. has in mind the snaky-haired Furies of Greek and Roman myth who were sometimes taken to represent the guilty conscience (cf. Lucretius, iii. 1011, 1018–19). The whole passage 983–1112 is rearranged, expurgated, and adapted from Lucretius, iv. 1008-1208.

1002   **great Design:** noble purpose.

1010   **rosy-bosom'd Spring:** cf. Milton, *Comus* 984–5.

1011   **Arch:** the sky.

1021   **vain:** empty.

1023   **Site:** 'It is taken by *Thomson* for posture, or situation of a thing with respect to itself: but improperly' (Johnson, citing 1022–4); cf. the 'proper' usage at *Su.* 159.

1028   **Romantic:** 'Fanciful; full of wild scenery' (Johnson, citing 1027–8); cf. *Su.* 459, 1375, *Au.* 880, *Wi. 260 Preface* 89 (Appendix B). See Logan Pearsall Smith, 'Four Romantic Words' in *Words and Idioms* (1925), pp. 66–134.

1029   **thrilling:** piercing; cf. *Au.* 200, 1003.

1035   shines through clouds in the eastern sky; cf. *Wi.* 15.

1037   **Hours:** cf. *Su.* 4 n.

1038   **Languish:** tender glance; cf. Pope, *Iliad* xviii. 50.

1039   **Bird of Eve:** nightingale. On the reason for the nightingale's woes cf. *Sp.* 601 n.

1060   **Impertinence:** 'Troublesomeness; intrusion' (Johnson).

1065   **waste:** to no purpose.

1067–73   Cf. Virgil, *Georgics*, iii. 258–63, in allusion to Leander, who used to swim the Hellespont to visit his mistress Hero, and was eventually drowned.

1070a (*30q*, 984)   **Bacchanal**: wild, ecstatic priestess or votary of the god Bacchus; cf. Ovid, *Metamorphoses* iii. 701–33, xi. 30–43.

1071   **outragious**: violent; cf. *PL* vii. 212.

1083   **yellow-tinging Plague**: jealousy.

1107   **warm**: amorous.

1109–12   **leads a Life . . . to waste.** Douglas Grant observes 'These lines were a curiously accurate prophecy of his own fate.' On T.'s unhappy, unrequited love for Elizabeth Young in the 1740s see Grant, pp. 198–244.

1113–76   Cf. *PL* iv. 750–70.

1123   **preventing**: anticipating. For the sentiment and some phraseology in 1121–5 cf. Pope, *Eloisa to Abelard* 93–7, and T.'s letter of advice to his sister on her marriage in 1740 (*Letters*, p. 132).

1139   **fair**: beauty; cf. *PL* ix. 608.

1161–5   Cf. T.'s letter to Elizabeth Young, 19 Apr. 1743: 'Competency with Contentment, a virtuous improved well-ordered Mind, right Affections, Friendship and Love, these give the truest Happiness, and these we may command.' (*Letters*, pp. 151–2).

1174   They will both die at the same time.

SUMMER

(*27*, *epigraph*)   Horace, *Odes* iii. xxix. 17–24: Already Andromeda's shining father reveals his hidden fires; already Procyon rages and the star of furious Leo, as the sun brings back the days of drought. Now with his listless flock the weary shepherd seeks the shade and stream and shaggy Silvanus' thickets, and the silent bank is forsaken by the straying breeze.

1   **Ether**: see *Sp.* 148 n.

2   Summer, like Spring (*Sp.* 1–4), is personified and makes a royal 'progress'; his masculine power is contrasted with Spring's feminine mildness.

4   **Hours**: in Greek mythology the goddesses who preside over the seasons and hours. As portresses of heaven or servants who yoke the chariot of the sun, they bring in the dawn; cf. Homer, *Iliad* v. 749, Ovid, *Metamorphoses* ii. 116–21, *PL* iv. 267–8, vi. 2–4, *Su.* 122.

12   **haunted**: i.e. by the Muses; cf. Milton, *L'Allegro* 129–30, *PL* iii. 26–8.

15   T. took the 'hint about personizing of Inspiration' from David Mallet (*Letters*, p. 45). In *Su.* 15–20 T. emphasizes the notion of the poet as creator; cf. *Su.* 192–6 and, perhaps, *Au.* 668–72, where inspiration is not personified and T. regards the poet as imitator and as translator of the book of Nature.

29   George Bubb Dodington (1691–1762), politician, poetaster, patron, and wit, was impressed by *Winter* (1726) and invited T. to dedicate

Summer (1727) to him. In 1730 he subscribed for twenty copies of the quarto *Seasons*. Edward Young (cf. *Au.* 667), Fielding, Glover, and Lyttelton (cf. *Sp.* 906) all made court to Dodington—as did T., who was a frequent visitor to his great house at Eastbury in Dorset (cf. *Au.* 655). For an account of Dodington and the opposition circle at Eastbury see John Carswell, *The Old Cause, Three Biographical Studies in Whiggism* (1954), pp. 131–265. Pope's sketches of Dodington's character, if less charitable than T.'s, are probably more faithful; cf. *Epistle to Arbuthnot* 231–48 and *Epistle to Burlington* 19–22. T. added lines 21–31 in *30q* to replace a prefatory prose dedication to Dodington (see Appendix B); he complimented Dodington also in a verse epistle *The Happy Man* (1729).

32–42 Cf. Gen. 1: 14 and 8: 22. Kepler and Newton had demonstrated that the planets are kept in their courses by a combination of transverse motion and the gravitational pull (or, as Kepler said, magnetic pull) of the sun; while Newton had shown that if the planets were projected with the correct initial velocities their present orbits would follow as a matter of course (cf. T.'s *Poem to Newton* 39–42). Physico-theologians of the period argued that gravitation proceeds from 'a Divine energy and impression', and that transverse motion 'can only be ascribed to the right hand of the most high God', who continues to preserve the solar system in its shape (Richard Bentley's Boyle Lectures, 1692, which were the first popularization of Newton's *Principia*). See *Background*, pp. 31–4. T.'s deletion of 'Machine' (*27*, 30) and his added allusion in *44* to God's hand emphasize, in accordance with Newton's views, that the constant presence of God is required to maintain order in the solar system; cf. also Shaftesbury, *Characteristicks* (1714), ii. 372–3.

43 alternate Twins: Gemini, third sign of the zodiac (see *Sp.* 26 n.), into which the sun enters about 21 May (about 10 May in T.'s day). The constellation Gemini was identified by classical astronomers with Castor and Polydeuces (Lat. Pollux), twin sons of Leda. When Castor was killed in battle, Polydeuces, who was immortal, asked to be allowed to die also, so Zeus granted that they should together spend alternate days in Heaven and Hades (or take turns to go to Hades); cf. Homer, *Odyssey* xi. 301–4, Ovid, *Fasti* v. 698–720. Servius, on Virgil, *Aeneid* vi. 121, suggests that the myth of Castor and Pollux relates to the Evening and the Morning Star, one of which sets as the other rises, but T. evidently has in mind the zodiacal sign; so 'alternate' refers only to the myth and not to any analogous astral phenomenon.

44 Cancer: the Crab, the fourth sign of the zodiac, into which the sun enters at the summer solstice on 21 or 22 June (*c.*10 June in T.'s day).

46 observant: 'Respectfully attentive' (Johnson); cf. Pope, *Odyssey* i. 342.

48a (*27*, 36) **elucent:** shining out, cf. Lucretius ii. 1051, Virgil, *Georgics* iv. 98; the word is not in *OED* and may have been coined by T. In *44* he prefers 'refulgent' (*Su.* 2) and 'effulgent' (*Su.* 135, 635), perhaps for their heroic associations with the *Aeneid*.

49 Ether: see *Sp.* 148 n.

55 Swell on the Sight: are revealed more distinctly.

56 smoaking Currents: rising mists; cf. Lucretius v. 463–4:

> exhalantque lacus nebulam fluviique perennes,
> ipsaque ut interdum tellus fumare videtur;

also vi. 523.

60 Passenger: traveller on foot; cf. Milton, *Comus* 39.

80 devious: 'Wandering; roving; rambling' (Johnson, citing 79–80).

81 The sun is personified making a royal progress, preceded by the Seasons (113, 121), the Hours (122), etc. Cf. Ps. 19: 4–6, *PL* vii. 370–3, and the famous fresco *Aurora* (1613) by Guido Reni; see Jean Hagstrum, *The Sister Arts* (Chicago, 1958), pp. 260–1 and plate xxix.

84 fluid Gold: cf. Mallet, *The Excursion* (1728), 41. For the Pythagorean notion that light is material (91), descending in liquid form from that fountain of light the sun, cf. Lucretius, v. 281–5, 592–603, and *PL* vii. 359–65. Cf. *Su.* 435, 453–5, 609, 659–61, *Au.* 958, 1095–1102, *Hymn* 68.

90–6 Cf. *PL* iii. 1–6, and Shaftesbury, *The Moralists*: 'our *Sun.* . . . Brightest Image and Representative of *the Almighty*!' (*Characteristicks* (1714), ii. 371). T.'s revision of 95–6 in *44* brings in God; cf. *Su.* 41–2 *Hymn* 66–7.

94 unessential: 'Void of real being' (Johnson); cf. *Sp.* 557, *PL* ii. 439.

97 attractive Force: gravitation, as evidence of God's continuing, loving presence within the universe; cf. *Su.* 32–42 n., and 'attractive Virtue', *PL* viii. 124.

100 Saturn was thought to be the outermost member of the solar system.

102 Can scarce be caught: because it is never above the horizon for more than two hours after sunset or for the same period before sunrise. Philosophic: of the scientist.

104 Informer: the sun, as 'best Image' (cf. *Hymn* 66) of God (cf. *Sp.* 860).

107 Lucretius (ii. 1052–76) had claimed that the infinite number of 'seeds' or atoms in boundless space must combine to form inhabited worlds other than our own, and Giordano Bruno likewise argued for a plurality of worlds, but in T.'s day the most influential statement of the theory was Bernard de Fontenelle's *Entretiens sur la Pluralité des Mondes* (1686), trans. Aphra Behn as *A Discovery of New Worlds* (1688). Cf. *PL* iii. 565–71, vii. 621–2, viii. 140–58, Blackmore, *The Creation* (1712), iii. 273–310, Prior, *Solomon* (1718), i. 512–35. For a full account of literature on the plurality of worlds see A. O. Lovejoy, *The Great Chain of Being* (Cambridge, Mass., 1936), chap. iv.

108 wait: are dependent.

109 unfettered Mind: disembodied spirit (of angelic beings).

110 daily Race: insects that live for a single day. On periphrases see *Sp.* 132 n.

117 Nations: of men.

118 Tribes: of animals and vegetables.

122 Hours: see *Su.* 4 n.; 'rosy-fingered' is Homer's epithet for dawn.

129+ (*27*, 120) **unwitholding:** cf. *Sp.* 46 n.

131–59 The theory in the ancient *Meteorologia*, attributed to Aristotle, that the penetrative force of the sun causes the growth and colouring of minerals was restated in Thomas Burnet's *Theory of the Earth* (1684) Book II, Chap. vi: 'Subterraneous things, metals and metallick Minerals, are Factitious, not Original bodies, coeval with the Earth; but are made in process of time, after long preparations and concoctions, by the action of the Sun within the bowels of the Earth.' Cf. *PL* iii. 583–6, 606–12, T.'s *Liberty* v. 13–14, Pope, *Windsor Forest* 396. Apparently Mallet gave T. a hint for *Su.* 140–59 (see *Letters*, p. 40), and cf. Blackmore, *The Creation* (1712), ii. 249–52:

> Now the bright Sun compacts the precious Stone,
> Imparting radiant Lustre, like his own;
> He tinctures Rubies with their rosy Hue,
> And on the Sapphire spreads a heavenly Blue.

134 Kinds: indicating that minerals grow and live like other objects of creation.

136–9 referring to metallic ores.

140 impregned: made fruitful; cf. *PL* iv. 500.

148 (*27*, 133) **grateful:** 'pleasing, delightful' (Johnson); cf. *Sp.* 271+ (*28*, 310), and Pope, *Pastorals*, Autumn, 74.

150 Tinct: 'Colour' (Johnson, citing 150–1): Lat. *tinctus*.

155 Newton had demonstrated that the colours of the spectrum blend into white light. T.'s description (140–59) runs through the spectrum as the colours emerge from the pure light of the diamond and return to the white light of the opal.

159 Site: position; cf. *Sp.* 1023 n.

162 relucent: 'Shining; transparent; pellucid' (Johnson, citing only 162–3); Lat. *relucens*.

163–70 Used as a motto by Turner for his painting *Dunstanburgh Castle, Sun-rise after a squally night* (exh. 1798), and by Constable for his *Hadleigh Castle* (exh. 1829). Turner substitutes 'Breaking' for 'Projecting' at 164. T. was a favourite poet of both painters.

164 Projecting Horror: casting a jagged shadow. Lat. *horrere*, to bristle.

176–81 Cf. *PL* iii. 3–6. Uncreated light is that light which is the divine

emanation itself, as distinct from physical light. For 'Smile' (179) cf. *Sp.*
84 and n. The entire passage, 81–184, enforces the central significance of
the sun—physically as the upholder of life, and spiritually because light
is the primary power in the universe and the Creator is light himself (176,
cf. *Hymn* 117).

184 Spheres: orbits.

186 Father: the revisions from 'POET' and 'MAKER' are increasingly
devotional. On 'POET' (27, 171), cf. *Sp.* 860.

185–96 T. agrees with many eighteenth-century preachers, philoso-
phers, and poets that 'the works of Nature everywhere sufficiently evidence
a Deity' (Locke); cf. *Hymn*. Furthermore, as God is the great artist or
author (cf. *Sp.* 859–60) and Nature is his art (cf. *Au.* 668–72; *Hymn* 23;
Browne, *Religio Medici*, Part 1, sect. 16; Shaftesbury, *Characteristicks*
(1714), ii. 372; Pope, *Essay on Man* i. 289), the best art that man can
attempt—albeit a feeble best (cf. *Sp.* 468–79)—is to read and translate the
sacred book of Nature.

205 Cf. *PL* ix. 426–7 (in the 1720 text, which reads 'blushing' for
'bushing').

206–8 Cf. *Au.* 1318 and Virgil, *Georgics* ii. 488–9; the echo is pointed
by a resonantly Virgilian word, 'gelid', cf. *Su.* 461, 682.

213 Shed by the Morn: cf. *Su.* 120–9.

216–9 That the sunflower follows the sun is a pertinacious poetic
fiction; cf. Ovid, *Metamorphoses* iv. 269–70.

223 Food: milk (expected by the cottage household).

232 vacant: 'Being at leisure; disengaged' (Johnson).

237 Summer-race: short-lived insects. On periphrases see *Sp.*
132 n.

241 reptile: 'Creeping upon many feet' (Johnson).

245 Tombs: chrysalises.

248 Parent: the sun.

267–80 Cf. John Philips, *The Splendid Shilling* (1705), 78–92. T.'s
mock-heroic tone gradually becomes clearer between lines 230 and 280.

287–317 'Every part of Matter is peopled; Every green Leaf swarms
with Inhabitants. There is scarce a single Humour in the Body of a Man,
or of any other Animal, in which our Glasses do not discover Myriads of
living Creatures. The Surface of Animals is also covered with other
Animals, which are in the same manner the Basis of other Animals that
live upon it; we find in the most solid Bodies, as in Marble itself, innumer-
able Cells and Cavities that are crouded with such imperceptible inhabi-
tants as are too little for the naked Eye to discover.' (Addison, *Spectator*
519, drawing on Fontenelle's *Plurality of Worlds;* cf. *Su.* 107 n.) 'If the
Eye were so acute as to rival the finest Microscopes, and to discern the
smallest Hair upon the leg of a Gnat, it would be a curse and not a Blessing

to us. . . . So likewise, if our Sense of Hearing were exalted proportionally to the former, what a miserable condition would Mankind be in? . . . we should have no quiet or sleep in the silentest nights and most solitary places; and we must inevitably be struck Deaf or Dead with the noise of a clap of Thunder.' (Richard Bentley, Boyle Lectures, 1692; cf. Locke, *Essay concerning Human Understanding*, II. xxiii. 12; Pope, *Essay on Man* i. 195–204.) These notions were often restated by eighteenth-century physico-theologians. See *Background*, pp. 48–52, for a full discussion. In revising *Su*. 287–317 for publication in *44*, T. deletes references to the great chain of being and to improvements in the microscope (*Sp*.28, 155–61), presumably because the first duplicates *Su*. 334 and the second contradicts *Su*. 288. The deletions may have been made in proof since a version of the earlier passage remains in manuscript.

301   downy Orchard: perhaps 'orchard in blossom', i.e. white and feathery as if with down; or perhaps 'down-covered fruit' (though *OED* cites no occurrence of orchard in that sense); cf. Dryden, *Virgil's Pastorals* ii. 72: 'downy Peaches'. T. may have been influenced by John Philips's description of an apple under the microscope: 'An inmate Orchat ev'ry Apple boasts' (*Cyder* i. 358).

318–28   This fable is from *Guardian* 70 (1713) by George Berkeley, but T. adds (in *44*) the information that Ignorance is female.

334   The chain of being was composed of 'an immense, or . . . infinite, number of links ranging in hierarchical order from the meagerest kind of existents, which barely escape non-existence, through "every possible" grade up to the *ens perfectissimum*—or . . . to the highest possible kind of creature, between which and the Absolute Being the disparity was assumed to be infinite—every one of them differing from that immediately above and that immediately below it by the "least possible" degree of difference.' (A. O. Lovejoy, *The Great Chain of Being* (Cambridge, Mass., 1936), p. 59.) Lovejoy's book surveys the whole subject with great learning. For near-contemporary statements of the notion of the chain of being cf. Locke, *Essay concerning Human Understanding* III. vi. 12; Addison, *Spectator* 519; Pope, *Essay on Man* i. 207–46; but the conception was Platonic and the idea prevalent in Western thought from the Middle Ages to the late eighteenth century. Cf. *Sp*. 378, *Su*. 1796–1805.

337a (*27*, *287*)   **Recoiling:** (transitive), driving back: *44* has the commoner intransitive usage.

342–51   Cf. *Sp*. 60–1, *Wi*. 638–45.

343   thwarting: cf. *Au*. 1113 n.

344   quivering Nations: dancing insects. On periphrases see *Sp*. 132 n.

351   Book of Life: record of the names of those who shall enjoy eternal life.

352–431   Georgical material added in the later editions (352–70 in *30q* and 371–431 in *44*), and typical of the georgic in combining an account of husbandry with pastoral idealism (e.g. 370, 400–4) and patriotism (423–31). In showing (423–31) that the farmer's activities support Britain's mercantile power, T. harmonizes simple rural scenes and national grandeur; cf. *Sp.* 32–77, *Au.* 43–150, Introduction p. xxvi.

355 Blown: caused to blossom.

356 swelling on the Sight: 'is an expression either unmeaning, or indelicate' (John Scott, *Critical Essays* (1785), p. 323). The maid is dressed in stays and skirt, with half-revealed breasts; a sly echo of *Su.* 55.

360 kind Oppression: i.e. the children are loaded with an uninjurious weight; cf. *PL* viii. 288.

361 Grain: grass gone to seed, i.e. hay; cf. *PL* ix. 450, 'smell of grain, or tedded grass'.

363 breathing: fragrant.

367 thick: numerous.

371 one diffusive Band: indicating that the villagers are spread out, yet acting in concert.

373 mazy: winding; cf. *Sp.* 577.

378 soft fearful People: sheep; cf. *Su.* 388, 417. On periphrases see *Sp.* 132 n.

387–99 'let the Weather be such, as may dry them soon after washing and warm the Ground against they lose their Fleece. . . . After the Wool is well cleaned, put your Sheep upon the lightest and highest Land you have, which will be a means of preserving the Wool clean, and in good Condition, till they are shorn; which Work of Shearing, may be done three or four Days after the Washing; observing at the shearing Time, to take care of winding the Wool, and laying it up clean and dry.' (Richard Bradley, *Gentleman and Farmer's Guide* (1729), p. 35.)

389 Treasures: fleeces (anticipating the wool harvest; cf. *Sp.* 112–13 on the corn harvest).

400–4 It was an ancient custom to hold a feast, presided over by a 'shepherd-king', to accompany the neighbourly activity of sheep-shearing. Such a feast (albeit with an unneighbourly conclusion) is referred to in 2 Sam. 13: 23–9. Drayton describes Cotswold shearing-festivals and shepherd-kings in his *Ninth Eclogue* (1606) and his *Poly-Olbion* (1613) song xiv; while John Brand, in *Observations on Popular Antiquities* (1772), asserts that shearing-feasts were still customary in southern England. T.'s pastoral queen (401) probably owes a suggestion to Perdita in Shakespeare, *Winter's Tale* IV. iv.

407 Vagrant: because shearing has temporarily removed the owner's mark from its side.

420 Care: rent; an ironic adaptation of *cura* in Virgil's *Georgics*—a Virgilian word for the tasks of the shepherd and farmer.

425 Stores: imports from the tropics.

430 Gallia: France. Though Britain did not declare war until March 1744 her ships were blockading Brest and Toulon before then. T.'s 'Rule Britannia' was first sung publicly on 1 Aug. 1740, during the masque *Alfred* by T. and Mallet.

432–97 Cf. Gay, *Rural Sports* (1720), i. 53–66.

437 dejected: cast down; cf. *Su*. 974, 1066.

440 cleaving: with surface cracked by heat.

453–5 For the notion of light as liquid see *Su*. 84 n.; cf. 'dazzling Deluge' (*Su*. 435).

458–63 Cf. Virgil, *Georgics* ii. 487–8; 'gelid', cf. *Su*. 206–8 n.

459 romantic: see *Sp*. 1028 n.

461 wrought: decorated with.

480–93 'A groupe worthy the pencil of Giacomo da Bassano.' (J. Warton, *Essay on the Genius and Writings of Pope* [i] (1756), p. 46.)

490 Front: face; cf. *Sp*. 880, *Au*. 14, 521.

491 incompos'd: discomposed; cf. *PL* ii. 989.

497 listening: (transitive); cf. *Su*. 1247, Milton, *Comus* 550.

498–505 Cf. Virgil, *Georgics* iii. 146–51.

506–15 Cf. Job 39: 19–21. T. sent a version of 506–15 to Aaron Hill in June 1726 (*Letters*, p. 39).

518 Quire: chancel; cf. Shakespeare, *Sonnet* 73: 4.

522–6 Cf. *Au*. 1030–6, and Shaftesbury's woodland rhapsody at the end of sect. i of *The Moralists* (1709) in *Characteristicks* ii. 390–1.

526–30 Cf. Milton, *Comus* 453–62.

538–63 T. acknowledged that Mallet gave him the hint for these woodland spirits (see *Letters*, p. 45), but cf. *PL* iv. 677–88 and Addison, *Spectator* 12: 'For my own Part, I am apt to join in Opinion with those who believe that all the Regions of Nature swarm with Spirits; and that we have Multitudes of Spectators on all our Actions, when we think ourselves most alone: but instead of terrifying myself with such a Notion, I am wonderfully pleased to think that I am always engaged with such an innumerable Society, in searching out the wonders of the Creation, and joining in the same Concert of Praise and Adoration.' Richard Wilson illustrated *Su*. 516–63 in his *Solitude*, several versions of which were painted from 1762 to 1778 (W. G. Constable, *Richard Wilson* (1953), p. 169).

546 Parent-Power: perhaps Nature, rather than God; cf. *Su*. 577, *Wi*. 106.

552a (27, 439) **commutual**: reciprocal, 'used only in poetry' (Johnson); cf. Shakespeare, *Hamlet* III. ii. 170.

556 Visionary Hour: supernatural beings are most likely to be encountered at noon or midnight; cf. Homer, *Odyssey*, iv. 400, 450, *PL* iv. 682.

564 Stanley: Miss Elizabeth Stanley. In 1740 T. wrote the epitaph upon her in Holyrood Church, Southampton, printed in T.'s *Poems on Several Occasions* (1750). Her mother (569) was daughter of Sir Hans Sloane, an early friend of T.

582–4 Cf. *Wi.* 603–8 and n.

591–606 The revisions in *44* enlarge the waterfall and offer a more favourable view of wild scenery; cf. 'aghast', 'with the rough Prospect tir'd' (*27*, 455, 467). In *27*, the waterfall is personified to point a parable of human misfortune.

595 prone: headlong; cf. *PL* v. 266.

604 infracted: 'To infract. To break' (Johnson, citing only 603–5); Lat. *infractus*.

607–11 Cf. *Sp.* 755–65 n.

611 tuneful: (replacing 'feathery' in *44* as a more appropriate epithet); on periphrases see *Sp.* 132 n.

614 Responsive: answering one another; cf. *Sp.* 201.

622–8 Cf. Milton, *Il Penseroso* 139–43.

626 Umbrage: foliage.

628+ (*27*, 632–42) Based on *Georgics* ii. 303–11 ('gummy Bark' translates *pingui cortice*). In Virgil a careless shepherd starts the fire; in T., the sun.

(*27*, 644–5) Cf. Deuteronomy 28: 23. T. adds 'rusty'.

(*27*, 651) **Barca:** one of the kingdoms of Barbary (Patrick Gordon, *Geography Anatomized* (4th edn., 1704, p. 317). T. took hints for his Sahara passage (*27*, 651–6) from the section 'Concerning Zaara or the Desert' in Gordon, pp. 323–4. See *Background*, pp. 144, 161.

628+ (*30q*, 718–49) The first English reference to a petrified city in North Africa seems to have been by Sir Kenelm Digby in *Mercurius Politicus* 334 (6 Nov. 1656). In 1728–9, when an envoy from Tripoli was resident in London, the story was revived, discussed, and elaborated in newspapers and journals; and one such elaborated 'dream' version, in the *Universal Spectator* 29 (26 Apr. 1729), was T.'s immediate source for the poses of his 'statue-folk', and suggested his analogy (742–9) with the story in Livy v. xxxix–xli. Cf. 'Memorial of *Cassem Aga*, the *Tripoli* ambassador at the court of *Great-Britain*, concerning the petrified city in *Africa*, two days journey south from *Onguela*, and seventeen days journey from *Tripoli* by *Caravan* to the South-east' in *Gentleman's Magazine* xvii (1747), 436; see *Background*, pp. 145–8. T. was fascinated by statuary (cf. *Liberty* iv. 134–214) and by 'human statues' (cf. *Su.* 1144–9a, 1217–22, 1344–9, *Wi.* 930–5) but he deleted *30q*, 718–49 from *44*, perhaps because he wished to reject the fabulous, since the story of the petrified city was discredited in Thomas Shaw, *Travels* (Oxford, 1738). See H. E. Hamilton, 'James Thomson's *Seasons*: Shifts in the Treatment of Popular Subject Matter', *ELH* xv (1948), 113.

(*30q*, 722) **Amusing**: engaging the (serious) attention.

(*30q*, 723) T. may have invented this 'scientific' explanation; cf. *Su.* 1092–116.

628+ (*27*, 657–62) T.'s footnote is almost word for word from Patrick Gordon, *Geography Anatomized* (4th edn., 1704), p. 324. The story was often told; see *Background*, pp. 144–5.

635–42 Parallels *Su.* 81–90, with differences appropriate to a tropical as distinct from a temperate sunrise.

641 footnote **general Breeze**: It is not true that rarefied air can push denser air before it—as T. recognizes later in the poem, cf. *Su.* 789–90. T.'s footnote, first printed in *44*, is based upon a clumsily worded explanation in Bernhard Varenius, *General Geography* (1733), i. 484–8; see *Background*, pp. 149–50.

646 Because of the sun's action; cf. *Su.* 131–59 n.

657–62 T. sees as one of the beneficent paradoxes of the harmonious natural order the fact that tropical fruits contain cooling juices. On light as liquid ('drink . . . redoubled Day', 659–61), see *Su.* 84 n.

659 **of . . . vital Spirit**: yielding life-sustaining fluids; cf. *PL* v. 484.

663 **Pomona**: Roman goddess of fruit-trees; cf. Ovid, *Metamorphoses* xiv. 623–771.

669 **Locust**: the very large courbaril tree of Guiana and the West Indies.

671 **Indian Fig**: The huge banyan tree whose extensive branches drop shoots which root and grow into trunks, so that one tree assumes the appearance of a dense and dark grove; cf. Pliny, *Natural History* xii. 22–3 and *PL* ix. 1101–10.

674 **verdant Cedar**: the cedar of Lebanon—in T.'s day an exotic, not to be planted in quantity in England before about 1760.

675 **Palmetos**: palm trees in general—not, as now, 'dwarf palms'.

677 **Cocoa**: coconut.

678 **Wine**: coconut milk.

679 **frantic**: intoxicating.

680 **Bacchus**: Roman god of wine.

683 **humble Station**: growing close to the ground.

685 **Anana**: properly 'ananas'—pineapple.

688 **tufty**: 'Adorned with tufts. A word of no authority' (Johnson, citing only 688–9); cf. *Sp.* 915 n.

694 **Flora**: ancient Italian goddess of flowers and fertility; cf. Ovid, *Fasti* v. 183–378.

703 **Solitude**: without man.

705 **fatning**: making fertile by irrigation, cf. *Sp.* 262.

707 diffus'd his train: his tail stretched out; cf. Milton, *Samson Agonistes* 118.

710 Behemoth: cf. Job 40: 15–24.

720 Theater: natural amphitheatre; cf. *PL* iv. 141–2, Dryden, *Aeneid* v. 377–8.

721 On the wisdom of elephants cf. Pliny, *Natural History* viii. 1–6.

728 mine . . . his Steps: trap by means of a camouflaged pit.

733 winding Umbrage: forests on the river banks; cf. *Su.* 626.

738–40 T. could have found the material for his footnote and other hints for 733–40 in accounts of the Jesuits' travels in Siam, trans. and reprinted in John Harris, *Compleat Collection of Voyages and Travels* (1705), ii. 468. See H. E. Hamilton, 'A Note on James Thomson's Sources', *Modern Language Notes* lxiii (1948), 46–8.

739 Because, as Newton had shown, sunlight is the source of colour.

742 Montezuma: 1466–1520, the last Aztec ruler of Mexico before it was conquered by Spain. The Aztecs wove feathers into a costly kind of cloth, and their soldiers ornamented their head-dresses and shields with feathers.

743–6 Cf. Milton, *Il Penseroso* 56–8. T. 'would sometimes listen a full hour at his window to the nightingales in *Richmond* gardens.' (Murdoch's 'Life' in *Works of Thomson* (1762), vol. i, p. xviii.) Line 745 is a quotation from Milton, *Upon the Circumcision* 5. Shakespeare described night as 'sober-suited' in *Romeo and Juliet* iv. ii. 11. For Philomel see *Sp.* 601 n.

750 Sennar: a kingdom and city in the upper Blue Nile valley, later part of the Sudan close to the Abyssinian border.

751 Nubian: Nubia was the ancient name for the upper Nile regions.

752 jealous: 'Suspiciously careful' (Johnson); cf. *PL* x. 478.

755–8 In the sixteenth and early seventeenth centuries Portuguese Jesuit missionaries sought to convert the Coptic Christians of Abyssinia to Rome; their success in converting the Emperor provoked a bloody civil war, the result of which was the complete exclusion of Europeans from Abyssinia. English translations of and commentaries upon Jesuits' travel accounts (cf. *Su.* 781–3 n.) usually made much of religious fanaticism, cruel imperialism, and commercial greed. Cf. *Liberty* iii. 251–6.

767 Sun-redoubling Valley: one that by reflecting the sun's rays from its side increases their heat.

768 middle Air: a cold vaporous region—the second of the three layers into which ancient and medieval philosophers divided the atmosphere; cf. *PL* i. 516, *Au.* 707–10 n.

773 Disdaining all Assault: because ringed by mountains.

781–3 Mount Amara 'is situate as the navil of that Ethiopian body, and centre of their Empire, under the Equinoctiall line, where the Sun may take his best view thereof, as not encountering in all his long journey with the like Theatre . . . the Sun himself so in love with the sight, that the first and last thing he vieweth in all those parts, is this hill.' (*Samuel Purchas, his Pilgrimage*, 1617, Book VII, chap. 5.) Lines 747–83 are based upon several geographical descriptions derived (like Johnson's *Rasselas*) from Jesuit missionaries' accounts, translations of some of which were reprinted in books listed in the *Sale Catalogue* of T.'s Library, e.g. *Travels of the Jesuits* (1714), John Ray, *Collection of Curious Travels* (1738), John Lockman, *Travels of the Jesuits* (1743). However, the paradisal overtones of T.'s description are mainly from Purchas and from *PL* iv. 280–4, with iv. 131–43. See *Background*, pp. 151–5.

788–802 Winds in the temperate zones drive clouds towards the tropics, where the air is warmer and therefore less dense (789–90, cf. *Su.* 641 n.). These clouds are condensed upon the Abyssinian, Himalayan, and other mountains to produce the monsoon rains. T.'s account is probably based on Antoine Pluche, *Spectacle de la Nature* (2nd edn., 1737), iii. 115–16, and on Lucretius, vi. 346–352, where it is asserted that thunder and lightning are caused by the collision of cloud-laden winds T., as usual, personifies natural phenomena. See *Background*, pp. 156–7.

803–5 Ancients and moderns alike had speculated about the source of the Nile (cf. Lucan, *Pharsalia* x. 172–331, Pliny, *Natural History* v. 51–4), and about the fact that it was the only river to flood in summer (cf. Lucretius, vi. 712–37, who repeats the opinions of early philosophers). T.'s account (806–21) is based upon that of the Jesuit Pedro Páez, as retold in various compilations (see *Su.* 781–3 n.), but refers only to the Blue Nile. The principal branch of the river is the White Nile, the source of which was determined by Speke in 1863. T. personifies the river without departing from geographical fact.

806   Gojam: a region of north-western Abyssinia.

808   Dambea: Lake Tana in Abyssinia.

816   devolves: 'To devolve. To roll down' (Johnson, citing 816–18); Lat. *devolvo.*

819   Nubian Rocks: the Cataracts, see *Su.* 751 n.

820   pours his Urn: the image is of a statue or other representation of the river-god, the reference is to the annual flooding of Lower Egypt; cf. T.'s *Liberty* iii. 251–2.

826 Coromandel is the east and Malabar the west coast of India.

827–8 The reference to lantern-flies in Siam comes from John Harris, *Collection of Voyages* (1705), ii. 465–8; see *Background*, p. 159.

828   Aurora: in Roman mythology the goddess of dawn, associated with a rosy colour, hence roses; cf. *Su.* 1326–7. The banks of the Indus would be rose-strewn only in its higher reaches, in Kashmir.

830–1 The monsoon floods making alluvial deposits on the land.

834   Oronoque: Orinoco

836 The native houses in trees were described in Raleigh's *Discovery of Guiana* (1596); see *Background*, pp. 159–60.

840 Orellana: named after its first navigator, Francisco de Orellana, a follower of Pizarro.

854 Pan: the Greek god of flocks, shepherds, and pastoral song. In a Christian legend (based on a story told by Plutarch) a mysterious cry 'The great Pan is dead' was heard about the time that Christ was born.

855 cruel Sons: Spanish and Portuguese.

856–9 The story that the currents of South American rivers carry fresh water many miles out to sea is told in *Purchas, his Pilgrimage* (1617), Book IX, chap. 1, and in many other travel books. T., typically, personifies ocean. For some account of all those geographical compilations—notably *Purchas* and Bernhard Varenius's *General Geography* (rev. by Isaac Newton, 1672)—which were drawn upon for this catalogue of rivers (803–59), see *Background*, pp. 155–60.

860–97 Though T.'s long exotic excursion (629–897, added in *44*) balances paradisal against horrific features of the tropics, his conclusion here, as in *Liberty* v. 8–47, is that the civilized arts of Europe are preferable to the barbarous nature of tropical regions. Cf. *Wi.* 587–93 n.

863 Ceres: Roman goddess of agriculture, cf. Ovid, *Fasti* iv. 393–620; here signifying harvest ('void of Pain', i.e. without labour). Cf. *PL* iv. 271, 'Which cost Ceres all that pain'; but T.'s is a dead phrase, beside Milton's.

869–70 Cf. *PL* i. 684–8, and T.'s *Liberty* v. 23–6.

871 Golconda: the town near Hyderabad in India where diamonds were brought to be cut and polished.

871 Potosi: the extremely rich silver-mining area in what is now Bolivia; 'sad' because the Spaniards treated their native labourers cruelly.

872 Children of the Sun: the Incas of ancient Peru worshipped the sun, of which their emperor was held to be a descendant.

898–907 The serpent guarding a spring comes from Lucan, *Pharsalia* ix. 607–10, with details from *PL* ix. 497–503, and from Virgil, *Aeneid* ii. 471–5 and *Georgics* ii. 153–4.

905 Thirst: thirsty creatures.

908 Minister of Fate: asp.

909 concocted: 'To concoct. To purify or sublime by heat; or heighten to perfection' (Johnson, citing 908–10). According to myth, the asp was formed by the sun's heat on a clot of Medusa's blood; cf. Lucan, *Pharsalia* ix. 700–5.

923 Mauritania: the Mediterranean coastal regions of what are now Morocco and western Algeria.

923 tufted Isles: oases; cf. *Sp.* 915 n.

925 King: lion.

934 thoughtless: free from care.

938 Atlas: see *Au.* 798 n.

939–50 T. developed this situation and repeated some of these expressions in Melisander's story in *Agamemnon* (1738), III. i.

946 Cf. *PL* ii. 636–7.

949 Cf. Milton, *Comus* 548.

952 stooping: declining.

954 Cato: Marcus Porcius Cato (95–46 BC), great-grandson of Cato the Censor (cf. *Su.* 1491 n.) and principal opponent of Julius Caesar in the Roman Civil Wars. He made a famous six-day march across the desert in 47 BC to join his allies at Utica, near modern Tunis, but, seeing their cause was hopeless and preferring his own death to Caesar's proffered favour, he committed suicide. Cf. Lucan, *Pharsalia* ix. As a model of Roman virtue Cato was often celebrated in English literature, notably in Addison's *Cato*, which was one of the first plays seen by T. after his arrival in London in 1725. Cf. *Wi.* 523.

954 Numidia: what is now eastern Algeria.

955 Campania: the fertile region around Naples.

956 Ausonia: Italy.

958 splendid Robber: Julius Caesar.

960 Cf. *Su.* 993, *Wi.* 67, 193, *Cas. Ind.* I. xliii. T.'s several references to demons (or other spirits) of the storm are indebted to the personifications of winds in classical mythology and to Biblical spirits.

961–77 T. took hints for his sandstorm from Lucan, *Pharsalia* ix. 455–92, perhaps by way of Addison, *Cato* II. vi. 51–7; but the burial of a caravan (instead of the soldiers in Lucan or the single soldier in Addison) and other details may be from Bernhard Varenius, *General Geography* (1733), i. 515–16: 'A thick black Cloud, mixed with fiery little Clouds (which are terrible to behold), bring Darkness in the Day, and on a sudden there breaks out a Storm, which is soon over; but it throws such a quantity of red Sand on the Land and Sea, that the *Arabians* say it sometimes buries whole Companies of Merchants and Travellers, with their Camels, *viz.* the Caravans.' 'Red Sand . . . carried up by the Wind . . . causes a red Colour to appear among the Clouds.' See *Background*, pp. 161–2.

970 Commov'd: 'To commove . . . to put into a violent motion' (Johnson, citing 968–9); Lat. *commoveo*.

974 dejected: down.

980 flexile: ' . . . obsequious to any power or impulse' (Johnson, citing 980–1).

983 radiant Line: Equator.

984–6 'Ecnephia(s)' is not in *OED* but is defined in Lewis and Short as 'a hurricane supposed to be produced by blasts from two opposite clouds'. Pliny defines the typhoon as a whirling ecnephias (*Natural History* ii. 131–2). T.'s immediate source for 980–1003 is Bernhard Varenius, *General Geography* (1733), i. 512–17. See *Background*, pp. 163–4.

989   of no Regard: unnoticeable.

993   Gale: 'A wind not tempestuous, yet stronger than a breeze (Johnson); cf. *Sp.* 478, 816, 873, *Su.* 1654.

998   Art: seamanship (in furling the sails).

1010   Lusitanian Prince: generally known as Henry the Navigator (1394–1460); Lusitania was the ancient name for Portugal.

1013–25   From Jean Barbot's 'Description of the Coasts of North and South Guinea' in Churchill's *Collection of Voyages*, v (1732), 225–6; see *Background*, p. 165. T.'s lines inspired Turner's painting *Slavers throwing overboard the Dead and Dying—Typhon coming on* (exh. 1840).

1014   threefold Fate: the shark has three rows of teeth. For 'Fate' as instrument of death, cf. Pope, *Iliad* i. 68, and *Su.* 1022, 1084, 1113, etc.

1028–30   Aristotle believed that insects such as fleas, flies, gnats, and mosquitoes could be spontaneously generated out of putrefying matter by the sun's vital heat. 'Breathes' (1030) may merely indicate that the clouds of destructive insects were wind-borne (cf. *Sp.* 120–2), but may allude to the process of generation, since, according to Aristotle, the *pneuma* (lit. breath, wind), i.e. the life-principle which lies within the semen of higher animals, is also present in the vital heat of the sun. (Aristotle, *On the Generation of Animals* I. i and III. xi; see Loeb edn., Appendix B, pp. 582–4.) Lucretius (vi. 1098–1102) claimed that pestilence arises from the earth, which gathers corruption when smitten by immoderate rain and sunshine.

1041   Admiral Vernon (1684–1757) commanded English attacks upon the Spanish West Indies in 1739–41. He earned great fame by taking Porto Bello (Panama) with only six ships, but his attempt in 1741 to take Cartagena (in what is now Colombia) failed—partly because of the onset of the plague described here by T., but mainly because of the incompetence of the military officers. The siege of Cartagena is described in Smollett's *Roderick Random* (1748), chaps. xxviii–xxxiv.

1045   beamless: unshining, or, perhaps, blind (referring to the Pythagorean theory of vision—that sight emanated from the eye).

1050   blank: pale; cf. *Wi.* 124, *PL* x. 656.

1050   Assistants: those present; cf. Dryden, *Theodore and Honoria* 306 (in *Fables*, 1700): 'The pale Assistants on each other star'd'.

1054   Nemesis: in Greek and Roman mythology the goddess of retribution, who punished insolence towards the gods. I have found no ancient reference to her as the mother of plague; usually she is represented as a virgin. Akenside, perhaps following T., represents Pain, the master of plagues, as 'Son of Nemesis' in *The Pleasures of Imagination* (1744), ii. 484–531.

1055 footnote Richard Mead, in *A Discourse on the Plague* (1720), claimed that the putrefaction of huge heaps of dead locusts in Africa caused plague. Thucydides said that the great plague of Athens began in Upper Ethiopia and spread to Egypt before it came to Greece. Lucretius (vi. 1141) wrote of plague arising from the inmost parts of Egypt. T.'s account (1052–91) is considerably influenced by the powerful description of the plague of Athens in Lucretius vi. 1090–1286 (based on Thucydides ii. 47–52); cf. Ovid, *Metamorphoses* vii. 523–613; Lucan, *Pharsalia* vi. 80–103. See *Background*, pp. 166–8.

1061 incumbent Cloud of Death: cf. Statius, *Thebaid* i. 645–8; *PL* i. 226; *Wi.* 924.

1065 angry Aspect: a position in the heavens that, according to astrologers, foretold disaster.

1066 Dejects: throws down; cf. *Su.* 437, 974, *Au.* 196.

1070 'The great Streets within the City . . . had Grass growing in them.' (Defoe, *Journal of the Plague Year*, ed. L. A. Landa, 1969, p. 101.) Cf. Pepys, *Diary*, 20 Sept. 1665. T.'s whole passage 1070–91 draws upon Defoe's *Journal of the Plague Year*, and upon arguments in the Preface to Richard Mead's *A Discourse on the Plague* (1720) against the policy of confining the families of plague-infected persons to their houses (as in England) or to a district within the *cordon sanitaire* (as in France).

1081 Savag'd: made cruel. 'A word not well authorized' (Johnson, citing only 1080–1).

1090 grim Guards: the *cordon sanitaire*.

1092–1116 Mineral caverns contained bituminous or sulphureous 'dry exhalations' (cf. Aristotle, *Meteorologia* ii. 9, Pliny, *Natural History* ii. 43) which might be ignited below ground to cause earthquakes and volcanic eruptions (cf. *PL* i. 233–5) or be drawn into the air as 'seeds of fire' (cf. Lucretius v. 460–6). When clouds laden with such seeds collided in a war of winds (*Su.* 1114–15, cf. Virgil, *Georgics* i. 318, *PL* ii. 714–18) thunder and lightning would ensue (cf. *PL* ii. 936–7). T.'s primary source was probably Lucretius vi. 96–422, and he made his own work a little more Lucretian in *44* by the deletion of God's 'high Command' (*Su.27*, 745). But see *Su.* 1171–1222 and n.

1093 Cf. *Su.* 628+ (*27*, 644–5) n.

1099 Aspiring: towering; cf. Spenser, *Ruines of Time* 408.

1103 lurid: 'Gloomy; dismal' (Johnson, citing only 1103–4).

1106 (*27*, 739) **damp Abrupt:** abyss full of explosive fire-damp. For 'Abrupt' as noun cf. *PL* ii. 409.

1109 fat: richly resinous.

1113 Touch: equivalent to 'touch-powder', continuing the explosive metaphor of 'Magazine' (1112, cf. *Wi.* 114). Cf. Isaac Hawkins Browne, *Imitation of Thomson*: 14–15 'illume / With the red touch of zeal-enkindling sheet'.

1116–25   Cf. Virgil, *Georgics* i. 356–9, 374–6.

1121   aërial Tribes: birds no longer freely ranging the air. On periphrases see *Sp.* 132 n.

1128   The parallel and contrast here with *Sp.* 161–2 and *Su.* 1233 draw attention to the different emotional implications of the storms.

1128–35a (*27*, 760)   Cf. *Ps.* 18: 13. Direct reference to God was deleted in *44* (cf. *Sp.* 861–4a (*28*, 813–18) n.), as T., in the interests of science, placed less emphasis on God as the Jehovah of the OT. See Introduction, p. xx.

1138   discloses: (intransitive), i.e. opens.

1144–9a (*27*, 778–87)   Perhaps based upon accounts in John Norton, *Natural History of Northamptonshire* (1712), p. 345, relevant passages of which are quoted in *Background*, p. 72.

1150–1a (*27*, 789)   Cf. *PL* i. 612–13, 'As when heaven's fire / Hath scath'd the forest oaks'.

1162   repercussive: 'Driven back; rebounding. Not proper' (Johnson, citing only 1162–5).

1168   Thulè: the name given by ancient geographers to a land north of Britain—perhaps Scandinavia or Iceland. T. is probably referring to the Shetlands here.

1168+ (*27*, 803–26)   Cf. Lucretius (v. 1216–23), who goes on to show that such fears of divine wrath are groundless, since thunderstorms are produced by natural causes. T. deleted these lines in *30q*; cf. *Su.* 1092–1116 n. and 1131 n., *Sp.* 860+ (*28*, 813–18) n.

1171–1222   The hint for this story probably came from newspaper reports of the two rustic lovers struck dead by lightning at Stanton Harcourt, Oxfordshire, in July 1718 (e.g. *Mist's Weekly Journal* 18 Aug. 1718), and from Pope's well-known epitaph upon the lovers. None of Pope's various detailed prose accounts are in print when T. published *Summer* (1727), but cf. *Correspondence of Pope*, ed. G. Sherburn (Oxford, 1956), i. 479. Lucretius (ii. 1090–1104, vi. 387–422), arguing against the notion that events in this world are controlled by divine agency, wrote ironically of the lightning bolt which misses the guilty and strikes the innocent. T.'s irony is directed against Celadon's simple view (1204–14) of a moral universe—an irony emphasized by the echo (1208–10) of Ps. 91: 5. T. makes no attempt to lessen the mystery of Heaven (1215), but, in the manner of the Book of Job (cf. *Wi.260*, Preface), shows God's power and man's incomprehension of God's purposes.

1195   instant: imminent.

1221   dissembled: simulated, cf. Dryden, *Aeneid* viii. 880. 'This is not the true signification' (Johnson). The conceit of a mourner turned by grief to the marble of a tomb was used in William Browne's famous *Epitaph* on the Countess of Pembroke (1621) and in Jonson's *Elegie on the Lady Jane Pawlet* (1631).

1222+ (*27*, 878) **commission'd**: cf. *Su*. 960.

(*27*, 879) **Pool**: whirlpool. Waterspouts (885) and whirlpools were caused by a sudden downward pressure of wind, cf. Lucretius vi. 423–50. T. deleted *27*, 877–89 from *30q*, perhaps because he had now elaborated another storm at sea in *Wi. 28*. See *Wi.* 153–74 and earlier variants.

1225 Sublimer: higher.

1233–42 Cf. *PL* ii. 492–9.

1240 serenes: makes calm; cf. *Sp.* 870.

1247 Gazing: (transitive) staring at; cf. *PL* viii. 258.

1248 meditate: (transitive) fix the attention upon; cf. *Au*. 670, Pope, *Windsor Forest* 102.

1248 Profound: depth; cf. *PL* ii. 980.

1259 keens: 'To keen. To sharpen. An unauthorized word' (Johnson, citing *Su*. 1259); cf. *Cas. Ind.* ii. l. 4.

1262 Illapse: 'Sudden attack; casual coming' (Johnson, citing 1262).

1264–8 The Roman arm may belong to Julius Caesar, who as a boy excelled in swimming, or to Romans in general, for swimming was one of the physical exercises practised in the Iuventus—the youth movement inaugurated by Augustus to provide pre-military training. The ideal of *mens sana in corpore sano* (1267–8, cf. Juvenal, *Satires* x. 356) is at least as old as the ancient Greeks, but T. offers unexpected—even quaint—support for it in the story of Damon and Musidora (1269–1370), added in *30q* and considerably revised in *44*.

1269–1370 The mock-heroic tone of 1285–7 perhaps refers to the unlucky chance by which Paris (cf. 1304) was called to make his judgement between the goddesses and set in train events which led to the fall of Troy. The version of T.'s story in *30q* is closer to the Judgement of Paris inasmuch as Damon sees three naked women who are likened to Juno (Hera), Pallas Athene, and the Cyprian goddess Aphrodite (*30q*, 994–1003). Whereas Paris found Aphrodite the most beautiful, Damon fixes his heart upon Musidora, the woman who corresponds to Athene, goddess of Wisdom. In *30q* T. represents Damon as a Stoic, devoted to 'false philosophy', who is humanized by a suddenly aroused love of beauty (984–6, 1032–7), but this scanty dress of philosophical instruction is flung away in *44*, where Damon becomes a lover, and T.'s appeal to prurience (1298–9) is simple and unashamed. Episodes in which a man spies upon women bathing are common in literature: cf. Actaeon (Ovid, *Metamorphoses* iii. 155–205), who is not humanized by the experience, and Sir Guyon (*Faerie Queene* ii. xii. 63–8), whose Stoicism remains unaffected. In Sidney, *New Arcadia* Book II (*Works* (14th edn., 1725), i. 245–8), Pyrocles, disguised as an Amazon, watches his mistress Philoclea and two other ladies bathing in the River Ladon, an Arcadian stream (cf. *Su*. 1301). The other hero of the *Arcadia* is called Musidorus, and much is made of lovers writing poems on sand, stone, and trees. Sacharissa and Amoret (cf.

30q, 989–90) are names of Waller's poetical mistresses; Amoret is a character in Spenser's *Faerie Queene* Book III. Grant, p. 102, suggests as T.'s possible source Samuel Croxall, 'On Florinda seen bathing', in *The Fair Circassian* (1720). Another possible source is Welsted's *Acon and Lavinia* (in *The Freethinker* 98 and 99, 27 Feb. and 2 Mar., 1718).

1288 Loves: Cupids, or frolicsome boy-gods of love; cf. Spenser, *Amoretti* xvi. 6.

1301 Arcadia: the mountainous district of central Greece where, in ancient times, Pan was worshipped. After it was mentioned in Virgil's *Eclogues* it came to be regarded as an ideal region of love and joy.

1315–20 Not surprisingly, Musidora was painted in this pose by many English artists, including Gainsborough and Etty.

1319 doubtful: causing apprehension; cf. T.'s *Agamemnon* (1738), III. i. 53.

1325 Crystal: clear water; cf. Denham, *Cooper's Hill* 322.

1327 Aurora: see *Su.* 828 n.

1347 footnote This statue was regarded as 'the standard of all female beauty' (Joseph Spence, *Polymetis* (1747), p. 66). T. describes it in *Liberty* iv (1736), 175–84. A drawing of the subject by Castelli was in T.'s *Sale Catalogue*. One of the four bathers in Kent's design for the plate to accompany *Summer* in *30q* (see p. xlix) is represented in the Venus de Medici pose. This bather was one of those removed when the 1738 octavo-size plates were re-engraved for use in 1744 (see Introduction, p. lxx).

1356 sudden: impetuous; cf. *PL* ii. 738. 'Not in use' (Johnson).

1364 Incumbent: leaning; cf. *Sp.* 41.

1364 silvan Pen: knife (The implausibility of Musidora's feat of carving suggests that T. may have regarded this whole episode as agreeable nonsense.)

1371 The sun is setting. T. wrote to David Mallet, 11 Aug. 1726, about *Summer*, 'I resolved to contract the season into a day.' (*Letters*, p. 45.)

1375 romantic: see *Sp.* 1028 n.

1383 pathetic: sympathetic.

1391 Sons of Interest: self-interested persons.

1391 Romance: 'A lie; a fiction. In common speech' (Johnson).

1393 Portico: the Painted Porch in ancient Athens where Zeno taught his philosophy.

1394 Lyceum: the garden with covered walks at Athens where Aristotle taught his philosophy.

1401 Amanda: see *Sp.* 483 n.

1408 Richmond Hill commanded one of the eighteenth century's most praised views. After 1736 T.'s home was in Kew Foot Lane, Richmond.

1410 Augusta: see *Sp.* 108 n.

1414 Contrast: juxtaposition of forms, colours, etc., as in painting.

1418–24 Harrington's retreat (1419) was Petersham Lodge, built in the 1720s for William Stanhope, Earl of Harrington. The pendent woods (1418) belonged to one of the very earliest English landscape gardens, laid out before 1713 by an earlier possessor of the estate—Henry Hyde, Earl of Rochester. Hyde's second daughter, Kitty, was the famous beauty and eccentric who married Charles Douglas (1698–1778), third Duke of Queensbury (referred to at line 1423). John Gay the poet lived with the Queensburys at Ham House (cf. 1420), near Twickenham, for the last four years of his life. The Duchess also befriended Congreve, Swift, Prior, Pope and T. Hyde's eldest surviving son was Henry, Viscount Cornbury (1710–53—referred to at line 1424), a High Church Tory MP, author, and friend of Bolingbroke, Pope, Swift, and T. Harrington, Cornbury, Queensbury, and Bolingbroke all subscribed to the 1730 quarto *Seasons*. The brilliant Ham House circle was a centre of opposition to Walpole and George II.

1427 Alexander Pope laid out a famous garden at his house in Twickenham, for the significance of which see Maynard Mack, *The Garden and the City* (Toronto, 1969). Pope fell fatally ill early in 1744, shortly before T. wrote these lines, and died 30 May. Cf. *Wi.* 550–4, *Liberty* v. 696–701.

1429–32 Henry Pelham (1696–1754), the Whig politician, was Secretary at War, Paymaster-General, and, from 1743 to his death, Prime Minister. His estate, Claremont (cf. 1429), at Esher on the River Mole in Surrey, had one of the most famous landscape gardens of the eighteenth century—laid out by Charles Bridgman and Vanbrugh before 1726 and later remodelled by William Kent; cf. Pope, *Epilogue to the Satires*, ii. 66–7. Kent's illustrations for the 1730 quarto *Seasons*, where in *Spring* he represents a Palladian villa standing directly in a natural landscape, pre-date his efforts as a gardener to realize such a composition on the ground. See Kenneth Woodbridge, 'William Kent as Landscape-Gardener', *Apollo* c (1974), 134–5.

1434 Achaia: the Roman province of southern Greece.

1434 Hesperia: 'western land'; a name for Italy.

1435–7 See Introduction p. xxx above. The whole passage 1371–1437 was first added in *44*, after T. had gone to live at Richmond.

1441 Smoke: blue haze (as in a Claude Lorrain landscape painting, cf. *Sp.* 950–62 n., *Cas. Ind.* I. xxxviii. 8.)

1442 Here begins a patriotic panegyric (1442–1619) highly characteristic of the eighteenth-century English georgic; the model is Virgil's praise of fruitful, prosperous Italy, the nurse of great men; cf. *Georgics* ii. 138–76. Until *44* T.'s panegyric followed the line corresponding to *Su.* 628 in the present edition. Between 1727 and 1744 the panegyric was nearly doubled in length, and, though the praise of Scotsmen was transferred to

Autumn in 1730 (cf. *Au.* 862–949 and n.), the number of English worthies was increased, gradually, through various editions. In 1727 there were nine—More, Bacon, Barrow, Tillotson, Boyle, Locke, Newton, Shakespeare, and Milton. In 1730 the preachers Barrow and Tillotson were withdrawn, and Sir Philip Sidney, Walsingham, Drake, Raleigh, Hampden, Algernon Sidney, Russell, and Ashley (i.e. Shaftesbury) added. In 1744 were added Alfred, the Edwards and Henrys, Spenser, and Chaucer. The completed list of names makes up a pantheon of English patriotism, liberty, enlightenment, and humanity, but the choice of politicians (and even of philosophers) betrays a strong Whig bias. It is significant that eleven of the men named by T. in this list were also commemorated in the Shrine of British Worthies (cf. *Au.* 1050 n.) which was gradually assembled at Stowe in the 1730s and early 40s.

1442–5 British Liberty the Queen of Arts scattering plenty—with the assistance of Property (1455) and gay Drudgery (1459)—is the political counterpart to Nature, whose liberality is referred to at, e.g., *Sp.* 98–9, 230–1, *Su.* 126–8.

1456 guarded: a revision in *44*, perhaps to remove the possible ambiguity of 'certain' (*27*, 512) and continue the thought of Property (1455) and Guardian-Oaks (material for warships, 1448).

1465 Sheet: sail; not what a sailor would call a sheet, cf. William Falconer, *The Shipwreck* (3rd edn., 1769) ii. 163 n.: 'The sheets, which are universally mistaken by the English poets and their readers, for the sails themselves, are no other than the ropes used to extend the *clues*, or lower corners of the sails to which they are attached.'

1470 listed Plain: literally, ground enclosed for jousting (cf. Milton, *Samson Agonistes* 1087), but T. means battlefield here.

1479–87 King Alfred and Edward the Black Prince were particular heroes of the Whig opposition. In *Craftsman* 478 (6 Sept. 1735) it was reported that Frederick, Prince of Wales, had commissioned a statue of King Alfred with an inscription in which Alfred was said to be '*the Founder of the Liberties and Commonwealth of England*', and also a statue of the Black Prince with an inscription promising that Frederick would make '*that amiable Prince the pattern of his own Conduct.*' Frederick is unmistakably represented under the guise of Prince Edward (later Edward I) as hero of T.'s *Edward and Eleonora* (1739), the public performance of which was banned by the Lord Chamberlain as seditious. Alfred is hero of the masque *Alfred* by T. and Mallet, commissioned by Frederick and performed privately before him in 1740; see Grant, pp. 169–94. Alfred, Edward III, and Henry V are praised in T.'s *Liberty* iv. 731–4, 840–67. I am not sure which other Henrys are intended at *Su.* 1484, but Henry I conquered Normandy and Henry II acquired a considerable part of France. Lyttelton was writing his long *History of Henry II* (1767–71) as early as 1741, three years before T. printed this passage.

1482 saint: canonize.

1488 More: Sir Thomas More (1478–1535), Lord Chancellor,

convicted of high treason and executed for his refusal to accept Henry VIII
as Supreme Head of the English Church. More appears in all versions of
T.'s list of worthies from *27*, but the qualifications implied in 'mistaken'
and 'useful' do not appear until *44*. 'Useful' is explained in *Liberty* iv
(1736), where T. writes of the suppression of the monasteries after which

> —wide-dispers'd, their useless fetid Wealth
> In graceful Labour bloom'd, and Fruits of Peace.　(908–9)

1491　Cato: The reference here may be to Cato the Censor (234–149
BC), patriot and fearless opponent of corruption and luxury in the Roman
republic, or, perhaps, to his great-grandson Cato of Utica, cf. *Su.* 954 n.

1491　Aristides: Aristides the Just (d. 468 BC), Athenian democratic
leader celebrated for rectitude, patriotism, and moderation. The intrigues
of Themistocles (cf. *Wi.* 464) brought about Aristides' ostracism, but
when he was allowed to return to Athens he assisted Themistocles with
service and advice in the war against Persia. Cf. *Wi.* 459.

1492　Cincinnatus: Lucius Quinctius Cincinnatus was the traditional
exemplar of early Roman pious frugality. In 458 BC, when the Roman
army was in danger of defeat, he was called from the plough and made
dictator; he defeated the enemy and returned to his farm. Cf. *Sp.* 60, *Wi.*
512.

1494　Walsingham: Sir Francis Walsingham (1536–90), diplomat and
statesman.

1496 During his circumnavigation of the world, 1577–80, Sir Francis
Drake captured or destroyed many Spanish ships.

1498　Maiden Reign: of Elizabeth I.

1499–1510 Sir Walter Raleigh wrote his *History of the World* while
imprisoned in the Tower of London (1603–15) on the unjust charge of
high treason. After the failure in 1618 of Raleigh's expedition to Guiana to
find gold for James I, the king placated the Spaniards by having Raleigh
executed in accordance with the sentence passed thirteen years earlier. T.'s
Whiggish detestation of the 'Coward-Reign' (1502) of James I emerges
even more strongly in *Liberty* iv (1736), 957–81.

1505–6a (*30q*, 586)　**retorted:** turned back, cf. Pope, *Iliad* xvii. 120.

1509　prov'd: experienced.

1511　Sidney: Sir Philip Sidney (1554–86), courtier, soldier, states-
man, poet, and novelist.

1513　Lover's Myrtle: see *Au.* 211–12 n.

1514　Hampden: John Hampden (1594–1643), Parliamentarian;
praised in *Liberty* iv. 1012–15.

1518 Seventeenth-century Parliamentarians who sought to limit the
king's prerogative claimed to be restoring a 'native freedom', i.e. the
ancient Saxon liberties of the people which had been lost at the Norman
Conquest. Cf. T., *Liberty* iv (1736), 689–762; see Christopher Hill, 'The
Norman Yoke', in *Puritanism and the Revolution* (1958), pp. 50–122.

1519 effulg'd: shone.

1520 late Time: the distant future.

1523 Russel: William, Lord Russell (1639–83), a republican, executed for complicity in the Rye House Plot; greatly admired in life and death by the Whigs. For 1522–3 cf. *Lycidas* 151.

1525 giddy Reign: of Charles II.

1528 Algernon Sidney (1622–83) was one of the judges at the trial of Charles I, was executed for his part in the Rye House Plot, and, like Russell, was a hero of the Whigs. Cf. *Liberty* iv. 1096. He is called the 'British Brutus' when he first appears in the poem, in *30q*, and in the revisions of *MS*, so the substitution of 'Cassius' was perhaps made in proof, possibly in the interests of euphony, and possibly to avoid confusion with Brutus the mythical founder of Britain. Like both of those upright murderers of Caesar, Sidney was a republican. The 'ancient' learning and freedom (1530–1) probably refer to Roman republicanism, but it is possible that Saxon freedom is also implied; see *Su.* 1518 n.

1535 Bacon: Francis Bacon (1561–1626), Lord Chancellor, was dismissed in 1621 for accepting bribes. T. praises him as a philosopher, particularly as the author of the *Novum Organum* (1620), the 'new instrument' which enunciated the inductive principles of experiment that have been the basis for most subsequent scientific investigation.

1542 the Stagyrite: Aristotle, native of the ancient Macedonian city of Stagira.

1542 Tully: Cicero; cf. *Wi.* 521.

1549–50 T. appears to disregard the sharp line of division that Bacon drew in his *Novum Organum* between human discovery and divine revelation. This notion of a progress of knowledge up the chain of being (cf. *Su.* 334 n.), in accordance with T.'s theory of vital ascent (see *Wi.* 603–8 n.), was introduced in *44*.

1551 The Third Earl of Shaftesbury (1671–1713) was the moral philosopher who taught that men possessed an intuitive moral sense which naturally inclined them to act benevolently towards all creatures around them; see *Sp.* 878–903 n. T.'s introduction of the heterodox Shaftesbury into his list of worthies in 1730, coupled with the expulsion of those orthodox divines Barrow and Tillotson (*27*, 539), perhaps indicates that his own religious position was shifting towards Deism.

1556 Boyle: Hon. Robert Boyle (1627–91), chemist, physicist, and theologian, and a founder of the Royal Society. In *44* T. deleted his earlier praise (*27*, 545) of the Boyle Lectures founded for the 'Proof of the Christian Religion against Atheists and other notorious Infidels' which were instituted under the terms of Boyle's will. Cf. Steele, *Guardian* 175 (1 Oct. 1713).

1559 A reference to Locke's *Essay concerning Human Understanding* (1690); cf. *Su.* 1788–805 nn.

1560–3 Newton might be described as 'pure Intelligence' because he sternly followed what he called the 'mathematical way' and would frame no hypotheses. His account of the system of the world in the *Principia* (1686–7) was abstract and schematic (no more and no less than a set of mathematical principles)—unlike the 'pictorial' representation of the world favoured by the so-called 'Mechanical Philosophers' of the earlier seventeenth century, Descartes, Hobbes, and Gassendi. Newton's principles were 'simple' because, as he said, 'Nature is wont to be simple, and always consonant to itself.' Cf. *Poem to Newton*, especially lines 68–90, and Introduction, p. xxii above.

1566 Shakespeare's 'wildness' (what Nicholas Rowe in his *Life of Shakespeare*, 1709, called his 'furor poeticus') was a commonplace of eighteenth-century criticism. Cf. Milton, *L'Allegro* 133–4.

1568 Dryden had declared that the powers of Homer and Virgil met and joined in Milton: 'Verses written under Mr. Milton's picture', *PL* (4th edn., 1688).

1572–5 T. praises those aspects of Spenser's verse that he sought to recapture in *The Castle of Indolence*.

1594 **She**: the soul.

1602 **Thou**: God.

1604–19 This description functions like a patriotic allegorical painting where—typical of this period and of T.—Public Zeal is in the foreground. Cf. the Power of Cultivation (*Su.* 1436 and Introduction p. xxx above), Liberty and the Queen of Arts (1442–3), Property (1455), and Drudgery (1459).

1607 The shedding of tears through smiles is common in romance; cf. Achilles Tatius, *Clitophon and Leucippe* VI. vii. 2; Sidney, *New Arcadia*, *Works* (14th edn., 1725), i. 2.

1620 **broadens**: 'I know not whether this word occurs, but in the following passage' (Johnson, citing 1620–1); but cf. *Wi.* 132. The sun broadens because its light, passing at a low angle through a broad belt of atmosphere, is refracted. T.'s revision of 1620–9 in *44* deletes Newtonian references to the solar spectrum (*27*, 942–4) in order to continue a personification with mythological elaboration.

1626 **Amphitritè**: wife of Poseidon the sea-god; her bower is the sea and her tending nymphs the Oceanids; cf. Ovid, *Fasti* v. 731, *Metamorphoses* i. 14.

1641–6 See *Sp.* 878–903 n.

1647 **Confess'd**: disclosed.

1647–54 John Scott (*Critical Essays* (1785), pp. 353–4) deplored the mingling of personification and natural description here, but the misalliance is less unhappy than in *Su.* 1620.

1649 **middle Air**: cf. *Su.* 768 n.

1654 Face of Things: cf. *Wi.* 57, *PL* v. 43.

1654–6 'A fresher Gale', etc., is quoted in the catalogue entry for Constable's *The Cornfield* (exh. 1826).

1660 Amusive: engaging the attention. Cf. *Sp.* 216.

1672–5 Cf. *PL* i. 781–8.

1686 Stygian: black as the River Styx in Hades (the infernal regions of classical mythology).

1687 erroneous: wandering. 'This circle, by being placed here, stopped much of the erroneous light' (Newton, *Opticks*, 1721, p. 91); cf. *PL* vii. 20.

1700 lambent Lightnings: shooting stars.

1703–29 T.'s description of a comet, introduced in *44* to occupy the place of the aurora borealis description (27, 1044–75) which was transferred to *Au.* in *30q*, could have been occasioned by the appearance of a conspicuous comet—the finest of its century—which was discovered on 9 December 1743 and reached its perihelion in March 1744 (*Notes and Queries*, 6 June 1896, pp. 443–4). There is no indication in *MS* that T. in the autumn of 1743 had any intention of adding a description of a comet to his poem.

1705 Worlds: the planets of distant stars (referring to the theory of a plurality of worlds, see *Su.* 107 n.).

1713 sequacious: 'Following; attendant' (Johnson, citing 1711–16).

1720–22 Cf. *Poem to Newton* 76-81.

1725–9 'The vapours which arise from the sun, the fixed stars, and the tails of the comets may meet at last with, and fall into, the atmospheres of the planets by their gravity; and there be condensed and turned into water and humid spirits . . . So fixed stars that have been gradually wasted by the light and vapours emitted from them for a long time may be recruited by comets that fall upon them; and from this fresh supply of new fuel those old stars, acquiring new splendour, may pass for new stars' (Newton, *Principia*, trans. Andrew Motte, 1729, ii. 387, 385). Here Newton, most uncharacteristically, has framed hypotheses; cf. *Su.* 1560–3 n. Mallet versified this hypothesis in *The Excursion* (1728), ii. 293–305. See *Background*, pp. 66–8.

1730 Philosophy: natural philosophy, i.e. science, which should tutor poetry; cf. *Su.* 1753.

1735–6 'Heavenly airs that are played to the departed souls of good men upon their first arrival in Paradise to wear out the impression of the last agonies.' (Addison, 'Visions of Mirzah,' *Spectator* 159.)

1744–52 Succinctly states the poet's dual interest in Nature. Cf. *Sp.* 111–13 n., 455 n.

1747 Essence: God; cf. *Sp.* 557.

1753–6   These lines (to 'never to die') were engraved on the monument erected to T. in Richmond church.

1754   **informs**: gives life to; cf. *Sp.* 860.

1758–81   Cf. *Au.* 43–150 n.

1788–99   This passage draws upon Locke's *Essay concerning Human Understanding*. Our first and simplest ideas are received passively from sensations (*Essay* II. i–v); the idea of perception is the first to result from our reflecting actively upon these simple ideas (*Essay* II. ix); reflecting further upon (compounding, ordering, dividing) our ideas, we may build up ever more complex ideas—some of them false and fantastical (*Essay*, Book II, cf. *Wi.* 609–16). However, God has set limits upon the extent of human knowledge (*Essay* IV. iii).

1789   **ideal Kingdom**: the mind, with its ideas, i.e. objects of understanding; cf. Locke, *Essay concerning Human Understanding*, I. i. 8.

1796–1805   T. incorporates Locke's psychology—as he incorporates Pythagoras' vegetarianism and the old notion of the great chain of being —into his theory of vital ascent or spiritual evolution; cf. *Sp.* 374–8 n., *Su.* 344 n., *Wi.* 603–8 n.

AUTUMN

1–3   Cf. Spenser, *Faerie Queene* VII ('Mutabilitie'), vii. 30.

3   **Doric Reed**: rustic pipe. The Doric dialect of ancient Greece was used by Theocritus in some of his idylls, and thereafter 'Doric' was often a synonym for the language of pastoral poetry or of country people.

4–5   See *Sp.* 563 n. and *Wi.* 694 n.

7   **Concocted**: ripened, cf. *Su.* 909.

9   **Onslow**: Arthur Onslow (1691–1768), Speaker of the House of Commons, 1727–61; patron of Richardson and Young as well as of T.

12   **Public Voice**: Parliament.

14   **Front**: face (Johnson, citing 13–14); cf. *Sp.* 880, *Su.* 490, *Au.* 521; Lat. *frons*.

16   **Maze of Eloquence**: agreeably winding river of words (cf. *Sp.* 577, *Su.* 606); T. repeats the phrase at *Wi.* 688–9 (also 'listening Senate' *Wi.* 680).

18   **pants for public Virtue**: desires to serve a worthy political cause. *Au.* 18–22 refer to *Britannia* (1729) and T.'s ambitions to write other political poems—ambitions fulfilled in *Liberty* (1735–6) and the plays.

23   **Virgin**: Virgo, the sixth sign of the zodiac, into which the sun enters about 23 August (about 12 August in T.'s day).

24   **Libra**: the Scales, the seventh sign of the zodiac, into which the sun enters at the autumnal equinox (22 or 23 Sept.)—hence 'equal scales', cf. Virgil, *Georgics* i. 208. Owing to the precession of the equinoxes (cf.

Sp. 26 n.) the sun's apparent path at the autumnal equinox would lie in T.'s day, as it lies at present, among the stars of the constellation Virgo, but T.'s zodiacal references are always to signs, not constellations.

43–150 As in *Sp.* 32–77, *Su.* 352–431, 1406–1619, a particular rural scene prompts T. to expansive, optimistic reflections on Britain's great- ness—in this case in the generalized form of a Whig myth of progress based on Lucretius, v. 925–1457, with hints of Virgil, *Georgics* i. 125–46. However, T. recognizes only the gains of progress, where Lucretius had recognized that material progress is accompanied by moral decay. The dominant verb in T.'s passage is raise (47, 76, 83, 119, 138); cf. rous'd (73), aspiring (117), shot up (125), heav'd (134), exalts (142). For a contrary view of progress see *Sp.* 242–335, *Au.* 1235–1351.

47–8 Cf. *Cas. Ind.* I. xi. 1, 'Outcast of Nature, Man!'

50 Cf. 'seeds of freedom', *Liberty* iii. 539–40; 'moral seeds', *Cas. Ind.* II. xi. 9. Lucretius refers to atoms, the first elements of all matter, as *semina rerum*. For the many kinds of 'seeds' in English nature-descriptive verse and scientific prose see Arthos, pp. 300–6. Locke, *Thoughts concern- ing Education* (1692), sect. 84, 100, likens the developing mind to a seed- plot.

58–9 On acorns as food of primitive man, cf. Virgil, *Georgics* i. 7; Horace, *Satires* I. iii. 99–102, Ovid, *Metamorphoses* i. 106.

97 **Public:** community or commonwealth.

116 **twining woody Haunts:** the constructing of wattle-huts.

121–33 Cf. Pope, *Windsor Forest* (1713), 219–24, 385–7. Britain's naval and mercantile strength was a favourite subject for early eighteenth- century poets; cf. *Sp.* 32–77 n. The reference in 130–3 is to the building and launching of a ship of the line—probably the most impressive in- dustrial spectacle of T.'s age. Between 1726 and 1730 T. lived near the Tower of London and could have gone to see launchings at the Royal Dockyards in Deptford.

125 **Sheet:** sail; cf. *Su.* 1465.

134 **magnific:** magnificent; cf. *PL* v. 773, x. 354.

135 **Luxury:** 'there is no Word more inconsistently used and capri- ciously applied to particular Actions or of more uncertain Meaning when denominating those Actions, than the Word *Luxury*.' (William Warburton, *Divine Legation of Moses* (1738), Book I, sect. 6.) T. uses the word pejor- atively at *Au.* 1249 and neutrally at *Sp.* 53.

143 'The thought of Winter—not a man in wintertime, but personified Winter—sitting by a social fire and being happy to hear the tempest ex- cluded, is somewhat difficult to grasp.' (P. M. Spacks, *The Varied God* (Berkeley and Los Angeles, 1959), p. 32.)

151–66 'Especially evocative of the details of' Poussin's painting *Summer: Ruth and Boaz*, according to Jeffry Spencer, *Heroic Nature* (Evanston, 1973), p. 275 n.

157   lusty: full of vigorous growth.

166   Spike: ear of corn (Johnson, citing 165–6); Lat. *spica*.

167–9   The instruction of Boaz to his reapers; cf. Ruth 2: 16. The story that follows, at lines 177–310, is modelled upon the Book of Ruth. John Nichols asserts in his edition of Welsted's *Works* (1787), p. xxiii, that Welsted's *Acon and Lavinia* (see *Su.* 1269–370 n.) gave the names for T.'s tale (Acon suggesting Acasto), and hints for *Au.* 192–4, 201–6, and *Su.* 1325–7. Welsted wrote a verse-epistle entitled *Palaemon to Caelia* (1717). Palaemon also occurs in Virgil, *Eclogues* iii, Chaucer, *The Knight's Tale*, and Shaftesbury, *The Moralists* (1709); Lavinia in the *Aeneid*, and Acasto in Ovid, *Fasti* i. 55.

176   faint: half-heartedly.

181–3, 189–91   This comparison between birds and human beings complements *Sp.* 680-6.

189   Nature's common Bounty: nuts, berries, etc., growing on common or waste land. In a birthday poem to Elizabeth Young T. refers to birds as 'Nature's Commoners' (*Letters*, p. 177); cf. 'Commoners of Nature', *Agamemnon* (1738), III. i. 9.

203–17a (*30q*, 211)   **deign their faith:** condescend to believe.

211–12   There are Biblical references to planting the lovely, fragrant myrtle in the wilderness; cf. Isaiah 41: 19, 55: 13. In classical mythology the tree was dedicated to Venus; cf. Pliny, *Natural History* xii. 3, and *Su.* 1513, 'Lover's Myrtle'.

220–3   Cf. the chorus describing the Golden Age in Act I of Tasso's *Aminta* (1593). For Arcadia see *Su.* 1301 n.

290–3   Before Lyttelton's revisions T. had allowed Acasto to offer his estate without attaching the condition of matrimony.

296–7   Enlightened benevolence is divinely raised above the vulgar joy because conscious of itself; cf. *Sp.* 878–903 n. Virgil, *Aeneid* v. 455, has *conscia virtus*, i.e. 'conscious valour'.

322   eddy in: collect as into an eddy.

333a (*30q*, 330)   **glomerating:** 'To glomerate. To gather into a ball or sphere' (Johnson). Cf. Virgil, *Georgics* i. 323–4: 'et foedam glomerant tempestatem imbribus atris / collectae ex alto nubes.' *Au.* 330–43 echo *Georgics* i. 322–7, 482–3, *Aeneid* ii. 496–7.

337   Red: T. may have in mind the red soil of the Cheviot region.

360–492   The hunting scenes are in the tradition of the English georgic and local poem; cf. Denham, *Cooper's Hill* (1668 edn.), 241–318, Pope, *Windsor Forest* (1713), 13–119, 147–58, John Philips, *Cyder* (1708), ii. 169–76, Gay, *Rural Sports* (1720), 289–342, 367–87, T's 'Of a Country Life', 67–89. However, in T.'s handling of this well-worn material an element of burlesque slowly emerges—to become quite plain with the mock-heroic 'O glorious he' (492) and the following drinking-scene.

363–71 The spaniel is trained to 'draw' (365) or 'set' the game, so that the birds remain immobile watching the dog until the huntsman has been able to cast a net over them; Cf. Pope, *Windsor Forest* 99–104, Gay, 'The setting-dog and the partridge', in *Fables*.

364 tainted Gale: light breeze imbued with the scent of an animal; cf. Pope, *Windsor Forest* 101, *Essay on Man* i. 214.

372–7 The rhythms convey the effect of surging flight broken by sudden death.

375 sounding: see *Sp.* 696 n.

395 gentle Days: days of calm weather—not during the gales described at *Au.* 311–59. 'Never take out your hounds on a very windy, or bad day' (Peter Beckford, *Thoughts on Hunting* (1781), letter ix).

404 chapt: cut short.

405 Lawn: glade; cf. *Sp.* 697.

408 Concoctive: ripening by heat; cf. *Su.* 909, *Au.* 7.

411–12 The hare 'has very prominent eyes, placed backwards in its head so that it can almost see behind it as it runs. These are never wholly closed, but as the animal is continually upon the watch it sleeps with them open' (Goldsmith, *History of Earth and Animated Nature* (1774), Book V, chap. ii).

416 sullen Openings: deep-toned barking of dogs; cf. *Sp.* 266.

426–57 All details of T.'s stag-hunt are modelled closely upon Denham, *Cooper's Hill* (1668 edn.), 241–318, except the tears at *Au.* 454 (from Shakespeare, *As You Like It* ii. i. 36–40), which contradict *Sp.* 349–51.

427 branching: antlered; cf. *Wi.* 818 and *PL* vii. 470.

440 circling thro': sweeping in a circle to pick up the scent again.

462 protended: held out in front; cf. Pope, *Iliad* xv. 888.

465 shaggy Foe: wolfhound. The last wolf in Scotland was killed in 1743, but wolves had disappeared from England probably two hundred years earlier (Anthony Dent, 'The Last of the Wolf', *History Today* xxiv (1974), 120–7). In 1730 wolves were still hunted regularly in many parts of Europe; cf. *Wi.* 389–413.

469 lighten: flash like lightning.

469 nervous: well-strung, sinewy.

472 nightly Robber: fox.

488 evolv'd: unrolled or made clear.

494 ghostly Halls of grey Renown: old-fashioned houses.

496 decent: fittingly (like 'graced', the word is used ironically).

497 antick Figures: old (and perhaps grotesque) portraits.

500 Thessalian Centaurs: fabulous creatures combining the body and legs of a horse with the torso, head, and arms of a man. Their legendary battle with the Lapithae, which occurred at a banquet after heavy drinking, is alluded to in mock-Miltonic descriptions of drinking-bouts by John Philips (*Cyder* (1708), ii. 476–9) and Gay (*Wine* (1708), 179), both of which furnished T. with hints for this passage. Thessaly is the part of north-eastern Greece south of Macedonia.

516 Maia: Roman goddess who gave her name to the month of May; cf. Ovid, *Fasti* v. 1.

517 diffus'd: stretched out; cf. *Su.* 707.

519 Strong ale, brewed in October and kept for several years to become even stronger, was regarded as the particular drink of those boorish, lesser country squires who were thought by many men to be the backbone of the Tory party. Defoe wrote pamphlets attacking Tory extremists under the name of the 'October Club'. Steele's *Tatler* 118 ridicules a Tory squire: 'All the hours he spent at home were in swilling himself with October and rehearsing the wonders he did in the field.' Cf. Addison, *Freeholder* 22.

521 Front: face (as usual in T.), cf. *Sp.* 880, *Su.* 490, *Au.* 14. The ale is personified.

528 Gammon: the game of backgammon.

531 'frequent' [i.e. 'crowded'] 'and full' is quoted from *PL* i. 797; 'divan' (originally an oriental council of state) is used to describe the council in Hell in *PL* x. 457 (and cf. *Su.27, 675*). T. makes other mock-heroic references to the Hellish assemblies in Milton's poem: e.g. 'perplexed' (542); cf. *PL* ii. 525; and *Au.* 550–2, cf. *PL* ii. 284–90.

539 Cf. John Philips, *Cyder* (1708), ii. 452–3.

554-5 Cf. Juvenal, *Satire* vi (trans. Dryden, 1693), 422–3.

558 Gazetteers: newspapers.

562 Cf. the lubber (Robin Goodfellow) lying asleep beside the fire in Milton's *L'Allegro* 110–2. On Lob in Shakespeare, *Midsummer Night's Dream* II. i. 16, Johnson comments '*Lob, Lubber, Looby, Lobcock*, all denote inactivity of body and dulness of mind.' T.'s Lubber Power is the personification of drunkenness, and, after Hunger and Thirst (512) and Whist (524), makes a fitting end to the allegorical pageant—a burlesque counterpart to such set-pieces as *Su.* 1604–19.

566 black: i.e. the colour of the clergyman's dress. In Hogarth's *A Midnight Modern Conversation* (engraved 1733) the parson appears least intoxicated in a company of drunkards. Socrates remains more sober than his flock at the end of Plato's *Symposium*.

570–609 These lines well exemplify a prevalent eighteenth-century attitude to what was called 'the fair sex', 'the weaker sex', or 'the sex'; cf. *Tatler* and *Spectator passim*. When T. wrote to his sister to give his consent to her forthcoming marriage in 1740 he said: 'The economy and gentle management of a family is woman's natural province, and from that her best praise arises' (*Letters*, p. 132).

575   spring: 'To pass by leaping. A barbarous use' (Johnson, citing 576–7).

587   nobler Game: cf. Young, *Love of Fame* (1728), satire v 'On Women', 114.

589–90   The hoop-petticoat was a frequent object of male satire; cf. Addison, *Tatler* 116 and frequently elsewhere in the *Tatler* and the *Spectator*.

595   Perhaps T. intended to write 'Disclosing in its every motion charm'.

597:   i.e. to embroider; cf. Cowper, *The Task* iv. 150–3.

598   tuneful Page: music score.

599–600   To lend ... Dainties: 'surely his diction is above his subject, if he meant the making of sweetmeats, conserves, and pickles' (John Scott, *Critical Essays* (1785), p. 337).

600–1   in their Race ... Life: educate their daughters.

612   close Array: perhaps 'close-fitting dress' which would not be caught on the tangling shrub, or perhaps 'closed ranks', so that individual girls would not be separated and lost in the thickets; cf. 'meet Array', *Au.* 1117.

620   ardent: shining; cf. *Au.* 691.

621   Melinda: identity unknown. In Sept. 1729 T. wrote affectionately of some unnamed woman, a neighbour of David Mallet's at Shawford near Winchester; see *Letters*, pp. 65–6.

626   Error: roving excursion, irregular course (Johnson); cf. *PL* iv. 239.

633   gentle Race: fruit.

644–51   *Cyder* (1708), written by John Philips (1676–1708) in imitation of Virgil's *Georgics*, describes, with patriotic digressions, the cultivation of cider apples and the making and the virtues of cider. Philips is 'second' (645) in importance to Milton (the 'British Muse' of *Wi.* 535) as a writer of blank verse. 'Rhyme-unfetter'd' (646) refers to Milton's remarks on the bondage of rhyme in his note on 'The Verse' prefacing *PL*.

645   Pomona: see *Su.* 663 n.

648   Silurian: Herefordshire; referring to the Silures, a British tribe who lived west of the River Severn in Roman Britain.

653   equal: moderately, because this is about the time of the equinox; cf. *Au.* 24 n.

655   For Dodington see *Su.* 29 n. His seat was Eastbury in Dorset, where a magnificent house was designed by Sir John Vanbrugh and gardens by Vanbrugh and Charles Bridgeman. When T. wrote *Au.* the house was still being built (cf. 662–4); it was not completed until 1738. As it proved too large and expensive for anyone to live in, it was partially dismantled soon after Dodington's death in 1762.

660 Dome: house; cf. *Sp.* 650. Eastbury had no 'dome' in the modern sense.

664 green: see *Sp.* 321 n.

667 The phrase referring to Edward Young (1683–1765) was added in *44*, after the first five books of his moralizing, eminently virtuous blank-verse poem in nine books, *Night Thoughts* (1742–5), had been published. Young acted as intermediary when Dodington offered patronage to T. (see Introduction, p. xlii above) and frequently visited Eastbury, where he wrote some of his poetry.

668–72 Cf. *Su.* 185–96 n.

670 meditate: (transitive); cf. *Su.* 1248, Milton, *Lycidas* 66, Virgil, *Eclogues* i. 2, vi. 8.

674 empurpled: see *Sp.* 110 n.

675–82 'Theme' (i.e. the book of Nature) is the subject of 'presents'. The hedonistic associations of the peach, vine, etc. are perhaps an unexpected development of 'moral song' (672), but T. found his fruits in Eden; cf. *PL* iv. 332–4, 307. On *Au.* 676–8, cf. 'the Sharpness of Vinegar consists in the Fierceness of the little Animals that bite you by the Tongue; not to name the Blue on Plumbs' (Bernard de Fontenelle, *Plurality of Worlds*, trans. 1688). See *Background*, p. 51.

683–706 A detour to the vineyards of France.

688–95 Grapes drink the sun's light and heat, which is stored and radiated by the rocky cliffs (cf. *Su.* 657–62 and n.). Their juice is exalted (694) because drawn upwards by the sun's heat (cf. *Sp.* 79–89 n.). The reference in *Au.* 691–2 is to black grapes and white.

691 ardent: shining; cf. *Au.* 620.

693 turgent Film: swelling skin.

693 living Dew: bloom.

702 rais'd: excited.

707–10 On warm autumn days the sun's heat draws up water vapour, but this is condensed by the layer of cool air in the middle sky (cf. *Su.* 768 n.), and so descends as fog.

708 Exhalations: evaporations; cf. Virgil, *Georgics* ii. 217.

711 On eighteenth-century man's new-found taste for the 'sublime' in external nature see M. H. Nicolson, *Mountain Gloom and Mountain Glory* (Ithaca, N.Y., 1959). Addison had written in *Spectator* 412 of the imagination's pleasure in 'greatness', i.e. vastness.

713 If the kingdoms are England and Scotland then T. is describing Carter Fell, which overlooked his early home. See C. V. Deane, *Aspects of Eighteenth-Century Nature Poetry* (Oxford, 1935), pp. 97–9.

722–7 These lines describe the effects of light refracted through a dense body of mist. For 723–4 cf. *Su.* 1620 n., *PL* i. 594–9; 'frights' implicitly contrasts the attitude of the fond sequacious herd with that of the enlightened few; cf. *Au.* 1103–37. Lines 725–7 refer to the magnified shadows of objects thrown by the low light of sunrise or sunset against a sheet of mist.

726 wilder'd: straying, puzzled; cf. Pope, *Statius, his Thebais* (1712), 589.

732 Hebrew Bard: Moses, who was inspired on mountain tops (cf. Exod. 3, 19, *PL* i. 6–10). T. implies that such divine inspiration was somehow linked with his experience of light and mist among mountains.

733 uncollected: i.e. by the sun. Light was created on the first day, the sun on the fourth; cf. Gen. 1: 1–19.

736–835 This account of the origin of lakes and rivers was much altered during T.'s revisions to the poem. In *30q* there was a passage of 42 lines offering an elaborate version of the old percolation theory, but in *44* this was reduced to 14 lines (743–56), when a long account of the new and correct theory (756–835) was first added. Man had long wondered whether the condensation of water vapour (the 'roving Mists' of 736) could furnish enough water to fill all the world's lakes and rivers. The ancient theory (743–56) was that the salt water of the oceans percolates through sand and gravel and is drawn eventually up to the mountain springs after all salt crystals have been strained out; cf. Lucretius v. 261–72. This notion was supported by Ecclesiastes 1: 7: 'All the rivers run into the sea; yet the sea is not full; unto the place from whence the rivers come, thither they return again.' Milton arranged the irrigation of the Garden of Eden by such porous action, cf. *PL* iv. 223–30. The ancient theory was still current in the early eighteenth century, where it may be found in, e.g., William Derham's very widely known and often reprinted *Physico-theology* (1713); but Pierre Perrault, in *De l'origine des fontaines* (1674), and Edmund Halley, in 'An Account of the Circulation of the Watry Vapours of the Sea, and of the Cause of Springs' in *Philosophical Transactions* xvii (1691), 468–73, had shown that condensation could, and did, account for all the supplies of fresh water. T. takes his objections to the percolation theory (756–72) and his account of those stratified pervious and impervious rocks which make subterranean reservoirs and conduits (807–28) from Antoine Pluche, *Spectacle de la Nature* (trans. 1733–9), iii. 90–8, 117–30. See *Background*, pp. 77–85. The old theory and the new were set out in dialogue form in Blackmore, *Creation* (1712), i. 508–73, and there is an allusion to the old theory in T.'s 'Paraphrase of Psalm civ' 22–3. In *Au.* 736–835 T.'s versified science combines Pluche's geology with Halley's hydrography to convey his constant message—the harmony of Nature (828–35), a notion reinforced by the faint but persistent anthropomorphism of the whole passage. For the repetitions of 'I see' (808–20) cf. *Sp.* 111–13 n. and Introduction, p. xxxi.

751 irriguous: see *Sp.* 495 n.

753 darkling: 'Being in the dark . . . a word merely poetical' (Johnson); cf. *Wi.* 536.

756–72a (*30q*, 770)   **Amelia:** (1711–86), second daughter of George II and Queen Caroline.

(*30q*, 774)   **Carolina:** Caroline (1683–1737), consort of George II. In 1730 she subscribed to *The Seasons* and accepted the dedication of T.'s *Sophonisba*. T. deleted *30q*, 764–74 from *44* as Caroline was now dead.

772   Deucalion: in Greek mythology a Titan who, like Noah, built a boat and saved himself and his wife from a flood sent by Zeus to destroy the whole race of sinful men; cf. Ovid, *Metamorphoses* i. 262–347.

783   Taurus: mountains running from south-west Asia Minor to Armenia.

783   Imaüs: a mountain range of central Asia mentioned by classical geographers and perhaps to be located in the Hindu Kush; cf. *PL* iii. 431–2, 'Imaus . . . Whose snowy ridge the roving Tartar bounds'.

784   sullen: dismal, cf. Pope, *Rape of the Lock* iv. 19.

785   Hemus: see *Au.* 1318n.

788   Dofrine Hills: 'which separate *Sweden* from *Norway*, arise near the South Promontory of *Norway*, and Proceed in several Ranges to the farthest Part of *Lapland*' (Bernhard Varenius, *General Geography* (1733), i. 137, cited in *Background*, p. 85).

790   Caucasus: 'The Mountains of *Caucasus* . . . extend themselves lengthway from the Confines of the *Caspian-Sea* towards the *Euxine-Sea* Black Sea. They are a sure Sea-Mark to those that sail in the *Caspian-Sea* to steer their Course by' (Varenius, i. 135, cited in *Background*, p. 86).

793 footnote   Taken almost word for word from Varenius, i. 136; see *Background*, p. 86. Ancient geographers located the Rhipaean mountains in northernmost Scythia, i.e. modern Siberia; cf. Virgil, *Georgics*, i. 240.

798   Atlas: mountains in N. Africa; cf. Herodotus, *History*, iv. 184, and Virgil, *Aeneid* iv. 246–51, for the identification of these mountains with the Titan who was condemned by Zeus to bear heaven on his head and hands. T.'s mention of Abyssinia immediately after Atlas may have been influenced by *Aeneid* iv. 480–3.

800   miny: subterranean.

801   compelling: driving or forcing together, Lat. *compellere*; (cloud-compelling is a Homeric epithet for Zeus).

802 footnote   Taken almost word for word from Varenius, i. 136; see *Background*, p. 86. Monomotapa, in the basin of the Zambezi river, was an important African empire at the time of the first Jesuit missions in the sixteenth century, but was broken up into tribal kingdoms in the mid-eighteenth century. The Mountains of the Moon were supposed, in T.'s day, to lie across the Equator in Central Africa.

803   Giant-Sons of Earth: in classical mythology the giant-sons of Ge, the Earth, were believed to be buried under volcanoes in Greece and Italy. T. extends this mythological reference to all mountains in the Old World, none of which was thought to be higher than the peaks of the Andes.

804 **dire:** because subject to earthquakes.

804 **Line:** Equator.

813 **bibulous:** absorbent of moisture (Johnson cites only this passage).

816 **guttur'd:** worn into channels by the action of water; cf. Shakespeare, *Othello* II. i. 69, 'The guttered rocks and congregated sands'. T.'s spelling preserves the connection with Lat. *guttur*, throat. T. has 'congregated' at *Au.* 823, cf. also *PL* vii. 307–8.

832 **fair-divided:** by rivers.

836–48 Pliny (*Natural History* x. 70–1) thought that swallows became torpid in winter, like bats, and this belief persisted into the eighteenth century even in the extravagant notion that flocks hibernated conglomerately under water in ponds. Gilbert White (*Natural History of Selborne* (1789), letters of 4 Aug., 4 Nov. 1767, etc.) allows the possibility that some swallows hibernate, but Defoe had correctly described the migration of swallows (*A Tour through Great Britain* i (1724), letter i, 'Suffolk').

849–52 An obstinate love of liberty among the Batavians and their descendants the Dutch was noted by many writers from Tacitus onwards. The diligence, too, of this people was emphasized in Sir William Temple's *Observations upon the United Provinces* (1673). The stork (*Au.* 853) was associated with liberty: 'The Dutch are very solicitous for the preservation of the stork in every part of their republic . . . They have even got an opinion that it will only live in a republic' (Goldsmith, *History of the Earth and Animated Nature* (1774), Part III, Book VI, Chap. iii). Cf. Savage, *The Wanderer* (1729), canto iv, lines 174–6.

853–61 This description may be taken from Richard Bradley, *A Philosophical Account of the Works of Nature* (1721), pp. 84–5; see *Background*, pp. 131–3; but cf. Pliny, *Natural History* x. 61–2 and *PL* vii. 425–30.

855 **liquid:** clear; cf. *Sp.* 452 and Pope, *Windsor Forest* 186. On 'liquid' as stock diction see Arthos pp. 237–47.

860 **figured:** in (wedge) formation; cf. Milton's simile of cranes that 'rang'd in figure wedge their way' (*PL* vii. 426).

862–5 Cf. T.'s *Britannia* 82–9 and *Liberty* iii. 227–9; inspired by Milton, *Lycidas* 154–8.

862–75 'Some of the lesser Isles [of Shetland] are so crouded with Variety of Sea-fowl that they darken the Air when they fly in great Numbers' (Martin Martin, *A Description of the Western Isles of Scotland*, second edn. (1716), pp. 374–5). Martin wrote also of the small size and variegated colours of Hebridean cattle, sheep and horses, and of dangerous climbs on the islands in search of birds' eggs. See *Background*, pp. 132–3.

864 **Thulè:** see *Su.* 1168 n.

867 **Nations:** of birds.

869 Cf. Milton, *Comus* 729.

877 Plumage: eider-down.

880 Caledonia: Roman name for North Britain, i.e. Scotland.

880 romantic: see *Sp.* 1028 n. T. recognizes that the 'romantic' quality attributed to landscape is a projection of the beholder's feelings.

882 diffusive: spreading widely (cf. *Su.* 851, 1752, *Wi.* 581), or, perhaps, shedding rain (drawn from the 'waving Main', *Au.* 881).

883 Breathing the Soul acute: manifesting the keen spirit of its people.

884 Incult: 'Uncultivated; untilled' (Johnson, citing only 883–5).

886 watry Wealth: fish. On periphrases see *Sp.* 132 n.

888 Cf. Milton, *Comus* 860.

890 Doric Reed: see *Au.* 3 n. It is a custom of pastoral poetry to associate the poet with a river near his birthplace or home. In T.'s case this river is the Jed in Roxburghshire.

893 Orca, Betubium: two of the northernmost promontories of the Scottish mainland were named Orcas and Berubium by the ancient geographer Ptolemy, and identified in Camden's *Britannia* (trans. Gibson, 1720) as Howburn and Urdehead.

896 Learning: Columba, Aidan, Cuthbert, and other evangelists of the sixth and seventh centuries.

896 Gothic Rage: barbarian invasions of the fifth century, particularly the sack of Rome in 410.

900 Wallace: Sir William Wallace, the Scottish statesman and general who successfully resisted Edward I's attempts to subdue Scotland, but was betrayed, and hanged, drawn, and quartered in 1305.

903–9 Scotland had for ages supplied, and would long continue to supply, the world with large numbers of emigrants and mercenary soldiers.

909 Boreal Morn: aurora borealis; cf. *Au.* 1108–37.

910–28 Many pamphlets appeared in the 1720s advocating improved agriculture, fisheries, and trade, and the development of woollen and linen manufactures in Scotland; see *Background*, pp. 135–6. The fortunes of the Scottish herring industry excited other poets, e.g. Defoe, *Caledonia* (1707), and John Lockman, *The Shetland Herring and Peruvian Goldmine* (1751). On that favourite early eighteenth-century poetic theme—praise of commerce and industry—see Bonamy Dobrée, 'The Theme of Patriotism in the Poetry of the Early Eighteenth Century', *Proceedings of the British Academy* xxxv (1949), 49–65.

913 late: distant, cf. *Su.* 1520.

918 Hyperborean: of the far north, cf. Virgil, *Georgics* iv. 517; according to ancient geographers the Hyperboreans lived north of the Rhipaean mountains, cf. *Au.* 792.

921   Batavian: Dutch; the Batavi were an ancient people living in part of what is now Holland.

922   finny Swarms: fish. On periphrases see *Sp.* 132 n.

927   Soul: national spirit.

929   John Campbell, second Duke of Argyll (1678–1743), was a distinguished soldier under Marlborough (cf. 937–8) and later commanded forces that crushed the Jacobite rebellion of 1715. He was one of the leading Scottish promoters of the Act of Union, and after the Union a prominent spokesman in the House of Lords for Scottish interests. The many contemporary tributes to his oratory (cf. 940–1) include one by Pope, *Epilogue to the Satires* ii. 86–7.

937   Throat: cf. Shakespeare, *Richard III* v. iv. 5, 'He fights,/Seeking for Richmond in the throat of death.' Johnson, citing *Au.* 937–8, defines 'throat' as 'The main road of any place'.

938   Tenier: Taisniere, the name of a wood near Malplaquet in Flanders, where the Duke of Argyll commanded the right wing in the battle of 11 Sept. 1709 and fought with great courage.

944   Duncan Forbes of Culloden (1685–1747), the much-respected MP and Scottish judge, befriended T. when the poet first came to London in 1725, and subscribed for five copies of the 1730 quarto. Forbes introduced improvements into Scottish agriculture and judicial processes, and sought to discourage the mischievous habit of tea-drinking. His son John was a close friend of T.; see *Cas. Ind.* i. lxii–lxiv.

952   Imbrown: make dark; cf. *PL* iv. 246.

952   dusk: dusky; cf. *PL* xi. 741.

957   light: lightly.

957-63   The upper atmosphere or ether (cf. *Sp.* 148 n.) is lightly shadowed, or 'fleeced', by cirrus clouds which stretch in thin streaks in all directions ('uncertain where to turn'); this is a sign that a change in the weather is coming. There is also a lower bank of clouds which absorb the sun's light and transmit some of it. The phenomenon is more clearly described in the first version of this passage; see 950–63a (*26f*, 29–33). For 'Wave', 'Current', and 'imbibe' (958–61) cf. *Su.* 84 n. The change of 'fleece' (958) from noun (*Wi.26f*, 29) to verb brings more movement into the scene. *Au.* 958 is the first citation in *OED* of the verb in this sense, 'To overspread as with a fleece; to dapple or fleck with fleece-like masses'; cf. *Cas. Ind.* i. xliv. 7.

950–63a (*26f*, 22)   At the autumnal equinox the sun's apparent course crosses the equator in a southerly direction.

967   Cf. Milton, *Comus* 6, 'low-thoughted care'.

970–1005   Cf. T.'s letter to Cranstoun (Letters, pp. 16–17), quoted in Introduction, p. xxxvi.

974a   Philomel: cf. Milton, *Il Penseroso* 56–7; see *Sp.* 601 n.

975–1003a (*26f*, 53–5)   Gilbert White listed woodcocks among winter birds of passage, observing that they appeared in the Selborne area 'about Old Michaelmas' (10 October), and that it was said they crossed the North Sea from Scandinavia on moonlit nights (*Natural History of Selborne* (1789), letters of 30 June 1769, 20 Dec. 1770, 12 Feb. 1772). Since the woodcock is seen only in winter T. removed all reference to this bird when most of *Wi.26f*, 17–111 was transferred to *Au*. in 1730. Cf. Pope, *Windsor-Forest* 125–8, Gay, *Rural Sports* ii. 349, *Trivia* i. 233–4.

1004–5   The various nervous disorders known as melancholy were thought to be found generally among men and women of high intelligence and sensitivity, so melancholy was sometimes called 'the wise disease'. 'All those who have become eminent in philosophy or politics or poetry or the arts are clearly melancholics' (Aristotle, *Problemata* xxx. 1). Dürer, in his engraving *Melencolia I*, had represented Melancholy as the presiding genius of art, while Milton's *Il Penseroso* (which prompted T.'s lines on Philosophic Melancholy) hailed her as 'goddess, sage and holy,/. . . O'erlaid with black, staid wisdom's hue'. In T. the melancholy mood is prompted by the autumnal 'desolated Prospect' (1003), but the lines following indicate that this melancholy is compounded of moral and aesthetic sensitivity and imagination, together with a hint of public virtue (*Au*. 1023–9), which was not one of the traditional associations of melancholy. T.'s personification, first introduced when the passage was transferred from *Wi*. to *Au*. in *30q*, represents Philosophic Melancholy as male—not female, as in Dürer, Milton, and elsewhere, e.g. Pope, *Eloisa to Abelard* 165. T.'s ecstatic, contemplative, wise Philosophic Melancholy probably found its final place in *Au*. because autumn was his 'inspiring' season (see *Hymn* 96 n.), but Empedocles had propounded a physiological reason for autumnal melancholy by asserting that in autumn the ascendant humour in man is black bile, which causes melancholy. (R. Klibansky, E. Panofsky, and F. Saxl, *Saturn and Melancholy* (1964), pp. 9–10.)

1006–29   Cf. *Sp*. 878–903 n.

1031   **visionary**: where visions will be seen; cf. *Su*. 556.

1037   An awkward transition to the new material (1037–81) added in *44*.

1039–40   The first half of the eighteenth century saw a mania, particularly among wealthy Whig lords, for the building or rebuilding of country houses.

1042   By 1744 (when lines 1037–81 were first added to *Au*.) the garden at Stowe, the Buckinghamshire estate of Lord Cobham, had been worked upon by Charles Bridgeman, Sir John Vanbrugh, James Gibbs, and William Kent. It covered over 400 acres and contained dozens of buildings, pillars, and other memorials to the persons and principles admired by Cobham's circle of opposition Whigs (cf. *Au*. 1050 n.). The garden was much admired in the eighteenth century (cf. Pope, *Epistle to Burlington* (1731), 65–70, and T.'s *Liberty* v (1736), 696–701), and often described, e.g. in Gilbert West, *Stowe, a Poem* (1732), Sarah Bridgeman

Plans of Stowe (1739), Anon., *A Description of Stowe* (1744). There are modern descriptions in Laurence Whistler, *The Imagination of Sir John Vanbrugh and his Fellow Artists* (London, 1954), chap. 7, and in *Apollo* xcvii (June 1973).

1043 Cyrus the Younger, who died in 401 BC leading an army in revolt against his brother Artaxerxes II, King of Persia, was 'not only a lord of gardens, but a manual planter thereof' (Sir Thomas Browne, *The Garden of Cyrus* (1658), chap. i). At Sardis on 'Ionia's shore', the central part of the west coast of Asia Minor, Cyrus created the famous garden, or 'paradise', described by Xenophon, *Oeconomicus* iv. 20–4, and by Browne.

1048 When this was first published (1744) the great years of William Pitt, the Elder (1708–78), as Secretary of State and Prime Minister were still to come, but he was already known as a fine orator and vigorous opponent of Walpole.

1050 Temple: William Kent's design for a Temple of Ancient Virtue first appeared in Isaac Ware's *Designs of Inigo Jones and others* (1735). When the Temple was built, shortly afterwards, it housed statues of Greek and Roman heroes only; while, as a form of concrete sarcasm, the contrasting Temple of Modern Virtue, built about the same time, was an empty, shapeless ruin. Probably T.'s footnote is wrong. Perhaps it should refer to the Shrine of British Worthies designed by Kent in the 1730s, which, over the years, came to contain busts of Alfred, the Black Prince, Elizabeth, William III, Raleigh, Drake, Sir Thomas Gresham, Hampden, Bacon, Locke, Newton, Shakespeare, Milton, Pope, Inigo Jones, and Sir John Barnard (an opponent of Walpole), or to the temple, designed by James Gibbs and built before 1732, in which some of those busts were originally housed; cf. *Su.* 1442 n. A third possibility is that T., making a less extravagant compliment, intended his note to refer to the Temple of Friendship, designed by Gibbs and completed in 1739, which actually did contain busts of Pitt and of other opposition politicians. See L. Whistler, M. Gibbon, and G. Clarke, *Stowe, a Guide to the Gardens* (rev. 1968), pp. 18–25.

1054–60 These lines allude to some of the principles of that informal 'landscape gardening' developed in eighteenth-century England. The garden was to be a 'regulated wild' (1055) or 'Nature methodized' (cf. Pope, *Essay on Criticism* 89—a text much quoted by gardeners). In thus regulating or methodizing 'common nature'—the actual landscape—the gardener sought 'the purest truth of Nature' (1058–9), that is, Nature as she must have been at the Creation, before man's fall degraded both the world and himself. Like other artists, gardeners 'should imitate the Divine Maker and form to themselves, as well as they are able, a model of the superior beauties and endeavour to amend and correct common nature and to represent it as it was first created' (Dryden's translation of Bellori in *A Parallel of Poetry and Painting* (1695); see *Essays of John Dryden*, ed. W. P. Ker (1926), ii. 118). The objects in a garden were intended to produce pleasing or inspiring associations in the mind of the beholder:

'objects should indeed be less calculated to strike the immediate eye, than the judgement or well-formed imagination, as in painting' (William Shenstone, 'Unconnected thoughts on Gardening', *Collected Works* (1765), ii. 112). The classical temples in their 'regulated' but natural-seeming settings at Stowe were intended to evoke the landscape of Greece and Rome (though the actual models were all Roman), while the dedications of these temples and the objects in them offered reminders of classical heroes and virtues (cf. 1055–6).

1056 Attic Land: Attica, the part of Greece around Athens.

1061–9 According to Lord Chesterfield, William Pitt had 'a most happy turn to poetry, but he seldom indulged and seldomer avowed it'. But T.'s reference in these lines may be to Pitt's already famous oratory (cf. 1065–9). T. had already drawn the 'tragic scene' (1062) three times, with *Sophonisba* (1730), *Agamemnon* (1738), and *Edward and Eleanora* (1739). Two more tragedies, *Tancred and Sigismunda* (1745) and *Coriolanus* (1749) were to come. 'Corruption' (1069) may well stand for Walpole, whom Pitt helped to bring down in 1742. T.'s tragedies were political, mostly anti-Walpole, pieces; cf. *Cas. Ind.* 1. xxxii. 6–9.

1064 decent: 'Becoming; fit; suitable' (Johnson); cf. *Au.* 496.

1070 The Elysian Fields, landscaped by William Kent about 1735, were the 'wildest' or least formal part of the garden at Stowe. Kent planted evergreens there—a comparatively new device in English gardens—to suggest the cypress groves of antiquity (cf. *Au.* 1055–6). In classical mythology Elysium was the place where heroes, patriots, and others favoured by the gods enjoyed after death a happy existence.

1072 Cobham: Sir Richard Temple, Viscount Cobham (1669–1749), soldier and politician, left Walpole's ministry in 1733 in order to cultivate his garden and a crop of gifted dissidents who became known as 'Boy Patriots' or 'Cobham's Cubs'. Prominent among these were Pitt (cf. *Au.* 1048) and Lyttelton (cf. *Sp.* 906). On *Au.* 1072–4, cf. Virgil, *Georgics* ii. 276–87; Marvell, *Upon Appleton House*, xxxvi–xlvi; and Pope's compliment to another soldier turned gardener, the Earl of Peterborough, in *Imitations of Horace*, Sat. II. i. 129–32.

1075–81 England was not prosecuting the War of the Austrian Succession with much vigour, and indeed had not declared war formally until Spring 1744. The preceding hostilities had produced no significant English victories apart from Porto Bello (cf. *Su.* 1041 n.) in 1739 and Dettingen in 1743.

1088–93 closely echo *PL* i. 287–91. For 'deluge' (1098) and 'tide' (1101) cf. *Su.* 84 n.

1093 optic Tube: telescope; cf. *PL* i. 288.

1096 Cf. Milton, *Il Penseroso* 72, *Comus* 332.

1097 Cerulean: blue sky; cf. Lucretius vi. 482, *caerula*.

1099 sky'd: 'Envelloped by the skies. This is unusual and un-authorised' (Johnson, citing only 1098–9).

1096–1102a (*26f*, 97–100)   Cf. *PL* v. 746–7, which also has 'impearls', cf. *260*, 98.

1109   Meteors: 'Any bodies in the air or sky that are of a flux and transitory nature' (Johnson). In this case T. refers to the aurora borealis. The aurora appears as variegated, flickering streamers of light radiating towards the northern horizon from a point between fifty and several hundred miles from the earth's surface ('High to the Crown of Heaven', 1111). Very fine examples were seen in northern Europe on 6 March 1716 and 19 Oct. 1726 (see *Background*, pp. 64–6), but the phenomenon was not 'new' (1137), since Aristotle, Seneca, and Pliny had all referred to it. For 1116–21 cf. *PL* ii. 533–8, Shakespeare, *Julius Caesar* II. ii. 19–20. T. goes on to draw his customary distinction between the reactions of the foolish herd and the enlightened few; cf. *Sp.* 210–17, *Su.* 1709–29.

1113   thwart: cross; cf. *Su.* 343, T.'s *Sophonisba* (1730), I. v. 10, and *PL* iv. 556–7, 'a shooting star/In autumn thwarts the night'.

1114   Ether: see *Sp.* 148 n.

1134   Inspect sage: wise insight.

1136   unfix'd: unexplained by man.

1143–4   On the power of light to kindle and create, see *Su.* 82–5, 104–11.

1152   Wild-fire: or *ignis fatuus*, is a phosphorescent light seen flitting over marshy ground, possibly due to spontaneous combustion of gas from decaying organic matter; cf. *PL* ix. 634–42.

1153   Moss: bog.

1162   Meteor: here St. Elmo's Fire—the glow accompanying discharges of atmospheric electricity which usually appears as a tip of light on the extremities of objects (such as ships' spars or the heads of horses and men) during stormy weather; cf. Virgil, *Aeneid* ii. 680–6 ('innoxia'), Shakespeare, *Tempest* I. ii. 196–201.

1169   This line was attached to Turner's *Frosty Morning* (exh. 1813).

1172–1200   'The common Way of killing the Bees and saving the Honey is to dig a Hole, hard by, a little bigger than the Bottom of the Hive, into which stick one or two Matches of Brimstone five or six Inches long, so that the Top of them may be even with the Surface Top of the Hole. The Matches being fired, gently and dexterously lift off the Hive, and set it over the Hole, and immediately close up the Hive at the Bottom, that none of the Smoke may get out, and in a few Minutes the Bees will be all dead' (John Laurence, *A New System of Agriculture* (1727), p. 108). Cf. Virgil, *Georgics* iv. 228–30. On T.'s anthropomorphic periphrases cf. *Sp.* 132 n.

1182   Domes: houses, but also alluding to the domed shape of beehives; cf. Virgil, *Georgics* iv. 159, *Au.* 660 n.

1183   convolv'd: rolled together (Johnson, citing 1181–3); cf. *Sp.* 837, *Su.* 343.

1201–7   Cf. *PL* i. 230–7. Palermo in Sicily was shaken by a violent earthquake on the night of 1 Sept. 1726.

1212   save what . . . brushes from the Plain: 'save what breeze brushes the filmy threads of evaporated dew from the fields.'

1214   ethereal Arch: upper sky, distinguished from 'sky' (1213), cf. *Sp.* 148 n.

1220   instant: imminent; cf. *Su.* 1195.

1221–34   'When the Fruits of the Earth are gather'd in, and laid in their proper Receptacles, it is common, in most of the Country Places, to provide a plentiful Supper for the *Harvest-Men*, and the Servants of the Family; which is called a *Harvest-Supper*' (Henry Bourne, *Antiquitates Vulgares* (Newcastle, 1725), p. 229).

1223   Toil-strung: given vigour by toil; cf. Dryden, *To John Driden* 89.

1226–30   Cf. Eustace Budgell, *Spectator* 161 (4 Sept. 1711).

1232–4   Cf. Stephen Duck, *The Thresher's Labour* (1730) concluding lines.

1235–1373   Modelled upon *Georgics* ii. 458–542. However, where Virgil describes principally the joys of the frugal, hardy, pious husbandman (with a short digression on the poet's own happiness in rural retirement), T. devotes his account of the 'happy man' almost wholly to the hedonist-philosopher-poet. Such an adaptation of Virgil's lines was extremely common in the eighteenth century: 'There is, indeed, scarcely any writer who has not celebrated the happiness of rural privacy' (Johnson, *Rambler*, 135). On such poetry of retirement see M.-S. Røstvig, *The Happy Man* (2 vols., rev. Oslo, 1962–8).

1244   mazy: intricately embroidered.

1249–50a (*30q*, 1145–6)   **Wine . . . gems:** i.e. the jewelled cup is brighter than the wine in it.

1260   greens: see *Sp.* 321 n.

1265   milky Drove: cattle (both elements in the periphrasis emphasize the cow's relation to man). On periphrases see *Sp.* 132 n.

1267   Chide: confused noise.

1278–86   This Virgilian theme became more urgent in eighteenth-century England as men grew concerned over the activities of West Indian planters and servants of the East India Company; cf. Burke, *Speech on the Impeachment of Warren Hastings* (1788), and the powerful lines in John Langhorne, *The Country Justice*, iii (1777), 76–83. T. displays a different attitude to trade in *Au.* 118–34.

1286   another Sun: cf. *Wi.* 893 n.

1294   iron Race: people living in an Iron Age (cf. *Sp.* 242–74 n.); T. implies that the contented country-dweller lives in something comparable to the Golden Age (cf. *Au.* 1349–51).

1311 Gems: see *Sp.* 196n.

1317 Tempè: see *Sp.* 909n.

1318 Hemus: Haemus, a mountain-range in Thrace celebrated by classical poets. Virgil refers to its cool, enclosed valleys, *Georgics* ii. 488; cf. *Au.* 785.

1329 hoary Waste Abrupt: sudden snowfall.

1337 Elates: 'To Elate. To exult; to heighten. An unusual sense' (Johnson, citing only 1337).

1352–73 Adapted and expanded from Virgil, *Georgics* ii. 475–86, which T. had reprinted and translated in the *Preface* to *260*, 101–25 (see Appendix B), with the significant difference that in the *Georgics* and T.'s *Preface* the Muses snatch the poet to their care, whereas in *Au.* Nature snatches the poet to Heaven. T. makes this philosophic rapture his climax, as Virgil does not. For the rhapsodic manner cf. *Wi.* 106–17n. For the 'chain of being' idea running through this passage cf. *Su.* 334n. For the human mind and its place in the rising system (1361–2) cf. *Su.* 1788–805 nn.

1367–9 The ancients thought that slowness of intellect might be caused by coldness of blood about the heart; cf. *Georgics* ii. 483–4.

1370 Inglorious: humble, cf. *Au.* 1073.

WINTER

(*26f, epigraph*) Virgil, *Georgics* ii. 321–2: The swift sun does not yet touch winter with his steeds. Now summer is waning.

Ovid, *Metamorphoses* ii. 30: Icy Winter, with white and shaggy locks.

(*260 28, epigraph*) Virgil, *Georgics* iii. 442–3: Winter, bristling with hoar frost.

1–16 Praised by the painter Constable in 1836 as 'a beautiful instance of the poet identifying his own feelings with external nature' (C. R. Leslie, *Memoirs of Constable*, ed. J. Mayne (1951), p. 328).

6 Cogenial: congenial, cf. *Sp.* 564a.

7 Morn of Life: T.'s boyhood in rural Roxburghshire, cf. Grant pp. 6–15.

15 Chambers of the South: the southern sky, cf. Job 9: 9.

16 smil'd: cf. *Sp.* 84n.

17–40 Added in 1730 to replace the prose dedication (see Appendix B); hence T. says he 'renews' his song after singing the other seasons (17–22). Spencer Compton (1673–1743), the Whig politician created Earl of Wilmington in 1730, was Speaker of the House of Commons when he received the dedication of the first edition of *Winter*. On Walpole's fall in 1742 he became Prime Minister—but in name only.

36 regularly: in accordance with rule or principle.

39 converting: turning, cf. Shakespeare, Sonnet vii.

42 Capricorn: the Goat, the tenth sign of the zodiac (cf. *Sp.* 26 n.), into which the sun enters at the winter solstice, 21 or 22 Dec. In *30q* T. mistakenly implies that Scorpio (the eighth sign) immediately precedes Capricorn.

42 Centaur-Archer: Sagittarius, the ninth sign of the zodiac, into which the sun enters about 22 Nov. For Centaur see *Au.* 500 n.

43 Aquarius: the Water-Carrier, the eleventh sign of the zodiac, into which the sun enters on 21 Jan.; cf. Virgil, *Georgics* iii. 304, 'cum frigidus olim/iam cadit extremoque inrorat Aquarius anno'; and, for 'inverted year', Horace, *Satires* i. i. 36, 'simul inversum contristat Aquarius annum'.

45 Ether: See *Sp.* 148 n.

46–9 Cf. *Su.* 1620 n., *Au.* 722–7 n.

57–60 Cf. Lucretius vi. 1090–102. The seeds of death and disease descend through the atmosphere as cloud or mist, or rise from the earth when it is soaked with moisture.

63–5 After harvest the stubble was ploughed in, and sheep were folded (hence 'untended') out in the field and fed with turnips ('wholesome Root') through the winter, so that their dung would restore the land's fertility. Defoe observed this practice in his *Tour*, vol. i (1724), Letter i, 'Suffolk'. This was part of the so-called 'Norfolk system' of husbandry which was spreading slowly into suitable parts of Britain in the eighteenth century.

66 moorish Fens: cf. Milton, *Comus* 432.

67 Cf. *Su.* 960 n.

72–80 Cf. Virgil, *Georgics* i. 322–31, praised by Dennis, Beattie, and other eighteenth-century critics as a classical example of sublimity. The 'Father' in Virgil is, of course, Jupiter, but T.'s conception is influenced by the OT Jehovah (e.g. Psalm 18: 9–13); cf. *Wi.* 197–201. The introduction of 'grumbling' (76) in *30q* and of 'joyless' (73) in *44* makes this a more personified description than that in *26f*.

80 Wanderers of Heaven: wild birds, as distinguished from 'household feathery People' (*Wi.* 87). On periphrases see *Sp.* 132 n.

98a chapt: fissured.

106–10 This passage may owe something to Milton's *Paradise Regained*, 'The Father . . . in whose hand all times and seasons roll' (iii. 186–7), but the tone and general cast of thought follow Theocles' famous outburst upon 'mighty *Nature*! Wise Substitute of *Providence*! impower'd *Creatress*!' in Shaftesbury's *The Moralists, a Philosophical Rhapsody* (1709), in *Characteristicks* ii. 345. This praise of Nature's hand, rather than God's, takes T. very close to 'natural religion' or deism. Cf. *Sp.* 556–62, *Au.* 1352, *Hymn* 1–3.

114 Magazines: cf. *Su.* 1112–13.

118–52 These signs of approaching storm appear, in different order, in Virgil, *Georgics* i. 450–6, 427–9, 351–92, 402–3. The spots at 119 (cf. *maculae, Georgics* i. 441, 454) are probably not sunspots but clouds, as in Virgil. 'Pensive (135) is possibly a mistranslation of *Georgics* i. 390: *pensa*, i.e. 'what is weighed out as a daily allotment or task' (referring to the amount of wool each girl had to card). The significance of 136–7 is that sudden, small gusts of draught which precede the storm cause the taper to gutter. The description of diffused light at 118–29 is compared to Elsheimer's painting *St. Paul in Malta* in Jeffry Spencer, *Heroic Nature* (Evanston, 1973), pp. 267–8, but no engraving of that painting was in T.'s *Sale Catalogue.*

124 Blank: white; cf. *Su.* 1050.

127 obtuse: dull, indistinct (continuing the metaphor of 'blunted', 125).

137–8 plumy Race, Tenants of the Sky: birds. On periphrases see *Sp.* 132 n.

148–84 In phrasing, detail, and sequence these two storm descriptions resemble lines 156–90 of the first of John Armstrong's 'Imitations of Shakespeare', first printed in his *Miscellanies* i (1770), 145–58, with a note saying that it was 'just finished' when T.'s *Winter* 1726 appeared. For 156–7 cf. *PL* vii. 212–13.

153–5a (*26f.* 162) **Fabrick:** edifice (cf. *PL* viii. 76). **pillar'd:** cf. Job 26: 11.

176 sturdy Sons: trees.

178 Aghast is defined in the glossary of obsolete terms in Hughes's edition of Spenser (1715).

182 Honours: foliage; cf. Virgil, *Georgics* ii. 404, Horace, *Epistles* xi. 5–6, Pope, *Windsor Forest* 221.

189 Dome: house; cf. *Su.* 1060, *Au.* 660.

191–3 Cf. *Su.* 960 n.

194 devoted: consigned to destruction; cf. *PL* v. 890, ix. 901, Pope's *Iliad* ii. 17, T.'s *Agamemnon* v. iii. 54.

195 Milton had personified wild Uproar; cf. *PL* iii. 710–11.

197–201 Cf. Ps. 18: 11, 104: 3; Mark 4: 39.

208 meddling Senses: contrast Wordsworth's 'meddling intellect' ('The Tables Turned' in *Lyrical Ballads,* 1798).

221 conscious Peace: cf. *Au.* 296 n.

223–40 Cf. Pope's *Iliad* xii. 331–44. T.'s third storm is more severe than its two predecessors at *Wi.* 72–80, 153–94, and is described without recourse to personification. 'Cherish'd' (232, introduced in *44*) indicates the beneficial function of snow in the natural system.

244 After the sheaves were threshed by flail in the barn the grain was winnowed, i.e. it was thrown up by shovels or sieves while a current of air passing between two opposite open doors (or generated by a large fan) blew away the chaff. At this time the barn doorways were besieged by birds hungry for the grain.

256–64 'Here the diction is parcel of the meaning. "Brown inhabitants" is a neat way of grouping creatures which inhabit the scene described and whose brownness is the most evident thing about them in the snow. "Bleating kind" is anything but an unthinking substitute for "sheep". T. is saying: we think of sheep as creatures who bleat, but they are silent enough in the snow; it is the dumb eye and not the voice that tells us of their despair' (G. Tillotson, 'Augustan Poetic Diction II', in *Augustan Studies* (1961) p. 42). Similarly, 'helpless charge' (265) directs our attention to the relationship between sheep and men. On periphrases see *Sp.* 132 n.

271   Waft: 'A floating body' (Johnson, citing only 268–71).

275   Wreath: plume of powdery snow blown by strong wind.

281   shag: make rough; cf. *Sp.* 910.

287   Nerves: the immediate instruments of motion and sensation (for the physiology of which see the reference at *Sp.* 904–64a (*28*, 865–76) n.); also, here, sinews; cf. *Au.* 469.

291   tufted: perhaps surrounded by a cluster of trees and bushes; cf. *Su.* 923, and Milton, *L'Allegro* 78, *Comus* 224.

311   officious: kind, doing good offices (Johnson); cf. *PL* viii. 99.

321   Perhaps Lyttelton thought 'Stretch'd out' more decorous (cf. *cubat*, 'lies', in Lucretius iii. 892, the source of this passage) than T.'s 'Unstretch'd' (*30q*), which indicated that the body was not decently laid out but had grown stiff in its horrible huddled position.

321   bleaching: growing white (Johnson, citing 317–21).

348–58   Cf. *Sp.* 878–903 n.

359 footnote   The first reports of a Parliamentary Committee appointed to investigate allegations of torture in English gaols were presented in March and May 1729, and provided ammunition for opponents of Walpole's government; so T.'s apostrophe 'Hail patriot-band' (*30q* 351, omitted from *44*) is slightly factious. Nine members of the Committee, including the chairman, James Oglethorpe (praised in T.'s *Liberty* v (1736), 645–6), and Arthur Onslow (dedicatee of *Autumn*), subscribed to the quarto *Seasons*; T.'s patron Charles Talbot, as Solicitor-General, prosecuted Thomas Bambridge, Warden of the Fleet Prison and most notorious of the 'detected monsters' (*30q* 353). Hogarth's painting of the Committee examining Bambridge is in the National Portrait Gallery. See A. D. McKillop, 'Thomson and the Jail Committee', *Studies in Philology*, xlvii (1950), 62–71.

384   Toils: snares, cf. *Au.* 1292.

405–6   For the belief that the lion instinctively reverences beauty cf. *Faerie Queene* I. III. v–vi.

414–23 Based on *An Account of the Glacieres or Ice Alps in Savoy* (February 1744) by William Windham and Peter Martel; relevant passages are quoted in *Background*, pp. 142–3.

415 Grisons: inhabitants of the mountainous eastern canton of Switzerland, noted for their happy simplicity.

431–3 Cf. 'Imagination . . . holds high converse with the Dead;/ Sages, or Poets' ('A Fragment', in Mallet's *Works* (1759), i. 52). Mallet and T. frequently exchanged poems and ideas from 1725 to 1727. Milton's *Il Penseroso* 77–119 furnished the hint for T.'s catalogue and its winter-evening setting (424–540); cf. also Pope, *Temple of Fame*, 151–243.

433–5 On the divine nature of humanity and social love see *Sp.* 878–903 n. Cf. *Wi.* 595 and n. T.'s choice of heroes shows that he was of Sir William Temple's opinion, that the first 'Rank in the pretensions to Heroick Virtue . . . has been allowed, to the wise Institution of just Orders and Laws, which frame safe and happy Governments in the World' ('Of Heroick Virtue' in *Miscellanea, the Second Part* (1692), p. 300).

437 long-liv'd Volume: probably Plutarch's *Parallel Lives* of Greeks and Romans. 11 of the 14 Greeks and 5 of the 11 Romans in T.'s catalogue of worthies (*Wi.* 439–540) are subjects of Plutarch's *Lives*.

439 Socrates (469–399 BC), the great moral philosopher of Athens, turned from the physical speculations of earlier thinkers in order to study virtue, which he equated with knowledge. He directed his own conduct by a divine voice, his *daimon*, which T. here equates with enlightened reason. Falsely accused of blasphemy and of corrupting Athenian youth, Socrates displayed fearless composure at his trial and while awaiting execution by poison. The oracle of Delphi called him 'wisest of mankind'. T. praises him in *Liberty* ii (1735), 227–40. Cf. Pope, *Temple of Fame* 170–3.

446 In *Liberty* ii. 159–63 T. calls Solon (*c.*640/635–*c.*560 BC) the 'mild Restorer' of Athenian democracy, and, in a footnote drawn from Rollin's *Histoire ancienne*, describes the institutions which curbed a lively people while preserving their freedom: 'The *Areopagus*, or Supreme Court of Judicature, which SOLON reform'd and improved: and the Council of *Four Hundred*, by him instituted. In this Council all Affairs of State were deliberated, before they came to be voted in the Assembly of the People.' Solon's '*tender* Laws' superseded the harsh code of Dracon.

452 smiling: rich; cf. *Sp.* 84 n.

453 Lycurgus, the legendary Spartan law-giver, promoted temperance and restrained luxury by many devices, including the prohibition of gold and silver. Some of the laws attributed to him may be dated about 600 BC. T. praises him in *Liberty* ii. 119–25, where Sparta is described as 'the sober, hard,/And Man-subduing City'.

457 Leonidas, King of Sparta, led the 6000 Greeks who, in 480 BC, held back a huge invading Persian army in the pass of Thermopylae, until his position was turned and he and many of his soldiers killed. He was regarded as a model of all the Spartan qualities valued by Lycurgus. Cf. *Liberty* ii. 172–5.

459 Aristides: see *Su.* 1491 n.

464 The strategy of the Athenian leader Themistocles (*c.*528–*c.*462 BC) brought victory over the Persians at Salamis in 480 BC, but after coming into conflict with Cimon, about 472 BC, he was ostracized, never to return to Athens.

466 Cimon (*c.*512–449 BC), was accused of incest in youth, helped Aristides form the Delian League of Greek states against Persia, and became the most powerful Athenian leader after the ostracism of Themistocles and the death of Aristides, 468 BC. He gained victories over the Persians by land and sea.

472 unequal: unworthy of the great men now to be named.

474 Timoleon (d. 336 BC), the Corinthian, conspired about 365 BC to kill his own brother Timophanes, who was trying to make himself tyrant; cf. Pope, *Temple of Fame* 162. In 1730 Bubb Dodington (cf. *Su.* 29) tried to persuade T. to write an epic poem on Timoleon; cf. *Letters*, pp. 74–5.

476 Pelopidas (d. 364 BC) held a command under his friend the brilliant military tactician Epaminondas (*c.*420–362 BC) when the latter led the Thebans to the victory over Sparta at Leuctra (371 BC) which gave Thebes supremacy in Greece until Epaminondas' death. Epaminondas is praised in T.'s *Liberty* ii. 468, and Pope's *Temple of Fame* 161.

481 The Athenian general and orator Phocion sought to prevent Athens from going to war with the Macedonia of Philip and Alexander the Great. In 318 BC he was sentenced to death by poison on a charge of treason. Cf. Pope, *Temple of Fame* 174. In stressing the contrast between Phocion's private and public characters T. appears to be drawing upon Rollin, *Histoire ancienne* (Paris, 1740), vii. 115–16.

488 Agis IV (*c.*262–241 BC), King of Sparta, attempted to cure his kingdom's ills by a return to Lycurgus' constitution, but was deposed and murdered. Cf. Pope, *Temple of Fame* 175.

491 Aratus of Sicyon in Achaea (271–213 BC), statesman and general, from 245 to 215 BC directed the Achaean League of Greek cities that had freed themselves from Macedonian rule. The League's affairs were administered by a Council composed of delegations from the cities in proportion to their population—an unusually advanced form of representative government for its day.

494 Philopoemen (*c.*250–183 BC) of Megalopolis in Arcadia, a highly successful general of the Achaean League who repeatedly defeated the Spartans, is often regarded as the last great man produced by Greece.

499 virtuous Times: of the first Roman kings and early Republic.

503 Numa, the legendary second king of Rome, is called a 'better founder' than Romulus the first king because his long reign was peaceful and enlightened. It was believed that he began the worship of Vesta,

Roman goddess of the blazing hearth. The virtue of ancient Rome is a major theme in T.'s *Liberty* parts i and iii.

504 Servius was according to legend the sixth king of Rome. To his reign, in the sixth century BC, were attributed certain forms of government that endured throughout the whole history of the Roman Republic.

507 The 'public father' was actually Lucius Junius Brutus, the nephew of Tarquinius Superbus, last king of Rome. After the expulsion of the Tarquins and the end of the Roman monarchy in 510 BC he became one of the first two Consuls, and in this office, it was said, sentenced to death his two sons, who had plotted to restore the Tarquins. T.'s footnote is wrong, but in *Liberty* i (1735), 88–9, where the phrasing of this description is anticipated, T. correctly identifies his hero as Lucius Junius Brutus.

510 Camillus, the Roman dictator and general of the early fourth century BC, was exiled but then recalled to lead the Romans to victory over the Gauls, the Volsci, and the Aequi.

511 Fabricius was three times Consul in the early third century BC, and a type of the old Roman frugality and integrity. In 280 BC he was the Republic's ambassador to the invading Greek king Pyrrhus, and, though poor, resisted all Pyrrhus' attempts to bribe him.

512 See *Su.* 1492 n. T. also refers to Cincinnatus at *Sp.* 58–65 and *Liberty* iii (1735), 143–7.

513 Regulus was consul in 267 and 256 BC, and one of the commanders of Roman expeditions to Africa in the First Punic War. He was captured, and in 250 BC the Carthaginians sent him with an embassy to Rome to propose peace, making him swear to return if negotiations failed; but he advised the Romans to continue the war, and returned to Carthage and a cruel death. There is a longer account of Regulus in T.'s *Liberty* iii 166–80.

517 Scipio: presumably Scipio Africanus Major (*c.*235–183 BC), who defeated Hannibal and broke the power of Carthage in the Second Punic War before spending his later years in retirement on his country estate in Campania. He appears in the *Lives* of Plutarch, particularly those of Flamininus and Fabius. The story of 'the Continence of Scipio', when he restored to her lover a beautiful princess he had captured, was frequently represented in post-Renaissance art; it is related in T.'s *Sophonisba* (1730), II. i. This is the Scipio praised in T.'s *Liberty* v (1736), 419–21, and *Cas. Ind.* I. xvii. 8–9. On the other hand it is possible that this reference at *Wi.* 517 is to Scipio Aemilianus Africanus Numantinus (184–129 BC), who wept over Carthage after he had destroyed it. A highly cultivated man, he was, in retirement, the centre of a brilliant literary and philosophical circle.

521 Marcus Tullius Cicero was often referred to as Tully by English writers down to the nineteenth century. Cicero's oratory helped to suppress Catiline's anarchist conspiracy, 63 BC. After Julius Caesar's death Cicero opposed the tyrannical ambitions of Mark Antony, who in 43 BC had him put to death. Cf. T.'s *Liberty* v (1736), 422–6.

522 rushing: rapidly declining.

523 Cato: of Utica; see *Su.* 954 n. Cato is called 'unconquer'd' in Pope, *Temple of Fame* 176.

524 Brutus: Marcus Junius Brutus (78–42 BC), the idealistic republican—friend and murderer of Julius Caesar.

532 Phoebus: Phoebus Apollo, in Roman mythology the god of healing, oracles, and prophecy. He appears in Virgil's *Eclogues* as patron of poetry and music. Cf. *Wi.* 660, *Cas. Ind.* i. vii. 4.

532 Mantuan Swain: Virgil; cf. *Sp.* 456.

534 Parent of Song: Homer was thought to have been the first poet. Cf. 'Father of Verse', Pope, *Temple of Fame*, 184; 'Fountain-Bard', T.'s *Liberty* ii (1735), 277.

535 British Muse: Milton; cf. *Su.* 1567–71.

536 Darkling: in the dark; cf. *Au.* 753. Milton was blind and Homer reputedly so.

537 those Shades: the Greek dramatists and lyric poets. T. described Attic drama as 'the Moral Scene' in *Liberty* ii. 279.

541 First: best.

546a Lycidas: probably Mallet, since 'Mallet' and 'Lycidas' are interchanged by T. in variant manuscript and printed versions of his 'Hymn on Solitude' between 1725 and 1748; see *The Castle of Indolence and Other Poems*, ed. A. D. McKillop (Lawrence, Kansas, 1961), pp. 120–7.

550–4 Cf. *Su.* 1427. Pope's translation of Homer's *Iliad* was published 1715–20, and his *Odyssey* 1725–6. He befriended T., who was introduced to him in 1725 by Duncan Forbes (cf. *Au.* 944). The compliment in 554 recognizes Pope's successful self-cultivation as the virtuous recluse or Horatian happy man at Twickenham. In reprinting *Wi.* 553–4 (slightly misquoted) among the 'Testimonies of Authors' in *The Dunciad* (1743) Pope repaid T.'s compliment by an allusion to the 'elegant and philosophical poem of the Seasons'.

555 James Hammond (1710–42), MP, equerry to the Prince of Wales, and poet, was one of the Cobham–Lyttelton–Pitt circle of 'youthful patriots' (*Wi.* 565, cf. *Au.* 1042–81 and notes, *Sp.* 906 n.), and died while on a visit to Stowe. His love elegies, published posthumously in 1743, were much admired (but not by Johnson, see *Lives of the Poets*, 'Hammond'). T. does not refer to the poetry in this tribute (555–71).

575–7 The first idea was the traditional interpretation of Gen. 1; cf. 2 Macc. 7: 28, 'God made [heaven and earth] of things that were not.' The second—that the material universe was created by God not out of nothing but out of his own being—was inferred and developed from Plato's suggestion in *Timaeus* 29 that the Creator formed the material world as a copy of an eternal pattern. This notion was elaborated by the first-century Jewish philosopher Philo (*De Opificio Mundi* v–vii), and was much discussed by seventeenth-century English theologians. It has been argued, from *PL* vii. 166–73 and from *De Doctrina Christiana* (not published till 1825), that Milton believed that God created the universe out of his own being (cf. Denis Saurat, *Milton: Man and Thinker*, rev. 1944).

579–82 Summarizes the intention of *The Seasons*.

583–7 T. could have found this notion in Shaftesbury's *Inquiry concerning Virtue* (1699), but the moral thought of the age was dominated by 'a firm persuasion of an omnipotent, omniscient, and most benign Universal Parent, disposing of all things in this system for the very best' (Francis Hutcheson, *System of Moral Philosophy* (1755), i. 215.) Cf. Pope, *Essay on Man* (1733–4), *passim*.

587 Historic Muse: Clio.

587–93 The influence of climate and other natural causes upon the national character and history of nations was a favourite topic for popular historians of the period; e.g. Sir William Temple, *Observations upon the United Provinces of the Netherlands* (1673), Goldsmith, *The Traveller* (1764).

590 smile: become rich; cf. *Sp.* 84 n., *Wi.* 452.

591 double Suns: probably the double harvest of *Au.* 915, rather than the double seasons of *Su.* 645.

594 Cf. Luke 24: 32.

595 Portion of Divinity: that godlike wisdom which is expressed in benevolence; cf. *Sp.* 878–903 and n., *Au.* 911–12, *Wi.* 433–5. In T.'s *Sophonisba* (1730), v. ii. 214, Masinissa refers to Scipio's benevolent wisdom as 'the divinity that breathes in thee'.

603–8 The old notion of the great chain of being (cf. *Su.* 334 n.) was reinterpreted in the seventeenth and eighteenth centuries to include the idea of progress in present and future states. So the future life may be seen as the infinite ascent of mind from stage to stage, and immortality as an endless extension of knowledge. For popular statements of this view see *Spectator* 111 and 237 by Addison, and 635 by Henry Grove. For modern accounts see A. O. Lovejoy, *The Great Chain of Being* (1936), chap. 9, and *Background*, pp. 21–5. T. wrote in a letter to William Cranstoun, 20 Oct. 1735: 'This, I think, we may be sure of: that a future State must be better than this; and so on through the never-ceasing Succession of future States; every one rising upon the last, an everlasting new Display of infinite Goodness' (*Letters*, p. 100). Cf. *Sp.* 336–78 n., *Su.* 1796–1805 n., *Hymn* 108–16, *Liberty*, iii (1735), 68–70, *Cas. Ind.* ii. lxiii. 3–5.

609–16 This conception of wit is in Locke, *An Essay concerning Human Understanding* ii. xi. 2, but T.'s distinction between wit and humour appears to be based on Corbyn Morris, *An Essay towards fixing the True Standards of Wit, Humour, Raillery, Satire and Ridicule* (1744). As usual, T.'s terms hover between personification and abstraction. Morris's *Essay* was published on 17 May, two months before printing of *44* (much revised in proof) was completed. T.'s earlier lines on humour (*30q*, 505–14) are crossed through in *MS*, but nothing is there substituted for them.

617–55 owe some hints to Milton's *L'Allegro* 100–38.

621–9 Cf. J. Philips, *Cyder* (1708) ii. 413–22.

628 respondent: in which the dancers arrange themselves in two facing rows.

630 intense: with strenuous effort.

645 mealy: powdered, cf. Shakespeare, *Troilus and Cressida* III. iii. 79. For the conventional insect figure of 638–45 cf. *Sp.* 60–1, *Su.* 342–8, *Cas. Ind.* I. li, *Letters*, pp. 139, 167–8.

647 Monimia: heroine of Thomas Otway's tragedy *The Orphan* (acted 1680).

648 Belvidera: heroine of Otway's tragedy *Venice Preserved* (acted 1682).

655 Bevil: T.'s footnote indicates that the hero of Steele's sentimental comedy was less well-known than the chief tragic characters of Shakespeare and Otway. In 'lifts her Strain' (653) T. recognizes that the drama of sensibility is a mixed genre; cf. Horace, *Ars Poetica* 93, 'vocem comoedia tollit', thus annotated by Richard Hurd, *Works* (1811), i. 37— 'Comedy, in the passionate parts, will admit of a tragic elevation.'

658 Springs: perhaps alluding to the minds and hearts of MPs 'touched' by the skill of Chesterfield's oratory, or perhaps to the finer feelings of all men influenced by his example, but the analogy here between springs in a machine and responsive, motivating organs or powers in a human being remains unclear; cf. *Sp.* 329–35 n.

659 Graces: in Greek mythology three goddesses who personify loveliness or grace.

660 Apollo: in Greek mythology the god of prophecy and light; cf. *Wi.* 532.

662 Cf. 'et praesidium et dulce decus', Horace, *Odes* I. i. 2.

664 Philip Dormer Stanhope, fourth Earl of Chesterfield (1694–1773), the politician, wit, and letter-writer. Like nearly every other politician commended in *The Seasons*, he was a leading member of the Prince of Wales's circle of Whigs opposed to Walpole and George II. He helped to engineer the fall of Walpole in 1742 but was still in opposition (cf. 669–70) when T.'s lines 656–90 were first printed in *44*. 680–1 probably allude to Chesterfield's speeches against the use of British money to defend Hanover. In Nov. 1744 he entered the government under Pelham (cf. *Su.* 1432). The fact that it is the Rural Muse who praises the highly polished, utterly urbane Lord Chesterfield indicates that there is no necessary connection between urban life and corruption.

675 Attic Point: Attic wit—from the acuity of ancient Athenians as talkers. Pope had paid the same compliment earlier, in *Epilogue to the Satires* (1738), 84–5.

687 Party: any political faction opposed to Chesterfield.

693 Serene: clear sky.

694 See *Sp.* 563 n. It was thought that 'a windy season and serene sky' favoured the production of nitre, 'and that the east and north winds only bring with them the primogenial acid of the air which saturates the alkaline sulphureous parts of the earth and converts them into nitre . . . long frosts and snows, especially after a hot summer mellow the ground and render it exceeding fertile, because the earth calcined and rendered alkaline by the summer heats is by the frost and snow abundantly supplied with an acid and rendered nitrous' (Anon., *The Rational Farmer* (1743), pp. 50–1). Cf. *Au.* 4–5, *Wi.* 706–8; John Philips, *Cyder* (1708), ii. n. 184–8; Blackmore, *Creation* (1712), ii. 277–94.

705–6 Cf. *Sp.* 111–13 n., but 'thoughtless Eye' also hints at T.'s usual distinction between the herd and the enlightened few.

706 concocted: solidified (but hinting, too, at the other meaning—'ripened', 'perfected', cf. *Su.* 909, *Au.* 7—and so indicating the fruitful part played by frost in the harmony of Nature).

707 vegetable Soul: here identified with nitre; see *Sp.* 563 n. and *Wi.* 694 n. Cf. *Curiosities in Nature and Art in Husbandry and Gardening* (1707), p. 27: 'A Plant . . . contains within itself a Principle of Life, which we may call Soul.'

709 stronger Glow: As gases are denser when cold than when hot, a fire in frosty weather would receive more oxygen than normally, and so would burn more strongly.

711 'The water which . . . snow yields when melted . . . is the purest' (Anon., *The Rational Farmer* (1743), p. 105).

714–20 'Cold and freezing seem to proceed from some saline substance floating in the air; we see that all salts, but more eminently some, mixed with ice prodigiously increase the effects and force of cold . . . Microscopical observations inform us that the figures of some salts, before they shoot into masses, are thin double-wedged . . . The dimensions of freezed bodies are increased by the insinuations of these crystal wedges in their pores, and the particles of congealed water are kept at some distance from one another by the figure of these crystals which in freezing insinuate themselves in their pores' (George Cheyne, *Philosophical Principles of Religion: Natural and Revealed* (1715), pp. 61–3). The microscope had revealed many variations in the shapes of snow crystals. See *Background*, p. 60.

716 illusive Fluid: spirit of wine, or ethyl alcohol, which was used in thermometers in T.'s day; for 'illusive' cf. Lat. *illudere*, to trick—'wine is a mocker' (Prov. 20: 1)—and *Sp.* 989 n. Members of a scientific expedition to Lapland in 1736–7 found that their spirit thermometers froze (Pierre Maupertuis, *The Figure of the Earth*, English trans. (1738), p. 85), but this must have been because the spirit of wine contained some water.

721 Steam'd: blown.

731a detruded: forced down; cf. *Sp.* 568.

733 double: increased to twice its usual loudness.

736 Swells: i.e. the sound swells.

754 plumy Wave: frost-coated trees having the appearance of feathers.

763 dissolv'd: dispersed; cf. *PL* ii. 506.

768 Batavia: Holland; cf. *Au.* 921 n.

771 then gay: because the Dutch were proverbially dull.

762–78a (*30q* 622) **cerule:** deep blue; cf. Lucretius v. 481: 'ponti plaga caerula tendit'.

(*30q* 627) **illuded:** made sport of; cf. *Wi.* 716. Perhaps T. removed the fallen skater in *44* because he thought the episode was too 'low'.

780–1 Cf. *Su.* 1620 n.

782 gelid: very cold, cf. Virgil, *Eclogue* x. 15 and Lucretius iii. 892; i.e. not the same meaning as in *Su.* 208, though no less evocative of Virgil and Roman poets generally.

804 Vast: (noun), cf. *PL* vi. 203.

809–14 Taken from Johannes Scheffer, *Lapponia* (1673, English trans. 1674), chap. xxix. Other parts of T.'s northern descriptions come from Scheffer; see *Background*, pp. 112–22.

814 freakt: variegated. 'A word, I suppose, Scotch, brought into England by *Thomson*' (Johnson, citing 810–14); but cf. Milton, *Lycidas* 144.

816–26 This method of hunting is described in Virgil, *Georgics* iii. 369–75.

818 branching: antlered; cf. *Au.* 427.

828 The substitution of 'shapeless' for 'shaggy' is perhaps influenced by Virgil's *informes ursi* in *Georgics* iii. 247, though it contradicts 'horrid' (i.e. bristling) in the following line.

831–3 The bear hibernates.

835 Boötes: the Waggoner, a bright star whose apparent position in the heavens is close to the Great Bear or Charles's Wain. As the Great Bear describes only a small circle around the pole it appears to move slowly; cf. Ovid, *Metamorphoses* ii. 176–7; 'Boote,/quamvis tardus eras'.

836 Caurus: cf. *Georgics* iii. 356, *Cas. Ind.* II. lxxviii. 4.

840–2 For the notion of the far north as the 'hive of nations' whose incursions into the declining Roman Empire reinvigorated an enfeebled Europe, see Jordanes, *Gothic History* iv. 1, Sir William Temple, 'Of Heroick Virtue' in *Miscellanea, the Second Part* (1692), and T.'s *Liberty* iii (1735), 510–38, iv (1736), 370–8.

843–50 Such idealization of the Lapps (cf. *Wi.* 877–86) is found in T.'s source—Olaf Rudbeck, *Lapland Illustrated*, appended to the 1704 edition of Scheffer's *Lapponia* (cf. *Wi.* 809–14 n.). See *Background*, pp. 116–22.

851–6 T. may have gained his information about the all-useful reindeer from Olaus Magnus, *A Compendious History of the Goths, Swedes and Vandals* (English trans. 1658), XVII. xii, which, like Rudbeck's book, idealizes the noble savages of the north.

857 marbled: hard, or perhaps smoothed.

859–64 The long winter night in the far north is illuminated by the aurora borealis (cf. *Au.* 1108–37), and by starlight and moonlight through clear skies, reflected from the snow. T. found this information in Scheffer's *Lapponia* (cf. *Wi.* 809–14 n.) and Pierre Maupertuis, *The Figure of the Earth* (English trans. 1738), p. 78. See *Background*, pp. 114–16.

867 Aurora: see *Su.* 1327.

871 spiral: circular. During the summer months in polar regions the sun never sets; in winter it never rises; cf. *Wi.* 797–8.

887 Tornea's Lake: Torne Lake in northern Sweden, near the border with Norway and at the head of the Tornio river which divides Sweden from Finland.

888 Hecla: the volcano in Iceland.

894–901 For the details of this personification see a description of the Italian Alps, translated from Silius Italicus, *Punica* iii. 477–92, in Addison, *Remarks on Several Parts of Italy* (rev. 1718), Letter xviii, 'Bolonia etc.' There are hints too from the Cave of Aeolus in Virgil, *Aeneid* i. 52–63.

902 Tartar's Coast: northern Siberia; cf. Mallet, *The Excursion* (1728), i. 336: 'Hence eastward to the Tartar's cruel coast.'

912–13a (*30q* 659–64) 'Near to the Land . . . some greater Ice-Mountains are seen . . . that stand firm on the shoar, and never melt at bottom, but increase every year higher and higher, by reason of the Snow that falls on them . . . and are never melted by the heat of the Sun at the Top . . . I once saw one of these pieces that was curiously workt and carved, as it were, by the Sea, like a Church with arched Windows and Pillars . . . on the incide thereof I saw the delicatest blew that can be imagined . . . The Sea dasheth against these Ice-fields, which occasioneth several fine Figures . . . like unto Mountains, Steeples, Tables, Chappels, and all sorts of Beasts' (Friedrich Martens, *Voyage into Spitzbergen and Greenland*, pp. 44, 46–7, 41, in *An Account of Several Late Voyages and Discoveries* (1711)). See *Background*, pp. 138–9. Martens was used by Pope in *The Temple of Fame*. Cf. Pope, *Essay on Criticism*, 232, 'Alps on Alps arise'; and cf. Mallet, *The Excursion* (1728), i. 324–9:

> Lo, hills of snow,
> Hill behind hill, and alp on alp, ascend,
> Pil'd up from oldest age, and to the sun
> Impenetrable; rising from afar
> In misty prospect dim, as if on air
> Each floating hill, an azure range of clouds.

918 wavy Rocks: frozen waves; cf. 'solid Billows' in Ambrose Philips's verse-letter on Copenhagen in *Tatler* 12.

924 incumbent: pressing with its weight. The echo of *PL* i. 226 is more forceful here than at *Sp.* 41 or *Su.* 1364.

925 footnote Willoughby and his crew entered an inlet, subsequently known as Arzina (cf. *Wi.* 930), near the present border between Norway and Russia, intending to pass the winter of 1553–4 there, but they were ill-provisioned, and all died. Their bodies were found some years afterwards, and Willoughby's journal was printed in Hakluyt's *Principal Navigations* and in many other collections. The description of the crew frozen in activity seems to be T.'s own, and is, of course, fictitious. Later attempts (cf. *Au.* 927–9) on the north-east passage were made by Pet and Jackson in 1580, by Barents in 1594–7, and by expeditions set in motion by Peter the Great and commanded by Vitus Baring in 1725–8 and 1740–1.

937 Oby: the river Ob', rising near the borders of Russia and Mongolia and flowing into the Arctic Ocean. Its mouth was surveyed in the 1720s as part of Peter the Great's efforts to find the north-east passage.

937 Last of Men: the Samoyeds and Ostyaks, whose subterranean winter lodgings and miserable barbarism were described in John Perry, *The State of Russia under the Present Czar* (1716), and Friedrich Christian Weber, *The Present State of Russia* (English trans. 1722–3); see *Background*, pp. 107–8. T.'s description owes something also to Virgil's less miserable Hyperboreans in *Georgics* iii. 349–83.

954 Gothic: barbarian.

955 Peter the Great (1672–1725), Tsar of Russia, travelled in 1697–8 through Western Europe to study government, commerce and industry, and even learned handicrafts in the shipbuilding yards of Holland and England (cf. *Wi.* 969). On his return home he reorganized his backward country's army, navy, civil government, education, social life, and culture. After he had captured part of the Baltic coast he founded in 1703 a new capital city, St. Petersburg (cf. 973); he planned to join the Baltic and the Black Sea by canals (cf. 975–6). Though Peter did eventually defeat Charles XII of Sweden (cf. 980 n.), he did not awe the Ottomans (cf. 980–1), for though he attacked Turkey in 1711 he was forced to accept a humiliating peace and loss of territory. There were many English tributes to Peter's achievements (e.g. in Steele's *Spectator* 139), but T.'s immediate source was probably Aaron Hill's *Plain Dealer* 106, 26 May 1725 (repr. 1734, ii. 407–15), which included quotations from Hill's earlier poem in praise of Peter, *The Northern-Star*. See A. D. McKillop, 'Peter the Great in Thomson's *Winter*', *Modern Language Notes* lxvii (1952), 28–31. For T.'s admiration for material progress, cf. *Au.* 43–130.

980 Alexander of the North: Charles XII (1682–1718), King of Sweden, the military genius who inflicted defeats in turn on Denmark, Russia, and Poland (1700–2). In 1708 he invaded Russia, but his army, severely weakened by the Russian winter, was annihilated at Poltava in 1709.

981 Othman's . . . Sons: Turks.

990 resolves: cf. Shakespeare, *Hamlet* I. ii. 130: 'melt, thaw, and resolve itself into a dew.'

1001–8 Cf. *PL* i. 207–8, ii. 285–90.

1005 tost: makes good sense, but may be a misprint for 'lost', the reading of all editions before *44*.

1014–16 Cf. T.'s juvenile 'Paraphrase of Psalm 104':

> Even the broad ocean, wherein do abide
> Monsters that flounce upon the boiling tide, . . .
> 'Tis there that Leviathan sports and plays   (92–3, 97).

Leviathan is the monster in Job 41, but here (1014), as frequently in modern literature, identified with the whale; for 'tempests' (1016) cf. *PL* vii. 412.

1027 tuneful Kingdom: birds. On periphrases see *Sp.* 132 n.

1028–46 Cf. Job 14: 1–15.

1049 Cf. *Sp.* 111–13 n.

1055 Cf. Acts 8: 23.

A HYMN

In the edition which Lyttelton prepared about 1758, but never published (see Introduction, p. xxvii above), this *Hymn* was omitted, because, as Lyttelton wrote in his Preface (see Appendix C below), 'it appears to good Judges that all the Matter and Thoughts in that Hymn are much better exprest in the Seasons themselves'; but it has appeared to some later judges that Lyttelton's real objection was to its supposed deistical tendency. T.'s *Hymn* is modelled in a general way upon *PL* v. 153–208 and Psalm 148, but restates and harmonizes many of the scientific, philosophical and religious notions introduced earlier in the poem.

1–3 Cf. *Wi.* 106–7 n. and Pope, *Essay on Man* i (1733), 267–80.

14–15a (*30q*, 17) **beamy:** 'Radiant; shining; emitting beams' (Johnson).

18–19 Cf. *PL* vi. 771.

21–7 Contradicts the attitude of *Sp.* 317–20: the *Hymn* corrects and extends limited views of Nature found earlier in the poem. On 'kind Art' (23) cf. *Su.* 185–96 n.

29 mighty Hand: cf. *Su.* 32–42 n.

31 Deep: the earth; cf. *Sp.* 79–80.

35 grateful: pleasing; cf. *Sp.* 735.

36 Springs of Life: cf. *Sp.* 329–45 n.

51 humid Maze: winding, divided brook; cf. *Su.* 373. On periphrases see *Sp.* 132 n.

58 Pencil: small brush; cf. Dryden, *Palemon and Arcite*, ii. 56, 'Nature's ready Pencil paints the Flow'rs'.

60 still: silent—indicating some correspondence between rhythmic movement and music; cf. Wordsworth, 'Airey-Force Valley' (1842): 'A soft eye-music of slow-waving boughs'.

63–5 Hint at a correspondence between light and music. This scene and its feeling (59–65) are finely caught by Samuel Palmer in his painting *Cornfield by Moonlight, with the Evening Star*.

66 Source of Day: the sun; cf. *Su.* 90–6 n.

68–9 For light as liquid cf. *Su.* 84 n.

79 Philomela: see *Sp.* 601 n.

96 Russets the Plain: parches the grass brown.

96 inspiring Autumn: cf. T. to Lyttelton, 14 July 1743: 'I think that season of the year the most pleasing, and the most poetical. The spirits are not then dissipated with the gaiety of Spring and the glaring light of Summer, but composed into a serious and tempered joy' (*Letters* p. 163).

96 gleams: with light reflected from ripe corn.

107 Newton's description of infinite space as 'the sensorium of the Godhead' is quoted by Addison, *Spectator* 565. In the *Hymn*, as in the whole of *The Seasons*, T. emphasizes God's immanence—never his transcendence; cf. *Sp.* 853–60, *Su.* 41–2, etc.

112 Cf. *Sp.* 84 n. and *Su.* 176–81 n. In the *Hymn* the subject of 'smiles' is raised progressively from a natural object, 'Forest' (6), to 'Creation' (81), to 'Universal Love' (112).

113 Sons: inhabitants, see *Su.* 107 n.

114 Cf. *Wi.* 1050–69 and T. to Elizabeth Young, 21 Jan. 1744: 'There is no real Evil in the whole general System of Things; it is only our Ignorance that makes it appear so, and Pain and Death but serve to unfold his gracious Purpose of Love' (*Letters*, p. 170).

118 expressive Silence: 'the sublime is sometimes attained by a total want of expression: and this may happen, when by silence . . . we are made to understand, that there is in the mind something too great for utterance' (James Beattie, 'Illustrations on Sublimity' in *Dissertations Moral and Critical* (1783), p. 633). Cf. *Longinus on the Sublime*, chap. ix, Beattie (*Dissertations*, p. 626) claimed that T.'s *Hymn*, except for 'an unguarded word or two', was in no way inferior to Milton's morning hymn in *PL* v. 153–208.

APPENDIX B

Sp.28 dedication

Countess of Hertford: see *Sp.* 5 n.

Sp.28 advertisement

T.'s proposals for a subscription edition of the Four Seasons were published in January 1728. *Spring* was published in June 1728.

Su.27 dedication

Mr. Dodington: see *Su.* 29 n.

Wi.26 f–28 dedication

According to Spence this dedication was written by Mallet; see Joseph Spence, *Observations*, ed. J. M. Osborn (Oxford, 1966), i. 370.

Sir Spencer Compton: see *Wi.* 17–40 n.

Wi.260 preface

11 Moses: Aaron Hill in the Preface to his poem *The Creation* (1720) had referred to the Pentateuch as the oldest and sublimest poem in the world, and declared that the art of poetry had been given to Moses by God.

17 amusing: engaging the attention. Addison in *Spectator* 321 says that Milton's account of angelic hymns in Eden 'is altogether Divine and inexpressibly amusing to the Imagination'.

24 Aesop's Ass: see 'The Dog and the Ass', Fable xxiv in John Ogilby, *The Fables of Aesop Paraphras'd* (1668).

33 Attacker of the Stage: William Law (1686–1761), whose *The absolute Unlawfulness of the Stage-Entertainment fully demonstrated* was published in March 1726.

76 Enthusiasm: 'a prophetick or poetical rage or fury, which transports the mind, raises and inflames the imagination, and makes it think and express things extraordinary and surprising' (Nathan Bailey, *Universal Etymological Dictionary* (1721)).

89 romantic: see *Sp.* 1028 n.

101–12 *Georgics* ii. 475–86.

114–25 Cf. *Au.* 1352–71.

128–9 press variant: see Introduction p. xxxix above.

143 Malloch: Mallet.

Wi.260 commendatory poems

See Introduction pp. xxxvii–xxxviii above.

INDEX TO THE INTRODUCTION AND COMMENTARY